THE HISTORY OF
WORLD PAINTING

THE HISTORY OF WORLD PAINTING

Edited by Hans L.C. Jaffé

Ancient and Classical Art	P.P. Kahane
The Middle Ages	P. Francastel
The Renaissance	G.C. Argan
The Seventeenth and Eighteenth Centuries	Michael Levey
The Nineteenth and Twentieth Centuries	Hans L.C. Jaffé
Far Eastern Art	H. Hetl-Kunze

NEW ORCHARD EDITIONS

POOLE   DORSET

This edition first published in Great Britain
1980
JUPITER BOOKS (LONDON) LIMITED
167 Hermitage Road, London N 4

ISBN 1 85079 026 4

Reprinted 1985
New Orchard Editions
Robert Rogers House
New Orchard
Poole Dorset BH15 1LU

Translated from the French, German, and Italian by Robert Erich Wolf.
Produced in the Netherlands.

contents

introduction

Hans L. C. Jaffé

It should surprise no one that the task of introducing this book, a book whose ambitious aim it is to survey a full 20,000 years of painting, should fall to the author responsible for the section which concludes it and which treats of the art of the past 150 years. Compared with the vast stretch of time preceding, these 150 years are no more than a moment in the historical sense of the word. In the span of human culture, and in their contribution to painting, these years are truly but a passing moment. And yet, they are also the fixed standpoint from which we today must view and comprehend the painting of the past both as history and as something of current significance to us. In Dutch, "moment" is *ogenblik*—the blink of an eye, and that is exactly what we are speaking of here: that instant of revelation which direct contact with a painting gives, and which the works of art reproduced in this book offer to the reader.

The way we look at painting and its forms and colors, the way we understand the painter's language, is determined for all of us by our familiarity with the art of our own time, by our contact with the world of forms that is our present-day reality. Like men in earlier times, we look at the painting of the past with contemporary eyes. Our point of view is that of our own art. No matter how we may try, we simply cannot be objective about this, we cannot enter into the mind of every artist of the past and look out through his eyes. We are men of today, and we view the past in our own fashion.

It goes without saying that purely as sense organs our eyes scarcely differ from those of our most remote ancestors. They are human eyes, instruments of human contact with the environment, like our ears, mouth, and other sense organs. But it is precisely this comparison that clarifies the essential problem: our mouths form sounds in the same way as those of thousands of years ago, and our ears do not hear any differently. But the speech made up of those sounds has changed, has developed, has followed quite different rules. The barrier between sensory perception and intellectual comprehension is a movable one in speech as in vision, and vision in its own way is equally a means of communication. We speak in the visual language of our own time, and this inevitably imposes certain limitations on our understanding of other types of visual language. And yet, it may well be that the visual languages of the past are more accessible to our understanding than the verbal languages of faraway peoples. Not that such understanding comes to us without effort. Far from it. It demands a certain measure of knowledge, of sympathy, of willingness to renounce, if only for a moment, the familiar secure bases of our normal modes of understanding. Otherwise we risk misunderstanding and misinterpreting everything we look at. That is because the visual language of earlier ages not only employed a vocabulary and a syntax which differ from ours, but also because it often dealt with quite different subjects, so remote from our experience that we can now scarcely conceive of them. Yet those subjects formed the basis of the visual concepts and mental attitudes of past ages, and as such were handed down to us in the substratum of our collective consciousness, our common stock of conceptual thought. This explains why it sometimes happens, when we look at artworks of the remote past, that we experience a sudden flash of recognition, a surprised feeling of familiarity, just as in reading books of legendary antiquity such as the Bible or the *Odyssey* we encounter traits of character that seem to have been known to us always. But to read such books we must know their language; we must be acquainted with their ways of expression in order to glean their content.

This is true also of our understanding of visual language. If we do not make the effort to understand the vocabulary of forms used in the past, we can be led into grave misconceptions. One of those misconceptions lies in seeking to bridge the gap between our contemporary point of view and the thought that lay behind an artwork at its origin by taking into account only the differing conception of the subject, of what is depicted. We know that such difficulties occur also in other non-representational arts: music of distant countries or past cultures is not immediately accessible to the modern ear. Music, painting, poetry, all the arts use a language which changes according to its own rules through the ages, and the notion that we can spontaneously grasp works of former times is ignorant if not downright presumptuous.

Our own historical period, the past 150 years, has on the one hand fostered such a misunderstanding, on the other hand stimulated our understanding of painting and the other arts of earlier times. One of the most important factors in this domain has been the founding of the first public art museums and the wide-ranging development which the character of those museums has undergone in the past 175 years. A museum, as an institution, presupposes that innumerable works of visual art, of painting in particular, have been removed from their original environments and brought together within a new category, that of pure art in its own right. Religious paintings that were originally designed to be objects of veneration and prayer on the altars of churches are now hung (and were in the past also) alongside portraits of men and women, of princes, public officials, or heroes of either intellectual or military distinction, and these in turn are adjacent to landscapes which may evoke the terrors of savage mountains or, again, may present clearly ordered and topographically accurate views of cities or places. Since the middle of the last century, those paintings, among which are many masterpieces, have been joined in the museums by objects unearthed in archaeological diggings: painted vases from Greece, the Hellenic islands, the Middle East and Italy, as well as Egyptian frescoes and, more recently, works from China, Japan, ancient Mesopotamia, and the early cultures of Pre-Columbian America.

The last century took to displaying together all these various works with the aim of showing the historical development of art and thereby also of man himself. What they were intended to reveal as a whole was a constantly recurring cycle of organic development which, it was thought, human life had undergone, a cycle of growth, maturity, and decline. For the nineteenth century, the mature phase—what was taken as the classical stage of each development—was represented by that kind of painting which most closely approximates the external appearances of reality. What was "natural"—meaning what corresponded to what everyone would recognize as resembling nature—was used as a measure of appreciation by which other styles could be dismissed as "barbarous," "primitive," "undisciplined," and the like.

Only around the beginning of our century were these notions of art history changed and more subtle distinctions introduced. The arrangement of artworks according to the time and place in which they were done was seen to have nothing in common with the notion of a development which followed a stereotyped pattern of crests and troughs of excellence. The idea of an organic development was replaced by the idea of the artist's independent will, and this was closely related to the new conceptions of style and pictorial language. Style in the visual arts was thenceforth conceived as a system of pictorial speech used by the artist and understood by the society to which he belonged. What came of this was an entirely different conception of the history of art—in our case, of painting—which no longer saw in the diverse forms a regular progression from the first tentative steps in learning a language, upward to its mastery (the classical period), and finally downward to its degeneration into formless stammering. The new conception, the one which underlies the present book, views the history of painting as a kind of symphonic score in which different instruments play their melodies at different times with their own unique timbres and their own melodic and rhythmic characteristics, sometimes closely bound to the other instruments, sometimes ranging at large so that the relationships can scarcely be made out. From time to time one of the instruments dominates, standing out compellingly above the ensemble, at other times several instruments unite in balanced harmony. It is typical of our present-day point of view of the history of painting that we no longer see the chronological succession of styles as the orderly working-out of an organic development—from birth to maturity to decline—but instead think of the consecutive

periods as movements in a symphony or sonata in which each movement (sometimes resembling, sometimes differing from, its predecessor) presents a new theme, develops it to its fullest resolution, and then rounds it off in musical fashion. Thus the present book is divided into chapters—into movements—which do not pretend to present complete closed organic cycles of development, but instead, through the clear working-out of certain themes and their structures, aim to make a contribution to the interpretation of the past, to the conception of the picture as an optical configuration of the dominant outlook on the world at some particular time.

The reader of this book must therefore take the point of view that in the various "movements" of this symphonic score works of painting give adequate expression to an ever-changing view of the world and of human existence. He must be convinced that painting too is a language, a means of communication in human culture, which is as effective as words themselves and in which—as Francastel has formulated it—thought and sign are identical.

This transformation in our way of thinking no longer places the emphasis on certain regularly recurring periods in art history that previous centuries deemed classical because of the life-likeness of their art, but much more on certain personalities or certain segments of phases at which time the leading motifs of the period emerge most purely and most convincingly. In place of the developmental approach to history, inspired by the organic growth and decay of life, modern art history deals with a process which considers the changing styles of painting to be the molds of a human style of living which the social and cultural structures of a period fill with visible form.

This shift of emphasis from organic cycle to symphonic score certainly did not arise by itself. The basis for it was laid when the notion of verisimilitude to nature was called into question, when the art of our century took the path from art as illustration to art as significant sign. This doubt cast on the old premises of the normative value of the image as a reflection of nature, this question of how much truth there really is in observable appearances, came about at the turn of the century. It resulted from new discoveries in science and philosophy and from certain technical developments which set before man a number of phenomena whose effects, although clearly perceptible, defy explanation by the evidence of man's senses. Electricity, radio, and the like are obvious examples of phenomena that cannot be elucidated by sensory data alone.

Yet another technological advance that took place at the end of the nineteenth century and the beginning of the twentieth challenged the utility, as a standard of art, of the "resemblance to nature" which had governed artistic thought in the nineteenth century both of its own art and that of the past. This was the invention and subsequent improvement of photography, a technical innovation which made it possible to seize the most fleeting image of the world of appearances, that world which corresponds to what we actually see, and to pin it down forever. Photography had a similar effect on the guiding principles of art history that the Industrial Revolution had, in the intellectual sphere, on history itself. A verisimilitude to nature which could be achieved by mechanical means as well as by art, a verisimilitude which in its technical perfection stood "beyond good and evil," beyond any subjective judgment, could no longer be the artist's unique goal, nor could the historian of art continue to accept it as a standard. The fundamental principle of the long-standing division of history into periods—the growth of a tendency toward resemblance to nature, its maturity, and finally its decadence—was no longer beyond question and had to give way to a new system of values.

The new scale of values of art history—which certainly today need no longer be thought of as new—was first proposed by the Viennese school, by personalities such as Alois Riegl and Max Dvořák. These men were much taken up with a certain historical approach which dominated all considerations of cultural history in their time. For them it was axiomatic that, in essence, all the cultural phenomena of a particular period were intimately related. Certainly they thought that, precisely in their own time, pictorial art was clearly freeing itself from the centuries-long bondage it had first had to theology, then to absolute monarchy, later to national states, and so on. But they emphasized the fact that painting had always played a part in the system of values of particular historical periods and that those systems of value had been fully embodied in the visual arts. One of the most impressive examples of this approach is Dvořák's masterly essay, "Idealismus und Naturalismus in der gotischen Skulptur und Malerei," published in 1918, in which he examined side by side the changes that occurred during the Middle Ages in its conception of the world, in its way of life, and in its art.

At somewhat the same time that these scholars were striving to formulate a historical approach which would take in the parallel currents of artistic thought, another scholar, Heinrich Wölfflin, went one step farther. For specific historical periods, in his case the Renaissance and the Baroque, he laid down basic principles of art history, fundamental characteristics based on the way people saw things and, therefore, governing the creation of their art at a particular time. Thereby the history of art became the history of style, and this meant a history of art that could dispense with the great names (this was the goal for a long time of an entire school of art historians). Art, for Wölfflin, was a language, the visual means of communication for men in any particular period, the means through which the problems of their period received expression in precisely the way and manner appropriate to that period. It was a language that everyone in such a period heard, understood, and spoke.

Only later, in fact shortly before World War II, a new approach arose which admittedly owed much to the study of the language of art but attributed much greater importance to the influence of personality and creative fantasy. The scholars of that generation were mostly Germans who had fled from the Nazi regime to the United States or England. They were convinced that a language does not simply exist but is in a constant state of evolution, and that it is precisely the poets—the artists—who create the language, who mold it into a vital, living unity. They inverted the previous point of view to the extent that, for them, the language of painting was no longer the precondition but, instead, the result of creative activity. Furthermore, they added to the understanding and knowledge of a painting an entirely new dimension: they did not focus only on the form in which the content was embodied at a particular period, but also on exactly what it was that the particular period aimed to express in depicting some specific subject. The method by which such questions are approached is called iconology; in the last few decades it has laid bare levels of meaning in painting that had been completely forgotten in the intervening time since the work was painted and had been quietly ignored by a method which concentrated exclusively on the formal aspects of art. Yet it was precisely the iconological factors which, in time past, had been fundamental in giving adequate expression to the spirit of the age. Present-day art history, as exemplified by the authors of this book, is again concerned with an artist's choice of a particular subject and with the mythological or emblematic references that may lurk behind an image. Modern scholars are convinced that in new historical epochs, in times when styles change, not only are traditional subjects seen and portrayed in different fashion, but different subjects are also chosen to be depicted. Thus it is not the form alone but the content as well that transforms the basic orientation of what is being communicated.

Here too the comparison of painting with a language—or, more accurately, with a series of languages—holds good. When iconology seeks to disclose the emblematic background of a picture, it is doing nothing different from what the linguistic sciences do when they try to reveal the original hidden meaning of some word which, on the surface, seems easy to understand. Such an approach also reveals a relationship between meaning and form, between sense and the guise it assumes.

11

Baudelaire took down from Delacroix certain highly significant phrases which even today, in an age when abstract painting has come to the fore, can provide the key for the comprehension of the visual arts: "Nature is no more than a dictionary." And he went on, "To grasp all the vast significance those words hold, one must call to mind the many ways in which we customarily use a dictionary. One looks up in it the meaning of a word, its origins and etymology, finally gets out of it all the elements needed for a sentence or a story; but no one has ever thought of a dictionary as a composition in the poetic sense of the term. The painters who follow the lead of their own imagination seek in their dictionaries those elements which correspond to their own conceptions, and then they confer on them an entirely new appearance in accord with their own personal natural bent. Others who lack imagination simply copy from the dictionary. The result is an evil vice, the vice of banality, which is the chief characteristic of those painters whose specialty makes them very much the kin of the so-called 'soulless nature painters'—for example, the landscape painters who generally consider it a triumph when they allow nothing of their own personalities to show. They look and copy what they see, and meanwhile forget to feel and to think."

The delimitation or definition of painting as a language which is implied in these sentences is relevant not only to Delacroix's own epoch, but to the entire history of painting. The words of that language are, for the most part, pre-existent, but the important element is just how a word is used, what meaning it takes on in association with other words. Nor is it entirely a matter of words taken from a dictionary, but rather of sentences and stories (compositions "in the poetic sense of the term," as Baudelaire put it), of exactly *what* is being said, of what the painter feels and thinks and aims to communicate to his fellow men. It is precisely in this sense that painting is a social tool of the greatest importance, and not only in times when most men were unable to read and write, and thus had no other means of exchanging information. In our times it is painting that translates the way we live and think into visible graphic signs which, for many of our contemporaries, communicate more clearly than worn-out, rigidly systematized words. Moreover, the pictorial language of painting, unlike the language of words, has never, throughout the millennia of its existence, been hemmed in by national frontiers. So true is this that it seems we may be at the threshold of an "optical age" (the title of a book by Karl Pawek) in which the visual language will steadily become of greater consequence than words, as well as being closer to reality. It is our age which rediscovered the significance of pictorial concepts in the unconscious, in the world of dreams. Surrealism and the art forms which have grown out of it have regained for human consciousness the many-

sidedness, the double, triple, sometimes quadruple meanings, of a pictorial "word." Even in the daily run of our lives we increasingly encounter pictures—that is, information conveyed by pictorial means—which not only communicate some fact, but also make us participate emotionally or spiritually in some experience, in some event. We owe this to magazines, television, and especially to that kind of photo-reportage which plunges us directly into the stream of the life around us and, from the confused flood of great and small events, singles out for us those images which are most pictorially striking. To this has recently been added the even stronger visual experience of color, which more than ever before has become an important factor in our daily lives.

Interest in painting, as reflected in the growing concern with reproductions of pictures, books on art, and the steadily increasing attendance at museums, also has its roots in present-day life, and these roots have certainly influenced our attitudes toward the history of painting. A history of that art written more than some fifty years ago would scarcely have included the beginnings of painting in prehistoric times. These early works were still considered not as part of the visual arts, but as data of interest only to the ethnologist. Not until the start of our century, with the discovery of so-called primitive art and its enthusiastic reception by painters such as Picasso, Derain, Matisse, Kirchner, and Nolde, was our range of appreciation broadened. What is more, a history of art written a half-century ago would have made no place for contemporary art, because it was felt that present times were too close to be part of history. The emphasis would even have been different as regards the art of the past. El Greco had just been rediscovered after long neglect, and this occurred because he fitted in with the spirit of Expressionism. Piero della Francesca was still virtually unknown, although now, since we have been schooled by Seurat to appreciate a similarly crystal-clear and disciplined art, we reckon him among the greatest masters of painting. In addition to purely historical relationships among the various schools of painting, scholars now perceived a number of what might be called "elective affinities," of kindred spirits whose work was given new significance because of their rapport with the creative activity of artists of our time. These were the artists of the past whom our modern painters would claim as their ancestors. Thus, Cézanne hailed Poussin because they had in common their concern with imposing order on the visible world, and the Expressionists found a predecessor in Mathias Grünewald and made pilgrimages to his Isenheim altarpiece. Every generation now claimed the right to select its own ancestors, to seek out those works of the past which anticipated its own aims and desires in respect to expression and form. Suddenly, more than ever before, painters' studios were full of reproductions of many kinds of art of the past. Laymen too have become fascinated with the pictorial language as their acquaintance with it has grown. If people began to acquire books on art, it was to have their personal "Museum without Walls," to arrive at a clearer consciousness of themselves and of the world they lived in. Through its increased accessibility, and because of the progress made in the techniques of reproduction, painting in recent decades has become a mirror of human culture in which each generation, every individual strives for self-discovery. Such a wide-ranging history of painting as the present volume therefore has meaning and importance not only for the historical sciences, but even more for our present-day cultural consciousness.

This is the basis on which the introductions were written and on which the works reproduced in these pages were chosen. Our aim has been to produce a compilation by means of which the changing language of painting can be followed through the centuries, with characteristic examples of the various periods selected and grouped in such a way as to bring out their true significance. Each author has aimed to bring out clearly the conception of voices within a polyphony which is typical of our approach to art history today. This means that the various voices which must always be singled out in every period have also to be exposed clearly to the reader. They must be differentiated one from the other and, at the same time, their interrelationships made clear. What emerges from this is a historical progression in which the several periods are not treated as oversimplified generalizations, and the course of history is not forced into a mechanical goose-stepping parade of styles and forms. As the reader follows the pictures from page to page, he will become involved in a dialectical process that encompasses not only the developments in a specific area of man's creative activity, but the history of humanity itself as it is mirrored in the forms of painting.

However, the reproductions do more than emphasize the immense diversity of that development, the dynamics of the voices which successively reveal their own existence as elements in a web of polyphony. They add enlarge-ments of carefully selected details that bring insight into the special structure of the pictorial language characteristic of each period and often of each separate voice. In such details, the factual content of a picture, its relation to some specific subject, may almost disappear, or at least be reduced to secondary importance. But in them the linguistic structure of painting is made completely clear, and one sees how the total picture was painstakingly built up from smaller elements, and from a basic design (in old terminology, design—*disegno*—was equivalent to drawing) which the artist conceived in advance. Details reveal how, in another type of work, the separate elements were welded together in the fire of the creative process so that the final structure gives the impression of having grown almost without plan in the course of the artist's work. Those separate elements of the structure are highly instructive and of great importance, because they coincide with types of linguistic usage which are connected with historical or personal traits of character. Modern techniques of reproduction have thereby placed in our hands a key to the essence of painting which is of such significance that art history must always be indebted to them.

There was yet another criterion in the selection of reproductions for this volume. An effort was made to avoid pictures which are too familiar and obvious and to replace them with others which are just as characteristic. However, the choice was not made on historical grounds alone, but in equal measure on a critical basis. The aim has been not merely to illustrate what happened in the course of 20,000 years of painting, but to lay before the reader a series of masterworks which will equip him with a measuring-rod of quality and excellence. In the great chain of artworks that have reached us from the past, and to which new links are constantly being added, the masterworks occupy a special place. Like a tuning fork, they give us the tone in all its purity, and on that pure tone we can erect scales of value. Only with that imaginary tuning fork in hand can we perceive the entire history of painting as one "opus," as something man himself has made, and view it, moreover, as a "work in progress" to which each new day in the history of mankind continues to bring its contribution.

13

ancient
and classical art

P. P. Kahane

Introduction

The cultures that we shall see in this opening chapter stretch out over vast periods of time, thousands of years in some cases, as well as over immense areas of our planet. It would be a hopeless undertaking (and to some extent a foolish one) even to try to establish any kind of over-all unity capable of taking in all the pictorial creations of those cultures: in this respect, these diverse cultures are quite unlike the epochs of European painting that follow the decline and fall of the ancient world, because the subsequent styles and schools of painting can and indeed must be considered a coherent body, for all that they differed markedly at different times and places. Furthermore, it serves no purpose to pretend that within the separate early cultures, Egypt's excepted, it is possible to trace the various stages of development through which their painting passed. What little has come down to us is the result of chance finds; in addition, the materials in which their painters worked were perishable or have survived only in poor condition. For these reasons we can here point out only selected examples, and we must be cautious in making any generalizations. The ground we stand on does not become really secure—again with the exception of Egypt, which is so rich in surviving monuments—until we arrive at the paintings which decorate Greek vases, Etruscan tombs, and the Roman dwellings in Pompeii and Herculaneum.

When we talk about a "painting" nowadays we usually mean easel paintings on wood or canvas as we find them in homes, churches, and museums, and with these we include the pictures on the walls of churches, palaces, and other public buildings. From the sociologist's point of view, the origins of easel painting have three main sources: the works in temples and, later, churches with their religious rites; in the palaces of the ruling group; and in the homes of aristocrats or, at a later date, of wealthy middle-class citizens. But of that sort of easel painting all that survives from antiquity are a few painted clay metopes from early Greek temples, and some small votive tablets (*pinakes*) in Archaic Greek style which likewise were painted on clay. We happen to know from the ancient writing which dealt with art, at least from the Early Classical period of Greece on, that paintings on wooden panels were occasionally made by outstanding painters, but we can only guess at what these looked like from what we can still see in Greek vase paintings, in Roman mural decorations in Pompeii and Herculaneum, or in Egyptian mummy portraits from Roman times.

If panel painting played a minor role in early cultures, what must painting have been like in the thousands of years which preceded Classical antiquity? Certainly there were wall paintings; we find them on rock cliffs and inside prehistoric caves, in temples and tombs, in the palaces of kings and great leaders, and in public edifices. But painting in ancient times was by no means restricted to panels and walls. There was, in fact, no sharp division between sculpture and painting: all kinds of sculpture, especially in relief, was painted; so also were certain architectural elements and clay vessels, and all those objects we now lump under "applied arts," including textiles and manuscripts.

We think today of a "picture" as a finite, delimited, usually two-dimensional unity, framed or unframed. Even wall painting in modern times may be no more than an easel painting enlarged beyond its usual, limited dimensions. But except for the ancient panel paintings of which we know so little, such a definition simply does not apply to the vast majority of prehistoric and ancient "pictures." A few examples: prehistoric rock paintings are complexes of figures or images more or less loosely linked, and these may extend over hundreds of yards of cave roofs and walls. Egyptian paintings in temple, tomb, or palace likewise are not isolated pictures, but ensembles that someone planned and laid out with great care. The same is true of Mesopotamian, Iranian, and Aegean "pictures," whether in temples or palaces.

These pictorial complexes all have in common the formal peculiarity that they are distributed over an extended area, and as such constitute large ensembles; they also have a certain unity of content. Most of these pictorial complexes are neither merely decorative, nor purely symbolic: they are, in fact, functional, having a purpose over and beyond decoration. There can hardly be any question as to the magical function of prehistoric animal pictures, and the reason for the paintings in Egyptian tombs is obvious: they were meant to guarantee for the deceased an untroubled existence in the after-life. The same is true of the *symposia*—the banquets—so common on the walls of Etruscan burial chambers. Indeed, it may well be that many of the mural decorations in the villas of wealthy Romans in Pompeii, Herculaneum, and similar places served higher ends, that is, to elevate earthly existence into a mythical, chiefly Dionysian, sphere.

From what has been said, it is easy to see (and one need not hide the fact) that photographs can often reproduce only small fragments of such large pictorial complexes. They cannot give a total picture of prehistoric or ancient Middle Eastern wall paintings, nor even of those of Hellenistic, Etruscan, and Roman times. Naturally the situation is better with painted objects of applied art, including Greek vase paintings. But these can never replace the many lost mural paintings—what would we know of ancient Egyptian culture if its wall paintings and reliefs had not survived?—because, compared with such monumental works, objects of applied art are less endowed with functional power, with a "message."

Writers on art have two ways of approaching a picture: the work can be *described* or it can be *interpreted*. But no one would pretend that a description of a picture, accurate and clear as it may be, can bring out all of its functional, symbolic, sociological, historical, and spiritual content, especially when it is a religious work, ritual monument, mythical scene, or a symbol, as is so often the case in the earliest artistic creations. On the other hand, the interpretation of the function or spiritual content of a picture can go astray, leading to irresponsible speculation. For these reasons, we have aimed in commenting on each of the pictures reproduced at presenting description and interpretation in just measure and, wherever possible, to make clear also the relevant historical and cultural backgrounds.

Prehistoric Painting

If we wish to understand how painting began, or art in general, we find ourselves faced with the problem of defining what we mean by "art." A few examples: can we consider artistic creations to be the designs tattooed on the human body to ward off evil or for some other magical purpose? or the imprints or outlines of human hands that we find on the walls of the oldest Franco-Cantabrian caves? If we rule out these two cases, we must still admit that the images of men and animals reproduced in our first three pages of pictures are magical-religious contrivances as well as aesthetic objects. The great majority of art works from the early epochs are fraught with significant content; and most of them were devised to accomplish some particular function, and for no other reason. Not that this in any way excludes aesthetic perfection: far from it, for art has never refused to be a willing handmaiden to magic, ritual, and religion.

Our first three pages of plates present four groups of prehistoric religious paintings from four different regions: the Franco-Cantabrian mountain area, eastern Spain, the Sahara, and southern Africa. Within the Franco-Cantabrian group we can make out three distinct phases or cultures which have been named after the localities in France where they were discovered: the Aurignacian, the earliest phase of the Upper Paleolithic period (c. 60/40,000–20,000 B.C.); the Solutrian, the next phase of the Upper Paleolithic (c. 30,000–20,000 B.C.); and the Magdalenian, which belongs to the late Upper Paleolithic (c. 20,000–10,000 B.C.). The eastern Spanish rock paintings are related in many ways to those of the Franco-Cantabrian region, but they nevertheless have many distinct peculiarities; and their style may have begun in the late Upper Paleolithic period and gone on through the Mesolithic (10/8000–3000 B.C.) into Neolithic times (in Europe, c. 3000–1800 B.C.). The date of the Sahara rock paintings is even less certain, many authorities considering that they began to be made in the Early Neolithic period (seventh century B.C. in the East) and continued to be turned out right up to the dawn of the Christian era. The beginning of rock painting in southern Africa still remains obscure: while many of the paintings date back to the end of the Ice Age (the Upper Paleolithic period), most of them were done later. Indeed, many were produced by the Bushmen, and one cannot simply rule out in advance the notion that Bushman art merely perpetuated a prehistoric tradition. As to whether these four cultural phases were, in fact, linked one to the other and, if so, to what extent, are questions often raised but as yet not satisfactorily answered.

Characteristic of Franco-Cantabrian rock painting is the preponderance of images of animals. This must reflect the thinking of a higher hunting culture in which the wild beast played a central role. In the eastern Spanish group, images of animals and men appear in equal numbers, and along with scenes of hunting there are others of war and dancing. This is the case in central Africa also; but, unexpectedly, animals predominate in southern Africa just as in the Franco-Cantabrian region.

Anyone who has seen these rock paintings, especially the early ones, is forever haunted by them. Just what do they really mean? Many explanations have been proposed, and two of these are distinctly enlightening and certainly not mutually exclusive. Both consider that the motive behind the works was sympathetic magic. According to one theory, these generally realistic images of wild animals were intended to help in hunting them down; the other theory claims that the images were a magical means of guaranteeing an ever greater supply of animals to be hunted. To understand fully these animal pictures, one must keep clearly in mind that the survival of primitive man depended entirely on his success as a hunter and on a bountiful supply of game always at hand. Obviously both of these theories as to the function of the images are predicated on totemism, and we cannot rule out the possibility that totemism began long before history.

It is interesting that many of the most impressive pictures of animals were painted in the deepest recesses of the caves and could only have been executed with the greatest difficulty, probably by the light of flickering torches. From this we can infer that these painted cave interiors were the locale for religious rites whereby men propitiated the spirits they feared or worshiped with magical dances and animal sacrifices. In the cave known as Les Trois Frères in Arièges in France there is a painting of a dancing man dressed in a stag's skin, and elsewhere have been found

Upper Paleolithic figurines of fertility goddesses. These confirm our idea of the significance of the rock paintings of animals and make it probable that they were, in fact, connected with magical rites.

The quite exceptional formal beauty of many prehistoric animal pictures should not lead us astray: the powerful impression they make arises, in the first place, from the inseparable bond between their formal perfection on the one hand and their dynamic function on the other.

Egyptian Painting

The art of ancient Egypt ranks high among the greatest cultural achievements of mankind. Most astounding of all is its longevity—a life-span of some 4,000 years throughout which a fundamental unity in style was maintained intact. Three factors explain such unusual consistency. The civilization of the Nile grew up in geographical isolation (Egypt was protected from invasion on all sides by desert, mountains, or sea) and it profited from an unshakable stability in its religious and political institutions. Its state rested solidly on a polytheistic religion administered by a priestly class and on the kingship of the pharaohs, whose divinity was beyond question. To this can be added certain permanent nonhistorical factors, intangible as they may be: the sun-drenched landscape of Egypt and the artistic genius of its ancient population. From the technical and stylistic point of view, the special character of Egyptian painting lies in the fact that it employed a purely linear style: it was, in essence, an art of drawing. Most probably this is because it grew out of a prehistoric style wherein everything was rendered in silhouette; but Egyptian painting also remained closely linked with Egyptian sculptured relief, and this, by nature, tends to render all figurative themes in terms of surfaces, without concern for the illusion of depth. Old Egyptian art was completely indifferent to perspective, space, and shading, it was purely an art of surfaces. The painter working at the order of the Pharaoh, his family, high officials, or priests was not expected to depict themes as aesthetic phenomena but, instead, to set down their objective reality, their existence as things. For this a completely linear style was most apt, and the object portrayed was rendered either in full profile or in strict frontality. Thus the external aspect of the object or person depicted was in no way clouded by the illusions of spacing and depth. The aim was toward a higher objective realism, not toward a naturalism based on appearances. And yet, despite this serenely objective orientation to which Egyptian art clung for thousands of years, that art, as everyone agrees, never lacked an extraordinary aesthetic fascination, for it had the finest artistic feeling for color and line. Nothing prevented subtle changes in style from occurring between one epoch and another, but the innovations that in fact were introduced did not violate the traditional objective unity of the art. Fundamentally they were changes of a quite different kind from those we are familiar with in the evolution of art in Europe.

Painting in the Ancient Middle East

In this chapter we shall examine the art of the ancient Middle East as it arose among the various peoples whose cultures at one time or another flourished within that vast area: the Sumerians first of all, then in turn the Babylonians of the first dynasty, the Mitannians, Canaanites, early Hittites, Neo-Babylonians, the Persians under the Achaemenid dynasty, and finally the sixth-century B.C. Phrygians in Anatolia.

The earliest cultural manifestations were the creation of the Sumerians, a people neither Semitic nor Indo-European, who appeared in southern Mesopotamia in the early fourth millennium B.C. They were the first to achieve what can be called a higher culture. Because of their invention of the art of writing in cuneiform characters they were able to set down accounts of their mythological and religious beliefs, and these exercised a fundamental influence on all the other civilizations of the Middle East, including those of the Hebrews and the Greeks. The latest cultural manifestations we shall discuss here are those of the great Persian empire, for with Alexander the Great's conquest and Hellenization of half the known world, the independent existence of the ancient states of the Middle East and their separate cultures was brought to an end.

In view of the multiplicity and diversity of the ancient Middle Eastern cultures—they ranged from those of small city-states to those of immense empires—one may well ask if we have any right to speak of them as a unity. Without wishing to press the point, we must insist on the fact that the foundation which the Sumerians laid, in their invention of writing and in their religious conceptions, became the dominant influence throughout the vast area. In the more restricted realm of painting, it must be kept in mind that from the Sumerians came also a great many artistic and technical traditions such as stud-mosaics, inlay work, painted ceramics, glazed tiles, and the contour style and the color range of wall paintings. Furthermore, traditions of arts and crafts are perpetuated chiefly in two ways. First, the regional traditions of craftsmen often continue unchanged for centuries unaffected by political changes, as was probably the case with the enamel technique of the Elamites, Neo-Babylonians, and Persians; and second, from imperial centers were diffused to the outlying regions specific artistic techniques, styles, and types of representation. Thus a certain continuity in artistic production was made possible regardless of whatever political upheavals took place.

Within the vast range of time to be considered here we must distinguish between "higher" and "lower" cultures, problematic as such judgments always must be. Even within a single culture qualitative differences are so marked between what we call art and what we call crafts that we are compelled to distinguish between "court" art (which includes religious art) and "peasant" or "folk" art, the art of utility, of handiwork or, as we put it now, "applied art." Wall paintings belong to the first class, to "high art," while painted ceramics (e.g., the pot reproduced on page 38) often fall into the second. But peasant pottery is frequently of great importance to us precisely because, through the centuries, it may perpetuate in simple pictorial form the most ancient myths, such as the Tree of Life on the Canaanite Megiddo vase (page 41). However, we must remember that there is no specific folk or peasant art in epochs or civilizations that gave rise to no cultural tensions between separate social classes: this was the case, for example, in ancient Egypt, whose culture was determined and dominated by the ruling Pharaoh; and it was true also—and this is a particularly apt example—of prehistoric times. The painted ceramics made between the sixth and fourth millennia B.C. must be considered "high art," unlike the utility products turned out by artisans of later periods in the Middle East.

Minoan and Mycenaean Painting

The Mycenaean kingdom was given its classic description in the Homeric epics. There has long been general agreement that the *Iliad* and the *Odyssey* did not receive the monumental final form given them by the Ionian poet Homer until the eighth century B.C., some five hundred years after the Trojan War, which had taken place around 1250–1230 B.C. The poet idealized the Mycenaean age: for him its kings, all of them, were great heroes, and he elevated the events of its history to great tragedies of destiny, forerunners of the Attic tragedy of the fifth century B.C. And yet, despite the poet's heroic transformations, the two epics contain much that seems valid as historical evidence; these elements had been carried down through the centuries in the rhapsodic recitations of bards or through other channels of oral tradition and must, in part at least, reach back as far as the Mycenaean epoch itself. What is more, to complement the richly poetic account of what took place, certain monuments survive. Of special importance are certain contemporary written documents. The soil of Crete and the Greek mainland has delivered up a great number of clay tablets with writing in two different systems which have been named Linear A and Linear B. As yet, only the documents in Linear B have been deciphered (by

M. Ventris and J. Chadwick, in 1956). Despite many still unsolved problems of decipherment and interpretation, what they have revealed is indeed epoch-making. The language of the Linear B tablets is Greek, but the characters are apparently based on the older and still undeciphered Linear A, whose language is not Greek (Semitic? Anatolian?) and seems to have died out in the first half of the fifteenth century B.C. So far the Linear A tablets have been found on Crete only; those in Linear B have been found chiefly on the Greek mainland, in Pylos and Mycenae for the most part but also on Crete, although as yet only in Knossos. What conclusions can be drawn—with all the necessary reservations—from these and the other not inconsiderable evidence available to us? First of all, that the Mycenaean Greeks (who may have been Homer's "Achaeans") colonized part of Crete in the course of the fourteenth century B.C. and, with minor modifications, adapted the Linear A script they found there to their own language, that of Eastern Greece, thereby creating Linear B. With the Dorian migrations which occurred in a series of waves throughout the twelfth century, the Mycenaean hegemony came to an end along with the Linear B script, first on the Greek mainland and then on Crete. But if the Mycenaean language and the Mycenaeans themselves were Greek, how can one explain the fundamental difference between Mycenaean style of painting, art, and handicrafts and the Geometric style of Greece? The Greek tribes who had migrated into Greece at the beginning of the second millennium B.C. were certainly at a lower level of civilization. Their contact with the widely diffused high culture of the Minoans of the period of the "new" palaces on Crete resulted in a thoroughgoing adoption of Cretan culture from around 1600 B.C. on, as is shown above all by the many shaft tombs found in Mycenae. This cultural symbiosis lasted until the Dorian migrations around 1200 B.C. Nevertheless, Mycenaean Hellas never wholly abandoned its original characteristics which are seen most clearly in architecture (n.b. the megaron, a large royal audience hall), in burial customs, in fortifications, and above all in its unbounded enthusiasm for hunting, war, and weapons. As the power of the Minoan civilization waned in the fifteenth, sixteenth, and seventeenth centuries B.C., the latent "Helladic" elements of the Greco-Mycenaean civilization again came to the fore, and it was those elements which, in the latest Mycenaean and sub-Mycenaean ceramics, paved the way for a Proto-Geometric and Geometric style of vase painting, diametrically opposed to that of the Minoan-Mycenaean culture.

Greek Painting

It is only with circumspection that one can make generalizations about the over-all character of Greek painting since a major part—perhaps the

19

best and most significant part—of mural and panel paintings are as good as lost to us forever.

True, in vase paintings we can make out many hints of what the free style in painting must have been, but in most cases the influence of that painting was not necessarily to the good: each of the styles had its own technique and rules, and each had its great merits which had nothing to do with those of the other. Vase painting was conceived by the Greeks as inseparably combined with the form of the vase. Furthermore, according to Greek ways of thinking the image painted on a vase had to be held within the limits allowable to vase decoration. As long as vase painting was confined to a flat solid silhouette style—either in black on the natural clay background, as in the black-figure style, or in red on a black ground, as in the red-figure style—the painting remained essentially decorative. But when, under the influence of large-scale painting, the vase painters aimed at effects of depth, modeling, and polychromy, the technical and stylistic harmony between vase image and vase form was then endangered and the autonomous development of the art of vase painting became diverted into ways alien to its true nature. Such crises occurred not infrequently and were especially intense under the influence of the large-scale painting of Polygnotus in the second quarter of the fifth century B.C. (see page 62, top), and again in the fourth century B.C. (see pages 64–66). Nevertheless, armed with their native artistic discretion and instinct, Greek vase painters were able over and over again to surmount such hazards. When, however, in the latter half of the fourth century B.C. Greek vase painting had reached and, indeed, transcended its full potential, its further development at last came to an end.

The virtually single-minded consistency of Greek vase painting from its beginning to its end is truly astonishing, even unique in the entire history of art. Like Greek sculpture and architecture, this branch of art went on to new triumphs from generation to generation, from one workshop to another, from one supreme master to the next. Such continuity in development can be explained by two concrete phenomena: on the one hand, the workshop traditions carried on by potters and painters; on the other, the constant striving of the painters to surpass their predecessors and their competitors. These were, in completely realistic terms, the factors responsible for what Jacob Burckhardt in his *History of Greek Culture* termed the "agonal element," the element of rivalry, competition, and emulation. In art as in life this was a dominant trait of Greek character and was the inner mechanism which linked the Greeks' truly exceptional native aesthetic genius to a deep-rooted ambition to attain ever greater heights. The vase painter was not content to adorn his vessels with ornamental and floral designs but ranged widely for his subjects,

taking them as he willed from the mythological tales of gods and heroes or from the modest happenings of everyday life. What that signified, in actual practice, becomes clear if we keep in mind that these "pictures" were not conceived in and for themselves but, rather, as decoration for vessels intended for domestic use or to be placed in tombs. They were never meant to be illustrations of Greek life and mythology but to be objects having a normal and necessary function in the daily activities of men. But this usage endowed the subject depicted with no less importance than the aesthetic form conferred on it, that is, its style, and this must never be forgotten when considering Greek vases: Greek art was the expression of a high civilization in which content and form were in equilibrium.

As a final factor, we should not overlook the political and commercial aspects which influenced Greek vase painting. It does not suffice merely to point to the political and cultural matrix in which the art developed, that is, the changing forms of Greek institutions—from monarchy to tyranny, then to oligarchy and democracy, until at last everything gave way to Hellenistic imperialism. The city-state culture in Greece itself and in its eastern and western colonies survived throughout all these changes right up to Hellenistic times. It was only then that Greek culture became cosmopolitan and the previously diverse local cultures expanded to become the culture of the entire world. Until the latter years of the fourth century B.C., when pan-Hellenism took sway, each of the many separate city-states had its own culture, its own styles of architecture, sculpture, and painting. Many of these local styles can be made out in vase painting since that art developed along parallel lines with the other arts in Athens in the ninth and eighth centuries, under the leadership of Corinth in the seventh and the first half of the sixth centuries, and, above all, in Athens in the sixth to fourth centuries before our modern era.

Etruscan Painting

From its first appearance in the late seventh century B.C. until its assimilation centuries later into the civilization of Rome and Italy, Etruscan painting stood in a special relationship to Greek art, a relationship of tension and opposition. Its continuous dependence on Greek prototypes, from Archaic to Hellenistic times, is first explained by the fact that the Etruscans originated in Asia Minor, the region serving both to separate and link the Near East and the Greek West. Then, after they settled in central Italy, there were steady cultural and trade relations between Etruscan and Greek cities. Finally, throughout Italy there was constant contact with Greek culture and civilization. When, despite this, Etruscan art remained essentially unclassical and even "barbarian," as the Greeks must have considered it, there were good and deep-rooted reasons. What may be the most accurate hypothesis takes account of the fact that Etruscan art was founded in the Villanova culture of the Iron Age, which was dominant in central Italy. The Villanova culture was the Italian branch of the so-called Urn Field cultures, themselves part of the Hallstatt culture of the older Iron Age of central and western Europe between the tenth and fifth centuries B.C. Thus, in addition to Etruria's ties and contact with Greece, an imposing heritage from prehistoric sources was also a local component of Etruscan art. The amalgamation of that prehistoric legacy with the continuous influence of Greek culture, and with the Etruscan-Oriental tradition in its religion and cult of the dead, accounts for the extraordinary flowering of Etruscan art. For anyone concerned with Greek painting, the Etruscan tomb pictures are of the utmost importance since they can provide—in a fragmentary and transformed guise, it is true—some notion of what the lost Greek panel paintings and wall paintings must have been like.

Roman Painting

Pompeii, after having been first an Etruscan, then a Samnite settlement in early historical times, came under Hellenizing influences and finally, in 80 B.C., became a Roman colony, a seaside town of delightful villas. But in A.D. 79 the long-dormant Vesuvius erupted and buried the entire town under an enormous layer of lava, a catastrophe which had the one fortunate result of preserving it intact through the ages. Around the middle of the eighteenth century excavations began, and they are still going on. To our modern world they have offered a picture of everyday life in Roman times, complete to the most homely details, and of Pompeiian art. As might be expected, nowhere else has such a rich store of Roman wall paintings been discovered, and it has taken the combined efforts of specialists in technical and stylistic analysis to put into order the thousands of murals now known. The paintings preserved range in time from the second century B.C. to A.D. 79. Like the preceding Etruscan civilization, Roman civilization was based on Greek culture which it modified, step by step, into its own "higher" civilization. The process becomes clear as we trace from stage to stage what actually took place in the literature and painting of Rome, although this is not easy. When scholars set out to explain the wall paintings and floor mosaics produced in the Roman Empire, especially those of Pompeii, they found that in studying virtually every detail they came up against the same question: Greek or Roman—what is owing to each of these? The answers have never been simple, even when it has been a matter of a Roman copy of a painting known to be Greek. Almost without exception both elements are present, although in differing measure.

In pre-Hellenistic Greece, wall painting had served an exclusively public function and was patronized by state or religious authorities. In the Roman Empire the well-to-do private citizen took over as patron of art. Pompeii is the classic example of this: the thousands of wall paintings there uncovered were nothing more than the interior decoration of villas owned by wealthy Romans. Traditions, fashions, and personal tastes alone determined the choice of pictures, their subject matter, and their style. It took some time for scholars to recognize that the only way to understand Pompeiian frescoes was to see them as part of an ensemble—not separate pictures but simply as elements of the total decoration of a room in a villa. Only thus can one reconstruct what the patron and the artist had in mind regarding both the relationship in subject matter between one picture and another and the distribution of the pictures in the available space. This condition, as we saw earlier, is true also of prehistoric and Egyptian ensembles.

In addition to the frescoes and mosaics from the three towns at the foot of Vesuvius—Pompeii, Herculaneum, and Stabia—we shall also look at a few works from Rome itself and paintings and mosaics in Italy and the Roman provinces made later than the eruption of Vesuvius. The examples presented here—too few, alas—will at least give some idea of the significant role played by painting and mosaic in the Roman Empire. From the vast number of works of Imperial times we have also selected three Egypto-Roman mummy portraits, an interesting genre for its artistic quality and for what it reveals of how people looked in the past. Mummy portraits are also important in rounding out our knowledge of the art of portraiture under the Empire for, despite the numerous sculptured likenesses, surprisingly few painted portraits from that period have survived.

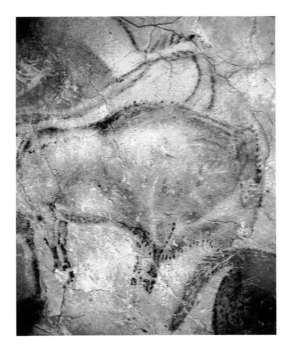

Standing Bison · Detail of a cave painting · Franco-Cantabrian, Upper Paleolithic period (High Magdalenian) · c. 13,500 B.C. · Altamira, Spain

Here a varicolored bison is surrounded by three others, whose hindparts are visible in our reproduction. The almost life-size bison is depicted in a characteristic position: it is standing, its great power concentrated in the massive upper body in contrast to the short thin legs. These varicolored images were first drawn in a fine outline, usually with a sharp flint, and then modeled in colors made from charcoal and red, yellow, and brown ocher. There is a fine balance between fidelity to nature and artistic form.

The Franco-Cantabrian cave paintings of southwest France and northern Spain date from around 13,500 B.C., that is, the late Ice Age, the high point of the reindeer-hunting culture. The now famous ceiling paintings in the caves of Altamira were discovered in 1879 by a five-year-old girl: following her father into the low-roofed cave, she noticed what a grown person obliged to stoop might easily overlook, paintings no more than five to six and three-quarters feet from the ground. The so-called Hall of Pictures, less than a hundred feet from the cave opening, contains twenty-five almost life-size polychrome pictures of animals. Farther along in the cave, whose total depth is around 885 feet, are other images of animals painted or incised on the rock walls. The cave painters exploited the irregularities of the rock surfaces to increase effects of plasticity and realism. While bison predominate among the colored or incised images of animals, there are also wild horses, does and stags, ibexes, boars, an occasional bull, and, more rarely, elk and wolves. They are scattered over the ceilings and walls with no recognizable attempt at scenographic unity. Besides these pictures of animals, the cave contains a variety of signs or symbols, such as groups of dots, club marks, ladder-like patterns; also imprints of human hands, like those found in caves elsewhere.

Cow and Small Horses · Detail of a cave painting · Franco-Cantabrian, Upper Paleolithic period (late Aurignacian-Perigordian), epoch of higher hunting culture · 15,000–10,000 B.C. · Right wall of axial gallery in the cave of Lascaux (Dordogne), France

A black cow gallops toward the left, and beneath there is a frieze of small horses. Above is the outline of a colossal head of a bull facing right.

Stags and Bulls · Detail of a cave painting · Franco-Cantabrian, Upper Paleolithic period (late Aurignacian-Perigordian), epoch of higher hunting culture · 15,000–10,000 B.C. · Left wall of the rotunda in the cave of Lascaux (Dordogne), France

Three small reddish-brown stags with immense spreading antlers gallop to the left between two colossal heads of bulls (cf. following plate). The antlers of the lower two stags are drawn in double perspective; this may be due merely to technical incapacity or, as in early Egyptian art, to an attempt to emphasize the important element of the antlers as much as possible. That approach, at the same time anti-naturalistic and realistic, is based on the desire to express a fundamental conception rather than on the attempt to capture the look of things as they are.

Bull and Cattle · Detail of a cave painting · Franco-Cantabrian, Upper Paleolithic period · 15,000–10,000 B.C. · Left wall of the rotunda in the cave at Lascaux (Dordogne), France

The large bull facing left is outlined in black, with horns in double perspective. It was drawn over earlier paintings of two reddish-brown wild cattle, much smaller in size. At the left is a group of small stags (cf. preceding plate), and above them is the head of a reddish-brown wild horse; at the upper left one sees the colossal head of a bull. Following this bull, at the right, is another bull not included in our photograph, the fourth large one in this principal hall of the cave. These four over-life-size pictures of bulls (which are as much as eighteen feet long) are executed in the same technique and style. Dominating the great hall in Lascaux, this group of images is one of the most impressive in all of prehistoric art.

Wounded Bison, Man, and Rhinoceros · Detail of a cave painting · Franco-Cantabrian, earliest Upper Paleolithic period. Lower gallery ("well") at lower end of the "apse" shaft in the cave at Lascaux (Dordogne), France

Here is a bison drawn in blackish-red outlines, horns lowered as if in attack, tail raised, mane bristling. A long barbed spear pierces him through, and his entrails burst out of his wounded flank. Outlined in red in front of the bison lies an ithyphallic man with a birdlike head, his arms and hands (four-fingered) stretched out. Below him lies a short barbed spear, and a barbed staff capped by a bird. On the left a rhinoceros facing left is likewise drawn in blackish-red outline.

The cave in Lascaux, which was discovered in 1940, lies above the valley of the Vézère near Montignac in the department of Dordogne in southwest France. Of all the Franco-Cantabrian caves, Lascaux and Altamira are certainly the most famous. The relationships in chronology, composition, and context among these images of animals have not yet been made clear, and they are obviously not uniform in technique or style. Nor are we sure of their significance. In any case, the Lascaux paintings cannot date from too far back in the long span covered by Franco-Cantabrian cave paintings, which ranges from 40,000 to 9000 B.C.

Doe, Stag, and Wild Goats · Detail of a cave painting · Mesolithic (in Europe, 10/9000–3000 B.C.) or Neolithic period (in Europe, 3000–1800 B.C.) · Second niche of a cave at Cuevas de la Araña (Province of Valencia), Spain

From top to bottom there are a running doe, a stag, and wild goats in flight. These reddish-brown silhouettes of animals do not have the feeling for movement and dynamic form and color of the Franco-Cantabrian paintings. Whereas the dominant role in cave paintings of the Franco-Cantabrian region is reserved for animals, in the caves of the Spanish Levant it is taken by man as hunter, warrior, and dancer, and the chief theme is the hunt. The date of the Spanish paintings is uncertain, but the evidence for placing them after the Ice Age includes the fact that, in contrast with the Franco-Cantabrian paintings of the Paleolithic Ice Age, they portray animals which may have survived after the great wave of cold had passed, among them red deer, fallow deer, elk, chamois, boars, wild goats, cattle, and horses.

23

Masked Negroid Woman · "Period of the Roundheaded Men" · Probably later than the early Neolithic period · Rock painting (modern copy) · Height, c. 27½" · Sefar, eastern Tassili massif, central Sahara Desert, Algeria

The woman wears ornaments below her knees and around her ankles and arms, and her only garment is a sash hanging from the waist to the knees. The object she holds with both hands may be some sort of vessel. Her round head and brown body color characterize the figure as Negroid, and this is both the earliest known depiction of a Negro and the earliest example of Negro art. The Negro art of the so-called Roundheaded Men began most likely in the second period of the late Neolithic, as outlined below, and seems to have been carried on over many thousands of years. The dating of the present painting is uncertain, but it seems to come from after the Bubalu period and therefore must be later than the early Neolithic. The central Sahara rock pictures fall into four periods. The first, named after the bubalu, a long-extinct species of buffalo, was most probably Neolithic but still within the Paleolithic tradition. Since the rhinoceros, hippopotamus, and buffalo are frequent in these pictures, the Sahara at that time must have been a well-watered, fertile, and densely populated region. The second period, that of the cattle herders, lasted from the fourth to the second millennium B.C., and the animals depicted are the same as in the earlier period. Along with hunting, however, men also engaged in agriculture and cattle breeding. The third period was that of the horse, at first as a beast of burden, then as a mount. It is in that period that we have pictures of warriors with Lybian feather headdresses, as in the preceding example, and this is when the thick-skinned race disappeared. Lastly there was the period of the camel, when the drying-up of the Sahara led to the horse's being replaced by the camel in Republican Roman times.

Running Warrior · "Period of the Horse" · Late 2nd millennium B.C.? · Rock engraving · Height, 17⅞" · Wadi Djerat in the Tassili massif, central Sahara Desert, Algeria

The silhouetted running warrior shooting his bow has three feathers on his head, like the Lybian warriors in Egyptian pictures. He wears a long loincloth girded at the waist and falling halfway down the thigh. The engraving technique used both for contours and surfaces recalls that of the so-called sunk reliefs of Egypt. The region of the Tassili massif where this was found stretches over some eighteen miles, and in it have been uncovered more than 4,000 rock engravings from various epochs.

Giraffes, Men, and Demons · Detail from a rock painting · Date uncertain, probably end of Bushman period of art · Cave of Silozwane in the Matapos, Southern Rhodesia, Africa

In these painted silhouettes of men and animals, some of whom are varicolored, the larger human figures are almost life-size. Depicted are two giraffes facing in opposite directions, and surrounded by human figures bearing burdens. In the right foreground is a tent. Above, from left to right, are two tall nude warriors with spears, then a white figure which has been interpreted as a masked demon, and finally a figure lying down. Below are many tiny men and animals of which some belong to several different strata of painting. The meaning of the picture has not yet been ascertained. It may record how a dark-skinned race, Negroid or Ethiopian, crowded the non-Negroid Bushmen out of their hunting lands in southeastern Africa and drove them into the desert-like Kalahari region of South Africa. According to Arabian sources, it appears that as recently as about a thousand years ago the Bushmen still inhabited South Africa as far north as the Zambesi River.

Dancer · From a wall painting · South Anatolian Early Neolithic Culture · c. 6000 B.C. · From the temple in Level III of Catal Hüyük, Turkey

The male figure, a monochromatic silhouette, wears a cap of leopardskin and around his hips a leopard pelt which swirls out as he dances. In his left hand he has a bow, in his right what may be a club. The gently fleeing figure is a detail from a wall painting which has a great many male figures likewise in monochromatic silhouette and, for the most part, in similar energetic movement. The figures are distributed through three zones and were painted at different times. It has been proposed that what is portrayed is a ceremonial dance, a hypothesis perhaps supported by the fact that in the same room there are pictures of a deer and a large bull. These wall frescoes were discovered in 1961 in a temple of the Early Neolithic period, that is, from around 6000 B.C. and in part even earlier. They are the earliest known paintings on the walls of a building, but much in them suggests that they are still related to prehistoric cave paintings.

Earthenware bowl with antelope design, from Hassuna near Mosul, Iraq · Samarra Culture · c. 5000 B.C. · Height, $3\frac{3}{8}''$; diameter, $9\frac{3}{4}''$ · Iraq Museum, Baghdad

The decoration inside the bowl consists of four geometrically stylized antelopes with wavy horns painted in reddish-brown monochrome on a light ground, and geometric designs on the rim, both outside and inside. Three pairs of holes bored through on either side of a crack are evidence that the vessel was broken and repaired at a time when it was still in use. The bowl belongs to a very early type of monochromatic painted pottery from northeastern Mesopotamia, the so-called Samarra ware, which is characterized by the decoration of the inside of the vessel with highly stylized human or animal figures in a rhythmic, usually twisting composition designed to follow the curve of the bowl. Samarra ware is among the first pottery types to have figurative decoration.

Flat earthenware vessel with geometrical designs on inner surface, from Arpachiyah · Halaf Culture of northern Mesopotamia · First half of 5th millennium B.C.

In the course of the fifth millennium, northwestern Mesopotamia developed an especially rich polychromatic ceramic style known as Tell Halaf ware. A good example of it is this thin-walled flat vessel decorated with a finely articulated rosette of leaves in the center, surrounded by geometrical and floral patterns. Such designs are obviously related to those used for textiles. The effect of a light shiny glaze was achieved by polishing the vessel after firing.

Painted bowl, from Chesm-i Ali near Teheran, Iran · Sialk II
period · c. 4000 B.C. · Diameter, 5″; height, 1¾″ · Metropolitan
Museum of Art, New York

The bowl is decorated inside with concentric circles
representing stylized ibex horns. It belongs to a type of
pottery named after one of the principal sites where ancient
Iranian ceramics have been found, Tepe Sialk, which lies
between Teheran and Isfahan.

Painted double-conical vessel, from Chesm-i Ali, near
Teheran, Iran · Sialk II period · Late 5th millennium B.C. ·
Archaeological Museum, Teheran

This almost spherical vessel has rows of zigzag motifs
grouped in separate fields. Like the preceding bowl, it is in
Sialk ware. Four principal phases of Sialk ware have been
distinguished: Period I (early fifth millennium B.C.), handmade pottery with crude geometrical ornamentation;
Period II (late fifth millennium), also handmade but with
various decorative motifs, either geometrical or combined
geometrical and animal; Period III (fourth millennium),
animals in friezes and fields, and the first depictions of
human figures in silhouette. The potter's wheel was introduced during that period and made possible more rapid
production as well as more precise forms with angular
profiles. Period IV (early third millennium) was marked by
the decadence of painted Sialk ware.

Bowl with geometrical designs, from Hacilar (Level I),
southwest Anatolia · Late Chalcolithic period · Late 4th
millennium B.C. · Museum, Ankara

This bowl with a steep, almost vertical rim is decorated on
its inner surface with geometrical patterns painted in
reddish-brown on a yellow ground in such a way that the
design can be "read" as reddish-brown on yellow or as
yellow on reddish-brown. The connection with wickerwork
which has been proposed has much justification. Of special
interest is the centrifugal composition built around a sharp-
angled rhomboid in the center, a motif typical of this type of
pottery; it is also reminiscent of the designs on Samarra
ware, except that in the latter the movement tends to be
twisted (see bowl with antelope design, page 25). This bowl
comes from the deepest and therefore earliest stratum of the
diggings in Hacilar.

High beaker with stylized animal patterns, from Susa, Iran · Susa A ware · c. 3500 B.C. · Archaeological Museum, Teheran

This thin-walled tall beaker is decorated with highly stylized motifs in monochrome brown. In the principal field there is a geometrically stylized ibex whose exaggeratedly long horns sweep up, back, and around to form a most effective circular frame for the enclosed geometrical design. The zone below the rim has a frieze of extremely stylized long-necked water fowl. It is difficult to say which is more admirable, the elegant shape of the beaker, the sure-handed laying-out of the ornamental motifs on its surfaces, or the sophisticated stylization of its quasi-abstract designs based on animal forms. Certainly patterns like this must be related to textiles. Innumerable such vessels were found in the more than 2,000 graves of the cemetery outside the walls of the Elamite capital Susa, and this type of pottery has been named Susa A, the first of four phases reaching from the fourth to the third millennium B.C. Such refinement of style in pottery tells us that Susa must have attained a high level of civilization in the fourth millennium.

Conical beaker, from Tall-i Bakun, Iran · c. 3500 B.C. · Diameter, 9⅞″; height, 9⅝″ · Archaeological Museum, Teheran

Here the monochromatic blackish decoration comprises geometrical forms filled with latticework, enclosed within upright or inverted sweeping curves which resemble garlands but are in fact, as we know from other vessels of this type, stylized abstractions of ibex horns. The classification to which this conical vessel belongs is therefore closely related to the Susa A ware shown above without however attaining the same high quality. The bowl was found in Tall-i Bakun, a large burial ground in the region of Persepolis.

Stemmed goblet, from Tepe Hissar (Damghan), northeast Iran · Hissar III period · c. 3500 B.C. · Diameter, 6″; height, 6¾″. University Museum, Philadelphia

The monochromatic decoration is made up of a blackish-brown frieze of leopards and a black-hatched zigzag band. The goblet comes from a site southeast of the Caspian Sea in Iran.

Head of a man, from Jericho, Jordan · Unbaked clay, about two-thirds life-size · c. 6000 B.C. · Palestine Archaeological Museum, Jerusalem, Jordan

In this head from a statue of a man the eyes are made of pieces of sea shell, and the hair and beard are painted in reddish-brown on a gray to clay-colored plaster undercoating. The unnatural flatness of the head shows that it was intended to be seen from the front only. Along with the head were found arms and legs which made possible the approximate reconstructions of this and other statues. There appear to have been two groups of three statues each, made up in both cases of a man, woman and child; it is not known if these figures represent gods or human beings. Coming from a period before baked-earthenware pottery was made in that region, these very unusual statues were built up in unbaked clay over a kind of armature of reeds. At the time they were made Jericho was already a small city, one of the oldest on earth, and in the Neolithic pre-ceramic stratum where this head was found there is also an edifice more or less like a *megaron*—a chief's house or primitive palace—which has quite rightly been identified as a temple.

Polychrome wall painting (detail), from a house in Teleilat Ghassul, valley of the Jordan River, Jordan · Chalcolithic epoch · Second half of 4th millennium B.C. · Modern reconstruction drawing · Istituto Biblico, Rome

Between 1929 and 1938 a Chalcolithic settlement was uncovered at Teleilat Ghassul in the Jordan valley southeast of Jericho. From it much information was gained as to the Near Eastern culture of the latter half of the fourth millennium. In many of the ruins of dwellings polychromatic wall paintings were found, among them the present example made up of a massive eight-pointed star surrounded by dragonlike animals, figures which may be human, masks, and a few geometrical designs. All of them were painted in strong colors: black and gray, light and dark red, yellow-brown and white. Many questions arise: is the star evidence of star worship? did the group of houses with wall paintings have some religious function? These and other questions suggested by the remains of this early urban civilization in the region between Egypt and Mesopotamia still await solution. Because of the poor state of preservation of the original, the reproduction here is a reconstruction.

Fragment of an ossuary with painted and modeled decoration, from Azor, Israel · Chalcolithic epoch · Second half of 4th millennium B.C. · Archaeological Museum, Jerusalem, Israel

A hundred or more earthenware ossuaries in the shape of houses have been found in graves of the Chalcolithic epoch in Azor, south of Tel Aviv. Most are in fragments, and the majority are painted and, in some cases, also have modeled decoration. Our fragment of such a house-shaped coffer for bones represents the pediment over the opening (note at the lower left the vestige of the doorjamb). House-shaped though it be it also has, oddly enough, a prominent projection clearly intended to be a nose since on either side there is a painted eye. Around these features there is a geometrical pattern which may be a stylization of palmetto leaves. It is not certain if this stylized face is to be interpreted as human or animal, though it is probably an eagle-owl. Be that as it may, it is obvious that the decoration of this ossuary must be understood as apotropaic, and is therefore "figurative" or "representational" in the modern sense.

Narrow-necked conical clay urn, from Burial Mound I, Gemeinlebarn, Lower Austria · Late Hallstatt period · c. 550–400 B.C. · Natural History Museum, Vienna

The urn is richly ornamented both with painted patterns and with small molded clay figurines set around its circumference. Such elaborate decoration tells us that the vessel was certainly not intended for domestic uses but, instead, for a higher purpose. It is, in fact, an urn for ashes and was found in the burial mound of a personage of high rank. This remarkable example from Lower Austria belongs to a southeastern European civilization called the Hallstatt Culture, after a center of Iron Age civilization in the Salzkammergut; the Hallstatt Culture flourished from around 900 to around 400 B.C. and, because of its salt mines, had commercial relations with the Mediterranean regions, especially northern Italy, Greece, and Anatolia. Influences from outside the area were grafted on to the local agricultural and hunting culture which itself continued to carry on its prehistoric tradition. Ethnographically the Hallstatt period's population was probably made up of Illyrians, Venetii, and Celts, and its culture was widely diffused into the northern Balkans, Hungary, Lower Austria, and all of the Alps; it extended as far north as Alsace and Burgundy, and as far south as northern Italy, especially around the Adriatic. This urn itself is in every respect extraordinary: in form it has a markedly protuberant central zone and a strongly emphasized conical neck and rim; and in decoration, especially the figurines disposed around the middle—a deer hunt with riders—and around the rim, where there is a circle of tiny birds. All of these elements suggest a prototype of metal rather than pottery. From the character of the figurines it is easy to deduce that the dead man whose ashes the urn contained was a hunter and certainly not a humble peasant.

Amphora, from the megaron in Dimini, Thessalia, central Greece · Sub-Neolithic epoch · First half of 3rd millennium B.C. · National Museum, Athens

This two-handled earthenware amphora is handmade and painted with blackish-brown and reddish-brown rectilinear and round patterns, mostly ribbons and spirals whose twisting movement follows the form of the rounded upper part of the vessel. One's first impression of the decoration as haphazard and disorganized changes on further acquaintance. It is true that straight lines and curves are freely combined, but they all serve the purpose of harmonizing with the three-dimensional form of the vessel. What is surprising is that this "organic" principle of decoration is not found as often as might be expected. Generally the painter of pottery sought to use ornamental patterns or images to discipline, so to speak, the form of the vessel; he therefore relied on horizontal friezes, ribbonlike compositions, or even well-defined picture areas (as in Greek vases) in order to convert the curved volumes of the vessel into a two-dimensional pictorial surface. The distribution of decoration on the present vase is, in principle, a more natural solution than that found in the more familiar types. This variety of pottery is called Dimini Style, after the site where it was first discovered, a locality in Thessalia on the Greek mainland; its principal patterns are bands and spirals reduced to their linear components. The amphora here reproduced was found in the megaron—the chief's house—in the hill citadel of Dimini itself.

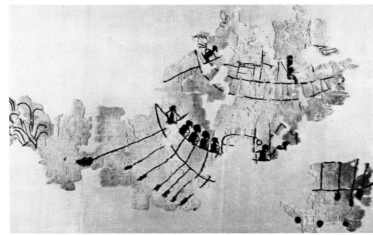

Hippopotamus Hunt · Fragment, from the burial ground at Gebelein, near Luxor and Thebes in Upper Egypt · Pre-Dynastic period · 4th millennium B.C. · Painting on linen · Height, c. 30⅜″ · Egyptian Museum, Turin

On this fragment of the oldest surviving textile painting, on a strip of brown linen, we see two barges of identical form, each with a double cabin in the middle and with a helmsman at the left using a long steering pole. The boats are drawn in outline, the figures in silhouette. In the upper and smaller boat there are only two figures, but the larger one below is fully manned by oarsmen. To the far left there is an area with vegetation typical of the Nile that serves as a kind of landscape setting. Obviously the boats should not be thought of as one above the other, but as alongside or near each other. The indifference to perspective that is characteristic of all Egyptian art is already manifest in this pre-Dynastic work, suggesting that this fundamental stylistic element was taken over from primitive prehistoric art. It was maintained unchanged until Egyptian art itself declined.

29

Royal Family. Old Kingdom, late Fourth Dynasty ·
c. 2613–2494 B.C. · Painted low relief · Tomb of Princess
Meresankh III, Giza

This painted low relief on the left wall of the entrance to the
tomb of Princess Meresankh III portrays the princess
between her mother Princess Hetep-heres II, who wears a
blond wig, and her son Prince Neb-em-akhet; behind the
prince, vertically disposed, are the other members of the
family, and in addition there are two small children to the
left of the princess. Translated into modern terms, we have
here a picture of the princess' intimate family. The Pharaohs,
to whom she and her mother were married, are conspicuous
by their absence; when we add to this the fact that the
princess was buried in her own separate tomb, we can
deduce the high place occupied by women in the earliest
times in Egypt. From the standpoint of art, this polychrome
family portrait is typical of the Old Kingdom in its combination of relief and wall painting, a combination anticipated in certain prehistoric rock pictures but achieving its
first and, so to speak, classical formulation in the early art
of Egypt.

Princess Meresankh III · Detail of the preceding plate

The black-haired princess wears a leopardskin (note the
leopard's head on her upper thigh) and two necklaces; she
holds the royal fly whisk as an emblem of authority (her
mother is likewise shown with the fly whisk in her hands
crossed over her breast). Princess Meresankh III was the
grandniece of the founder of the dynasty, Pharaoh Sneferu;
the niece of the Pharaoh Cheops who built the great pyramid
in Giza; the daughter of the Crown Prince Ka-wab, who
died young; and the consort of the Pharaoh Chephren,
whose pyramid in Giza is only slightly smaller than that of
Cheops and who had the great Sphinx, the watcher of the
pyramid temple, hewn out of rock. But despite her great
distinction, the princess gives precedence to her mother,
the widow of Crown Prince Ka-wab and later the consort of
Pharaoh Radedef.

Prince Rahotep and His Consort Nofret · From the tomb of the
Prince in Medum · Old Kingdom, early Fourth Dynasty ·
c. 2613–2494 B.C. · Painted limestone statues · Height, $47\frac{1}{4}''$ ·
Museum, Cairo

Among the most significant achievements of the Old
Kingdom is this pair of painted limestone portrait statues
found in the tomb of Prince Rahotep ("Worshiper of the
Sun"), apparently the son of Sneferu, founder of the dynasty.
He is portrayed along with his consort Nofret ("The
Beautiful" or "The Good"). Here the art of characterization
is truly extraordinary: color, anatomy, and expression all
combine toward that end. The dark-skinned prince, wearing
only a loincloth, is robust in physique with athletic shoulders,
arms, and legs. He is in marked contrast to the pale fine-bred
princess, whose voluptuous figure is emphasized by her
close-fitting white garment. His masculine strength is
further expressed by his hands rolled into fists, while she
holds her delicately articulated right hand flat across her
chest. A narrow band from which hangs an amulet encircles
the prince's thick-set neck; a broad collar covers hers, and as
further ornament she wears over her black wig a circlet
studded with flowers and rosettes. Especially lifelike are the
eyes, which are insets of pale rock crystal made even more
prominent by black outlining and by the dark eyebrows,
likewise inset. Strikingly realistic as these effects are, other
features are still archaic: the figures are sculpturally heavy,
and the heads, torsos, arms, and legs are rigid and taut.

Men Bearing Offerings (detail) · Old Kingdom, Sixth Dynasty · c. 2345–2181 B.C. · Painted limestone relief frieze · Tomb of Mehu, Saqqara

Each man leads an animal—from right to left a calf, a goat, and a gazelle—and each has both hands full of offerings. The one at the far right carries a live goose and a basket of fish, and the others carry fowl (dead or alive), baskets of fish, fruit, jars of honey or figs, or, in the case of the second man from the right, lotus flowers. The name of each man is given in hieroglyphs. The tawny-skinned black-haired bearers, with their almost white loincloths and gifts, stand out sharply against the darker background, and it should be noted how small are the animals in proportion to the men. The meaning of such a scene as the decoration of a tomb is perfectly clear: this is the nourishment which the dead man will consume throughout eternity, for the dead must lack for nothing if they are to rest in peace.

Portrait of a Judge · From the chapel of Mehu the Judge, in Giza · Old Kingdom, late Fifth Dynasty · c. 2494–2345 B.C. · Fragment of a painted relief · Museum of Fine Arts, Boston

This fragment was originally part of a large painted polychrome wall relief in the chapel of Mehu the Judge (not to be confused with the tomb of Mehu in Saqqara, in our preceding example). The entire relief depicted a fishing scene in the marshes, a frequent theme in tomb murals because it guaranteed that the deceased would continue his favorite sport in the other world. In Egypt fish were speared with a harpoon, and the man here holds one at shoulder-height. Part of the hieroglyphic inscription that has survived explains the meaning of the scene; another part gives the name of the deceased, who was the oldest of the judges and the secretary of the privy council in the great court of judgment, as well as a priest of Maât, the goddess of Truth. The judge is portrayed here with his ceremonial wig, a wide ornamental collar, and the short close-cropped beard which was the distinguishing mark of eminent personages.

Fishermen Setting Out a Net · Old Kingdom, Sixth Dynasty · c. 2345–2181 B.C. · Part of a painted relief · Tomb of Ptahiruka, Saqqara

On this section of a polychrome painted relief there are two distinct zones: the lower contains a hieroglyphic inscription, the upper has scenes of setting out a net and of fishing. Wall paintings in tombs of this period depict all the various activities the deceased might wish to continue in afterlife.

Portrait of Neferti-abet · From the royal burial ground in Giza · Old Kingdom, Fourth Dynasty · c. 2613–2494 B.C. · Painted limestone slab · The Louvre, Paris

The dead Princess Neferti-abet is portrayed seated on a backless, lion-legged stool. She wears a ceremonial wig and a close-fitting leopardskin dress which leaves her right shoulder bare. Before her are offerings of food: on the table are sliced loaves of bread set up on end; under the table are heads of a goose, ox, and antelope, along with a drinking vessel and other objects. Close to her head is a vase for libations. At first such offerings of food for the deceased were actually placed in the tomb, but later were simply painted and an inventory written out. Thus in the rectangle filling the upper right area there is an inventory, in hieroglyphs, of all the offerings intended to accompany the dead princess into the other world. This simple but clear and colorful picture of a typical princess—certainly not a portrait in the modern sense—dates from the time of Cheops, Chephren, and Mycerinus, the great builders of the pyramids at Giza.

Sacrifice of a Bull · Detail of a wall painting · First Intermediate Period, Seventh to Tenth Dynasties · c. 2258–2040 B.C. · Tomb of Ataker in Gebelein, near Luxor and Thebes, Upper Egypt

This wall painting is divided into two sections by a painted frame of black strips whose horizontals serve also as bases for the two scenes. In the upper field we see the sarcophagus of the deceased which was probably carved from a tree trunk according to the practice in the Middle Kingdom. It is painted yellow, with a horizontal white stripe through the middle which has pictographs appealing to the good will of the jackal-god Anubis, patron of mummification and protector of burial grounds. At the right, below this stripe, are two eyes, the "unmoving eyes of Horus" which were called "udjat": the dead man, whose head rested at that end of the sarcophagus, was supposed to be able to observe everything going on around him through these painted eyes. In the lower field is depicted the sacrifice of a bull in honor of the dead man. The black-spotted white bull has been thrown on its back and its four legs are bound together and held by a servant, while a second servant slits the bull's neck with a flint knife and lets the blood pour out on the ground.

Prince Sirenpowet II and His Son · Wall painting · Twelfth Dynasty · 1991–1786 B.C. · Rock tomb of Sirenpowet II in Aswan

Prince Sirenpowet II was a contemporary of Pharaoh Amenemhat II who reigned from 1929 to 1895 B.C. The dead man sits on a lion-legged stool, his left hand reaching out to a table heaped with food of which can be made out clusters of grapes, a goose covered by a palm branch, the thigh of an ox, and a calf's head, along with small loaves of bread. In front of the table is a low stand with four drinking vessels. At the right we see the prince's son bringing three lotus blossoms to his dead father. The name of the reigning Pharaoh is within a cartouche in the accompanying inscription, which also praises the prince's son. The picture is framed by a decorative painted pattern and occupies a prominent position in the rock tomb, a niche at the end of the long entrance corridor where it is visible from far off. To the left and right of this painting are two others, one with the dead man and his mother and another in which he is accompanied by his son and wife.

Fishing and Bird Hunting · Fragment of a wall painting · Middle Kingdom, Twelfth Dynasty · 1991–1786 B.C. · Tomb of Antefoker in Thebes

This painting depicting scenes from the daily life of the dead man includes this view of fishermen; in what is obviously a happy mood, they draw in with animated gestures a net full of fish. Below them is a second net, a draw-net fixed fast and pulled taut, in which flutter all sorts of marsh birds including wild ducks, geese, ibis, and flamingos. The rope holding this net is clasped on the right by three men (not included in this reproduction). From the inscription above the scene we learn the titles of the deceased: "Prince, chancellor of the northern region, sole friend of the king, grandee of the king of the north. . . . "

Sacred Asps and an Inscription · Detail of a painted relief frieze · New Kingdom, Eighteenth Dynasty · c. 1490 B.C. · Funerary temple of Queen Hatshepsut, Deir el-Bahari, near Thebes

In the funerary chapel of Thutmose I (1525– c. 1512 B.C.) there is a wall painting which was damaged during the reign of Thutmose III. It depicts Queen Hatshepsut (1503–1482 B.C.) bringing an offering to the vulture-headed god Sokaris, who is described in the inscription as "Sokaris, great god, lord of the secret place. . . " The significance of the painting is made clearer by the painted relief frieze above it, which is illustrated here. Over the inscription runs a horizontal band decorated with yellow stars symbolizing the heavens, and this band is topped by an ornamental framing border showing a frieze of sacred asps. Each wears on its head the horns of the cow-goddess Hathor with a red solar disk between them. Separating the asps are, alternately, the cruciform sign of Ankh, symbol of life, and the sign of Djed, symbol of permanence. Combined, these hieroglyphs give the name Queen Hatshepsut. The funerary chapel of Thutmose I is in the upper terrace of the funerary temple of his daughter Hatshepsut in the Theban necropolis of Deir el-Bahari, which was built at the order of Queen Hatshepsut by her chancellor Senmut around 1490 B.C.

Ramesses I between the Gods Horus and Anubis · Detail of a wall painting · New Kingdom, Nineteenth Dynasty · c. 1312 B.C. · Tomb of Ramesses I, Valley of the Kings, near Thebes

In the middle stands the dead Pharaoh Ramesses I (1314–1312 B.C.). He is welcomed with expressive gestures by the two gods and addressed in "the word of Anubis Imi-ut." "Imi-ut" is one of the titles of the jackal-headed Anubis, the god who presides over the preparation of the mummy and usually appears with Osiris in the judgment hall of the realm of the dead. The hawk-headed god to the left is Horus, son of Osiris and Isis: "the word of Horus, son of Isis, great god, lord of the highlands, protector of the son of both lands under Osiris." King and gods alike wear the usual loincloth and a pectoral ornament around the neck. Horus wears the double-crown symbolizing the union of Upper and Lower Egypt. As a pictorial theme the judgment of the dead was a creation of the New Kingdom although the idea itself was already current in the Old Kingdom.

Most of the great edifices in Thebes belong to the Nineteenth and Twentieth Dynasties, and the great architectural accomplishments of that epoch began under Ramesses I, the first ruler of the Nineteenth Dynasty, which endured from 1314 to 1200 B.C.

Celebration for the Dead in the Other World · Detail of a wall painting · New Kingdom, Eighteenth Dynasty 1567–1320 B.C. · Tomb of Rekhmere, Thebes

In three friezes are portrayed the celebrations for the dead in the afterworld as depicted in the tomb of Rekhmere, a high dignitary under Thutmose III (1504–1450 B.C.) and Amenhotep II (1450–1425 B.C.). The two upper friezes contain only white-clad women, the lower frieze men whose reddish-brown body coloring contrasts with that of the women above. The middle frieze, here illustrated, is devoted to music and dance. At the right two maidens kneel on a mat, observing the scene while breathing in the perfume of lotus blossoms. In front of them two girls beat time with their hands for a dancer who holds a hand-drum, her body moving gracefully to the music of the girls at the left who play harp and lute. The inscription tells us what the three musicians are singing. The first sings "Spread balsam on the hair of Maât [the goddess of Truth and Justice who weighs the souls of the dead] for health and life are with her"; the second, "O Amon [the dominant god of the New Kingdom], the sky is lifted up for thee, the ground trod for thee, Ptah [the death-god of Memphis] erects with his two hands a chapel as a resting place for thee"; and the third, "Come, O North Wind, I saw thee when thou wert in thy tower."

Musicians at the Celebrations for the Dead in the Other World · Detail of a wall painting · New Kingdom, Eighteenth Dynasty · 1567–1320 B.C. · Tomb of Nakht, Thebes

In this second detail from the tomb of Nakht, a graceful trio of musicians play the harp, lute, and double-oboe. Like the young maidservant in the frieze above, the girl in the middle is almost nude. Her head turns back to the oboe player behind her as if in a sudden movement, and as a consequence her upper body is twisted forward. Quite unexpectedly the painter did not hesitate to depict this double movement combining the frontal position with the profile head and legs, which is completely unconventional in Egyptian art. In many ways the Eighteenth Dynasty was marked by a certain relaxation in the traditional Egyptian stylistic principles. This new freedom reached its high point some fifty to sixty years later in the art of Amarna (see page 36) although it never really broke the bonds of the archaic style that ruled so long in Egypt (unlike Greece, where a new classical style replaced the archaic in the fifth century B.C.). Various circumstances led to this change in Egyptian art, among them the urbane refinement of the new royal residence and metropolis of Thebes, and also the imperial character of Eighteenth-Dynasty Egypt beginning with Thutmose III. To these must be added the extraordinary encouragement given to art and architecture by the Pharaohs beginning with Queen Hatshepsut, and, finally, the more rationalistic and realistic spirit of the age.

Court Ladies at the Celebrations for the Dead in the Other World · Detail of a wall painting · New Kingdom, Eighteenth Dynasty · 1567–1320 B.C. · Tomb of Nakht, Thebes

This and the next example are from the wall paintings in the tomb of Nakht, a priest of the Theban Amon and court official under Amenhotep II (1450–1425 B.C.). Here six elegantly dressed young women in a comfortable kneeling position listen to the music of a blind harp player (not included here). Those at the right indulge their other senses, breathing in the perfume of flowers and fruits (tomatoes, more elegantly known as "love-apples"). Meanwhile an almost nude girl, smaller in scale, adjusts the earrings of the three women at the left.

Woman Dressing · Detail from a wall painting · New Kingdom, Eighteenth Dynasty · 1567–1320 B.C. · Tomb of Djeser-ka-rê-seneb, Thebes

Djeser-ka-rê-seneb, from whose tomb this picture comes, was an administrative official of the granary under Pharaoh Thutmose IV (1425–1417 B.C.). Here we see two maids adorning a court lady in preparation for the festivities for the dead in the other world. She sits on a low lion-legged chair with a backrest. One maid arranges the strands of her mistress's hair, the other brings a wreath of flowers in her right hand, a lotus in her left. All three, lady and maids alike, wear around their straight black hair a circlet with a flower, and on top of their heads is a cone filled with scented oil of myrrh. All, but especially the lady, wear ornaments in their ears and around the neck and arms. On the left, vine tendrils coil down over large jars set on openwork stands, each jar bearing the cruciform sign for Life (Ankh).

Wailing Women in a Funeral Procession · Detail from a wall painting · New Kingdom, Eighteenth Dynasty · c. 1370 B.C. · Tomb of Ramose, Thebes

Ramose was a minister under the Pharaohs Amenhotep III and Amenhotep IV (Akhenaten). With cries of lamentation, arms and hands stretching upward in grief, hair hanging, breasts bared, cheeks streaked with tears, the women mourners (among whom there is a naked child) fulfill their sorrowful task. There is highly effective contrast in color and movement between the steady tranquil pace of the men on the left who carry the sarcophagus (not included here) and the vibrating restless gestures of the black-haired mourning women in their long white draperies. Many other aspects of Ramose's funeral procession are recorded in wall paintings in his tomb. He seems to have died during the first years of the reign of Amenhotep IV (1379–1362 B.C.), which would explain why the tomb was left unfinished, for the new Pharaoh shortly transferred his court from Thebes to Tell el-Amarna.

A Garden · Detail of a wall painting · New Kingdom, Eighteenth Dynasty · 1567–1320 B.C. · Tomb of Minnakht, Thebes

This wall painting from the tomb of Minnakht, overseer of the granaries of Upper and Lower Egypt under Thutmose III (1504–1450 B.C.), gives us a good idea of the conventions employed by Egyptian artists. Here we see the garden of the dead man. There is a small pavilion on the left, and a rectangular artificial pond on which floats a sailboat with a cabin and a single sailor aboard. To either side of the pond are shade trees and palms. In the center of the picture a staircase bordered by tall vases planted with creepers leads up to a small group of buildings on the right.
Egyptian painters of the past represented only two dimensions, the third—depth—being virtually nonexistent in their art. Because of this, they flattened out, as it were, into a single plane all three-demensional objects in their drawing or painting on flat surfaces. Thus trees, boats, figures, and the like were of necessity rendered in full profile: in the present picture are combined an aerial view of a ground plan and profile or side views of persons and things. Any suggestions of perspective are studiously avoided in order to depict each object with the fullest possible clarity.

Wild Duck in the Marshes · Plaque from the floor of the palace in Tell el-Amarna · New Kingdom, Eighteenth Dynasty · 1567–1320 B.C. · Tempera on stucco. Museum, Cairo

This stucco plaque painted in tempera comes from the floor of the palace of Amenhotep IV-Akhenaten (1379–1362 B.C.). Its depiction of a wild duck starting up from a marsh thicket of bulrushes and lotus plants seems to contradict the description of Egyptian painting just above. Instead of a neatly laid-out, rigorously objective manner of representation, here we have a style which at first glance seems to deserve the term "impressionist." How to explain this? It may be that this entirely unexpected conception with its strong feeling for nature was connected with the spirit of what is called the Amarna Culture, itself a product of the deeper revolution that took place under Akhenaten when he brought into being a new solar religion. The sculptors and painters who decorated the temple of the Sun in Karnak, and the palaces in Tell el-Amarna, abandoned the traditional Egyptian ideal of beauty and returned to nature as a guide, seeking to pin down what was ephemeral, accidental, and individual even when it might be ugly, as might be said, in fact, of many portraits of the Pharaoh and the royal family.

A Princely Couple · Painted relief plaque in stone (soapstone?), from Tell el-Amarna · New Kingdom, Eighteenth Dynasty, period of Akhenaten · 1379–1362 B.C. · State Museums, Berlin-Dahlem

This princely pair was once believed to be Pharoah Akhenaten and his consort Nofretete, but is now thought to be another couple from his court, chiefly because Nofretete in her portraits usually wears the high headdress we see in the next example. Recent studies suggest that the persons pictured may be Prince Smenkh-ka-râ, Akhenaten's younger brother, and Princess Merit-Amon. As a token of her love, the princess offers the prince two mandragora blossoms while holding in her left hand a small bouquet. Both are dressed in ceremonial costumes of fine pleated linen in the height of Amarna fashion, and they wear the royal sacred asp on their foreheads. Her hair is combed back, making her cranium seem especially elongated, while the prince, supporting his weight on a staff, wears a short wig from the back of which two broad bands fall freely.

Portrait of Queen Nofretete · New Kingdom, Eighteenth Dynasty · 1567–1320 B.C. · Painted limestone statue · Height, 18⅞″ · State Museums, Berlin-Dahlem

Queen Nofretete (whose name means "The Beautiful One is come") was the consort of Pharaoh Akhenaten (1379–1362 B.C.), the creator of a new solar religion and builder of the royal residence in Tell el-Amarna. Ever since this painted portrait head was displayed to the public in the Berlin Museum, it has been considered one of the most fascinating artistic creations in the world, comparable in its way to the *Mona Lisa* by Leonardo da Vinci. Here technical and artistic perfection and precision go hand in hand with the incomparable charm of an unquestionably regal female personality. The artistic value of the portrait is in no wise lessened by knowing that it was found in the model room of the court sculptor Thutmosis in Tell el-Amarna and is generally believed to be nothing more than a workshop model, though executed with the utmost care. Evidence for this is that such busts were used in Egypt exclusively as models and teaching examples, but there is also the fact that the right eye, made of rock crystal, appears to have been set in as an experiment while the left was simply indicated in white. The unusually high form of the crown has never been found in portraits of other Egyptian queens. Although a sculptured piece, this head has been included here as an outstanding example of polychrome painting on sculpture.

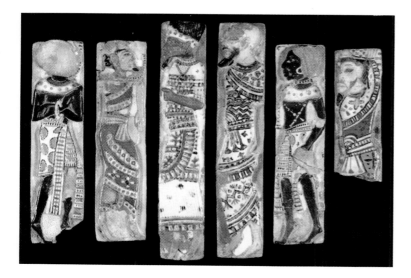

Foreigners · Glazed faience tiles, from Medinet Habu, near Thebes · New Kingdom, Twentieth Dynasty · 1200–1085 B.C.; time of Ramesses III, 1198–1166 B.C. · Museum of Fine Arts, Boston

These faience tiles came from the great palace of Ramesses III in Medinet Habu near Thebes. As early as the Third Dynasty, in the first half of the third millennium, tiles like these were used as wall-covering in the tombs and palaces of the Pharaohs and sometimes also as inlays in the royal furniture. These varicolored tiles brightened entire walls, but their special attraction lay in their subject matter. Often they portrayed the dignitaries of the peoples subjugated by Egypt in lands ranging from Africa to Mesopotamia, and as such were a means of proclaiming the military glory of the conquering Pharaohs. The Egyptians achieved astonishing realism in characterizing diverse ethnic types and in representing the details of the splendid costumes worn by the foreign personages. Black skin coloring (as in the figure at the far left and the second from the right) generally defined the person as Nubian, red skin as Philistine (third from the left), yellow as Syrian (second from the left), and baldness (third from right) as Amorite.

Acrobatic Dancer · Painted clay shard (ostrakon), probably from Thebes (Deir el-Medineh) · New Kingdom, Eighteenth to Twentieth Dynasties · 1567–1085 B.C. · Height, 4½″ · Egyptian Museum, Turin

The lithe body in a full back-bend is naked except for a patterned cloth around the hips. The movement of the body and the hair streaming down show with what great skill and artistic taste the artist has observed nature. In all probability this tiny masterpiece was found in the region of Thebes, most likely in Deir el-Medineh, which lies between the great funerary temples of the Pharaohs and the Valley of Kings: there lived the so-called Servants of the Abode of Maât, the goddess of truth and justice, weigher of souls in the cult of the dead. Among the "servants" were artists and craftsmen, and it may be that this shard, masterly as it is, was actually no more than a workshop sketch, or an experiment like the bust of Nofretete. Dancing figures are found throughout Egyptian art from prehistoric times to the latest period, and they range from the ritual dances of the early epoch to acrobatic spectacles staged for the guests at banquets.

The Judgment of the Dead (Psychostasis) · Illustration from the Book of the Dead of Hunefer · New Kingdom, Nineteenth Dynasty, period of Seti I · 1313–1301 B.C. · Tempera on papyrus · British Museum, London

Our final example of Egyptian art is part of an illustration from a Book of the Dead, painted on papyrus, showing the judgment of souls. Above are some of the judges attending the inquiry (not all forty-two are seen here). In the principal scene below, reading from left to right, we see the dead man being led in by Anubis, the weighing of his heart, Thot delivering his judgment, and Horus presenting the dead man, now accepted by the judges, to Osiris, lord of the other world (not included here). In the course of the inquiry, the dead man speaks the following words which are given in hieroglyphs: "I have begun no evil against any man, I have ill-treated no beast . . . nor have I blasphemed against God. . ." The ordeal completed successfully, the dead man may enter into Paradise and enjoy its delights in peace.

War · Detail from the Standard of Ur · Sumerian · 2750–2650 B.C. · Inlay of yellow shells and reddish limestone on lapis lazuli · Height, 8″ · British Museum, London

This and the next example are from two rectangular inlaid plaques which have been given the name "Standard of Ur" because of their subject, War and Peace. Here we see part of the three-zoned plaque depicting war. In the center of the upper zone appears the Sumerian king, larger than the other figures, and behind him, in the portion reproduced here, his entourage or family who are followed by the royal chariot pulled by two mules with the charioteer afoot holding the reins. On the other side prisoners with bound hands are led before the victorious king. In the middle zone at the left are the serried ranks of helmeted Sumerian spearbearers marching against the defeated enemy who flee before them. The lower zone, not included, shows four Sumerian war chariots triumphantly assaulting the enemy forces.

Peace · Detail from the Standard of Ur · Sumerian · 2750–2650 B.C. · Inlay of yellow shells and reddish limestone on lapis lazuli · Height, 8″ · British Museum, London

The upper zone of the plaque devoted to the pleasures of peace shows the dignitaries of the Sumerian court drinking a toast to the victorious king. Their festivities are enlivened by music. A male instrumentalist plays a harp decorated with a bull's head while a woman sings, holding her hands in the position characteristic of singers everywhere and at all times. The two lower zones are concerned with the booty of war, which includes oxen, sheep, and goats. Typical of the so-called minor arts in Sumeria are inlay work and the silhouette style, the latter especially effective in making the figures stand out against the background. The discovery of the royal necropolis in Ur in the 1920s was an epoch-making event for Middle Eastern archaeology, and Sumerian culture has since taken a prominent place in world history.

Painted earthenware pot · Iran, Tepe Giyan Culture IV, 3rd millennium B.C. · Height, 19¾″ · The Louvre, Paris

This spherical vessel with sloping shoulders and rimmed wide mouth is painted in monochrome brown with a frieze of ibexes around the shoulder and with geometrical rows of ornamental motifs. Although the stylized animals and the rectangular lattice pattern undeniably contribute a certain charm to the shape of the vessel, it is clear that this pottery style has become rather clumsy and its decoration overly rigid, especially as compared with the ceramics from the fifth and fourth millennia examined above. It cannot be denied that there was a decline in the potter's art in Mesopotamia in the third millennium B.C., that is, in the early dynastic Sumerian period and the Akkadian period which followed it—especially when one remembers that in the same epoch metalworking reached great heights in the urban centers. Further evidence of such a decline is the provincial character of various other kinds of craft objects. This vessel belongs to a class called Giyan Ware IV, after the principal site in Iran where it has been found.

Fisherman · Detail of a wall painting from the palace of King Zimrilim, Mari · Time of Hammurabi · First quarter of 18th century B.C. · National Museum, Aleppo

The French expeditions in 1934–39 and 1951–55 uncovered the very important ruins of Mari, an ancient center in the Middle Euphrates area in what is now Syria. Their findings showed that the city had played a dominant role in Middle Eastern culture at two separate epochs: in the pre-Sargon period at the beginning of the third millennium B.C., and in the Amorite period in the early second millennium. This and the next three examples from the royal palace represent the second of the two main phases in the history of Mari. The second golden age of the city did not last long. Around 1760 B.C. its political independence and cultural achievements were interrupted when it was conquered and devastated by Hammurabi, King of Babylon (1792–1750 B.C.). Later, the city regained a certain importance as an Assyrian military colony, but it then disappeared entirely from the stage of history.

Here we have a glimpse of everyday life in Mari. A bearded fisherman in a blue loincloth and short yellow mantle returns home carrying his catch suspended from a pole resting on his shoulder. The figure is painted in a forceful style with strong black outlines and lively coloring comprising blue, red, yellow, black, and flesh tones against a brown background.

Warrior · Detail of a wall painting from the palace of King Zimrilim, Mari. Time of Hammurabi · First quarter of 18th century B.C. · National Museum, Aleppo

Imposing temples, palaces, dwellings, and tombs were unearthed in Mari along with some 25,000 tablets in cuneiform script from the diplomatic and commercial archives of the state. The innumerable statues and wall paintings found at the site furnish us with a complete cross-section of the art and culture of Mari. Here, in contrast to the homely character of the preceding example, we are in the thick of battle. A warrior in white hood and chinstrap, dressed in a short yellow mantle and white loincloth, brandishes a spear although he himself has been run through by two spears or arrows. Although the two paintings differ in character, the warrior and the fisherman resemble each other in the forceful, colorful style in which they are portrayed.

Sacrificial Scene · Detail of a wall painting from the palace of King Zimrilim, Mari · Time of Hammurabi · First quarter of 18th century B.C. · Total dimensions, $19\frac{5}{8} \times 17\frac{3}{4}''$ · National Museum, Aleppo

More than one style is present in the art of Mari. Conservative elements predominate in the Akkadian tradition and are sometimes carried to a point of mannerist refinement, but nevertheless original creations are not lacking. Thus, this and the next example are quite different in style from the two preceding. In this scene of sacrifice we see a bearded man in leather hood and a cape with wide tongue-like trimming. Alongside him is the head of a bull. While the style is not as flexible and relaxed as in our preceding examples, the same firm contours are visible.

Sacrificial Scene · Detail of a wall painting from the palace of King Zimrilim, Mari. Time of Hammurabi · First quarter of 18th century B.C. · Total dimensions: length, 53″; height, 31½″ · The Louvre, Paris

The same can be said of the style of this second sacrificial scene. The large hand with an armband belongs to a towering male figure, probably the priest-king. To the left of this dominating figure (which has survived only in part) four smaller figures and a bull are disposed on two levels. On the lower level we can see the upper part of the smaller figure, with a fringed drapery and high white hood. A disk-like amulet hangs from a chain around his neck, and in his left hand he holds a slender white staff.

Only in Mari have the accidents of time preserved wall paintings from the first Babylonian dynasty, but everything we know indicates that in other great palaces of the time there were similar decorations on the walls of reception halls, rooms of state, and dwelling quarters. As far as their state of conservation permits us to judge, the wall paintings in Mari which exploit traditional themes are stiff and conventional in style, whereas those devoted to narrating actual events are fresh in conception and even, it seems, quite original. The four details reproduced here all belong to the latter type.

In style, many of these wall paintings have been quite rightly compared with those in the palaces in Crete.

Painted faience beaker with woman's head, from Ugarit (present-day Ras Shamra), northern Syria · Mittanian culture · c. 1300 B.C. · The Louvre, Paris

The beaker with a woman's face in painted high relief brings us to the golden age of Levantine culture, the latter half of the second millennium B.C. It has been proposed, on good though as yet unproved grounds, that the very striking face, which obviously represents the ideal of beauty of the time, may have some connection with the Syrian Magna Mater and her son Adonis, the seasonal god who each year died and was resurrected. Such a symbolic interpretation appears to be borne out by the fact that this beaker and others of the same type were found in tombs. This kind of beaker, in faience with relief decoration, is found over a wide area—in Ugarit in northern Syria, in Tell Abu Hawam north of Haifa, in Enkomi on Cyprus, in Rhodes, and also in the Mesopotamian centers of Mari, Assur, and Ur. Such wide diffusion shows what an international character the Levantine urban civilization assumed in the Mittanian sphere of cultural influence around 1300 B.C., a period now well known to us from innumerable diggings but above all from the royal archives of the fourteenth century B.C., found in Tell el-Amarna and Ugarit.

Column with cone mosaics, from the Terrace of Pillars in the temple of Innin, Uruk (present-day Warka), southern Mesopotamia · Uruk stratum IV, Early Sumerian I · Late 4th-early 3rd millennium B.C. · Partly displayed in the Museum, Baghdad, partly in the Middle East Museum, Berlin

These early architectural mosaics were used on columns, half-columns, and walls in the outer court of the temple of the goddess Innin in Uruk (called Erech in the Bible). They were composed of innumerable cone-shaped studs of baked clay with black, red, and white glazed heads, imbedded into the thick sun-dried bricks of the walls and columns in such a way as to create fascinating varicolored geometrical designs which recall those of textiles and were perhaps inspired by plaited wall mats. Their function was not merely decorative, for they protected the bricks from damage by weather. To cover the walls and columns of this court hundreds of thousands of these mosaic cones were required, and such an extraordinary effort can only be explained in terms of the special significance of the edifice itself. The sanctuary of Eanna ("The House of Heaven") was dedicated to the Sumerian mother goddess and queen of heaven Innin (the Ishtar of the Babylonians and Assyrians). It was not only the chief sanctuary of Uruk but also of all the Sumerian lands. The temple was found in the fourth stratum of the diggings which has been identified as Early Sumerian I, the epoch during which Sumeria achieved a cultural level whose significance for the entire Middle East and for the future development of mankind is now generally recognized.

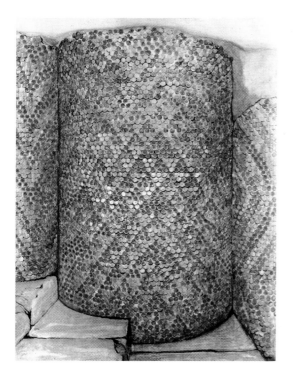

The Megiddo Vase, from Tomb 912 D, Megiddo, Israel ·
Late Bronze Age, Canaanite period · c. 1300 B.C. · Oriental
Institute, University of Chicago

Roughly contemporary with the preceding vase is this
double-conical clay canister from Megiddo (the biblical
Armageddon), but the two vessels reflect different aspects of
a single Levantine culture. The so-called Megiddo vase is
decorated with a great many animals in geometrical silhouette style, loosely grouped around a Tree of Life whose
branches can be made out on the left in our photograph;
a ram nibbles at its fruit. The reverse side is similarly
decorated with rams and birds, and underneath the handle
there is a crab. The theme of the Tree of Life surrounded by
the beasts of the earth, air, and water is found on a not inconsiderable number of Canaanite pottery vessels of the late
Bronze and early Iron Ages. The beaker in the preceding
example is a product of a highly developed Levantine urban
culture and is in what can be termed a naturalistic style,
whereas the present vase is a piece of folk art and its style is
virtually abstract. This is understandable, since it is chiefly
in folk art, which often finds its most natural expression in
homely unpretentious pottery, that primeval religious myths
such as the Tree of Life are perpetuated through the
centuries.

Demon and Griffons · Fragment of a glazed clay tile, from
Susa · Neo-Elamite · c. 10th–9th century B.C. · The Louvre,
Paris

Originally this glazed tile must have had a symmetrical
design with a bird-footed demon standing on two griffons
couchant and probably clutching them with his hands (the
lower part of the left-hand one survives). The theme of the
Master or Mistress of the Beasts (or Heroes) presented in a
heraldic arrangement is a very ancient one in the Middle
East; it can be traced in many variants from as far back as
early Sumeria through all the epochs and cultures of the
ancient world. This tile comes from Susa, the capital of the
Elamites, which at the start of the tenth century B.C., after a
significant and eventful history, entered upon a third phase,
the Neo-Elamite. That phase was in turn brought to an end
around 640 B.C. when the city fell to the Assyrians; their
hold, however, was broken in 550 B.C. by Cyrus, king of the
Persians. Under Darius I and his followers, Susa became the
capital of the Persian empire until finally it was taken by
Alexander the Great. It is likely that the technique of
coloring and glazing tiles was invented by the Elamites in
the late second millennium B.C. and spread to the neigh-
boring states of Assur, Babylon, and Persia, which carried
the technique to unprecedented heights (see page 43).

Beaked jug, from Tepe Sialk, central Iran · Iron Age,
Period B · 10th–9th century B.C. · Height, 5⅛″ · Archaeological Museum, Teheran

This graceful pottery jug with a long beak-like lip and
monochrome wine-red designs comes from the early Iron
Age Burial Ground B in Tepe Sialk, a settlement on the
central Iranian plateau. The painted decoration includes
figurative and abstract designs freely disposed over the
surface of the vessel. The depictions of animals are in a style
peculiar to Iranian figured vase paintings of the Iron Age:
a free, somewhat unsteady stance of the animals, with necks
sunk almost to the horizontal; ibexes shown with horns
lowered; and hawks viewed from below. But invariably
there was a *horror vacui*—a revulsion against any unadorned
surfaces—which led the painter to fill up the empty areas
with geometrical designs. This trait of Elamite work of the
Iron Age is shared by many other geometrical styles, not
only in Iran but as far west as Anatolia and the eastern
Mediterranean regions under Greek cultural influence.

A Bearded Man · From Susa · Early 1st millennium B.C. (?) · Painted terracotta head · Height, 9½″ · The Louvre, Paris

Along with two famous bronze sculptures from the latter half of the second millennium B.C.—the portrait statue in the Louvre of Napir-asu, consort of Untashgal, king of the Elamites (second half of the thirteenth century B.C.), and the bearded head in the Metropolitan Museum, New York—the present head is the most significant surviving piece of Elamite sculpture. The terracotta head still has abundant traces of its original paint, and its high qualities are obvious: freshness of approach, concentration in expression, maturity of style, technical virtuosity in contrasting the rough texture of hair, eyebrows, and beard with the sleekness of the skin. If the paint on the eyeballs was restored, the head would give an extraordinary impression of vitality, though the question must remain open as to whether or not it is an actual portrait. For lack of similar Elamite heads from the late second and early first millennium B.C. with which to compare it, it has not been possible to give this work a definite date.

Dignitary at an Official Audience · Detail of a wall painting from the governor's palace, Til Barsip (present-day Tell Ahmar), northern Mesopotamia · Neo-Assyrian epoch, probably the reign of Tiglathpileser III (c. 745–727 B.C.) · Height, 16″ · Museum, Aleppo (modern copy by L. Cavro)

From the time of Assurbanipal II on (883–859 B.C.), all the Assyrian rulers decorated the official state chambers and courts of their palaces with stone reliefs and wall paintings, and the doors of those rooms with bronze strips ornamented with figures. The most famous of the Neo-Assyrian palaces are in Nimrud, Balawat, Til Barsip, Khorsabad, and Nineveh. There main techniques were used to decorate walls: (1) orthostatic stone plaques, the most frequent technique; (2) glazed relief tiles (forerunners of the Neo-Babylonian and Persian enameled relief tiles) sometimes replaced these, or painted and glazed terracotta plaques; (3) wall paintings in fresco, mostly over a base of plaques. All three techniques have in common the use of varicolored painting, and as we know from the traces of paint remaining, even the famous Assyrian stone reliefs were originally painted.

Dignitaries at an Official Audience · Detail of a wall painting from the governor's palace, Til Barsip (present-day Tell Ahmar), northern Mesopotamia · Neo-Assyrian epoch, probably the reign of Tiglathpileser III (c. 745–727 B.C.) · Height, 16″ · Museum, Aleppo (modern copy by L. Cavro)

The decoration of Assyrian palaces served a high function, the glorification of the king, and its imagery comprised not only the ceremonial acts of the ruler in his palace but also his private diversions, especially hunting. Reproduced here and in the preceding example are dignitaries of the Assyrian court as portrayed in a wall painting from the governor's palace in Til Barsip, a town on one of the sources of the Euphrates in northern Mesopotamia. The high officials are in attendance at an audience given by the king, probably Tiglathpileser III, who on another part of the painting appears in ceremonial vestments receiving tribute bearers whose leader has thrown himself down at the monarch's feet. A row of bearded older dignitaries and beardless younger ones stands before the king in what seems to be a hierarchical order with the Great Eunuch in the second position and behind him the two bearded men seen here. Behind the throne are court officials and soldiers returned from a successful campaign and delivering their booty to the king.

The Ishtar Gate of Babylon · Neo-Babylonian epoch, time of Nebuchadnezzar II, king of Babylon (604–562 B.C.) · Middle East Museum, Berlin (reconstruction utilizing fragments of original glazed tiles)

The outer façade of the double gate flanked by imposing towers is faced with glazed bricks forming reliefs of bulls and dragons spaced at regular intervals. This elaborate structure was certainly no mere city gate but rather a passageway through the double walls of the city; it was used only for a special purpose, namely, for processions from the temple of Marduk, the patron god of the city, which was within the walls, to the special building outside the walls, the New Year's festival hall (not yet discovered but presumed to have once existed there). The inner façades of the walls of the processional passage are likewise faced with glazed tiles on which lions are depicted in relief. The lion was sacred to Ishtar, the bull to the weather-god Adad, the dragon to Marduk. In a cuneiform inscription sixty-one lines long, Nebuchadnezzar describes the architectural enterprises undertaken during his reign, among them the Ishtar Gate in the vicinity of which the inscription was found. He refers to the glazed bricks used as background for the reliefs as "blue stones."

A Winged Bull · Colored enameled brick relief from the palace of the Achaemenid Great King in Susa · Reign of Darius I · 522–486 B.C. · Height of bull, 54″ · The Louvre, Paris

This and the next relief come from the palace of the Achaemenid Great King in Susa, the residence city of the Achaemenid dynasty in the Persian province of Elam. An inscription was found there in which Darius I recounts his architectural achievements. After invoking the Persian god Ahuramazda, Darius proclaims: "This is the palace I built in Susa. Its decoration was brought from far-off places... The Babylonians formed the sun-baked bricks. The cedarwood was brought from the Mountain of Lebanon ... the yakà wood from Gandhara [a province in northwest Pakistan] and Karmania [present-day Kirman]. The gold came from Sardis and Bactria, the precious gems lapis lazuli and carnelian from Sogdiana [a Persian district in Turkestan], turquoise from Chorasmia [in Central Asia], silver and ebony from Egypt. The material to decorate the walls came from Ionia, the ivory from Ethiopia, Sind [in the Indus region], and Arachosia [a satrapy of the old Persian empire]. The stone pillars were brought from [a quarry near] Abiradus in Elam, the stonemasons were Ionians [Eastern Greeks] and from Sardis, the goldsmiths were Medes and Egyptians, the woodworkers from Sardis and Egypt, those who fashioned the bricks Babylonians, those who decorated the walls Medes and Egyptians. In Susa a truly extraordinary work was set these men and carried out. May Ahuramazda protect me and my father Hysdaspes and my land." The royal document gives us a realistic glimpse into the imperial culture of the Persian Great Kingdom.

A Member of the Royal Bodyguard · Colored enameled brick relief from the palace of the Achaemenid Great King in Susa · Reign of Artaxerxes II · 404–359 B.C. · Height of figure, 58″ · The Louvre, Paris

The portrait of a member of the imperial bodyguard comes from the same palace as the winged bull but was done a century or so later, when further building was carried out under Artaxerxes II.

43

Fragment (upper portion only) of a large vessel with poly-chrome decoration in relief, from Bitik, near Ankara · Hittite · c. 1400 B.C. · Height of fragment (not reproduced in its entirety), 14⅜″ · Archaeological Museum, Ankara

On this fragment of a large thick-walled vessel with relief decoration painted in wine-red and yellow we see two seated figures, a man at the left and a woman opposite who is completely enveloped in a mantle from head to toes. They appear to be involved in an unveiling rite, and it seems significant that the man holds out to the woman a drinking bowl. This type of representation of what may be a mythical marriage ceremony became especially popular in Archaic Greek art and was designated as a "sacred marriage." There are two other relief friezes below on the fragment, one visible in part here, depicting bearers of offerings and musicians. The style recalls that of the orthostatic reliefs in basalt on the city walls of Alaca Hüzük, which date from the height of the Hittite empire (1450–1200 B.C.).

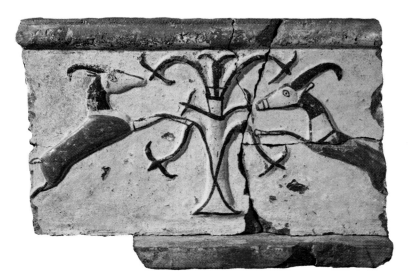

Tree of Life Flanked by Two Ibexes · Terracotta plaque from an architectural frieze, from Gordrion (Phrygia) · 6th century B.C. · 10½ × 17⅛″ · Archaeological Museum, Ankara

The projecting borders on this polychrome painted plaque are evidence that it was originally part of the roof decoration of a public building. The stylized Tree of Life is flanked on either side by similarly stylized ibexes in the heraldic com-position that was in great favor in the Middle East from ancient times on and was later taken over by Greece. As in the preceding plaque, the style here mingles traits from the Middle East and from Eastern Greece. Gordrion, where it was found, was the center of Phrygian culture in the archaic period.

Two Warriors · Terracotta plaque from an architectural frieze, from Pazarli, north of Boghazköy, northern Anatolia · Phrygian · Latter half of 6th century B.C. · Height, 17⅞″; length, 17¾″; thickness, 3⅛″ · Archaeological Museum, Ankara

Two warriors march toward the left armed with helmets, shields, and spears; they are dressed in garments whose richly ornamented borders can be made out below the shields, which themselves are decorated with geometrical designs. The warriors are painted in tones of red. Other plaques exist from this or a closely related frieze. Although unearthed in a region under Hittite influence, the style is neither entirely Middle Eastern nor Phrygian; it combines stylistic elements typical of both the Middle East and Eastern Greece in what is, admittedly, a rather provincial manner. It is, in fact, this provincial character which makes the style seem more archaic than it may actually be.

Beaked clay jug with mottled decoration, from Vassiliki, eastern Crete · Vassiliki Style, Early Minoan II · Second half of 3rd millennium B.C. · Height, $13\frac{1}{4}$″

This and the next three examples will give an idea of the character and development of Cretan pottery from the second half of the third to the second half of the second millennium B.C. Here we have a jug with a high open spout in the shape of a bird's beak. The button-like eyes between the beak and the handle show that the potter aimed deliberately at a zoomorphic character. The jug comes from the Early Minoan epoch in the early Bronze Age; the date is also borne out by the very unusual decoration of amorphous dark blotches on a relatively lighter ground which was probably an attempt to imitate, by burning the pot unevenly, the varicolored streaked stone that was also used for vessels in and around Crete at the same time. This type of pottery is called Vassiliki Style after the site in eastern Crete where it was found.

Beaked clay jug with vegetable design, from the Old Palace in Phaestos · Kamares Style, Middle Minoan II · 1850–1700 B.C. · Height, $10\frac{5}{8}$″

This jug, like the preceding one, has button-like eyes between the handle and the spout. Its polychrome decoration is based both on abstract and vegetable forms and is very appropriate to the high-swelling shape of the vessel, lending it a dynamic movement. Vessels of this type were found in great numbers in the Old Palaces of Phaestos and Knossos but most of all in the famous grotto of Kamares on Mount Ida dedicated to Ilithyia, the goddess who assisted in childbirth; this much admired type of pottery is therefore called Kamares Ware. Examples exported to Egypt permit us to date it in the Twelfth Dynasty which is equivalent to the Middle Minoan II period.

Two-handled clay jug with floral design, from the New Palace in Hagia Triada · Late Floral Style, Late Minoan I · c. 1500 B.C. · Height, $6\frac{1}{2}$″

The painting in brown on a lighter ground on this two-handled jug with horizontal beaked spout reveals that in time vase painting developed a decided turn toward naturalism. It has been observed that painters in this Floral Style aimed at a more naturalistic effect by laying on color more thickly for certain of the leaves. Innumerable vessels of the same period reproduce in naturalistic style either plants or marine animals, such as fish, octopuses, starfish, and mussels.

45

Three-handled clay amphora decorated with papyrus plant designs, from the New Palace in Knossos · Palace Style, Late Minoan II · c. 1450–1400 B.C. · Height, 30¾"

This large three-handled storage jar brings us to the end of a development: the naturalistic vegetable and marine designs of the preceding styles have hardened into purely ornamental decoration. Here we have six tufts of papyrus (the plant had been introduced into Crete from Egypt) and between them amorphous so-called sand surfaces. For the most part such vessels have been found in the New Palace in Knossos which accounts for the name given to the style.

The stylistic evolution is perfectly clear. After the early Vassiliki Style, in which the forms cannot be called specifically Cretan but whose painting imitates the appearance of early Cretan vessels in stone, a genuine Cretan style came into being with Kamares Ware. As so often in the development of cultures, the later stages did not fulfill the potential of the earlier stages: even in technique Kamares pottery is superior to that of later periods in Crete. In a third phase, both elements latent in the Kamares style—abstraction and naturalism—were carried further: whether purely ornamental, or naturalistic with plants and animals, the designs are clear and simple but they lack the fascinating dynamic inherent in Kamares decoration. Increased ornamental rigidity characterizes the fourth and last phase, the Palace Style.

Female head called "*La Petite Parisienne*" · Fragment of a wall painting in the hall of state, New Palace, Knossos · Late Minoan I · 1550–1450 B.C. · Height, c. 9⅞" · Archaeological Museum, Heraklion, Crete

On Cretan vases of the Minoan period, there are plants or animals as well as abstract motifs, but never human beings. In Minoan times the depiction of gods and men, the highest theme of art, was apparently reserved to wall paintings in the palaces. Innumerable fragments of these have survived, most of them from the New Palace in Knossos which has been dated between 1600 and 1400 B.C. On this fragment there is an attractive, elegantly dressed young lady whose charm has won for her the sobriquet of "la petite Parisienne." In accordance with the stylistic principles of Egyptian and Near Eastern painting, the figure is in profile but the exaggeratedly oversize eye is presented frontally; the entire figure is firmly outlined. Whatever its similarities to other styles, this head remains unmistakably Cretan. Painted in quick strokes with a well-developed feeling for coloristic effects, it is fresh and spontaneous, a quality which has led to its being described—not too correctly, it may be said—as "impressionistic" and which also explains why such an art should have influenced Egyptian wall painting, especially that in Tell el-Amarna (cf. page 36, top). Other fragments from the same wall painting have been reconstructed more or less approximately into a scene with young men and women standing or seated on folding stools arranged in two registers separated by horizontal bands.

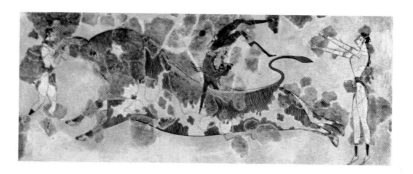

"*The Toreador Fresco*" (much restored) · Fragment of a wall painting from a court in the east wing of the New Palace, Knossos · Late Minoan I · 1550–1450 B.C. · Height including borders, 31½" · Archaeological Museum, Heraklion, Crete

We know that bull-vaulting was an important part of Cretan religious practice from the many depictions of it, especially on seal-rings, but exactly what took place is still a mystery. A young acrobat (the dark skin coloring identifies him as masculine) performs a back somersault over a wildly charging bull while two young girls look on, clad only in loincloths but richly bejeweled. The composition is at one and the same time full of movement and firmly balanced. To avoid erroneous associations with present-day bullfights, it should be remarked that Cretan games with bulls were performed without weapons and no blood was shed.

Sacrificial Scene · Side panel of a stone sarcophagus painted in fresco, from a tomb near the palace of Hagia Triada, Crete · Beginning of Late Minoan III · c. 1400 B.C. · Length, 53⅞″ · Archaeological Museum, Heraklion, Crete

There are many unsolved problems connected with the sarcophagus from which this and the next frescoed side panel come. Both are scenes of sacrifice. Here, from the center toward the left, move two women and a man (identifiable by his brown skin coloring). Each woman bears a vessel containing some liquid to a larger mixing vat that is placed between two columns, each crowned by a double-axe and a bird. The first woman empties her vessel into the vat, the second appears to be a princess or possibly a priestess because of her crown, and the man following them plays the lyre. In the opposite direction move three men who bear calves and a model of a boat to another—apparently armless —man standing in front of an edifice which is probably his tomb. If this strange figure at the right is really a dead man, then he must be the invisible observer of his own burial ceremonies.

Sacrificial Scene · Side panel of a stone sarcophagus painted in fresco, from a tomb near the palace of Hagia Triada, Crete · Beginning of Late Minoan III · c. 1400 B.C. · Length, 53⅞″ · Archaeological Museum, Heraklion, Crete

The other longitudinal side panel of the sarcophagus shows another scene of sacrifice unrolling from left to right. From the left, in part destroyed, are five women, once again led by a princess. In the center is the sacrificial altar with a bull bound upon it, his blood running into a bucket. Behind the altar stands a musician playing an aulos. Farther right, a woman lays offerings on an altar, and beyond this is some sort of sacred edifice crowned with double-horns and a holy tree. On each of the two smaller sides of the sarcophagus, not reproduced here, there is a chariot: one contains two women and is drawn by two horses; the other also carries two women who seem to be goddesses, and their chariot is drawn by two winged griffons over which flies a fantastic bird. The questions raised by this sarcophagus have not as yet received conclusive answers. Are all four pictures meant to constitute a significant unity? Are the sacrifices offered to a dead mortal or to the gods? What is the role of the divinities who certainly appear on at least the second of the smaller sides?

Lion Hunt · Detail of the blade of a bronze dagger with inlay in gold, silver, and black niello, from shaft grave IV in grave circle A, Mycenae · First half of 16th century B.C. · Length of whole, 9⅜″ · National Museum, Athens

Running down the upper side of this bronze dagger blade is a strip of black niello (compounded of copper, lead, and sulphur) serving as the ground for an inlaid gold and silver miniature of a lion hunt. Four scantily clad hoplites and an archer strike with arrows and spears at a powerful lion who, wounded by a spear, turns on his attackers in a swift lunge. The first warrior, who has wounded the lion, has been knocked down; the second hides behind a large shield shaped like the figure 8 and, backed by his three companions, hurls his lance at the beast. Two other lions farther down the blade, not reproduced here, flee from the scene. On the other face of the blade, the ornamental strip inlaid in the same technique shows a lion stalking a gazelle. The 8-shaped shield, the narrow waists of the slender warriors and their animated movements, and above all the virtuoso style and technical mastery suggest that this and similar daggers found in shaft graves of the first half of the sixteenth century B.C. in Mycenae must have been made by Cretans. Probably the daggers were commissioned by Mycenaean princes who, unlike the Cretan nobles, delighted in hunting, war, and weapons.

47

Bust of a Woman · Fragment of a wall painting (heavily restored), from the palace at Tiryns · 1400 B.C. or later · Height, c. 11¾″ · National Museum, Athens

The preceding picture was in Cretan style but treated a typical mainland Mycenaean theme, hunting and warriors. This fragment of a heavily restored wall painting shows, in contrast, a Cretan theme—a religious procession of women, possibly priestesses—executed in typically Cretan guise as emphasized by the hairdressing and costumes. Yet, in spite of its richly varied coloring, it is in the hard, almost dry style characteristic of Mycenaean mainland art. The great number of fragments surviving from this procession of full-length, almost life-size female figures allows us to reconstruct its original composition: two rows of women bearing offerings approach each other solemnly against a blue background, their steps directed toward something in the middle of the fresco which can no longer be made out. The mural dates from around 1400 B.C. or later, the second period of building of the palace in the celebrated citadel which Homer acclaimed as "Tiryns with its walls." Here is a significant contrast: on the Mycenaean mainland there were mighty citadels, on the island of Crete open palaces.

Female statue head, profile view, from Mycenae · Late Mycenaean · Polychrome painting on stucco over limestone · Height, 6⅝″ · National Museum, Athens

Surprisingly enough, neither the Cretan-Minoan nor the Mycenaean civilizations produced any significant number of large three-dimensional stone statues. One of the most authoritative experts on the period says, "There was no monumental sculpture in Crete. . . One cannot really speak of a true monumental art in Crete. Only wall paintings along with the stucco reliefs related to them were developed there." That is why the almost life-size polychrome stone head pictured here and in the next photograph is so significant: it is the only large-scale stone sculpture of the Mycenaean epoch known so far, except for the lions on the famous Lion Gate in Mycenae from the fourteenth or thirteenth centuries B.C. which are relief sculpture subordinated to an architectural function.

Female statue head, front view, from Mycenae · Late Mycenaean · Polychrome painting on stucco over limestone · Height, 6⅝″ · National Museum, Athens

Because of the wide circlet around the forehead ("stephane"), this head, which surely cannot date from earlier than the late Mycenaean period, is considered to be that of a woman. Stylized curls in symmetrical arrangement fall across the brow. The three rosettes made of dots on the cheeks and chin are quite unusual; they have not been properly explained unless they are, as has been suggested, tattoo marks. Despite its marked stylization, the head makes a not inconsiderable impression. The body from which it has been broken off has unfortunately not been preserved, but it has been proposed that the figure may have been a sphinx—a female head on a lion's body—since depictions of sphinxes in gold and ivory are known to us from Mycenaean sources.

Women on a Balcony · Fragment of a fresco, from grave circle A in Mycenae · 15th century B.C. · Length, 5¼″ · National Museum, Athens

At first glance this and the next small fragment of fresco could be taken for Cretan. Their freshness of color, style, composition, and subject matter remind us inevitably of the so-called impressionistic style of many frescoes from the time of the New Palace in Knossos such as the "*Petite Parisienne*" (see page 46). However, the fact that both fragments come from Mycenae tells us that the cultural relations between Crete and the Mycenaean mainland were not one-sided: Cretan artists and craftsmen served Mycenaean masters on the mainland and treated local Mycenaean themes in the style and technique native to Crete until such time as Mycenae finally developed its own artists. This small fresco which gives the impression of having been dashed down all at one go is generally dated early, in the fifteenth century B.C.; it was found in a grave circle in Mycenae, though it obviously was not part of the decoration of a grave. It depicts women seated in a kind of loggia or veranda observing some sort of scene, probably of a religious nature. Above them hang white garlands, each suspended from two double-axes.

Three Donkey-headed Demons · Fragment of a fresco, from Mycenae · Late Mycenaean · 15th–14th century B.C. · Length, 4½″ · National Museum, Athens

The subject here has not yet been explained satisfactorily. Three human figures with horned donkey heads carry, suspended from a long pole resting on their shoulders, some not easily identifiable beast of prey. Certain scholars interpret these donkey heads as masks of the kind used much later, in the fifth century B.C., for Attic comedy, but others think they belong to demons, a Minoan-Maycenaean variant of the Egyptian hippopotamus-goddess Ta-urt.

The Warrior Vase · Detail of a clay krater, from the House of the Warrior Vase in the citadel of Mycenae · 1200 B.C. or somewhat later · Height, 16⅛″ · National Museum, Athens

Concerning the cultural level of which this vase is a product, an authority on the Minoan-Mycenaean epoch has remarked, "No more palaces were being built, no one any longer had his house decorated with paintings, no poet praised Mycenae as rich in gold." It was the time, around 1200 B.C. or somewhat later, of the transition from the Bronze to the Iron Age, from the Mycenaean to the Geometric style. Here we see part of the frieze which encircles a tall krater unearthed by Schliemann himself. Six bearded warriors march off to battle in coats of mail and horned leather helmets, carrying lances and kidney-shaped shields. Behind them a woman in a dark wool garment raises her right hand in sorrowful farewell. It was only at the end of the Minoan-Mycenaean epoch that human figures appeared on pottery on both the mainland and Crete, although they were much more frequent on the so-called Levanto-Helladic kraters, especially those from Cyprus and Rhodes. The decline in aesthetic quality in late Mycenaean vases is explained by the decline of an aristocratic high culture to a peasant folk art which, as we shall see, eventually reached its own high point in Geometric style vase painting.

49

Attic Proto-Geometric clay amphora with geometrical designs, found in Athens · Proto-Geometric period · 10th century B.C. · Height, c. 15¾″

During the twelfth century B.C., Mycenaean civilization declined along with its citadels and palaces, wall paintings, metalwork and pottery. For some two hundred years thereafter all of Greece sank into cultural apathy. But around 1000 B.C. there were fresh stirrings, and a new culture began to take shape which has been called Geometric, after the style of vase decoration then current. It started in the early tenth century with the Proto-Geometric preparatory phase shown here, and it developed with remarkable consistency during Homeric times—the ninth and eighth centuries B.C.—into the well-differentiated ornamental-figurative Geometric style we shall see in the next three vases.

Almost every Greek region, that is, every city-state, produced its own Geometric style of vase decoration, but by far the richest and most significant for the future was that of Attica, which is why all four examples seen here have been chosen from that region. Only in Attica can we follow step by step the formation of the Geometric style from its forerunners, the Late-Mycenaean, Sub-Mycenaean, and Proto-Geometric styles. For the archaeologist and historian it is truly a fascinating and unique experience to be able, for once, to trace every phase of the transition from one epoch, the Bronze Age, to the next, the Iron Age, within such a restricted area as Attica and in a form as humble as the everyday pottery utensils made for dwellings and tombs. The result is surprising enough: despite innumerable links with Mycenaean and sub-Mycenaean ceramics, and despite a perfectly clear-cut tradition in pottery-making, the vases that came into being in the Proto-Geometric and Geometric periods were entirely new.

Here, for example, we have a large-bellied amphora with two handles. It was found in a grave of the Proto-Geometric epoch in Athens. Vessels of this type were used chiefly as funerary urns and played an important part in the cult of the dead. What is so attractive here is the graceful but well-proportioned compactness of the form, the clear structure of its separate stereometric parts, and the precision of its geometrical decoration which fits the vessel's form while at the same time dividing the surface into clearly distinguished separate horizontal zones. Comparing it with a typical Minoan-Mycenaean vessel (page 46), we realize that a diametrically opposite aesthetic feeling for form and decoration has taken over; here are not seen the curving, upward-sweeping lines of plants and animals typical of the "organic" character of Minoan-Mycenaean decoration, which was in fundamental harmony with the actual forms of vases used in that period.

Attic Geometric clay krater with lid, decorated with geometrical patterns and horses, from the ancient necropolis of Dipylon in Athens · Geometric period, "severe phase" · Second half of 9th century B.C. · Height, 22½″ · The Louvre, Paris

In form and decoration this vessel, probably a funerary urn, represents the so-called severe phase of the Attic Geometric style. Everything we noticed in the preceding vessel is carried here to a more severe point of perfection. The geometrical patterns are laid out in distinct tiers from top to bottom, and no areas are left uncovered. The patterns can for the most part be read in two ways, as dark on light or as light on dark. Such a rigorous system of decoration is not at all in contradiction with the rounded shape of the vessel but, in fact, fits it perfectly. Even the black silhouettes of the human and animal figures presented in well-defined separate fields are in harmony with the purely flat and linear geometric designs.

Corpse Lying in State (Prothesis) · Detail of an Attic Geometric funerary amphora, from the ancient necropolis of Dipylon in Athens · Geometric period (mature Geometric style) · First half of 8th century B.C. · Height of entire vase, 61″ · National Museum, Athens

This detail comes from the most famous vase of the Geometric period, a tall funerary amphora which was once a monument on a grave in the Dipylon. Its perforated base tells us that it also served to hold offerings of wine. At the level of the handles on the front, in accord with the function of the vessel, is depicted the lying-in-state (prothesis) of the dead man attended by his mourning family and friends. This is executed entirely in the Geometric style at its most mature.

Chariot Procession · Attic Geometric clay funerary krater, from the Dipylon in Athens · Geometric period (late Geometric style) · Second half of 8th century B.C. · Height, 48″ · Metropolitan Museum of Art, New York

In the late phase of the Geometric style, the latter half of the eighth century B.C., there was a relaxation in the previous ornamental severity and a new emphasis on figuration. On this very large funerary krater it is the figurative scenes which, in fact, dominate. In an upper zone there is a corpse lying in state, and below this a procession of chariots and heavily armed warriors very much like Homer's description in the *Iliad* of the funeral games in honor of Patroclus.

Chariots and Riders · Detail of a frieze on an amphora, from Attica · Attributed to the Analatos Painter · Proto-Attic style · Early 7th century B.C. · Height of entire vase, 31⅞″ · The Louvre, Paris

While the preceding urn, for all its relaxation in patterning and its emphasis on figuration, remains within the limits of the Geometric style, the present amphora makes clear the direction that the development of the late Geometric style was bound to take. The pure silhouette style began to change: contour outlining was broken up, areas were increasingly left free, more and more details such as eyes, features, draperies, and the like were stressed. Clear evidence of this is found in the faces of the charioteers which, alternately, are done in Geometric silhouette style and in Post-Geometric outlining. The geometric motifs which still dominated the mature phase of the style begin now to be restricted to filling up the areas where there are no figures and to form purely decorative horizontal bands of secondary importance. Where once the form of the vase and its painted decoration made up an indissoluble unity, this organic link began to be loosened in the late Geometric period. The shape of the vessel is overly slender and its neck is disproportionately long and at the same time wide; these features show, along with certain orientalizing traits of the decoration, that the Attic Geometric style has been left behind and that this work belongs rather to what can be called the Proto-Attic style, a new pictorial language which began in the seventh century B.C.

Heracles Slaying Nessus · Painting on the neck of a funerary amphora, from the Dipylon in Athens · By the so-called Nessus Painter · Proto-Attic period · Last quarter of 7th century B.C. · Height of entire amphora, 48″; height of the painting on neck, c. 10⅝″ · National Museum, Athens

Compared with this vase painting, the two preceding seem merely tentative efforts to depict human figures and animals. However rich in promise was the folk-art stage of the earlier Greek culture, here we have entered fully into the archaic phase of a higher Greek civilization. What is depicted is the slaying of a shaggy-bearded monster, the centaur Nessus ("Netos" as the inscription reads in Early Attic), by the "civilized" strong man Heracles, the heroic destroyer of everything barbaric. Heracles is, of course, within his rights, since the centaur had tried to ravish the hero's young bride Deianeira. With images such as this was ushered in the full-fledged narrative style of black-figure vase painting. The new style was characterized by dramatic concentration, rejection of everything not essential, well-balanced composition, and—despite the limitations of the silhouette technique—a feeling for plastic volume.

The "Macmillan Aryballos" with three miniature friezes, from Thebes (Boeotia) · Middle Proto-Corinthian · c. 650 B.C. · Height, 2½″ · British Museum, London

This lovely miniature perfume vase from the Corinthian workshops is among the finest examples of Greek pottery. It is understandable why perfume flasks in this and similar style should have been eagerly sought after in the world market of the time. Made for export, they have been found in all the coastal settlements of the Mediterranean and the Black Sea. In point of time as well as of development, the pottery of the Proto-Corinthian phase came between the two preceding vases, and such pottery unquestionably made a fundamental contribution to the evolution of the Attic black-figure vase style. Both form and decoration of this tiny vase were conceived with consummate elegance and certainty, and the superbly modeled lion's head with gaping jaws which forms the neck and mouth of the vessel gives an impression of monumental scale despite its miniature dimensions. The decoration is divided into separate zones: a garland of lotus palmettes on the shoulder, then in the principal frieze a battle scene with eighteen hoplites in energetic movement, followed by a smaller frieze with a horse race and a still smaller one with a hare hunt, and finally a circlet of rays to round off the foot. The new black-figure style proves itself an ideal technique for decoration.

Three Goddesses (?) · Fragment of a polychrome painted clay metope, from the temple of Apollo in Thermum, Aetolia · Corinthian · Latter half of 7th century B.C. · National Museum, Athens

On this metope are represented three white-clad women enthroned, in all likelihood a trio of goddesses. Interestingly enough, the metope was restored in Hellenistic times and much repainted. Its upper part is missing.

Chelidon and Aëdon Killing Itylus · Detail of a polychrome painted clay metope, from the temple of Apollo in Thermum, Aetolia · Corinthian · Second half of 7th century B.C. · Original dimensions, 31½ × 31½″; surviving right half, 17⅞″ · National Museum, Athens

There can be no doubt that Proto-Corinthian polychrome vase painting in small and even miniature formats (cf. plates top left and right) borrowed such basic elements as polychrome and free composition from Corinthian wall paintings of the same period. Some idea of the lost Corinthian wall paintings can be gleaned from the painted clay metopes in the temple of Apollo in Thermum, one of the earliest Doric temples. Here and in the preceding plate are two of them, not equally well preserved. They were painted on baked reddish clay in the same colors as the Proto-Corinthian vases: light orange for flesh-tones of men, white for women, black for hair, beards and eyebrows, lilac for garments and other details, yellow for the background. Because the coarse clay used for these plaques made it impossible to sketch the figures, as was done on pottery at that time, the figures were outlined in black and the colors laid on flatly, without modeling. The close relationship between wall and vase painting makes it highly likely that the same painters did both.

Like the stone metopes of Archaic and Classical temples, composition in the early painted metopes was as a rule restricted to groups of two or three figures in relatively large dimensions, and the subjects were taken from Greek mythology. On this metope, part of whose better-preserved right half is reproduced here, two women sit before a table on which, as we know from the myth, a small boy lies. Above the woman is seen her name, in High-Archaic Greek script which runs from right to left: she is Chelidon, sister of Aëdon. According to the gruesome myth, the husband of Aëdon ravished her sister Chelidon and, to prevent betrayal, cut out her tongue. Despite this, the girl succeeded in communicating the terrible story to Aëdon. As revenge, the two women slaughtered Itylus (or Itys), Aëdon's son, and set the cadaver before the child's father as a meal. When this thoroughly wicked gentleman understood what the sisters had done, he tried to put both of them to death, but the gods intervened and metamorphosed all three into sad-singing birds. On our metope it is Chelidon's murder of the child which is presented rather than the denouement: it is frequent in Greek depictions of myths to show the grisly event leading to the tragic catastrophe.

This delicate painting on a wine jug shares with the decoration on the Macmillan aryballos (page 52) its style, small dimensions, polychromy, incised contours, and linear drawing of details within the figures. The stylistic resemblances are such that both vases, as well as certain others, have been attributed to the workshop of an artist called the Macmillan Painter, a Proto-Corinthian workshop active around the middle of the seventh century B.C. The decoration is in three figured friezes: the lowest and smallest depicts a hare hunt; the middle one the Judgment of Paris, along with a procession of chariots and horsemen and a lion hunt; the upper one contains the battle scene reproduced here. In this detail we see from left to right a phalanx of heavily armed foot-soldiers being led into battle by an unarmed young musician playing the aulos. On the right two enemy phalanxes clash, four in one group against five in the other, their spearheads crossing between the rows of soldiers. It is hard to say which is more admirable, the precise rendering of all details despite the miniature format, or the harmonious decoration, or the vigor with which the scene is portrayed.

Wine jug with friezes, from Kamiros, Rhodes · Transition between Proto-Corinthian and Corinthian styles · c. 640–625 B.C. · Height, 7⅞″ · Ashmolean Museum, Oxford

No less impressive than the painting on Corinthian vases is their form. Here we are struck first of all by the pleasing equilibrium of the vessel's shape. But hand in hand with the balanced form goes a balanced distribution of the colors in the separate zones in such a manner that the lights, darks, and polychromy of the animal silhouettes blend together like figures in a carpet. Indeed, it has often been claimed that textiles exerted an influence on the orientalizing designs of Greek pottery. In the transitional phase represented by this vessel, with its two friezes of animals separated by a polychrome scale pattern, the way was prepared for a more conventionalized type of representation of animals. This led in turn, in the succeeding Corinthian style (625–550 B.C.), to a mechanical and rigid manner contrasting unfavorably with the much fresher Proto-Corinthian way of depicting animals. One reason for this change was certainly the mass production of pottery in Corinth aimed at the export trade.

Animals and *Leavetaking of a Hero from His Bride* · Details of friezes from a column krater, from Caere, in Etruria (present-day Cerveteri, Italy) · By the so-called Three-Maiden Painter · Late Corinthian style · c. 575–550 B.C. · Height of entire vase, 16¾″ · Vatican Museum, Rome

The upper frieze is richly filled with a mythological scene in which a hero and his bride aboard a chariot are presented, in a full-blown narrative style exploiting all the technical resources of the Late Corinthian style. The composition is masterly in technique though somewhat cold and pompous with its repeated groups of three maidens under a single mantle (it is from this motif that the anonymous master gets his name). But in comparison the simpler, purely decorative lower frieze of stereotyped groups of panthers and rams seems old-fashioned and stiff. It is clear that competition from the many-figured black-figure style of vase painting (cf. pages 55–57) spelled the end of the purely ornamental Corinthian animal friezes.

53

Amphora with shoulder handles, decorated with orientalizing animal motifs found in Grave 7, Thera, Cyclades Islands · Heraldic Group style, Cycladic (probably Naxian) · c. mid-7th century B.C. · Height, 32¼" · National Museum, Athens

In its form this amphora remains within the Geometric tradition, but its decoration and the style of the animals on the neck and handle area place the vessel decisively in the orientalizing style of the middle of the seventh century. It was found on the island of Thera in the southern Cyclades and is typical of Cycladic vase painting, which developed much more slowly than that of the mainland centers of Athens and Corinth. The painting on Cycladic Post-Geometric orientalizing vessels is light and fluent, even when the motifs are borrowed from a very ancient Middle-Eastern tradition as is the case of the heraldic group of lions in the middle of the neck, a theme going back to the old Tree of Life flanked by animals. Along with a number of other vases of the same style and composition, this amphora is classified as Heraldic Group and its origin is ascribed to Naxos by many scholars.

Pitcher with trefoil mouth and red elbow handle, from Rhodes · Late Wild Goat style · End of 7th century B.C. · Height, 13" · Museum Antiker Kleinkunst, Munich

Dominating the Eastern Greek vase styles of the second half of the seventh century B.C. was a type of jug decorated with friezes of wild goats. The motif accounts for the designation "Wild Goat style"; the style is pleasing as decoration without aiming at any high artistic end and was probably influenced by Oriental textiles of the time. On the trefoil-shaped mouth of this vase is an eye, giving the jug a zoomorphic character; on the neck is a frieze of ornamental Greek-key patterns; on the shoulder is a wild goat running and a goose, along with ornamental motifs which fill the rest of the space; then comes a more regular Greek-key pattern which can be read as light on dark, or vice versa; and at the bottom a circlet of rays. Such unpretentious Wild Goat pottery was widely exported from its center on Rhodes to the Cyclades, Syria, Palestine, Asia Minor, Egypt (Naucratis), the Black Sea region, and even to the Rhodian colonies in Sicily as well as to far-distant Marseilles.

Amphora decorated with a running man and a vegetable pattern, from Kamiros on Rhodes · By the so-called Painter of the Running Man · Fikellura style · c. 540 B.C. · Height, 13⅜" · British Museum, London

This compact amphora is painted in red over a light-colored slip. There is a net-like pattern of vegetation on the neck, a garland of pomegranates on the shoulder, and a complex floral design below the handles. These latter ornaments provide a compositional balance to the freer movement of the athletic running figures on the front and back of the vessel. Except for a few lines on the face and body, this running man is rendered entirely in silhouette. His movement unfolds on a surface plane, not in depth. The painter of the two preceding vases felt compelled to fill all empty areas with some kind of ornamentation, but the artist here shows exceptional skill in placing a human figure in empty space without so much as a base line to set the stage. The figure of the runner is brilliantly if freely drawn. Vases of this and related styles have been found on Rhodes, Samos, Delos, and Aegina, but also at Naucratis in Egypt, on Cyprus, and along the Black Sea coastline. They are called Fikellura ware after the first place where they were discovered in Rhodes. Fikellura ware was produced from the second to the last quarter of the sixth century B.C., and a series of vases in that style have been attributed to the workshop of the so-called Painter of the Running Man and dated around 540 B.C.

Potnia Theron, "Mistress of the Beasts" and *Ajax Carrying the Dead Achilles* · Detail from the handle of the "François Vase," found in a tomb at Clusium in Etruria (present-day Chiusi, Italy) · Signed by the painter Kleitias and the potter Ergotimos · Attic · c. 570 B.C. · Height of entire vase, 26″ · Archaeological Museum, Florence

Our next three pages are devoted to Attic black-figure vase painting of the sixth century B.C. On page 50 we saw the steps which led to this style in Attica, and on pages 51 and 52 those which took place in Corinth. Corinthian vase painting of the seventh century inclined more to polychrome figures and Attic to black figures, but both used a good deal of hatching and drawing within the figure. The late seventh-century Nessus Vase we saw earlier (page 51) was the outstanding forerunner of Attic black-figure vases and already contained all the essential elements of the style in its techniques, artistic approach, and subject matter.

The next stage of development is represented by these two small pictures on one of the curved handles of the justly celebrated François Vase, named after A. François who discovered it in 1845 in an Etruscan tomb in Italy. The decoration of the vase is made up of six mythological friezes that include over two hundred figures painted in the most delicate miniature style. It constitutes a veritable compendium of Attic vase painting and of the mythological subjects most popular around 570 B.C. The masterpiece is signed: "Ergotimos made me, Kleitias painted me." For all their archaic stiffness, the two pictures reproduced here are thoroughly monumental in style. Above is the winged Potnia Theron, "Mistress of the Beasts," clasping two lions, an ancient Near Eastern motif which made its way through Asia Minor and Crete into Greece; there, as time went on, it came to represent the huntress-goddess Artemis. Below this heraldic motif is a tragic scene from the *Iliad* with Ajax removing the dead body of the "godly Achilles" from the thick of battle. This juxtaposition of a theme derived from the East with one from Homer's epic can stand as a symbol of the entire Archaic Greek culture.

Hen and Cocks · Attic tripod bowl · Attic black-figure Little Master style · Third quarter of 6th century B.C. · The Louvre, Paris

The third and richest stage of development of the Attic black-figure style came in the third quarter of the sixth century. The miniature narrative style of the François Vase was taken over by artists now called the Little Masters, who carried the style to a high level of narrative power and decorative subtlety. This and the next drinking bowl (kylix) are decorated with groups of figures on the lip, but the handle area has only abstract ornamentation. Often there are also scenes or ornamental elements on the inner surface of such bowls. The painted composition, either black or polychrome on a light background, is designed to fit tightly into the space reserved for it.

The Birth of Athena · Detail of an Attic tripod bowl · Signed by the potter Phrynos · Attic black-figure Little Master style · c. 550 B.C. · British Museum, London

Here, in the same style, is represented the myth of the birth of Athena. Aided by Hephaistos, Father Zeus gives birth through his head to the fully armed goddess. The scene is portrayed with a wonderfully mordant harshness and a typically Mediterranean exuberance of gestures which is and certainly must have been meant to be humorous. Not visible here are two inscriptions: one on the handle area reads "Hail to thee, drink from me, so be it!"; the other on the reverse of the bowl gives the name of the potter Phrynos.

Dionysus and Two Maenads · On a neck amphora, from Vulci, Etruria, in Italy · Signed by the potter Amasis, decorated by the so-called Amasis Painter · Attic black-figure style · c. 540 B.C. · Height of vase, 13″ · Cabinet des Médailles, Bibliothèque Nationale, Paris

On this amphora, whose charm lies in both its form and decoration (the lid does not belong to it), we see Dionysus, the god of wine, holding his drinking bowl, a kantharos. Two dancing maenads approach him, their arms around each other's shoulders. One of them offers the god a rabbit which he welcomes with outstretched hand. The inscription names Amasis as the potter; it is likely, if not certain, that Amasis was also the painter of this and other vases with the same signature, so they are attributed to the "Amasis Painter" who worked from around 560 B.C. to after 530.

Hephaistos Brought Back to Olympus by Dionysus · Detail of a frieze on a column krater · By the painter Lydos · Attic black-figure style · c. 550 B.C. · Height of entire vessel 27¼″; diameter, 22⅞–23⅜″ · Metropolitan Museum of Art, New York

The myth depicted on this large krater concerns Hephaistos, who was born lame and therefore cast down from Olympus by his mother Hera. On earth he became a smith and for many years produced works of surpassing ingenuity in the various arts. To avenge himself on his mother, he sent her a golden throne with springs concealed in the arms which, when she sat in it, closed on her in such a way that no one could release her. Desperate, the gods decided that willingly or not Hephaistos must return to Olympus to liberate Hera. It finally fell to Dionysus to get him drunk and bring him back, and this is the amusing scene presented here. Reeling drunk, a drinking horn in his hand, the wily smith makes his way to Olympus astride a mule attended by the boisterous company of the satyrs and maenads of Dionysus, who himself appears on the other side of the vase. The painter who produced this masterwork between 550 and 540 B.C. signed himself "the Lydian," the man from Lydia, a kingdom in Asia Minor from which he may have emigrated to settle in the flourishing Athens of the time of Pisistratus.

Dionysus in His Boat · Interior of an "eye cup," from Vulci, in Etruria · Signed by Exekias · Attic black-figure style · c. 535 B.C. · Diameter, 4⅛″ · Museum Antiker Kleinkunst, Munich

Without doubt the greatest master of the mature phase of the black-figure style, which lasted from around 550 to 525 B.C., was Exekias whose signature appears as master-potter on eleven vases and on two of them as painter. On the basis of the style of those two vases, a number of other vases and painted clay tablets have been attributed to him. Exekias combines the monumental style of the Nessus Vase (page 51) with the narrative powers of Kleitias (page 55, top); but at the same time he unites the decorative subtlety of Kleitias and of the Amasis Painter (at left) with the precision and dignity of many Attic black-figure vases. In each and every painting Exekias employs the most subtle psychological observation to synthesize these disparate elements into an astonishing whole the atmosphere of which is best defined by the Greek word "ethos." To appreciate fully the greatness of Exekias one must recognize the formal perfection of his vessels no less than the perfection of their painting. This is true above all of the picture on the inner surface of this eye cup. It can be described best in the words of a modern authority on Exekias: "The image on the inner surface is absolutely unique. It fills the entire round area. A luminous orange-red glaze has been spread over the entire ground, and on it is depicted in black-figure technique a ship with white sails in which Dionysus lies stretched out. Around the mast twine vine tendrils, and the ship gliding through the water is surrounded by frisky dolphins reputed to be the metamorphosed souls of Tyrrhenian pirates. The entire image is replete with a god-like majesty, and yet it is suffused with a mood of lyricism."

Scene of Mourning · Fragment of a clay tablet (pinax), from a tomb in Athens · By Exekias · Attic black-figure style · c. 540 B.C. · Original dimensions of this and other pinakes found with it: length, 16⅞"; height, 14⅝" · State Museums, Berlin-Dahlem

This is one of a number of similar clay tablets found in a tomb in Athens, all by Exekias and all concerned with burial rites: the lamentation for the dead, the gathering of the mourners, the funeral chariot, the funeral procession. The column on this fragment indicates that the scene is the interior of a dwelling. To the left there is a mourning woman who pulls out her hair, to the right an old man identified by an inscription as Ares, who expresses his grief by placing one hand on his head. For all its humble simplicity, this is a touching portrayal of sorrow.

Homecoming of Castor and Pollux from the Hunt · On an amphora, from Vulci, Etruria · Signed by Exekias as potter and painter · Attic black-figure style · 540–530 B.C. · Height, 24" · Vatican Museum, Rome

Most of this severe but elegant amphora by Exekias is covered by a gleaming metallic varnish. On both back and front a well-defined area is reserved for the paintings. Here we have the return from the hunt of Zeus' sons, the Dioscuri, Castor standing behind the horse, Pollux at the far left. They are welcomed home by their mortal parents: Tyndareos, at the head of the horse, and Leda, presenting them with flowers, on the left. There is something touching about the excited antics of the faithful dog at the left, and there is a youngster who brings his master a chair, fresh garments, and a flask of body oil.

Leda · Detail of preceding amphora by Exekias · Vatican Museum, Rome

In the picture on this amphora one feels the atmosphere of the courts of the tyrants at the time of Pisistratus. It is worthy of note that each of the figures, even the horse, has its parallel among the Attic marble statues and grave steles of the mature Archaic period.

Arkesilas Overseeing the Weighing and Packing of Wool (?) ·
On the inner surface of a high-stemmed drinking cup, from
Vulci, in Etruria · By the so-called Arkesilas Painter · Poly-
chrome Laconian style · c. 560–530 B.C. · Height of vase,
7⅞"; diameter, including handle, 15" · Cabinet des Médailles,
Bibliothèque Nationale, Paris

This and the next two examples continue the series (see
page 54) of vases not in Attic black-figure style. Comparison of these with Attic black-figure vases (pages 51,
right, and 55–57) suffices to reveal the immense difference in
quality between the two styles. The non-Attic vases were
either mere local imitations of Attic types, as in the plate
below, or provincial creations which are for the most part
interesting, often impressive, and even, sometimes, amusing;
but they are comparatively coarse in conception or primarily
decorative, and generally painted in polychromy, like this
and the next plate. There are, of course, occasional masterly
achievements among them. Here we have the polychrome
interior of a drinking bowl with inscriptions identifying
the various details. The principal figure, labeled Arkesilas
and thought until recently to be Arkesilas II, King of
Cyrene (569–568 B.C.), is long-haired and bearded, wearing
a broad-brimmed conical hat and holding a scepter. Seated
beneath a sunshade, he watches a group of men busily
weighing a mass of something white (which may be the
silphium plant or, probably, wool) on a large pair of scales.
The goods are weighed, packed (on the right), and stored
away in a repository below, which is separated from the
scene above by a horizontal line. This vessel and several in
a similar style were for a long time considered to be Cyrenaic
because of this portrayal of Arkesilas, but they have since
been found in Sparta and their designation changed accordingly. In fact, the present scene has recently been
reinterpreted, and with good reason, as purely Spartan,
since the inscriptions are in Laconian script and Arkesilas
is a good Spartan name. This type of vase was distributed
chiefly in the western Mediterranean basin.

Heracles, Cerberus, and Eurystheus · Detail of a hydria, from
Caere, in Etruria (present-day Cerveteri, Italy) · Eastern
Greek polychrome style · c. 530–510 B.C. · Height of entire
vessel, 16⅞" · The Louvre, Paris

Here is a fantastic mythological scene. As one of the twelve
labors set Heracles by his master Eurystheus, lord of Argos,
he was sent to Hades to carry off the Hound of Hell Cerberus. We see the hero in a lionskin brandishing a club in
his right hand and holding the monster by a leash. Eurystheus, in his fright, has jumped into a large storage jar and
raises his hands in horror at the dreadful sight—the hero's
perfect revenge on his taskmaster. Meant as a terrifying
scene, it nevertheless is portrayed with broad humor. Some
thirty hydrias—three-handled water jugs more than fifteen
inches tall—have been found in the Etrurian settlements of
Caere and Vulci in Italy and, as a class, named for the principal site, Caere. They are attributed to a workshop active
between 530 and 510 B.C. Whether they were actually made
in Caere or imported, the artist must have been a Greek and
most probably an Eastern Greek.

Mask of Dionysus · On an "eye cup" · Chalcidian black-figure
style · Second half of 6th century B.C. · The Louvre, Paris

The use to which this vessel was put is clearly shown by
by the mask of Dionysus, god of wine. The impressive head
is flanked by two large eyes which may have religious
significance. The rest of the surface is covered with vine
tendrils appropriate to the main subject. Such "eye cups"
were especially popular in Athens and Chalcis in the second
half of the sixth century.

Heracles and Cerberus · On an amphora, from Vulci, in Etruria · By the so-called Andokides Painter, from the workshop of the potter Andokides · Red-figure style · c. 510 B.C. · Height of entire vessel, 23⅛″ · The Louvre, Paris

In the masterpieces by Exekias and the Amasis Painter the Attic black-figure style attained its ultimate height. It is therefore not surprising that the highly developed pottery industry of Athens set out to find new means of stimulating the demand at home and abroad. Most vases being painted in black on a reddish-colored ground, it was thought that something new must be invented: the result was the red-figure style. After being lightly sketched in, figures were left in the natural red of the baked clay, and the black glaze previously used for the figures was relegated to the background. Details were left in the background-black or else drawn in with a fine brush in brown or, at times, lilac-red. In the black-figure style details had been incised with a graver's needle, but with the new approach the fine lines could be in relief by the use of the brush. The decisive innovation in the red-figure style was that it was no longer necessary to work in flat silhouette, and the way was opened to new possibilities in the representation of man and his "ethos."

Here we have the same scene as that in the preceding vase, but the mood is quite different. With a calm and reassuring gesture Heracles puts chains on the Hound of Hell while behind him his divine patroness Athena, in full war-dress, stands looking on. In its main lines the conception has much in common with the style and ethical feeling of Exekias—in fact, there are red-figured copies or imitations of black-figured works by Exekias. These were done by the Andokides Painter, the name given to the outstanding artist in the workshop of the potter Andokides, and they are evidence of the close link between the two vase painters. It may well be that the new red-figure technique was invented between 530 and 520 B.C. in this same Andokides' workshop, and it is of interest to note that a number of vases from that workshop are painted in red-figure style on one side, in black-figure on the other. This happens to be the case with the reverse of the present amphora; it is in black-figure style, and was certainly not done by the Andokides Painter.

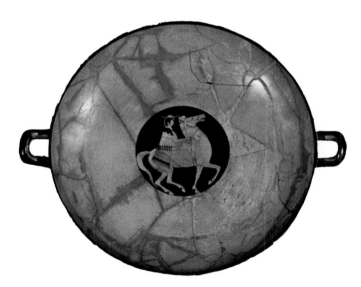

"The Handsome Leagros" · Interior of a drinking bowl · Signed by the painter Euphronios · Red-figure style · 510–500 B.C. · Diameter, 16⅞″ · Museum Antiker Kleinkunst, Munich

The elegant young horseman is identified in the inscription as "the handsome Leagros," an Athenian youth celebrated on more than fifty vases turned out between 510 and 500 B.C.

Theseus Slaying the Minotaur and *A Drinking Bout* · Friezes on the exterior of a drinking bowl, from Vulci, in Etruria · Signed by the painter Epiktetos · Red-figure style · c. 520 B.C. · Diameter, c. 11⅜″ · British Museum, London

On one side of the frieze on this drinking bowl Theseus slays the Minotaur, on the other there is a riotous drinking bout, a *komos*. Epiktetos, the painter who signed the bowl, started around 520 B.C. in the black-figure technique and went on to the new red-figure style. This bowl is a fine example of a harmonious relationship between the form of the vase and its painting, and no less notable is the decorative effect of its red figures in rhythmic motion against the gleaming black background.

Maenad in Ecstasy · Detail from a Dionysiac scene on an amphora, from Vulci, in Etruria · By the Kleophrades Painter (now known as Epiktetos II) · Red-figure style · c. 500–490 B.C. · Height of entire vessel, 22″ · Museum Antiker Kleinkunst, Munich

The painting from which this detail is taken shows a full-face satyr, playing an aulos, between two maenads in ecstasy striding away from the center. This maenad from the left side has blond hair and a lilac-colored garland. Caught up in her transport, her head is flung back, her lips lightly parted, and she shoulders a thyrsus, the staff borne by the votaries of Dionysus. A deerskin hangs across her right shoulder, a snake writhes around her left arm. We are in the presence of the great expressive style of Late Archaic red-figured vase painting, a style completely capable of communicating the new ethical feeling. The painter of this vase was for long called the Kleophrades Painter, after the master-potter of that name with whom he worked; but since a signature has been found on a vase in this style he is now known as Epiktetos II, to distinguish him from the painter of the same name we have already encountered. More than a hundred vases can be attributed to him, and his development can be followed from around 500 to after 480 B.C.

The End of the Party · Interior of a drinking bowl, from Vulci, in Etruria · Signed by the potter Brygos, painted by the Brygos Painter · Red-figure style · c. 490 B.C. · Diameter, 6⅛″ · University Museum, Würzburg

The two figures undoubtedly represent an intimate scene following the bacchanale depicted on the exterior of the vessel, a komos in which bearded men, youths, and maidens join in dancing and carousing to the sound of music. Here a young man leaning on his staff surrenders himself to the ministrations of a maiden who holds his drink-sodden head. The two figures are encompassed in the round medallion with a wonderful naturalness, and the prosaic, not very appetizing scene of the youth heaving up his drink is presented with unexpected grace and dignified reserve. There is no doubt that the perfection of this image is not just a matter of its consummate form but lies also in the tender movements of the hands and—a typical Greek trait, this—of the maiden's body. The bowl is signed by the potter Brygos, a very prolific vase painter of the second and third decades of the fifth century, and here we see the master at the summit of his achievement, around 490 B.C. The movements of the bodies and draperies are rendered with extraordinary sureness and the human expression with the most subtle lifelikeness. One step more and we shall have arrived at a truly Classical art.

Preparing for the Bath · Interior of a drinking bowl · By the painter Douris · Red-figure style · c. 470–460 B.C. · Metropolitan Museum of Art, New York

What makes this painting so attractive is its elegance of composition and technique. Two nude, well-formed young women are seen laying their carefully folded clothes on two stools. The larger of the two is drawn in full profile, the other in a serpentine pose with torso in frontal position and legs and head in profile. The result is an entirely convincing picture of human bodies moving in space, and with it the Archaic style has been left behind once and for all and we are at the threshold of High Classical art. The painter responsible for this fine image was Douris, one of the best-known names in Greek vase painting, to whom something like two hundred vase pictures have been attributed. We can judge here what mastery he achieved in the decoration of interiors of bowls during his long career. He began around 500 B.C. in the Late Archaic style, reached his maturity around 495–480, and despite a certain academic conservatism, retained to the last (470–460 B.C.) his capacity to assimilate each new development that took place in vase painting. This is proved by the present example whose style is already unmistakably Classical. There is much to be learned from a comparison of this with other bowl paintings such as "*The Handsome Leagros*" (page 59) from 510–500 B.C. and *The End of the Party* (at left) from around 490.

Vase in the form of a woman's head, from Tarquinia, in Etruria · By the potter Charinos · c. 500 B.C. · Height, 8¼″ · National Museum, Tarquinia

This and the next vase come from around 500 B.C., and their hard, strained, rather mannered style is typical of the Late Archaic period. This remarkable drinking vessel is in the shape of a woman's head capped by a crown, a *polos*. There is marked stylization of the eyes, eyebrows, and mouth as well as of the hair which bulges over the forehead in a hair net. A handle, not visible here, reaches from the top of the crown to the back of the head, and on it is incised the name of the potter Charinos. A number of similar vases in the shape of women's or Negroes' heads are attributed to his workshops. The present example is among the earliest of his products and also one of the first head-shaped vessels made in Attica where they were produced from around 500 to 420 B.C. In style this pottery head is related to the heads of figures in marble done at the same time for the Acropolis in Athens.

King Croesus on the Pyre · Shoulder amphora, from Vulci (?), in Etruria · Painted by the potter Myson · Red-figure style · c. 500 B.C. · Height of vessel, 23″ · The Louvre, Paris

This is one of the few Greek vase paintings of an historical subject: the burning of King Croesus of Lydia on the pyre, an event which took place almost fifty years before this vase was made. The story is told by Pindar, Bacchylides, and Herodotus: Croesus was celebrated among the Greeks as an immensely wealthy king, the donor of splendid gifts to the temples in Ephesus and in Delphi, whose oracle he is known to have consulted on several occasions. In 547 B.C. he was vanquished by the Persian king Cyrus and condemned to be burned alive. But a rain, said to be sent by Apollo, put out the fire and saved Croesus' life. On the vase we see Croesus with the scepter in his left hand enthroned on the pyre and offering wine to the god in a golden bowl. One of his own servants—not, as might be expected, a Persian—kindles the fire. The Late Archaic style of Myson is slightly mannered and, in fact, led to the mannerist orientation which prevailed in red-figure vase painting until after the middle of the fifth century; the chief exponent of this style was a pupil of Myson's known as the Pan Painter.

Pallas Athena · On a lidded shoulder amphora · By the Berlin Painter · Red-figure style · c. 480 B.C. · Collection Ciba, Basel, Switzerland

The tall slender figure of Athena stands out against the gleaming black glaze of the amphora with consummate clarity, gracefulness, and sense of scale. She is poised on a band delicately ornamented with a palmette pattern, and with her right hand she reaches out a wine jug to Heracles who appears on the opposite side of the vase. In its conception the goddess is much as she appears in temple statues, fully armed with helmet, aegis, spear, and elaborately decorated shield. The author of this masterpiece is known as the Berlin Painter because of an amphora in the Berlin Museum closely related to this in form and style. He decorated over two hundred vases in his long career which ran from the last years of the sixth century to around 460 B.C. In a vase painting such as this one, executed around 480 B.C., we can observe the gradual transition from the Late Archaic to the Classical style. Characteristic both of this great painter and of the style of his time are a harmonious flow of lines, a sober controlled movement, and a preference for the single figure which often, as here, is matched by another on the opposite face of the vase. It has been suggested that the Berlin Painter did not limit himself to vases but also did large-scale paintings.

61

This and the two examples following represent the Age of Pericles, the Classical period of Greek art and culture. These vase paintings surely reflect what was being done in wall and panel paintings at the same time. In ancient writings about art, especially those by Theophrastus, Pliny, and Pausanius, the greatest wall and panel painter of early Classical times was held to be Polygnotus of Thasos. Of his celebrated and highly important murals in Athens, Thespiae, Plataea, and Delphi we know no more than what the ancient descriptions recount. Certain traits were singled out as Polygnotus' special achievements: (1) women are portrayed in transparent garments; (2) mouths are painted open (3) with teeth showing; (4) in contrast to the rigid Archaic style, facial expressions are varied; (5) figures are no longer set up like a frieze on a single base-line but are distributed, alone or in groups, across the picture surface in no fixed order and with all the diversity of a natural landscape; (6) what he seeks to bring out above all is an ethical content, an emphatic but nevertheless idealized characterization of the human being. Even in our small detail we can make out most of the characteristics the literary sources ascribe to Polygnotus, and there can be no doubt that this vase painting was indebted to some large wall or panel picture of the time. The sculpturesque repose of the figures and their relationships to each other, not based on their actions but rather on their expressive qualities and relative positions, are what distinguish this vase painting from the preceding works. But this was certainly not the independent invention of some vase painter. Whoever he was—he has been called the Niobid Painter because of the painting on the other side of this krater—he did this vase between 455 and 450 B.C., and this was during the lifetime of Polygnotus. This vase is traditionally but incorrectly called the Argonaut Krater.

Scene of Leavetaking · On a stamnos, from Vulci, in Etruria · By the Kleophon Painter · Red-figure style · c. 430 B.C. · Height of vessel, 17¾″ · Museum Antiker Kleinkunst, Munich

The decoration on this jar ranks among the most mature creations from the time of the Parthenon. With the most subtle means of expression it portrays a warrior taking leave of his wife in the presence of his father and mother (or sister). The restrained sorrow of the two is brought out with incomparable expressiveness: she bows her head in mute grief, he fixes her with his eyes while holding aloft a bowl with the farewell libation.

Achilles · Detail of an amphora, from Vulci, in Etruria · By the Achilles Painter · Red-figure style · 445–440 B.C. · Height of entire vessel, 23⅝″ · Vatican Museum, Rome

Like the Athena we saw earlier (page 61), Achilles is presented in full figure standing on an ornamental strip, his gaze directed at Briseis who is portrayed on the opposite side of the vase. The similarity between the two compositions is explained by the fact that the so-called Achilles Painter was a pupil of the Berlin Painter. The style of his mature work has much in common with that of the Parthenon frieze, and of the famous bronze statue of the *Doryphorus* by Polyclitus of Argos (the statue may, in fact, represent Achilles). In any case, the Achilles Painter was certainly one of the greatest artists of antiquity, and from his hand we have something like ninety red-figured vases plus almost a hundred white-ground lekythoi (see *A Muse*, page 63).

A Muse · Detail of a white-ground lekythos, from the tomb of a girl in Attica · By the Achilles Painter · c. 445 B.C. · Height of vessel, 14½″ · Private collection, Lugano, Switzerland

Among the most significant creations of Classical Greek painting of the second half of the fifth century are the Attic white-ground lekythoi in general, and those by the Achilles Painter in particular. A lekythos is a vase with cylindrical body and long neck; in it was kept the consecrated oil used to anoint the dead, and it was buried with them. These vases may have black-figured, red-figured, or white-ground paintings. For the latter, the reddish clay was covered by a white slip on which the figures were outlined in fine lines of golden brown, black, or mat and then painted in with various colors, especially yellow, rose, and dark red. Here we have a Muse playing a kithara on Mount Helicon, as an inscription makes clear, and at the upper left there is a so-called "lover's inscription": "Axiopeithes, son of Alkimachos, is beautiful." At the Muse's feet is a nightingale which, in the words of Aristophanes, "sings with the Muses." To the left, not included here, stands a second Muse. In both style and quality, this picture by the Achilles Painter, whom we encountered before (page 62), ranks with the contemporary friezes on the Parthenon.

Dead Warrior in Front of His Tomb · Detail of a white-ground lekythos, from Eretria (Boeotia) · By "Group R," close to the style of the Reed Painter · End of 5th century B.C. · Height of vessel, 18⅞″ · National Museum, Athens

In the middle of the fifth century B.C., white-ground lekythoi began to be painted with funerary scenes. In this detail we see a young warrior seated before his own tomb. His expression is melancholy and touching. At his right stands a youth, at his left (hardly visible here) a maiden. Behind the tomb rises the grave stele with blue molding, crowned by a gable and acroteria. In style the painting resembles that of the famous Reed Painter who worked at the end of the fifth century. There is remarkable freedom in the brushwork: lines are brushed in as in a sketch, the colors are lightly washed across the surface, and the seated warrior is slumped in three-quarter profile, all features that combine to lend depth to the composition and plastic volume to the figures. The style of this and other later white-ground lekythoi differs from that of all the vase paintings we have examined so far, and it is difficult to explain this free style except as the result of influence from large-scale painting. Because of this, the name of Parrhasios is often cited, since he was the celebrated artist who renewed the style of wall painting in the last decades of the fifth century.

The Myth of Phaon · Detail of a hydria, from Populonia, in Etruria · By the Meidias Painter · Red-figure style · 410 B.C. · Height of entire vessel, 18½″ · Archaeological Museum, Florence

On the right is the handsome Phaon playing a lyre and looking over his shoulder at Demonassa who offers him a golden diadem. From the left the small winged boy Himeros ("Longing") flies toward him with open arms. Farther left there are two nymphs, of whom one is seen here. The myth recounts that the goddess Aphrodite (a bit of her chariot can be made out above Phaon) transformed the ugly old boatman Phaon into a handsome youth because he ferried her without payment across the straits of Lesbos although she presented herself in the guise of an ancient crone. Here we see him seated beneath an arch of laurel together with the beautiful Demonassa and surrounded by gods and nymphs. The Meidias Painter carried on the Phidian style of the Parthenon pediments, but with him that lavish but controlled style took on a mannerism having an entirely personal stamp: a fantastic play of beautiful bodies, some in transparent garments; gestures that are studied; extreme refinement in the treatment of draperies; and abundant use of gold-colored details such as diadems, necklaces, bracelets, and the love god's wings. It is the sensuous world of Aphrodite which reigns over the art of this master. He was active in the last two decades of the fifth century, but the influence of "Meidian mannerism" extended far into the fourth century.

63

Dionysus and Ariadne among Actors · On a volute-handled krater, from Ruvo (Apulia), Italy · By the Pronomos Painter · Red-figure style · c. 400 B.C. · Height of vessel, 29½″ · National Museum, Naples

This and the next two vases represent the Late Classical and Post-Classical styles of the late fifth and the fourth centuries B.C. With the disastrous conclusion of the Peloponnesian War in 404 B.C. there was a halt in production of Attic vases and, therefore, in their export to southern Italy and southern Russia (Kerch in the Crimea). When Athens began to return to normal in the early fourth century, it found that its chief markets in both west and east had taken to producing their own vases, often under Attic influence.

The luxurious vase pictured here, with its high ornamental volute-handles, is notable for its elaborate form and its use of both red-figured and polychrome decoration. However, its real importance lies in its subject matter more than in its intrinsic artistic quality. The vase is typical of Attic vase painting after the Meidias Painter. Whoever the artist of this painting was, he has become known as the Pronomos Painter because of the figure of the aulos-player and actor Pronomos, seen seated in the lower register of the decoration; the fame of this actor has been handed down in literary sources. Although most of the individual figures are identified by inscriptions, the interpretation of the whole remains puzzling in many particulars. Generally the painting has been thought to depict a satyr play, with the Lord of the Theater, Dionysus, in company with Ariadne, portrayed in the center of the upper register and surrounded by the chorus of the satyr play. The chorus consists mostly of naked young satyrs, some of whom carry bearded satyr masks, as well as, at the upper right, Papposilenos, the stock comic old man. Further, we can identify through the inscriptions the poet Demetrios, seated at the lower left, then Pronomos himself, and standing near him the lyre-player Charinos. In the upper register there are three richly dressed figures holding masks in their hands: to the left of Dionysus is King Laomedon, to the right of Ariadne is the king's daughter Hesione with the winged Himeros, and next to her is Hercules her rescuer. All three of these mythological personages appear in the trappings of actors in tragedy. Odd as this motley company may be, it is not impossible that a vase painting could encompass such a curious mixture of actors, costumed for their roles, together with the mythological personages whose parts they take. In any event, because there are several vase paintings contemporary with this and closely related to it in subject matter, it is thought that there must have been a common prototype in some wall painting done around 400 B.C.

Dionysus and Maenads · Detail of a volute-handled krater, from Ceglio del Campo (Apulia), Italy · By the Karneia Painter · Italiote red-figure style · c. 410 B.C. · Height of entire vessel, 28⅜″ · National Archaeological Museum, Taranto

This is an outstanding example of the red-figured vase painting done in Italy at the end of the development of Greek vase painting. The detail shows the youthful Dionysus in company of maenads dancing and making music.

The Capture of Thetis by Peleus · On a pelike, from Kamiros, Rhodes · By the Marsyas Painter · Red-figure polychrome Kerch style · Third quarter of 4th century B.C. · Height of vessel, 16¾″ · British Museum, London

This vase made in Kerch in the Crimea combines the red-figure technique with polychromy (white, gold, blue, green). The sea-nymph Thetis is surprised in her bath and captured by Peleus. The hero is accompanied here by the winged Eros, and the capture takes place in the presence of Aphrodite, seated at the right, and the Nereids. The impression of spatial depth and plasticity is due to the use of the various colors, to lines which are broken up, and to ingenious foreshortening and torsion. With this vase we arrive at the ultimate step in the development of red-figured Greek vase painting.

Lion Hunt · Detail of frieze of the Sarcophagus of Alexander, from the royal necropolis in Sidon · Attic · End of 4th century B.C. · Polychrome painted marble · Height of frieze, 23″ · Archaeological Museum, Istanbul

The Hellenistic period, which lasted from the reign of Alexander the Great in the last third of the fourth century B.C. to that of Augustus (27 B.C.—A.D. 14), ushered in a new epoch in which Greek art and culture spread over the entire *orbis terrarum*, and itself came under the influence of various Eastern cultures. What resulted was a world art under the hegemony of the Hellenistic empire. Hellenistic art flourished in the leading cities of the wideflung regions of the Alexandrian and post-Alexandrian empires, among them the Macedonian residence-city of Pella (see plates below), Athens (at right), Alexandria, various towns in southern Italy and Sicily (see following page), and Pergamum, Miletus, Epidauros, and Antiochia. It was during that time that vase painting declined to an insignificant craft, after having exhausted itself in the Late Classical style of the fourth century: in general, it was satisfied to turn out attractive forms with unpretentious ornamental decoration. Wall and panel painting, however, were another matter. Although only a few original examples have come down to us, Hellenistic art in those forms must have been of great importance; we gather this from ancient writings about art but also, and more significantly, from the mass of indirect evidence, such as copies in mosaic or paint that were done at a later period, especially those found in Pompeii. The most famous of these is the mosaic depiction of one of Alexander's battles which was discovered in the House of the Faun in Pompeii and is now in the National Museum at Naples. In all likelihood it was a conscientious copy in mosaic of a celebrated wall painting made almost within Alexander's own lifetime. Probably in accord with the original, only four colors—black, red, white, yellow—were used in the mosaic. The lost original was painted by Philoxenus of Eretria around 300 B.C. at the order of the ruler of Athens, Kassandros. It depicted the clash between Alexander and the Persian king Darius in the Battle of Issus, which took place in 333 B.C.

It has been proposed that one of the reliefs on the so-called Sarcophagus of Alexander, found in the royal necropolis in the Phoenician city of Sidon, may depict the same battle. This is far from certain, but the section that shows Alexander defeating a Persian prince corresponds to that part of the mosaic. On the relief pictured here we have a detail from one of the long sides of the sarcophagus depicting a lion hunt. The frieze is Attic work of great delicacy from the end of the fourth century, and this marble relief is included here because of the traces which remain of its original rich coloring in blue, red, violet, and yellow.

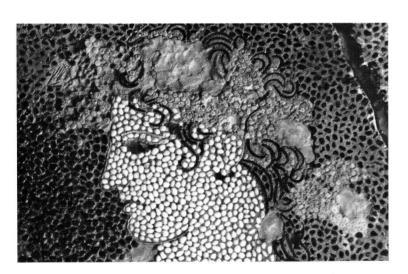

Head of Dionysus · Detail of a mosaic floor · End of 4th century B.C. · Museum, Pella (Macedonia)

This and the next example introduce us to the early stage of the art of mosaic. They come from a floor in Pella, the birthplace of Alexander the Great and the residence-city of the Macedonian kings. Such mosaics made from natural colored pebbles can be traced back as far as the late fifth century B.C.; they are found in Olympia and in Olynthus in Macedonia, dating from before and around the middle of the fourth century, and in Alexandria and Pella from the end of that century. The splendid head seen here is a detail from a mosaic showing Dionysus riding on a panther.

Huntsman · Detail of a mosaic floor · End of 4th century B.C. · Height, 84⅛″; total length of mosaic, 132¼″ · Museum, Pella (Macedonia)

The huntsman is part of a mosaic floor depicting a lion hunt. The sculptural quality of the figure is truly astonishing and is due in part to the lead stripping that emphasizes the contours in certain places. The limitations of the medium—pebbles, with their small range of natural colors —explain why this type of mosaic has played no great role in the history of art.

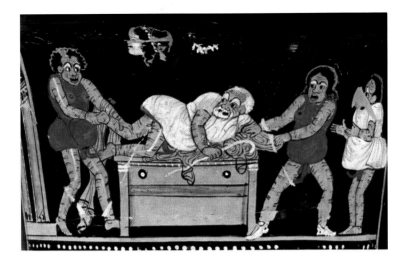

Mime Scene · Detail of a krater, from Nola (Lucania), Italy ·
By the painter Asteas · Polychrome style of Paestum ·
c. mid-4th century B.C. · Height of entire vessel, 14⅝″ ·
State Museums, Berlin-Dahlem

A new theme appears in the late phase of vase painting:
scenes from the southern Italiote vulgar comedy which
was acted by mimes. On a stage supported by white columns, not visible here, two comic characters, Gymnilos
and Kosilos, struggle to drag an old miser off the money
chest to which he clings in desperation while his servant
stands by helplessly, knees quaking. The broad humor
and rich characterization typical of the bawdy pranks of
the southern Italian burlesque plays, the *phlyakes*, are well
expressed in this vase painting. These low comedies often
made fun of the noble themes of the epics and mythology,
though in the present case we seem to have a sort of
thieves' comedy. The painter of this and other "Phlyax
vases" was one Asteas, who was active in Paestum between
360 and 330 B.C. The style of the Phlyax vases was the last
creative contribution of Greek vase painting to Late
Classical art.

Maiden · On a lekanis, from a tomb on the island of Lipari
off northwest Sicily · By the Lipari Painter · Polychrome
style of Lipari · Last quarter of 4th century B.C. · Diameter,
5⅞″ · Museo Eoliano, Lipari, Italy

In form, color, subject matter, and style, this and the next
example are entirely different from the Greek vases and vase
paintings in the red-figured style of Classical stamp. They
belong to a new world, the Hellenistic. Both vases are
mannered and, one might say, "baroque" in form and pictorial decoration, both show influences from the vessels in
precious metals which Hellenistic times especially favored.
Here we have a special type of covered dish called lekanis,
with elegant metal handles. On the cover, in delicate mat
tones of brown, white, and blue, are three half-nude
maidens; one of them is a winged Nike, who offers up a
girdle, the symbol of virginity. It appears from this that the
vessels were used for wedding gifts. Many bowls of this
same type found on the island of Lipari permit us to speak
of a distinct Lipari style and of a Lipari Painter active in the
last quarter of the fourth century B.C.

Lidded krater with painted and relief decoration, from
Centuripe, Sicily · Polychrome style of Centuripe · 3rd
century B.C. · Height of vessel, 22″ · Institute for Classical
Archaeology, Catania, Italy

This very ornate vessel is richly decorated with relief work
and polychrome painting. On the vault of the lid there is
the twisting tail of a sea-panther surrounded by frisking
dolphins; on the body of the vessel a woman sits on a chair
with elaborately turned legs, while two serving maids attend
her with sunshade and fans. Probably this was meant as
a picture of a deceased woman, since similar scenes are
found on tomb reliefs. The over-all impression given by
the delicate tones of blue, yellow, and gold against the
rose-red background is like that of the fresco art found in
Alexandria and Pompeii. Such vessels were made in
Hellenistic times in the ancient town of Centuripae in Sicily.

Sphinx · Part of the wall covering of a tomb chamber in La Banditaccia near Cerveteri · Orientalizing phase of the Etruscan Archaic style (c. 700–475 B.C.) · Before the middle of 6th century B.C. · Polychrome painted clay plaque · British Museum, London

This and four other polychrome painted clay plaques, called the Boccanera slabs after their discoverer, came from an Etruscan tomb near Cerveteri (the ancient Caere) where they served as wall covering. Two of them show a crouching sphinx with crescent-shaped wings. On the other three there are friezes with a total of nine elaborately dressed figures, male and female, representing in all likelihood a religious ceremony. The sphinx—a winged lion with human head—entered Cretan-Mycenaean culture from Egypt by way of the Near East, primarily from the Syrian and Phoenician cultures. It was a familiar motif on Greek vases and art objects by the late eighth century. Although as time went on the Greeks transformed the motif into one of considerable charm, it never lost completely the traits that reveal the Eastern origin of both its form and content. The present depiction is unthinkable without some eastern Greek prototype, but the Etruscan style—which, as has been said, is "full of character but coarsens the eastern Greek elegance"—is evident in both form and coloring. What we have here, then, is a product of the orientalizing phase of the earliest style of the Etruscans.

Two Bearded Men and a Tiny Winged Creature · From a tomb in Cerveteri ("Campana Group") · Ionian-Etruscan phase of the Etruscan Archaic style (c. 700–475 B.C.) · Third quarter of 6th century B.C. · Polychrome painted clay plaque · The Louvre, Paris

To the second phase of Etruscan panel and wall painting belong the pictures from a series of tombs of which the most famous are the group containing the so-called Campana slabs, originating in Cerveteri, plus five tombs in Tarquinia identified respectively as the Tomb of the Bulls, of the Augurs, of the Lionesses, of the Hunting and Fishing Party, and of the Baron. In all of them the style shows the mixture of Eastern Greek-Ionian and local Etruscan elements typical of the last third of the sixth century B.C. Their subject matter likewise is drawn from both Greek and Etruscan sources and is often very difficult to explain. Thus, on the basis of one Campana slab (not reproduced here) which shows a winged youth bearing away a woman, the over-all theme is held by some to be the carrying-off of the deceased by a spirit of death into the Beyond, but by others to be Iphigenia led forth to the sacrifice.

Ritual Dance · Detail of a wall painting from the back wall of the Tomb of the Lionesses, Tarquinia · Ionian-Etruscan phase of the Etruscan Archaic style (c. 700–475 B.C.) · c. 530 B.C. · The Louvre, Paris

Especially impressive is the dance scene with youths and maidens in the Tomb of the Lionesses. The athletic pair are caught up in an ecstatic rhythm. The brown-skinned, blond-haired youth clutches a golden jug in his left hand, while the light-colored maiden, wearing a transparent garment, makes an unusual gesture, raising two fingers of her left hand, which probably has some ritual significance. The other paintings in this tomb include, on the long wall, two men reclining at a meal and, on the entrance wall above a niche for the funerary urn, men and women dancing and making music around an enormous jar. There can be no doubt that these funeral banquets and ritual dances have to do with the Etruscan cult of the dead. The paintings of the tomb show the Ionian-Etruscan style at its highest point. Rhythm and ecstatic movements are expressed here in an incomparable manner with vital energy and, at the same time, graceful elegance.

67

Mourning Figures · Wall painting · Ionian-Etruscan phase of the Etruscan Archaic style (c. 700–475 B.C.) · c. 530–520 B.C. · Tomb of the Augurs, Tarquinia

On the back wall of the so-called Tomb of the Augurs is a *trompe l'oeil* painted door flanked by two bearded men in priestly vestments. Each man has one hand raised to the head in sign of mourning and the other hand stretched out in sign of welcome. Plants and birds around them indicate that the scene takes place out-of-doors. On both long walls in the tomb are scenes from the funeral games in honor of the deceased, with wrestling bouts, dances, and the like. Of special interest are two masked male figures with pointed hats, one of whom seems engaged in a ritual dance while the other lassoes and seizes a third man who is blindfolded and defenseless. The first figure is identified by an Etruscan inscription as *phersu* (from which derives the Latin word *persona*), that is, a "masked person" in the Etruscan funeral games. Perhaps this scene represents the intermediate step between the Greek funeral *agon* and the Roman gladiator contests, which were introduced into Rome from Etruria in the third century B.C.

Mourning Man · Detail of the preceding plate

In style the fresco cycle of the Tomb of the Augurs is especially significant since it takes its subject matter entirely from the daily activities of the Etruscans. Certainly one cannot call the style "naturalistic," but it is based on a realistic observation which is carried further here than in any Greek painting before Hellenistic times.

Dancing Youth · Detail of a wall painting from the Tomb of the Triclinium, Tarquinia · Atticizing phase of Greco-Etruscan painting (c. 475–400 B.C.) · 470–460 B.C. · National Museum, Tarquinia

A number of Etruscan tomb paintings reveal an affinity in style with Attic vase paintings of the latter phase of the Archaic style, dated in the first third of the fifth century B.C. Since the Etruscan stylistic development must inevitably have been in the wake of the Attic, the murals in this tomb have been dated in the end of that phase. As in the paintings from the Tomb of the Lionesses (page 67), there is also a banquet scene with guests reclining on couches—*triclinia*—while musicians and dancers entertain them. And yet, however similar in subject matter, the two friezes are a world apart in style. What was dramatic force and ecstasy (though not lacking in grace) in the earlier painting here becomes lyricism and charm. The powerful realism of the early work is transformed into an almost sentimental, dream-like musical sweetness. The artist who did this mural may have been a Greek who adapted his art to Etruscan taste, or a native Etruscan who grew up in the technical and stylistic tradition of Tarquinia; in any case, Etruscan and Greek stylistic elements are here present in equal measure.

Battle of the Amazons · End slab of a sarcophagus, from a tomb in Tarquinia · Classical phase of Greco-Etruscan style (c. 475–330 B.C.) · c. mid-4th century B.C. · Tempera on marble from Asia Minor · Archaeological Museum, Florence

In this and the next two examples we see two phases of Greco-Etruscan painting in the service of the cult of the dead, the first two representing the Classical phase, the third the Hellenistic. Etruscan sarcophagi and ossuaries with sculptured decoration are extremely numerous, but painted ones very rare. On the end panel seen here, as on the other three sides, are scenes from an Amazonomachy—a battle of Amazons—with four-wheeled chariots and animated battle episodes painted in tempera on marble imported from Asia Minor. The colors—pale lilac, blue, yellow, reddish-brown, white, and black—are unusually well preserved. We see here three figures in the conventional poses of combat: in the middle a bearded Greek with helmet, armor, and shield has been wounded through the thigh by a spear and is attacked from either side by Amazons in long garments. Typical of this Classical style are the feeling for plastic volumes, the foreshortening that appears in the right leg of the kneeling warrior, and the pathos in the expression of the Greek fighting for his life. The same stylistic traits are found in the contemporary Apulian vase paintings, many of which were done in the workshops of Taranto. This suggests that this artist may have been a Greek living in southern Italy, which was called Magna Grecia, or perhaps an Etruscan who had studied with him.

Head of Velia, Wife of Arnth Velcha · Detail of a wall painting · Classical phase of Greco-Etruscan style (c. 475–330 B.C.) · c. 400 B.C. or somewhat later (?) · Tomb of Orcus, Tarquinia

This head, Classical in character, belongs to a now-fragmentary frieze in the first and earliest chamber of the Tomb of Orcus ("Hades") in Tarquinia. The name of the woman is given in an Etruscan inscription, and the tomb seems to have been used for aristocratic families of Tarquinia among whom the Velcha family must have held a prominent position. Although the painting is fragmentary, we can surmise that the woman, together with her husband, must have been reclining on couches before a table, as in the next example. The face is lightly touched with red on the cheeks, eyelids, nostrils, and folds of skin on the neck. Realism and idealism combine here in a truly Classical manner, and the head is not a portrait in the modern sense but remains within the limits of a general characterization. The dating is controversial, ranging from the end of the fifth century B.C. to the early third century B.C., but seems to be around 400 B.C. or somewhat later.

Banquet of the Dead · Detail of a wall painting · Hellenistic phase of Greco-Etruscan style · First half of 3rd century B.C. · Tomb of the Shields, Tarquinia

Members of the aristocratic family of the Velcha were also buried in the Tomb of the Shields. Two banquets of the dead are depicted there, of which this is one. The dead man, Larth Velcha, crowned with laurel, reclines on a couch with his wife Velia Seitithi sitting alongside him. The table is set with bowls brimming with food and fruit, and near it stands a small serving-maid holding a fan. Velia offers her husband a fruit with her right hand and touches his shoulder lovingly with her left. The gaze she directs at her dead husband is intent and sorrowful, but his eyes seem already lost in the other world. Comparison with the late-Classical Etruscan examples in the two preceding plates reveals that this early Hellenistic picture is already remote from the Greek character of earlier Etruscan art. A number of elements clearly define the new style: the intensity of the facial expressions, a certain naturalism (there may be already some attempt to individualize portraits, as in the man's nose and beard), a partiality for combining three-quarter view or profile heads with frontally posed torso and above all the new technique of painting that is seen in the woman's drapery and in the food on the table. This technique appears alongside the old linear outline technique and shows that a new period has set in, the Hellenistic-Roman. The picture is dated in the first half of the third century B.C., at which time Rome had almost completed its political overthrow of the Etruscan city-states.

Relatively little has been preserved of pre-Roman wall painting in the regions south of Rome (Samnium, Campania, Lucania), although there remain a good many vase paintings in Hellenizing style using red-figured or polychrome technique (see page 66). Most of the wall painting we do have is of great interest for its subject matter, but artistically it is either conventionally schematic or naturalistic in a provincial manner. However, this and the next example are far above the average of Italiote painting on panels, walls, and vases. Here we see eight of the thirty-six women who are depicted in a ceremonial dance of mourning on six sections of a long frieze found in a tomb in Apulia. In both movement and color—white, black, red, yellow, and blue—it is a truly fascinating work. At three places the continuous circle of women hand in hand is broken, in one case by a woman facing left, then by two youths, finally by a young lyre-player and a woman. This painting is too little known and it unquestionably ranks among the most impressive funeral scenes that have come down to us from Antiquity.

Warriors Returning from Battle · Detail of a frieze, from a tomb at the Porta Aurea, Paestum · Italiote · Second half of 4th century B.C. · Average height, 29½″ · National Museum, Naples

Unlike the great majority of Etruscan and Italiote paintings, this work does not have to do with the cult of the dead but, instead, is a subject from contemporary history. Two Samnitic-Lucanian warriors are seen returning from battle. Not included in our detail are a woman offering a drinking vessel to the standard-bearer (part of the bowl is visible on the left) and, on the right, an armed warrior on horseback behind whom is a man in a white mantle. This parade-like group can serve as a vivid illustration to the account by Titus Livius of the Samnite war against Rome; he describes the contrast of the uncouth Roman legionnaires with the splendidly outfitted Samnites in white tunics, gleaming armor, polished shields, and, as here, feathered and horned helmets and bright banners. It has been possible to fix the date of this painting between 330–310 B.C., that is, during the second Samnite war with Rome (328–304 B.C.), because by a lucky chance Hellenizing vases of that period from Paestum were found in the same tomb.

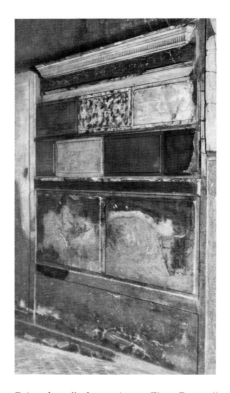

In the 1880s a degree of order was established in the great mass of Pompeiian wall paintings already known. On the basis of Vitruvius' handbook on architecture, which dates from around 25 B.C., the paintings were classified into four "styles" or, more accurately, systems of decoration. Here we have an example of the First Style; this can be traced back as far as the second century B.C., and died out around 80 B.C. To create the impression that the walls were faced with slabs of marble, they were coated with glossy stucco that was built up in relief; this surface was then painted. First Style painting is a non-figurative type of decoration that is also called Incrustation Style or Structural Style. Decorative systems in anticipation of it can be found everywhere in the Hellenistic world: the Black Sea regions, Asia Minor (Priene), Attica, the Greek islands of Delos, Thera, and Aegina, and southern Italy. Basically, the character of the First Style is pre-Roman, i.e., Hellenistic.

Painted wall decoration · Second Pompeiian Style, phase Ib · c. 70/50–15 B.C. · Villa of the Mysteries, Pompeii

In the Second Style was created an independent pictorial idiom. Its first appearance coincides with the transformation of Pompeii into a Roman colony, around 80 B.C. However, there were anticipations of it in the capital itself which suggests that the style was, in fact, a creation of urban Rome. Here we see a corner of a room in the Villa of the Mysteries. What appears to be constructed architecture is really painted architecture, an illusion, *trompe l'oeil*. At the upper left is seen the upper part of a fantastic round building. The rectangular wall panels below are no longer built up in stucco as in the First Style but are entirely painted. The wall itself loses its identity as a wall and becomes a kind of screen on which lavish richly colored architectural motifs give the illusion of three-dimensional columns, Corinthian capitals, and projecting cornices. Irresistibly the eye is decieved into seeing depth on a flat surface. That illusion of depth is achieved by an axial perspective in which, as has been said, "all foreshortened lines of the structures meet in a vertical central axis rather than in a central vanishing point" (central perspective was unknown to the ancients). By means of such illusions the occupants of these relatively small rooms could enjoy the impression of dwelling in some sumptuous Hellenistic royal palace. The illusionistic architecture was further enhanced by "organic" forms, that is eye-deceiving depictions of what seem to be friezes or representational pictures hanging on the walls. The Second Style, which is divided into various phases, began around 80 B.C. under Sulla and lasted until approximately 15 B.C., the time of Augustus. A great many of the largest and most important villas in Pompeii and Rome were decorated in that style.

Painted wall with monochrome landscape, from Pompeii · Third Pompeiian Style · c. 15 B.C.–A.D. 60 · National Museum, Naples

It must have been during the reign of Emperor Augustus that a new fashion in interior decoration set in. In the Third Style, as pictured here, flat wall decoration replaced the architectonic illusion of space. The new illusion consisted of painting a wall in such a way that there seemed to be panel paintings set into it. Those paintings copied Greek prototypes or modified them to suit the taste of the time. In metal utensils, relief ceramics, blown glass vessels, and cameos of the late Augustan and early Claudian periods we find the same fine flair for decorative forms which reminds us irresistibly of the craftsmanly character of Art Nouveau in the early years of our own century. The Third Style finally exhausted itself after seventy years, more or less, of pouring out fresh variants and playfully decorative innovations.

Painted wall, detail of a fragment, from Herculaneum · Fourth Pompeiian Style · c. A.D. 60–79 · National Museum, Naples

During Nero's reign (A.D. 54–68), the classical surface decoration of the Third Style began to break down. The newer Fourth Style combined elements from the fully developed Third Style with fantastic architectural illusions of deep space. The framing curtain now directly suggests a theater proscenium, and the theatrical impression is strengthened by the tragic mask on the propylon in the center. Looking at this brilliantly painted decoration one cannot help recalling the scenographic designs by Bibbiena or Piranesi in the Baroque era.

71

ALEXANDROS OF ATHENS *The Knucklebone Players* · From Herculaneum · 1st century B.C., copy of a lost work of the 5th century B.C. · Painted marble panel (pinax) · 16½ × 15″ · National Museum, Naples

This and the next five examples from Pompeii, Herculaneum, and Rome, whether painted or in mosaic, are almost certainly imitations of original paintings from Classical or Hellenistic Greece. As we have already pointed out, this in no way means that they can be considered faithful copies. Here we have a small painting on marble which is signed by Alexandros of Athens, presumably the copyist and not the original artist. In it we rediscover the special atmosphere of works from the second half of the fifth century B.C. Its style and painterly technique, with shading on the draperies, have much in common with the pictures on fully developed white-ground lekythoi (see page 63). Each of the five women is identified by an inscription: Leto, Niobe, and her daughter Phoebe stand in the background, while the young girls Aglaia and Hileaira kneel in the foreground intent on a game of knucklebones. The imposing figure of the goddess Leto, mother of Apollo and Artemis ("the very picture of outraged majesty," someone has called her), reacts with icy reserve to Niobe's effort to take her hand as a gesture of appeasement. Niobe herself, the middle figure, makes her gesture with great reluctance, prodded by her daughter. For various reasons it has been doubted that the two groups were taken from the same original: for one thing, the names Aglaia and Hileaira do not figure in the myth of Niobe; for another, the standing figures have been disproportionately heightened by the copyist to leave room for the kneeling figures in the foreground. It seems likely that the Greek copyist attempted to heighten the interest of the original three-figure composition by introducing the foreground group.

Perseus and Andromeda · Wall painting from the House of the Dioscuri, Pompeii · Fourth Pompeiian Style · c. A.D. 65–70 · 48 × 39½″ · National Museum, Naples

Andromeda's mother foolishly boasted of her daughter's beauty to the Nereids, the Daughters of the Sea, who complained to Poseidon; he unleashed a flood upon the land and with it a frightful dragon. The oracle decreed that salvation could come only if Andromeda were delivered up to the monster, but at the last moment she was rescued by Prince Perseus. In our painting the grim myth has been debased into a love story with a fairy-tale prince and a true-to-life princess. With an elegant gesture she sets to rights her beautifully draped silk garment, and with grace and dignity permits the handsome youth to take her off to a more hospitable locale for their first chat. Such a reduction of a myth to human terms would have been unthinkable before Hellenistic times, and the attitudes current in Rome in the period of the Fourth Style must have influenced this conception. The same theme, with minor variants in the composition, was frequently painted in Pompeii, which permits us to conclude that all the versions must go back to some Greek prototype; probably it was the picture Pliny mentioned as being by the famous painter Nikias.

Alexander the Great in Combat · Detail of the *Battle of Issus*, from the House of the Faun, Pompeii · Late Hellenistic copy in the First to Second Pompeiian Styles · c. 80 B.C. · Mosaic · Height of whole, 8′ 10¾″ · National Museum, Naples

The largest villa in Pompeii, having a surface area exceeding that of the Hellenistic royal palace in Pergamum, is the House of the Faun, named from the bronze statuette of a dancing faun found there. In major respects its decoration still belongs to the First Style, of the second to early first century B.C.; this explains why the principal medium used was still mosaic. The most important of the mosaics, the *Battle of Issus*, is also the most famous antique mosaic that has survived to our day.

A great event found here its worthy expression in art: the great king with all his heroic energy comes face to face with the "barbarian" king who is both royal and human. In his encyclopedic *Natural History*, Pliny the Elder (A.D.23/24–79 —he perished in the eruption of Vesuvius) mentions an outstanding painting by Philoxenus of Eretria depicting the battle between Alexander and Darius which was done at the order of King Cassander of Macedonia (317–297 B.C.). That painting is almost generally conceded to have been the prototype for this mosaic. Especially convincing is the fact that the mosaic uses only four colors—white, yellow, red, and black (no blue)—and this is the palette used by various great painters of the fourth century B.C.; among these were Apelles and Nicomachus, and the latter was the teacher of Philoxenus of Eretria, the presumed author of the original battle-picture. The mosaic technique used is strong evidence that the copy was executed in Pompeii itself. But how could a mosaic artist in Pompeii have copied a large-scale panel painting in the possession of the Macedonian court? Here again a literary source helps: it is highly likely that the painting was brought to Rome as booty by the consul L. Aemilius Paullus Macedonicus after his victory over King Perseus of Macedonia in 167 B.C. According to certain authorities, the mosaic was executed in the transitional period between the First and Second Pompeiian Styles, around 80 B.C.

DIOSCURIDES OF SAMOS *Street Musicians* · Mosaic from the Villa of Cicero, Pompeii · Copy in the Third Pompeiian Style (15 B.C.–A.D. 60) of a Hellenistic painting of the 3rd or 2nd century B.C. · Height, 16½″ · National Museum, Naples

Here we are in a quite different world, that of humble street musicians. A masked woman followed by a dwarf accompanies on the aulos two plump male dancers who play clappers and a hand drum. The scene takes place on a small stage and represents an interlude in a theater performance. The brightly colored naturalistic style leaves no doubt that the original must have been a Hellenistic painting of the period of the Attic New Comedy. This mosaic has as its companion-piece *The Visit to the Wise Woman.* In this and the three preceding examples we can see how far the cosmopolitan character of the Hellenistic and Roman epochs went beyond the accepted repertory of subject matter and the representational modes of the Classical period: we have seen a myth transformed into a mere episode of gallantry, goddesses stooping to express human feelings, an historical event in which Greek heroism clashed with Barbarian humanity, and in this mosaic, a glimpse of the lower classes of the theatrical world.

Marine Life · Floor mosaic from the House of the Faun, Pompeii · Probably a copy in Second Pompeiian Style of a Hellenistic painting · 33½ × 33½″ · National Museum, Naples

In this and the example reproduced below we have two further aspects of the new repertory: the world of animals here, and humor in the next. Technically both pieces are brilliantly skillful specimens of the art of mosaic, whatever the original paintings from which they were copied may have been. The several variants of this marine composition, one of which is in the House of the Faun in Pompeii, show the popularity of subjects drawn from natural history as well as the decline of the art since the Hellenistic fish paintings of the second century B.C. To the present-day viewer there is special fascination in the large prawn at the upper border, the shark between a nautilus and a large squid, and the fight between a lobster and an octopus in the center. In the middle of the left-hand margin there is a small rock on which perches a bird watching for prey, and two smaller rocks appear at the bottom.

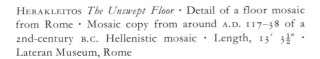

HERAKLEITOS *The Unswept Floor* · Detail of a floor mosaic from Rome · Mosaic copy from around A.D. 117–38 of a 2nd-century B.C. Hellenistic mosaic · Length, 13′ 3½″ · Lateran Museum, Rome

Of the large floor mosaic from which this detail comes only fragments survive which made up the border around a lost central picture. It once occupied the middle of the floor in a square room roughly thirty-five feet on each side in a dwelling within the Aurelian walls south of the Aventine Hill. When this highly significant mosaic was unearthed in Rome itself in 1833, the Vatican took possession of it, and it now adorns a floor in the Lateran Palace. External evidence points to the time of Hadrian (A.D. 117–38) for the origin of this mosaic signed by Herakleitos, but it was most likely a copy of a lost second-century B.C. Hellenistic original which a passage in Pliny suggests was by Sosos of Pergamum. Pliny praises Sosos as the designer of mosaic decorations so naturalistic that every object portrayed seems to cast a shadow. He mentions specifically one in a house in Pergamum as depicting "an unswept floor." Our detail, roughly a tenth of the surviving fragments of this mosaic, shows all sorts of remains of food strewn across a floor, each with its own shadow. The "show-piece" of this *tour de force* is the mouse nibbling at a nut in the lower center.

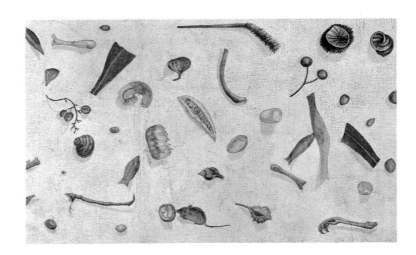

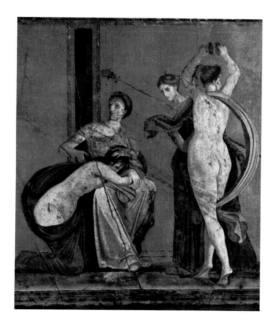

Scene of Divination · Detail of wall painting, Villa of the Mysteries, Pompeii (see next plate)

At the feet of the divine pair Dionysus (Bacchus) and Ariadne sits old Silenus, his fine Socrates-like head crowned with laurel. A young satyr stares intently into the jug Silenus holds, while a second satyr brandishes aloft a demoniac Silenus-mask. This seems to be a form of divination by mirror in which the liquid in the jug reflects future events. The mask and the head of Silenus himself are juxtaposed in a contrast somewhat akin to that of the two dancing women on the right in the preceding illustration.

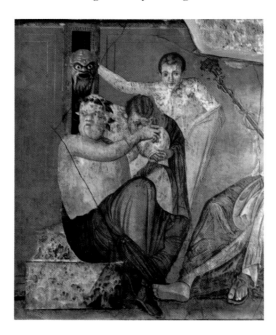

Left wall and main wall, Villa of the Mysteries, Pompeii

On the left-hand wall we see the preparations for the ceremony of initiation; on the principal wall are the scene of divination, Dionysus and Ariadne, and a kneeling torch-bearer. It can be said that much of the entire cycle, in both style and iconography, suggests that it was copied from some original that may have been done in Pergamum in the second century B.C. It appears that, like the Pompeiians, the kings of Pergamum had private rooms set aside in their palaces for the worship of Dionysus. In any event, such "Arcadian" mysteries seem to have been a link between Hellenistic Greece and the educated Romans of the first century B.C.

Flagellant and Dancers · Detail of a wall painting · Period of the Second Pompeiian Style (c. 50 B.C.), after an unknown original of the 2nd century B.C. (?) · Tempera · Height of frieze, 10′ 10¼″ · Villa of the Mysteries, Pompeii

Leaving Pompeii by the city gate leading to Herculaneum, among the funerary monuments lining the road is one belonging to the Istacidius family, wealthy Pompeiians of Roman origin, who seem to have owned the nearby dwelling known as the Villa of the Mysteries. The character and significance of this and similar *villae urbanae* of well-to-do Romans in the second and first centuries B.C. have been described in this way: "A wealthy urban society wished to enjoy to the full the pleasures of country life without any of its discomforts and so, in line with the culture it had acquired from Greece, turned to nature. The Romans' feeling for landscape was sentimental, like that of all city-dwellers. The same may be said about the relationship of that society to the great god of Nature who, together with his followers, is portrayed on the walls of the Villa of the Mysteries."

The room containing the famous frescoes of the Mysteries is surprisingly small, about twenty-nine by nineteen feet. Yet the pictures constitute the most significant cycle that survives to us, not only in Pompeii but from all of ancient painting. It contains twenty-nine almost life-size figures against a red background. A dark violet border runs above the top of the pictures all around the room, and the frieze and high base consist of marble incrustation imitated in paint according to the Second Style of the first century B.C. No less impressive than the color is the statuesque plasticity of the figures and groups. Ignorant as we are—to our great loss—of what wall painting was really like in Greece, here we are irresistibly reminded of the Greek relief friezes we do know.

These three illustrations include about half of the complete cycle. Ever since its discovery the interpretation of its complex symbolic content has been a problem for archaeologists and historians of religion, and there is still no general agreement on many questions. Nevertheless, it is accepted today that the subject concerns the initiation of a bride into the Dionysiac-Bacchic mysteries. Three distinct but interconnected themes can be made out: the bride and her mother (not reproduced here); the preparations for the rites (plate below, which shows the left-hand wall up to the lyre-player); and the god Dionysus himself, with Ariadne and his followers (see also the plate below, which includes the central group on the main wall). The cycle falls into certain separate groups having a relationship to each other which was perfectly clear to the inhabitants of the villa, though to us today it has not given up all its secrets. Immortals and mortals—exclusively women—are involved together in the initiation rite.

Here we see two groups. To the right two women, one richly clad, the other naked, dance to the clashing of cymbals, possessed by Dionysian ecstasy. On the left, a maiden buries her head in the lap of a seated woman who bares the girl's back in readiness for the whip of a female demon (the corner figure of the adjacent wall, not visible here). This appears to be a rite in which fertility is guaranteed by beating with the "rod of life."

Medea Preparing to Slay Her Children · Detail of a wall painting, from Herculaneum · Copy in Fourth Pompeiian Style (A.D. 70–79), after a Hellenistic original · Height, 53⅞″ · National Museum, Naples

Inevitably one is reminded here of Hellenistic draped statues. That this is a copy of a lost painting is strongly suggested by the fact that other copies have been found in Pompeii and Stabia. The subject in itself is of great interest, since it goes back to Euripides' celebrated play *Medea* in which Medea, abandoned by her husband Jason, resolves on vengeance and puts to death their two young sons. Like the three great monologues of Euripides' play, the painter here brings into powerful relief the deep inner conflict of Medea as wife and mother. Racked with grief, she gazes at the children (their figures have not survived in this version), wrings her hands, and holds the sword in readiness. Many authorities trace this masterly copy back to a lost early Hellenistic painting from around 280 B.C. Others, following a clue in Pliny, identify it with a *Medea* by Timomachos of Byzantium, a contemporary of Julius Caesar's; Timomachus was paid eighteen talents—around 80,000 dollars—for two paintings, one of Medea and one of Ajax, to be placed in the temple of Venus Genetrix in Rome.

Europa and the Bull · Wall painting from the House of the Punished Cupid, Pompeii · Third Pompeiian Style · c. A.D. 10 · Freely imitated from a Hellenistic prototype · Height, 57⅛″ · National Museum, Naples

Five wall paintings from the same house, including this one, are so closely related in style that it can be assumed they were done by the same artist. The figures are disposed in a loosely symmetrical pyramidal composition set against a kind of theatrical backdrop of architecture or landscape. The style is polished, Classical, and perfectly traditional in its choice of types and subjects. This accords well with the general character of the time they were painted, the late Augustan phase of the Third Style.

At play with her companions on the Phoenician shore, Europa, the daughter of Phoenix, was abducted by Zeus disguised as a bull. He carried her across the sea to Crete where she bore him Minos, Rhadamanthos, and Sarpedon. Here the bull god seems almost human—dignified, and even attractive. The maiden sits proudly on his mighty back while one of her companions caresses the beast. The pillars, columns, and theatrical-like fantastic landscape all contribute to the pathetic and mysterious character of the scene.

Girl Picking Flowers (Primavera) · Wall painting from Stabia · Third Pompeiian Style · 15 B.C.–A.D. 60 · Height, 12¼″ · National Museum, Naples

This utterly charming figure has turned the heads of more than one prominent archaeologist. She may have represented a particular personage from ancient mythology; she is, however, affectionately known as "Primavera" because she not only seems to be gathering the first flowers of Spring, but also because there is a hint of Botticelli in her delicate beauty and grace. Seen from the back, she clasps with her left hand a basket of flowers; with her right she plucks a blossoming branch. Her sleeveless chiton has slipped low on her arm to reveal a lovely shoulder, and the folds of the light garment suggest the flowing lines of her body. The floating mantle adds an ethereal buoyancy to her moving figure. She glides lightly and elusively away, her face concealed except for the soft oval of her cheek. Her mysterious allure would remain undiminished even if her identity were to be discovered.

The painting is a mature product of the late Augustan-Neronian period, and this accords with the fact that it comes from a villa in the Third Style located in Stabia near Pompeii. If not the style, the theme at least—for all that it has not yet been pinned down—is Greek in character, since in the same house were found three similar paintings of isolated figures which can be identified as Medea, Leda and the swan, and Artemis-Diana with her bow.

Odysseus at the Entrance to Hades · Detail of the Odyssey Landscapes frieze, from a house in Rome · Second Pompeiian Style · Probably after a Hellenistic original of the 2nd or early 1st century B.C. · Dimensions: total height of frieze surviving, 5′; total length of frieze surviving, c. 45′; original length, c. 65′ · Vatican Library, Rome

The eye plunges deep into a fantastic rocky landscape with a broad expanse of sea in the background. The scene illustrates Book XI of the *Odyssey*, in which Odysseus visits the underworld. To the left is his ship with sails set. Two nude figures sprawl on the foreground rocks, personifications of a mountain and of the River Styx. A livid light bathes the sorrowful group of the dead. Odysseus is the only living figure in the midst of the shades, who are identified by Greek inscriptions as Teiresias, Eurylochus, Perimedes, Phaedra, Ariadne, and Leda. On the rocks in the background is Odysseus' dead companion Elpenor. Interesting as these literary accessories may be, they are only incidental to the pictorial quality of these seven landscapes. With its feeling for depth and its effects of light and color contrast, the series contains the finest landscapes that have come down to us from antiquity. The frieze was unearthed in 1848–49 in a first-century B.C. house on the Esquiline Hill in Rome, where it was installed eleven feet above floor level. The pilasters (not illustrated here) separating the scenes are in the Second Style. The mythological figures in the scenes were without doubt borrowed from Greek art, but the landscape as such must stem from Hellenistic pictures in the manner of theater décor, as developed in the course of the second century B.C. (see also those in the plates on page 71). The effects of spatial depth, color, and light in these scenes had great influence on Roman landscape and architectural painting.

Bucolic Landscape · Wall painting from Pompeii · Third to Fourth Pompeiian Style · Mid-1st century A.D. · Height, 9″ · National Museum, Naples

This small wall painting, only nine inches high, is one of many landscapes of similar style and content that decorated the walls of the nature-hungry owners of Roman villas in Pompeii. A fantastic landscape, it includes rocks in the distance, a succession of temple-like buildings and a sanctuary in the middleground, and a herm with two torches in the foreground. A herd of cattle grazes in a meadow on the right, and a shepherd leads a goat over a bridge on the left. It is a bucolic idyl and it must have delighted the eyes of a weary city-dweller. The painting is a little masterpiece, painted with full consciousness of the charm of an idyllic landscape and of the requirements of the so-called sacred landscape. One sees the brilliant play of colors, the contrasts of light and shade, and the depth of space; the style is that of a form of impressionism. There were sacred landscapes from the time of the early Augustan age mentioned by Vitruvius, and this accords with the examples still extant today; Pliny designated a certain Ludius (or Studius), a contemporary of Augustus, as the inventor of bucolic landscape painting. All the early sacred landscapes show a light color scheme and aerial perspective. This painting, with its strong accents of color and form, probably belongs to the late Third or the Fourth Style.

View of a Harbor · Wall painting from Stabia · Fourth Pompeiian Style · A.D. 60–79 · Height, 9½″ · National Museum, Naples

Despite its small format and its loosely brushed-in impressionistic technique, this picture has a wealth of fine detail. Apart from the greenish-blue of the almost transparent water, the picture is made up of whitish touches against a lilac-brown ground. In the foreground is a rocky island with a lighthouse or obelisk-like monument guarding the harbor entrance, and one can make out the figures of two fishermen. Three rowboats approach from the right. In the middle ground, a pier with a latticed railing and statues set on columns encloses the entrance to the harbor. The pier extends from a point of land on which is a row of small gabled structures alongside a series of crenelated towers and, at the far right, a gate opening on a street where perhaps some figures can be seen. The inner harbor containing four large ships is defined by a shore on which stand several tall columns bearing statues, and at the left there is another pier. The harbor mouth is dominated on the left by an imposing building with colonnades. In the background is the city itself with temples, arches, and villas. The thin blue streaks in the distant background are the sky, and the striking feature of the entire picture is its high horizon line, giving the effect of a view from above. Such an impressionistic approach does not aim at topographic accuracy. In style this little picture from Stabia, one of the oldest villa-cities on the gulf of Naples, is entirely Roman, specifically that of the period of the Fourth Style.

Nile Scene · Detail of a mosaic from Praeneste (present-day Palestrina) · Reign of Sulla (80–75 B.C.) or of Septimius Severus (A.D. 193–211) · Marble mosaic · Total dimensions, 17′ 2¾″ × 21′ 6¼″ · Archaeological Museum, Palestrina

This large mosaic, now heavily restored, was discovered in the seventeenth century in the absidal hall of the temple of Fortuna in Praeneste, a town in Latium. There are two separate sections. The lower one, not reproduced here, shows innumerable hunters and animals (identified by Greek inscriptions) in a flooded rocky Egyptian landscape. The upper one, of which we see here the lower left quarter, has crocodiles and hippopotamuses, a manned boat with a cabin, birds perched on jutting points of rocks, and in the background a temple with priests and worshipers. The subject of the work has been variously interpreted as the Nile in flood and as a symbolic portrayal of all of Egypt in a bird's-eye view. The dating likewise is controversial. In his *Natural History* Pliny speaks of tapestry-like mosaics brought into Italy at the instigation of Sulla (80–75 B.C.), one of which was installed in the temple of Fortuna in Praeneste. But was that our present Nile mosaic? On stylistic grounds certain scholars prefer to connect it with the *Nature of Animals* by the Stoic writer Aelianus, who was high priest in the same temple during the reign of Septimius Severus (193–211).

Still Life with Fruit · Wall painting from the House of Julia Felix, Pompeii · Roman, Fourth Pompeiian Style, time of Vespasian (A.D. 69–79) · 27½ × 42½″ · National Museum, Naples

Almost everyone on first seeing this still life calls it a masterpiece worthy of Cézanne. The subject is simple enough: vessels and fruit placed on a step-like structure. Vitruvius, the author of the handbook on architecture from around A.D. 25, designates such still lifes with the Greek word *xenia*, gifts for guests: "When the Greeks had house guests they were invited to the family table on the first day only; thereafter they were given the ingredients to prepare their own meals, and the food thus provided was called *xenia* and so were pictures depicting such food." It is very likely that the Romans took over from the Greeks the custom itself, its designation, and the Hellenistic style of still-life painting. Our picture, by no means an isolated example, is aesthetically rather puzzling: there are certain inconsistencies—the arrangement of the steps and the amphora leaning without visible support—which are difficult to reconcile with the masterly treatment of composition and color. One wonders if these seemingly merely decorative pieces may not have placed aesthetic values above naturalistic imitation, rather like the case of modern art since Cézanne.

Cupids as Goldsmiths · Detail of a painted frieze · Roman, Fourth Pompeiian Style · c. A.D. 63 · House of the Vettii, Pompeii

While the House of the Faun (see page 72) and the Villa of the Mysteries (see pages 71 and 74) are certainly the most impressive dwellings from the early period in Pompeii, the House of the Vettii is the most attractive from the last years of the town. The owner was apparently a freedman who had risen in his station in life. Unerring powers of observation and a supreme mastery of the medium, allied with delightful humor and exquisite taste in decoration, characterize the famous friezes of the Cupids; these are, to all intents and purposes, purely Roman in style. In them are depicted glimpses of everyday life: goldsmiths here, on others are weavers and sellers of garlands, makers and marketers of oil, clothmakers, vintners, traders, and the like. But there is no hint of banality in the friezes, for the tradesman and craftsmen in these scenes are tiny winged Amors, male and female, who belong both to this world and to the higher sphere which itself is the earthy realm of Father Bacchus. The friezes were executed shortly after the earthquake of A.D. 63.

Portrait of a Young Girl · From Pompeii · Roman, late Third to Fourth Pompeiian Style · Diameter, 11⅞″ · National Museum, Naples

Archaeologists have long been fascinated by the personality of this girl who holds in her left hand an oblong writing tablet (a *tetraptychon*), and in her right a stylus held to her lips, her eyes seemingly lost in a dream. Many have wondered just who she may have been, and she has been given fanciful names such as "Sappho" or "The Poetess"—but also "Young Matron Bringing Her Household Accounts up to Date." On the basis of her hair style, with curls and gold hair net, the picture has been dated in the time of the Claudians or Flavians. The cool-toned colors, the painterly treatment, the controlled suppleness of transitions in color and form are all outstanding. What is perhaps more interesting than the identity of the sitter is the function of the picture: could it be a commemorative portrait of a girl who died young?

Double-portrait of the Attorney Terentius Neo and his Wife · From a house in Insula 7, Pompeii · Roman, Fourth Pompeiian Style · Shortly before A.D. 79 · 23½ × 20½″ · National Museum, Naples

The house from which this double-portrait came was first thought to be owned by the master baker Pacuvius Proculus and his wife, and this painting to be their portrait; but it is now understood that the bakery, which still survives, was set up at a later date. Scholars believe that the portrait shows the attorney Terentius Neo and his wife. Both are dressed in tunic and mantle. He rests his chin on a parchment scroll with a red seal, probably some sort of legal document, while she, with a similar gesture, holds a writing stylus to her lips and has a hinged writing tablet (a *diptychon*) opened toward the viewer. The young woman with her rosy complexion and large brown eyes wears a similar hair style to that of the girl in our preceding example. For all that the man is a little uncouth and not very attractive, his portrait is as lifelike as his wife's. Unlike the preceding portrait of a young girl, which may be a funerary painting, this seems to be a genuine family portrait intended to adorn a house. Since the decoration of the House of Neo was not completed at the time of the disastrous eruption, the painting can be dated shortly before A.D. 79.

Mummy case and portrait of Artemidorus, from the Roman cemetery of Harawa in the Faiyum, near Cairo · 2nd century A.D. · British Museum, London

In this, one of the best-preserved mummy cases known, ancient Egyptian and Roman elements are fully combined. The case is decorated with gilded silhouettes of the Egyptian divinities of death—among them Osiris, Isis, Anubis, the hawk-headed Horus, the serpents of Uraeus—while the portrait in encaustic is purely Roman and, on stylistic grounds, can be dated in the second century A.D. The youth wears a golden laurel wreath, a Greco-Egyptian symbol of death. Across the case in fine gold Greek letters is written "Artemidorus, farewell!"

Mummy portrait of a bearded young man, from the Roman cemetery of Hawara in the Faiyum, near Cairo · Hadrianic-Antonine period · 2nd century A.D. · Encaustic · $16\frac{7}{8} \times 8\frac{5}{8}''$ · Museum, Cairo

This is a highly realistic portrait of a man who, though bearded, is still young. It was done in encaustic, that is, with pulverized pigments in a medium of hot wax applied to a wooden panel by means of heated irons. The completed panel was set into the head of a mummy case. Here the man wears a white tunic with a *clavus*, a decoration in the form of purple bands which was a sign of wealth, though not necessarily of social position, in the eastern provinces of the Roman Empire. Over the tunic he wears a white drape, the *pallium*. The head is presented almost frontally, in contrast to the turn of the torso. As in most mummy portraits, the most striking feature is the unnaturally large eyes, a trait typical of images of the dead in many different epochs. The naturalistic style is sufficient evidence that this, like most mummy portraits, was an actual likeness of the dead man. What links the approximately six hundred known mummy portraits into a distinct class is their common origin in a few districts of Egypt—notably the Faiyum in the Nile Delta, some forty-three miles from Cairo. In those districts there were many settlements of Greco-Romans, Jews, and Christians. This explains why these mummy portraits combined traditional Egyptian elements with Roman traits such as naturalism in portraiture.

Portrait of a bearded man · 3rd-4th century A.D. · Painting on gold leaf over glass · Diameter, c. 2″ · Archaeological Museum, Arezzo

This masterwork of the art of portraiture carries us beyond the chronological limits set for the first section of this book, but it is a perfect example of the naturalistic portrait as developed in the Imperial Rome of the first and second centuries of our era. Fundamentally different from Pompeiian portraits, it has an aloof dignity, an air of remoteness; this accords with its different function, since it is a solemn official portrait. Its aesthetic perfection is due not only to artistic and technical mastery but also to the luster of its material. Typical of early Byzantine art is this "gold-glass" technique in which gold leaf is laid over glass, the drawing incised into the gold and painted, and a second transparent glass laid over it as protection. Numerous miniature portraits in *fondo d'oro* were done in this period. The art of the time was a court art partial to luxury, to precious materials; its artistic style was stamped with a new remoteness that was expressive of an aristocratic government and a religion set above and beyond the homely accidents of human existence.

Head of Abraham · Detail of a floor mosaic, from the synagogue of Beth-Alfa (Palestine) · 6th century A.D. · Mosaic of colored stones · Kibbutz Hefzeba, Israel

In this Palestinian floor mosaic we see the head, a shoulder, and an arm of Abraham as he prepares to sacrifice his son Isaac. The personages are indentified by Hebrew inscriptions. Abraham's left hand seizing the boy is visible, and the blade of the sacrificial knife beneath it. Abraham inclines his bearded head before the voice of God commanding "Slay him not" (inscribed in Hebrew). The style may be called childlike, primitive, or provincial: it is the translation of a Biblical story that was known to everyone into an image designed to be understood by everyone, a work of folk art illustrating the unconditional faith of the patriarch in his God and in his God's goodness, justice, and love for His chosen people. The floor mosaic, which also contains representations of the Zodiac and of the Torah, comes from the sixth-century synagogue of Beth-Alfa in Galilee. In this work of unadulterated folk art can be observed the transition from direct narrative to symbolic representation in both form and content. Faced with this naïve creation of common man, the magnificent achievements of Greco-Roman art—all their numberless manifestations of a high civilization—pale into an episode of an almost forgotten past: here we stand at the threshold of the Middle Ages.

the middle ages

P. Francastel

The whole notion of the "Middle Ages" bids fair to go out of fashion. It belongs to ways of thinking of other ages than ours. Men felt in the Renaissance that, after dark centuries of ignorance, they were reforging the link with the only form of civilization which had permitted man to express the eternal values inherent in human nature: the classical past. In the nineteenth century, when Western man was beginning to think of himself as the standard-bearer of evolution and progress rather than as a mere detail in a history of dates and facts, the historian Michelet still insisted that there were three contrasting phases: the first developing according to the natural order of history; the second, a grandiose adventure of the spirit led on by the mirage of the invisible; and the third—come to triumph after the French Revolution—presaging for a second time a new development in the natural order of life.

The West has not only conquered the planet by force of arms, it has also convinced all mankind of the superiority of its intellectual techniques as the one way to grasp and hold control of the terrestrial stage where man acts out his gallant epic. But this means also that the West can never again view itself in quite the same perspectives as of old. In the first place, the very act of imposing on other peoples its own modes of technical organization as the sole guide to prosperity has led the West to discover that in the realm of knowledge there exist other values, other modalities than its own. Simultaneously, it has deepened the understanding to be gained by its native methods of reflection and analysis and has also transformed its own grasp of problems on the levels of both physical causality and conceptual relationships. Embracing an incredibly multiplied number of phenomena both in time and space, extending its knowledge to both the infinitely great and the infinitely minute, the West has armed itself during the past half century with new tools of thought as well as new techniques of action.

The result: our past appears to us in new perspectives. It is no longer possible for us to carry on with the idea that the development of human consciousness has taken place in a straight line only, and that that line has been the only valid form of thought throughout all time and for all men and all societies. One of the casualties has been the notion of the "Middle Ages," at least in the sense the term has had for the past five centuries and in spite of whatever bits and pieces of lasting truth it may still express.

The text you have in hand has no ambition to rewrite the history of a whole millennium. Much more modest, it wishes only to tell about artworks produced in the West between the birth of the Christian world and the Italian Renaissance, and it still thinks of that "rebirth" as a time which initiated a new mastery of thought and generated a universalism comparable only to that of the ancient classical world and, even more, to that of Neolithic times when a single culture budded everywhere on our planet.

Certainly these few pages cannot provide a complete gallery of all the significant artworks of those twelve or fourteen centuries of development and change. The mere act of selecting them would demand long and patient study based on a new and special view of history. What is more, by their very nature there are limitations on the works that can be reproduced. Stained glass can really be shown only schematically, with no more than its lines and composition brought out clearly. No reproduction, however fine, can ever bring out the fact that, in a church enshrined by a shell of colored glass, the function of the windows is not to offer to the eyes merely another set of scenes to decipher, similar to and interchangeable with those displayed in cycles of frescoes or miniatures; rather, those windows are there to bring to life the interior space of the church with its hourly metamorphoses in light and expressiveness. It is unfortunate, but true, that a reproduction necessarily detaches one element from the ensemble for which it was conceived and thereby alters the appearance and meaning of any artwork. An album of images such as this cannot pretend to put into your grasp ensembles as they truly are or were, but only to furnish a key to let you into their few corners which are most easily accessible to our present state of understanding.

In our times, the image is *à la mode*. There is no dearth of books which make an ever larger place for the image as a clue to how things were in past ages. There are writers who fancy they have revealed something about art when they include in their books a great number of fragmentary reproductions of details as corroboration of events and principles already amply documented in their written sources. True, one can never avoid isolating the parts from the whole—by definition impossible to represent—when one tries to bring out those elements one judges significant for one's own attempt to interpret the values of the past. But it must always be kept in mind that the books we create cannot really reconstruct ensembles now dispersed and forever lost to us in their original state, and this despite the fact that the eye gives us the means to grasp aspects of reality, past or present, inaccessible to all other procedures of observation and study. And yet, if we toy with the notion that any and every fragment of figurative art belongs to a universal museum in which it may be switched about as fancy wills from one civilization to another, with no thought for the role it played or plays within a determined system, and if we blithely ignore the simple fact that to understand any work of art involves understanding the logic indigenous to the milieu which made it and to which it once belonged, we merely accumulate documents without gaining any insight either into the original value of such works or into what they can reveal of the mechanisms of thought characteristic of a limited and well-defined period in history. In the final analysis then, one derives from those artworks no more than the substratum our age holds in common with all other ages; history is shrunken to an exercise in artificial and sterile erudition in which the very notion is lost of reconstructing the wholes belonging to other times or places, together with any possibility of understanding how men's thoughts have guided their hands.

Our aim in this book is not so pretentious. Allowing for the inevitable limitations on procuring photographs of every work we should have liked to include, we have kept our choice to paintings, in the broader sense of the word: that is, to mosaics, frescoes, miniatures, and the portable pictures on wood which were the ancestors of modern easel paintings. On the other hand, we have not been content with merely a garland of what today are taken to be the "world's great paintings." Instead, we have selected in such a way as to disclose the guiding thread for those who wish to go farther and deeper. On the basis of what has been said above, I hope to show that in the course of the period between the end of the ancient world and the full upsurge (rather than the bare beginnings) of the Italian Renaissance, the function of painting changed at least twice. I do not personally consider figurative art as the external manifestation of a universal faculty all men possess and utilize in the same fashion and for the same purposes in all societies, past and present. Thus it seemed to me that this book offered a happy occasion to show in a modest way, but with precision, the value of painting as an instrument of culture, as a visual expression of thought.

* * *

In its earliest phase, medieval painting and Christian painting were one and the same. Certainly the Christians did not all at once work out an original new system of figurative representation. As always happens, to express new values they employed the old means society already had at hand. The first Christians were converted pagans; their painting likewise was a pagan painting diverted from its contemporaneous significance. This meant that the artists' first task was to work out a new iconography. Where they were able to speak their faith boldly and aloud—in the catacombs—they established new symbolic signs for their new creed. The usual inscriptions on tombs soon came to be accompanied by visual symbols: first, conventional figures posed as if in prayer; then more specific attributes; finally—very soon as a matter of fact—genuine pictorial images such as the

Good Shepherd and the Virgin and Child came to embody the key moments of the legend which was gradually taking shape. From the outset Christian painting expressed above all the fundamental belief in another existence in which the individual believer does not lose his identity. In the catacombs such painting was buried from the public eye as Egyptian painting once had been, but unlike Egyptian painting it represented a common destiny and as a result was highly generalized in character. Only very much later did it depict particular saints, the witnesses to a faith which, at the start, was spread as a direct message from the original proselytes. It was a painting of faith and hope, the tangible expression of a spiritual attitude. Later it was employed to make the rites more vivid, as well as, in addition to the rites themselves, the events and acts by which faith manifested itself more and more: first the sacred writings were illustrated, then the heroic deeds of the faithful were commemorated. After having begun as an expression of man's inward hope, Christian painting went on to bear witness, to enshrine tradition and history. It became, then, a new intellectual system modifying both the individual representation of destiny as well as the causality of the acts men perform. In short, it helped give stability first to a state of mind, a spiritual tradition, and then to the entire tradition of the faithful. In this way it created both a durable record of human feeling and a history quite apart from official history. It offered to artists—and through them to the faithful—a painstakingly worked-out repertory of attitudes and events which could have meaning only for the initiated. It is not surprising, therefore, that at the outset Christian painting consisted of only the scantiest subject matter. But in time it became the immense common depository of the concepts and memories of individuals who were otherwise strangers to each other in all their ways of doing and of thinking. As a consequence, Christian painting presents not a documentation of the manners, modes of life, and outward actions of the society which brought it into being, but the working-out of a system of communicable signs and symbols whose secret cannot be grasped by the uninitiated.

Not that Christian art rejected the means of pagan painting to achieve this end. The Christian painters of the first epoch were Roman in dress and manners, and lived in dwellings decorated in Hellenistic styles, and they kept up the techniques and figurative elements the dominant civilization equipped them with. Since their first task was not to furnish the powers-that-be with new art forms designed to persuade the masses to specific thoughts or acts, at the outset the painters did not even try to depict any society other than the civil society of their time. Later, when Christianity became the official creed of the Roman Empire, it was only natural that art should aspire to express the imperial will, which was to guarantee the conversion of all contemporary society with the minimum possible disturbance to things as they were. That is why, in Rome as in Salonica, the first great ensembles exposed to public gaze show us the Romans changed in their hearts, as it were, but not in their outward aspects. In the mosaics of San Lorenzo in Milan the Ancestors of Christ are draped in togas, as is Moses in the mosaics of Santa Maria Maggiore in Rome. It took centuries for a very small number of symbols to become immediately comprehensible to the public. For in no epoch does a figurative art develop merely through the rapid proliferation of its signs and motifs. Styles are based on a deepening of the possibilities opened up by a system, not on the dissemination throughout a culture of certain signs arrived at by an intellectual principle whereby everyone can translate at sight and automatically those signs into elements filled with meaning. For this reason, Christian art was concerned neither with illusionism nor with startling innovations. On the contrary, it became a conventional code in which, over and over again, a very few essential themes and figurative formulas were more and more deeply explored.

From its beginnings, however, Christian painting hesitated between two paths. Alien as it was to any kind of illusionism and to realism, it began by giving material form to certain intellectual concepts, by visualizing them, as it were. From that point it went on to recount the events which were part of a history at that time still "modern." For a millennium the Christian legend was to play the role played by Homer's poetry or the Vedas in other civilizations or, to a lesser degree but in like manner, by the French romances of the Round Table. As it happened, those epics were transmitted through literary and not pictorial channels, and the question arises as to how much the extraordinary hold Christianity came to exercise may have been due to the fact that, by preference, it utilized visual images to implant its message in the minds of men.

At the outset, Christian painting—a secret, indeed a stealthy art—made use of the frescoed wall painting as its means of expression. In its earliest phase it did not seek to profit from the abundant resources of contemporary art, restricting itself in the catacombs to fixing a small number of simple, isolated images with no concern for the decoration of the total environment. As a second step it had recourse to the art of mosaic. Once the Church had made its peace with the Roman Empire, Christian art became the official art and benefited from the wealth that power brought. At the same time, its content changed. Instead of recording the intimate hopes of the faithful, it proclaimed aloud the doctrine of power. The hidden art became a public art and expressed the will of great princes to establish among their peoples a single unified belief. Very soon, as in Ravenna, it held up before the Christian flock the register of all those virtues considered indispensable to social cohesion. Rather than insisting on the purely religious bond which unites each of us to the Unknown, it gave concrete form to the positive truths on which rests the solidarity of the members of a well-disciplined social body. In the mosaics of Ravenna the Emperor was held up as a necessary factor in the right sort of belief, during a long period in which divergent orthodoxies clashed head on. As generations slipped by, art became more of an instrument of intellectual understanding than a soul-stirring witness to the timorous but often heroic faith of individuals that it once had been.

It is no more than fair to insist on the high quality of Christian mosaics of the earliest Middle Ages. In Rome, Salonica, and Ravenna, a technique was worked out during four centuries which was far superior to that of any known works during antiquity. The artists employed color with consummate mastery and created ensembles whose beauty is quite independent of their intellectual message. Indeed, the beauty of those great ensembles is entirely unlike the immobile and serene perfection of classical Greek art, but it is as high a summit of the emotional power of fascination that the representation in color of an imaginary universe always carries with it. The splendor of Christian mosaics surpasses by far what the technique of antiquity could achieve and bears witness to the high spirituality of the age. Today, through our familiarity with this art, we have at last come to understand that the innumerable quarrels of the theologians—so "Byzantine" to the modern mind—were the expression of brave controversies in which individuals not only staked everything on the acceptance or rejection of some doctrinal definition, but also brought into play their spiritual being. Theology in that age was man's central concern, as humanism and mathematics were later to become and, in our time, physics and its various ways of depicting the universe. With no more than tiny cubes of marble subtly cut and matched, artists succeeded in preserving for us some reflection of the glory of Justinian and Theodora; at the same time, they made tangible to us a system which, for all its hierarchies, set up a perfectly organic conception of the universe. It would be ingratitude on our part to fail to recognize that in those few images, easy to comprehend as well as deeply expressive, they bequeathed to us documents of their age unmatched by anything we can read in the chronicles and texts of the time. A rigid religion based on the terror of men in awe before the ministers of a God who was not satisfied with promising them fair judgment at the end, but lay upon them the burden of submitting meekly here on earth to all His rites and rituals—what a vast change from the simple faith of the catacombs! Implicit already in the first centuries of our era is the second phase of Christian art.

* * *

Between the fourth and eighth centuries, painting was at first militant, then triumphant; first the expression of the hopes for the miraculous of a minority of believers, later the finest tool of government in the hands of a theocracy that sought to impose at least some fugitive unity on its subjects. This unity was made the more necessary on the spiritual level by the fragility of the political ties which bound men to each other. Although as early as the fifth century invasions had broken the frontiers of the Empire, the Roman world continued to absorb new peoples, thanks chiefly to that religion rooted in the common people and tinged with the miraculous which Rome had seen fit to adopt when the time was ripe. The last bastions were not shattered until the eighth century, and then only by a new wave of invasions brought on by the awakening of the Arab world, and by the pressure of Central Asia on the Middle East. Only then did the unity of the Mediterranean world fall asunder and the ties which held society together go slack. The general splintering of the world led also to the splintering and definitive collapse of the framework of Christian culture inasmuch as it had made of its institutions one basic element of human order. Material ruin decimated the workshops of the refined art of mosaic, intellectual ruin destroyed the last vestiges of unity in the ancient world.

Then, for more than five centuries, there were no more great undertakings comparable to those which were the glory of Salonica and Ravenna. And yet, curious as it seems, the great art of mosaic was not destined to disappear. After a few centuries it would once again produce splendid works, as soon as a semblance of organization was set up after the expulsion of the invading hordes. In the twelfth century in Venice, as in Sicily and Constantinople and later, in the fourteenth century, in Greece, new and admirable monumental ensembles were created that were the direct continuation of the great Byzantine works of the century of Justinian. No human tradition is ever wholly lost in the sands of time when cataclysms strike, nothing disappears merely because it is worn out. Humanity forgets nothing. Values suffer eternal eclipse only when replaced by other values. Man does not humbly efface himself save when other men impose a new and alien order on the places he has settled and cherished. One of the great errors of the science of history is to seek chronological dividing-posts between civilizations. At no time does a society live entirely in the past or in the future, and the present is never anything but a fragile equilibrium between the two. Thus, though Christian imagery had been evolved in the historic period when the state religion, Christianity, was incarnated in works proclaiming the triumph of dogma, for many centuries it was still able to engender new masterpieces wherever a civil organization more or less faithfully modeled after the former type came into being.

And yet it is also true that a new form of culture and of Christian art began to take shape, beginning in the eighth and ninth centuries. This form was destined to have a no less lengthy and brilliant future. In the West, Christian art of this second phase belonged to a clerical civilization, and it manifested itself first in manuscript illuminations, then in frescoes.

Just as no civilization can vanish suddenly, neither can it emerge unprepared. It simply does not happen that on some particular day and by some stroke of genius a society can invent the form and content of a new culture. Evolution is continuous; man never tosses away *en masse* all the cultural apparatus on hand. Every object, every form, every symbol constitutes a point of encounter and interpenetration of many levels of consciousness combined in diverse modes of significance and with variable aims. When one has shown that a particular graphic device or practice had already been conceived within a particular system, one cannot conclude that one has thereby disclosed the source of new ideas, the prototype which inspired a new culture. The elements are not what counts, but only how they are put together. Some practice, device, or object which within a particular context played no more than a secondary role suddenly becomes the basic principle of a new organization incarnating new and original values full of promise for the future. In this way, the clerical civilization which arose in the West early in the eighth century borrowed most of its tools from the past, but to each of these tools it imparted a new significance because it had itself instituted a new human order on both the intellectual and social planes.

It was certainly not Carolingian civilization that invented manuscripts. But it is beyond question that it was that civilization which made them the chief instrument for the dissemination of learning. The true revolution in the Occident dates from the time when in the monasteries—the only centers of organization and the only repositories of learning during the dark centuries of the breakup of the Empire and invasions from abroad —it was discovered that everything known could be preserved and transmitted in texts and images. It was then (and, in particular, in the entourage of Charlemagne) that Western civilization— modern civilization—found the way to its astonishing future. At that time the West was neither more advantageously situated nor more advanced than other civilizations. But it did understand the power that derives from pinning down facts and from the effective presentation of the truth, or of what passes for truth. With the organization of the scriptoria—workshops of scribes—and the imposition of the Carolingian script, Charlemagne gave to the West the first two weapons for its conquest of intellectual leadership. We still write in the script he championed, and it is but a short time since we have ceased to look at the world as he did. Gutenberg and the development of engraving, six centuries later, mark the moment when those two chief instruments of the concrete culture of the spirit became widely diffused and our modern world began. But credit for the actual invention, the innovation, belongs to the Carolingian world, and not by accident. Quite the contrary. It was the result of the coming together of the finest minds of a time, and it had the merit of discovering some of those simple things to which men, after a few centuries of familiarity, have become so accustomed that they no longer even notice them. So true is this that today certain younger historians catering to the popular taste can dare to assert in flashy vacuous writings that history could well do without Charlemagne, that too much, to their way of thinking, has been made of him.

The need to restore culture to a ravaged world even while it was still strife-torn made the value of books much more evident, and this was recognized as early as the seventh century. This was a period of missionary zeal, set upon rescuing the essential values from oblivion. The Irish monks already looked on books as one and the same thing as the Word of the Gospels. For them a book was a treasure, something with an existence of its own, living and personal. As early as this was launched the process of identification of thought with its vehicle, the sign. Linked with the Roman tradition, the Irish monks took one of the very first steps toward the Carolingian renaissance. A second step was taken a little later, in Northumbria, toward a closer bond between the graphic character of the image and script itself. But it was at the court of Charlemagne that men foregathered from England, Ireland, Italy, Spain, and France, from the banks of the Loire as from those of the Rhine. It was these men who gave the impulse not to a mere revival of antique culture but, rather, to the possibility of something new, a different and unique culture. From that standpoint, it is clear that, although the term "renaissance" applies less accurately to the Carolingian revival than to the later Humanist movement, this in no way detracts—indeed, quite the contrary—from the great creative achievement of the epoch. Within the Carolingian perspective, which was that of a Christian Empire, there could be no question of a return to the culture of pagan antiquity: men dreamed of Constantine, not Augustus, and they sought to fasten on what was permanent, not to cancel out a cycle of history. For the Carolingians there could be only a single Truth. The conflicts which were to arise between the ecclesiastical and military powers were not a question of the proper sharing of authority but, instead, of which single authority should triumph in the end.

Just as in the first phase, painting in the new period was to play a role so much the greater because the number of sources of learning were few. With no more than the Scriptures to go on, iconography could not depend on a diversity of themes but only on the high quality of the work achieved. In complete opposition to the ideal of monumental painting, the Carolingian clerks created in their manuscript illuminations an art which, although in a different context, is as perfect as sculpture in antiquity or painting in modern times. They invented an exemplary form of art, addressing themselves to a limited number of readers and working in a small format. Not satisfied with literal illustration of the texts, they constructed compositions which, for all their small dimensions, were as rich in complexity and as perfect as the great ensembles in mosaic or fresco. What they created was a major art, as easel painting, however small in size, was later to become. In time, the art of miniatures, whose highest achievements spread over at least seven centuries, became more diversified, ranging from literal commentary on a text to virtually independent compositions. Like mosaic, the Carolingian miniature came to constitute one of the summits of pictorial art.

And yet this is not the whole story. Miniature painting was not the only form of art in the Western Middle Ages. Very soon Western clerics, reluctant to settle for the snugness of their monasteries and not overly enchanted by the hermit's life, joined in the efforts of cultured, politically minded laymen: they quit their confining walls to win over and organize the populace, at least to the extent the secular authorities had done. From this stemmed a reciprocal exchange of influences which transformed the clergy, as well as the masses they were leading toward the City of God by means of their organization of the City of Man. This was not, as later, an equilibrium between two truths, but rather an integration of two orders reflecting a single common source and aspiration. As early as the tenth century, and parallel with the development of the refined art of the miniaturist, a popular, folk-oriented art sprang up on church walls to proclaim the doctrine of faith to the eyes of all. In their graphic approach, expression, linkage of scenes, treatment of space by expansion or concentration—the same system of exploitation of the image to embody basic beliefs held sway in both arts.

* * *

In the twelfth century the third phase of this history began and was marked by the development of the fresco and, finally, of the individual picture. Not that there was any break between the painting of the second phase—of the Carolingian Empire and the feudal struggles—and that of the third. Gothic civilization grew out of Romanesque civilization, which itself was an extension of Carolingian culture. Nevertheless, in the fourteenth century the success of a clerical culture, coupled with economic and political advances in the West, created the conditions for a new organization of power. What is more, it suggested to artists and their patrons new subject matter as well as new modes of presentation. Alongside the military powers—that is, the emperors and kings—and the clergy—Rome and the proselytizing militia of the Dominicans and Franciscans (the latter quickly brought into line) —a third, secular, power asserted itself: the middle classes, with their strength massed in cities whose fortune depended on theirs. The result: the range broadened in feeling and in subject matter that was open to art. The innovations of the fourteenth century seem, outwardly at least, inconsistent with each other. The preaching of the first Franciscans kindled a blazing mysticism in which for the first time the ancient intimate dialogue of the human soul with the One God of the Gospels was resumed; but at the same time the century expressed heartily its delight in the good things of the earth. Fashions and domestic decoration and the way things should be done became interesting in themselves for the citydwellers who were the new patrons of art. Meanwhile, the militant religious orders implanted their doctrine of the active life, of salvation through practice rather than contemplative illumination. But however diverse its aims, Gothic art was to enjoy great unity for a long time.

What is so interesting in the development of fourteenth-century painting is the question of the real motivations inherent in it which caused artists, during the first twenty years of the following century, to depart from the Giottesque idiom in favor of that developed by Van Eyck, the Master of Flémalle, and the miniaturists of the French court. This has remained one of the obscure points in history because until now no one has approached it objectively. Starting with an incontrovertible fact—that in Florence around 1425 there was a sudden break brought about by Masaccio's personal genius—historians have neglected the study of the art of the preceding century in and for itself. The academic doctrine enthroned in the nineteenth century propounded the absurd notion that Italian painting of the fifteenth and sixteenth centuries was "realistic." It never occurred to those academics that linear perspective is in no way a practical procedure for the "photographic" representation of the external world as it may exist independently of human consciousness. Perspective is, in fact, no more than a clever studio trick making it easy to repeat certain models having high stylistic qualities which do not in any way imply that the models have achieved absolute objectivity. Any and every representation of the universe necessarily is based on a selection of significant elements. Even hypothetically there cannot exist a total vision outside of human perspectives nor outside the perspectives of man at a given stage in his history. One should not confuse the realism— factual but partial—of plastic figuration with another kind of realism (in itself almost inconceivable), that of an art which would make man the equal of the Creator of the universe or, more precisely, which would require of man the capacity to observe reality not only as his own senses grasp it, but also as it must appear to the creatures beyond number which populate or have populated earth and the heavens. Every art is selective. For that reason it is linked to the demands of a particular way of understanding, and of a need for action determined both by the knowledge and by the powers of a particular society at a particular time and in a particular geographical region. And this is precisely why we can look to painting for information about the social world, but not for the immutable secret of the infinite universe.

There was no precise break between the Gothic world and the Renaissance. Masaccio borrowed from his contemporaries the theoretical and imaginative material for his art, and it took a century before the equilibrium of the two worlds was definitively upset. Gothic culture was international, and included both Giotto and Gentile da Fabriano. The art and the culture of fifteenth-century Europe were developed in the workshops connected with the French court and the Burgundian dukes as much as in the *botteghe* of Florence. Beyond question, it was Masaccio and Brunelleschi who introduced those problems which later, at the start of the sixteenth century in the Rome of Leo X, gave rise to a conception of painting destined to remain the absolute standard for generations to come. But it is simply unthinkable that our age, which, as we stated at the outset, has a wider vision of a vaster history, should retain such a standard. Whether we wish to understand better the fragmentary but effective solutions discovered by the Renaissance, or the Gothic origins of those solutions, or the role of the West within a universal context, it is absolutely indispensable that we reconsider the problem of what part was played by the international workshops of the entire fourteenth century. It was those workshops which brought into being that efficacious though limited culture which conferred on the West, however briefly, the mastery of the globe, although it did not and could not give the assurance of having penetrated the ultimate secrets of the universe. When such a study has been undertaken, it is probable that our present chronological divisions will lose both their meaning and their value and that we shall perceive a new continuity between Middle Ages and Renaissance. This will entail also our giving up, right from the start, our notion that the Western countries, France and Italy above all, constituted separate hubs of civilization linked to each other by no more than sporadic and ephemeral bonds. A finer, more penetrating knowledge of Western painting leads to the conclusion that we must study it as one of the major factors in civilization. As such, it can spread out before our eyes the fundamental customs, traditions, and structures of institutional and speculative thought that united the entire Western world.

Virgin and Child (?) · 3rd century · Fresco · Catacomb of Priscilla, Rome

This fresco in one of the great Roman catacombs was made, beyond doubt, before the recognition of the Church by Constantine. A secret art in a secret place, it was intended not to impress and overwhelm the masses but, instead, to affirm on a wall tomb, above his mortal remains, the faith and hope of a dead Christian—a functional art if there ever was one. Rather than the usual figure of a praying man or women symbolic of the deceased's personality, often found elsewhere, here we have one of the first images in which Christian art strove to give material form to the Divine. Is it a Virgin and Child or, as some think, the Church, mother of the faithful? Here we are at the first step in the creation of a system of new signs and symbols quite unlike anything known before.

An Ancestor of Christ · 4th century · Mosaic · Chapel of St. Aquilino, San Lorenzo, Milan

This small chapel, an annex to the great church, was perhaps originally a baptistery of the Arians. Entirely decorated with mosaics around A.D. 350, under Constantine III, it is one of the first attempts to create a complete ensemble of symbols summing up Christian doctrine. No longer concerned merely with the personal bond between the believer and his God, what is shown here is the intellectual system on which rests the institution of the Church in relation to its origins and traditions. Christ is enthroned in the center between Sts. Peter and Paul and surrounded by the Patriarchs, Apostles, and Martyrs—all the witnesses to His earthly mission. Traces of other depictions survive: Elijah in his chariot, the Good Shepherd with His sheep. The two principal currents of Christian iconography are already laid down here: narrative and symbolism.

Christ in Glory · Early 5th and 8th centuries · Mosaic · Santa Pudenziana, Rome

An old description allows us to date this admirable mosaic in the reign of Pope Innocent I (401–7). It has come down through fifteen centuries in a comparatively satisfactory state of preservation, although when it was restored at the end of the eighth century two of the twelve Apostles and the two edges of the composition were lost. Nevertheless, the work remains perfectly coherent and without serious alterations. We see Christ enthroned surrounded by the Apostles and the allegorical figures of the New Law and the Old (later, these were personified as Church and Synagogue). The inscription DOMINUS CONSERVATOR ECCLESIAE PUDENTIANAE names Christ Himself as patron of the sanctuary, but behind Him there is also a view of the Heavenly Jerusalem with features borrowed from the real city (the Holy Sepulcher and the Church of the Ascension). From Milan to Rome the doctrine of the Latin Fathers of the Church was beginning to be preached in images.

The Empress Theodora · 6th century · Mosaic · Church of San Vitale, Ravenna

The mausoleum of Galla Placidia was the work of the nobility, the baptistery that of the clergy. A century later, under Justinian, the church of San Vitale was built through the initiative of the Archbishop Ecclesius (522–32) and his successors Urcinius (533–36) and Victor (538–45), and completed before 547 by Maximinian, whose episcopal throne still survives. The edifice was conceived after a visit to Constantinople, and its plan recalls those of the churches of St. John in Hebdomon and of Sts. Sergius and Bacchus. Its decoration, however, is entirely in the style of Ravenna with, in the choir, Justinian and Theodora taking their places on either side of Christ as His leading servants and representatives on earth. The new church was financed by the wealthy banker Julianus Argentarius—the Scrovegni of the time—who, however, unlike Giotto's patron, was apparently more concerned with getting into the good graces of his earthly rulers than with winning eternal grace from the Church. The Christ Pantocrator in the vault of the apse, Abel, Isaac, Moses, and Melchizedek on the sides, fade into minor roles alongside the imperial splendor: not the least remarkable trait of this décor is the fact that the Empress is placed on an exalted plane with the great Biblical heroes. This is one of the summits of the art of mosaic, and the richness of its color in no way detracts from the monumentality of the ensemble.

Detail is shown on next pages

Story of Moses · 5th century · Mosaic · Basilica of Santa Maria Maggiore, Rome

There survive great ensembles of the mosaics with which Pope Sixtus III (432–40) endowed the basilica on the Esquiline hill which replaced that of Pope Liberius (352–66), founder of the first church dedicated to the Virgin. Over thirty of the original forty-two mosaics have been preserved. The Marian dogma had been proclaimed by the Council of Ephesus in 431, but here the scenes from the life of the Virgin on the triumphal arch and around the apse are still associated with subjects from the Old and New Testaments, the Apocalypse, and the life of Christ. Abraham, Jacob, Moses, and Joshua serve as witnesses to the Redeemer, but there are no saints, since these mosaics date from before the time when saints were depicted. In this scene of the revolt of the Hebrews against Moses, the technique is pictorial and entirely Occidental in conception. Here narrative was introduced into monumental art, contrary to contemporary practice in Byzantium: in the West, the need of proving was more urgent than the need to dominate.

Sts. Onesiphorus and Porphyrios · 6th century · Mosaic · Church of Hagios Georgios (St. George), Salonica

Sometime between 306 and 334 the Emperor Galerius constructed a rotunda in close proximity to a triumphal arch at the entrance to Salonica. Around 390 Theodosius transformed it into a palace church and had the interior decorated with mosaics after having surrounded the church with a circular gallery. In the center of the cupola soars Christ in the company of angels, and the drum is decorated with figures of saints against a background of architecture in the Fourth Pompeian style which must date from no earlier than the sixth century. The niches are adorned with flowers, fruit, and birds, and the saints are those of the Eastern Church calendar. The décor is obviously related to Persian art and to what was later to become the Moslem style. It is evident that in Salonica in the fifth and sixth centuries there existed a *koine*, a common mode, in which the forms, however Hellenistic they might be, were as much dependent on Roman and Latin developments as on those of the East. It is difficult to pin down the liturgical significance of the themes in the central motif: they might represent either the Fountain of Life or abstract designs in conformity with the iconoclastic doctrine. The feeling for space is entirely different from that of Rome as typified by Santa Maria Maggiore: here space is suggested but not rendered tangible.

The Good Shepherd · 5th century · Mosaic · Mausoleum of Galla Placidia, Ravenna

Western counterpart to the Church of St. George in Salonica, this delightful monument was probably begun as the Chapel of the Holy Cross for the palace of Constantius III (d. 421). It was completed around 425 by his successors, Honorius (d. 423) and Valentinian III, respectively brother and son of Galla Placidia who, at her death in 450, was without doubt buried with her husband and her brother. The mausoleum is surprisingly well preserved, and even the light still filters through windowpanes of alabaster. Depicted are Christ as the Good Shepherd gathering souls to Him and, in addition, St. Lawrence with the Cross and the Book, the tunic and the keys—once again the two approaches: symbol and figure. Already certain principles were set down here from which Christian iconography was scarcely ever to stray, and these show the role played by the theologians in the programs they worked out and in the church they guided. But however similar in principle such ensembles as this may be with the decorations of Santa Pudenziana in Rome, not only the work but even its underlying spirit are entirely transformed by a different technique, a different style, a different artist, and the demands placed on art by different patrons.

The Baptism of Christ · 5th century · Mosaic · Cupola, Baptistery of the Orthodox, Ravenna

The elements we found in Salonica and in the mausoleum of Galla Placidia appear again here. Once more there is an evocation of the universe itself, but here, in line with the function of the edifice, everything centers around the baptism of Jesus. The principal composition, the Baptism, which is entirely in mosaic, fills the cupola and continues down to the level of the walls where there are two more tiers of decoration; the higher of these is sculpted, and recalls the system used in the church of St. George in Salonica but differs by being in relief. The images in the outer circle of the cupola are not figures but thrones and altars. Thus, as in Salonica, symbolic objects rather than human representations are used here, and this reflects the famous dispute over iconoclasm as well as the relationship between Christian art in the East and that of Islam. The individual components of the vocabulary of images were not devised anew for each new work but rather were drawn in each epoch from an ancient repertory as much as they were invented: what counted was the way they were put together, the montage, what we call the structure or composition.

One of the Three Magi · Detail of a nave frieze · 6th century · Mosaic · Basilica of Sant'Apollinare Nuovo, Ravenna

Erected under Theodoric around 504 as the chapel of his palace, the edifice was consecrated to the Orthodox cult under Bishop Agnello (557–70) and placed under the patronage of St. Martin *"in-ciel-d'oro."* When, in the ninth century, the relics belonging to Sant'Apollinare in Classe were transferred to this church, its name was changed to the "new" church of St. Apollinaris. The mosaic decoration of the upper tier—Christ and the Passion, the Virgin enthroned with four angels—dates from the time of Theodoric. The middle tier, between the windows, has a line of thirty-two figures of apostles and patriarchs, sixteen on each wall. The lowest tier was executed when the church was reconverted to Orthodoxy about 560, except for the Virgin enthroned and the four angels around her toward whom winds a procession of the three Magi followed by the Virgin Martyrs. Near the entrance of the church a view of the port of Classis commemorates the transfer of the relics and the new significance of the edifice, while on the opposite wall a cortège of martyrs proceeds toward Christ on His throne flanked by four angels. These mosaics, almost contemporary with those of San Vitale, are among the finest produced by the Ravenna workshops, indulging neither in the coloristic impressionism of the beginning of the century nor in the somewhat arid style of the mosaics at Classe.

St. Apollinaris and the Transfiguration · 6th century · Mosaic · Basilica of Sant'Apollinare in Classe, Ravenna

This church was founded by Archbishop Urcinius (533–36) and completed before 549 by the wealthy Julianus, both of them agents of the imperial reconquest of the territory of Ravenna, local partisans of the policy of imperial unity. They were among those who, in the provinces, actively aided in Justinian's great reconsolidation of the Empire, viewing the undertaking not as an annexation of Italy by Byzantium but, instead, as a revival of the ancient Roman dignity to be won by force of arms. However, the mosaic decoration of this church was not completed until more than a century later, around 675, in the time of the bishop Reparatus and of Constantine Pogonatos. It is interesting to compare this apse with the Good Shepherd in the mausoleum of Galla Placidia (page 92): here, in striving for artistic unity, both the symbolic and the figurative elements are relegated to less important parts of the edifice. San Vitale represents a summit of art, a classical high point, whereas in this church the first warnings of an impending academicism make themselves felt.

St. Demetrius between Prefect Leontius and Bishop John · 7th century · Mosaic · Basilica of St. Demetrius, Salonica

To round out the series of representative mosaics, this work of the seventh century is typical of the moment when imaginative invention came to a halt. Erected around 412–13 under Leontius, Prefect of Illyria, then destroyed between 629 and 634, and rebuilt by the bishop John (d. 649), the church was razed by a fire in 1917. In 1907 extensive mosaic decoration had been discovered, but of it no more survived the fire than the portraits of Sts. Demetrius and Sergius and this picture of St. Demetrius between the two founders of the church. A comparison of the virtually hieratic style of these figures with those of the Church of St. George in the same city (see page 92) shows the strength of the local "School"; it also reveals the variety that is possible in an art like mosaic in which, with identical means, works as different as those in Santa Pudenziana in Rome and those in Ravenna could be created. This tells us much about the basic character of the mosaic art and also how styles tend to end in academicism.

Story of Adam, from the Ashburnham Pentateuch · North Africa or Spain · 6th century · Manuscript illumination · Ms. nouv. acq. lat. 2334, Bibliothèque Nationale, Paris

This precious manuscript of only nineteen pages seems to date from the sixth century. Together with the Rossano codex, it reveals the transition from the antique style of miniature painting to the more narrative forms of the Western Middle Ages. The brilliance of the coloring contrasts with the minute detail and complexity of the drawing. In other famous manuscripts of the same period, in particular the two Virgil manuscripts in the Vatican and the Vienna Genesis, one finds again the Roman tradition of large-scale compositions which reappears in Byzantium in the ninth-century Macedonian renaissance. Here, on the contrary, the style is no longer based on the reduction of a monumentally conceived composition into a miniature but, instead, on the exploitation of line itself. Such an art was not aimed at impressing multitudes, but rather at speaking to the learned clerk as he pored over the texts. In these crowded scenes from the Pentateuch, the first five books of the Old Testament, one catches glimpses of the daily life of a society concerned with integrating its faith and its behavior into a living whole.

Christ before Pilate, from a Book of Gospels (Codex Rossanensis) · 6th century · Manuscript illumination · Treasury of the Cathedral, Rossano

The principle adopted for the decoration of this New Testament manuscript—only the Gospels of Matthew and Mark survive—differs from that used in the Ashburnham Pentateuch, but the elements are identical. Richness and brilliance are achieved here by the purple background, and a series of scenes directly illustrates the text. The approach invented by the artists of the catacombs reappears here in a new form; henceforth it was continually to interact with that other approach which inspired the great monumental decorations. The lavishing of purple, a precious and costly material, on the pages of the manuscript gave it a value to which the clerics were not indifferent. Such a manuscript represented for the clergy a capital as tangible as, say, real estate, and it was also deemed fitting that the word of God should be enshrined in such a valuable object. A final note of interest: images such as these provided the basis for another form of evocation of the Biblical stories—they were soon to give rise, by way of paraliturgical chants and ceremonies, to the religious theater.

St. Luke, from the presumed St. Augustine Bible · Roman · 6th century · Manuscript illumination · Ms. 286, Library of Corpus Christi College, Cambridge, England

Pope Gregory the Great sent this manuscript of the Gospels to St. Augustine, his representative in England and missionary bishop at Canterbury. It bears witness to the importance of the transitional period of the sixth century in which, just before the irruption of Islam, the West laid down the bases of its achievement. Note the analogies of the framework with the cupola of St. George in Salonica (page 89), and also how the small scenes to the sides resemble elements of the Ashburnham Pentateuch (page 94) as well as of the cloisonné enamels which began to appear at that time. There existed in the sixth century a Mediterranean civilization which here and there elaborated elements borrowed from pagan tradition to fit the new beliefs. Thus miniatures became a complement to the monumental wall decorations and lavish arts which were by no means confined to Byzantium alone. This manuscript seems to have contained originally some hundred images illustrating the text step by step.

St. Matthew, from the Book of Durrow · 7th century · Iona (?) · Manuscript illumination · Ms. A.4.5, Trinity College, Dublin

Here, on another page of the same manuscript, is an even more complex problem. It is often said that the outstanding trait of Irish art was the integration of the human figure into a system of ornamental design, the subordination of man to geometry. But this opinion seems to me to be based on a modern conception of geometry. For the men of the seventh century, every sign, each animal or arabesque, had a significance, was part of the system of knowledge of an age in which legend and learning had not yet grown apart. But, besides this, it seems evident that the Irish artist depicted the Evangelist dressed as he is here not merely to integrate him into the network of linear forms. We know that the Irish missionaries who went about preaching the Gospel wore garments which earned them the epithet of "the Striped Ones." Most likely, then, their garments, especially their liturgical vestments, became, as it were, the badge of their calling, symbolizing it in both color and design. So the problem disappears when we read the language of these symbols as it was meant to be read. The figure of St. Matthew here is "realistic": he is depicted as a monk who spreads abroad the sacred message. Once again, as in the page of ornament, the Book and the image are explained by the Word.

Ornamental Page, from the Book of Durrow · 7th century · Iona (?) · Manuscript illumination · Ms. A.4.5, Trinity College, Dublin

In the seventh century, while the Mediterranean art centers were declining, the first important workshops began to appear in northern Europe. Obviously those workshops profited from what had been achieved in the Mediterranean, but they interpreted it in their own fashion. In particular, the monasteries on the Irish coasts and in Northumbria created a purely native style which spread into western Europe at the time of the great expansion of the monastic system under St. Columbanus. Much emphasis has been placed on the integration of Celtic ornamentation into the Irish idiom, and certainly a page like this cannot be accounted for without reference to the style of the Celts, especially their metalwork. And yet it is difficult to explain why, in the middle of the book, a Gospel, there should appear a purely ornamental design. I think that here the image serves a double function, as it did in the Rossano Gospels: the page of plaitwork corresponds to the purple background in the latter codex, but richness of work is here substituted for richness of material. This is in itself significant: it should not be forgotten that for the monks on the island of Iona the Book, the word of God, was itself a treasure and that for them both prayer and labor were equally consecrated to the Lord.

The Letters XPI, from the Book of Kells · 8th century · Ireland · Manuscript illumination · Ms. A.i.6, Trinity College, Dublin

It is on this manuscript that most of the usual definitions of the Irish style are based. Here, the principle of ambivalence —of interpretation on different levels—gives way to fusion, to integration, to ambiguity as to the exact significance of those interpretations. Tiny realistic scenes, animals, and figures are wound into the coils of the arabesques. The decorative element predominates; ornamentation is no longer a material value in itself that can be likened to an act of devotion on the part of the scribe; a book is no longer cherished as a repository of the word of God but is considered an instrument to transmit texts. The elements are subjected to a scheme of values and no longer thought to have equal importance, however complex and individual their forms, in conveying the fundamental aim of the artist. Just as style took the place of invention in monumental decoration in fresco and mosaic, so also in the art of illumination an academic phase set in around the seventh and eighth centuries: the second age of Christian art was drawing to a close. The creative life of Anglo-Saxon Christendom began when St. Augustine introduced books from Rome in the sixth century; in the eighth century, one of his successors, Abbot Benedict Biscop, made five journeys to Italy to bring back manuscripts executed in Rome: it is always the initial breakthrough which is creative.

Symbol of St. Mark, from the Gospels of Echternach · c. 690 · Ireland (?) · Manuscript illumination · Ms. lat. 9389, Bibliothèque Nationale, Paris

This magnificent volume was executed for St. Willibrord. Here is another proof of the delicate and flexible relationship which, in this style, unites the three aspects of an image: linear drawing, specific content, ulterior meaning. The Evangelist is presented here not as a man who spreads the Gospel but as a symbolic animal in line with a tradition dating back to St. Jerome. The inscription IMAGO LEONIS shows us that for the miniaturist himself there was a problem in an image not merely borrowed from life but representative of an object having symbolic value. Thus, contrary to general opinion, the key to Irish miniature art does not lie in the subordination of the human figure to abstract arabesques but, rather, in a flexible relationship between concrete and imaginative values. It is false to say that the *Lion of St. Mark* is formed by the repetition of a single element and that the form is broken up: the image is rendered in volume by an over-all modeling which is prior to and independent of the ornamental decoration. The entire surface of the page is modulated by admirable procedures which convey a graphic ambivalence that is parallel to the subtle relationship between the image and the object.

GODESCALC *Christ Enthroned*, from the Gospels of Godescalc, made for Charlemagne and his wife Hildegarde · 781–83 · Manuscript illumination · Ms. nouv. acq. lat. 1203, Bibliothèque Nationale, Paris

Written out between 781 and 783 for the great emperor by the clerk Godescalc, this admirable volume on purple parchment uses gold letters in uncial script (except for the dedication, which is in Carolingian characters but likewise in gold). At the beginning of the book one finds the four Evangelists, Christ, and the Fountain of Life; Christ is enthroned like the Evangelists and like them holding a book. This is still a civilization of clerks based on the Book, that is, on tradition, though the tradition has broadened to include recollections of the Roman Empire. Godescalc's figure of Christ is evidently related to contemporary work in ivory and gold. A new mode, distinct from that of Byzantium, is in formation, often on the same bases but with a changed spirit. The Godescalc Gospels is still a precious object inhabited by the Word, but, at the same time, the enthroned Evangelists are placed in front of cities, and the Fountain of Life underlines the autonomy of the two worlds whose respective mediators are Christ and the Emperor. The play of ambivalences no longer occurs between image and form but between those who, on earth, administer the divine legacy.

The Fountain of Life, from the Gospels of Saint-Médard of Soissons · Palace School (Ada group), beginning of 9th century · Manuscript illumination · Ms. lat. 8850, Bibliothèque Nationale, Paris

In this fine work, the most luxurious of the Palatine series, the usual introductory figure of Christ is replaced by the Celestial Jerusalem with the attributes of the Evangelists and the twenty-four Elders of the Apocalypse adoring the Lamb. The volume was given to Angilbert in 827 by Louis the Debonair and his wife, and it seems to have belonged to Charlemagne, though the manuscript is monastic or ecclesiastic, unlike that prepared for the Emperor's personal use. Heading the canon tables is a Fountain of Life, as in Godescalc's Gospels, which may well be the first appearance in the West of this Oriental motif. The decoration is related to that in the Church of St. George in Salonica as well as to the mosaic of the Good Shepherd in Ravenna (page 92). A double convention is developing here, one of themes and one of forms; but the play of combinations always reveals an aim distinct from the customary iconographic program. Power and glory, the government of men, or their death and judgment are each set forth in turn, in a precise relationship with the owner of the book.

St. Luke, from the Gospels of Saint-Médard of Soissons · Palace School (Ada group), beginning of 9th century · Manuscript illumination · Ms. lat. 8850, Bibliothèque Nationale, Paris

An additional page from the same fine manuscript may help to clarify the preceding statements. Here the Evangelist is shown presenting his book on the pages of which are written some of the key words of his gospel. In Godescalc's manuscript, as in most books of the Carolingian period, the Evangelist was depicted in the act of writing his text; thus the variation here is not without significance. In the new Carolingian society, the cleric was the scribe, and on him depended the order of the society: he acted and he advised, and was no longer a mere onlooker. But in the monasteries the chief task remained the preservation and dissemination of the sacred legacy on which human order is founded. It is in the choice of subjects and significant elements that we can discover how the functions of books and images differed in different times and places.

St. Luke, from the Gospels of Ebbo · School of Rheims, beginning of 9th century · Manuscript illumination · Ms. 1, Bibliothèque Municipale, Épernay

This beautiful manuscript was offered by Abbot Pierre of Hautvillers to Ebbo, Archbishop of Rheims from 816 to 845. It is entirely written in Carolingian minuscule letters in gold. The text is adorned with pedimented borders for the canon tables and with full-page miniatures depicting the Evangelists. At the start of each Gospel, there is a large ornamental gilded and painted initial letter. The St. Luke seen here constitutes a document of the greatest interest for Carolingian graphic art. There are many illustrations—among the most famous are those in the Utrecht Psalter—in which the image has a cursive character very close to handwriting itself. In this instance that kind of drawing is elevated into a deliberate stylistic procedure. The depiction of the bull is not without humor, and in the treatment of costume the striving for stylistic effect clearly dominates over symbolic intent. The entire picture is conceived no longer as a sign strictly tied to the literal and allegorical meaning of the image but rather as a work of art interesting in and for itself. Carolingian miniature art disposed of many technical and figurative approaches, from which the artists seem quite deliberately to have picked and chosen.

The Emperor Lothair, from the Gospels of Lothair · School of Tours, 849–51 · Manuscript illumination · Ms. lat. 266, Bibliothèque Nationale, Paris

This Bible was executed by a certain Sigualis at the order of Lothair. Following the portrait of the Emperor on his throne, there is, on the next page, Christ blessing, as in Godescalc's Gospels, in this case surrounded by the attributes of the Evangelists. Then follow the canon tables and the Gospels, each of which is preceded by a list of chapters framed like the canon tables, by a figure of the Evangelist, and by a full-page initial in gold. Another step has been taken: the earthly Prince takes precedence over the King of Heaven—and this gives us the first portrait in the history of medieval France. As royal power weakened, the royal person was made the more of, however much his rule might be challenged. Moreover, the separation between earthly and heavenly powers is marked even on the theoretical level: it is no longer the Evangelists who, by virtue of their writings, direct the disposition of the human order as distinct from the order of nature which is symbolized by the Fountain of Life; now the temporal sovereign determines all, though his authority no longer derives only from divine right. Here we witness the arrival of secular government on the scene.

Presentation of the Book to the Emperor Charles the Bald, from the Vivian Bible · Saint-Martin of Tours, or Marmoutiers, 849–51 · Manuscript illumination · Ms. lat. 1, Bibliothèque Nationale, Paris

This manuscript was prepared by order of Count Vivian Abbot of Saint-Martin in Tours in 845 and of Marmoutiers in 846. In this miniature—one of the first depictions of such a presentation ceremony—Vivian is escorted by members of the clergy of his two abbeys and followed by, we presume, the scribes of this Bible: Amand, Sigualis, and Agregarius. The celestial powers do not directly intervene; they look on from the top of the triumphal arch surmounting the King's throne. The King is surrounded by his lay counselors, while his warriors are somewhat apart. Unlike the portrait in the Gospels of Lothair, here the emperor is more than the mere instrument of secular power, and his court conforms more to the authentic Carolingian tradition. The prominence of the clergy is in accord with the theory of the three orders of the state: nobles, warriors, clergy, all grouped around the throne. The hand of God guarantees the legitimacy of a social system that is no longer immutable and based only on sacred authority.

St. Gregory, from a Sacramentary · School of Corbie, end of 9th century · Manuscript illumination · Ms. lat. 1141, Bibliothèque Nationale, Paris

This volume is a Sacramentary and contains only the Common Preface and the canon tables. There are five full-page illuminations: the coronation of a prince between two haloed ecclesiastics; this illustration, St. Gregory inspired by the Holy Ghost to write his Sacramentary; Christ in Glory surrounded by angels and saints and the symbols of the Evangelists; the heavenly court gathered about Christ the Master of Heaven and Earth. At St. Gregory's feet two scribes rummage in a chest of books. The Saint is enthroned like Christ or the emperor, a fact which tells us that power no longer belongs solely to the Incarnate Word but to learning itself—i.e., to the clergy: in this modern world, then, the prince is not the only vessel of the power of God. It will be noted that the Saint appears to be hidden behind a curtain which one of the clerks lifts to catch a glimpse of the Holy Ghost, and the perspective organization is quite unlike the treatment we have seen heretofore. The sensitive use of color is admirable and the rendering of volumes truly masterly. Within a century, from the Christ of Godescalc's Gospels to this St. Gregory, a style was formed and developed.

The Prayer of Hannah, from the Paris Psalter · Constantinople, 9th century · Manuscript illumination · Ms. gr. 139, Bibliothèque Nationale, Paris

It is interesting to compare the Carolingian productions in the ninth century with those from Byzantium. In Byzantium the conflict with the Iconoclasts—those opposed to depicting Christ and the highest mysteries—did not end until 843, and the creative period leading to the Macedonian renaissance was therefore later than that of the West: between 880 and the beginning of the tenth century. The first manifestations were mosaics, in particular the famous ones in Santa Sophia in Constantinople: one, over the entrance door to the narthex, shows Emperor Leo VI, the Wise, prostrate at the feet of the enthroned Christ between two medallions, of the Virgin and of an angel (in Heaven, therefore); the other, over the south door, shows the Virgin enthroned with the Child on her lap between the Emperors Constantine the Great and Justinian. Both of these are "imperial" images in which the divine right of kings is asserted much more succinctly than in the West. In addition there are many manuscripts from this period among which some, like the well-known Kludhov Psalter, provide a marginal commentary with tiny scenes illustrating and framing the text. The treatment is entirely different from that used in the Utrecht Psalter and the Ebbo Gospels (page 97): not linear in approach, the tiny picturesque episodes are rendered by colored contours.

The Prayer of Isaiah, from the Paris Psalter · Constantinople, 9th century · Manuscript illumination · Ms. gr. 139, Bibliothèque Nationale, Paris

The Macedonian renaissance drew inspiration from antiquity, and the West had nothing comparable to show. The two miniatures reproduced here, the *Prayer of Hannah* and the *Prayer of Isaiah*, have much in common with those in manuscripts of late antiquity and are remarkable examples of a renaissance in the strict sense of the term, such as was virtually unknown to the Western world. They have been included here to show how pictures can sum up the different human climates in which artworks are produced. Where Byzantium strove to preserve and restore the glorious past by maintaining the intellectual and social framework of the Empire, the West, even when it took up the concept of empire, based its action on a thoroughgoing revision of the relationships between men and men, and between men and things.

The Massacre of the Innocents, from the Codex Egberti · Reichenau, 10th century · Manuscript illumination · Codex 24, Municipal Library, Trier

At the end of the tenth century a new renaissance, the Ottonian, brought forth a new style that was first centered in Lorraine. Otto the Great (936–73) was supporting a movement of monastic reform with the aim of creating an entente between Crown and Church against the feudal lords. The state abbeys, Fulda, Regensburg, and St. Maximin in Trier, thereby became the center of a cultural revival inspired by the example of the Carolingian renaissance. The chancellery and scriptoria created a remarkable series of great illuminated manuscripts. No abbey could compete in this with Reichenau on Lake Constance, whose first abbot, Rudmann (972–84), founded a scriptorium in which an individual style developed very rapidly. Its scribes worked mostly for the princes of the imperial church—Gero, Archbishop of Cologne, and Egbert, Archbishop of Trier— the latter a great connoisseur who moreover had his own scriptorium at Trier. For him a famous psalter was illuminated at Reichenau (now in the Archaeological Museum, Cividale del Friuli) and a volume of pericopes (passages from the Gospels for various religious feasts) as a gift from two monks of that abbey. It is interesting to note that the weeping women in this *Massacre of the Innocents* are much like those at the funeral pyre of Dido in the Vatican Virgil manuscript from the fourth century. The source is common to both the Paris Psalter and this Codex Egberti.

St. Luke, from the Gospel Book of Otto III · Reichenau, c. 1000 · Manuscript illumination · Ms. Clm. 4453, Bayerische Staatsbibliothek, Munich

Rudmann was succeeded as head of the abbey of Reichenau by Witigowo (985–97), and it was then that the Ottonian style reached its height. Here and in the next plate we have two specimens from that workshop to show once again that creativity flowers in diversity rather than in unity, and that the range of means available to artists was greater than that of the procedures they actually employed. The St. Luke is framed by architecture similar to that in the Corbie miniature of St. Gregory (page 98), but the revelation is expressed here with extraordinary power. The Evangelist is enthroned in the empyrean, holding on his lap the Earthly City, and seated on the Rainbow of the Alliance, triumphant and prophetic. The image of his thought, that is usually in the form of the book placed on the Evangelist's lap, bursts forth from his arms and head. And the kings of the earth are no more than those of the Bible: warders of the Divine Law.

St. Peter Receiving the Keys, from the Pericope of Henry II · Reichenau, beginning of 11th century · Manuscript illumination · Ms. Clm. 4452, Bayerische Staatsbibliothek, Munich

The St. Luke of the Gospel Book of Otto III represents the highest degree of animation achieved by the Reichenau workshops under the Ottonians. The Pericope of Henry II presents complementary evidence as to the aesthetic treatment of light. Composition and gestures are simplified, all attention is concentrated on the painting itself. In it there is an enthusiastic return to the gold backgrounds of Carolingian art, a concern with the book as a precious object. But, using that point of departure, the Reichenau artists worked out their own system. The juxtaposition on the deep gold background of light colors in a much simplified linear setting; the choice of lilac, sea green, sandy yellows, off-whites (all of them rare colors at that time and throughout the Middle Ages); the partition of the background into bands suggestive of space—all of these factors reveal an exceptionally refined science of the spatial values inherent in color. Had the experiments of Reichenau been adopted as the basis for visual culture, a quite different path might have been taken by Western painting.

St. John, from the so-called Grimbald Gospels · School of Winchester, beginning of 11th century · Manuscript illumination · Ms. Add. 34890, British Museum, London

Parallel with the Ottonian renaissance, another center grew up in the West during the tenth century: England. As early as the end of the ninth century, while repairing the ravages of the Viking invasions, King Alfred called to his court a monk of Saint-Bertin, Grimbald, to serve as his Alcuin. Alfred's grandson Aethelstan (925–39), and then King Edgar (959–75), likewise encouraged the monastic reform undertaken by Bishops Dunstan, Oswald, and Aethelwold in conjunction with the Frankish monasteries. They also supported the scriptoria at Winchester, and thus began a second brilliant period in miniature art in the wake of the Carolingian renaissance and reform, and of the seventh- and eighth-century works in Ireland. The Winchester masterworks, the Benedictional of Aethelwold and the so-called Grimbald Gospels, are in a style directly derived from the graphic idiom of the School of Rheims and the Gospels of Ebbo. In contrast with the School of Reichenau, composition here is a function of line and arabesque, even when the coloring becomes iridescent and brilliant. In the final analysis, the Winchester style is less antique and more Carolingian in flavor than is the Ottonian.

100

The Nativity, from the Missal of Archbishop Robert · School of Winchester, c. 1008 · Manuscript illumination · Ms. Y.6, Bibliothèque Publique, Rouen

Robert, Archbishop of Canterbury, driven from his see in 1052, fled to Jumièges to live out his last years. It is thought that he brought with him this manuscript and a Pontifical that is also now in Rouen. The two books were produced during the best period at Winchester, the end of the tenth century, at the same time as the Benedictional of Aethelwold and the Grimbald Gospels. This composition is interesting not only as an example of the marvelous art of the English workshops of the time, but also because it combines a typically Carolingian framework with a type of spatial organization destined for a remarkable future. The superposition of the two episodes of the narrative and, above all, their respective positions in a hierarchy introduced a tradition which was to continue until the time of Fouquet.

The Three Marys at the Sepulcher, from a Pontifical · School of Winchester (?), c. 971–84 · Manuscript illumination · Ms. 369, Bibliothèque Publique, Rouen

This miniature, from the second of the two books probably brought to Jumièges by the exiled archbishop, reveals how the English style, with its unitary and majestic composition in the Carolingian spirit, developed toward an attitude closer to actual visual experience. Like the *Nativity* in the preceding reproduction, this picture doubtless owes something to the paraliturgical dramas presented first inside, later outside, the church. Following a figurative phase in which the style stems from an idea, from a thought made visible, there develops another phase in which the clergy fulfills its missionary function by addressing the congregation in more familiar language.

The Building of the Tower of Babel, from the Metrical Paraphrase of Pentateuch and Joshua, by Aelfric · 11th century · Manuscript illumination · Cotton Ms. Claud. B. iv, British Museum, London

Parallel with the development of the Winchester style, there was another remarkable current in eleventh-century English illumination. No doubt it would be an exaggeration to suggest that this current reflects folk and national influences, but it certainly differs from the official style of the time. No longer, as in Ottonian art, does the image symbolize the relations between the various forces; instead, it directly illustrates the text in hand. Of the two permanent possibilities for Christian art this is the image as visual equivalent of a text; the other is the image as a synthetic expression of the meaning of the text. In another famous manuscript, a paraphrase of the poems of the bard Caedmon (Bodleian Library, Oxford), there is further use of a whole repertory of iconography, diffused throughout the Mediterranean regions and especially in Spain, which imitates but does not strictly follow the Byzantine monastic miniatures. The giant Nembroch who builds the tower in the present example had to be named to be recognized, but everyone could understand immediately the everyday labor of the masons. We must keep in mind, however, that the ladder and the door had traditional symbolic meanings far beyond their direct representation.

101

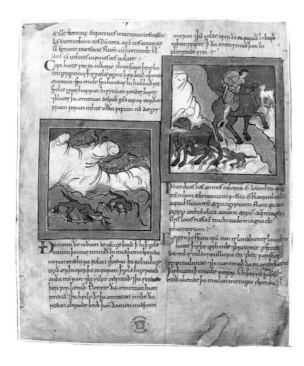

The Land of the Great Ant Hills, from *Marvels of the East* (Astronomical Treatise) · Durham (?), c. 1030 · Manuscript illumination · Cotton Ms. Tib. B. v, British Museum, London

This manuscript, which may be almost contemporary with the preceding ones, testifies to the wide range of culture in England at the close of the early Middle Ages. As is known, there were very few works of secular inspiration, and this account of a voyage is in its way an anticipation of the marvelous tales of Marco Polo as well as of the voyages of Gulliver—an informative document but, at the same time, full of feeling. The linear style is not abandoned but it is combined with other effects, in large part no doubt because the illuminator was working outside of a constraining tradition. Every style implies a certain sacrifice of free invention, and an out-of-the-way manuscript proves that a too-perfect style cannot sum up the entire culture in any epoch.

Christ and the Twenty-four Elders, from the Apocalypse of Beatus · Saint-Sever (Gascony), between 1028 and 1072 · Manuscript illumination · Ms. lat. 8878, Bibliothèque Nationale, Paris

The choice of this double plate aims at showing two stylistic factors: how the rules for dividing the illustrated surface carry across centuries and schools but do not, for all that, determine the spirit and character of the image; and how iconography was revitalized in the eleventh century. Here the eternal problem of the proportioning of powers between Heaven and Earth has been left behind, and that of the direct manifestation of the mysteries has been introduced: evidence of a new and more immediate relationship between clergy and congregation. There is a striking parallelism between the formulas that are being elaborated in this manuscript and those which soon prevailed in monumental sculpture: artists express in any medium the deepest significances of their epochs. It will be noticed that the other two images reproduced from this manuscript divide the figurative space according to the narrative, whereas here the single vision has imposed a spatial unity.

The Woman on the Beast, from the Apocalypse of Beatus · Saint-Sever (Gascony), between 1028 and 1072 · Manuscript illumination · Ms. lat. 8878, Bibliothèque Nationale, Paris

This book was written and illustrated in the time of Abbot Gregory Muntaner. One Stefanus Garsia signed his name on a column of folio six, but it is not certain that he was the painter or, in any case, the only painter. The illuminations in this manuscript are particularly numerous and are intended to illustrate the text in detail as it unfolds. To say that this style is popular or folklike would be as inexact as in the case of the manuscript of Aelfric (page 101). Once again we are faced with opposing conceptions in miniature art, paraphrase as against symbolism; and these are the eternal alternatives of all art throughout the ages. The book itself is of very high intellectual quality; this Commentary on the Apocalypse was neither first conceived nor written at Saint-Sever, however: the monk Beatus died in the monastery of Liebana in Spain around 798, and many illustrated versions of his work were made.

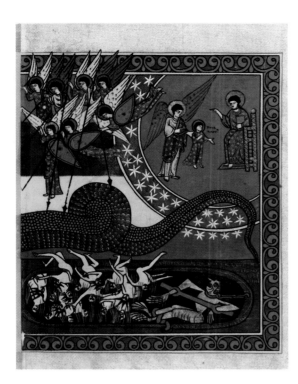

The War of the Angels, from the Apocalypse of Beatus Saint-Sever (Gascony), between 1028 and 1072 · Manuscript illumination · Ms. lat. 8878, Bibliothèque Nationale, Paris

In a series of images the painter laid out the various events of the War in Heaven: first the encounter and what ensued, then, with victory won, the Beast and one of its symbolic allies imprisoned in Hell. The war of the angels is less realistic and less violent, but the Beast and the Fallen Souls are depicted with great immediacy and are not confined within the dividing bands. The insertion of a second division, the circle surrounded by stars, juxtaposes opposing worlds —Heaven, Earth, and Hell—and the presentation of the Just Soul emphasizes that opposition. There is as much skill in these methods of partitioning space as there was in the treatment of light by the artists of Reichenau, or in the linear approach of Winchester. But the best comparison would be with the manuscript of Aelfric (page 101), since both styles are linked to the same Mediterranean traditions and have the same concern with illustrating a text in detail.

The Conquest of England by the Normans: Death of the Brothers of King Harold · Detail from the Bayeux Tapestry · Caen, c. 1070 · Treasury of the Cathedral, Bayeux

The Earth · Detail from an Exultet Roll · Bari, 11th century · Manuscript illumination · Archives of the Cathedral, Bari

For the eleventh century there was a real and important problem involved in the transformation of the spoken sign into a visual sign, that is, word into image. This is well exemplified in certain scrolls in southern Italy in which a number of scenes are arranged one above the other, each illustrating a text which is upside down in relation to the image. The present picture explains this odd procedure. It refers to the morning of Holy Saturday at the moment of benediction of the Paschal candle; from the pulpit the deacon intones the hymn *Exultet jam angelica turba coelorum*, holding in both hands the scroll which he unrolls before the congregation. Thus the faithful can look at the pictures right side up, while the deacon reads aloud his text with its musical neumes. We see here that images were presented differently when they were intended to be looked at by the crowd of the faithful, and when they were meant to be studied in the silence of the cloister.

It is incorrect to present, as is usually done, the Exultet rolls as isolated examples of the major problem in the early Romanesque period: the new relationship between text and image. The celebrated embroidery presumed to be by Queen Mathilda recounts in more than sixty episodes the expedition across the Channel by William the Conqueror and his victory over Harold. In contrast to the Bari Exultet roll, this text serves only to comment upon or, more precisely, to corroborate the image; the reversal of functions is also contrary to the practice in previous periods, when it was the task of artists to comment on the text, to give material form to the Word. Here is proof of a change in the forms of culture in the Western world occurring between the tenth and the twelfth century, a change much like the one we are experiencing today.

The Fall of Man, from an Octateuch · Byzantine, 12th century · Manuscript illumination · Cod. 8, Topkapi Palace Museum, Istanbul

A second example of a friezelike composition, here used to separate the episodes of a narrative, is furnished by this manuscript typical of the last phase of the Macedonian renaissance. It is the more interesting in that, for once, we find in the East a reminiscence, faint as it may be, of a Western work. In two copies of the so-called Moutier-Granval Bible the story of the Original Sin is recounted in very similar fashion: the same principle of representing figures, the same partitioning, the same rhythmic scansion of the trees. Since this procedure is also found in many Romanesque frescoes, no doubt there existed "models" which circulated throughout the Eastern and Western regions of the Mediterranean basin. This present example is not a development of the picturesque popular style of the Byzantine monastery workshops but an instance in a sequence that goes back to a conservative pictorial tradition.

The Entry of Christ into Jerusalem · School of Monte Cassino, c. 1060 · Fresco · Basilica, Sant'Angelo in Formis (Capua)

Space prevents reproducing here the many works of the ninth and tenth centuries which, in mural art as in manuscript illumination, helped to maintain a tradition common to Byzantium and the Roman and Carolingian West. In fresco painting the dialogue between East and West went on, and the interplay of influences never permits us to define the particular schools with exactitude, but only to detect their traces within individual works. The Romanesque fresco—the next great step in the history of medieval painting after the mosaic—did not constitute a closed world. At the same time that the first Roman workshops were becoming active, this particularly significant cycle was painted in Sant'Angelo in Formis. A little later, around 1070, Desiderius, the great abbot of Monte Cassino, was to call in other artists from Constantinople. All of this suggests the high diversification of art at this time. Furthermore, parallel influences from southern Italy can also be seen. The situation can be summed up as being less a question of Western versions of Byzantine prototypes than of eclectic, international workshops which, each in its way, perpetuated the various styles prevailing at the end of antiquity.

Christ the King Enthroned in the Heavenly City · Lombard school, end of 11th century · Fresco · Sanctuary of San Pietro al Monte, Civate (Como)

The date of these frescoes is much debated, and some place them as late as mid-twelfth century. Since the style is traditional, the problem is of secondary importance. What counts is that here, as in Sant'Angelo (preceding plate) and at Saint-Savin (page 106), an entire church has been decorated with frescoes. In content, they bring together the grandiose apocalyptic vision and the paradisiac City of God according to St. Augustine. Many elements recall themes and solutions used in miniatures: among the other frescoes in the church are the Rivers of Paradise and the Combat of the Archangel Michael with the Dragon. One cannot simply ascribe these works to Byzantine influence. From one workshop to another the proportion of such influences varied. Here the problem of the treatment of depth resembles that in the *St. Gregory* of the Corbie Sacramentary and in the presentation scene in the Vivian Bible (page 98) rather than that in Eastern mosaics. However, it is less important to note in each individual case the interpenetration of cultures than to ferret out the seeds of the future.

The Prophet Jeremiah · Lombard school, 1007 (?) · Fresco · Church of San Vincenzo, Galliano (Cantù)

From the point of view indicated in the preceding comment, this fresco cycle from the region of Lake Como is particularly interesting. The church was consecrated in 1007 by a cleric, Ariberto d'Intimiano, who became Archbishop of Milan in 1018 and whose likeness is now in the Ambrosiana in Milan. In the apse there is a theophany, an apparition of Christ: Christ standing, Roman fashion, appears to the prophets Jeremiah and Ezekiel. With its mixture of Roman and biblical iconographies, was its model Byzantine Greek or Palestinian Paleo-Christian? Below the theophany are several scenes from the life of St. Vincenzo, the patron saint of the church: a hagiographic cycle replacing the traditional evangelical series. All this contributes to the great interest of this ensemble and makes it a good example of the new values coming in at that time. Moreover, one can make out several hands at work in the painting with differences in workmanship, and the personalities of the various artists constitute a point of interest that takes us beyond the conventions that they hold in common.

The Annunciation of Ustyug · Detail of an icon · Novgorod workshop, beginning of 12th century · Tempera on wood · 93¾ × 66½″ · Tretyakov Gallery, Moscow

This famous painting is one of the few surviving from the first period of Russian culture. The standing angel stretches his hand toward the Virgin who stands on a podium and who has an unusual iconographic note: in her breast is seen a haloed image of the Child to be born to her. Above, a mandorla, now mutilated, contains the enthroned Christ. The angel's head has much character in both its features and its plastic treatment. The Byzantine hieratic quality is softened by a sentiment closer to that of the women represented in the Nea Moni in Chios than to that of the workshops in Constantinople.

Adam Naming the Animals · Umbrian school, end of 12th century · Fresco · Abbey of San Pietro, Ferentillo (Terni)

Along with Lombardy, central Italy in the twelfth century was the stronghold of a conservative tradition. In those regions can also be found the link between monumental fresco art and Gothic tapestry. In compositions such as this, one finds reminiscences not only of mural painting of the preceding centuries, but also of certain series of miniatures related to those in the Apocalypse of Saint-Sever (pages 102–3). The fact that, at this date, the figures are still disposed somewhat pell-mell against the background contrasts with the effort made elsewhere—in France and Spain notably—to bring order into the monumental ensembles. This is one reason why Romanesque mural painting is best studied in examples from France.

The Prayer of Enoch · c. 1100 (?) · Fresco · Nave vault, Abbey Church, Saint-Savin (Vienne)

Founded in the ninth century and rebuilt by the abbot Eudes who died about 1050, the church was embellished with frescoes apparently in the last years of the eleventh and the first years of the twelfth century. The decoration covers the crypt, the vault of the nave, the choir, the bell-steeple porch, and the gallery. The iconographic program is of un-rivaled richness: the Bible from Genesis to Moses, the Apocalypse, the Passion, Prophets and Saints, and the lives of Sts. Savin and Cyprian. Here we have the first great monumental achievement in the West. No doubt many artists—or, indeed, many teams of artists—must have worked on this ensemble, and yet the unity of conception is unmistakable and ushers in a new age. The great compositions in the nave are obviously related to the mural paintings of Oberzell at Reichenau, for example, but their wide scope of subject matter and plan was unmatched else-where in the Western world of the time. What is more, the expressive power of the images attained a level which left far behind, once and for all, the hieratic character that was more and more in favor in the Byzantine world.

The Building of the Tower of Babel · c. 1100 (?) · Fresco · Nave vault, Abbey Church, Saint-Savin (Vienne)

It is impossible to describe adequately the tremendous effort which went into the decoration of Saint-Savin. Begun in part even before the building was finished, the frescoes were carried on concurrently with the construction. No-where else is image more intimately linked to architecture: painting here brings the stones themselves to life. Men strove to make this entire monument into an object both precious and replete with life, very much as the Irish miniaturists conceived the Book to be a living treasure incarnating the word of God. But it is the style which is especially out-standing: the figures are at the same time stylized and animated; their liveliness is achieved without any attempt at realism; they are the visualization of thought in action. Moreover, there is perfect equilibrium between what might be called the rhetoric of the forms and the purely plastic quality of the ensemble.

Noah's Ark · c. 1100 (?) · Fresco · Nave vault, Abbey Church, Saint-Savin (Vienne)

We cannot here go into one of the most interesting problems Saint-Savin presents, that of the order in which the frescoes of the vault were meant to be read. The barrel vault was originally intended to be smooth, without trans-verse ribs after the third span, for the distance that was needed to recount the New Testament stories. However, this plan was abandoned, together with the larger project of decorating the whole church like a kind of jewel box, as in the Orient. Instead, decoration was concentrated at key points; but this made it impossible to unfold a great narrative across an entire wall. This architectonic problem explains why sculpture and miniature eventually supplanted fresco painting. The image reproduced here, if compared with such contemporary works as the capitals in the Church of La Daurade in Toulouse, reveals that all share a single principle of representation that affects iconography, over-all programs, and choice of techniques.

The Creation of Man and the Temptation · First half of 12th century · Fresco, detached from the interior of the Hermitage of Vera Cruz, Maderuelo (Segovia) · The Prado, Madrid

This is an interesting example of how similar problems may find entirely distinct solutions: as in Saint-Savin, the problem was to cover a vault. Here, too, the borrowings from the traditional repertory of motifs are flagrant, and in this fresco we have a composition which anticipates the sculptured portals of the Romanesque. On the other hand, while the style of the figure of Christ may be related to the figures in Saint-Savin, the Adam and Eve are wholly Byzantine. Twelfth-century Spain acted as a kind of divide, a watershed between the world of fully developed traditional forms and the new world in which Romanesque formulas were beginning to find existence. This comparison reveals the degree to which Spanish culture was marked by contacts not only with Islam but also with the entire eastern basin of the Mediterranean.

David and Goliath · c. 1123 · Fresco, detached from the interior of the Church of Santa María, Tahull (Lerida) · Museo de Arte de Cataluña, Barcelona

The frescoes of this little church hidden away in the mountains represent the Mozarabic tradition in its purest form. Comparison of this composition with the miniatures in the Apocalypse of Saint-Sever (pages 102-3) shows how this vein of local inspiration differs from the authentic Byzantine current. Once again one sees the application of the same stylistic principles to different techniques and the range of colors—the basic means—that is common, on the whole, to workshops during the period. Only four colors are used: white, black, ocher, and vermilion; to the frescoes in the apse are added blue and orange. An archaic note is provided by the short tunic; the fashion for long garments had set in as far back as the 1090s, and it was promptly adopted in the Saint-Savin frescoes. Figure styles provide a sensitive index to the developing phases of a culture: in Saint-Savin is recorded, in fact, the birth of the great Aquitaine civilization.

Decorative Figure · End of 11th century (?) · Fresco · Crypt, Church of Saint-Nicolas, Tavant (Indre-et-Loire)

Devastated by fire in 1070, the town was not rebuilt until around 1124. This crypt which is completely covered with frescoes is, however, an entirely separate construction from the church and was probably built earlier; it is unlikely that it was subsequently dug beneath the church since the style of the frescoes has much in common with the Carolingian. Here again is a transitional work in which can be glimpsed the birth of the Romanesque-Gothic civilization destined to triumph throughout the Western world. Like the crypt in Auxerre, this tiny crypt combines sculptured capitals with frescoed walls. It is still conceived as a jewel box covered with illustrations which are held together less by a narrative thread than by their symbolic meaning: the struggle between good and evil within the human soul, aided by the example of the Scriptures. Red and yellow ocher, reddish-brown and green earth on whitewash, sometimes with parallel bands—these are the same principles that prevail a little later in Catalonia. The composition and technique are, as in Tahull, a continuation of an earlier tradition, but the actual treatment of the frescoes leaves no doubt that Tavant lies close to Saint-Savin.

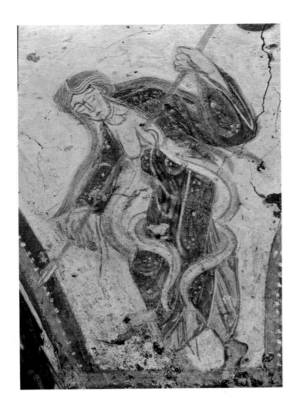

Luxuria · End of 11th century (?) · Fresco · Crypt, Church of Saint-Nicolas, Tavant (Indre-et-Loire)

The *Decorative Figure* of page 107 and this figure of *Luxuria* occupy analogous positions on a spandrel of the crypt. Seing them side by side emphasizes how innovations may arise within a system without immediately altering the system as a whole. The decorative figure suggests in striking fashion not movement as such (in the sense of the term applied to the Tahull frescoes or to Carolingian art), but the animation of the personage depicted; this generates a movement which, being no longer the direct object of attention, may consequently be most faithfully expressed by entirely unrealistic methods. In these two instances there is a very clear separation between the geometrical construction of the figures and their presence (more exactly than their volume) in space. A few strokes determining the axis of the image are juxtaposed with patches of color creating depth. This brings about the same discord between representation by line and by color that occurs in the famous apples by Cézanne; it gives rise to a richness of vision that obliges the viewer to re-create the image rather than to perceive it directly.

Virgin in Majesty · End of 12th century · Fresco · Apse vault of crypt, Church of Notre-Dame, Montmorillon (Vienne)

In this church, which belonged to the diocese of Saint-Savin, one sees how, within a century, a compromise took place in the Romanesque style on the eve of a new inspiration, Gothic stained glass. Here we are not far from the first Sienese Madonnas. The links with Byzantine taste remain obvious, but what counts, I think, is the double current at the start of the twelfth century, deriving from Saint-Savin on the one hand, from Berzé-la-Ville on the other, and both developing autonomously. Here the Virgin kisses the Child's hand while He places His other on the crowned head of one of the six female saints flanking the mandorla, witnesses to His triumph. Who is that saint? St. Catherine of Alexandria, whose martyrdom is commemorated below? or the personification of the Church? Formerly the figure had a silvered face, now black as the Shulamite's in the Song of Songs. But it was St. Catherine who was pledged in the mystic marriage. Probably the composition was meant to be ambiguous, combining certain aspects of both meanings. In the Saint's hand a white stone refers to the Apocalypse and the transformation brought about in the person who receives it, but this might signify either the sanctification of Catherine or the Church replacing the Synagogue.

Martyrdom of St. Vincent · c. 1100–1109 (?) · Fresco · Apse wall of upper chapel, Castle of the Monks, Berzé-la-Ville (Saône-et-Loire)

The frescoes in this little Cluniac priory present another problem in the relations between western France and Byzantium: influence from Monte Cassino? from the Ottonians? was a lectionary of Cluny used as model? Together with a great Christ in Majesty in the half-dome of the apse, there are numerous Western saints. The organization of the subject matter is not too unlike that at Tavant or Saint-Savin, but the treatment is quite different. Furthermore, the fresco technique here is not the same as that used in western France. It is instead in the Greek manner with multiple coats of paint as prescribed in the well-known treatise of Dionysius of Fournas, a monk at Mount Athos: two coats of yellow and whitewash; the drawing traced out in red lines; a black background heightened by blue; a blacker contour line for the figures; finally the colors. This is a slow and laborious process quite unlike the fresco technique soon to triumph in the Occident.

Martyrdom of St. James · End of 12th century · Fresco ·
Saint-Jacques-des-Guérets (Loir-et-Cher)

This church belonged to the abbey of Saint-Georges-du-
Bois (Sarthe), held by the regular canons of St. Augustine.
The original decoration must quickly have seemed out-of-
date, for it was covered over with new frescoes during the
thirteenth century. The Massacre of the Innocents, the
Nativity, Crucifixion, Christ in Glory, Sts. George and

Augustine, Paradise, Pride and Wrath—here we are far
from the orderly program of Saint-Savin: the Gothic with
its *Summae* of all knowledge has set in, the Romanesque
having given up any attempt at system in its ensembles.
While clinging to certain Romanesque conventions, this
style introduced innovations: mauves, coppery yellows,
green touched with yellow, and an approach both realistic
and expressionistic. The figures are both sharply cut out,
like certain Carolingian silhouettes, and manneristic.
Detail is shown on next pages

109

A Saint · End of 12th century · Fresco · Apse vault of crypt, Church of Notre-Dame, Montmorillon (Vienne)

The group of six female saints who flank the Virgin in majesty had many predecessors, notably at Notre-Dame-la-Grande at Poitiers and Castel Sant'Elia near Viterbo. The garments of the saints with their long trailing sleeves date them at the end of the twelfth century. However, the colors —ocher, green, violet—and, even more, the backgrounds with alternating bands of white and gray-blue belong to the Romanesque spectrum rather than the Gothic. Just as the Elders of the Apocalypse are associated in this church with the female saints, so the two styles also intermingle. This figure of a saint is an offspring of the images at Tavant. But, throughout, there is more skill than invention: enthusiastic imagination gives way to elegant reserve. By rejecting nothing, an art always becomes perfected—and impoverished.

St. Paul and the Viper · End of 12th century · Fresco · Chapel of St. Anselm, Christ Church Cathedral, Canterbury (Kent)

Only two chapels in this cathedral have preserved their twelfth-century frescoes, the chapel of St. Andrew from around 1130 and that of St. Anselm from after 1174. In the latter, there remains only the story of St. Paul in Malta (biblical Melita): while laying sticks on a fire, "there came a viper out of the heat, and fastened on his hand . . . and he shook off the beast into the fire, and felt no harm." The composition is admirable, and there is highly subtle modeling of the face and of the costume which is in the fashion of those at Saint-Savin. The range of colors recalls the Winchester miniatures, and also the frescoes recently discovered in the monastery at Sigena in Spain; however, in either case it would be an oversimplification to speak of Byzantine influence. The human westernized character of the *St. Paul* is evident; for the rest, we have scarcely begun to explore the relationships between the various modes of the West, in particular the contacts between Mozarabic Spain and the Irish monasteries.

Christ Pantocrator between Emperor Constantine IX Monomachus and Empress Zoë · 1028–42 · Mosaic · South gallery, Hagia Sophia, Constantinople

After the Iconoclastic opposition was put down in 843, many sovereigns were depicted rendering homage to Christ or the Virgin, and by the eleventh century the formula had become stereotyped. Byzantium remained faithful to the mosaic technique, while the West preferred frescoes and probably not merely for reasons of economy. I have already stressed the gradual weakening in the West of the concept of the artwork as a rare and precious object in favor of an approach which exploited the images as a free commentary. Doubtless at the start the hieratic character of these images was linked in the East to a certain striving for dignity, like the Roman ideal of impassivity in representing magistrates; but it also soon became no more than a rigid sign, a fixed motif, in consequence of the history of the Eastern Empire.

Virgin and Child between Emperor John II Comnenos and Empress Irene · c. 1118 · Mosaic · South gallery, Hagia Sophia, Constantinople

In this mosaic the head of the Emperor was changed three times—proof of the functional character of this art. The vestments with their liturgical significance came to be more important than the personages they clothed. Moreover, from one section of the mosaic to the next the manner becomes more arid and hard. Only the head of the Virgin was treated with some originality. These were official portraits, and it would be wrong to judge an age only by the portraits and devotional imagery it produced. But the portraits are nevertheless real, while the figure of the Virgin, for all that it is of finer quality, is an icon. Stylistic invention and the technique of execution are at odds here.

St. John the Baptist · End of 12th century · Mosaic · South gallery, Hagia Sophia, Constantinople

This beautiful mosaic is part of a *Deësis*: Christ stands in the center flanked by the Virgin and St. John, a curious iconography implying a kind of synthesis of the themes of the Pantocrator and the Pietà. Most likely this fine work with its striking sensitivity dates from after the Crusades. Compared with the first great icon devoted to Mary, the Virgin of Vladimir in the Tretiakov Gallery, Moscow, dated c. 1125, the pictorial technique here stands out in contrast to the linear stylization which was to become traditional in the Eastern world. In any event, there seems to have been no direct influence from the West. Instead, this work seems to reveal the possibilities that mosaic still offered to artisans of admirable sensitivity although the restrictions of a stereotyped iconography forced their art into academicism.

St. Justus (detail) · Constantinople workshop (?), end of 11th century · Painting on silk · Cathedral of San Giusto, Trieste

To permit a more precise comparison between the different forms of influence—or, better, of relationships—between the West and Byzantium in the eleventh and twelfth centuries, here is a detail of a full-length figure of a saint painted on silk. His name is written on both sides of his halo in Latin characters, but the style recalls the Byzantine ivories of the so-called Court School. The painting may have been done by a master working for some Latin dignitary. In any case, it is interesting that while certain effects of modeling, notably the relationship between the light and heavy parts of the costume, recall the technique of the Canterbury *St. Paul* (page 112), on the other hand everything in the general attitude and facial expression here is totally different from the Canterbury painting. We have arrived at a period in which two cultures have evolved from what was surely a common base; now more and more they go their separate ways.

113

Virgin and Child (Theotokos) · 12th century · Mosaic · Cathedral, Torcello

Built on the island of Torcello in the Venetian lagoon, the basilica of Torcello was first decorated with frescoed figures of saints of which the few traces discovered are markedly Byzantine in style. Later, in the twelfth century, the decoration was transformed into mosaic by workshops still Byzantine in tradition—it was another two centuries before native workshops developed in the area. The figure of the Virgin is unforgettable, a completely personal creation in contrast with the other, doubtless almost contemporary, mosaic on the west wall of the basilica, a Last Judgment whose crowded folklike character is, to say the least, lively and amusing. The Last Judgment is a work of folk imagery, but the great Virgin of Torcello is one of the summits of mosaic art. For my part, I do not think this use of empty space to symbolize the ethereal infinity can be related to anything in Byzantine style. It must certainly have derived from a profound understanding of a mystical concept that has here been given truly inspired form, a form which remained as unique and isolated as the dramatic art of Chios (see plate below left).

The Three Marys at the Foot of the Cross · Detail from a *Crucifixion* · Middle of 12th century · Mosaic · West wall, Church of Nea Moni (the New Monastery), Chios

That the hieratic and increasingly stereotyped character of Byzantine art resulted from intellectual conditions rather than from purely technical or stylistic factors is again confirmed by this fine mosaic which makes an interesting comparison with those in the galleries of Hagia Sophia in Constantinople (pages 112–13). The gold background is archaic, but the feeling expressed must have struck its contemporaries as very modern, so different is it from the *Deësis* in Hagia Sophia: not intimate emotion but, instead, drama. The range of rare and refined colors testifies to the capabilities of the workshop which produced it, provincial though it may have been; but its technique is entirely unlike that of the *Deësis*: there is simplification and sharp contrasts of effects instead of fine gradations and subtle modeling. In fact, the style of Chios is much closer to the logic of mosaic art than is the sensitivity used in rendering the *Deësis*.

Noah Sends the Raven and the Dove Out upon the Waters · 12th century · Mosaic · Narthex, Basilica of San Marco, Venice

Rather than from Torcello, this and the next three examples are chosen from San Marco in Venice where one can follow the development of technique and style. In the twelfth century Byzantine or Byzantine-influenced workshops decorated the small cupolas of the narthex, using illustrations from a sixth-century Greek Bible as their models. What is remarkable here is the perfect equilibrium between narrative content and monumental style. In general, in Byzantine art the small episodes are commentaries on a text. Here, the anecdote is part of a pictorial ensemble, and its meaning is immediately understandable even without the accompanying inscriptions. The markedly linear depiction of the waters is balanced by the massive sculpturesque bulk of the Ark.

114

The Bringing of the Body of St. Mark to Venice · 12th century · Mosaic · Wall, south bay, Basilica of San Marco, Venice

Before achieving an independent style, the Venetian workshops strove to manifest their personality by an individual approach to iconography, to subject matter. The legend of St. Mark provided them with an original theme which they exploited with all the care necessary in recounting events less universally familiar. Both the inscription and the image function as commentary on the legend. Here, the soul of the Saint whose body lies lifeless in the boat is given material form, guiding the seamen who can only submit to his will. Over and beyond the story itself, this picture exemplifies the Venetian boast that Providence had chosen their city out of all the cities of the eastern Mediterranean, and above all Alexandria, to receive the body and the patronage of St. Mark.

The Building of the Tower of Babel · 12th century · Mosaic · Narthex, Basilica of San Marco, Venice

It is an interesting fact that different techniques and styles were practiced in periods that were quite close in time, or even within the same workshops. This mosaic should be compared with the English miniature on the same subject (page 101). Once again we see that one style was popular, folklike, and overtly narrative in contrast to another which was practiced in the great centers where scribes prepared fine manuscripts for the clergy: the first had to do with paraphrases of texts, the second led to imposing Sacramentaries and Pontificals. In this mosaic, there is evidence of a narrative tradition both persistent and highly international: in short, the difference between the two kinds of art was a matter of their respective aims and not of the capabilities of those who made them.

The Banquet of Herod · 14th century · Mosaic · Wall, Baptistery, Basilica of San Marco, Venice

In the course of the fourteenth century, precisely when Italian artists were elsewhere laying down modern principles of figuration which made their way only very slowly to Venice, the mosaic workshops in that city were practicing a style infinitely more Byzantine than that of the twelfth century. Comparison of this mosaic with the frescoes of Cavallini at Assisi or of Giotto—all much earlier in date— shows that the Byzantine style dies slowly, frozen into more and more faithful imitation of old forms and with no real innovations. Another example of a Byzantine style ending in academicism can be found in Constantinople itself, in the decoration of the Kariye Camii.

115

Christ as the Pantocrator · 1148 · Mosaic · Apse, Cathedral, Cefalù

The Norman kings of Sicily, Roger II in particular, founded and erected in a very short span of time enormous edifices with interiors sumptuously decorated with mosaics in the Byzantine manner. Their taste was highly eclectic, for they were rulers by virtue of conquest, and not natives of the land they governed. They built Latin edifices, adorned them in Byzantine fashion, and covered the ceilings with sta- lactites as the Moslems did. From this cultural melting pot was to develop in the next century the civilization of the Hohenstaufens, a high point in the history of Western thought. In the cathedral of Cefalù the Byzantine style of the mosaics is out of keeping with the classical character suggested by the basilican plan of the edifice. The individual components remain pure Byzantine; for my part, however, I feel that in Cefalù as in Torcello there is an exploitation of surfaces and volumes—especially evident in the Pantocrator and the Virgin (the latter recalling that of Torcello)— which aims at an impression of relief and, in fact, at an illusionism alien to the Byzantine spirit.

The Nativity · 1132–40 · Mosaic · Nave wall, Palatine Chapel, Norman Palace, Palermo

Founded by Roger II in 1132 and consecrated in 1140, this chapel has a Latin plan, but its mosaic decoration is more Byzantine than that of the Cathedral built a few years later; expecially remarkable is the gallery of the "Fathers of the Church," one of the masterpieces of Byzantine style. Nevertheless, certain elements reflect the adaptation of the cycle to a new architectural setting. A composition such as the *Nativity* deserves separate study in itself. It opens the way to the speculations underlying a large part of medieval painting in Italy. Infinitely rich in iconography, it faces up to what later became a major problem, the co-ordination of spatial and temporal factors. We have become so accustomed to the pictorial conventions devised in the West between the twelfth and fourteenth centuries that it is hard to realize that here we have a true imaginative creation. The admirable unity in the chapel is furthered through the harmony of colors.

GIUNTA PISANO (documented 1236–54) *Crucifix* · Before 1236 · 37 × 28¼″ · Painted wooden cross from the Church of San Ranierino, Pisa · Museo Nazionale, Pisa

The painted crucifix is a transposition into wood of the Byzantine reliquaries made in the form of a cross in gold or silver and embellished with enamels depicting biblical scenes, in which the relics were enshrined in small decorated receptacles fixed at the lateral extremities of the cross. These jewel-box-like containers inspired the earliest form and type of decoration of the squared-off extremities of thirteenth- century Italian crosses. Here then is a new genre of art: born out of a need for economy—wood was less costly than precious metals—the painted crucifix, for all that the material was less elegant, gave rise to new aesthetic possibilities and a wider dissemination of works of art. The dead Christ on the Cross (the eyes here are closed) is a motif whose earliest example may date from the ninth century in Byzantium. In thirteenth-century Italy it enjoyed increasing favor in connection with the Franciscan ideas then current, and eventually replaced the motif of Christ as the Triumphant Pantocrator which, at that time, was the dominant feature of Byzantine apses.

Virgin and Child · Florentine school, second half of 13th century · Tempera on panel · Museo Bandini, Fiesole

This panel may have been part of a larger ensemble. Frontal, rigid, holding the Child who blesses in the manner of the Greek rite, the Madonna resembles the Byzantine Virgins of the Nicopea type who hold the Child in a shield (or in place of a shield) like the pagan Nikes, the goddesses of Victory. This Madonna is proof that in the second half of the thirteenth century Florence had not yet shaken off the Byzantine domination which had prevailed since the sixth century; and also that Florence was still far behind Pisa, which had begun to liberate itself two generations earlier, and with a refinement unmatched by any other city in Italy. Be that as it may, the power of this image suggests—certainly more than the so-called "Madonna with Large Eyes" of Siena to which it is related—that already a local temperament was beginning to assert itself and to shake off traditional academic formulas.

THE MASTER OF THE BARDI ST. FRANCIS *Altarpiece of St. Francis* · c. 1250 (?) · Tempera on panel · 92 × 50″ · Santa Croce, Florence

Here we have the basic type of altarpiece of the period: the vertical component of a painted crucifix (see plate at left) has been extended to either side to create, in this case, a long vertical rectangle; the lateral areas thus formed are divided into compartments extending to the top and bottom of the panel; each compartment contains a small scene from the life of the holy personage depicted in the center. Here that personage is St. Francis, the ideal saint of the epoch, who according to the doctrine of his Order was the second incarnation of Christ on earth. Already transformed into an official and authoritarian figure, St. Francis is no longer the ecstatic innocent of the earliest depictions, although the twenty scenes from his life, such as the Sermon to the Birds, still stress his fraternal humility.

BONAVENTURA BERLINGHIERI (c. 1215–after 1274) *A Miracle of St. Francis* · One scene from an altarpiece of St. Francis · 1235 · Tempera on panel · San Francesco, Pescia

This panel comes from an altarpiece almost identical with that reproduced in the plate at left. By comparing them we can learn what is common to the style and what unique to the individual artist. Taken out of its context, this scene of a miracle of the Saint seems remarkably more advanced in style than those of the Master of the Bardi St. Francis and of the Pisan artist reproduced on the next page; this is not a matter of superior quality but of a different spirit. At this early date this artist has faced problems of perspective which were to be posed again in very similar terms a century later. Most of the problems which preoccupied artists at the beginning of the Quattrocento had been, to all intents and purposes, already envisaged by the so-called primitives of the Trecento. There exists a third altarpiece, similar to the two presented here, which is by Pierino of Pisa.

117

ANONYMOUS PISAN PAINTER (MASTER OF THE SAN MATTEO CRUCIFIX) *Pietà* · Compartment from a painted crucifix · Between 1200 and 1230 · Tempera on parchment, attached to wood · Museo Nazionale, Pisa

When crucifixes came to be painted on wood, it became necessary to broaden the central upright; the wider panel thus created came soon to be embellished, either with standing figures (the Virgin and St. John), decorative motifs, or compartments with narrative scenes. In turn, these panels gave rise to the square or rectangular altarpiece; the cross could be replaced by a large figure of a saint, surrounded by small scenes recalling the memorable acts of his life. Here, since the central figure is Christ, the six compartments are devoted to His life and Passion. This *Pietà* has been chosen because of the extraordinary quality of its composition, draftsmanship, and coloring; it gives some idea of the high achievement of Pisan art in the first half of the thirteenth century, a period too often undervalued by historians.

Follower of GUIDO DA SIENA *Altarpiece of St. Peter* · c. 1280 · Tempera on panel · 32¼ × 65″ · Pinacoteca Nazionale, Siena

The great altar frontals, such as the one dedicated to Mary Magdalen now in the Accademia of Florence, were fixed in place and intended for churches only. For private chapels in homes or for a usage which consisted of placing the painting below a table, smaller types were needed like this portable altarpiece *(paliotto)* dedicated to St. Peter. A seated figure fits this small format better than a standing one; thus, the saint enthroned became a feature of portable altars and, eventually, even of large altar paintings with, naturally, suitable enlargement of the figure. This St. Peter, still somewhat hieratic in manner, is surrounded by four episodes from his life that are in much freer and more animated style, and by two scenes from the life of the Virgin. The presence of the Virgin suggests that this *paliotto* was perhaps intended for a private chapel.

Eliezer and Rebecca (?), from the Psalter of St. Louis · Parisian workshop, between 1253 and 1270 · Manuscript illumination · Ms. lat. 10525, Bibliothèque Nationale, Paris

This psalter according to the rite of Sainte-Chapelle was executed for the King and embellished with seventy-eight full-page illuminations on facing pages with the explanatory texts on the blank back pages. It is worth comparing these admirable compositions with the contemporary paintings produced in Italy, which are too often considered without reference to the great currents of European culture in the period. In the thirteenth century, the great art of painting was French, which is to say Parisian. Gothic painting is not best expressed in frescoes but in miniatures and stained glass: the art is offered on the one hand to the admiration of everyone, on the other, to the small number of cultured persons, but it is the same taste which is revealed. Gothic civilization was the great form of medieval art—and its center was north of the Alps.

Abraham and the Three Angels, from the Psalter of St. Louis ·
Parisian workshop, between 1253 and 1270 · Manuscript
illumination · Ms. lat. 10525, Bibliothèque Nationale, Paris

Here is a second example of this admirable art, to stress the
perfect and exceptional harmony in all techniques in this
remarkable period of the history of the arts. The im-
pressiveness of architecture and stained glass was matched
by an art of drawing which went hand in hand with masterful use of color. The Tree of Life continues the old
Romanesque tradition but also anticipates Piero della
Francesca, nor was the still life mastered by the Italians until
the next century. The episodes are at the same time interre-
lated and distinct. This painter possessed an art of figurative
exposition never again equaled. Here we have a marvelous
example of a visual culture in full possession of its own means.

Calendar Frontispiece, from the Psalter of Paris · Parisian
workshop, c. 1223 · Manuscript illumination · Ms. 1186,
Bibliothèque de l'Arsénal, Paris

Intended for a woman of the royal house, this psalter was
also part of the Treasury of the Sainte-Chapelle. It includes a
calendar and twenty-five full-page illuminations. Preceding
the calendar is this miniature in which we see a scribe, a
mathematician, and an astronomer holding an astrolabe:
where once had figured the Evangelist—vessel and witness
of the Divine Word—now appear scientists who explore the
universe. Their learning no doubt has an astrological flavor,
but it is no less true that with their eyes fixed on the
heavens, in the midst of nature symbolized by the trees,
these men confront the precepts of divine science with the
data of direct observation. This psalter is divided into ten
parts; this is according to the usage in England and the
Northern countries and, like the markedly linear treatment
of the figures, it belongs to the traditions of a region which,
until the fifteenth century, was the center of civilization.

Coppo di Marcovaldo (documented 1260–85) *Crucifix* ·
Between 1260 and 1265 · Tempera on panel · 116 × 97″ ·
Museo Civico, San Gimignano

Among the crowd of anonymous Sienese and Florentine
artists in the second half of the thirteenth century, Coppo is
one of the first whose personality can be pinned down. A
native Florentine, he took part in the battle of Montaperti
on September 4, 1260, was taken prisoner by the Sienese,
and remained for some time in their city where he received
certain commissions: a *Madonna Enthroned* for the church of
the Servites in Siena, and this *Crucifix* for San Gimignano.
Repatriated, he did for Florence the mosaic *Last Judgment* in
the Baptistery (see page 125) and, together with Meliore, a
Madonna for Santa Maria Maggiore; in addition, he painted
a *Madonna* for the Servites in Orvieto and a *Crucifix* for the
cathedral of Pistoia between 1265 and 1274. Far from
attempting to throw off the Byzantine tradition, he
revitalized it by a remarkable intensification which contrasts with the earlier stereotyped treatment in Florentine
art. His icons streaked with gold, his angels treated like
arabesques to which he adds his own kind of expressionism
gleaned perhaps from German miniatures—these make of
him the leader in a neo-Hellenic revival.

MASTER OF VICO L'ABATE *The Miracle of the Bull*, from the altar frontal of the Archangel Michael · c. 1260 · Tempera on panel · Church of Sant'Angelo, Vico l'Abate, near Florence

The anonymous and perhaps provincial artist who painted this altar frontal likewise profited from the new Eastern science favored by Coppo but, less learned and less powerful, he injected into it naïve and spontaneous accents which lend it a quite special savor. If in Coppo's *Crucifix* the figure of Christ is already conventionalized, and if what is personal to Coppo is only to be found in the small panels and the Christ in benediction at the apex, here the entire painting is more homogeneous and infused throughout with the same creative vigor evident in the single panel reproduced. Everything is a pretext for this artist to make what we call today a "bit of painting": the humorously treated bull, the thick plant in the foreground (more conspicuous than the animal around which the story centers), the rock at once both contorted and smooth, the self-possessed attitudes of the personages, their plump individualized faces. This same devotion to detail reappeared later in the milieu of Verona, from which Pisanello came.

MELIORE *The Crucifixion of St. Peter with Three Women* · Detail from an altarpiece of the Virgin and Child, flanked by Sts. Peter and Paul · 1271 · Tempera on panel · Church of San Leolino, Panzano (Tuscany)

Quite unlike the Master of Vico l'Abate, the Florentine Meliore, who collaborated with Coppo di Marcovaldo on the great *Last Judgment* of the Baptistery of Florence (see page 125), intensified his expressionism to the point of tragedy: rhythmical figures disproportionately elongated, angels with profoundly intent expressions and cruel mouths. Meliore was taken prisoner, like Coppo, at the battle of Montaperti in 1260; more sensitive than his illustrious master to the ecstatic and visionary aspect of the Sienese temperament, he carried it over into his own works. In 1271 he signed the altarpiece of which this panel is a part; its central portion, the enthroned Virgin framed by Sts. Peter and Paul and four small compartments, is still in Panzano near Siena, while the ogive arch painted with a blessing Christ very much in the latest Byzantine manner is in the Uffizi in Florence.

GUIDO DA SIENA *Virgin in Majesty* · Central panel of an altarpiece · 1262 (?) · Tempera on panel · Palazzo Pubblico, Siena

Guido da Siena, reputed the master and ancestor of the entire Sienese school, is known only through this fine painting restored and repainted in the early fourteenth century by an artist in Duccio's circle, perhaps by Duccio himself. The name of Guido can be read on it along with a date which seems to be 1221: for stylistic reasons and historical probability, it is generally dated around 1262 when analogous works appear. For the same reasons another Madonna in the Pinacoteca of Siena is attributed to Guido, with the same date, this one cut down to half-length but otherwise better preserved. Names and dates aside, the two paintings mark the moment when the Byzantine-influenced style attained in Siena, more than elsewhere, an unsurpassed degree of refinement which had far repercussions—even after the Byzantine manner was entirely rejected—on the Madonnas painted in Siena and Tuscany.

ROMAN MASTER *The Original Sin: Adam* · c. 1290–95 ·
Fresco · Upper Church, Basilica of San Francesco, Assisi

In the third quarter of the thirteenth century, Florence went
through a Byzantine revival as a result of improved
acquaintance with the art of Crete, the Balkans, and Sicily.
Siena in this period continued to refine on the Byzantine
tradition by lending its own characteristic temperament.
Meanwhile, Rome turned back to its own original fountain-
head, ancient art. In Assisi, among the cohort of painters who
rushed in from every artistic center of Italy, the Romans
played an important role, even if they remain anonymous.
Granted that fresco had replaced mosaic as wooden painted
crosses had taken the place of metalwork crucifixes, and for
the same reasons, but fresco had already been a Roman
tradition in the first Christian catacomb paintings of the
third to sixth centuries. Moreover, it was probably through
the intermediary of Early Christian art, itself so close to
ancient art, rather than by direct study of pagan models that
the Roman artists rediscovered the classical vein which
reappeared in their painting after an absence of centuries.

PIETRO CAVALLINI (active c. 1270–1330) *Apostle* · c. 1293 ·
Fresco · Church of Santa Cecilia in Trastevere, Rome

This figure is one of the twelve Apostles who, with the
Virgin and St. John the Baptist, surround Christ in the Last
Judgment, the surviving section of what was once an
extensive decoration. Attributed by Lorenzo Ghiberti,
along with the rest of the decoration, to Cavallini, whose
native origins are not known, this figure is less supple than
those by the Roman painters at Assisi; but in compensation
it displays a robustness which, at that period, could only
come from contact—direct or indirect—with the art of
antiquity. Its rigidity may be due to the fact that the artist
was more used to working in mosaic of which he seems to
have been a specialist, as attested by the fragments of
decoration surviving in Santa Maria in Trastevere in Rome.
The authenticity of these is vouchsafed by a biography of
Cavallini written by Cardinal Jacopo Stefaneschi, brother
of the donor of the decoration.

The Twenty-four Elders of the Apocalypse · c. 1255 · Fresco ·
Apse of crypt, Cathedral, Anagni

Along with Assisi and Rome, Anagni—a city made notorious
a little later by the attempt against Pope Boniface VIII
committed in the name of Philip the Fair—offers another
example of great mural decoration in Italy at the time when
France was developing the art of stained glass. It is also one
of the last examples of extensive mural decoration in the
spirit of the old traditional style and iconography; soon,
with Giotto, there was to be more stress on narrative. Here,
in this monumental cycle commemorating the dedication of
the church and the acquisition of its relics, we find an
ultimate summation. It shows man the microcosm in his
mystical relations with the destinies of the universe, the
same comprehensive program found on the great
Romanesque portals such as Beaulieu and Saint-Denis.
Painting is still concerned with cosmic symbols; later it was
to give concrete form to legends, The saints and the deeds
of mankind were more and more to interpose themselves
between God and man.

121

JACOPO TORRITI (or DA TORRITA) *The Coronation of the Virgin* · 1295 · Mosaic · Main apse, Basilica of Santa Maria Maggiore, Rome

The signature and date on this mosaic are the only documents we possess for this artist except for the signature placed in 1291 on the apse mosaic in San Giovanni Laterano, Rome; the latter mosaic, entirely remade, can no longer tell us anything about his way of working. Today it is thought that he was perhaps responsible for certain of the frescoes in Roman style in Assisi but that, in any event, he started out like Cavallini by restoring fifth-century Roman frescoes and gained from them his knowledge of an art still inspired by antiquity. This *Coronation*, like other thirteenth-century mosaics, strives to respect the style—realistic and adopting small scenes in the open air—still visible in certain vestiges of fifth-century decoration which remained in place and are not greatly removed from the style of Pompeii.

Last Judgment · End of 13th century · Mosaic · Cupola, Baptistery of San Giovanni, Florence

This great work was conceived, as in Byzantine churches, as a veritable microcosm in which a celestial hierarchy presides over Genesis, the Passion, events from the Old and New Testaments, and finally an overwhelming Last Judgment; it was certainly made by a team of artists, not by one man alone. In this universe swarming with details, placed too high to be easily analyzed, the center of interest is the Christ of Judgment enthroned in glory on the rainbow of the Apocalypse and, with a broad gesture, separating the Good from the Bad among the resurrected dead at His feet. The figure has often been attributed to Cimabue, but Carlo Ragghianti's suggestion of Coppo di Marcovaldo, probably assisted by Meliore, seems quite valid. To whomever the mosaics in the Baptistery of Florence may be due, one can say without hesitation that they belong to a current opposed to that of the apse mosaic of Santa Maria Maggiore in Rome: they are Byzantine and in no way Roman.

CIMABUE (CENNI DI PEPO) (1240/50–1302/3) *Crucifix* · Before 1270 (?) · Tempera on wood · 11′ × 8′11″ · Church of San Domenico, Arezzo

While the collaboration of Cimabue in the Baptistery of Florence is no more than a probability, there is general agreement in attributing to him this *Crucifix* which he would have painted at a time when he was still much involved in the Byzantine current of Coppo. In any event, his affinities with Coppo, whose work was always a little cold and formal, are limited to the technical conception. Even in such youthful efforts, Cimabue was concerned above all with expression, seeking to reveal in both human figures and objects the dominant and single idea behind them. Among all the Christs of the epoch, those of Cimabue are the supreme example of the Christ who suffers beyond death itself.

GIOTTO DI BONDONE (c. 1266–1337) *The Kiss of Judas* ·
1304–5 · Fresco · Scrovegni Chapel, Padua

It is in this masterly fresco that Giotto reveals the full
measure of his quintessential humanism outside of which all
his less fundamental explorations—and these he by no
means avoided—must appear merely incidental. Here, in the
absence of any setting, the fraction of space left unfilled by
figures is animated only by the lances and blazing torches
which are dependent on the hands that hold them. There is a
single plastic motif: the bringing into relief of the principal
figures in the compact crowd. There is also a single emotional motif: the contrasts between the falsely fraternal gesture
of Judas, Jesus' awareness of it that is expressed in His face,
the panic of the Apostles, and the vulgar brutality of the
myrmidons of the law eager for their prey. A true artist,
Giotto shows here that he could express himself as well in
dramatic intensity as in that serene but never frigid mood
which so often is his.

Detail is shown on next pages

CIMABUE *Virgin and Child with Angels and St. Francis* · 1282–1301 · Fresco · Lower Church, Basilica of San Francesco, Assisi

It was Vasari who first attached the name of Cimabue to this fresco which Ghiberti had given to Cavallini; today, opinion unanimously assigns it to Cimabue. If there has been uncertainty, it was because the gap between the two artists tended to lessen in the period of Cimabue's maturity when he increasingly abandoned Byzantine formalism in favor of greater freedom in the means of expression. Those means were adapted with remarkable consistency to the artist's fundamental concern with bringing out the chief emotional and ideological characteristics of his personages: here the Virgin is doubly maternal, mother not only to the divine Infant but also to the humble and human St. Francis, the second incarnation of Jesus. The soft coloring and the velvety treatment of what already deserves the name of chiaroscuro aid alike in softening an implacable divinity in favor of a more human truth.

CIMABUE *St. Luke* · 1282–1301 · Fresco · Crossing, Upper Church, Basilica of San Francesco, Assisi

For the four sections of the cupola, placed very high, each of which is devoted to one of the Evangelists, Cimabue went back to a linear treatment more easily decipherable at a great distance; he also reverts a conception of space which, without imitating that of the Romans, no less clearly renders the three dimensions of the cities over which reign Luke, Matthew, Mark, and John, each of them identified by a legible inscription as well as by his small conventional symbol. The large city which supersedes the symbol was an innovation in monumental art and must certainly have derived from manuscript illuminations whose style, moreover, is imitated here.

GIOTTO DI BONDONE (c. 1266–1337) *The Stigmatization of St. Francis* · c. 1296–1304 · Fresco · Upper Church, Basilica of San Francesco, Assisi

According to Riccobaldo of Ferrara and Vasari, Giotto went to Assisi at the invitation of Giovanni di Muro, general of the Franciscan order between 1296 and 1304. So it is probably between those dates, most likely about 1297, that the artist's arrival in the city of St. Francis took place, although he seems to have visited it about 1295. After much debate it is now generally agreed that it was in fact Giotto, no doubt with the aid of a large group of students, who during his second sojourn in the city executed the twenty-eight frescoes in the Upper Church which illustrate the life of St. Francis. Before Giotto there had been numerous interpretations, painted and written, of the legend of the Saint; Giotto gives us a conception that is ideologically official, but artistically very new. This and the following example, the *Confirmation*, have been chosen because they demonstrate better than the other frescoes the synthesis of these two normally contradictory aspects in this complex work.

GIOTTO DI BONDONE *The Confirmation of the Franciscan Rule by Pope Honorius III* · c. 1296–1304 · Fresco · Upper Church, Basilica of San Francesco, Assisi

Like the *Stigmatization*, this fresco was conceived to assert to the world the rank of St. Francis in the hierarchy—in this case, on earth; in the preceding example, in Heaven. The stigmata received by the Saint are the proof that he relived on earth the same existence as Christ and that he is therefore, after Christ, the most important personage in the universe. The present fresco reassures us of his good relations with the Church of Rome, which many then current aspects of the Franciscan legend might have led the faithful to doubt, as might also the continued existence of the Spiritualist sect of the Friars Minor, generally considered heretical. Over and beyond such ecclesiastical concerns, both of these works, especially in the treatment of the draped figure as inspired by French and Pisan sculpture, constitute a breakthrough to a new art destined to depart from the established tradition, an art of which Giotto himself in his subsequent works was to be the principal agent.

GIOTTO DI BONDONE *The Dream of Joachim* · 1304–5 · Fresco · Scrovegni Chapel, Padua

Even more than at Assisi, the sculptural quality of Giotto's figures is evident in his frescoes for the chapel of Enrico Scrovegni, known as the Arena Chapel because it was built on the ruins of an ancient amphitheater. Enveloped—shrouded, rather, in a manner that makes us think of French funeral monuments—in the ample folds of a cloak with broadly modeled surfaces, the figure of Joachim sleeping is like a block of stone, compact, scarcely altered by the sculptor's tools, much like the statues of Giovanni Pisano who, as it happened, was himself at Giotto's side during the work on the chapel. The few years between the Assisi frescoes and those at Padua have sufficed not only to ripen Giotto's talent but also to make him conscious of the path his quest had to pursue.

GIOTTO DI BONDONE *The Presentation of the Virgin in the Temple* · 1304–5 · Fresco · Scrovegni Chapel, Padua

The progression of any development is always partial. If at times Giotto concentrated entirely on the human figure, at others he continued to include, unmodified, many elements of setting belonging to the authentic Byzantine repertory of images and in particular to that of Sicily: the imaginary stylized rock of *The Dream of Joachim*; the small marble edifice, scarcely more than a shell, with its slender columns, which represents here the Temple; still others which set the stage for most of his narrative scenes. As a matter of fact, the juxtaposition of the two approaches enhances the effect, as here where the fragility of the architectural setting only makes the natural weight of the human figure so much more evident. There is one true invention here, however, in the depiction of architecture: the bare steps of the staircase, with all their solidity, on which poises the tiny figure of Mary—the motif was to survive and to be repeated with great effect as late as Titian and Tintoretto.

127

GIOTTO DI BONDONE *The Entry into Jerusalem* · 1304–5 · Fresco · Scrovegni Chapel, Padua

The Entry into Jerusalem is a subject that has much to offer the painter. It requires a variety of picturesque elements which blend nicely: a city or its gate, a procession and a counterprocession, a cloak spread out, trees, a donkey. For this reason the subject had been popular since early times, and all its elements had become virtually obligatory, fixed by a long-standing tradition. Giotto kept them all, but far from aiming at merely picturesque effect, as Duccio did in the same subject painted at the same time, Giotto condensed the conventional elements to the minimum and treated them as simple signs, mere indications: the city gate is barely visible in the corner, the boys gathering palm branches are relegated to the background, the two processions do not straggle off into space, the cloak covers no more than a bit of the path. All interest is focused on the majestic figure of Christ and on His mount and, above all, on the dramatic encounter.

GIOTTO DI BONDONE *Last Judgment* · 1305 or 1306 · Fresco · Scrovegni Chapel, Padua

It was probably some time after the completion of the frescoes devoted to Joachim, Mary, and Christ, and after the celebrations of the feast of the Virgin of the Arena in 1305, that Giotto culminated his work with this *Last Judgment*, which stretches across the entire entrance wall of the chapel. Crowning all, Paradise; in the center, the Christ of Judgment and a row of Apostles; below, the Elect and the Damned. In the foreground, offering his chapel to the Virgin, is Enrico Scrovegni, son of the patrician Rinaldo Scrovegni, the usurer Dante thrust into the seventh circle of his Inferno, and this explains the origin of the chapel: to obtain pardon for their ill-gotten fortune, the Scrovegni family was commanded to atone by building an expiatory chapel. The over-all plan of the fresco is of special interest for its perspective treatment of the fan-shaped ranks of haloed angels' heads on either side of the window, and also for the architectural *trompe l'oeil* separation of Heaven and Earth, the first of a long series of such illusionary renderings in the decoration of large wall surfaces.

GIOTTO DI BONDONE *The Burial of St. Francis* · Between 1317 and 1320 · Fresco · Bardi Chapel, Basilica of Santa Croce, Florence

Established in Florence, famous, wealthy, and admired, Giotto received many commissions to decorate the private chapels the greatest families of Florence were privileged to set up in the transept of Santa Croce, which was, along with the Dominicans' Santa Maria Novella, the most important church of the city and the official seat of monastic and papal Franciscanism. Four of these were decorated by Giotto's workshop: the Bardi, Peruzzi, Giugni, and Tosinghi chapels, but only the frescoes of the first two have survived; completely whitewashed over, they were not discovered until 1841. Very much restored since, they still have much to tell us, if only about the choice of subjects and the ultra-official type of composition in favor at the time. The frescoes constitute, in fact, an apologia for Franciscanism, which had made its peace with the Church of Rome by complete submission. In any case, this burial scene is a masterpiece of composition whose measured rhythm could well be envied by many a great classical artist.

DUCCIO DI BUONINSEGNA (c. 1250/60–1319) (?) *Virgin and Child with Two Angels* · c. 1283 · Tempera on panel · Church of Santi Salvatore e Cirino, Badia a Isola (Tuscany)

Whether the Master of Badia a Isola was Duccio himself at his beginnings, or a disciple of Cimabue working at the time the great Sienese was young, this *Virgin* has qualities which reflect a great artistic personality. In any event, it is not an isolated work but one of a long line of enthroned Madonnas which, no longer of the frontal hieratic type long favored in Byzantine Italy, are in three-quarter profile bending down toward the Infant. The series begins with the Virgin in the Accademia in Florence, goes on to that of the Carmine in Siena and those in Perugia and Arezzo, continues with Guido and the Madonnas Coppo painted for the Servites of Siena and Orvieto, to culminate in the celebrated *Rucellai Madonna*, now recognized as Duccio's, and in that by Cimabue in the Louvre. All of them are seated on a throne as monumental as a church—this throne is, in fact, a symbol of the Church. But the Madonna of Badia carries over from the past her mantle streaked with gold, the Child who blesses in the Greek fashion, and the two angels who must always, according to the tradition of Constantinople, attend the Virgin.

DUCCIO DI BUONINSEGNA *The Virgin in Majesty* · Central panel of the front of the Maestà Altarpiece · 1308–11 · Tempera on panel · 84 × 157″ · Museo dell'Opera del Duomo, Siena

This central panel of the renowned altarpiece from the Siena Cathedral has a Virgin of the same type seated on a monumental throne, but she has developed, become more supple, and the Child has become a believable infant. The Byzantine attributes have been discarded, although the style remains close to the Greek. The two angels have increased to twenty, a heavenly court, and the court is rounded out by ten saints, among whom are the patron of Siena, St. Catherine, and four saint-protectors of the city. And yet this Queen in the center of her court, with the twelve Apostles as guard of honor, is nonetheless a younger sister to the Madonna at Badia a Isola and to all those preceding her. The *Maestà* was commissioned from Duccio in 1308 by the Commune of Siena to be placed in the Cathedral. The day it was finished, it was borne in triumph to its new home by an ecstatic populace: Duccio's fame was assured.

DUCCIO DI BUONINSEGNA *The Virgin Borne to Her Sepulcher* · Superstructure of the Maestà Altarpiece · 1308–11 · Tempera on panel · 21¾ × 19¾″ · Museo dell'Opera del Duomo, Siena

The life and death of this Queen reigning over a heavenly court are recounted in six scenes. Such scenes had become virtually obligatory ever since the early crucifixes and altarpieces of saints with accessory narrative panels. But in the *Maestà* the expanse required for the great court—both ideologically and pictorially an innovation at the time—created a problem: to place the narrative scenes at the sides of these ranks of figures would mean breaking both the style and the significance of the composition. Therefore Duccio had the happy thought of placing them all at the top of the altarpiece to form a large superstructure (which was later detached from the rest of the painting). This innovation was later followed only in part: although altarpieces were more and more given a decorative superstructure, the theme was generally confined to the Annunciation or to isolated figures without narrative scenes.

129

DUCCIO DI BUONINSEGNA *The Apparition of Christ through a Closed Door* · Panel from the back of the Maestà Altarpiece · 1308–11 · Tempera on panel · Museo dell'Opera del Duomo, Siena

Duccio's great altarpiece is unique in that it was meant to be viewed from both front and back. This innovation was not taken up by others, doubtless because of the difficulties of installing such an altarpiece in a chapel. One wonders if the notion may not have come from the famous *Pala d'Oro*, the gold altarpiece in San Marco in Venice, the contacts between Siena and Venice having certainly been more extensive and more frequent at the time than has hitherto been recognized. The back of the *Maestà* is entirely devoted to scenes from the life of Jesus. No attribute sets Him apart from the Apostles, but He is recognizable from one scene to the other by His red robe and blue mantle. However, for the apparitions after the Resurrection, Duccio had recourse to another procedure: the risen Christ is clothed in a gold-streaked mantle in accord with the Byzantine tradition. Thus, to indicate the transformation from the human to the divine, Duccio dipped back into Byzantine art, still considered more noble and, in any case, most effective in representing the extraspatial character of God.

DUCCIO DI BUONINSEGNA *The Flight into Egypt* · Panel from the predella of the Maestà Altarpiece · 1308–11 · Tempera on panel · Museo dell'Opera del Duomo, Siena

The predella—a row of small square or rectangular panels generally of uneven number (three, five, or seven) placed below the central panel of an altarpiece as a sort of dado or pedestal—became the favored location for small narrative scenes. Although Duccio had already made use of the superstructure for these, he also utilized the predella. Small scenes on the predella on the back of the *Maestà* continued the account of the life of Christ, while on the front others, separated by figures of prophets, were devoted to the Virgin. The seventeen panels known to have survived have been dispersed to various museums, but whatever others there were have disappeared. *The Flight into Egypt*, one of seven remaining in Siena, has a picturesque character entirely alien to the severity of the main central panel, although Duccio, unlike other artists, lavished on it the same highly controlled drawing and the same painstaking execution as on the principal section of his altarpiece.

DUCCIO DI BUONINSEGNA *The Entry into Jerusalem* · Panel from the back of the Maestà Altarpiece · 1308–11 · Tempera on panel · Museo dell'Opera del Duomo, Siena

Of the twenty-six compartments on the back, three of larger dimensions form the center of the composition: *The Crucifixion*, *The Kiss of Judas*, and *The Prayer on the Mount of Olives*. Although installed at the far left side, *The Entry into Jerusalem* likewise is almost twice the size of the other compartments. Compared with Giotto's treatment of the same subject (page 128), this *Entry* employs all those illustrative elements which had become traditional, but nevertheless reveals that something quite different could be made out of them. Duccio does not emphasize the figure of Christ but, instead, the city, the procession, the landscape, and the spread-out cloak, and he disposes them all in depth, distributed throughout the various planes, and this well in advance of any hint of later theories as to how space should be represented.

DUCCIO DI BUONINSEGNA *Jesus before Annas* and *The First Denial of Peter* · Panel from the back of the Maestà Altarpiece · 1308–11 · Tempera on panel · Museo dell'Opera del Duomo, Siena

We have seen in *The Entry into Jerusalem* that Duccio, like Giotto, when he wished to was perfectly capable of presenting a view of a city in quite satisfactory perspective. This seems to prove that the theories of linear perspective of the following century did no more than codify usages long known even if not systematically exploited. Here we have not an exterior but two interiors superimposed. Their cuboid, scenic, and perspective character is perfectly well brought out: note the staircase which carries the eye upward, the arcade below with its glimpse of the entrance, and the ceiling of the upper room. Nevertheless, it may well be that this practice was reserved to minor types of painting, to small scenes, while the "noble" style appropriate to large central panels continued to call for the Byzantine manner.

DUCCIO DI BUONINSEGNA *The Rucellai Madonna* · 1285 (?) · Tempera on panel · 14′ 9⅛″ × 9′ 6⅛″ · Uffizi Gallery, Florence

First attributed to Cimabue, this Madonna was finally recognized as the painting which the Confraternity of the Laudes of the Dominican Church of Santa Maria Novella in Florence had commissioned from Duccio in 1285, thereby crowning the fame of a painter who, having come from Siena, was considered an outsider. The painting was found in the chapel in Santa Maria Novella which had belonged to the Rucellai family, and this accounts for the name currently given to it. One can see how far the painter had come from the Madonna at Badia a Isola, and how close he was already to the Virgin in the central panel of the *Maestà*: the mantle no longer has Byzantine gold streaks to symbolize folds in the drapery, and those folds are now carefully worked out for plastic form and suppleness. The angels—of which Byzantine tradition had always required two—have been multiplied threefold. The rigid and monumental superstructure of the throne has been replaced by a curtain falling in draped folds. The Infant is no longer a tiny adult and, without yet being truly a baby, is at least a child. In all, there is an as yet timid step toward greater flexibility, and the rejection of the immutable canons Italian art had passively accepted under the sway of the Byzantine tradition and which, in fact, it had too often interpreted with an unadventurous respect not always justified by Byzantine art itself.

SIMONE MARTINI (c. 1282–1344) *Guidoriccio Ricci da Fogliano* · 1328 · Fresco · Palazzo Pubblico, Siena

Four years before Duccio's death in 1319, another *Maestà* adorned the walls of a hall in the palace of the commune, the work of the young Simone Martini. To have been awarded such an official commission during Duccio's lifetime, the artist must already have gained a considerable reputation. His fame grew: an invitation from the King of Naples, commissions from Pisa and Orvieto, capped in Siena itself by yet another assignment for the communal palace, this fresco. Since Duccio's heyday the world had changed, the barrier separating the realms of East and West had been crossed. The Western world was the world of the Crusades, not long past but already legendary. What the city fathers had in mind was a simple votive painting, a victory trophy of thanks from the thriving commercial middle-class city to a captain-at-arms, the *condottiere* Guidoriccio, who had conquered for it the two castles we see in the fresco. But for this simple task the artist conceived a veritable poetic incarnation of the chivalric ideal of the Western Middle Ages—the finest masterpiece of Sienese painting.

131

SIMONE MARTINI *St. Martin Renouncing the Sword* · Detail from the cycle of the Life of St. Martin · 1326–28 or 1328–30 or both in two separate working periods · Fresco · Lower Church, Basilica of San Francesco, Assisi

The Siena and Assisi frescoes have much in common, although it is not known if the latter were done first or perhaps in two phases, before and after the work in Siena. The Assisi frescoes portray the same world of chivalry, which was no longer a reality though it continued to excite the nostalgia of an artist who, living in the most commercially minded city of Italy, nevertheless thought of himself as a great gentleman, a lord even, and behaved accordingly. It seems likely that he acquired such tastes during his stay at the court of Robert of Anjou in Naples, because before then he was said to be sober in manner with perhaps just a touch of affectation. His talent was at ease in either attitude, but the pleasure he took in conjuring up military dress and trappings, encampments, lances, and helmets—which here make their first brilliant tumultuous entry into Italian art—is more evident in these frescoes than in works like the polyptychs for Pisa and Orvieto which belong to an ancient tradition.

SIMONE MARTINI *The Annunciation* (detail) · 1333 · Tempera on panel · Uffizi Gallery, Florence

This polyptych, dated and signed by both Simone Martini and Lippo Memmi, who probably did the wings, was formerly in the Chapel of St. Ansano in the Siena Cathedral. Was it because it was conceived as an altarpiece, like the polyptych in Pisa, that Simone, who had set his frescoes for Assisi and Siena against a radiant blue sky, settled here for the conventional gold background? Whatever the reason, the background is the only concession to the old Byzantine tradition in the delightful central panel; its fluid and somewhat mannered drawing and its fluttering drapery seem Baroque before the fact. But perhaps there is something Byzantine in Simone's very personal interpretation of the Virgin of the Annunciation as an *ancilla Domini*, as Byzantium considered her to be even after the West had proclaimed her Queen. Surely the artist must have had his own opinion, since his Handmaiden of God is both timid and palpitant with life, and this indeed transcends the tradition of any country, of any time.

SIMONE MARTINI *The Way to Calvary* · c. 1342 · Tempera on panel · 9¾ × 6¼″ · The Louvre, Paris

It is thought that this panel, together with another now in Berlin and four in the Antwerp Museum, was part of a portable polyptych which once belonged to Cardinal Stefaneschi. It must have been done at Avignon, where Simone lived from 1340 until his death in July, 1344, and where he painted frescoes on the façade of Notre-Dame-des-Doms, now half ruined. This panel is of interest for two reasons. Better than the damaged frescoes it reveals the hold Provençal art took on the style of the Sienese master, both in the transformation of his color, which has become flickering here, and in a certain jaggedness of line not unrelated to the Gothic art of Flanders and France. And also in this small panel we find the beginnings and crystallization of an iconographic theme later repeated, almost unchanged, by many artists until it culminated in the *Calvary* of the Spanish Chapel in Florence.

SIMONE MARTINI (?) *The Blessed Agostino Novello Saves a Child Fallen from Its Cradle* · Panel from a triptych · c. 1330 · Tempera on panel · Church of Sant'Agostino, Siena

Had Simone once before succumbed to the fascinations of the folk style? The large votive painting of the miracles of the Blessed Agostino Novello, a saintly hermit-knight, is not always conceded to be by Simone, and certainly its technique seems a serious obstacle to such an attribution. Still, it is a tempting hypothesis that our painter, innovator that he was, might also have introduced such new folklike themes, whose naïve freshness is so unlike the solemn nobility of previous Sienese art. The beds with their bright patterned covers are very much in Simone's taste, and even if he himself was not the painter, the inspiration certainly came from him, so that if the notion of an artist's "circle" ever has any meaning, it unquestionably does in this case.

PIETRO LORENZETTI (d. 1348?) (?) *Scene from the Life of the Blessed Umiltà*, from the altarpiece of the Blessed Umiltà · 1316 (?) · Tempera on panel · 17½ × 12½" · Uffizi Gallery, Florence

This delightful altar painting, whose various scenes are now dispersed between Florence and Berlin, recounts the life of a woman of medieval times who was beatified. She was Rosanese Negosanti, spouse of Ugolotto Caccianemici, who lived in Faenza and founded there the Order of the Daughters of Vallombrosa, herself assuming the name in religion of "Humility." Drawing inspiration from Giotto and with a certain just moderation typical of Florence, but also with a refinement seemingly unique to Siena at that time, this painting's authorship has been hotly debated, and even the date inscribed on it has been questioned. What seems certain is that it is not by some minor master, as Vasari claimed, but by an artist of considerable talent, probably one whose youthful works are little known. It has finally been awarded to Pietro Lorenzetti, of whose activities before 1320 we have no precise knowledge. This is not entirely convincing, but no satisfactory counterproposal has ever been made.

PIETRO LORENZETTI *Virgin and Child* · c. 1326–30 · Fresco · Lower Church, Basilica of San Francesco, Assisi

The first sure evidence of Pietro Lorenzetti is in a polyptych made for Arezzo, signed and dated 1320. Its central panel contains a Madonna of the Hodegitria type, wearing a mantle similar to those coming into fashion at the court of Burgundy. On the basis of that picture plus another polyptych, signed and dated 1329 and painted for the monastery of the Carmelites at Siena, a number of attributions have been made to Lorenzetti, who is, without doubt, the artist most difficult to pin down of his entire century. These attributions include the frescoes in the left transept of the Lower Church in Assisi. More or less contemporary with Simone Martini's frescoes in the same church, they are radically different in spirit. Their severe expressionism, with no indulgence in the merely picturesque, gave rise to a current which, in the next century, was to constitute one of the most striking and typical aspects of Sienese art in its ultimate phase.

133

PIETRO LORENZETTI *The Deposition from the Cross* · c. 1326–30 · Fresco · Lower Church, Basilica of San Francesco, Assisi

In the same transept, on the end wall and alongside an *Entombment*, this *Deposition* belongs to a not very extensive cycle on the Passion which begins with a large *Crucifixion*. The tragic expressionism favored by this painter takes on greater breadth here than elsewhere in his work, and no longer derives only from a particular treatment of faces and expressions, as in the *Virgin and Child* (page 133), but also from contortion of the lines of the bodies and from the exaggerated proportions of those details the artist wishes to stress. The focus is on the shattered, twisted body of Christ, but the emotional impact is accentuated by the grouping of the other figures into a dynamic pyramid shape within which lines are broken at right angles as well as by the asymmetry of the group in relation to the Cross in the center.

PIETRO LORENZETTI *The Birth of the Virgin* · Two panels from an altarpiece · 1342 · Tempera on panel · Museo dell'Opera del Duomo, Siena

Thirteen years separate this triptych from the altarpiece for the Carmelites, thirteen years during which, to judge by a *Maestà* from as late as 1340, Pietro went on painting his enthroned Virgins who, for all that they are organized according to the conventions of the "noble" style, are surprisingly sensitive and even petulant in expression. What explains the abrupt change of style in this panel, which is signed and is therefore certainly by Pietro? The example of Simone Martini? Of his brother Ambrogio? The wish to be "up-to-date"? Or simply the awakening of tendencies long dormant in him, already hinted at in the Carmine predella, and to which he finally gave free rein at a time when the public was beginning to concede that a genre scene could also be the main subject of a picture?

PIETRO LORENZETTI *St. Albert Gives the Carmelite Rule to St. Brocardo* · Central predella panel from the polyptych for the Church of the Carmine · 1329 · Pinacoteca, Siena

Pietro Lorenzetti, who duly signed this polyptych, did not always avoid the picturesque note but, as was the custom, reserved it for the predella, which in this work is placed below a queenly Virgin enthroned, magnificent in style albeit a little stiff and formal. It is exceptional to find in the predella a subject as important as the consignment of the Rule, the most important event in the history of a religious order, but despite the solemnity of the theme, Pietro went so far as to place alongside a splendid and rigorously disposed procession a number of picturesque details, some drawn from observation of everyday reality, some from the creative fancy without which no artist can be considered complete. Here such details introduce a more pleasant note into Lorenzetti's somber tragic universe.

AMBROGIO LORENZETTI (d. 1348?) *Virgin of the Milk* · c. 1320 · Tempera on panel · $35\frac{1}{2} \times 17\frac{3}{4}''$ · Seminary of San Francesco, Siena

Pietro's brother Ambrogio had long been aware of what was happening. If this charming Virgin nursing a frail Child is attributed to him, it is precisely because the general tendency of his temperament was quite opposite to that of his brother and, in a sense, was rather more like Simone Martini's in its love for detail and lavish costume. To this he added his own taste for things observed in everyday life, though he never failed to interpret these in his own imaginative fashion, as here. True, like all the painters of the first half of the fourteenth century, even in his full maturity he at times had to bow to the taste of a conservative clientele, especially when commissions came from monasteries. This is why, as late as 1342, he turned out the very conventional *Presentation at the Temple*, now in the Uffizi, and continued to produce from time to time the standard enthroned Virgins. Yet he never failed to introduce some personal note: a cluster of flowers in the lap of a girlish saint, a bright-patterned carpet, some lively gesture of the Infant.

AMBROGIO LORENZETTI *The Submission of St. Louis of Toulouse* · c. 1331 · Fresco · San Francesco, Siena

In his youth Ambrogio went to Florence, and that experience no doubt had some influence on this fresco and its companion piece, all that remain of the decorations of the cloister of San Francesco, which were transported to the interior of the church in 1517 when the cloister was demolished. We know the authorship through Ghiberti, and if he was especially enthusiastic about this work it was certainly because he recognized in it traits characteristic of his native Florence. Not that there is servile imitation of Giotto, but rather an application of theories no doubt current in Florentine circles, theories which were perhaps already concerned with cubic space; how to represent it on a two-dimensional surface, how to dispose various planes in depth. Much more than with Giotto, one finds here a deliberate use of these notions. Despite its conscious concern with theory, the fresco reveals an audacity and breadth of vision which justify its attribution to the great innovator of Siena.

AMBROGIO LORENZETTI *The Effects of Good Government on the City* (portion) · c. 1338 · Fresco · Palazzo Pubblico, Siena

A few years later Ambrogio turned his back on the too-constricting example of Florence to reveal the true measure of his own independent genius. Wishing to proclaim its desire for peace, the commune of Siena commissioned from him a fresco for the town hall, an allegory of Good Government and its beneficial effects on city and countryside. Ambrogio undertook to do what no Italian painter before him had so much as thought of doing: to *depict*, rather than to symbolize by conventional means, a city and a landscape. And yet, there must be no confusion about the term "depict": what he produced was an intellectual realization in which real elements were organized not according to what could be observed but rather on the basis of an intellectual evocation of something everyone knew. Where a Giotto or a Simone Martini let city or country be symbolized by some edifice or a tree so that it was no more than background or stage setting, Ambrogio totally transformed traditional values to create a cityscape and a landscape with an existence of their own.

135

This is another aspect of Ambrogio's depiction of the city. The preceding portion showed how the city rises out of the countryside, how they are linked and interdependent. Here we have the city itself, inspired no doubt by Siena, with its tall buildings crammed within battlements in typical medieval fashion. It is not unlikely that certain buildings were painted "from life," and the appearance of tall towers lording over the urban complex, if not exact in its details, is most probably, at least in over-all effect, much like what Siena must have looked like observed from some particular viewpoint. But anyone who tries to take it as a realistic picture of the old city finds it impossible to pin down the spot from which it was painted. The city is seen both from above and below: an intellectual viewpoint, not a real one.

AMBROGIO LORENZETTI *The Effect of Good Government on the City* (continuation) · c. 1338 · Fresco · Palazzo Pubblico, Siena

In a continuously unrolling picture, following the depiction of the city with its manifold activities, comes a view of the country around Siena represented in the same arbitrary manner which organizes real observed elements—hills and brick kilns, fields and roads—in a concise view, intellectually conceived but recognizable. In evoking with evident pleasure the commercial, rural, and folk activities of these places, Ambrogio's taste shows itself quite unlike that of a Simone Martini still caught up in dreams of chivalry. What he obviously enjoyed painting was the joyous bustle of a people working hard at building the city's future, and he left to his pupils the less attractive task of the companion fresco which shows war as the effect of bad government and which, had he so desired, could have been the pretext for a display of military pomp and splendor.

PACINO DI BONAGUIDA (active first quarter of 14th century) *The Tree of the Holy Cross* · Tempera on panel · 99¼ × 60¾" · Accademia, Florence

We have seen that in Siena there was a diversity of artistic trends due in equal measure to the tastes and temperaments of individual artists and to the demands of the particular public for which they painted. Besides, the same artist might work in both the "noble style" inherited from Byzantine art and an individual and path-breaking style. This was true in Florence also. This painting by a contemporary of Giotto proves that an archaic current lingered on alongside the revolutionary efforts of the great master and his pupils. Its interest is chiefly iconographic: inspired by the *Lignum Vitae* of St. Bonaventure and attributed to Pacino because of stylistic similarities to a polyptych of the Crucifixion he signed and dated, this picture illustrates a doctrine and a legend and was to be the prototype for a long series of productions of the same sort.

TADDEO GADDI (d. c. 1366) *The Nativity* · c. 1332–34 ·
Tempera on panel · Medallion from the sacristy chests of
Santa Croce · Accademia, Florence

This docile pupil of Giotto, considered after his master's
death the best painter in Florence, likewise executed together with his workshop a *Tree of Life* inspired by St.
Bonaventure. But his crowning work was the frescoes in
the Baroncelli Chapel in the Basilica of Santa Croce and,
probably around the same time, twenty-six quadrilobate
medallions and two half-lunettes for the sacristy cupboards
in the same church, today scattered through various museums. In this idyllic image the artist's chief concern is with
a pleasing arrangement of figurative elements by now well
fixed in the standard repertory of painters of Christian
subjects. It shows how Giotto's art became transformed by
his best disciples. We are told that Sienese influence counted
for much in this, but we might just as well admit that those
who follow obediently in a great man's path end up, inevitably, as not very creative academics.

MASTER OF THE VAULTS OF SAN FRANCESCO *The Nativity* ·
Before 1325 · Fresco · Lower Church, Basilica of San
Francesco, Assisi

A few years earlier, another painter of Giotto's circle, whose
name has not come down to us, treated the same theme on
the vaults of the Lower Church of San Francesco in Assisi.
His version has the same idyllic character but deserves
credit for being the first. The delicious freshness of its
coloring and its spontaneous and charming naïveté com-
pensate for its dependence on a master of more forceful
personality. In any case, that dependence is less complete
than Taddeo Gaddi's, or at least less servile. While certain
elements such as the rock and the manger and a figure like
the St. Joseph derive from Giotto, the artist also kept in
mind the blues and the golden haloes of the miniature
painters and the way they grouped angels into clusters and
arabesques. A personal invention, the little foreground inset
of the Birth of the Virgin, does much toward making this
work both complex and highly attractive.

ANDREA DI CIONE ARCAGNOLO, called ORCAGNA (docu-
mented 1343–68) *Christ Conferring Authority on St. Peter and
Thomas Aquinas* · 1357 · Tempera on panel · Santa Maria
Novella, Florence

Commissioned by the great Strozzi family from the prosperous workshop of the Cione, and signed by the workshop
master usually known as Orcagna, this altarpiece takes us
out of the Francescan climate so dominant in the Florentine
paintings we have been looking at. The times had changed.
The Dominicans claimed that the terrible plague which
decimated the population of Florence was a punishment
from God and that they alone knew the secret of protecting
the city from a second onslaught of such a calamity. This
gave them the upper hand over the Franciscans who, in
addition, were still hampered by the heterodoxy of their
minor orders. This altarpiece made for Santa Maria Novella,
the Dominican stronghold, is above all a doctrinal procla-
mation asserting the excellence of the Dominican order:
Christ enthroned bestows a book on St. Thomas Aquinas,
the second patron of the Order after St. Dominic, and the
keys of Paradise on St. Peter, symbol of the Church of
Rome, thereby symbolizing the perfect agreement between
the two forces.

ANDREA DA FIRENZE (documented 1343–77) *The Government of the Church* · c. 1366–67 · Fresco · Spanish Chapel, Santa Maria Novella, Florence

While Pisa was satisfied to commission pictures from those artists of Florence or Milan or Bologna who had taken to wandering about to wherever work was available, the more energetic city of Florence preferred to exert a more active control. For a new chapel, founded by the husband of a plague victim and later used as the chapter house of the Dominican order, a grandiose decoration was ordered to illustrate how the punishment of God could be avoided: under the auspices of the solemn Order, preaching brothers —depicted both in human form and as the dogs of the Lord (*Domini Canes*)—go off in search of the faithful, whom they lead in gracious procession step by step to the very Gates of Paradise guarded by St. Peter and dominated by the Christ of Judgment. The very happy solution by which the artist triumphed over the difficulties in laying out such a complex subject wins him a place among the great painters.

GHERARDO STARNINA (c. 1360/65–1409/13) (?) *Thebaid* · Tempera on panel · $29\frac{1}{2} \times 81\frac{7}{8}''$ · Uffizi Gallery, Florence

Along with the message of active devotion they preached in Florence, the Dominicans in a city like Pisa, by then a Florentine province but with tendencies toward mysticism, gave their support to an anchoritic and contemplative movement in order to cut the ground out from under the Benedictines. The latter had painters who specialized in depicting their saints, Anthony the Hermit and Jerome, and among them was Gherardo Starnina, to whom is now attributed this curious picture long believed to be by Lorenzo Monaco. It has much in common with the fresco on the same subject in the Camposanto of Pisa, by Francesco Traini, whom some still consider the author of this picture despite its very different technique. Like the various cycles on the Triumph of Death which were inspired by the plague, these pictures and many writings on the same theme proclaim that salvation is to be found only in a contemplative life withdrawn from the world.

GIOVANNI DA MILANO (documented 1350–69) *The Birth of the Virgin* · 1365 · Fresco · Rinuccini Chapel, Santa Croce, Florence

Some artists, like Orcagna, Andrea da Firenze, and Starnina, placed themselves at the service of the religious orders. Others, such as this Giovanni who came from Milan, accepted commissions from any source and were more concerned with a fresh approach to traditional themes than with religious or political doctrines. In this curious and touching painting, Giovanni entirely renewed the subject of the Birth of the Virgin, which had tended to remain frozen in the form given it by Pietro Lorenzetti. Not only has the old iconographic disposition been supplanted here by another, but the astonishing stylization of the figures (which anticipate those of Piero della Francesca) and the exploitation of arm movements to enliven a neutral space suggest a strong individual artistic personality. Giovanni was finally eclipsed by Piero della Francesca, whose style is more static, and since his personal synthesis of the static and the dynamic was not explored by later artists, he seems to us today somewhat archaic.

ANDREA DA FIRENZE *The Road to Calvary* (detail) · c. 1366–67 · Fresco · Spanish Chapel, Santa Maria Novella, Florence

The talent of Andrea is confirmed by this fragment from another fresco in the Spanish Chapel which depicts the Passion of Christ in the great span of a half-circle. Compared with works of the preceding generation—those of Pietro Lorenzetti in Assisi or of Barna in Siena—this work impresses us by the extraordinary mastery with which it fills the difficult area of the great arch of the back wall of the chapel. In the center of the composition Calvary spreads out beneath a vast sky, and on the ground there is a veritable swarm of figures—a real innovation in Italian art. It seems almost as if the next step could only be Mantegna's art, and yet it took almost a century for the lessons of this precursor to be assimilated. In this detail from the base of the arch it is the approach of Giovanni da Milano which is applied. Not before Masolino (see page 151) was anything like this great open composition attempted again, and until then the usual practice was to crowd together a great many highly animated figures to suggest a great space.

BARTOLO DI FREDI (c. 1330–c. 1409/10) *The Adoration of the Magi* · c. 1370 · Tempera on panel · 82¾ × 69″ · Pinacoteca, Siena

In the wake of the brilliant upsurge of Sienese art in the first half of the fourteenth century with the Lorenzettis and Simone Martini, there developed a school of painting in that city which, without attaining the creative power of the great innovators, nevertheless kept alive the values of what, by the second generation, had already become a tradition. Among those artists—Barna, Andrea Vanni, Luca di Tommè—the most vital was certainly Bartolo di Fredi, gifted as he was with an incontestable sensitivity as a colorist. Between the two spurts of Sienese genius—that of the first half of the fourteenth century and that of the beginning of the fifteenth (including Sassetta, Giovanni di Paolo, and the anonymous Masters of Asciano and of the St. Anthony), which was to last until Sienese art finally capitulated before the style of Florence—Bartolo di Fredi, working in a rather lusterless period, bridged the gap between two high points and guaranteed a quite respectable continuity to local painting.

The Dormition of the Virgin (detail) · Novgorod workshop, 12th–13th centuries · Tempera on panel · Tretyakov Gallery, Moscow

Dating from more than a half century after *The Annunciation of Ustyug* (page 105), this monumental composition, also painted in tempera on wood, tells us much about the still poorly understood characteristics of Russian icons. It will be noted that movement was very soon added to the inward expression of the figures without, however, taking its place as it usually did elsewhere. The great simplicity of means and, above all, of effects, and the emphasis on individualism in the faces, which contrasts with the hieratic rigor of the attitudes, confer on this work a character of greatness. Nevertheless, the icon remains an image summoning men to prayer, a type of figuration entirely unlike that of the Occidental miniature.

139

The Journey to Bethlehem · 14th century · Mosaic · Narthex, Church of the Saviour in Chora (Kariye Camii), Istanbul

Our chronological survey of the monuments of medieval painting helps us to trace the conservative line to which certain of them belong. The decoration of the narthex of the Church of the Saviour in Chora constitutes a great cycle, highly successful as a whole. The finesse and virtuosity of the Byzantine mosaic artists remained remarkable, but a century after their high point it becomes obvious that their conception of an image derived from the miniaturists, and that thenceforth the avant-garde was to be found elsewhere, in the Italian workshops and those of the French court. However perfect the rendering, it cannot conceal the immobility of the conception or the traditionalism of the figurative elements used.

Christ in Limbo · 14th century · Mosaic · Church of the Saviour in Chora (Kariye Camii), Istanbul

The decoration of the edifice includes two great cycles, one the story of Jesus and Mary, the other the miracles of Christ. There are unmistakably two manners, two workshops, and although they worked with different means they were both less concerned with theological matters than with clear exposition of the narrative. Thus, the fact that notions from the Apocrypha are introduced is less striking than the contrast in the two manners, one related to the dominant style in the Western Mediterranean, the other to Greek and Slavic art. Further, in one of the series a painterly approach is exploited, rather than the techniques more appropriate to mosaic.

The Nativity · 14th century · Fresco · Church of Peripleptos, Mistra

The frescoes in Mistra were executed in the fourteenth century for the despots of Morea. To understand them, one must keep in mind their setting: they loom up out of darkness on the vaults of tiny churches and were designed to be viewed from below at the proper angle. What is interesting here is the transition in the Eastern Mediterranean from the Greek school—the *maniera greca*—to the icon. This same composition is found in many Russian works, and apparently such models were disseminated widely by itinerant workshops, as was also the case in the West.

ANDREI RUBLEV *The Trinity* · 1422–27 · Tempera on panel · 55½ × 44½″ · From the Monastery of the Trinity-and-St.-Sergius at Zagorsk, near Moscow · Tretyakov Gallery, Moscow

Contemporary of Masolino, the Limbourg brothers, and the Master of Flémalle, Andrei Rublev represents the great Eastern tradition in the waning Middle Ages. Two centuries after *The Dormition of the Virgin* (page 139), Russian art returned to a vision stripped of all striving for effect. The same subject was treated in Paris in the thirteenth century (page 119, top) in an entirely different spirit. The work of Rublev is not inspired by a written text but by a living thought. Monumentality is achieved by an organization of space and an equilibrium between planes of color which were to remain unknown in the West until modern times.

The Annunciation · Icon from the Church of St. Clement, Ohrid · 16th century · Tempera on panel · Museum, Skopje, Yugoslavia

Comparison of this *Annunciation* with that of Ustyug (page 105) shows how widely apart in feeling they are and also how an art can evolve within a system which is both unified and diversified and still remain faithful to a set style. In place of a simple face-to-face confrontation of the two personages, here they are infused with animation and surrounded by a wealth of accessories. The architectural element defines the setting as a church. References and associations spring from the narrative and action and not, as in the past, from meditation on an article of faith. The central concern is no longer the communication of a thought but the perpetuation of an iconographic tradition. Moreover, there were numerous intermediate stages in which the beginning and end of a cycle were in contradiction.

Martyrdom of St. George · c. 1300 · Fresco · Chapel of the Rosary (formerly of St. George), Cathedral, Clermont-Ferrand

This fragment of mural painting is of great interest in both content and technique. St. George, the saint and hero and knight who led the Crusaders to the walls of Jerusalem, is shown at the moment of his ascension rather than of his martyrdom. This is the first appearance of the demigod type of figure later typical of Donatello, and the first—and surprisingly early—conception modeled after the antique. Certainly it lacks perspective, but it does resolve the problem of mental vision in movement and, unlike the Parisian miniature style, challenges us to reconsider the question of the "Gothic" sources of the Renaissance.

The Burial of St. John the Baptist · 1354–62 · Fresco · Chartreuse, Villeneuve-lès-Avignon

The Chapel of St. John the Baptist was the initial edifice around which the great Carthusian monastery was built. Its frescoes form a complete cycle recently attributed to the Italian Matteo Giovanetti. In any event, they have some connection with the foliage-design tapestries of northern France, and the recent discovery of the frescoes of Simone Martini, who died in 1344, proves the existence of a Franco-Italian center of great influence. Was not the culture of Petrarch and Giotto born of contacts between France and Italy?

GIRARD D'ORLÉANS *Portrait of John II the Good* · c. 1360–64 · Tempera on panel · 23¼ × 14¼″ · The Louvre, Paris

To this artist is also attributed the famous painted altarcloth from Narbonne which includes portraits of Charles V and his Queen. The two works indicate the King's interest in art as ornament for the royal chapels and palaces. Here we have one of the first portraits as such in the history of post-classical art. The subject is portrayed with astonishing presence, and the work certainly owes something to the statues and tomb sculpture of the time. Besides, it is one of the very first easel paintings known. It opens the way to one of the realistic phases of Western art not so much for its style as such as in its aims.

The Adoration of the Magi · Parisian workshop, c. 1380 (?) · Tempera on panel · 19½ × 12″ · Museo Nazionale, Florence

This wing from a small diptych known as the *Bargello Altarpiece* is halfway between the Parisian miniatures of the thirteenth century and Gentile da Fabriano, and is a perfect illustration of the international style of the end of the fourteenth century. Scholars one after the other have spoken of relationships with Siena, Bohemia, Flanders, or Avignon, and this in itself testifies to a common style throughout Europe dominated by the taste and intellectual culture of Paris. Not that we wish to propose any limiting definition on this art, but it is clear that its eclectic formation and very wide diffusion were both guaranteed by the French nobility.

Christ Bearing the Cross · School of Avignon, c. 1390 ·
Tempera on panel · 15 × 11″ · The Louvre, Paris

Comparison of this work with the preceding clarifies what
was said there. The over-all tonality and a greater breadth in
drawing recall the style of the *Burial of St. John* from
Avignon and of Simone Martini. The influence of the international style was widespread: in England, for example,
it appears in the Wilton Diptych. Rather than insisting on
Parisian workshops, one should speak of the princely style
of the French court, not only the model of the time but
the rallying point for artists as much as for great lords.

MELCHIOR BROEDERLAM *The Circumcision* and *The Flight into
Egypt* · Right wing of the Champmol Altarpiece · 1394–99 ·
Tempera on panel · 64 × 51″ · Musée Magnin, Dijon

It is interesting to pick out in this and the following pictures
the elements they have in common: the Fountain of Life as
in the Limbourg brothers, the architecture like that of the
Master of Flémalle, the rock formations of the Italians right
up to the end of the Quattrocento. It was not the Florentines
who laid down the first bases of modern art. Between the
Parisian, Sienese, and Florentine style of 1360–80 and the
Renaissance of Masaccio and Van Eyck, there came a generation which throughout Europe exchanged themes and
suggestions.

MELCHIOR BROEDERLAM *The Annunciation* and *The Visitation* · Left wing of the Champmol Altarpiece · 1394–99 ·
Tempera on panel · 64 × 51″ · Musée Magnin, Dijon

This altarpiece was painted at Ypres for the only French
princes who came close to creating another cultural center
than Paris, the Burgundians. Toward the close of the fourteenth century a genuine tradition was established in the
lands between Bruges and Dijon, which was to disappear
finally with the decline of the Dukes of Burgundy and make
way for the triumph of Italy. Despite the similarity of
figurative material, it is certain that here we are in another
artistic climate than that of Paris. The composition is less all
of one piece; the coloring is richer; architectural motifs play
a more important role, especially because they exploit space
in depth and thereby anticipate the great scientific codifi-
cation of the Italian Quattrocento.

JEAN MALOUEL *The Small Pietà* · c. 1400 · Tempera on panel · The Louvre, Paris

Between Broederlam and Bellechose, the official painter of the Dukes of Burgundy at Dijon, was Malouel. The two *Pietàs* attributed to him, the Small and the Great, show how much Burgundian art was indebted to that of Paris. For some years now it has been suggested that the *Madonna* in the Berlin Museum may also be by him. That picture is itself most exceptional and as much a unique innovation as the portrait of John the Good, since it is painted with tempera on canvas instead of board. Most probably it was in the circle of the dukes of the royal house of France that portable paintings destined not for altars, but intended merely as separate devotional images, became common, and this was owing to the itinerant living habits which also led the nobility to sponsor tapestry workshops.

HENRI BELLECHOSE *Altarpiece of the Martyrdom of St. Denis* · 1416 · Tempera on panel · 63¼ × 82½″ · The Louvre, Paris

Bellechose had just succeeded Malouel as painter to Jean Sans Peur when he was charged with completing this unfinished altarpiece. With it a new generation appears. Compared with the *Christ Bearing the Cross* of Avignon (page 143), this work is still very Parisian, and its character is traditional in contrast to Broederlam's style. Parisian style of this period must be sought elsewhere, in miniatures and tapestries.

HENNEQUIN OF BRUGES and NICOLAS BATAILLE *The Whore of Babylon*, from the Apocalypse Tapestries · 1373–79 · Château, Angers

Duke Louis I of Anjou borrowed from the royal library of Charles V a manuscript of the Apocalypse as model for this marvelous set of tapestries in which are summed up the learning and taste of the last Gothic generations. They were finally bestowed on the Cathedral of Angers by King René, as the most precious testimony to the prestige of his house. In them a veritable world of dreams unfolds before us. It must be kept in mind that in those times men occupied austere dwellings that were enlivened by tapestries with foliage designs which they even transported with them on their travels. In this set, tapestries with blue and rose backgrounds alternate, and there are both realism and mystery in them. Tapestry, miniatures, and stained glass were the basis for one of the greatest periods in the history of painting.

The Lady and the Unicorn · End of 15th century · Tapestry · Musée de Cluny, Paris

Although this work is very much later in date than the others in this chapter, it has been included as a concrete reminder that the Middle Ages did not die out suddenly at the start of the fifteenth century, either in men's tastes or in their ways of thinking. Executed for the Le Vistes and the Guillards, great lawyers of the region of Lyons, these splendid tapestries combine the theme of the symbolic figuration of the five senses with the by then legendary subject of the magic hunt. The Middle Ages faded away into legend, but for a long time the visual stuff for works of the imagination continued to be medieval.

MASTER OF THE HOURS OF BOUCICAUT *The Vigil of the Dead*, from the Book of Hours of the Maréchal de Boucicaut · c. 1410–15 · Miniature · Musée Jacquemart-André, Paris

Between 1380 and 1422, under Charles VI, Paris, or more correctly the French court, was more than ever the most refined art center of Europe. Duc Jean de Berry in particular was a great patron of artists, and it was through him that, in rivalry with the Burgundians, the French workshops continued their creative activity. André Beauneveu, Jacquemart de Hesdin, Jacques Coene, Jean Malouel, the Limbourg brothers, and the anonymous Masters of the Hours of Boucicaut and of Rohan are in no way inferior to an Orcagna, an Andrea da Firenze, a Giovanni de' Grassi. But the study of the great international currents of the fourteenth century has not even yet been attempted.

MASTER OF THE HOURS OF BOUCICAUT *The Visitation*, from the Book of Hours of the Maréchal de Boucicaut · c. 1410–15 · Miniature · Musée Jacquemart-André, Paris

Among the painters of the Duc de Berry, this master is one of the least recognized although his works are of immense interest. It is obvious here that, long before Masolino and Masaccio, knowledge of linear perspective was spreading throughout Europe. There is no need to stress the virtuosity of the way it is associated here with other ways of representing space, or how the iridescent sky and chiaroscuro anticipate all of the solutions of the entire Quattrocento.

145

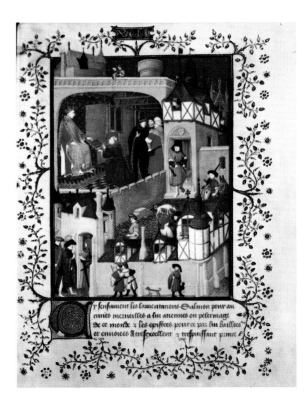

The Book of Hours of Boucicaut includes forty-five large illuminations, the Pierre Salmon book twenty-seven, and there are still others by this master, all revealing a very rich pictorial language. This scene of the presentation of the book to its patron owes something to the theater for its conception; and it contrasts markedly with the preceding examples because of its simultaneous exposition of scenes occurring at different times. Evidently in this milieu no attempt was made to impose a single method. This was an art directed to readers of lively intelligence, and figurative means became limited only when times changed and there came about a change in the aims of art and in its public.

The Limbourg brothers *The Month of June : Paris and the Palace*, from *Les Très Riches Heures du Duc de Berry* · 1413–16 · Miniature · Musée Condé, Chantilly

Natives of the Gelder region and perhaps nephews of Malouel, the Limbourg brothers were in the service of the Duke of Burgundy from 1402 to 1404, then for a time in the Paris workshops, and after 1410 employed by the Duc de Berry. To them we owe certain masterpieces of miniature art which were also of capital importance in the development of the international style of the beginning of the fifteenth century. Jean de Berry was not only one of the most lavish art patrons in history, but was also wise enough to gather around him representatives of the most progressive art of his time. It was at his court that the convergence of all contemporary styles—Italian, Flemish, Burgundian, from Altichiero to Jacques Coene, from Michelino da Besozzo and Giovanni de' Grassi to Beauneveu and Jacquemart de Hesdin—was best realized, and it was there that the solutions were found which, very shortly after the Duc's death in 1416, were to result in the great Franco-Flemish and Italian works of the early Quattrocento.

The Limbourg brothers *The Month of July : Poitiers and the Palace*, from *Les Très Riches Heures du Duc de Berry* · 1413–16 · · Miniature · Musée Condé, Chantilly

This book of hours presents a synthesis of the medieval system of intellectual representation with modern pictorial techniques. On the one hand, the astrological calendar expresses the relationship of man to the universe of which he is one element indissolubly attached to the whole. On the other, the direct interest in the depiction of men's activities, the importance placed on the organic connection of the picture with the entire page, the evocation of the transparency of air, all these belong to a system of values destined to sustain the modern age. The comparison of these two related subjects is significant: they use the same figurative scheme, but the first of them is free of all reference to traditional figurative material which might hold any meaning independent of the direct depiction of the real world.

146

MASTER OF THE HOURS OF ROHAN *The Dead Man before His Judge*, from *Les Heures de Rohan* · c. 1420 · Miniature · Ms. lat. 9471, Bibliothèque Nationale, Paris

It is beyond our scope to present examples from all the works produced at the courts of the Dukes, but alongside the skillful compositions of the Master of the Hours of Boucicaut and the picturesque scenes of the Limbourg brothers we cannot omit this striking expressionistic page, archaic perhaps in its over-all design and lack of spatial depth, but at the same time a presage, both in sentiment and in the extraordinary realism of the dying man, of the most modern manifestations of Western art in the succeeding centuries. Once again we see that Occidental culture has exploited no more than a tiny number of the possibilities open to it.

STEFANO DA VERONA (1374–after 1438) *Madonna of the Rose Garden* · c. 1395–1400 (?) · Tempera on panel · $50\frac{3}{4} \times 37\frac{1}{2}''$ · Castelvecchio, Verona

This version of the Madonna of Humility, seated on the ground in a closed and intimate garden, seems most unusual in Italian art, whose usual repertory of decorative motifs includes neither the flowered greensward, the little garden, the bird-winged angels, nor the birds themselves. True, the Master of Vico l'Abate had attempted to draw attention to incidental notes borrowed from nature and not indispensable to the story depicted, but his approach was quite different: his details are magnified, isolated, and expressive, whereas here they are abundant, finely worked out, and entwined in arabesques recalling the goldsmith's craft or a certain type of tapestry. This technique comes from the North, from the Parisian miniature, the tapestries of Arras, and the reliquaries of the Meuse valley, and it reached Italy by way of Avignon perhaps and with Venice as intermediary. It was to give rise to a very special style which predominated in Verona up to the time of Paolo Veronese and which, in its turn, influenced Rhenish art.

STEFANO DA VERONA *The Adoration of the Magi* · 1435 · Tempera on panel · The Brera, Milan

This work, the only one Stefano signed and dated, serves along with two frescoes signed but not dated as the basis for all other attributions to him. It is of particular importance as evidence of the Verona milieu from which Pisanello came, a milieu still not very well known but, apparently, a thriving center where new ideas from everywhere—the North, Lombardy, Venice, Florence—were eagerly discussed. This painting reveals the impact of such diverse influences and how they were harmonized. In it we see how the aging Stefano came under the sway of the Umbrian painter Gentile da Fabriano, dead by then but famed throughout Italy for his *Adoration of the Magi* of 1423. Obvious as the borrowings from Gentile are (compare the plate at the bottom of the following page), it seems that for the scene of homage the artist turned back to the painting on the same subject by Bartolo di Fredi of Siena (page 139).

147

GENTILE DA FABRIANO (c. 1370–1427) *St. Dominic* · Detail from the polyptych of Valle Romita · c. 1400 · Tempera on panel · The Brera, Milan

In his first works Gentile was not yet equipped with the vast culture which later was to permit him to deal with the procedures and sentiments of the past as if they were his own and, at the same time, to assimilate and give visual form to the most recent viewpoints on art and history. Though his talent expressed itself with as much vivacity in his simple youthful pictures as in the complex works of his maturity, the basic means he used were quite different. This polyptych, executed for a monastery of Observants near his native Fabriano, shows that around 1400 Gentile was still no more than a limited provincial painter who seems to have had affinities with Verona of the time before Pisanello. Nevertheless, and this he owed only to his own personal gifts, he was able to endow his personages with an esoteric spirituality while at the same time playing with consummate mastery with oppositions of broad simple volumes and carefully studied naturalistic details.

GENTILE DA FABRIANO *The Adoration of the Magi* · 1423 · Tempera on panel · 9′ 10⅛″ × 9′ 3″ · Uffizi Gallery, Florence

Gentile had numerous bonds with both Venice and Verona, as well as with Florence, Siena, and Lombardy. This altarpiece, his masterwork, is at one and the same time a synthesis of all his hesitations before diverse ways and also a masterful demonstration that a great artist can overcome all such confusions, even if he never finds the single solution to sweep them all away. Gentile wished to sacrifice nothing of the treasures accumulated in his peripatetic life: neither the splendor of Venice, last vestige of the Byzantinism it loved; nor Sienese density and expressionism as seen in the procession here; nor the humanism of Florence as reflected in the foreground figures; nor Veronese naturalism, which he raised to a high point here in the dogs, horses, camels, the ass, and the ox; nor finally the latest innovation, the rationalistic perspective he applied within the lunettes of the gold frame and in the predella. Such a mixture might easily have resulted in disaster. It did not, and this masterpiece comes to us as the product of a great talent and a vast personal culture.

GENTILE DA FABRIANO *The Presentation in the Temple*, from the predella of the altarpiece at left · 1423 · Tempera on panel · 10¼ × 24″ · The Louvre, Paris

The predella of the *Adoration* was dismembered, and one of its panels is now in the Louvre. In Gentile's time, as in the past, the predella continued to be the chosen site for avantgarde experiment: audacious essays, innovations too daring for the main body of an altarpiece—which had to be in a noble style consecrated by tradition—these were relegated to the predella. When the noble style was still Byzantine-influenced and hieratic, the predella was used for flights of fancy, but in Gentile's time it was the Gothic with all its romanticism and fantasy which was deemed noble, and so the independence and progressivism typical of the predella took the form of "scientific" rigor. These carefully organized architectural elements with something of the antique about them, these elongated, stylized, and impassive figures which in a few years would be promoted to the place of honor—the central panels of altarpieces—all prove that in forward-looking circles there was already concern with perspective and the revival of the antique, though it was not until around the middle of the century that they finally came to be considered essential.

GENTILE DA FABRIANO *The Young King* · Detail from *The Adoration of the Magi* · 1423 · Tempera on panel · Uffizi Gallery, Florence

Between Gentile's *St. Dominic* (opposite page) and this *Young King* intervened the influence of Venice. Before 1408 Gentile spent a long time there, and while Venice itself profited from what he could teach it, there is no doubt that, for his part, throughout his life he retained the mark left on him by his years in that city. Later he lived in Brescia, where he was caught up in the Lombard craze for the French romances of chivalry and the fashions of the court of Burgundy. Finally, he must certainly have been familiar with Sienese art. All these diverse experiences are concentrated in the figure of the young king: he is dressed in a knight's costume recalling the sumptuousness of Burgundian attire, and wears a haloed crown glistening with jewels like those Simone Martini painted for his saints. Here this theatrical vision of knights-of-old was not conjured up as a real knight, but rather to lend glory to the young son of the powerful Strozzi family, which held the reins of industry in Florence and which commissioned this altarpiece.

MASTER OF ASCIANO *The Birth of the Virgin* · c. 1430–40 · Tempera on panel · $87\frac{3}{8} \times 62\frac{1}{4}''$ · Museum, Asciano

To emphasize the international character of the system of representation in favor throughout Europe in the first third of the fifteenth century, we have placed side by side here works from Italy and Flanders. This anonymous painting from Asciano carries on the creative effort of the Sienese, who are incorrectly judged archaic because they perpetuated certain medieval values. This work takes up again the theme of a painting by Pietro Lorenzetti, and of a fresco he and his brother did for the hospital of the Scala in Siena. There are air and space in this picture and perspective, a figure draped in gold brocade in the fashion of Burgundy, a bird-winged angel gleaming in the entrance; these new elements serve to re-create that climate of intimacy and domestic peace which, though with other means, was another aspect of the Sienese genius. Further, the warm-cool quality of the coloring makes of it a work unique in its time.

MASTER OF FLEMALLE *The Marriage of the Virgin* · c. 1425 · Tempera on panel · $30\frac{3}{4} \times 35\frac{1}{2}''$ · The Prado, Madrid

At almost the same time but at the other end of Europe, another anonymous master painted this picture, which is in many ways both like and unlike the preceding. It belongs to a group of works which are highly problematical: are they by Robert Campin, Rogier van der Weyden in his youth, someone else, or several artists? The one sure fact is that, alongside the Van Eycks and before 1430, when we find Rogier in full possession of his gifts, there was a Northern style which carried out the same experiments as the Italians in pushing still further the ultimate discoveries of the international workshops of the waning Middle Ages. A key work, the so-called *Mérode Altarpiece*, is much closer than the *Nativity* of the Master of Flémalle to the painting in Asciano in terms of structure, although it is also more related to the Van Eycks and, despite its incomparable quality, less revealing of the difficulties the innovators had to overcome.

149

MASTER OF FLÉMALLE *The Nativity* · c. 1430 · Tempera on panel · 34¼ × 27⅝″ · Musée des Beaux-Arts, Dijon

Comparison of this and the preceding painting shows the hesitations experienced in this milieu. In *The Marriage of the Virgin* two episodes are juxtaposed and, in line with medieval tradition, the events of the narrative are set forth in separate scenes, as are also the two aspects of vision which bring together the interior and exterior of an edifice whose portal is that of the Church of the Sablon in Brussels and whose choir is an imaginary Jerusalem. The unity of the picture depends therefore on intellectual associations. In the present painting, however, optical integration is pushed further. The approach remains intellectual, but it has sloughed off the tradition of simultaneous events. The unity of the world of the senses was soon to supplant the unity of the world of thought.

MASOLINO DA PANICALE (1383–1440/47) *The Foundation of Santa Maria Maggiore* · c. 1430 · Tempera on panel · 56¾ × 29⅞″ · Museo di Capodimonte, Naples

A duality in time determines the composition here, but in a different way than in *The Marriage of the Virgin* by the Master of Flémalle. Furthermore, a duality of place here accompanies the duality of time. The celestial vision is set in a qualitative, unmeasured, typically medieval space, while the earthly vision is one of the first Italian examples of linear perspective governed by a single vanishing point. We must remember that Masolino's work in the Brancacci Chapel in Florence dates from 1424–27, by which time Jan van Eyck had already painted the Book of Hours in Turin and probably the *Virgin* in the Louvre. Nor can it be supposed that the invention of linear perspective and modern notions of space were achieved suddenly in 1425 by the Florentines. Renaissance art was the product of an international culture which grew out of the last experiments of the Gothic; moreover, it did not restrict itself to a single approach.

MASOLINO *Herod's Banquet* · 1435 · Fresco · Baptistery, Castiglione Olona

Even a few years later, in the period following Masaccio's death when he was full master of his own art, Masolino continued to combine very modern and very traditional elements of representation. The open loggia in the foreground goes back to the setting for the Tabitha episode in the Brancacci Chapel frescoes, while the colonnade resembles the earliest architectural exploits of Michelozzo in Venice and in the monastery of San Marco in Florence. These elements clash with a background which is not governed by the same principle and is less integrated than in Flemish paintings. What orders the imagination of artists is not merely an ability to look at the universe and then transfer what is seen to a two-dimensional surface by means of tricks of illusion. Rather, and much more important, it is a matter of how they conceive the association of elements containing inherent significance and how they articulate them within a whole.

MASOLINO *The Crucifixion* · 1428–31 · Fresco · San Clemente, Rome

Dated between 1428 and 1431, and therefore earlier than the *Banquet*, this admirable work is infinitely more modern and more integrated in the direction to be taken by the so-called Grand Style of the future. Yet it was executed for the same patron, Cardinal Castiglione, and moreover recalls the approach of Andrea da Firenze in the 1360s in a similar monumental fresco (page 139). To produce true art, artists need more than a handy system. Not before Mantegna's *Crucifixion*, from about 1460, did the principle of open space in a landscape which dips and rises again become one of the standard solutions of modern art. For at least two generations, painters explored a diversity of approaches before arriving finally at systems which, soon after, turned into academic formulas.

LORENZO VENEZIANO (documented 1356–72) *The Annunciation* · Central panel of a polyptych · 1359 · Tempera on panel · 49⅝ × 29½″ · Accademia, Venice

It was only in the generation following Paolo Veneziano, the first truly Venetian painter, that the local Byzantinism began to become less clear-cut. A style developed which was more fluid but also heavier and rather flaccid. As yet Venice took no more from International Gothic than its way of treating draperies and a certain suppleness in posing figures, but not its sparkling vivacity. And yet, for all that Venice had so much difficulty in sloughing off the Byzantine character it prized so highly and is therefore commonly dismissed as "backward" at the precise moment it was about to take off to new heights, the fact is that once again it was in advance in iconography: this Virgin of the Annunciation is no longer the humble handmaid of God as in Byzantium and Siena (Martini's is of exactly the same date), but instead is a queen as in Western art, and the angel here is not the agitated emissary of Heaven bearing an order, but a submissive messenger who bows before the future Mother of Christ.

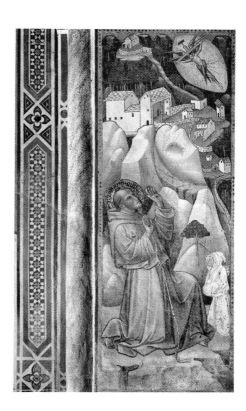

CENNI DI FRANCESCO DI SER CENNI *The Stigmatization of St. Francis* · 1410 · Fresco · San Francesco, Volterra

A provincial current rolled on undisturbed while in Siena, Venice, Umbria, and Lombardy there was coming into being an international style whose substance was drawn from the fashions, manners, and knightly sports of the princely courts of France, Burgundy, Aquitaine, and northern Italy. Although still rooted in Giotto, as time passed and new artistic modes gained the upper hand that current nevertheless liberated itself from rigorous servility to the great master, and became a popular and folkloristic expression with a certain often naïve and spontaneous charm of its own. Agnolo Gaddi, Taddeo's son, was the leader in this trend, setting up in Florence a large workshop which churned out pictures one after the other for anyone who would buy. Cenni di Francesco followed his lead, but, working alone, without assistants, his paintings were much more personal. In this fresco, where the figure of the Saint is borrowed from Giotto, he gave free rein to his gift for observation to construct this delightful vertical background in which a city and a desert are tumbled together like children's playthings.

151

St. Michael · Detail from a *Last Judgment* · Auvergnat workshop, 1405 · Tempera on panel · Collegiate Church, Ennezat (Puy-de-Dôme)

We have chosen to place this picture between those examples which illustrate the Florentine tradition and the first manifestations of a genuinely Venetian style, and those others which show how Siena made one last effort to revitalize the medieval heritage rather than reject it. In opposition to the styles of the French court, it reveals that in France as in Italy provincial workshops continued to cling to a truly academic medievalism. Bestowed by a canon of Auvergne on his church, this vast composition inspired by the Apocalypse offers something like an ultimate summing up of the old traditional figurative themes, though these had more often been treated in sculpture over portals of cathedrals than in paint. In France the chief accomplishments of the Gothic style were in stained glass and miniatures. Obviously, any survey limited to painting must distort the true state of affairs, and it has not been possible here to consider even the entirety of medieval painting in every single aspect and, least of all, when it utilized vast dimensions.

SASSETTA (STEFANO DI GIOVANNI DI CONSOLO) (1392?–1450) *The Journey of the Magi* · c. 1430 · Tempera on panel · 9 × 12″ · The Metropolitan Museum of Art, New York

The resurgence of Sienese painting took place before and after the middle of the fifteenth century. Among the greatly gifted painters responsible for it—Giovanni di Paolo, Sano di Pietro, the anonymous Masters of the Osservanza, of Asciano, and of the Life of St. Anthony—the most famous, Sassetta, was also the one who studied most attentively and conscientiously the Florentine innovations in linear perspective. Although he did not adhere to them, they were not entirely banned from his work. In this picture, Sassetta's attitude toward the Florentine experiments is revealed by his attempt to create an impression of spatial depth. However, the effect is not attained by the means favored in Florence, that is, perspective lines meeting at a fixed point in infinity plus a horizon line carefully established and set low. Instead, Sassetta uses empirical means with an invisible but high horizon line, and much of the charm of the picture is due to this approach.

SASSETTA *St. Anthony in the Wilderness* · Before 1450 · Tempera on panel · 17¾ × 13⅜″ · Collection Robert Lehman, New York

The same high horizon line characterizes this masterpiece of Sienese Quattrocento painting. It strives to synthesize the notion of distance—a modern conception—with the precepts of the Trecento to which the artist, for all his individuality, obviously remained very much attached. In seeking to reconcile them, the artist discovered the possibilities of curved space (all the lines determining space are curved: the horizon, the clouds, the road leading to the church). Like Fouquet at the same time in France, he thereby showed that there were other means of rendering space than linear perspective, and that medieval optics were quite capable of working out a system of vision in depth not based on linear construction and of three-dimensional space which is not cuboid. If today we consider this system archaic, it is because later the other approach prevailed. However, in the light of current research we are obliged to admit its internal consistency, which makes it as valid as the system to which it gave way in the Renaissance.

MASTER OF TREBON *The Resurrection* · c. 1380 · Tempera on panel · 52 × 36″ · National Gallery, Prague

This work, once in the Augustinian monastery at Trebon, is included as an indication of the diverse paths taken in this period. It has not been possible to show the various national aspects of the Gothic in all their diversity within the over-all unity, but it must be kept in mind that in the fourteenth and fifteenth centuries Gothic civilization touched every corner of Europe. From Portugal to Riga and from Cyprus to Portugal, there was a common Occidental culture at the very moment when new forces were about to write finis to universal beliefs and social and economic conditions built up slowly during the preceding centuries. Bohemia in particular, linked as it was with the French court, enjoyed a brilliant Gothic culture. This painting was chosen because it shows brilliantly how national geniuses found their individual expression within one of the most consistent systems of thought the world has known.

PISANELLO (ANTONIO DI PUCCI) (before 1395–1455) *The Vision of St. Eustace* · Before 1450 · Tempera on panel · 21½ × 25¾″ · National Gallery, London

While resistance to Florentine rationalism was strongest and most systematic in Siena, because of its attachment to a past more glorious than that of other regions, it was also present in such places as Verona, which, although not indifferent to new ideas, sought them out from the most remote sources. Pisanello was perfectly capable of exploiting the Florentine experiments when he wished, but his natural bent was to the romantic and, at times, even mystic art of chivalry faded into legend, and to this he joined a courtly style which he himself brought to its highest development. This painting, unanimously attributed to him, disdains all spatial and scientific considerations. It is set in a mystical environment not otherwise defined and yet well characterized, and is, above all, a pretext for studies of animals and the knight's costume, favorite concerns of this artist whose numerous sketches of animals and costumes are among his chief claims to glory.

PISANELLO *Portrait of Ginevra d'Este* (?) · 1438–40 · Tempera on panel · 17 × 11¾″ · The Louvre, Paris

This marvelous portrait reveals the favorite preoccupations of Pisanello. The profile in silhouette as if cut out by a knife blade, as in the medals of which he also was a great master; the slight displacement from an axis, with the head in full and the body in three-quarter profile; the costume and headdress painstakingly studied and admirably rendered; the background of flowering shrubs; the butterflies —all of these are conceived as pictorial elements and are fitted together entirely as functions of their internal relationships and with no concern for anecdote or situation. As in the *St. Eustace*, the picture is built up on the basis of its own logic, which is that of a proper relationship between forms and colors. In this way, it creates a world in itself undisturbed by any connection with the world outside the picture. When Florence took to imitating Pisanello's approach to portraiture, it reduced this conception to a simpler scheme, substituting a neutral background for this living one and thereby eliminating the rapport between the person portrayed and his setting.

153

MASTER OF THE PIETÀ OF VILLENEUVE-LÈS-AVIGNON *Pietà* ·
c. 1460 · Tempera on panel · 63¾ × 85⅞″ · The Louvre, Paris

While the Italians, by a series of compromises, were striving
to renew the Gothic style which was still vital but already
condemned by the rise of a point of view less sensitive to
inspiration than to reason, the last Gothic workshops in
France were marking the end of the system which had been
dominant in Europe for three hundred years. With absolute
mastery of the rhythm of line and relief, supreme decora-
tiveness of forms, and consummate simplicity in rendering
a variety of expressions, the plastic thought of the Gothic
produced this final masterwork before disappearing. The
fact remains that this painting is still closely related to
sculpture. If the Gothic had to bow out before a new style,
perhaps it was because, having inspired admirable works in
all media, it remained too dependent on its specific techniques. In contrast, the new art, often of lesser quality,
emphasized the intellectual bases of a system of thought
that took pride in manipulating the stuff of nature rather
than in working out a style impregnated with the mirages
of a universe conceived in accord with man's own modes
of feeling.

the renaissance

G. C. Argan

The fifteenth century marks the beginning of the modern era in the visual arts. Three centuries earlier, the artistic climate of East and West had undergone the same sharp cleavage that the doctrine of St. Thomas Aquinas had produced in the spheres of science and philosophy. In art, too, Western Europe awakened to a sense of its own history and laid claim to a tradition of its own. In Romanesque art it asserted its descent from Latin civilization, while in Gothic art it expressed the dramatic reality of its own times. During the fifteenth century "historical" man defined his place in the world around him. He constructed the mental framework for a direct experience of reality and established his position as *subject* in relation to nature as *object*. From then on, art ceased to be a material means for setting forth transcendent, spiritual truths. In Italy, Cennino Cennini, an early-fifteenth-century theoretician still imbued with the Gothic tradition, maintained that a painter must render visible what one cannot see; Leon Battista Alberti, a mid-fifteenth-century theoretician of the "new art," maintained that to an artist all that counts is what one sees.

The term "Renaissance," when used to indicate the sum total of fifteenth- and sixteenth-century culture, means the rebirth of the art and philosophy of antiquity in the thought and action of modern man, for it was then that artists began to study the monuments of ancient Rome—either directly, by making archaeological diggings and taking measurements and more often by copying ancient sculptures in drawings, or indirectly through ancient literature, especially the works of Vitruvius. Princes began to collect antiques, artists reverted to historical and mythological subjects, and scholars wrote theoretical treatises, especially on architecture. At first this interest in the art and thought of the ancients seemed to conflict with the Christian faith. Soon, however, a compromise was reached: even though the ancients had been denied the Divine Revelation, God in His mercy granted them the capability to acquire a perfect knowledge of nature and through that a natural philosophy and a system of ethics which enabled them to attain a sense of the Creator through His creations. Consequently, for these first Renaissance humanists, the study of nature and the study of antiquity were identical, or at least were two paths leading to the same goal—artistic perfection. They did not even have to study the ancient monuments directly: rather than being a storehouse or repertory of forms and examples, antiquity became a dimension of the spirit.

As a rule, art historians consider that Italy was the cradle of the Renaissance—Florence from the first decades of the fifteenth century and Venice from its middle years. The end of the Renaissance is usually fixed at about the middle of the sixteenth century, when the taste for Mannerism spread throughout Europe, a conception of art as an unquenched thirst for an unattainable ideal of beauty rather than as a positive knowledge and representation of the world. Thus, the Renaissance is seen as a typically Italian historical phenomenon, and the revivified artistic currents that developed outside Italy are seen as the outcome of a progressive diffusion of Italian culture.

Undoubtedly, that phenomenon occurred earlier in Italy than in other countries. There it reached a more impressive development and was accompanied and sustained by a vaster scholarly activity in the fields of theory, history, and literature. The treatises of Leon Battista Alberti, Piero della Francesca, Francesco di Giorgio Martini, and Leonardo da Vinci (to mention only the most important) equated artistic activity with science: science based on geometry and mathematics, which were considered the logical explanations of the rational structure of the universe, or on the direct, methodical study of nature. Mantegna, a philologist and archaeologist as well as an artist, held that the foundation of art was actually an ancient science (in other words, that art began as a science). In their treatises, the sixteenth-century architects Serlio, Palladio, and Vignola placed a knowledge of ancient monuments on a par with that of the laws of statics or the science of constructions. Venetians like Paolo Pini and Ludovico Dolce asserted that painting based on our natural feeling for light and color was no less intellectual than that of the Florentines and Romans (which was based on drawing), because the result was always a true, if not a *truer*, knowledge of nature. Once art had achieved the status of a science, the artist was no longer a craftsman respected for a skill acquired through a long practical tradition but a scholar whom the ruling classes could use not only for their undertakings in the sphere of art but also for their civil and military activities.

There is no denying that during those two centuries Italy held the leading position in European art, but it would be a serious mistake to consider the Renaissance an exclusively Italian phenomenon. Although the Renaissance began in Italy and had its major center there, it was, on the whole, a European movement and indeed one of the ideological foundation stones of modern Europe. The Renaissance was not the product of a single current of ideas but resulted from a concourse of ideological and cultural trends that were often divergent and sometimes even conflicting.

In the fifteenth century Jan van Eyck was no less "modern" than Masaccio, just as in the sixteenth Dürer was no less a classical "humanist" than Raphael. While Michelangelo saw in Flemish art the diametrical opposite of his own esthetic ideal, Leonardo felt that it had a certain affinity with his analytical spirit. Thus, the very antithesis of the realism of Bruegel to Michelangelo's formal idealism seems like the dual polarity of the same cultural cycle.

It is true that in the fifteenth century the first national schools of painting sprang up amid the "international" Gothic that had spread throughout Europe. Writers of that period stressed the antithesis of Italian (or "Latin") to "German" (or Northern) art, in which certain Gothic themes and motifs still played an active, if not a paramount, part until late in the following century. But it was typical of the new Europe that it was the result of different and sometimes contrasting cultural and political forces in search of equilibrium.

Moreover, artistic relations were close and exchanges frequent. In the fifteenth century Flemish painters like Rogier van der Weyden and Justus of Ghent and French painters like Jean Fouquet had already visited Italy and worked there. And the influx was greater in the sixteenth century, when it was due, as in the case of Dürer, to the precise intention of establishing a contact between the two cultures. Masolino went to Hungary to work; Leonardo settled in France early in the sixteenth century. A little later the presence of Andrea del Sarto, Rosso Fiorentino, Niccolò dell'Abate, Benvenuto Cellini, and other Italian artists made Fontainebleau the center from which Mannerism—now an international movement—radiated in all directions. Tuscan Mannerists like Pontormo and Beccafumi took many of their themes and motifs from Northern art.

Characteristic of the Renaissance throughout Europe was the principle that the artist's task was research rather than the mere development of traditional themes, techniques, and styles. The artist must be original; his work must be "invention." Techniques were incessantly renewed by the exchange of individual experience in order to cope with the demand for new means of expression. Since all research must have an object, the first problem that arose was the representation of space, which is an essential element of nature. Medieval philosophy had elaborated a science of optics and an esthetics considered to be the theory of beauty; since art represented beauty but had also to be seen, the concrete relation between optics and art was one's vision of the work of art. Now, instead, the work of art had come to represent what the artist saw, hence, the vision of reality was a function of the mind and no longer merely of the eye; the vision of space was the intellectual vision of reality.

Perspective is the law that governs the vision and the representation of space by means of geometrical construction. It was conceived by Brunelleschi as the principle for the rational distribution of architectural elements in space. Very soon, however, it became the science of vision, and its purpose the "objective" representation of space. In painting, which is the representation of human actions, perspective establishes a homogeneous, unitary vision of space and results in a homogeneous, simultaneous representation of the action. The latter is caught at the moment of maximum intensity, when all motives and causes are resolved in the actual gestures of the figures; hence, it is seen as "historical" action. A representation constructed in accordance with the laws of perspective creates the conditions for perfect unity of time and place, thus eliminating all unessentials. The highest examples of this total elimination of descriptive or anecdotal detail and the reduction of the figures to their plastic or spatial essence are the frescoes Masaccio painted in Santa Maria del Carmine in Florence in 1427. Obviously, this search for plastic and spatial essence eliminates all the stylistic devices of rhythm, form, and color in which the traditional conception of beauty found expression.

In Flanders the works of Jan van Eyck revealed a conception of space diametrically opposed to that of his contemporary Masaccio but equally clear and consistent. His vision was panoramic and mostly from above, as we can see in the large altarpiece of the Adoration of the Mystic Lamb, at Ghent (1426–32); it avoids the use of receding planes and thus permits the representation of the slightest detail. In this type of perspective, which sets no limit on magnitude, there are no distinct planes, no vanishing lines, and no points of sight or convergence, and the colors do not vary with the position of an object in space. Every point of this continuous, boundless space has the same value and, insofar as it draws and fixes the attention of the spectator, constitutes the center of the universe; all objects, however distant, are always in perfect focus, and the qualities of the local colors help to identify them. Such a conception, which takes stock separately of every object and its details, might be termed "nominalistic" or "analytical"; it is certainly at the opposite pole to Masaccio's synthetic vision but satisfies the same demand for an "objective" vision of reality.

The relation that, formulated in these terms, was merely dialectical soon became historical. The representation of a "theoretical" space reached its culminating point in Paolo Uccello, that "fanatic" of perspective, but Fra Angelico occasionally achieved solutions of the space-light relation very close to those of Van Eyck. However responsive he was to the new ideas, he based his painting on an esthetic that was still Thomistic, so that he could not accept a space unrelated to light and to objective appearances. Still less could he accept that space as a condition for representing an action governed not by Divine Providence but solely by the human will. Thus, the Florentine painters were faced with the problem of reconciling ideal space with the space of empirical experience. Attempts to solve this problem can be clearly seen in the works of Filippo Lippi, Andrea del Castagno, and Domenico Veneziano, but it was Piero della Francesca who reached, not a compromise, but a grandiose synthesis of idea and experience, of intellectual truth and the truth of faith, of rational certainty and dogmatic

157

certainty. And it was only after Piero that the Venetian Giovanni Bellini succeeded in representing space by means of "tone," which is the relation of color to light. After the light-form-color synthesis realized by Piero, Florentine painters had only two alternatives: they could deviate from the perspective conception of space, as did Botticelli, or they could restate the problem of space in the totally different context of experimental analysis, as did Leonardo. He was one of the first to appreciate Flemish painting for its landscape potential.

Of course, the spatial conception of Van Eyck, the Master of Flémalle, and Dirk Bouts was still a development of medieval optic space. But it is significant that the Flemish vision of space, especially after Memling's first historic contacts with Italy, tended to approach that of the Italians. Conversely, the Italian artists tended to accept, to an ever greater degree, the results of empirical experience and even some elements of a typical Flemish vision. At the end of the fifteenth century and the beginning of the sixteenth—that is, just when the Italians were becoming more interested in Northern art—the first theories of perspective based on Italian models began to appear in Northern Europe. Jean Pélerin's *De artificiali perspectiva* was published at Toul in 1505 and immediately translated and published in Germany. (The title obviously alludes to an opposite *perspectiva communis* based not on mathematics but on optics.) During the second half of the fifteenth century as French a painter as Jean Fouquet—perhaps after seeing works by Piero della Francesca in Italy—tended clearly to geometrize forms in order to make them comply with his ideal of perfection and correspondingly sought for a supernatural quality in color and light.

In the theoretical writings of the Renaissance, "beauty" had ceased to be an abstract harmony of lines and colors and had become the ideal form of nature, as viewed and represented by the ancients; hence, the question of beauty was inseparable from that of space. And just as perspective space was a representation of nature by means of a structure of proportional planes, so the human figure which ideally inhabited that space was constructed in accordance with a sum of metric relations or a system of proportions. Albrecht Dürer was the first to formulate a complete theory of the proportions of the human body, and his theory loses no whit of its originality for deriving in part from Italian sources that have not yet been identified. He also compiled a treatise on perspective, but it is less a theory of space than a collection of practical hints to guide the painter in his work. In the same way, his theory of proportions is a collection of rules and might be called a grammar of the language of figure painting. According to Dürer, every natural form, beginning with space itself, had its own laws of proportion, its own beauty, and the universe was made up of different perfections, each separately identified. Space did not include all things in a single law but harmonized their diverse perfections.

In Italy, instead, the great masters of the early *cinquecento* shared the same concept of beauty. After Fra Angelico's neo-Thomistic experiment, the first to take "beauty" as his aim was Botticelli. His ideal of an incorporeal, almost unattainable beauty, apparent only as the expression of the artist's loftiest aim, was clearly that of the neo-Platonists Marsilio Ficino and Pico della Mirandola. For Leonardo, beauty no longer derived from antique exemplars, but from the intimate fusion of the human image in nature and the painter's way of feeling and expressing that cosmic unity. For Raphael, beauty was the choice, among nature's infinite aspects, of the most regular forms—the reconstruction, so to speak, of an ideal form of the universe from the infinite fragmentary reflections offered by reality. Michelangelo reverted to the neo-Platonic ideal and saw beauty as the pure "idea" laboriously separated from the dross of matter. For Correggio, beauty lay in "natural" movements and postures, in the "grace" of a gesture or a smile. The Venetians, starting with Giorgione, attained beauty rather by the juxtaposition and modulation of their colors than by drawing; and writers like Dolce and Pino explicitly assert that this sensuous beauty is no less legitimate than the intellectual beauty extolled by the Florentines and Romans. But even outside Italy and apart from Dürer's specifically esthetic research, the aspiration toward a paragon of beauty is clear to see in the works of Cranach and Altdorfer, in Grünewald's dramatic mysticism, in the School of Fontainebleau, and in the first Flemish *italianisants*. The Mannerists united and fused all these researches, legitimatizing every module of beauty so long as it was attained through drawing, which they considered to be the typical medium of artistic creation.

In the second half of the century it was universally recognized throughout Europe that art was not a means of expressing a religious or secular ideal but an independent activity, and therefore that the aim and object of the artist's activity was art itself. This explains the founding of artists' associations. These first academies, unlike the earlier guilds, were not devoted to defending the artists' interest but to promoting the independent development of art by organized teaching and by other means. It also explains why the Church, at the Council of Trent, endeavored to destroy this independence and reassert art's religious finality.

If art is independent and its object is beauty, the corollary is that the artist is free in his choice of subject matter. By the beginning of the fifteenth century, art had already broken loose not only from the laws of iconography but also from its traditions. Even scenes from the lives of Christ and the saints were represented as events that had actually occurred. But the need to "invent" the figuration and present the action in a well-defined space, where the story could not be divided into "episodes" (as in medieval tradition), focused the painter's interest on the real world around him and on the society in which he lived. The development of portraiture during the fifteenth century is evidence of this general trend toward formal objectivity. The figurations of classical antiquity, and still more the "themes" that could be derived from ancient sources, supplied a great variety of motifs; and, since antiquity was regarded as the age of wisdom revealed in the forms of nature, reference to it was nearly always accompanied by allegorical allusions.

Since art was the representation of nature in its outer appearance and innermost significance, allegory became one of the typical procedures of artistic "invention." What artists call the "difficulty" of art is precisely the discovery of the significant content under the outer form. Here too artists' views that seem divergent are, in the ultimate analysis, complementary. Bosch was a contemporary of Botticelli's, and the works of both are equally saturated with allegorical content and significance. For Bosch, the significance is something that lies beneath natural appearances and is revealed in nightmare images and an obsession with ugliness; for Botticelli it is something that lies above natural appearances and is revealed in images of ecstasy and an obsession (if that is the right word) with beauty. But their views are parallel, as are those of Michelangelo and Bruegel later in the sixteenth century. The same theme, namely mankind's collective destiny and the difficulty of its redemption from sin, is expressed by Michelangelo in titanic figures spasmodically tensed in the effort to free spirit from matter and by Bruegel in the resignation of humble folk to their fate of sin and folly. But these antitheses around the same conceptual core, or at least linked with the same metaphysical and moral problem, enriched the painter's store of themes with all the potential of the human imagination. Hence, there was the need to set limits, fix categories, and separate the different directions of research. The distinction between portraiture, landscape, and still life that became an essential feature of seventeenth-century art can already be observed in the sixteenth century.

Thus, the artist's newly found "professional status" stressed the importance of the method, or means of expression—technique, in the broadest sense of the term. Drawing was the technique of formal invention. According to the Italian theorists, drawing was the artist's ideal form, a priori, and the common root of all the arts; painting, sculpture, and architecture were arts of drawing because they grew from that common root and were merely different functional techniques for the realization of the idea. For German and Flemish artists, drawing was the technique for subtly recording what they saw, making a precise analysis of reality, and studying the idea within that

reality. Drawing was felt to be a medium capable of producing a finished work of art, not only a preliminary stage. Consequently, drawings were soon in great demand by connoisseurs—a new class that grew ever more numerous, radically altering the former patron-artist relationship.

Drawing, as the technique of formal ideation and invention, was classified as "theory" and distinguished from the pictorial execution, which was classified as "practice," but it proved difficult to maintain a sharp distinction between theory and practice. The chiaroscuro of fifteenth-century Tuscan and Roman painters is an intermediate stage between drawing and painting; and it was not long before the Venetians, first among them Giorgione, realized that, in order to construct a form by means of color values, one must sacrifice precision of line. The constructive value, however, defines the form and so remains drawing; therefore, drawing must express these color-light relationships even without the use of pigment. Hence, in the extremely free drawings by Titian and Tintoretto, the lines define not so much the plastic masses as the extent and quality of the areas of color and light. In Dürer's drawings, too, and still more in Grünewald's, the intense, nervous, vibrant line expresses the quest for a tension which is not merely formal but also chromatic. Moreover, analytical drawings such as the Flemish cannot be separated from the qualities of color and light; as with the Venetians, color becomes an essential part of the drawing. The apparently unfinished type of painting, with rapid touches of color and intense effects of light, that developed during the late sixteenth century, and not only in Venice, is also linked to this conception of drawing as linework capable of revealing the movement of the figure. Thus, practice too is vindicated on the level of the ideal values of art, and every phase of the execution of a painting becomes a phase of the artistic expression.

The conception of painting as "invention" obviously hinders the transmitting of technical experience from one generation to the next. In fact, the two generations of the Renaissance were characterized by a rapid transformation of media and technical procedures. The most important was the changeover from painting in tempera to painting in oils. Although Italy can boast many examples of the use of oily solvents for colored pigments, early authors agree in attributing the invention of oil painting to the Flemings. This agreement proves that technique was linked with certain stylistic modes and particularly with the typical mellowness and sensitivity to light of the colors in Flemish paintings. There is also a connection between the growing taste for blended tones and warm effects of color and light, and the technique of applying the paint in transparent glazes; these glazes give the paint the solidity and warmth of living flesh, atmospheric depth, and an infinite range of gradation and variation. 159

Another factor was the substitution of panel by canvas, which offers the brush a taut yet elastic surface that fosters a supple, fresh touch.

A profound transformation also took place in the teaching of art. The artist was no longer a craftsman who learned his trade in the master's workshop by collaborating in the execution of his works but a man of culture educated by the study of history. Institutes were founded for the systematic training of "professional" artists. The first academies—one was the Academy of Drawing established in Florence in 1563 through the initiative of a group of artists led by Giorgio Vasari—were chiefly sodalities for the defense of the artist's interests in place of the former companies and corporations. Soon, however, instruction prevailed over organization, and in 1565 Federico Zuccari proposed that the Florentine Academy should keep theoretical teaching separate from practical or technical instruction. Zuccari was the heart and soul of the Roman Academy of St. Luke, which adopted its statutes in 1579 and very soon became a cultural center where artists discussed not only practical and professional matters but artistic problems as well. The Italian example was followed in the seventeenth century by the French, who set up the Academy of Painting and Sculpture in Paris (1635) and the Academy of France in Rome (1666) for the specific purpose of helping young artists study classical antiquity. In the eighteenth century were founded the Royal Academy in London (1768) and the Academy of San Fernando in Madrid (1752; already proposed by Velázquez in the previous century).

The development, side by side with the artists' own activity, of a genuine art criticism quite distinct from treatise writing was no less important. At the beginning of the sixteenth century, artists and men of letters already engaged in heated discussions on the value and finality of art as well as on the superiority of painting to sculpture, or vice versa. Men of letters collaborated with artists by supplying them with the programs for their large decorative cycles and with themes and classical sources for their allegorical figurations. Such men were also the first to comment on, and often to celebrate, a work of art. An artist's works—and his life, too, for that matter—came to be considered a subject for the historian on a par with the achievements of great statesmen or authors. Giorgio Vasari's monumental series of "Lives" was undoubtedly the first attempt to turn the history of art into the history of artists. And since the figure of a great artist is inseparable from that of the "master," namely, from the historical consequences of his work, history of art took the shape of a history of artistic "schools." Vasari's views were still conditioned by the doctrine that art went through three successive phases: growth, summit, and decline. He assumed that growth started at the end of the thirteenth century, when Giotto broke loose from the Byzantine tradition; that the summit was represented by Michelangelo; and that decline was indicated by Mannerism (although Vasari was a Mannerist himself). But in Venice, in Titian's cultural orbit, Pietro Aretino, Pino, and Dolce had already prepared the way for what might be termed a "criticism of taste," which aimed at the direct valuation of the pictorial qualities of a work, independently of the rules and doctrines of the classicists.

The development of a theory and criticism of art—a phenomenon that very soon spread to Germany, the Low Countries, and France—is no mere collateral aspect of Renaissance art in Europe. Rather is it an essential trait, for the really novel factor in the artistic climate of the fifteenth and sixteenth centuries was that a thorough consciousness of the value and finality of art led to the appreciation of the artist's activity. Conversely, the realization of the value of the artist's activity cannot be separated from the consciousness of the finality of art in relation to society and to the great ideal themes on which it rests. Hence, strong ties bound art (though as a separate, independent activity) to scientific research and the will to acquire an objective knowledge of the universe, to religious ideals and conflicts, and to history and politics. Thus one may say that, from the historical point of view, Renaissance art is not merely a chapter in European history but one of the essential factors in the ideological and cultural formation of modern Europe.

MASACCIO (1401–28) *Crucifixion* · Pediment of the Pisa polyptych · 1426 · Tempera on panel · 30¼ × 25⅝″ · National Gallery of Capodimonte, Naples

This Florentine painter, who died in Rome when still very young, was responsible for the greatest of all artistic revolutions, for Masaccio marks the beginning of the Renaissance. Little is known about his training, and his earliest works already reveal a personality at once original, authoritative, and at loggerheads with the style of his day. He must, however, have known Brunelleschi's novel conception of perspective space because his very first works show that he saw the human figure as a mass moving in a space modeled by its gestures.

MASACCIO *The Expulsion of Adam and Eve from Paradise* · 1427 · Fresco · Santa Maria del Carmine, Florence

These frescoes relate the most important events in the life of St. Peter but they are also a compendium of the story of the human race from the Creation to the spread of Christ's message throughout the world. Masolino, a timid, aristocratic painter, was soon won over by the indomitable vigor of his youthful companion. The world Masaccio depicted is no longer the transcendent, immaterial world of the Middle Ages but the three-dimensional world of reality. This he achieved by strictly scientific perspective and impartial, truly terrestrial light.

MASACCIO *The Tribute Money* (detail) · 1427 · Fresco · Santa Maria del Carmine, Florence

Masaccio further developed his conception of the figure-space relationship in the fresco cycle he painted side by side with Masolino in the Brancacci Chapel, Florence. What is new here is the rigorous moral commitment that caused him to simplify his composition, eliminating all superfluous decoration and every element that might distract attention from the essential action. The "heroic" development of Florentine painting as the representation of human actions stemmed from Masaccio's closed, austere vision.

MASACCIO *St. Peter Healing the Sick with His Shadow* (detail) · 1427 · Fresco · Santa Maria del Carmine, Florence

In these frescoes Masaccio relates the vicissitudes of a new humanity, which he situates, as we have seen, in a new space. It is not a race of gods, for he was a realist, but a race of supermen rendered transcendent by suffering and the consciousness of suffering. His figures are so true to life that art historians still search them for portraits of the artist or his contemporaries. But Masaccio avoided trite descriptions and commonplace anecdotes, for he aimed higher than mere human affairs.

MASACCIO *St. Peter Baptizing* (detail) · 1427 · Fresco · Santa Maria del Carmine, Florence

Masaccio has also been called a "classicist," and this quality may perhaps be observed in isolated compositions where the human figures have the importance of architectural elements. But his types do more than merely reflect the condition of fifteenth-century townsmen; they recall antique statues of philosophers, immovably rooted with their gaze fixed on an infinite distance.

MASOLINO DA PANICALE (1384–after 1435) and MASACCIO (1401–28) · *Sts. Jerome and John the Baptist* · Detail of the Santa Maria Maggiore triptych · 1428 · Tempera on panel · 44⅞ × 20⅞″ · National Gallery, London

Masolino, though shackled to the Late Gothic tradition, seems to have been attracted into Masaccio's orbit between 1427 and 1430. In his later works, such as the frescoes at Castiglione d'Olona, he reverted to the line and color harmonies of what might be called "Renaissance Gothic." He and Masaccio worked together on the *Miracle of the Snow*, another part of the Santa Maria Maggiore triptych, and the panel reproduced here was probably commenced by Masaccio and finished by Masolino. Vasari reports that Michelangelo admired this work.

FRA ANGELICO (1387–1455) *The Beheading of Sts. Cosmas and Damian* · Predella of the altarpiece from San Marco, Florence · 1438–40 · Tempera on panel · 14⅛ × 18⅛″ · The Louvre, Paris

After Masaccio's revolution, there was a trend towards preserving art's religious character and finality while reexamining the fundamental principles of the artist's vision. Its major representative was Fra Angelico, a Dominican friar who aimed at embodying in his painting the esthetic canons of Thomistic philosophy—immaterial purity of form, luminous clarity of color, and harmonious beauty of proportions.

FRA ANGELICO *Lamentation for the Dead Christ* · 1436–40 · Tempera on panel · 41¾ × 64⅝″ · San Marco Museum, Florence

Although Fra Angelico's art is generally looked upon as mystical and inspired, both its subject matter and its forms are saturated with doctrine. And, in fact, he influenced later developments hardly less than did Masaccio and other painters committed to the new formal researches. According to Bernard Berenson, Fra Angelico was not a man of the Renaissance but a belated follower of Giotto. In my view, his construction of space (particularly in the Chapel of Pope Nicholas V in the Vatican) is the most logical outcome of Masaccio's discoveries.

FRA ANGELICO *Annunciation* · c.1440 · Fresco · San Marco Museum, Florence

Fra Angelico painted frescoes in the cells in the Convent of St. Mark before he went to Rome. They display a new symbolistic atmosphere that almost amounts to a reversion to the Middle Ages. But we must not forget that these pictures were designed to be the subjects of the monks' daily meditations, not to be works of art for the public eye. Note the progressive simplification of architecture, landscape, and figures, which are reduced to essentials in order not to trouble the rapt pathos of the Gospel Story.

FILIPPO LIPPI *Madonna and Child with Two Angels* · c. 1460 · Tempera on panel · $37\frac{3}{8} \times 24\frac{3}{8}''$ · Uffizi Gallery, Florence

In pictures of this type, the chiaroscuro becomes a slow gradation of pale, mostly cold, colors (silvery grays). This naturalism, less doctrinarian and examplary than Fra Angelico's, resulted in a new feeling for the portrayal of natural sentiments and the bodily gestures that express them. In 1434 Lippi worked at Padua, where his presence acted as a stimulus to the new Venetian School. This is not the least of his merits.

FILIPPO LIPPI (1406–69) *Madonna and Child with Angels and Sts. Frediano and Augustine* · c. 1440 · Tempera on panel · $85\frac{3}{8} \times 96\frac{1}{8}''$ · The Louvre, Paris

Lippi's first teacher was Lorenzo Monaco, but later he was influenced equally by Masaccio and Fra Angelico. In his first dated work (the *Tarquinia Madonna*, 1437) the impact of Masaccio's statuesque figures has crystallized in the use of contour lines to define the masses, revealing the influence of Donatello's sculpture. By means of Donatello's "flattened relief" (in which the illusion of depth is obtained by means of light effects) Lippi was led to transform perspective planes into planes of light.

DOMENICO VENEZIANO (c. 1400–61) *St. John in the Desert* · Predella of the altarpiece from Santa Lucia dei Magnoli, Florence · c. 1445 · Tempera on panel · $11\frac{1}{8} \times 12\frac{3}{4}''$ · National Gallery of Art, Washington, D.C. (The Samuel H. Kress Collection)

This painter probably received his training in northern Italy and changed his idiom through contact with Tuscan art. Though not much is known about him, he is important as one of the first who sought to reconcile the strictly perspective, linear conception of space with the space of actual experience, which is filled with light. This aim is best achieved in the great altarpiece for Santa Lucia dei Magnoli, where the sculptural, translucent form is produced by the fabric of luminous colors.

163

PAOLO UCCELLO (1397–1475) *St. George and the Dragon* ·
Canvas · $22\frac{1}{8} \times 29\frac{1}{8}''$ · Jacquemart André Museum, Paris

Paolo Uccello was one of the first Florentine painters to
realize the importance of the formal revolution accomplished by Masaccio, Donatello, and Brunelleschi. In 1425
he worked in Venice, where he and, later, Andrea del
Castagno introduced the modern forms of the Tuscan
Renaissance. That he was a theoretician of perspective is
proved not only by documentary evidence but also by a
number of his drawings. In his paintings, too, his major
aim was to achieve a strictly geometrical construction of
space and insert his figures in a clear composition of planes.

ANTONIO DEL POLLAIUOLO (1429–98) *Apollo and Daphne* ·
c. 1475 · Tempera on panel · $11\frac{5}{8} \times 7\frac{7}{8}''$ · National Gallery,
London

Pollaiuolo was a Florentine sculptor and painter who
studied under Donatello and Andrea del Castagno. His
paintings reveal quite clearly the influence of Baldovinetti,
particularly in the landscape backgrounds. A characteristic
trait is the sharp, vigorous drawing, in which the strong
outlines suffice to define plastic masses. Pollaiuolo initiated
the new attitude of Florentine Renaissance artists toward
antiquity, whose literature and works of art they considered
to be a source of ideas rather than the basis of historical
experience.

ANDREA DEL CASTAGNO (c. 1421–57) *David* · c. 1450 · Tem-
pera on leather · $45\frac{1}{2} \times 30\frac{1}{4} \times 16\frac{1}{8}''$ · National Gallery of
Art, Washington, D.C.

This Florentine painter was one of the leading adherents
of Masaccio's formal revolution, but he also felt the influence of Donatello. In his paintings he aimed not only
at representing perspective space and forms in bold relief
but also at relating form to light. His plastic-luminous
masses are defined by hard, sharp contours. This makes
him one of the first and greatest representatives of the
Florentine School of drawing.

PAOLO UCCELLO *The Legend of the Profanation of the Host*
(detail of a predella) · 1467–69 · Tempera on panel ·
$16\frac{1}{2} \times 138\frac{1}{4}''$ · Ducal Palace, Urbino

Francastel recently observed that this late work marks a
regression in Paolo Uccello's mode of rendering space. The
predella is divided into six scenes; but they are not united
by a common perspective, and each scene stands alone. Note
the exquisite, unnatural colors laid on in ample planes and
harmonized by the rarefied, diffused light. The six acts
of this mystery play are full of drama; there is no catharsis.

164

ANDREA DEL CASTAGNO *The Condottiere Pippo Spano*, from the cycle of *Famous Men* formerly in the Carducci Pandolfini Villa at Legnaia · c. 1450 · Fresco · Refectory of Sant' Apollonia, Florence

Andrea del Castagno also worked in Venice, particularly in the Chapel of San Tarasio in San Zaccaria. What he did there influenced the Paduan School and even Mantegna, thus contributing to the spread of Tuscan forms on the Venetian mainland. His most important work still extant is the fresco decoration of the refectory in the Convent of Sant' Apollonia in Florence (1445–50).

PIERO DELLA FRANCESCA (c. 1416–92) *Nativity* · c. 1475 · Tempera on panel · 49⅝ × 48⅜″ · National Gallery, London

Little is known about the artistic training of this great master, who was responsible for the triumph of the Renaissance style in central Italy. In 1439 he worked in Florence with Andrea del Castagno and Domenico Veneziano on the frescoes in Sant'Egidio, now lost; Domenico was probably his master. He certainly studied Masaccio and Fra Angelico, striving to attain a synthesis of perspective space and luminous space, of plastic form and color. This late work, executed after the Arezzo frescoes, clearly reveals a Flemish influence.

PIERO DELLA FRANCESCA *The Reception of the Queen of Sheba* (detail) · 1452–66 · Fresco · San Francesco, Arezzo

Piero's vision, at once geometrical and luminous, was completely formed by the time he painted these frescoes at Arezzo. The perfection of the forms reveals the spatial structures, the light, and the color of reality. In 1448 Piero was at Ferrara, perhaps meeting Rogier van der Weyden. But the chief center of his activity was Urbino, where his formal doctrine was the springhead of a cultural current that reached as far as Raphael and Bramante. He was also a theoretician and his treatise *De prospectiva pingendi* is the most valid attempt to place pictorial vision on a totally scientific basis.

PIERO DELLA FRANCESCA *The Defeat of Chosroes* (detail) · 1452–66 · Fresco · San Francesco, Arezzo

Even in battle scenes like this Piero never departed from his "Apollonian" attitude to the world—that sense of fatality, of expectation without hope, for which his art has been termed "ineloquent." Centered in the tireless study of space, that art lacks the time factor, which is so intrinsic in our human experience. But his figures are certainly not merely pure, immaterial "ideas" (in the Platonic sense); they are real men and women sublimated with the help of geometry and spatial syntax.

165

PIERO DELLA FRANCESCA *Constantine's Dream* (detail) ·
1452–66 · Fresco · San Francesco, Arezzo

In this scene Piero has undertaken a theme wholly alien to
his art—the "nocturne." There is no overestimating his
importance in Italian art. In Central Italy he was less understood, but his example had a decisive impact on the Venetians. It led Giovanni Bellini and Antonello da Messina to
the study of landscape and the utmost simplification of
nature in geometrical rhythms.

ANDREA MANTEGNA (1431–1506) *St. Sebastian* · c. 1470 ·
Tempera on canvas, 101⅛ × 55⅞″ · The Louvre, Paris

Mantegna is the first Renaissance artist of Northern Italy.
He was influenced less by Squarcione than by the painting
of Andrea del Castagno and the sculpture of Donatello.
Mantegna advocated a severe classicism based on the art
and literature of the ancients. His ideal was historical
painting, and in his eyes history comprised not only the
experience of the past but also the study of nature and the
dramatic, sometimes tragic, experience of the present.

ANDREA MANTEGNA · *Bridal Chamber* (Camera degli
Sposi, detail) · 1472–74 · Fresco · Palazzo Ducale, Mantua

The technique used for this work (tempera on plaster) is
quite rare and rather unreliable. The wall covering in
gilded and tooled leather helped to make the chamber a
precious casket. The decoration of the vaulted ceiling with
medallions of Roman emperors and groups of animals and
cherubs offsets the historical narrative developed on the
walls beneath. This blend of mythology and ancient history,
of natural idyl and modern chronicle, is the most fascinating
feature of Mantegna's "painted chamber"—an effective
synthesis of all the features of a stage setting.

ANDREA MANTEGNA *Madonna with Sts. John the Baptist and
Mary Magdalen* · c. 1500 · Tempera on canvas · 54⅜ × 45¾″
· National Gallery, London

Everything in Mantegna's work is as clear as the statement
of a logical, philosophical truth. The forms are crystalline,
perspective space is visible to the farthest horizons, and the
figures are shown in full action. The ancient world may be
the world of history, that is, of eternal causes, but those
remote causes have their effects in the present. Hence,
history supplies not placid catharsis but moral responsibility.

166

PIERO DELLA FRANCESCA (c. 1416–92) *The Resurrection of Christ* · c. 1462 · Fresco · Palazzo Comunale, Sansepolcro

"Here too Piero had occasion to present a moment, indeed the most triumphal moment, of the Christian myth; and he did so apparently without greatly deviating from the traditional setting. . . He framed the scene in a barely hinted, exquisite architecture of Corinthian columns. Behind them, backed by a tender brown, dappled tree—evidence of a season of difficult transition—stands the risen Christ, shockingly silvan, almost bovine; rugged as a tough Umbrian peasant, he has paused on the edge of the tomb to survey his worldly estates. . . And now at last we discover the four guards brilliantly illuminated from the side by an invincible shaft of sunlight, dozing like players in an orchestra during the intervals of the music. . . And if these four armed men appear, at first glance, to have fallen back at Christ's resurrection like the four quarters of a fruit, we soon realize that they possess the same stupendous metaphorical naturalness which is also displayed in certain passages at Arezzo. . . The guard on the left, whose schematic profile has the simplicity of a sculptured relief, recalls those on the sides of the 'Ludovisi Throne.' But the third dimension is restored by the barometer exactly immersed in the shadows of the folds; and more still by the fact that this figure, instead of having a rhythmic correspondence at the opposite side, differs from all the rest." (R. Longhi)

Detail is shown on next pages

167

ANTONELLO DA MESSINA (c. 1430–79) · *The Virgin of the Annunciation* · c. 1470 · Oil on panel · 16⅞ × 12⅝″ · Alte Pinakothek, Munich

Antonello got his training in the artistic climate of Naples, which was strongly influenced by Flemish art. Later he felt the impact of Piero della Francesca and Mantegna. It is largely due to him that Venetian painting overcame Mantegna's sculptural harshness and strove for atmospheric and tonal values. In his own work the geometrical masses and the perspective space of the backgrounds seem to be imbued and enveloped by light that softens the contours and blends the colors.

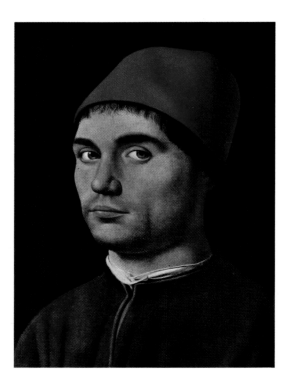

ANTONELLO DA MESSINA *Presumed Self-Portrait* · c. 1470 Oil on panel · 13⅜ × 9⅞″ · National Gallery, London

Antonello's incisive, steely portraits give a clear idea of the sitter's character (aggressive in the example in Cefalù, cynical in that in New York, melancholy in this work in London). They are a triumph of pure forms—cylinders and spheres in space. And here we can see how intensely he studied Piero della Francesca. Even the combination of man and nature in his last portrait (Berlin-Dahlem, State Museums) had already been tried out by Piero.

ANTONELLO DA MESSINA *St. Sebastian* · c. 1475 · Oil on panel (transferred to canvas) · 67⅜ × 33½″ · State Picture Gallery, Dresden

One feels in this masterpiece that Antonello has left behind the Flemish influence for a new spatial construction. He has not lost his love for inanimate objects—that is, for the world—but the perspective and arrangement of those objects place them in a different, typically Renaissance space. A column, the module for the columnar composition, corresponds to the supine figure in the middle distance, itself a human module that alludes to the perspective. The contrast between the saint and the workaday world around him could not be more striking.

GIOVANNI BELLINI (c. 1430–1516) *Madonna and Child* · c. 1475 · Oil on panel · 32¼ × 24⅝″ · Brera Gallery, Milan

This greatest of early Venetian painters was the son of Jacopo Bellini and the brother of Gentile, both of whom were masters of the Late Gothic School in Venice. He worked with his father until the latter's death in 1470, and drew close to his contemporary (and brother-in-law) Mantegna, whose hard, sharp contours he borrowed. The *Brera Madonna*, which originally had a gold background, belongs to this first period and is obviously close to Mantegna, but it also has the warmth of more intimate and refined tones.

GIOVANNI BELLINI *Portrait of an Unknown Man* · c. 1480 ·
Oil on canvas · 12⅝ × 10¼″ · The Louvre, Paris

In his second period Giovanni Bellini approached the ideas
of Piero della Francesca through the intermediary, Antonello da Messina. He no longer probed nature with relent-
less harshness but interpreted it with spacious, luminous
fluidity and an extremely consistent openness that anticipates Giorgione. Venetian critics like Marco Boschini
already noted the transition in his painting from winter fog
to springtime sunlight. As a portraitist Bellini excelled
Antonello in his rendering of atmosphere. He broke the
bonds that shackled man to geometry and proposed a new
contact with sunny nature.

VITTORE CARPACCIO (c.1455–1526) *The Scribe* · Detail from
The Ambassadors' Leave-Taking in the St. Ursula cycle ·
1490–95 · Oil on canvas · 110¼ × 99⅝″ · Academy of
Fine Arts, Venice

Carpaccio, a Venetian contemporary of Giovanni Bellini,
was fond of painting lively stories situated in a luminous
space. This first cycle, the life of St. Ursula, was followed
by a second cycle, the life of St. George, in the Scuola
degli Schiavoni, which was started in 1502; the second is
more important for its independence of iconographic
tradition and its vigorous pictorial and narrative notation.
Carpaccio gave Venetian painting the discursive quality
and vivid observation of nature that continued to be
among its major traits in the sixteenth century.

VITTORE CARPACCIO *The Courtesans* · c. 1510 · Oil on panel ·
37 × 25⅛″ · Correr Museum, Venice

GIOVANNI BELLINI *Sacred Allegory* · c. 1487 · Oil on panel ·
28¾ × 46⅞″ · Uffizi Gallery, Florence

In his landscape, Bellini's realism develops into a stringent
argument on behalf of nature and a primeval, uncorrupted
world where humanity rediscovers joy in work and not
only (as it had in the Middle Ages) in mystic contemplation.

There is no doubt of Carpaccio's contacts with Urbino and
Ferrara, and many obscure features of his art could be
explained by a journey to the Papal court in Rome. His
cycles and his isolated pictures reveal a "familiar" approach
to life and art. But Carpaccio was not a fifteenth-century
"naïve" painter, because he possessed an active, up-to-date
culture. Under his brush history turns into fable, legend
into idyl, and religion into a fascinating mythology.

CIMA DA CONEGLIANO (1459– c.1517) *St. Helena* · c. 1490 · Panel · 15¾ × 12⅝″ · National Gallery of Art, Washington, D.C. (The Samuel H. Kress Collection)

This follower of Bellini and Mantegna worked in Vicenza and Venice. His ample, balanced forms situated in an airy, atmospheric space made him famous before he was eclipsed by Titian's dominating personality. Cima was no mere rustic, provincial "Madonna-painter": he frequently came close to drama, all his pictures display a very cultivated (almost archaistic) classicism, and his vision of nature is truly bucolic, worthy of a Virgil.

COSIMO TURA (c. 1430–95) *Madonna and Child, with the Annunciation* · c. 1452 · Panel · 20¾ × 14⅝″ · National Gallery of Art, Washington, D.C. (The Samuel H. Kress Collection)

Tura was the first and greatest painter of the Ferrarese School. He received his training at Padua beside his contemporary Mantegna and fell very strongly under the influence of Donatello. At the beginning of his career he may have taken a hand in the Palazzo Schifanoia frescoes in Ferrara. There is no mistaking his manner: the line, taut as steel wire, tortures the forms but at the same time enhances the gemlike quality of the color. His style is at once intensely dramatic and sublimely elegant. The Ferrarese School was also subject to Flemish and German influences.

FRANCESCO DEL COSSA (1435–77) *St. Lucy* · Part of a polyptych · c. 1474 · Panel · 31¼ × 22″ · National Gallery of Art, Washington, D.C. (The Samuel H. Kress Collection)

This Ferrarese painter softened Tura's rigid, broken line into a firm contour that defines the plastic masses of the figures. He expanded space and filled it to the farthest horizon with a clear, luminous atmosphere. This gives his figures a monumental quality that recalls Mantegna and Donatello. Cossa was the connecting link between the schools of Ferrara and Bologna.

ERCOLE DE' ROBERTI (c. 1450–96) *Giovanni Il Bentivoglio* · c. 1474 · Panel · 21¼ × 15″ · National Gallery of Art, Washington, D.C. (The Samuel H. Kress Collection)

This disciple of Tura's worked with Cossa at Palazzo Schifanoia in Ferrara and was certainly in touch with Mantegna and Giovanni Bellini. From the first artist he borrowed his monumental conception (as seen in his Brera altarpiece of 1480); from the second a more lively, luminous sense of color. His spare, dry portraits are reminiscent of ancient medals and of Pisanello's sharp profiles. After Roberti the School of Ferrara was represented by the impoverished art of Lorenzo Costa, Francesco Francia's hybrid languors, and the aristocratic whimsicality of Amico Aspertini.

ALESSO BALDOVINETTI, ascribed to (1426–99) *Portrait of a Lady* · Tempera on panel · 24 × 15¾″ · National Gallery, London

Baldovinetti was the first, and Botticelli the greatest, of the new generation of painters that appeared in Florence during the second half of the fifteenth century. Baldovinetti seems to have been the only one really to grasp Piero della Francesca's unique message, in representing scenes where the landscape predominates. He received his training from Fra Angelico, in whose footsteps he developed a delicate intimacy, rejecting the "eloquent" manner of Andrea del Castagno and Pollaiuolo.

BENOZZO GOZZOLI (1420–97) *Journey of the Magi* · 1459 · Fresco · Medici Chapel, Medici-Riccardi Palace, Florence

Gozzoli was one of Fra Angelico's assistants in his frescoes in the Convent of San Marco in Florence and the Chapel of Pope Nicholas V in the Vatican. He was undoubtedly Fra Angelico's greatest disciple, though his interests were more mundane than religious. This made him a keen observer and a vivid narrator, and he embellished his stories with graceful figures and brilliant, harmonious colors.

ANDREA DEL VERROCCHIO (1435–88) and LEONARDO DA VINCI (1452–1519) *The Baptism of Christ* · c. 1475 · Tempera on panel · 69⅝ × 59⅜″ · Uffizi Gallery, Florence

Verrocchio, sculptor, goldsmith, and painter, was the master who taught Botticelli and Leonardo. His paintings, though excellent, are not very numerous; but he exerted an enormous influence on Florentine art around 1470. In this *Baptism* he was assisted by the young Leonardo, who painted the angel in profile that holds Christ's tunic and the open, hazy landscape.

SANDRO BOTTICELLI (1445–1510) *Portrait of a Man with the Medal of Cosimo de' Medici the Elder* · c. 1463 · Tempera on panel · 22⅝ × 17⅜″ · Uffizi Gallery, Florence

After studying under Filippo Lippi and Verrocchio, Botticelli entered the service of the Medici in 1474, where he found his place beside Poliziano and Marsilio Ficino. His art is based on linear rhythms that give his pictures an inner movement, a sort of perpetual counterpoint which keeps the form from becoming stable and definite. The line suddenly turns, twists, and stops; it is never steady and unbroken and therefore never becomes "form." The convolutions of form imply the convolutions of content; or rather, the allegorical subject matter gives the content the value of beauty—one might say a secret form revealed in the image.

SANDRO BOTTICELLI *Adoration of the Magi* · c. 1477 · Tempera on panel · 43⅝ × 52¾" · Uffizi Gallery, Florence

Botticelli's painting marks a crisis in the grand figural compositions produced earlier during the fifteenth century; a crisis in the conception of space and perspective; a crisis in the form, in the sense of knowledge or representation of nature; a crisis in the "story" as a dramatic rendering of human actions; a crisis in the moral and religious character of art; and a crisis in the social position of the artist as a representative of a superior category of craftsmen.

SANDRO BOTTICELLI *The Birth of Venus* · c. 1485 · Tempera on panel · 67⅞ × 109⅝" · Uffizi Gallery, Florence

Like Leonardo, Botticelli approached the problem of light from the neo-Platonic viewpoint; neither artist seems to have asked himself how man reacts to the phenomenon of light. Botticelli stressed its transparency by eliminating all material substance. Leonardo instead studied the atmosphere. Leonardo's solution is based on experience; Botticelli's is wholly intellectual.

SANDRO BOTTICELLI *La Primavera* (detail) · c. 1477 · Tempera on panel · 79⅞ × 123⅝" · Uffizi Gallery, Florence

This picture is an epitome of Botticelli's poetic vision. The forms of the Three Graces are neither concealed nor revealed by their transparent, floating veils. One cannot tell whether the movement of the figures is defined by their bodies or by the veils nor whether these latter sway with the movement of the dance or flutter in the breeze. The three figures are clothed in air.

SANDRO BOTTICELLI *Altarpiece of San Barnaba* (detail) · Tempera on panel · 105½ × 110¼" · Uffizi Gallery, Florence

All of Botticelli's works display the "furor" mentioned by Marsilio Ficino (who held that love of beauty was a sort of Orphic rite and the artist an initiate). This is most true of those that mark the religious crisis he experienced between 1480 and 1490. But even when deeply perturbed by Savonarola's harsh doctrine, he could never imagine a world shorn of imagery and an art incapable of discovering and revealing it. That crisis found its dramatic denouement in the *Descent from the Cross* in Munich, the *Crucifixion* in Cambridge, Mass., and the *Nativity* in London.

FILIPPINO LIPPI (1457–1504) *The Story of Lucretia* (detail) · c. 1480 · Tempera on panel · 16⅛ × 49⅝″ · Pitti Palace, Florence

Filippino Lippi was a pupil of Botticelli's and worked on the frescoes begun by Masolino and Masaccio in Santa Maria del Carmine in Florence. In Lippi, owing perhaps to some Flemish influence, Botticelli's lyrical, dreamy linear style degenerates to a restless, exuberant, disorderly expressionism. Often, however, he remains a sentimentalist who chooses indifferently for his subjects the most sublime themes of religion or the humbler themes from mythology.

DOMENICO GHIRLANDAIO (1449–94) *Portrait of an Old Man and a Boy* · Tempera on panel · 24⅜ × 18⅛″ · The Louvre, Paris

This Florentine painter was a pupil of Baldovinetti but was influenced by Verrocchio. His masterpieces include frescoes in the parish church at San Gimignano, in the Sistine Chapel in Rome, and in the Choir of Santa Maria Novella in Florence. Ghirlandaio was the last of the great narrative painters of fifteenth-century Florence. He invented nothing but utilized the new forms of Tuscan art to make a richer, more flexible language for describing the society of his day.

PIERO DI COSIMO (1462–1521) *The Death of Procris* (detail) · c. 1510 · Tempera on panel · 25⅝ × 72⅛″ · National Gallery, London

Piero started out as a fresco painter beside his master, Cosimo Rosselli, in the Sistine Chapel in Rome (1481). He is known chiefly for a series of mythological pictures that rank among the most interesting interpretations of ancient authors produced at the end of the fifteenth century. He saw classical antiquity as a fabulous world in which civilization was born and made its first steps—a mythical world that was the cradle of human sentiments, as represented, for example, in this eleg ac rendering of the *Death of Procris*.

PIERO DI COSIMO *Simonetta Vespucci* · c. 1477 · Tempera on panel · 22⅜ × 16½″ · Condé Museum, Chantilly

This is more than a mere portrait: it is a complex, mystery-laden allegory. The stormy sky, the contrast between the leafless and the leafy trees, the necklace in the shape of a serpent, all allude to the young girl's untimely death. Piero di Cosimo was greatly attracted to allegory and liked to give his allegories a moral content. For example, his five pictures representing the beginning of the human race: first, all harmony and brotherly love, then progressively more bestial.

175

PERUGINO (1445–1523) *Madonna and Saints* · c. 1493 ·
Panel · 31½ × 26″ · The Louvre, Paris

Perugino studied under Verrocchio in Florence, but the
works of his first period have disappeared and little is
known of his early training. Very soon, however, he formed
a style of his own and produced a type of devotional painting that met with great success: large figures in the foreground in ecstatic, adoring attitudes, against spacious,
faraway backgrounds. His conception of space included at
once perspective and atmosphere; his method of composition was based on the contrast between close-up figures and
perspective backgrounds. A typical example of this is
Christ Giving the Keys to St. Peter in the Sistine Chapel (1481),
which had a decisive influence on Raphael.

PERUGINO *St. Michael* · Portion of the Pavia polyptych ·
1496–99 · Panel · 49⅝ × 22⅞″ · National Gallery, London

Perugino's masterpiece is the fresco cycle in the Collegio
del Cambio, Perugia (1497–1500), where he extolled the
cardinal virtues in portraits of famous men. As Heinrich
Wölfflin wrote in 1898, "Perugino modulates the line in a
manner that nobody had taught him. He is not only much
simpler than the Florentines; he also has a sense of serenity,
of life that flows calmly, which contrasts strongly with the
Tuscan painters' dynamic manner and the formal affectation
of the late fifteenth-century style."

LUCA SIGNORELLI (1450–1523) *Madonna with St. John the
Baptist and Prophets* · c. 1490 · Panel · 68⅞ × 47″ · Uffizi
Gallery, Florence

Signorelli received his training in the ambiance of Piero
della Francesca, and later from Pollaiuolo in Florence. The
vigorous structural drawing of his figures is most evident in
his masterpieces, the frescoes of the *Last Judgment* and the
Stories of the Antichrist in Orvieto Cathedral. The bodies
are modeled with an amazingly sure hand, as if wrought in
bronze or iron. His treatment of the human form had a
great impact on Michelangelo, who seems to echo not only
Signorelli's sculptural vigor but also his moral intention
and pessimistic view of the world.

JAN VAN EYCK (c. 1390–1441) *The Virgin in the Church* ·
c. 1425 · Oil on panel · 12⅝ × 5½″ · State Museums,
Berlin-Dahlem

Van Eyck was the first great master of the Flemish School
in the fifteenth century. The extent of his collaboration
with his brother Hubert is still under discussion. Our
earliest information about him dates from 1422, and his
masterpiece, the polyptych of the *Adoration of the Mystic
Lamb* at Ghent, was finished ten years later. Although his
work is apparently linked more closely with the Late
Gothic tradition, Van Eyck was no less a revolutionary in
Flanders than Masaccio was in Florence.

JAN VAN EYCK *The Adoration of the Mystic Lamb* (detail) ·
1425–32 · Oil on panel · 137⅞ × 181½″ · Cathedral of
St. Bavo, Ghent

Its huge size and the incredibly complicated story it tells
make the polyptych at Ghent more like a triumphal fresco
cycle through which blows an apocalyptic hurricane. Here
Van Eyck has depicted the workaday world, the world of
chivalry, and the world of the Church in the early fifteenth
century, all within a unique complex that has a genuine
Renaissance quality; I cannot subscribe to Huizinga's thesis
that Van Eyck was a medieval artist.

JAN VAN EYCK *The Donor Jodocus Vijd* (detail) · Exterior
of one wing of the polyptych · c. 1425–32 · Oil on panel ·
Cathedral of St. Bavo, Ghent

Van Eyck was one of the most complete figures of the
Renaissance. I agree, although maintaining that Van Eyck
was not merely an objective realist, with the opinion expressed by M. J. Friedländer: "His gaze is so penetrating
that it reconstructs the human body visible under its
clothing. . . . He knows cloth like a weaver, architecture like
a master mason, the earth like a geographer, its flora like
a botanist."

JAN VAN EYCK *The Lucca Madonna* · c. 1455 · Oil on panel ·
25¾ × 19½″ · Städel Institute, Frankfurt

Here Our Lady is no longer a gigantic apparition symbolizing
the whole Christian Church (as she is in *The Virgin in the
Church*); she has assumed a more human, familiar size. It is
no mere chance that the flower-decked throne stands halfway
between the niche with the utensils and the window that
admits a serene, earthly light: the Virgin has taken up her
place between the symbols of the sacred liturgy and the
open sky of this world of ours. A few touches suffice to
revalue or transfigure a traditional or a too-familiar convention.

JAN VAN EYCK *The Madonna of Chancellor Rolin* · c. 1435 ·
Oil on panel · 26 × 24⅜″ · The Louvre, Paris

The new sense of space is matched by a new conception of
light, color, and line. These new values of form and color
make Jan van Eyck one of the major figures of what may
be termed the European Renaissance. "Van Eyck discovers
the eternity of things in a universe that is as constant, clear,
and hard as crystal. In his art there is no evolution in the
real sense of the word. He repeats himself and in so doing
reasserts his ideal. . . . Van Eyck's greatness lies in the limits
he consciously sets himself and in his incessant quest for
a new, monumental, expressive form of the universe."
(Tolnay)

177

JAN VAN EYCK *The Madonna of Canon van der Paele* (detail) · 1436 · Oil on panel · 26 × 24⅜″ · The Louvre, Paris

It is high time to reject once and for all the application to Van Eyck of the term "realist." He interprets nature in his own way, for nature is not so capillary, meticulous, and absurd as his prodigious eye sees it. The subjects and objects he studies are no less remote from nature than an abstract picture may be—because he does not copy but creates a new reality that has the definition of certain terrifying premonitory dreams. Van Eyck's revolt against the Middle Ages consisted in holding that the empirical world—though indeed a particular aspect of it—is well worth depicting and contemplating.

MASTER OF FLÉMALLE (ROBERT CAMPIN) (1378/9–1444) *Madonna and Child before a Fire Screen* · c. 1420–30 · Panel · 24¾ × 18⅞″ · National Gallery, London

This painter worked at Tournai during Van Eyck's youth; his name, the Master of Flémalle, comes from four pictures in the Städel Institute in Frankfurt that were believed to come from an abbey of Flémalle-les-Liège, although it actually never existed. While his identity is still under discussion, the most probable hypothesis is that he was Robert Campin, a French painter who worked throughout Flanders. His work has a definitely statuesque quality that may be the influence of sculpture which, thanks to the work of Claus Sluter, flourished during those years.

ROGIER VAN DER WEYDEN (c. 1400–64) *Portrait of a Knight* · c. 1460 · Panel · 14⅝ × 10⅞″ · Royal Museum of Fine Arts, Brussels

The greatest Flemish painter after Van Eyck during the first half of the fifteenth century. He traveled to Italy in 1450 for the Holy Year and worked at the court of the Duke of Ferrara, exerting a great influence on the Ferrarese School. He not only painted many sacred compositions in which intense dramatic feeling is combined with the utmost severity of form but he was also one of the greatest portraitists. In Rogier van der Weyden Flemish art attained a draftsmanship in no way inferior to the Florentine though directed rather toward the analysis of detail than toward spatial unity.

ROGIER VAN DER WEYDEN *Portrait of a Lady* · c. 1460 · Panel · 14⅛ × 10⅝″ · National Gallery, London

The Master of Flémalle had a great influence on Van der Weyden's artistic development, but Gothic sculpture, so imbued with popular instinct and cordial expressionism, also played its part. He produced a whole portrait gallery of men with sad gestures and women bent with fatalism. A comparison with Van Eyck's solemn, self-reliant sitters enables us to grasp this new atmosphere of uncertainty and suspense.

JAN VAN EYCK (c. 1390–1441) · *Giovanni Arnolfini and His Wife* · Signed and dated 1434 · Oil on panel · $28\frac{1}{4} \times 23\frac{1}{2}''$ · National Gallery, London

"Giovanni Arnolfini and Jeanne Cenami ... apparently considered their marriage as a very private affair and chose to have it commemorated in a picture which shows them taking the marital vow in the hallowed seclusion of their bridal chamber—a picture that is both a double portrait and

a marriage certificate. And this explains that curious wording of the signature: 'Johannes de Eyck fuit hic' ('Jan van Eyck was here') ... The artist has set down his signature—lettered in the flourished script normally used for legal documents—as a witness rather than as a painter. In fact, we see him in the mirror entering the room in the company of another gentleman who may be interpreted as a second witness." (Erwin Panofsky, *Early Netherlandish Painting*, Vol. 1, Harvard University Press)

Detail is shown on next pages

179

Johannes de eyck fuit hic
·1434·

PETRUS CHRISTUS (c. 1410–72/3) *St. Eligius Receiving a Betrothed Couple* · 1449 · Oil on panel · 38⅝ × 33½″ · Lehman Collection, New York

This painter was trained in the school of Jan van Eyck but evolved toward the more draftsmanlike style of Rogier van der Weyden. He may have spent some time in Italy, but one cannot accept the hypothesis (based on the faulty reading of a document) that he was in touch with Antonello da Messina. His most personal work is the enigmatic *Portrait of a Boy*, now in Berlin. In other pictures, such as the one reproduced here, he merely pushes Van Eyck's objective analysis to extremes.

DIRK BOUTS (c. 1415–75) *Ordeal of the Countess* (detail) · 1468–73 · Panel · 127⅝ × 71⅝″ · Royal Museum of Fine Arts, Brussels

Bouts, who was of Dutch extraction, studied in Brussels under Rogier van der Weyden and has his place in the Flemish School of painting. The two triptychs, *Scenes from the Life of the Virgin* in the Prado and the *Descent from the Cross* in Granada Cathedral, were youthful works. His masterpiece is perhaps the *Last Supper* in St. Pierre at Louvain, which he painted between 1464 and 1467.

HUGO VAN DER GOES (c. 1440–82) *Adoration of the Shepherds* (detail) · From the Portinari triptych · c. 1475–78 · Panel · 96½ × 228⅜″ · Uffizi Gallery, Florence

Van der Goes was one of the leading Flemish painters of the second half of the fifteenth century. In 1475 he entered the Augustinian order. He received his artistic training under the influence of Rogier van der Weyden and had an important bearing on the evolution of painting in Florence towards the end of the *quattrocento*. The large triptych executed for Tommaso Portinari, the Medici agent in Bruges, strongly influenced Ghirlandaio and Filippino Lippi, thus contributing to the transformation of taste in Tuscany at that time. The exquisite, yet monumental work sums up the fifteenth century and portends the solemnity of the sixteenth.

HANS MEMLING (c. 1435–94) *Portrait of an Italian* · 1470 · Panel · 10¼ × 7⅞″ · Royal Museum of Fine Arts, Antwerp

Van der Weyden was the greatest influence on Memling's artistic formation. His major works, painted about 1480, are the *Shrine of St. Ursula* and the *Adoration of the Magi*, both in St. John's Hospital, Bruges, and the *Seven Joys of the Virgin* in the Alte Pinakothek, Munich. During his later years he approached, though only superficially, the forms of the Tuscan and Umbrian Schools. From 1465 on he lived at Bruges, where his workshop was the most prosperous in the town and he was one of its wealthiest citizens.

HANS MEMLING *Veronica with the Sudarium* · c. 1480 ·
13⅝ × 9⅜″ · Collection Baron Thyssen, Lugano

Memling's art is pure, ecstatic contemplation; it has its
problems, however, though they are not apparent at first
sight. Carping critics call him shallow because he belonged
to the wealthy middle class. But I am convinced that Memling, though not a genius, was a unique phenomenon in the
history of Flemish art. Elegy need not be less important
than tragedy, nor middle-class qualities less valuable than
heroism or divinity.

JUSTUS VAN GHENT (c. 1430–80) *Triptych of the Crucifixion*
(detail) · c. 1465 · Panel · 85 × 67¼″ · Cathedral of St.
Bavo, Ghent

A Flemish painter who worked first in Antwerp and later
at Ghent. In 1473 he was called to the court of Urbino,
where he stayed until 1475 and produced his most important
work, the *Communion of the Apostles*, assisted perhaps by the
Spanish painter Pedro Berruguete. It reveals the impact of
Piero della Francesca's luminous perspective on the Flemish
conception of space, resulting in a monumentality
that is new in Flemish art. Panofsky says of Justus van
Ghent, "The Rogierian principle of rhythmic concatenation
is reconciled with the Boutsian principle of free development in depth."

HANS MEMLING *The Descent from the Cross* · c. 1485 · Panel ·
19⅝ × 13¾″ · Royal Chapel, Cathedral, Granada

His painting is pervaded by a slender thread of sentimentality, and in its concentration on the inner life of his characters it might be termed "decadent." This explains how the
St. Ursula reliquary fascinated so restless and melancholy
a spirit as Rodenbach in *Bruges-la-Morte* : "Martyrdom is
accompanied by painted melodies. Infinitely sweet indeed
is this death of the virgins, grouped like a bouquet of
azaleas on the galley that is dropping anchor and will
become their tomb. . . . Oh angelic comprehension of martyrdom: Oh heavenly vision of a painter who had no less
piety than genius."

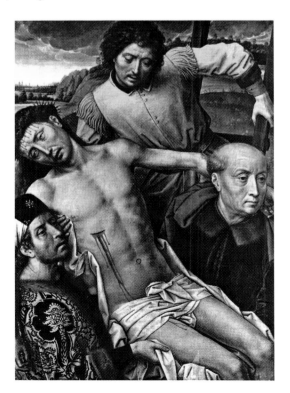

GERARD DAVID (c. 1460–1523) *The Descent from the Cross* ·
Panel · 24⅞ × 24⅜″ · National Gallery, London

David was born in Holland but worked at Bruges after
1484. In 1498 he painted the Judgment panels for the town
hall at Bruges; between 1500 and 1507, the *Baptism of
Christ* (Bruges, Museum). In David, as in Memling, the
Flemish love of detail is compensated by a more compact,
sculptural form. Flemish "naturalism" was ready, by the
sixteenth century, for contact with the spatial researches
made by the Italians.

GERARD DAVID *The Annunciation* · Panel · 16⅛ × 12⅝″ · Städel Institute, Frankfurt

The intensified sculptural quality of David's painting may be derived from a possible visit to Italy (about the first decade of the sixteenth century). But his fundamental uncertainty displays the dangerous risk that later came to a head in Mannerist art. He was a skillful, sentimental eclectic, but he had few subjects and fewer ideas of his own. There is little documentary evidence of David's activity as a miniaturist—here too he followed in Memling's footsteps—but he is credited with a Book of Hours in the Escorial as well as Queen Isabella's Breviary in the British Museum.

HIERONYMUS BOSCH (c. 1435–1516) *The Vagabond* · Detail of exterior wing of triptych *The Hay Wagon* · c. 1470 · Oil and tempera on panel · 53⅛ × 18⅛″ · The Prado, Madrid

Little is known with certainty of this extraordinary character, but at an early date he became famous even outside his own country. Francesco Guicciardini, the great Florentine historian, called him "most noble, marvelous inventor of things fantastic and bizarre." Some forty works by Bosch are still extant, and these are no less mysterious than their author. In Bosch's heyday Flanders still labored under the heritage of the Middle Ages. Wealth brought vice in its train, and the common people became more and more corrupt. A host of moralists and reformers opposed this degeneracy: Erasmus of Rotterdam and Hieronymus Bosch were among the greatest and most severe of these.

HIERONYMUS BOSCH *Fragment of a Last Judgment* (detail) · c. 1490 · Panel · 23⅝ × 44⅞″ · Alte Pinakothek, Munich

Bosch combined mysticism with a vein of magic—two streams of thought and often two ways of life that were decisive for his time. Hence, he was not, as many believe, either a bizarre, casual painter or a precursor of the Surrealists; the group to which he belonged was not out of touch with the events and ethics of their day.

HIERONYMUS BOSCH *The Adoration of the Magi* · Triptych · c. 1495 · Panel · 53⅞ × 54⅜″ · The Prado, Madrid

Bosch's lifetime coincided with a period of spiritual and social crisis in Flanders, to which artists reacted by stressing their individualism. Bosch, too, produced an extremely personal art, so imbued with doctrine as to be often incomprehensible. By opposing what is evil and demonic in the world he came gradually to exalt that demonism. *The Ship of Fools* and the *Cure of Folly* are pictures that match the cultural climate of that day. In 1494 Sebastian Brant wrote a poem entitled *The Ship of Fools;* in 1511 Erasmus published his *In Praise of Folly.*

184

HIERONYMUS BOSCH *The Temptation of St. Anthony* (detail) ·
Triptych · c. 1500 · Panel · 51⅝ × 86⅝″ · National Museum of Ancient Art, Lisbon

Critics have long taken a passionate interest in the catalogue of Bosch's works, for none of them is dated, few are signed, and there are endless copies. His themes are allegorical and universal, like the *Last Judgment* or the *Garden of Delight*. Other works of his deal with man's infinite weakness and solitude: the *Seven Capital Sins*, the *Hay Wagon* (an allegory of human life), and the *Temptation of St. Anthony*. Bosch's painted nightmares had an important influence on Bruegel, the greatest genius among Flemish sixteenth-century painters.

HIERONYMUS BOSCH *Christ Carrying the Cross* (detail) ·
c. 1505 · Panel · 29⅛ × 31⅞″ · Museum of Fine Arts, Ghent

Bosch forces us to believe in his demonic apparations because our eyes are familiar with every detail of that absurd world. What is new is the odd context in which those slices of reality are situated and the reversal of the normal proportions. The transformation of large into small and vice versa reflects a controversy that is not only moral and religious but social and political as well. Yet it is always the tireless study of nature that provides the means for attaining the supernatural.

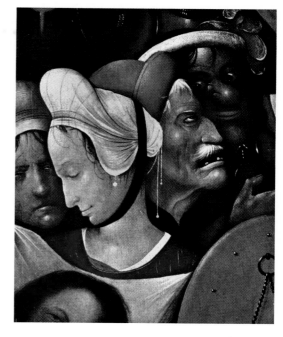

HIERONYMUS BOSCH *Christ Carrying the Cross* (detail) ·
c. 1505 · Panel · 29⅛ × 31⅞″ · Museum of Fine Arts, Ghent

Bosch derived his wealth of symbolic material chiefly from the mysterious field of alchemy, which had degenerated from an aristocratic science to a popular superstition. The huge egg that appears in many of these figurations is the culminating point of an alchemic chain, but the animals and even the colors have a hidden meaning. Hence, Bosch's painting is not capricious but subtly calculated; it is governed by iconographic rules at least as strict as those usual in religious art.

LUIS DALMAU (active 1428–60) *The Madonna of the Councilors* (detail) · 1445 · Panel · Catalan Museum of Fine Arts, Barcelona

Dalmau, born in Spain, was sent to Flanders by Alfonso of Aragon in 1431 and there became a pupil of Jan van Eyck. This was a decisive factor in his painting, as in that of other Spanish artists, such as Jacomart Baço and Juan Reixach of the School of Valencia. Lacking a pictorial idiom of their own, many fifteenth-century Spanish painters adopted the styles of Flanders or Italy.

185

JAIME HUGUET (c. 1415–92) *St. Bernardine* (detail) · Retable of the Guild of Mat and Glass Workers · 1467–69 · Panel · 89 × 65⅛″ · Cathedral, Barcelona

Huguet was a Catalan and worked mostly in Barcelona. Gentleness and harshness appear side by side in his works, which reveal a certain Italian influence—Gherardo Starnina was in Spain late in the fourteenth century—but always combined with the study of Flemish models. Art historians have even seen reminiscences of Sienese and Umbrian art in his refined figures, but he really belongs rather to the variegated stream of the international Gothic, as evidenced by such "florid" works as the *St. George* in the Catalan Museum of Fine Arts in Barcelona.

PEDRO BERRUGUETE (c. 1450–1504) *St. Dominic and the Albigensians* · Detail from the Retable of St. Dominic · c. 1490 · Panel · 66½ × 29⅞″ · The Prado, Madrid

Italy was also a decisive factor in the formation of Berruguete. He worked at Urbino for Duke Federigo of Montefeltro from 1472 to 1482 and left several pictures of famous men besides a very searching portrait of the duke himself. His collaborator at Urbino was the Flemish painter Justus van Ghent. Berruguete took what he had learnt in Italy back with him to Spain, but very few works of his are still extant there. The most important is this polyptych (now dismantled and displayed in the Prado) for the Dominican church of Santo Tomas at Avila.

BARTOLOME BERMEJO (second half of the fifteenth century) *The Madonna of Canon Despla* (detail) · 1490 · Oil on panel · 72⅞ × 78¾″ · Cathedral Museum, Barcelona

Bermejo certainly received his training in Italy. At Acqui there is a *Madonna of Monserrat* signed Bartolomeus Rubeus —even in his signature the painter was anxious to assert his Latin descent. Bermejo's work, which stands on the highest level of Spanish fifteenth-century art, is characterized by the figures, either solemn (for example *St. Dominic Enthroned*, in the Prado) or grim (as in this detail).

ANYE BRU (active c. 1473–1507) *Martyrdom of St. Cugat* (detail) · 1502–06 · Panel · Catalan Museum of Fine Arts, Barcelona

Anye Bru, who was of German descent—perhaps his real name was Hans Brun—worked mostly in Catalonia. He was a truly international painter: we can trace Italian, Flemish, and French influences. Yet it would be quite wrong to call him an eclectic. He combined a solid, serene sculptural quality, which is typically Italian, with an expressionistic pathos derived from the German art.

NUNO GONÇALVES (active 1450–71) *Polyptych of the Adoration of St. Vincent* (detail) · c. 1460 · Panel · 81½ × 50⅜" · National Museum of Ancient Art, Lisbon

Gonçalves was a Portuguese painter who won fame at the court of Alfonso V of Spain. This work in Lisbon, perhaps the only one still extant, was admired late in the sixteenth century by Francisco de Hollanda as one of the greatest masterpieces of Portuguese art. In the densely populated polyptych the saint is surrounded not only by the royal family and the authorities but also by the common people; it is thus a choral representation of the life of his day.

ENGUERRAND QUARTON OR CHARENTON (c. 1410–c. 1466) *The Coronation of the Virgin* (detail) · 1453–54 · Panel · 72⅛ × 86⅝" · Hospice, Villeneuve-les-Avignon

Quarton has been linked with Piero della Francesca, but in reality he was wholly medieval and archaistic. In this altarpiece, for instance, the summarily depicted coronation is balanced by groups of worshipers who are barely individualized, and the long sketchy landscape is reduced to essentials. The tide of "expressionism" that had flooded France early in the century—as exemplified by the extraordinary master who painted the *Grandes Heures du Duc de Rouen*—has ebbed. And the rustic yet courtly style of the Limbourg brothers, who decorated the *Très Riches Heures du Duc de Berry* in the second decade, is a thing of the past.

JEAN FOUQUET (c. 1415–c. 1480) *The Melun Diptych* (detail) · c. 1452 · Panel · 37⅜ × 33⅞" · Royal Museum of Fine Arts, Antwerp

Fouquet is the greatest representative of French painting in the fifteenth century. In 1445 or thereabouts he was in Italy, where he was greatly impressed by the art of Fra Angelico. He probably also saw paintings by Piero della Francesca because in his own works delicate, luminous color is combined with the quest for geometrical regularity of form. But this is due rather to his refined taste than to a precise study of masses and perspective. Rhythm of line and color is the basis of his art.

JEAN FOUQUET *The Fall of Jericho* · Miniature from the *Antiquités Judaïques* by Flavius Josephus · c. 1475 · Parchment · 8¼ × 7⅛" · Bibliothèque Nationale, Paris

Fouquet also won fame as a miniaturist. In addition to the *Antiquités Judaïques*, noteworthy are Etienne Chevalier's Book of Hours in the Condé Museum at Chantilly and the Boccaccio in the Munich Library. These scenes very often rise above the level of trite illustration to excel many works of greater pretensions. The School of Avignon flourished at the time of Jean Fouquet. Its major representatives were the Master of the Avignon *Pietà*, Nicolas Froment, whose realism borders on the grotesque, and the Master of Moulins, the most interesting French painter after Fouquet.

KONRAD WITZ (1398–c. 1445) *David and Abishai* · c. 1435 · Panel · 39⅜ × 31½″ · Museum of Art, Basel

In the fifteenth century German painting was still bound up with the international Gothic style. The Swiss Konrad Witz revolted against the medieval tradition in favor of a new vision of nature and a sculptural rendering of human form, which are the typical traits of the German artistic idiom. In his works the isolated figures are often plotted against a gold ground but often, too, against an open landscape that stretches to the horizon (for example, the *Miraculous Draught of Fishes* in the Geneva Museum, an actual view of Lake Geneva). What has been ascribed to contacts with Antonello da Messina is more probably due to the two artists' parallel experience and interpretation of Flemish works.

STEFAN LOCHNER (c. 1410–51) *The Madonna of the Rose Bush* · c. 1450 · Panel · 19⅞ × 15¾″ · Wallraf Richartz Musem, Cologne

Lochner was a lyrical painter in the Late Gothic tradition. The realistic trend toward the end of his life did not contradict the delicate poetic vein of this singer of cherubs, maidens, and flowering fields. Lochner has his place in the Italian line of Stefano da Zevio, Pisanello, and Gentile da Fabriano. This refined mode of painting was abandoned by Lucas Moser in favor of daring perspectives, and by Hans Multscher, who stressed the sculptural quality of his forms. But the major painter of the Colmar School is Martin Schongauer, more famous for his engravings.

MICHAEL PACHER (c. 1430–98) *Madonna and Child Enthroned with Saints* · c. 1485 · Panel · 15⅞ × 15½″ · National Gallery, London

Pacher was a native of the Val Pusteria, a district half Austrian and half Italian. His art too is divided between the influences of Padua and Venice—he was certainly familiar with Mantegna's work—and of congenial German art. German tradition has it that he was also a wood carver. Pacher, here rustic and bizarre, there rational and refined, marks the peak of German painting in the fifteenth century.

LEONARDO DA VINCI (1452–1519) *Portrait of a Woman (Ginevra dei Benci?)* · c. 1478 · Panel · 16½ × 14⅝″ · Liechtenstein Gallery, Vaduz

Leonardo is one of the greatest representatives of Renaissance art and of Italian culture in general. He was a theoretician of painting, sculpture, and architecture, a student of mechanics, hydraulics, botany, and anatomy. His writings —mostly notes for vast treatises that were never written— are the foundation stone of modern science, which rejects dogmas and systems and relies entirely on the direct observation of natural phenomena. An interest in the analytical observation of nature is a trait common to scientists and artists alike.

LEONARDO DA VINCI *The Virgin of the Rocks* (detail) ·
c. 1490 · Panel (now transferred to canvas) · 77⅞ × 48¼″ ·
The Louvre, Paris

The major centers of Leonardo's activity were Florence
(where he was trained by Verrocchio and to which he
returned early in the sixteenth century), Milan, and France
(where he emigrated in 1512). His paintings reveal a new
vision of reality and a new conception of formal beauty.
Their most typical trait is the blending of forms and colors
in the atmosphere. In other works, such as the lost cartoon
for the *Battle of Anghiari* in Florence, he studied in minutest
detail the movements of the figures and the reflection of
sentiments and passions in bodily attitudes and facial expressions.

LEONARDO DA VINCI *The Virgin of the Rocks* · 1483–c. 1508
· Panel · 74⅜ × 46⅞″ · National Gallery, London

This work is not entirely by the master's hand but was
painted in collaboration with the De' Predis brothers. Here
the ineffable mystery of an ambivalent and not always
benign nature is congealed and crystallized by an excessive
rationalism that stifles the poetic quality of something
"unfinished." As Goethe said, Leonardo "never yielded to
the ultimate impulse of his original, incomparable talent
and, curbing all spontaneous and fortuitous transport,
insisted that every brushstroke be pondered and pondered
again."

LEONARDO DA VINCI *Mona Lisa* · c. 1503–7 · Panel ·
30⅜ × 20⅞″ · The Louvre, Paris

This work, vaguely decadent and crepuscular, has inspired
an infinite number of analyses, harrowing and rapturous,
mystic and erotic. Walter Pater's labored study is an especially pathological case: "She is older than the rocks
among which she sits; like the vampire, she has been dead
many times and learned the secrets of the grave; and has
been a diver in deep seas and keeps their fallen day about
her; and trafficked for strange webs with Eastern merchants;
and, as Leda, was the mother of Helen of Troy, and, as
Saint Anne, the mother of Mary; and all this has been to
her but as the sound of lyres and flutes."

LEONARDO DA VINCI *The Madonna and Child with St. Anne
and St. John* · c. 1510 · Panel · 66⅛ × 44⅛″ · The Louvre,
Paris

Eugène Delacroix had an artist's intuition of the odd symbiosis of technique and art, science and simplicity, in
Leonardo's painting. He says in his diary, "This man,
whose manner is so characteristic, is devoid of 'rhetoric.'
Always observant of nature and ceaselessly referring to it,
he never copies it himself. The most learned of masters is
also the most artless, and neither of his two rivals, Michelangelo and Raphael, deserves that praise as he does."

LEONARDO DA VINCI *Bacchus* · c. 1506 · Canvas · 69⅝ × 45¼″ · The Louvre, Paris

It is interesting to know what Rubens, an artist at the antipode of Leonardo's Apollonian, "classic" conception, thought of him. "Leonardo," he said, "began by examining everything in the light of a scientific theory, whose laws he applied to the subject he wished to represent. He gave every object the fittest and most lifelike aspect, and exalted majesty to the point where it becomes divine. His rule in rendering an expression was to catch and hold the imagination with essentials rather than confuse it with minute details, and in this, he strove to be neither prodigal nor niggardly."

GIOVANNI ANTONIO BOLTRAFFIO (1467–1516) *Portrait of a Woman Called "La Belle Ferronnière"* · 1495 · Panel · 24⅜ × 17⅞″ · The Louvre, Paris

This picture was formerly attributed to Leonardo. It serves to show how the master's art was travestied by the Milanese School, the first to adopt his manner of painting. In place of delicate chiaroscuro there is a heavy contrast of lights and shadows; in place of subtle psychological study a pleasure in the superficial; depth gives way to a flatness that is quite involuntary. Boltraffio, a *cinquecento* artist, seems to have the same instinct for geometry that Antonello da Messina had in the *quattrocento*.

AMBROGIO DE' PREDIS (c. 1455–1508) *Portrait of the Musician Franchino Gaffurio* · c. 1495 · Panel · 16⅞ × 12⅛″ · Pinacoteca Ambrosiana, Milan

This Lombard disciple of Leonardo assimilated better than his fellows the master's formal conception of blended chiaroscuro and his taste for psychological analysis. But, like all great masters, Leonardo was fated not to be completely understood even by his own pupils. Andrea Solario, Cesare da Sesto, and Bernardino Luini all reverted to a provincialism that made them languid, sentimental storytellers, while Giampietrino clearly contaminated Leonardo's lesson with Flemish elements.

SODOMA (1477–1549) *St. Sebastian* · Standard of the Confraternity of St. Sebastian in Camollia, at Siena · 1525 · Canvas · 82⅝ × 57½″ · Pitti Palace, Florence

Sodoma, a native of Vercelli, first studied under Martino Spanzotti but was chiefly influenced by Leonardo. He spent nearly all his working life in Siena, where he grafted onto Leonardo's blended chiaroscuro a variety of artistic influences—Filippino Lippi, Fra Bartolommeo, and especially Raphael. His frescoes with the stories of Alexander the Great in the Farnesina in Rome are the clearest proof of this eclecticism, which did not prevent him from attaining a high artistic level.

DONATO BRAMANTE (1444–1514) *Man at Arms* · Fresco transferred to canvas · Brera Gallery, Milan

Bramante was born at Urbino and fell under the influence of Laurana, Francesco di Giorgio, and Piero della Francesca. When he reached Milan, about 1480, he modified his severe, ultra-rational architectural vision in contact with Leonardo da Vinci. His painting has an extremely robust constructional power and a balance that is perfectly suited to the noble figures of heroes with which he decorated the palace of the Panigarola family in Milan. The bold statuesque masses of the glorious warriors and learned scholars stand out against a severe architectural background.

BRAMANTINO (1455–1536) *Crucifixion* · Canvas · 146½ × 106¼″ · Brera Gallery, Milan

Bramantino learned his trade from the pictorial examples of Foppa and Butinone, but he also studied Bramante's monumental compositions. These contrasting and complementary influences are clearly visible in, for example, a youthful work such as the *Nativity*. But the pale, somber colors soon became lively and bright, especially after Bramantino's journey to Rome, where he may have studied works by Melozzo da Forlì and Piero della Francesca. Particularly worthy of note are his cartoons of the Months for tapestries commissioned by Trivulzio; they are mature and monumental.

GAUDENZIO FERRARI (c. 1475–1546) *Concert of Angels* (detail) · 1535–36 · Fresco in the cupola of the Sanctuary at Saronno

This Piedmontese painter, who worked mostly in Lombardy, was no mere eclectic always ready to borrow from Leonardo, Bramantino, Dürer, or Perugino. His manner, homely and blunt, violent and scathing, made him a very original artist. In works such as this, Ferrari seems to have deliberately abandoned the artistic climate of his day for a timeless art that has permanent validity because it is very close to popular taste, which never changes.

RAPHAEL (1483–1520) *The Three Graces* · c. 1500 · Panel · 6⅝ × 6⅝″ · Condé Museum, Chantilly

Raphael, Leonardo, and Michelangelo are the three major representatives of High Renaissance painting. Raphael was first apprenticed to Timoteo Viti and Perugino. In Florence during the first years of the sixteenth century he studied works by Leonardo and Michelangelo. In 1508 he went to Rome, where he decorated the famous *Stanze* in the Vatican for Pope Julius II and his successor Leo X. Towards the end of his life, after the rise of Sebastiano del Piombo, Raphael enriched his palette with the more robust colors of the Venetians.

191

RAPHAEL *Portrait of a Man* · c. 1503 · Panel · 17⅜ × 12⅛″ ·
Borghese Gallery, Rome

In Raphael's works the almost spontaneous poetry of forms
and colors is accompanied by a clear, rational study of composition. "His beauties are the beauties of the mind, not of
the eyes; hence, they are not felt at once by the eyes, but
only after they have penetrated to the mind." (Mengs)
His many portraits display a splendid balance of mind and
body. The silvery gray, orange, or vermilion tones are
accompanied by a vigorous, vibrant manner that mirrors
the moral, social, and cultural condition of the most important men of the period.

RAPHAEL *The School of Athens* · 1508–c. 1511 · Fresco ·
Stanza della Segnatura, The Vatican, Rome

Taine saw in Raphael the "unique blessing of a twofold
education which, after first showing him Christian innocence and purity, made him feel pagan joy and strength."
These two poles combined to produce an incredible,
Olympian calm. It is ruffled at times by a display of official
pomp; at others by an undercurrent of legend and play, as in
many of his Holy Families. Very rarely indeed it is troubled
by ambiguous touches of sentimentality.

RAPHAEL *The Miracle of Bolsena* (detail) · 1512–14 · Fresco ·
Stanza di Eliodoro, The Vatican, Rome

Raphael was no less an original artist for the many influences
to which he submitted: they all added up to a poetic vision
that was wholly classical. The effort to identify form and
space and give form its full sculptural roundness is but one
aspect of Raphael's art. His chief concern was to render with
absolute clarity religious truths, natural phenomena, and
historical events. This art, as the palpable representation of
all reality, both visible and invisible, is the ideal expression
of Catholic dogma—impossible to prove yet perfectly
logical—before the Reformation.

RAPHAEL *The Sistine Madonna* · c. 1513–16 · Canvas
104⅜ × 77⅛″ · State Picture Gallery, Dresden

This work, which, since Burckhardt, has been considered
the highest achievement any painter ever attained, might
be taken as the emblem of Italian Renaissance painting. Its
extraordinarily airy and scenic conception is due less to a
pre-Baroque feeling for the limitless and the theatrical than
to precise perspective-spatial considerations: therefore, it
still lies within the ambient of the Renaissance. Actually, the
picture simulates a window open to the sky. It was painted
for the altar of San Sisto in Piacenza.

ANDREA DEL SARTO (1486–1530) *Stories of Joseph* · Panel · 38⅝ × 53⅛″ · Pitti Palace, Florence

This Florentine painter, a pupil of Piero di Cosimo, initiated the style known as Mannerism. He was one of the first to aim directly at a "beauty" that combined all the qualities and aspects of nature, as defined by the artists of that day. He sought to merge strong plastic relief with harmoniously fused colors, architecturally balanced composition with intense expression of emotion. In 1519 he brought the new style of Italian painting to the court of Francis I of France.

MICHELANGELO BUONARROTI *The Creation of Man* (detail) · Ceiling of the Sistine Chapel · 1508–12 · Fresco · The Vatican, Rome

The Doni roundel in the Uffizi is an example of the first phase of Michelangelo's quest, while he was still in Florence. In 1508 he embarked on the huge task of decorating the ceiling of the Sistine Chapel in Rome with scenes from Genesis. There he sought to achieve a synthesis of the painted architectural structure and the figures, all inserted between the strong architectural cornices.

MICHELANGELO BUONARROTI (1475–1564) *The Holy Family* · c. 1503–05 · Panel · Diam. 47¼″ · Uffizi Gallery, Florence

Michelangelo—painter, sculptor, architect, and poet— dominates all sixteenth-century art in Italy by his extraordinary sculptural vision and the depth of his intellect. He considered painting inferior to sculpture because it was more liable to the illusions of the senses, and in his paintings he sought to satisfy the sculptor's ideal. In keeping with his neo-Platonic philosophy, Michelangelo held that drawing was the highest form of art because it was the pure, immaterial expression of the "idea." Hence, his aim was to achieve a synthesis of all the arts—he considered them mere manual skills—to obtain the ideal result.

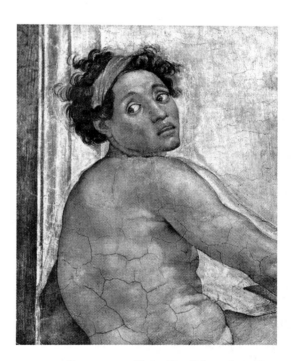

MICHELANGELO BUONARROTI *Nude* · Detail from the ceiling of the Sistine Chapel · 1508–12 · Fresco · The Vatican, Rome

The ceiling of the Sistine Chapel is the explosive text that served as a primer for the rising generation of Florentine Mannerists, until Michelangelo's *Last Judgment* offered one still more explosive. It gave rise to the myth of Michelangelo's sublime "manner," which is based on the most dreadful moral anguish and yet inspired his followers to mere formalistic repetitions. Here, owing to a reversed sort of Copernican revolution, interest is no longer focused outside man but precisely in the human figure, considered to be the seat of spirit and matter, of being and non-being, of boundless aspirations and inevitable humiliations. These contortions of mind and spirit are reflected in the canon of the "figura serpentinata."

MICHELANGELO BUONARROTI *Judith and Holophernes* (detail) · Spandrel of ceiling of the Sistine Chapel · 1508–12 · Fresco · The Vatican, Rome

The ceiling of the Sistine Chapel relates the long history and prehistory of humanity before the Redemption. The ten biblical scenes synthesize the origin of man and the chain of sin that was born with him. The Redemption is represented symbolically in the four spandrels containing the prefigurations of the Passion; it is also announced by rugged prophets, severe sibyls, and Christ's wrathful ancestors, who seem to be in the throes of a cosmic anguish. The entire composition should, perhaps, be interpreted in neo-Platonic terms—there are, in fact, obvious references to Plato's *Phaedo*—as man's slow ascent toward knowledge and therefore toward salvation.

MICHELANGELO BUONARROTI *Last Judgment* (detail) · West wall of the Sistine Chapel · 1536–41 · Fresco · The Vatican, Rome

Michelangelo started to think of the *Last Judgment*—though his first idea may have been to paint a Resurrection—at the suggestion of Pope Paul III in 1534. The cartoon was ready in the following year. The composition is visualized as a single, compact, overflowing mass of figures that fall and rise in a whirling rhythm of perpetual motion. Architectural or naturalistic space is totally lacking: it is merely suggested by the human module—exalted and triumphant, or tragic and despairing. In this epic of the Last Day, Michelangelo has incorporated forms and allegories, lights and emotions, doubts and certainties, desires and frustrated hopes.

MICHELANGELO BUONARROTI *Conversion of St. Paul* and *Crucifixion of St. Peter* · 1542–50 · Fresco · Pauline Chapel, The Vatican, Rome

The two frescoes in the Pauline Chapel represent not the tragedy of a judgment without appeal but the luminous catharsis (in the *Conversion of St. Paul*) and the anguishing consummation (in the *Crucifixion of St. Peter*) that mark the passage to a higher life, whether in this world or the next. Emotions are inflated and passions attain the grotesque as the composition condenses in hallucinating wildness, its forms crystallizing in an attenuated Mannerism. The color apparently extinguished in earthy tones suddenly flares up in unbelievably delicate iridescences. Michelangelo's meditation on the highest of spiritual themes is pervaded with the despair of his poems on death.

PONTORMO (1494–1556) *Portrait of Ugolino Martelli* · c. 1540 · Oil on panel · $36\frac{1}{4} \times 27\frac{1}{8}''$ · National Gallery of Art, Washington, D.C. (The Samuel H. Kress Collection)

Pontormo, a Florentine pupil of Andrea del Sarto, was the ablest of the Tuscan Mannerists. He did not actually copy Michelangelo's forms but rather followed his laborious quest for an ideal form surpassing all traditional canons of beauty. In this quest Pontormo was aided by a knowledge of German art. In his art one notes a melancholy contemplation of life, an eroticism pushed to the ultimate consequences. His nocturnal vision of the world is also a halfhearted aspiration towards classicism.

ROSSO FIORENTINO (1495–1540) *Moses and the Daughters of Jethro* · c. 1520 · Oil on canvas · 63 × 46⅛″ · Uffizi Gallery, Florence

Rosso, an outstanding exponent of Tuscan Mannerism, also worked in France. Only a limited group of works by Rosso are known, except for the partly ruined fresco cycle in the Fontainebleau Castle, but all are of a very high order. Michelangelo's influence is clear to see, especially after 1520, in pictures like this one. Pontormo's hopelessness has given way to an aristocratic intellectualism combined with a passion for experiment. Rosso went so far as to dig up corpses for his anatomical studies.

BRONZINO (1503–72) *Eleonora of Toledo and Her Son* · c. 1545 · Oil on panel · 45¼ × 37¾″ · Uffizi Gallery, Florence

In the Florentine School Bronzino is the representative of pure reason. In his pictures color gives way to firmly defined form. His portraits are sculptured by the light, and idealized in severe geometrical arrangements. The whole family of the Medici granddukes sat to Bronzino, who gradually refined his painting to the point where it became the synthesis of pure "ideas" in the neo-Platonic sense. His portraits constitute a splendid gallery of frigid icons: they lack only a gold background in place of the blue or gray.

CORREGGIO (c. 1489–1534) *Jupiter and Antiope* · c. 1525 · Oil on canvas · 74⅞ × 48⅞″ · The Louvre, Paris

Correggio is one of the great masters of the Italian Renaissance, and the founder of the Emilian School of painting in the sixteenth century. His artistic formation is unknown, and the first phase of his activity reveals a strong influence of Mantegna's Mantuan period. But in the Camera di San Paolo at Parma he developed Mantegna's classical themes in a more humanistic, literary style. The impact of Leonardo's delicate atmospheric chiaroscuro further attenuated the rigid modeling and classicistic severity Correggio had learned from Mantegna.

CORREGGIO *Adoration of the Shepherds*, also known as "*La Notte*" · c. 1530 · Oil on panel · 100¾ × 74″ · State Picture Gallery, Dresden

Correggio's frescoes in the cathedral of Parma and the church of St. John the Evangelist reveal a new influence—that of Raphael and Michelangelo, whose works he saw in Rome between 1517 and 1520. Though his art is made up of many cultural ingredients, all of his paintings are harmonies in the unity of a style based on modulated rhythms of curved lines, on colors at once rich and almost dissolved in the luminous atmosphere, and on daring formal arrangements that make his figures move freely in space.

195

CORREGGIO *The Madonna with Sts. George, Gemignano, Peter Martyr, and John the Baptist* · c. 1530 · Oil on panel · 112¼ × 74⅞″ · State Picture Gallery, Dresden

Correggio transformed the Renaissance ideal of beauty into an ideal of "grace" that had a decisive impact on the Emilian School. Much later, that ideal prompted Stendhal to formulate his important observations on the contrast between "romantic" beauty and "classic" beauty. The formal movement that makes Correggio a precursor of Baroque art is never external but forms an integral part of his talent.

PARMIGIANINO (1504–40) *The Madonna of the Long Neck* · 1534–40 · Oil on panel · 85 × 52″ · Uffizi Gallery, Florence

This contemporary of Correggio's also worked at Parma. He distilled the essential qualities of Correggio's style, developing the line in rhythms of the utmost elegance and condensing the color in rich, exquisite shades. The *Madonna and Saints* in the Uffizi was painted earlier in Rome for Pope Clement VII in 1523; it proves with what noble eclecticism Parmigianino assimilated the teaching of Michelangelo and Raphael. His encounter with Rosso Fiorentino also had a strong impact on his artistic evolution. The frescoes of Diana and Acteon in the castle of Fontanellato near Parma are an original development of the classical theme that Correggio had employed in his decoration of the Camera di San Paolo.

DOSSO DOSSI (1479–1542) *Circe the Sorceress* · c. 1530 · Oil on canvas · 69¼ × 68½″ · Borghese Gallery, Rome

Dossi studied in Venice, where he chiefly adopted Giorgione's tonal manner. Raphael's work, which he saw in Rome, was also a decisive influence. It must not be forgotten, however, that Dossi belongs to the extremely rich and aristocratic tradition of Ferrara, within which he represents the magical, fabulous element. That tradition was literary as well as pictorial: Ariosto was both the historian and the mythographer of the Ferrarese "courtly" world.

DOMENICO BECCAFUMI (1485–1551) *The Archangel Michael* · 1524–30 · Oil on panel · 137 × 88⅝″ · Santa Maria del Carmine, Siena

The influence of Perugino is clear to see in Beccafumi's early works. Then he went to Rome, where he studied Michelangelo, and later was in touch with Sodoma and Fra Bartolommeo. Beccafumi combines a quest for monumentality and space with violent, smoky colors that produce brilliant flashes of light amid the heavy shadows. His works are full of northern motifs, hallucinatory visions, and curious forms; these take the form of contrasts of grandiose and fragile figures, sudden transitions from darkness to light and changes of color tones in the light.

GIORGIONE (c. 1477–1510) *The Adoration of the Shepherds* (detail) · c. 1498 · Oil on panel · 35⅞ × 43¾″ · National Gallery of Art, Washington, D.C. (The Samuel H. Kress Collection)

This great master, who studied under Giovanni Bellini, was the herald of Venetian sixteenth-century painting. Very few of his works are still extant but there are enough to prove that in every aspect his art was entirely new. Starting with the subject matter, which is often linked with the philosophical and literary trends of Padua University and bears witness to a novel conception of nature and of man's relationship to the world around him, Giorgione conceived a picture as a "poem," a mysterious moment filled with suspense, as if in expectation of some decisive natural event.

GIORGIONE *The Madonna with Sts. Francis and Liberale* · c. 1500 · Oil on panel · 78¾ × 59⅞″ · Church of San Liberale, Castelfranco Veneto

Other essentials of Giorgione's vision are the shrewd interpretation of character, the representation of space by tonal relations of light-drenched colors, and the loose handling that sacrifices firm contours to delicate effects of atmosphere and light. Titian, the greatest of Venetian sixteenth-century painters, took as his point of departure Giorgione's deeply committed art.

GIORGIONE *The Three Philosophers* · c. 1505 · Oil on canvas · 47⅝ × 55½″ · Kunsthistorisches Museum, Vienna

Music, as Walter Pater remarked, was perhaps more important for Giorgione than for any other artist. This statement applies less to his subject matter than to the rhapsodic composition of his pictures. His great love of scenery stemmed from Giovanni Bellini, who was perhaps the first painter to compose modern landscapes. Giorgione's reputation with posterity is based on a very small number of works, but they suffice to make us see him as a painter who was at once dreamer and scientist (after the manner of Leonardo), idyllic sentimentalist and rational philosopher.

GIORGIONE *Gipsy and Soldier*, also known as "*The Tempest*" · c. 1506 · Oil on canvas · 30⅝ × 28⅞″ · Academy of Fine Arts, Venice

Many of Giorgione's pictures are statements of a thesis, for he places immaterial beings, both divine and human, in vast landscapes as if to suggest that contact with nature is the only way to salvation. The so-called *Tempest* may perhaps be a scene from the life of Moses—as Calvesi proposes—but we shall never cease to be astonished by the magical, almost mysterious climate that emanates from these ruinous buildings, enigmatic figures, and threatening skies. Not satisfied with copying nature, Giorgione invented a new nature to be contemplated with new eyes. He was not only a painter but a poet and a philosopher as well.

197

GIORGIONE *Sleeping Venus* · 1508–10 · Oil on canvas · 42¾ × 68⅞″ · State Picture Gallery, Dresden

In certain pictures executed between 1505 and 1510 Giorgione and Titian worked side by side, and it is quite impossible to give to each his own. Besides the frescoes in the Fondaco dei Tedeschi (Venice), the *Fête Champêtre* in the Louvre (Paris), and the *Concert* in the Pitti Palace (Florence), they include this dreaming nude. This group of hedonistic works contrasts oddly with such works as the ruthless *Portrait of an Old Woman* (Academy of Fine Arts, Venice), which is an indictment of the ravages of time. Their common factor is perhaps Horace's "carpe diem," a warning to enjoy the good things of life before it is too late.

SEBASTIANO DEL PIOMBO (1485–1547) *Pietà* · c. 1516 · Oil on panel · 106¼ × 74¾″ · Museo Civico, Viterbo

This Venetian painter, a pupil of Giovanni Bellini and Cima da Conegliano, was strongly influenced by Giorgione. It was he who finished the *Three Philosophers*. In 1511 he went to Rome, where he felt the impact of Michelangelo's vigorous drawing and sought to reconcile it with the tonal coloring of the Venetians. He often succeeds in creating an atmosphere of drama by isolating his figures in the tragic solitude of nature. The livid skies and hallucinatory scenery of some of his works count among the first examples of suggesting landscape as a state of mind. Their subjects may be religious (as in this *Pietà*) or mythological (as in the *Death of Adonis* in the Uffizi).

TITIAN (c. 1480–1576) *The Penitent Magdalen* · c. 1530 · Oil on panel · 33½ × 26¾″ · Pitti Palace, Florence

Titian was certainly the greatest exponent of the Venetian School in the sixteenth century. After studying under Giovanni Bellini, he was Giorgione's closest follower. But it was not long before he abandoned the latter's elegiac melancholy and sought a more robust classicism, and a monumental composition based essentially on tonal coloring. He exerted a decisive influence on Venetian painters in the sixteenth and seventeenth centuries.

TITIAN *Portrait of a Lady*, also known as "*La Bella*" · 1536 · Oil on panel · 39½ × 29½″ · Pitti Palace, Florence

Titian painted hundreds of pictures on an infinity of subjects, which are now dispersed throughout the whole world. His career could be traced through his successive commissions. When the generation of Bellini and Carpaccio drew to a close, and after Giorgione's untimely death, he became the official painter of Venice. From 1516 to 1529 he worked for the Estense court in Ferrara, producing among other pictures his famous Bacchanals; from 1525 to 1536 for the Gonzaga court in Mantua; and from 1532 to 1545 for the della Rovere court in Urbino. It was during this latter period that he painted the captivating "*Bella*" in the Pitti Palace.

TITIAN (c. 1480–1576) *Sacred and Profane Love* · c. 1515 · Oil on canvas · 46½ × 109⅞″ · Borghese Gallery, Rome

The two maidens seated at the sarcophagus are not natural persons but gracious deities native to the soil, the waters, and the trees of an idyllic land—the most succulent fruits of that terrestrial season. The slowly setting sun marks the passage of a magic hour, an immemorial period of time. The ancient sarcophagus, to which the quietly bubbling spring lends a tenuous animation amid a harmonious nature, also seems to allude to a time and space in which the only possible occurrences are the pulses and pauses of light and shade, their intensification and attenuation, their identification with the color. The space is tonal, painterly, not because the rhythm of the perspective is transferred to the color harmonies but because it is open as far as the vibrations of the color can reach, because every tone is matched by other tones and every human accent rouses concordant echoes in nature. Breaks in the context of tones are supplied by the slender stems and dark foliage of the trees silhouetted against the bright sky—pauses in a space measured by the intensity of the echoes roused by the high-pitched, long-held notes of color. This painting is not an abstraction of reality in an exemplary form; it is the story of an emotion that grows and spreads to nature, on which it casts so strong a light that it is tantamount to love of nature. Here form is but the touch of the brush exploited to its ultimate consequences, the accent of light and color that vibrates endlessly in the wide open space.

Detail is shown on next pages

199

TITIAN *Danaë* · 1553 · Oil on canvas · 50⅜ × 70⅛″ · The Prado, Madrid

In 1545–46 Titian stayed in Rome, where he worked for Pope Paul III. He met Michelangelo and painted portraits of the Pope, the cardinals, and men of letters (e.g., Pietro Bembo). This *Danaë*, painted for Ottavio Farnese, prompted Michelangelo's famous phrase, "What a pity these Venetians don't know how to draw!" The experience of Roman art, especially that of Raphael and Michelangelo, led Titian to give his forms greater vigor but did nothing to weaken his natural vision of color and light. On the contrary, as his compositions become more dramatic, the effects of color and light become more intense.

TITIAN *The Fall of Man* · c. 1570 · Oil on canvas · 114⅛ × 73¼″ · The Prado, Madrid

During the last years of Titian's life his forms are carved by light, dissolved in rapid gleams of color that give an astonishingly modern impression. The great themes of history, religion, and mythology are enveloped in an atmosphere of tragic desperation. Hallucinatory, sulfurous skies, rent by flashes of lightning, brood over scenes of death or torment (from the *Martyrdom of St. Sebastian* to the *Crowning with Thorns*, from the *Death of Lucretia* to the *Flaying of Marsyas*). In his youth Titian had painted legends and myths in idyllic or passionate accents; in his old age he lost his smile and death cast its shadow on the magical world of myth (or, as here, on the enchantment of the Garden of Eden). In his last masterpiece, the *Descent from the Cross* that he painted for his own tomb, tragedy swoops in a roaring dive to rise again with the desperate force of catharsis.

TITIAN *Self-Portrait* · c. 1562 · Oil on canvas · 33⅞ × 25⅝″ · The Prado, Madrid

During the last thirty years of his life Titian worked for the kings of Spain, first Charles V (of whom he did some magnificent portraits) and then Philip II (to whom he sent several mythological pictures that he called "poems"). Titian was not only the "pure" painter who fascinated Delacroix; nor was it his mission to leave a dramatic message for future artists: his place in the history of art is very much his own. It was due to him that art ceased to be a laborious handicraft and became a respected profession, one might almost say an instrument of diplomacy.

PALMA VECCHIO (1480–1528) *The Meeting of Jacob and Rachel* · c. 1525 · Oil on canvas · 57½ × 98⅜″ · State Picture Gallery, Dresden

A follower of Giorgione, Palma Vecchio long remained true to the master's manner. But his interpretation is rather pallid and conventional and lacks the spark of genius. It is only in his last works that he seems to have observed the novelty of Titian's composition and coloring, as witnessed by the triptych in Santa Maria Formosa (Venice) and the portraits, mostly female, he painted at that time.

LORENZO LOTTO (1480–1556) *Portrait of an Old Man* (detail) · c. 1544 · Oil on canvas · 35⅜ × 29½″ · Brera Gallery, Milan

Lotto was probably born in Venice, but he traveled the length and breadth of Italy, from Venetia to Lombardy, from the Marches to Rome. His painting, which was first in the manner of Bellini and the Vivarinis, is a curious blend of the cultured and the popular. His art is not "naïve" and provincial, as many people believe, but extremely refined and aristocratic. Without Lotto there would be no Brescian School, and his influence was preponderant in Lombardy until the contemplative earthiness of Caravaggio's early work.

JACOPO BASSANO (JACOPO DA PONTE) (c. 1510–92) *St. Roch Visiting the Plague-Stricken* (detail) · 1575 · Oil on canvas · 137¾ × 82¾″ · Brera Gallery, Milan

This native of the Venetian mainland was long credited with inventing the realistic, popular genre picture. In reality, his novel manner of rendering religious subjects by setting them amid scenes from everyday life is linked with the novelty of his style. After first experiencing Pordenone's influence and a still closer contact with the Mannerists, he developed a new conception of pictorial space. His sharp, broken line, disrupting the unity of the form and exposing it to a violent light, is mingled with the pigment to produce a unity of painterly texture never before achieved.

GIOVANNI BATTISTA MORONI (c. 1525–78) *Portrait of a Tailor* · Oil on canvas · 37 × 29⅛″ · National Gallery, London

Moroni, a native of Bergamo, was chiefly a portrait painter. He is very important because he abandoned the courtly or heroic tradition of portraiture and gave it a social role, what might be called a "middle-class" character. In his severe altarpieces the simple composition and cool colors are contrasted with a dynamic conception that resembles Titian's.

TINTORETTO (1518–94) *Susanna and the Elders* · c. 1560 · Oil on canvas · 76 × 95⅝″ · Kunsthistorisches Museum Vienna

Ridolfi assures us that Tintoretto studied in Titian's workshop, but there is certainly little of Titian in his pictures, whether early or late. Important influences were Jacopo Sansovino, Schiavone, and the Mannerists of the Florentine-Roman School. Tintoretto's own contribution is his love of movement and contrasted light. Indeed, in his most famous works, what heightens the contrasts of light and shade is precisely the vertiginous movement.

TINTORETTO *The Three Graces* · 1578 · Oil on canvas · 57½ × 61" · Ducal Palace, Venice

After studying Michelangelo—he is known to have copied plaster casts of the figures in the Medici Chapel in Florence—Tintoretto came across the untrammeled poetry of Paolo Veronese's art, whose bright light and wide open spaces he has adopted here. Critics have often associated these pictures with the names of Manet and Renoir. But they are exceptions: the characteristic trait of Tintoretto's enormous oeuvre is the vast range of dramatic composition. To emphasize the muscular vigor of his dynamic figures, he employed a violent lighting that throws sudden flashes of light on the salient forms.

TINTORETTO *Christ in the House of Martha and Mary* · c. 1580 · Oil on canvas · 66⅝ × 57⅛" · Alte Pinakothek, Munich

Tintoretto painted this picture while he was producing his masterpiece, the huge cycle in the Scuola di San Rocco in Venice (1564–87). The enormous size of the vast work inspired him with a truly cosmic vision. Iconography is forgotten, composition is dissolved in light and shadow, all is drama. The inspiration is genuinely pre-Romantic. Tragedy, which many critics see here, is really absent; but we can feel it slowly approach.

VERONESE (1528–88) *St. Mennas* · Detail of the organ shutter from San Gemigniano in Venice · c. 1560 · Oil on canvas · 97¼ × 48" · Estense Gallery, Modena

Veronese received his training in Verona but worked in Venice. Parmigianino's elegant draftsmanship was an important influence. He was an eloquent, fertile painter who did historical pictures, portraits, and large-scale decorative works; above all he was a magnificent colorist. In his frescoes and canvases the color is laid on in ample compositions, mostly viewed from below to allow the figures, which are often boldly foreshortened, a freer projection into the air and light.

VERONESE *Infidelity* · c. 1565 · Oil on canvas · 74¾ × 74¾" · National Gallery, London

Unlike Titian, who harmonized his colors in low, golden tones, Veronese favored the higher ranges and bright colors. The silvery light, instead of falling on the forms, appears to be emitted by the refined color harmonies. Veronese's masterpiece is the fresco decoration in the Villa Barbaro at Maser, which brings Palladio's solemn architecture to life. Here the painter has become a magician: he opens up *trompe l'oeil* vistas, evokes Olympus and the elements, alternates the most fantastic allegories with the most realistic scenes from daily life.

VERONESE *The Crucifixion* · c. 1575 · Oil on canvas · 40⅛ × 40⅛″ · The Louvre, Paris

Modern critics have called Veronese the first "pure" painter, and Cézanne mentioned him as one of his favorites. In 1573, when he painted the *Supper in the House of Levi* (now in the Venice Academy), he was summoned to defend himself before the tribunal of the Inquisition. He had put in his picture jesters, German halberdiers, parrots, Negroes, and drunken men. His plea makes him a precursor of "art for art's sake": "We painters take the same liberties as poets and fools. If any room is left in a picture I fill it with figures to suit my whim." He was acquitted.

ALBRECHT DÜRER (1471–1528) *Portrait of the Painter's Father* · 1497 · Canvas · 20⅛ × 15¾″ · National Gallery, London

Dürer, one of the most eminent figures of the European Renaissance, was trained in the tradition of the German illustrators under Michael Wolgemut in Nuremberg. He went to Venice for the first time in 1494 and returned there in 1505 and in 1507. In his oeuvre, paintings and graphic works are equally important. The dramatic scenes of the Passion and the profound symbolic visions of the Apocalypse reveal a new sense of volume due in part to Italian influence and in part to his own theories on perspective and the proportions of space and form.

ALBRECHT DÜRER *Self-Portrait* · 1498 · Panel · 20¼ × 15⅞″ · The Prado, Madrid

Dürer's oeuvre embodies a whole new humanistic culture, which differs from that of the great Italians of the sixteenth century but has a no less historical and philosophical foundation. But his classicism is the expression of an almost religious aspiration rather than of actual historical experience. For Dürer antiquity is the region of profound thinking, of nature, and of symbols; but it is attained through the dramatic experience of the Christian faith and the constant harassing thought of sin and death.

ALBRECHT DÜRER *Fife Player and Drummer* · One section of the Jabach Altar · c. 1505 · Oil on panel · 37 × 20⅛″ · Wallraf Richartz Museum, Cologne

Dürer's attitude to religion had an important bearing on his artistic vision. At first he was close to the humanism of Erasmus, later increasingly committed to the ideals of Luther's Reformation. He was also a great writer, a poet, a student of scientific and experimental problems, an inventor of systems of fortification, and an author of treatises on art. His universality puts him on a par with Leonardo da Vinci.

ALBRECHT DÜRER *The Adoration of the Magi* · 1504 · Panel ·
37¾ × 44⅝″ · Uffizi Gallery, Florence

Dürer's first works were painted in the Gothic style, but
the courage of the exile proved his salvation. The urge
towards the South was a myth that maintained its validity
until Goethe's day. Among his graphic works must be
mentioned the cycle of the *Apocalypse*, which he treated
with popular, evangelical feeling. It was the age of witch
hunts, the Inquisition, the Peasants' War in Bavaria, and
great social ills. In these woodcuts Dürer synthesizes an
atmosphere of despair and of expectation for the end of the
world.

ALBRECHT DÜRER *Madonna and Child* · 1512 · Panel ·
19¼ × 14⅝″ · Kunsthistorisches Museum, Vienna

Dürer did some forty watercolors that have a place of their
own in his oeuvre. Critics have gone so far as to speak of
"Impressionism" in connection with these travel jottings.
But it is among his copper engravings, which are less
"popular" than his woodcuts, that we find Dürer's masterpieces—portraits (*Melanchthon, Pirckheimer, Erasmus*),
pure fantasies (*Knight, Death, and Devil, Melancholy*), magic
spells and alchemists' dreams (the *Doctor's Dream*, the
206   *Sea Monster*).

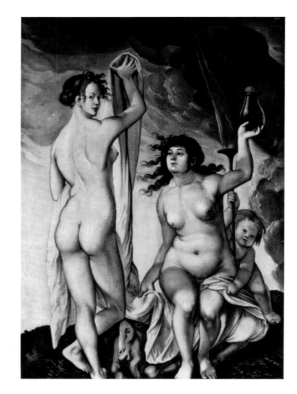

HANS BALDUNG GRIEN (c. 1480–1545) *Sacred and Profane
Love* · 1523 · Panel · 25⅝ × 18⅛″ · Städel Institute,
Frankfurt

Like his friend Dürer, Baldung was committed to the new
"Italian humanism." His figures are drawn in accordance
with the new laws of proportion and conform to an ideal
canon of "beauty." But in the mind of this northern humanist
the concepts of history and nature evoke the thought
of the flight of time and the brevity of life, the sense of sin
and death. He is fascinated by the motif of Death embracing
and seducing a young woman, namely, the theme that death
is the sole reality, whereas beauty is a vain illusion.

LUCAS CRANACH THE ELDER (1472–1553) *Judith with the
Head of Holophernes* · Panel · 33⅞ × 23⅜″ · Kunsthistorisches Museum, Vienna

The elder Cranach was the most important German painter,
after Dürer, of the early sixteenth century; he is noteworthy, too, for having joined the Reformation. He was
almost ostentatiously insensitive to the new formal
researches of Dürer and Altdorfer and continued to employ
the intense linearity and brilliant "local" coloring of the
Gothic tradition. But in his choice of subject matter he
adopted many motifs of the new German humanists, which
he linked with the tenets of the Reformation.

LUCAS CRANACH THE ELDER *The Judgment of Paris* · Panel · $40\frac{1}{8} \times 27\frac{7}{8}''$ · Metropolitan Museum of Art, New York

Cranach studied Dürer's engravings, but preferred idyl or elegy to drama. From 1505 until his death he worked at the court of Frederick the Wise, Elector of Saxony, but he always remained a free-lance artist and never became a courtier. At first sight, Cranach seems less universal than Dürer and less inclined to drama and pathos than Grünewald, but his painting is so rich and varied that he deserves a place among the three "Magi" of German sixteenth-century art.

LUCAS CRANACH THE ELDER *The Nymph of Spring* · Palitz Collection, New York

Cranach's painting is modulated and rhythmical; his extremely elegant profiles recall the firmness of Japanese prints, not Gothic vagueness. That is why he does not excel in portraits and religious pictures but is at his best in refined erotic subjects. The women he depicted, though the last word in refinement, do not conform to the classic canons of beauty, for he is not concerned with representing "Womanhood" or "Beauty" but a diabolical quality or a cold, provocative sensuality. And when he paints a Venus, we can sense his nostalgia for the pagan world.

MATHIAS GRÜNEWALD (c.1460–1528) *The Crucifixion* · Detail from the Isenheim Altar · 1512–15 · Panel · $105\frac{7}{8} \times 120\frac{7}{8}''$ · Unterlinden Museum, Colmar

Grünewald and Dürer were the great German painters of the sixteenth century, but Grünewald had no contact whatsoever with formal classical culture. The essential quality of his painting is the extreme dramatic tension of religious inspiration and the dual trend towards disconsolate realism and sublime transcendentalism. He was a mystic and a visionary; his use of color and light was more symbolic than naturalistic, but their violent contrasts make the gestures and expressions of his figures all the more tragic.

MATHIAS GRÜNEWALD *The Nativity* · Detail from the Isenheim Altar · 1512–15 · Panel · $105\frac{7}{8} \times 120\frac{7}{8}''$ · Unterlinden Museum, Colmar

Grünewald was not widely known during his lifetime and was rediscovered only a half century ago. In the Isenheim altarpiece he treated the same subjects as other painters of his day—the *Passion of Christ*, the *Temptation of the Hermit*, the *Joys of the Virgin*, the *Triumph of Heaven*. But Grünewald seems to exaggerate every aspect of reality; he sees Hell on all sides and the Devil constantly intervening in human affairs.

207

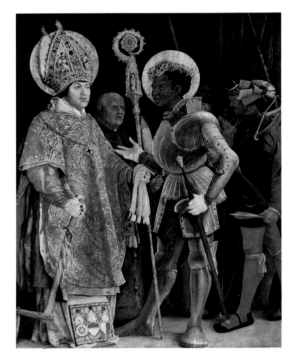

MATHIAS GRÜNEWALD *Debate between Sts. Erasmus and Maurice* · 1520–22 · Panel · 89 × 69¼″ · Alte Pinakothek, Munich

Grünewald was a splendid draftsman and gave his line the same sharpness and violence we observe in his contrasts of color and light. Indeed, the taut, broken, violent line intensifies the colors and light, giving the figures an inner energy that frequently develops into a wild excitement. His first known work, the *Mocking of Christ*, in Munich, has surprising points of contact with the fantasies of Hieronymus Bosch, which could also be explained by his knowledge of Leonardo's burlesque *"capricci."*

HANS HOLBEIN THE YOUNGER (1497–1543) *Portrait cf the Artist's Wife with Katharina and Philipp* · c. 1528 · Paper (later glued on panel) · 31½ × 25⅝″ · Museum of Art, Basel

The younger Holbein was certainly in touch with Lombard painting between 1518 and 1519, perhaps also with Lotto and the Venetians. After 1519 he worked mostly in Basel, where he deviated more and more from the harsh lines and colors of the German tradition. A work like the *Christ in the Tomb* in Basel (which so greatly impressed Dostoevsky) could not have been painted without an Italian prototype such as Marco Basaiti's picture in Venice. In his well-balanced altarpieces Holbein frequently adopted the arrangement Giorgione employed in his Castelfranco altarpiece.

HANS HOLBEIN THE YOUNGER *Portrait of Henry VIII* · 1540 · Panel · 34⅞ × 29⅜″ · National Gallery, Rome

In 1526 Holbein went to London at Thomas More's invitation and stayed there for two years. In 1532, when the Reformation deprived him of a livelihood in Basel, he went back to England, where he died of the plague in 1543. He did a quantity of portraits of the king and his queens, of bishops, courtiers, and foreigners, and in 1536 he was appointed official painter to the English court. His severe, piercing vision gave English painting a decisive impulse, just as Van Dyck's stately style did a century later.

ALBRECHT ALTDORFER (c. 1480–1538) *Battle of Issus* (detail) · 1529 · Panel · 55½ × 47⅛″ · Alte Pinakothek, Munich

Altdorfer's naturalism is charged with allegorical, even esoteric overtones and in his fantastic visions ancient history blends with medieval legend. He was the first great painter of landscapes (with and without figures). These prove that he knew the laws of Italian perspective, but he used it only to multiply indefinitely the succession of his images. The figures in his religious and historical pictures are small and find their place within nature's limitless variety.

QUENTIN MASSYS (c. 1455–1530) *Canon Stephen Gardiner* · c. 1520 · Panel · 28¾ × 23⅝″ · Liechtenstein Gallery, Vaduz

Massys was a musician and a man of culture who counted such famous men as David, Erasmus, and Dürer among his friends. His chiaroscuro recalls Leonardo's but, though he certainly traveled in Italy, he always maintained his independence. His very original grotesque and ironical pictures —e.g., the *Ill-Assorted Couple* (Paris, private collection) and the *Usurers* (Rome, Doria Pamphili Gallery)—are so close to caricature that one is led to believe that he knew those of Leonardo.

MABUSE (JAN GOSSAERT) (c. 1480–c. 1534) *Danaë* · 1527 · Panel · 44⅞ × 37⅜″ · Alte Pinakothek, Munich

This Flemish painter is important on account of transmitting his contacts with Italian artistic culture. He went to Italy in 1508 and worked as a miniaturist on the Grimani Breviary. From Leonardo he learned to paint wide spaces and plastic fullness of form, but that did not deter him from the meticulous study of detail. He was the first painter in austere Flanders to adopt mythological themes, and this led him very often to insert nude figures in his pictures. The cold light that bathes his mythological figures gives them a timeless quality.

JOACHIM PATINIR (c. 1480–1524) *Rest on the Flight into Egypt* (detail) · Canvas · 47⅝ × 69⅝″ · The Prado, Madrid

Patinir was a Fleming who may have studied under David and worked as a landscape painter in collaboration with Joos van Cleve and Quentin Massys. He was one of the first great Flemish landscape painters and is noteworthy for his sense of atmosphere. His views, painted mostly in blue tones, were admired by Dürer. Patinir sees man as immersed in the cosmos and he paints the world from above in order to depict the broadest possible area of it. His profound vision of nature recalls Bosch's fantasies, and his "psychological" landscapes—e.g., his innumerable *Temptations*—have a pre-Romantic tone.

BERNARD VAN ORLEY (1488–1541) *Portrait of Doctor Georg Zelle* · 1519 · Panel · 15⅛ × 12⅜″ · Royal Museum of Fine Arts, Brussels

Van Orley is the leading representative of the Flemish "Romanists." At an early age he saw Raphael's tapestry cartoons. The tapestry cartoons of hunting scenes that he later made for the Emperor Maximilian (now in the Louvre) show a more decided tendency toward the Baroque. Although he misunderstood Raphael and Michelangelo, reminiscences of them occur in all his monumental works. There is greater originality in his portraits, where he keeps to the more intimate Flemish tradition.

LUCAS VAN LEYDEN (1495–1533) *Card Players* · c. 1511 ·
Panel · 13⅜ × 18¾ · Collection Earl of Pembroke, Wilton
House, Salisbury, England

Lucas van Leyden was greatly praised by Dürer, who
painted his portrait. He often breaks loose from moral and
allegorical themes to become a disillusioned observer of
everyday life—a vision inherited by the Dutch "little
masters" of the seventeenth century. His painting is extraordinarily incisive and economical—a quality due to his
experience of engraving on copper and wood. The *Last
Judgment*, of 1526, is a monumental work in which he synthesized the Gothic tradition and the Michelangelesque
style. It was certainly through Van Orley that Lucas van
Leyden assimilated the Italian influence.

JAN VAN SCOREL (1495–1562) *Mary Magdelen* · 1529 · Canvas · 26⅜ × 29⅞" · Rijksmuseum, Amsterdam

A "Romanist" like his master Mabuse, and far removed
from Lucas van Leyden, Jan van Scorel worked chiefly in
Antwerp as a portrait painter and played an important part
in the development of Flemish painting in the direction of
the Italians' spacious conception of color. In 1522 he was
summoned to Rome by his compatriot Pope Adrian IV to
succeed Raphael as Superintendent of Antiquities. He
painted a great many portraits; one of the most noteworthy
is that of his mistress, Agata van Schoonhoven, in the Doria
Pamphili Gallery in Rome.

MAERTEN VAN HEEMSKERCK (1498–1574) *Portrait of Anna
Codde* · 1529 · Panel · 33⅛ × 25⅝" · Rijksmuseum, Amsterdam

This painter and engraver is the most interesting of the
Dutch "Romanists" for his rigid forms in bold relief, his
crude, violent colors, his expressive figures, and the novelty
of his compositions. He traveled in Italy, where he particularly admired Michelangelo and the Mannerists. In Rome
he did engravings of ancient and contemporary monuments, which are also very important as documents. His
Self-Portrait with the Coliseum (1533, at Cambridge) is very
revealing of either his sense of man's littleness or his
nostalgia for classical antiquity.

ANTONIS MOR (1519–76/7) *Portrait of Mary Tudor* · 1554 ·
Canvas · 39 × 33⅛" · The Prado, Madrid

This Flemish painter was Dutch by birth and studied under
Jan van Scorel. He went to Rome in 1550, then to Spain,
to Utrecht, and, finally, to England. Visibly influenced by
Italian painting and especially by Parmigianino, he was a
keen-eyed portraitist, capable of rendering every shade of
character with his supple line and refined colors. He vied
with Titian as portrait painter to the courts of Portugal and
Spain.

PIETER BRUEGEL THE ELDER (1525/30–69) *The Blind Leading the Blind* · 1568 · Tempera on canvas · $33\frac{7}{8} \times 60\frac{5}{8}''$ · National Gallery of Capodimonte, Naples

There is no alternative in Bruegel's world: all men are equal in blindness and folly, and the more they attempt to use cunning and fraud, the more they appear to be the supine slaves of fate, for men are born to be rogues and cheats. Kings, bishops, soldiers, burghers, and peasants, all bear the same guilt and share the same fate. This picture of the blind is almost emblematic. When the first falls, all the others must fall too, not because of a logical sequence of cause and effect but of a simple, yet inevitable, chain of accidents. How many of Bruegel's figures wear their caps over their eyes to show that the world goes blindfold! They are not blind but, like the ostrich, they bury their heads in the sand so as not to see or be seen. In fact, all men are hypocrites; in this world even virtue is but knavery and malice. And all men are fools because vice and folly are one. And this folly is no longer good-natured and kindly, a sort of providential condition of social intercourse like that praised by Erasmus, for the Lutheran tidal wave has overthrown the order on which society was based, destroyed the conventions that made manners gentle and cohabitation pleasant, and contrasted the utter baseness of man with the sublime excellence of God. The humanity painted by Bruegel seems free to the point of license, yet that license, which is not freedom but slavery, obliges it to repeat the gestures it has always made in order to attest in every act that its punishment is deserved. *Detail is shown on next pages*

211

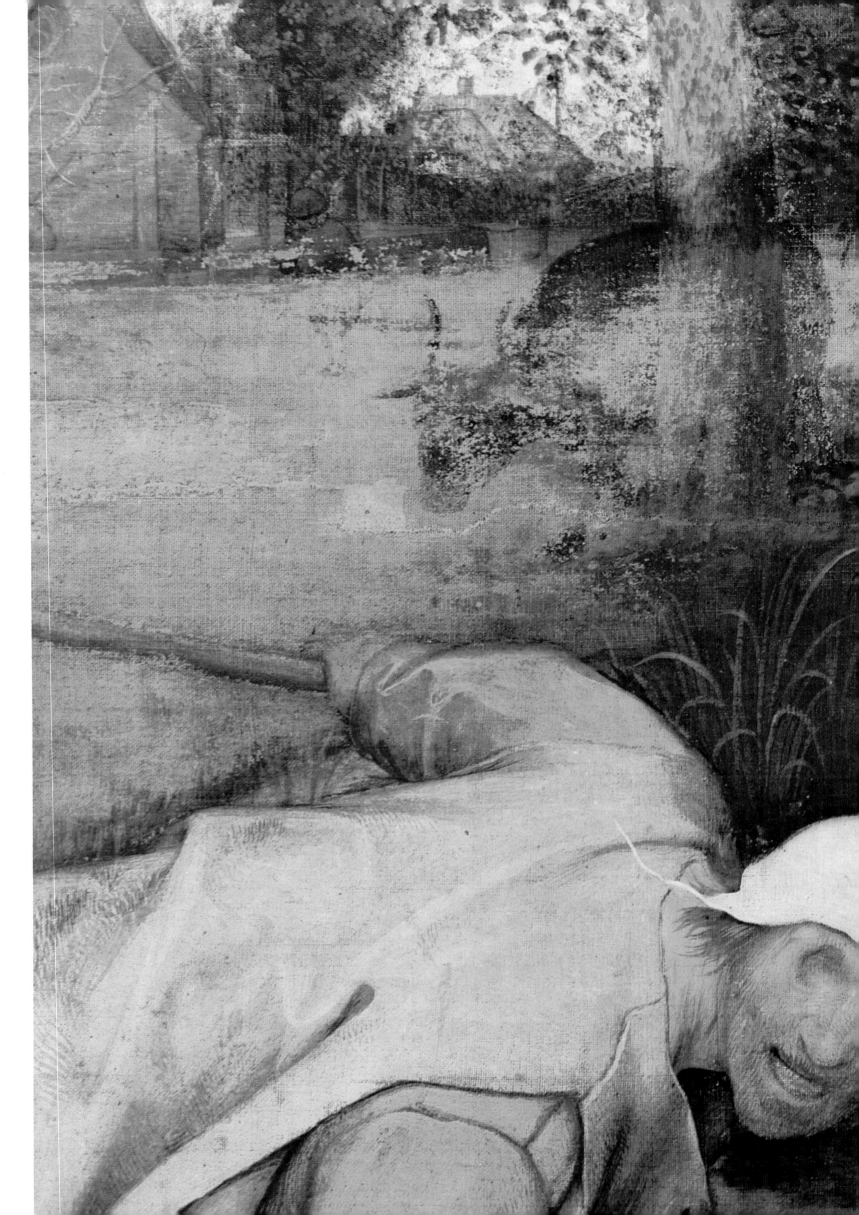

JOACHIM BEUCKELAAR (c. 1530–74) *The Egg Vendor* · 1565 ·
Panel · 49⅝ × 31⅞″ · Royal Museum of Fine Arts, Antwerp

Beuckelaar was born and lived in Antwerp, where he worked
side by side with Pieter Aertsen. He excelled in genre
pictures and especially in still lifes, in which he used a
broad handling and lively colors. He influenced Italian
painting, especially in the North. Beuckelaar took his
themes—peddlers, market gardeners, housewives, domestic
animals—from the everyday life of the lower classes. His
painting, though not of an elevated tone, often attains a
fluent facility that presages the seventeenth century and
Rubens.

PIETER BRUEGEL THE ELDER *Hunters in the Snow*, or *February*
· 1565 · Tempera on panel · 46⅛ × 63¾″ · Kunsthistorisches Museum, Vienna

Bruegel not only created a new style, whose apparently
cursory manner suited the country people he depicted, he
was also a tireless inventor of new subjects. He took his
themes from popular religion, proverbs, almanacs, and the
biblical parables beloved of the people. But he was more
than a painter of facile anecdotes and the chronicler of a
depressed humanity: he was deeply interested in social and
political affairs.

PIETER BRUEGEL THE ELDER (1525/30–69) *The Tower of
Babel* · c. 1563 · Tempera on panel · 44⅞ × 61″ · Kunsthistorisches Museum, Vienna

Little is known of Bruegel's life, but his works prove that
Bosch made a lasting impression on him. In 1551 he went
to Italy—visiting Rome, Naples, and perhaps Sicily too—
and he undoubtedly came into contact with Leonardo's
work. Bruegel's landscapes are no mere decorative back-
drops; they are an active component in the vicissitudes of
the miserable humanity he portrayed with fraternal sympathy. When he tried his hand at a difficult subject like the
Tower of Babel, he used a tone at once homely and legendary. His aim was not to write history but to tell a tale.

PIETER BRUEGEL THE ELDER *The Harvest*, or *August* ·
1565 · Tempera on panel · 46⅛ × 63″ · Metropolitan
Museum of Art, New York

The seasons follow each other with the implacable rhythm
of time and death, but also of resurrection—exactly as in
pagan mythology. And Bruegel seems to warn us in the
tones of a gospel parable or a "memento mori." Bosch
described a grotesque, diabolical world, which he identified
with a metaphysical sphere; Bruegel, instead, seeks out the
diabolical and grotesque aspects of life here on earth. He is
a moralist, though as a rule he leaves us to draw the moral of
his parables.

JEAN CLOUET (c. 1485–1540) *Portrait of Francis I* · c. 1535 · Panel · 37⅞ × 29⅛" · The Louvre, Paris

Jean Clouet was the first of a family of portrait painters famous for an extreme refinement of drawing and color. Particularly worthy of note are his portrait drawings and sketches. He also painted *Francis I on Horseback* (Florence, Uffizi Gallery). But he never pierced his sitters' outer shell nor attempted a psychological interpretation, for he was concerned only with elegance and decoration. It should be borne in mind that in the sixteenth century the French were still building cathedrals in the international Gothic style.

SCHOOL OF FONTAINEBLEAU (about the middle of the sixteenth century) *Diana the Huntress* · c. 1550 · Panel · 74⅞ × 52⅜" · The Louvre, Paris

Francis I started to build the castle of Fontainebleau in 1528, when he was released from imprisonment. From 1533 to 1534 the pictorial decoration was entrusted to Rosso Fiorentino and Primaticcio. The ballroom frescoed by the latter was built under Henry II; Luca Penni, Bagnacavallo, and Niccolò dell'Abbate also lent a hand. Fontainebleau played an essential part in the history of Mannerism and the spread of classicist culture in France and the rest of Europe.

SCHOOL OF FONTAINEBLEAU *Venus, Mars, and Cupid* · Panel · 38⅝ × 31½" · The Petit Palais Museum, Paris

Fontainebleau produced a very active school of painters who followed in the footsteps of the Italian Mannerists. Its major representatives are Antoine Caron, an intellectual whose pictures recreated a fairytale vision of ancient Rome, and Jean Cousin, a sensualist and libertine. Many of the most interesting works of this school are by unknown painters, for instance, those grouped under the name of "Master of Flora," in which Italianism is dissolved in a languid, decadent style of the utmost refinement.

215

the seventeenth
and eighteenth centuries

Michael Levey

The new fabric of the seventeenth and eighteenth centuries was woven from a rich Italian Renaissance past, dominated right up to 1800 by the giant *cinquecento* figures of Raphael and Titian. Over this period there was gradual change rather than a break at any specific point. Titian seems to merge into Tintoretto, who already constructs a highly personal but Baroque world; the same is true of El Greco, whose stormy visionary art may be taken either as a final manifestation of the Renaissance or as a prelude to the full Baroque of the seventeenth century.

But there was a significant shift before the end of the sixteenth century, a shift destined to have important effects on nearly all the great European artists of the subsequent period. The finest flower of the Venetian Renaissance was withering: it expired with the death of Tintoretto in 1594. In the following year Annibale Carracci left his native Bologna for Rome where he was to settle. Already the other great North Italian painter, Caravaggio, was working in Rome. In 1600 Rubens arrived in Italy, and in the following year he visited Rome for the first time. Thus, by the beginning of the seventeenth century, Rome held a trinity of talent in three artists who stand as the founder-figures and representatives of their century.

As the century progressed Rome became more firmly entrenched as the artistic capital, not merely of Italy, but of all Europe. Venice retained the prestige of its great past; the sixteenth-century Venetian school exercised enormous and significant influence on virtually every great seventeenth-century painter. An oscillation was set up between the two poles, Venice and Rome. Sometimes they could be synthesized, but often they were directly opposed, and their dichotomy was expressed in such quarrels as those over color and drawing, or nature versus antiquity. The contribution of Venice remained, however, in the past, for during the seventeenth century it utterly failed to produce a great painter and only temporarily accommodated great painters from elsewhere. Rome was the modern meeting place of living talents, the most active center of patronage. Through it there passed Rubens and Van Dyck and Velázquez; Claude and Poussin settled there, as did Elsheimer. Of leading native painters, the Carracci and Caravaggio were succeeded there by the generation of Domenichino, Reni, and Pietro da Cortona; and they in turn by Carlo Maratta, whose long career brings us well into the eighteenth century. For a hundred years Rome held the hegemony.

Although Rome was the dominant seventeenth-century city, it did not impose any specifically Roman style. Rather, it accommodated all styles and extremes, ranging from the almost rudely naturalistic to elevated classicism. It was as much the city of the Bambocciants painters, with their predilection for genre, as it was the city of Sacchi and Poussin. Between these extremes Rome fostered a style of exciting, colorful, decorative art that was given the name of Baroque. In fact, the classical and the Baroque were not in clear-cut opposition to each other. They shared a common origin in the work of Annibale Carracci for the Farnese Gallery. Here, although the large frescoes are conceived as dignified easel pictures, the general effect of the elaborate medallions, *putti*, stucco figures, etc., is certainly Baroque in its illusionism. The curved ceiling is thought of as a long tunnel of painted canvas open at the corners to show the sky beyond. This feigning of space became typical of Baroque decoration and culminated in the aerial visions of Tiepolo in the eighteenth century. From Annibale Carracci there stemmed the two streams of imaginative history painting: the exuberant Baroque and the calmly classical—both very different from the powerful new naturalism of which Caravaggio was virtually the creator. It was here that a real division lay.

Caravaggio came to Rome with the earthy realistic tradition of North Italy behind him. His powerful, emotional, but highly realistic paintings immediately caused a sensation and had an influence which reverberated throughout Europe. While the Baroque conceives a world of almost delirious dreams, allegories, and mythologies (both sacred and profane), the art of Caravaggio is intensely concerned with ordinary humanity, with life on this earth; biblical stories are interpreted by him with vivid emphasis on the sheer facts—whether it be the humble birth of Christ or the bloody moment of St. John the Baptist's execution. This attachment to truth, the truth of things seen, gave painting a new function when it moved on to record the everyday facts about the world. Rembrandt and the whole Dutch School, Velázquez and Zurbarán, the Le Nain brothers, Rubens, all extend the actual subject matter of painting, very much as the philosophers and scientists of the period were extending knowledge about man and nature. The seventeenth century was conscious of challenging those medieval assumptions which had continued to guide Renaissance man—and this was as much of a rebellion as Caravaggio's artistic one. The truths expressed by Galileo were deliberately contradicted by the Church, which broke the man but was eventually unable to resist his conclusions. Outside Italy religion was concerned more with justifying itself on moral than on miraculous grounds, and it is significant that Locke should write not only the *Essay Concerning Humane Understanding*, but also *The Reasonableness of Christianity*. With the coming of the eighteenth century, reason and reality in painting were to start struggling against the Baroque, and would ultimately triumph.

Caravaggio's work naturally appealed to many northern painters also, bred in the Protestant tradition as well as in the tradition of pungently realistic painting. Though he did not positively teach, he was in effect the master of a whole school of Italian artists, at Naples as well as Rome, and of the Spaniard Ribera as well. French and Dutch painters returned to their native lands to practice a Caravaggesque realism. Landscape had already become a subject for art in the work of Altdorfer and Pieter Bruegel the Elder. In Caravaggio's Rome, the German Elsheimer played an important part in creating intimate, poetic, but realistic small pictures of landscapes where the whole atmosphere is sensitively observed. He influenced Rubens, who was also his close friend, and later Claude. In his miniature-like way, he revolutionized landscape painting in Italy, emphasizing the facts of the natural world as Caravaggio emphasized those of ordinary humanity.

While Caravaggio asserted the new, Annibale Carracci was partly asserting the traditional. The influence of Raphael was strong in him, and stronger still in his pupils. Unlike Caravaggio, he was a gifted teacher. The classical elements in his style are emphasized and reiterated by Domenichino (who came from Bologna to work near him in Rome) and Domenichino in turn was to exercise a decisive effect on Poussin's art. This was a tranquil, somewhat withdrawn world in which the painter was often more at ease in private commissions for small pictures than in large-scale decorations. A more confident and public classicism was expressed by Guido Reni, trained in the Carracci Academy at Bologna, whose late work is a positive triumph of the calm and cool-colored.

But also studying as a young man under Annibale Carracci was Lanfranco who, along with Pietro da Cortona, created the high Roman Baroque style of the seventeenth century. It is epitomized, on a vast scale, by Cortona's ceiling for the Palazzo Barberini in which he glorifies the Barberini family in allusion and allegory, and involves the whole cosmos with its fortunes. This style was to travel outside Italy too—had already traveled earlier in Rubens' work—but required princely patrons and large-scale areas to make its full effect. Even more audacious illusionistic effects were to be devised by artists like Padre Pozzo. The eighteenth century was to see these tendencies developed, not so much in Italy as in Germany and Austria—the last flights from the real into the dizzily irrational.

In seventeenth-century Italy the oscillating tendencies between naturalism and the "High" style, between Titian and Raphael, are most clearly seen in the work of Guercino. He was, significantly, not to establish himself successfully at Rome and had to retire from the center to the periphery. His early work is strongly Venetian in color and handling, and often charmingly realistic. It probably seemed somewhat undignified to Roman eyes, and Guercino returned in 1623 to his native Cento, near Bologna. In the subsequent years he evolved from his Venetian manner a calmer and more classical style, based very strongly on Reni. After Reni's death in 1642, Guercino moved to Bologna and painted in a completely classical, idealized manner, from which all the fire and poetry had fled. In him Raphael had conquered Titian; but it had not been a victory for art.

One genius was able to assimilate without difficulty the lessons of these two great men: Rubens. In the same way, he was able to draw from the two artistic streams of Caravaggio and Annibale Carracci to such an extent that it might be said paradoxically that he was the greatest Italian painter of the century. He is undoubtedly the most typical figure of the period, with a tremendous Baroque invention combined with a tremendous grasp on reality. It is symbolically right that he should have been an active traveler in Spain, France, England, and one whose art was in demand wherever he went. Rubens drew together all the strands from the past and from the early years of the seventeenth century. He became in turn a founder-figure exercising tremendous influence on the great artists who eventually came after, and exercising it far beyond his own century. He is the master of Watteau in the eighteenth century, and of Delacroix in the nineteenth.

His immediate influence in his native Flanders stimulated a whole school of followers and imitators, mostly caricaturing his vigor and realism. Only Van Dyck escaped in another direction, again under direct impressions of Italian art, into a fluent and refined painting which is less vigorous than Rubens' and more wistfully romantic. Van Dyck tends to adorn rather than explore truth, and he remains perhaps the least typical seventeenth-century painter—certainly the least typical northern painter. Strong attachment to the facts of life in Flanders is the root of Teniers' art; his peasant scenes are unprettified (but often sensitively painted). They are more sober than Bruegel's and are part of the whole European movement toward recording reality which reaches its culmination in Holland.

Here the Baroque made little appeal. Instead it was Caravaggism, brought back from Italy by artists like Terbrugghen; and the Catholic city of Utrecht was a center for this style. Honthorst, too, had been influenced by Caravaggio in Rome, and he settled at Utrecht, becoming one of the few internationally known Dutch painters of this day. In Holland it is Caravaggism, tamed and made to have less of an assault on the emotions, which leads on to the work of Vermeer. It is contained in Rembrandt, the pupil of Lastman who worked in Rome in the first decade of the seventeenth century and who was formed by the pictures of Elsheimer and Caravaggio.

Rembrandt himself is the solitary exception among the great seventeenth-century painters in

219

that he never visited Italy. But the Italian influence was inescapable and, indeed, was welcomed by him. He owed no allegiance specifically to Rome. Like Rubens, he too assimilated rather more from Titian than from Raphael. But elements from both were in his art: for his *Self-Portrait* of 1640 in the National Gallery in London, he borrowed from Raphael's *Castiglione* as well as from Titian. There is even a period of Baroque drama in Rembrandt. His refusal to travel is expressive of the deep attachment of his art to the life and conditions of his native country. All the categories of Dutch art—landscape, portrait, still life, genre—are contained in Rembrandt's work. His drawings reveal the sheer range of his art almost better than do his paintings. He is forever re-creating his environment, his family, and himself. A whole existence can be reconstructed from Rembrandt's art: a private, often unhappy life, but, thanks to art, always vivid. Rembrandt's reality is increasingly a psychological one. His early paintings show him fascinated by the appearance of things and people; light dramatically illumines surfaces. But gradually he goes beneath the surface appearance; the lighting is less abrupt and more subtle in its exploration. His portraits become less showy and more responsive to the sitter as a thinking, suffering human being. Life is no longer a record of outward fact, but an experience savored within.

For lesser Dutch painters technical competence combined with observation to produce an art that clearly mirrored outward facts—the placid landscape, the ever present sea, the market place, the breakfast table. These, too, present an unparalleled report, in pictures, of the painter's environment. Dutch patrons asked in effect to be reassured that what they saw was seen by their artists, too. They were less concerned with feeling, and only certain painters—like Ruisdael—were able to record natural phenomena with any vein of poetry. In Vermeer it is almost a super-reality which has replaced the ordinary: an environment in which shapes are painted with appreciation of their abstract beauty—preluding the beautiful abstracted reality of Braque.

Vermeer seems to belong with that grave philosophical exploration of reality that is the seventeenth century's preoccupation, and more profoundly personal to it than the outward display of the Baroque. It is the same nearly mathematical effect that in Spain was achieved by Zurbarán, but which is equally present in Velázquez. He too looks to the world about him for his subject matter. His few mythological pictures simply put ancient Greece onto solid seventeenth-century Spanish earth. Although Velázquez painted with Titianesque freedom, the results are more pondered and grave. Reality is observed with a detachment that is scientific. The painter steps back from the sitter and scrutinizes him or her to produce an effect of absolute verisimilitude, itself achieved only by an effort of will. Although the final result in a painting by Velázquez gives a powerful sense of logic and rightness and truth, these have been reached only through experiment. Thus it is probably quite wrong to identify the dispassionate appearance of Velázquez' pictures with dispassion in the painter himself. It might even be that he had a natural impulse to record the immediate impression on his senses—for which he was superbly gifted—but controlled this impulse in the search for a "truth" that was more than immediate. The authority of his pictures comes from this rigor; each object is placed with an exact sense of interval and space. Fluency in the actual paint conceals thought and gives everything a deceptively improvised air. In Zurbarán there is a heavy application of paint which increases the air of timelessness and gravity; reality is formalized much more patently than in Velázquez. Even Murillo, though much sweeter and more decorative, is attached to the realistic tendency of the century; his once popular genre pictures have a strong basis of fact in everyday street scenes. If he prettifies poverty and low life, he is at least aware of it.

Flanders, Holland, and Spain were all separated from Italy by geography or politics, but France was closely bound to Italy by uneasy proximity and by religion. These were the two countries which most fruitfully practiced artistic exchange. Italian painters were active in Paris, while both Claude and Poussin preferred Rome to their own country. French painting presents the same divisions as Italian painting at the period. An early generation of French painters, including Valentin and Vouet, worked in Rome and took back Caravaggism to France. There evolved a specifically French realism, represented by Georges de La Tour (who probably owed something to the Utrecht painters), and by the Le Nain brothers. In them religious subjects are treated as humble genre, while genre itself takes on the dignity of showing the poor as they are: neither funny nor to be sentimentalized. There are no anecdotes, but simply depictions of peasant life.

The Le Nain brothers and La Tour remained obscure painters. They represent the opposite of the state Baroque style which reached its most sumptuous flowering under Louis XIV. Vouet's decorative abilities found full scope in rich private houses and the royal palaces, and this French Baroque continued under his pupil Lebrun, whose chief work is the decoration of the Hall of Mirrors (Galerie des Glaces) at Versailles. This style was not interrupted in 1700 and is the forerunner of the Rococo in France.

By remaining in Rome, Poussin and Claude detached themselves from state patronage; they had the freedom of being *déraciné* and they created their own highly personal solutions. Poussin moved away from the first Romantic influence of Venetian painting to a much more cerebral, classical type of picture—the most classical ever created. It is strongly based on reality, and Poussin showed a preference for history over mythology. It was with almost archaeological intent that he re-created the antique world, and with profoundly philosophic implications. While he schematized and formalized the real—people and buildings and landscape—it always remained alive and never became insipid. In a more obvious way Claude poeticized reality. Sustained for subject matter entirely by the Roman Campagna, Claude drew his inspiration from nature, though what he finally created was vision blended with fact. Both painters ignored the brilliantly colored, exciting Baroque world that was being created in the Rome they lived in, and without overtly rebelling against society, asserted the artist's right to paint what he wishes.

It is an irony that by the end of the seventeenth century the movement of *Poussinisme* should have stood for a restrictive attitude to painting and thus have been brought into antagonism with the movement of *Rubénisme*. Yet, beneath these names, it was really the old dichotomy. Nature was now more important than antiquity, and draftsmanship more important than color. Throughout early eighteenth-century Europe, *Rubénisme* triumphed, standing for that tail end of the Baroque whirlwind that is the Rococo. The shift in Italy was back to Venice, where a new renaissance was taking place: Canaletto, Guardi, Rosalba Carriera, the Ricci, Pellegrini, Piazzetta, and, most triumphant of all, Tiepolo, showed that Venice again had painters who could serve the world. Simultaneously, Paris felt an impetus to new freedom, and the death of Louis XIV in 1715 accelerated the process. Venice and Paris were in close artistic contact in these early years. France produced one genius to enshrine the new freedom, Watteau: himself drawing on the twin sources of Rubens and the Italian tradition, but creating one positive new category of picture, the *fête galante*, in which mood is more important than subject. Watteau intimates, without actually proclaiming, the death of the history picture. His work has no elevated moral lesson; it is not usually on a large scale, and his patrons were private people, often his friends. What separates it from the charming but trivial contemporary decorators in France and Italy is its serious psychological and emotional power; for all its miniature scale it is always concerned with people, not puppets. It may be set, as it were, in a theater—but it is the theater of the human heart.

Meanwhile, Rococo decorators flourished. The Italians, especially the Venetians, were everywhere in demand: more were employed outside Italy than in it. Germany and Austria were particularly receptive to the Rococo and produced their own superb Rococo architecture, as well as talented painters like Maulpertsch to decorate its interiors. Germany offered to Tiepolo the greatest opportunity—and he made magnificent use of it—when he frescoed the Prince-Bishop's Palace at Würzburg in 1750-53. Though he painted Apollo, the sun-god, in full glory at the center of his ceilings, in fact twilight was quickly to follow. Tiepolo represents the apogee of the Baroque—and its end. His radiant people, so at home as they float in the clouds of enchanted skies, are the last inhabitants of that sphere. Mythologizing was about to end. Morality was to demand "truth" in art, and the Rococo was to be condemned as false.

In France the career of Boucher runs nearly parallel to Tiepolo's. Both were to be condemned by advanced tàste before their deaths in 1770. Boucher's gallant, charming, and decorative pictures do not quite create a convincing climate of their own, but they celebrate a dream of voluptuousness and artifice. His people are not supposed to be real; they are so many beautiful bodies, ripe as fruit and with the same bloom, arranged to give the spectator pleasure. Boucher has no other standard but to please. His landscapes are equally disposed so as to delight—created to look not like the real countryside, but like a playful countryside made out of silk and feathers. Truth gives place to decorative emphasis. The landscapes are as much a deception as the visionary skies painted by Rococo artists on real ceilings: feigning the existence of what everyone knows does not exist.

Such a mood was increasingly out of accord with eighteenth-century enlightenment. The previous century had produced a vast body of pictures which conveyed facts about our ordinary and visible environment. Now the eighteenth century wanted pictures which would combine with progressive opinion and the other arts to teach man how he should live in the world he had made.

It was in England—so much admired politically by the European intelligentsia—that the first painter of modern moral subjects was to be produced: William Hogarth. Hogarth was influenced by the lively touch of the French Rococo painters, and tried to emulate the Italian Baroque history painters. But his best and most influential pictures were those scenes of topical life which narrated a complete moral story—positive novels in paint. Thus painting took on an engaged tone and purpose. It was dealing with the reality of life, satirizing the bad and praising the good; above all, it had recovered some purpose. In recovering this it did not always matter how artistically good the actual pictures were. This confusion of morals and art is one reason why the elaborate but badly painted story-telling compositions of Greuze were greeted with such praise by Diderot and his contemporaries. Greuze had no ability to satirize; his penchant was rather for sentimental depictions of village life which were meant to touch the heart. In fact, they were as false as the very pictures by Boucher which Diderot castigated; but their professed intention made them seem morally better.

221

Although it is hard to pardon Greuze for his ambiguous attitude toward his milkmaids and village girls with their artfully disarranged clothing, it is easy to appreciate the urgent feeling of intelligent people that art must come down to the ground and concern itself with the human condition. The eighteenth century inspired the painter to express this humanity without posturing, and without any program of revolt. Chardin, exemplifying this attitude, has in his genre scenes all the integrity of Poussin's art, and the same rigorous control, subordinating reality to a beautifully plotted scheme. Chardin painted with a heavy yet smooth brush stroke, which gives every object its weight, its place, and which somehow seems to capture its essence. He asserts permanence after the fluidity of the Rococo. Time stops; nothing moves; forever a woman holds a shopping bag, a boy blows a bubble, a child reads. No lesson is preached, but life is seen as at once intensely intimate and humble. In his still lifes Chardin transcends again the trivia of assorted objects, making a formal pattern and a satisfying subject out of two apples, a copper pan, and a white earthenware jug.

As the Rococo was really only the tail end of the Baroque, so its growing rival, the Neoclassic, was really the tail end of seventeenth-century classicism—with a sting in the shape of David. Rome had remained largely unaffected by the Rococo. It was ready to harbor the Neoclassic movement, first apparent in Batoni, gathering strength with Mengs, and then in full force under David. It was in Rome in 1785 that David created and exhibited *The Oath of the Horatii*, seen and immediately applauded by artists of all nations. Here at last was dignified reality, combined with a moral lesson from the great days of a great republic. It asserted truths, both visual and moral, in its attempted accuracy of detail and noble patriotic sentiment. It is a consciously revolutionary picture, and a few years later the revolution was to come, with David one of its most eager participants. Europe underwent an emotional upheaval which left artists clinging not to programs, but to their own consciousnesses. Society existed as something to withdraw from completely, and the Romantic, utterly private vision takes the place of moral lessons.

The eighteenth century's interest in humanity made it naturally responsive to portraiture. Portraits were no longer restricted to being of upper-class and royal sitters; everyone was painted, and painted *en déshabillé*, or working, or relaxing among friends. State portraits and allegorical ones, like those of Nattier, increasingly seemed too pompous and unreal. Most of the Neoclassicists—such as Batoni, Mengs, and, supremely, David—were good portrait painters. In England the relaxed and graceful genius of Gainsborough represents the quintessence of the civilized, unassertive portrait. His men and women, though at times more elegant than in reality, never try to impose their characters; they descend from Van Dyck in their easy negligence. Reynolds is more concerned to state something about his sitters, to make each portrait a comment on character. They play in art their roles in life and, paradoxically, this leads on to the Romantic portraiture of Lawrence and the early nineteenth century where each sitter acts out his personal drama; and Napoleon poses as the world conqueror.

The last great eighteenth-century painter, the first of the nineteenth century, is Goya. He, too, is obsessed by humanity, mocking of its vices, but angry as well. The penetration seen in his portraits (themselves influenced partly by mezzotints of English eighteenth-century work) and his refusal to be imposed on by outward rank reach biting revolutionary depths. He moves from the decorative genre of his early work into closer contact with people, recording man's brutality to man, and the cruelty of the French invaders of Spain who yet were welcome after the Bourbon monarchy. Thus he—alone of eighteenth-century painters—reached down into the psychological dilemma of mankind. All those professions of wanting to be good and noble did not impose on Goya; he knew that reason is always struggling with the blackness of the human heart. His etchings and drawings reveal what humanity is really like; and he holds up a mirror not to the superficiality of daily life, but to the real reality of existence: its urge to destroy. His last pictures portray the nightmare of a world gone mad, a world we can recognize only too clearly as modern and our own.

EL GRECO (1541–1614) *St. John the Evangelist* · Detail from
The Crucifixion · 1594–1604 · Oil on canvas · 35¼ × 30⅜″ ·
The Prado, Madrid

El Greco represents the fusion of several High Renaissance styles into a personal style that strongly preludes the
Baroque. A stormy spirituality agitates the emotional
figure of St. John who seems to have no more substance
than a candle flame, wrapped in a strange drapery and with
a single flame-like hand raised in horror. The certainties
of High Renaissance classicism have been exchanged for a
deliberately disturbed art. El Greco, born in Crete, had
trained in Venice and must have been influenced by Tintoretto. In 1577 he is recorded at Toledo where he lived until
his death. His increasingly mystic and private pictures
reveal the mind of an artist working in isolation.

EL GRECO *Cardinal Juan de Tavera* · 1609–14 · Oil on canvas ·
40⅛ × 32⅝″ · Hospital of St. John the Baptist, Toledo

This portrait is a late work by El Greco and remains in the
Hospital of St. John the Baptist at Toledo. While it is
certainly a vivid portrayal, and may be a good likeness of the
sitter, the picture is instinct with the painter's personality.
It is probable that El Greco used Tavera's death mask
for the portrait, as Tavera had died in 1545. A moon-
blanched light illumines the long bony head and turns
pale the stiff folds of the cardinal's cape. He rests his hand
on a heavy book which lies horizontally on a table that
slopes steeply toward the spectator. The effect is to increase
the sense of height: the sitter narrows to this tall thin
figure, topped by that white luminous face with its haunted
eyes, dark in the cadaverous eye sockets.

EL GRECO *The Virgin* · Detail from *The Holy Family* · Oil
on canvas · 44⅛ × 41⅜″ · Hospital of St. John the Baptist,
Toledo

An earlier painting than *Cardinal Tavera*, *The Virgin* shows
El Greco still very conscious of his Venetian training.
The color is less mysterious than it later becomes, and there
is something of Bassano, as well as Tintoretto, in the almost
roughly sketched-in features, the brush strokes of the hair
and the crackling folds of drapery round the Virgin's head.
The lighting is less erratic and emotional than in many
other pictures by El Greco.

EL GRECO *The Crucifixion* · 1590–95 · Oil on canvas ·
70 × 42½″ · Zuloaga Museum, Zumaya

Before El Greco, Tintoretto had conceived the Crucifixion as virtually a Baroque drama in which the whole
world seems gathered at Calvary. This concept is borrowed
but transformed by El Greco. The figure of Christ on the
Cross fills the whole composition, giving an effect of his
being thrust into the sky, raised far above the bleak earth
and the tiny departing soldiers. It is a moment of utter
isolation for Christ. But the cosmos expresses something
of this tremendous moment of its Creator's Crucifixion.
The black sky is riven by jagged cracks of light; the earth
seems shaken by the event. The elements are involved in
drama even while Christ turns his eyes to heaven.

EL GRECO *St. John's Vision of the Apocalypse* · c. 1613 · Oil on canvas · 88⅛ × 76⅜″ · Metropolitan Museum of Art, New York

El Greco naturally responded to the visionary. The allusive, highly pictorial imagery of the Apocalypse inspired him to effortless fantasy, reworking St. John's narrative in his own highly charged terms. St. John himself is seen at the left almost crucified by emotion, while in a lunar landscape those "who have come out of great tribulation" receive white robes. The robes are like ectoplasm, windy vaporous shapes similar to the vague clouds that fill the sky. A wind seems to shake all the gesticulating forms. Old ideas of formal composition have been replaced by this dynamic painting where emotion has dictated the lopsided design. St. John is almost as visionary as what he sees: the whole scene has been heightened, literally, by the tall figures, and then given an eerie quality by sulfurous green lighting which wavers over flesh and draperies.

ANNIBALE CARRACCI (1560–1609) *Venus and Adonis* · Oil on canvas · 85⅜ × 96⅞″ · Kunsthistorisches Museum, Vienna

Annibale Carracci, the greatest of the Carracci, the Bolognese family of painters, is the earliest of the creators of the Baroque. His style was woven out of elements from the great *cinquecento* artists who had preceded him, among them Raphael, the Venetians, and Correggio. *Venus and Adonis* shows what he evolved out of this heritage, making an art highly colored and dignified, despite playful touches. The whole subject here is an homage to Venetian painting, but the cupid at the left is clearly inspired by Correggio. The actual draftsmanship is, however, very much more careful than in a Venetian picture, the poses are carefully studied, and the result is an almost sculptural plasticity in the bodies of Venus and, especially, Adonis.

ANNIBALE CARRACCI *Silenus and Pan* · Tempera on wood · 14 × 32″ · National Gallery, London

This picture shows, on a small scale, the decorative gifts of Annibale at their height. It comes from a harpsichord—being part of the keyboard lid—and the subject of music is thus appropriate. Almost certainly it was painted at Rome, but the original fortunate owner of the harpsichord is not known. On the walls of the Farnese Gallery Annibale had shown how effortlessly he could devise a large-scale scheme of decoration and enter the classical, mythological world. With equal ease he depicts here the silvery rustic setting where the young god plays his pipes to the ogling, lecherous Silenus. It is an Arcadian atmosphere that he captures, artificial but highly decorative, and painted in dry tempera to give the effect of fresco.

ANNIBALE CARRACCI *Domine, Quo Vadis?* · Oil on wood · 30 × 21″ · National Gallery, London

Rome gave new dignity to Annibale Carracci's art. It remained no less painterly but its impetuous qualities were restrained. Detail was broadened and simplified under the direct contact with Raphael's work, and a classicizing tendency becomes quite patent. The broad polished draperies of the *Domine, Quo Vadis?*, the unparticularized cross, and—above all—the careful posing of the two figures, reveal the new classical strain. Everything is tightly organized. It is hard to say how Annibale himself would have developed this aspect of his art, for his increasing ill-health and premature death prevented him from playing the personal part to which his talent entitled him. It was left to his pupils to finish many of his late pictures and to develop the form of classicism which is particularly associated with Domenichino.

ANNIBALE CARRACCI *Flight into Egypt* · c. 1603 · Oil on canvas · 47½ × 88½″ · Doria Pamphili Gallery, Rome

This lunette is among Annibale's late works in Rome, one of the series of sacred subjects planned by him for the chapel of the Palazzo Aldobrandini, but of which he himself executed only this single one; the remainder were the work of his pupils Domenichino and Albani. While there is strong poetry in the group of the Holy Family—the donkey having been given a temporary respite from carrying anyone—the landscape has become more important and insistent than in the *Domine, Quo Vadis?* for example. It is a completely organized spatial scene in which the eye is led down to the water, across it, and over the undulating slopes to the satisfying square buildings on the far hill. This is a new type of art, preluding not only Domenichino, but the great achievements of Poussin and Claude when they too settled in Rome some years later.

CARAVAGGIO *The Fortuneteller* · Oil on canvas · 39 × 51⅝″ · The Louvre, Paris

The Giorgionesque tradition of sitters in fancy dress is here taken up by Caravaggio and reworked in his own idiom. The actual painting is a deliberate piece of virtuosity, with brilliant handling of white—a color which always appealed to Caravaggio—and with positive enjoyment in the showy effect of rich velvet, feathers, and linen. The boy is of a type particularly appealing to the painter: he and very similar models also appear in other pictures. Here he is dressed up as a gallant, and the act of having his fortune read is given a consciously erotic overtone as the girl exchanges glances with him. Absolute simplicity of background helps to concentrate attention on this encounter, and an ordinary moment of daily life is heightened by psychological tension.

CARAVAGGIO (1573–1610) *A Basket of Fruit* · c. 1590 · Oil on canvas · 18 × 25½″ · Pinacoteca Ambrosiana, Milan

The abrupt naturalism that enters seventeenth-century art with Michelangelo Merisi da Caravaggio is proclaimed by this painting. Although the ground has been repainted, there can be no doubt that this is not a fragment but a picture in its own right. The subject of still life—which was to become so popular in the seventeenth century—was already created by Caravaggio in Rome about 1596. He had been born in the small Lombard town of Caravaggio, whence his name, and trained in Milan. Like nearly every other great artist of the period, he was attracted to Rome where his first important patron was Cardinal del Monte, for whom this still life was painted. Caravaggio paints all the textures of leaves, fruit, basket, with *trompe l'oeil* realism, deliberately thrusting the objects forward in the picture plane so that the effect is of an actual basket, heavy with fruit, placed on a real ledge just in front of the spectator.

CARAVAGGIO *Boy with a Basket of Fruit* · c. 1610 · Oil on canvas · 26 × 20⅝″ · Borghese Gallery, Rome

Caravaggio's interest in daily life is not indiscriminate. It was only certain aspects which attracted him. Even when his models are beggar boys, they have been refined into something deliberately glamorous, as rich in their way as the fruit they often carry. These early pictures—like the present one—are not ambitious as compositions. The figure is usually alone, shown only half-length and seldom in action. But part of Caravaggio's revolutionary realism comes from choosing such ordinary sitters and making the subject of this picture no more than that of a boy with a basket of fruit. No longer does the painter restrict himself to religious pictures or portraits of respectable citizens. Although Caravaggio himself was violent and quarrelsome, he found important patrons and his pictures were sought after.

225

CARAVAGGIO *David with Goliath's Head* · c. 1606 · Oil on canvas · 26 × 25⅝″ · Borghese Gallery, Rome

Caravaggio's later pictures, of which this is one, show the marked evolution of his art. There is no longer a hard clear light bathing every object, but a thick dusky twilight from which figures emerge with poignancy. Feeling is emphasized in a new and emotional way. Here David seems to suffer from his deed of killing Goliath. He is not triumphant but mournful as he gazes at the giant's head—a head which is traditionally thought to be a portrait of Caravaggio himself. The actual painting too has become muted and less aggressive; enamel-bright colors have given way to these subtle tones where the whites are grayish. The paint is laid on thinly, to suit this quiet mood. The effect is a fresh revolution in religious painting, anticipating the achievements of Rembrandt.

ADAM ELSHEIMER (1578–1610) *Tobias and the Angel* · Oil on copper · 7½ × 10¾″ · National Gallery, London

Adam Elsheimer brought his own revolution to Rome in the early years of the seventeenth century. Born in Germany, he traveled to Venice and then settled in Rome where he was to die prematurely. In his short working life he created a new type of landscape art in small pictures where the figures are subordinated to the setting and where the setting is romantic, natural landscape observed with subtle feeling for atmosphere. He responded particularly to twilit and night scenes and to the poetry of dark woodlands and overshadowed water. In this picture Tobias and the angel return home through such a quiet countryside, delineated down to the minute details of plants and leaves. This is probably one of Elsheimer's last pictures, where the figures gain new importance in the composition. Elsheimer was a friend of Rubens and an influence on Claude.

DOMENICHINO (1581–1641) *Girl with a Unicorn* · c. 1602 · Fresco · Farnese Palace, Rome

Domenichino was one of the leading pupils of Annibale Carracci in Rome, working with him on the frescoes for the Farnese Palace in the opening years of the seventeenth century. *Girl with a Unicorn* is one of Domenichino's frescoes done at this early date and is one of his most spontaneously attractive works. There is already apparent in it something of Domenichino's tender, melancholy style. His art is happiest when not concerned with action but with idealizing figures and landscape into calmly classical compositions— and it was to have a considerable impact on Poussin. Domenichino's own nature was withdrawn and somewhat difficult. His art was out of sympathy with the Baroque exuberance that was coming into fashion in the later part of his life. He retired from Rome to work at Naples, but his last commission there was hindered by the jealousy of Neapolitan painters.

DOMENICO FETTI (c. 1589–1623) *The Good Samaritan* · Oil on wood · 23⅝ × 17″ · Metropolitan Museum of Art, New York

Born in Rome, Domenico Fetti was influenced first by Caravaggio and Elsheimer. By 1613 he had settled in Mantua where the Gonzaga collection of Venetian pictures, particularly, must have influenced him, and also Rubens' pictures. In the last year or two of his brief life he was living in Venice, where he died. His most original paintings are small-scale works, usually illustrations of the Parables (as here). He repeated these compositions in several versions, and *The Good Samaritan* is one of the most frequently repeated. The subject is treated in a simple, direct way as pure genre, with emphasis on the landscape setting.

GUERCINO (1591–1666) *The Incredulity of St. Thomas* · Oil on canvas · 45½ × 55½″ · National Gallery, London

Francesco Barbieri, called Guercino, was born at Cento, near Bologna, and he spent a considerable portion of his working life there. His art also lies outside the main currents of the seventeenth century, being blended partly from Caravaggio and from the sixteenth-century Venetians. His later pictures are inspired by the example of Guido Reni and aim at a calmer and more classical manner. His early pictures—like *The Incredulity of St. Thomas*—have opulent coloring and a richly handled paint surface. There is a direct emotional "attack" in the dramatic, moving depiction of the shadowy Apostle thrusting his fingers into the wound on Christ's brightly lit body. The composition is itself a drama of contrast between light and darkness, echoed by the tender yielding expression of Christ and the jutting, almost aggressive profile of St. Thomas. The picture has all the vigor of the full Baroque.

BERNARDO CAVALLINO (1622–54) *St. Cecilia* · 1645 · Oil on canvas · 24⅜ × 19⅝″ · National Museum, Naples

Bernardo Cavallino lived and worked at Naples but his art is not typically Neapolitan. Its refined and personal nature seems a reflection of the painter's own, and its delicate tonality is very unlike the harsh chiaroscuro of most Neapolitan artists. Cavallino's figures have an elegant, elongated grace and are posed with almost exaggerated refinement. St. Cecilia becomes expressionistic in her attitude as the angel appears to her. Little is known about Cavallino's life and the evolution of his art. *St. Cecilia* is his only signed and dated picture, and well represents the silvery grace of an art that was still evolving when plague killed the artist.

BERNARDO STROZZI (1581–1644) *Man Blowing a Fife* · c. 1623–25 · Oil on canvas · 34¼ × 26¾″ · Rosso Palace, Genoa

Strozzi might almost be a northern painter, judging from his pictures, and the influence of Rubens on him was decisive. Strozzi was born and trained in Genoa, but later settled in Venice. His vigorous northern style is patent in the picture here, with its emphasis on a sort of rustic realism. The almost uncouth pose of the wrinkled, puffing old man has a vigor that is nearly ludicrous. He blows his wooden, countrified instrument at the spectator in arresting fashion, and the picture is noisy with the sound. Like Caravaggio, and like so many of his contemporaries, Strozzi is anxious to record the ordinary, humble reality that he knows—and record it in the most effective way.

ORAZIO GENTILESCHI (1563–1639) *The Luteplayer* · c. 1626 · Oil on canvas · 56⅝ × 51⅛″ · National Gallery of Art, Washington, D.C.

Orazio Gentileschi is one of the few painters influenced by Caravaggio who actually knew Caravaggio personally. But his art had little of the great painter's force. From Caravaggio he acquired an interest in textures and an ability to use white—as in the present picture—with decorative effect. Gentileschi was in fact hardly more than a pleasing decorator with a certain response to color. Even the luteplayer is strangely disengaged, playing her lute at an awkward angle—not so much playing as posing with it. Gentileschi's brightly colored, not too serious style was successful far beyond Italy: he worked at the royal courts of France and England and was important as a disseminator of the Caravaggesque style throughout Europe.

PIETRO DA CORTONA (1596–1669) Sketch for a detail of the Barberini Ceiling · c. 1629–37 · National Gallery of Ancient Art, Rome

The great creator of Baroque painting at Rome is Pietro da Cortona and the great monument of this style is the colossal ceiling frescoed by him in the palace of the Barberini during the reign of the Barberini Pope, Urban VIII. The ceiling is really an elaborate, allegorized glorification of Urban, through whom Divine Providence is shown achieving its end. It was begun in 1633 and not completed until six years later. It shows evil being overcome everywhere and the aims of the Papacy being fulfilled, but its real concern is with the power and glory of the Barberini family rather than any spiritual aim. In its general effect the ceiling is splendid to the point of confusion. It is an almost hysterical assertion of glory, and aims to stun rather than to persuade.

SALVATOR ROSA (1615–73) *Mercury and the Woodman* · Oil on canvas · 49½ × 79½″ · National Gallery, London

Rosa was once one of the most famous seventeenth-century painters, particularly popular during the subsequent century for his wild, romantic scenes. He was born in Naples and worked in Rome and also in Tuscany. His fame came partly from his poetry and satires, and his lively nature, as well as from his pictures. Thundery landscapes like *Mercury and the Woodman* show how intensely he responded to the wildest poetry of nature and to the associations of lonely countryside. The figures are unimportant in this eerie scene of tangled foliage and jagged broken tree trunks, in which nature seems to grow more desolate and savage even while we gaze. It is exactly this *frisson* of the picturesque that the eighteenth century especially enjoyed.

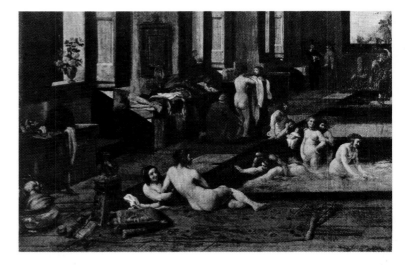

MICHELANGELO CERQUOZZI (1600–1660) *The Women's Bath* · Oil on canvas · After 1647 · Collections Marquise Eleonora Incisa, Rome

Cerquozzi reveals the ordinary, unpompous aspect of life and art in seventeenth-century Rome. In addition to the creations of classicism and the Baroque, there existed this stubborn vein of art which resolutely concerned itself with the depictions of such ordinary events as merrymaking and market scenes. This was also part of the heritage from Caravaggio and, though despised in some academic circles, it found plenty of patrons in Rome. In fact, *The Women's Bath* cannot be a real scene but is a fantasy perhaps inspired by some traveler's tale of the Orient. It was owned by Cardinal Flavio Chigi, nephew of Pope Alexander VII, and probably the most influential patron in Rome in the late 1650s. The architectural setting is by Viviano Codazzi (c. 1602–72), who collaborated with Cerquozzi on other pictures.

LUCA GIORDANO (1632–1705) *Apotheosis of St. Januarius* · Oil on canvas · 42 × 31¾″ · National Gallery, London

Luca Giordano is the Italian artist who bridges the Baroque and Rococo. Endlessly inventive and incredibly prolific, he dashed up and down Italy, decorating churches and palaces in a style that became progressively more light-hearted and air-borne. He was born in Naples and returned there finally in 1702 after a period of activity in Spain. The present picture is the *modello* for a large altarpiece painted for the Neapolitans' church at Rome, showing the patron saint of Naples. All Giordano's brilliance of color, speed of execution, and vitality is compressed into it. The angel positively hurtles toward the saint, bearing the palm of his martyrdom, and everything centers on this moment of divine intervention when heaven involves itself with the affairs of man. It is exactly this sort of vision which was to be so popular with Rococo painters in the early eighteenth century.

PETER PAUL RUBENS (1577–1640) *Marie de' Medici* · 1622–25
· Oil on canvas · 51¼ × 42½″ · The Prado, Madrid

For Marie de' Medici Rubens painted the great series of
pictures of her life allegorized, and he also painted her
portrait. There is nothing allegorized or high-flown about
this direct portrayal, which does not disguise the Queen's
plump silliness. Yet, without flattery, Rubens invests her
with great dignity—emphasized by the plain setting and
unadorned black dress. There is something assured about
the sitter's pose and the great sweep of crisp ruff which
frames her face. Indeed, the ruff is really the secret of the
picture: a fan of half-transparent linen which by its sheer
size imposes itself as a design over the whole picture area.

PETER PAUL RUBENS *Le Coup de Lance (Christ on the Cross)* ·
c. 1620 · Oil on canvas · 122⅛ × 68½″ · Royal Museum of
Fine Arts, Antwerp

Rubens' altarpieces for Flemish churches reveal not only
what he had learned in Italy as a young man but how he
created his own version of the Baroque style wherein drama
is combined with powerful plasticity. His full maturity is
represented by the famous *Coup de Lance*, the emotional
impact of which is strengthened by its huge size. The moment chosen is at once brutal and poignant: the Virgin
virtually faints away as Longinus, the centurion, pierces
Christ's side in a tremendous gesture of force. Nothing in
the composition is at rest except the slack body of the
crucified Christ. About him twist the thieves, his grieving
followers, the pawing horses—contrasting with the absolute
and hopeless repose of death.

PETER PAUL RUBENS *Rape of the Daughters of Leucippus* ·
c. 1615–16 · Oil on canvas · 87½ × 82¼″ · The Old Pinakothek, Munich

Although Rubens painted so many altarpieces and religious
pictures, he was perhaps more at ease in a classical pagan
world where his own sheer delight in life could find its
most lyrical expression. The exuberance of this rape communicates itself to the excited horses and even to the sunny
landscape. The daughters of Leucippus are almost too
splendidly robust in their distress and are giving their
captors a great deal of trouble. Rubens responds delightedly
to the expanses of blonde flesh, set off against the brown
skins of the men and made more creamy still by the glowing
draperies of gold and crimson. The picture is decoration but
it is dynamic decoration, spontaneous for all its large scale.

PETER PAUL RUBENS *Helena Fourment and Her Children* · Oil
on wood · 44½ × 32¼″ · The Louvre, Paris

Rubens' first wife died in 1627 and three years later he
married a girl of sixteen, Helena Fourment, who became
the inspiration of much of his late work. He painted her
and her children often, with breath-taking directness and
affection. The present picture is just such a masterpiece,
intimate, tender without sentimentality, and painted with
indescribable vividness. Apart from the red chair, there is no
strong color in the picture—and this would probably have
remained so even if it had been finished. In most ways it *is*
finished, for Rubens' rapid grasp on reality is sufficient for
us to complete mentally what he has only hastily sketched
in—like the lower part of the chair. The concept of the picture is quite simple, and the mood almost pensive. The
mother is absorbed by her son and it is only he who turns,
bright-eyed, to gaze out from the circle of her arms.

229

PETER PAUL RUBENS *Landscape with a Tower* · 1635 · Oil on canvas · 11 × 14¾″ · Ashmolean Museum, Oxford

Religious pictures, mythologies, portraits—these did not exhaust the range of Rubens' genius. Himself the owner of a country house, the Château of Steen, he became a painter also of landscapes. In fact he had probably always responded to the atmospheric possibilities of landscape painting ever since his early years in Italy when he had known and greatly admired Elsheimer. His own landscapes are sometimes large panoramic views; sometimes, as here, they are more simple and direct, and on a smaller scale. The tradition of landscape painting was not new in northern Europe and Rubens had a great predecessor in Pieter Bruegel the Elder. But Rubens is more than an observer of nature: his response is almost empathy, and in his pictures all nature seems invested with that vitality which positively breathes from everything—animate or inanimate—that he painted.

ANTHONY VAN DYCK (1599–1641) *Henrietta Maria with Her Dwarf* · c. 1633 · Oil on canvas · 86¼ × 53⅛″ · National Gallery of Art, Washington, D.C.

Van Dyck is always associated with the English court of Charles I, although he did not settle in England until 1632 and had become restless to leave during the period just before his death. It is true that Charles and Henrietta gave Van Dyck some of his finest opportunities, and he repaid them by a splendid series of portraits. The graceful dissembling quality of his art is well conveyed in this full-length painting of the Queen with her dwarf, Sir Geoffrey Hudson. For all its suggestion of relaxation and outdoor ease, the portrait manages to remind us casually that the sitter is royal—the crown obtrudes on the rich folds of curtain at the right.

ANTHONY VAN DYCK *Maria de Raet* (detail) · Oil on canvas · 83¾ × 47¾″ · The Wallace Collection, London

This portrait is full length in the original and is paired with a full-length portrait of the sitter's husband, Philippe Le Roy. Both pictures are among Van Dyck's finest work and they date from the period in Flanders before 1632. Van Dyck's own nervous sensibility is reflected in the present picture with its almost disturbed painting of the elaborate lace collar and the foaming agitated frills at Maria de Raet's wrists. She holds with long elegant hands a feathery fan, painted with the same nervous energy as the curls of her blond hair. The portrait has a restless and melancholy air which is perhaps partly Van Dyck's own. Everything is refined where Rubens would have made it robust. Although Van Dyck was Rubens' greatest pupil, the two men were very different artists.

ANTHONY VAN DYCK *Charles II of England as a Boy* · Detail from *The Children of Charles I* · 1635 · Oil on canvas · 59⅜ × 60⅝″ · Sabauda Gallery, Turin

The complete composition shows Prince Charles (later Charles II) at full length, standing with his brother James (later James II) and his sister Mary. They were the three eldest children of Charles I and the picture was painted in 1635, when Prince Charles was five years old, for the royal court of Savoy at Turin (where the picture has remained). Van Dyck has beautifully solved the problem of combining childhood and royalty; the young prince is already isolated by his importance, as heir to the throne, but given a pet dog to rest his hand on. His clothes, despite their richness, reveal his babyhood. He still wears long skirts instead of breeches, and it is known that Charles I was angry with Van Dyck for painting him in this childish costume. Another portrait of the three children was executed in the same year and in this Prince Charles wears adult clothes.

PETER PAUL RUBENS (1577–1640) *The Judgment of Paris*, and detail of the head of Venus · Oil on panel · $57\frac{1}{8} \times 76\frac{3}{8}''$ · National Gallery, London

Rubens is the first great northerner of the seventeenth century to return from Italy and create a new style built on what he had learned there. He was back in Antwerp in 1608 and in the years that followed he soon achieved a European reputation as a diplomat as well as a painter, traveling in both capacities in Spain, England, and France. Yet his art remains profoundly Flemish. *The Judgment of Paris* is a Greek story retold in the setting of Flanders. The goddesses themselves are not classically beautiful, but opulent bourgeoises of ample charm. Rubens treats the whole thing with a hint of humor—like Juno's peacock hissing at the dog crouched between the legs of Paris who has awarded the golden apple to Venus. Actually, Juno as painted by Rubens really deserves to win it, for her pose is marvelous, as is the painting of her flesh set off by the crimson furred cloak.

Suitably enough for the winner of the golden apple, Venus under Rubens' brush becomes golden. The artist's mastery of paint is seen in the clotted medium which richly conveys the pearl-adorned blond hair and then is diluted for the creamy skin. More than flesh is evoked. The confident brush strokes give a pulsating sense of vitality to a profile that seems virtually to breathe.

Detail is shown on next pages

ANTHONY VAN DYCK *William, Prince of Orange, and Princess Mary of England* · Oil on canvas · 41¼ × 55⅞″ · Rijksmuseum, Amsterdam

This double portrait celebrates the betrothal in 1641 of Charles I's ten-year-old daughter to the young Prince of Orange. The event took place in London and at the same time the Prince gave his bride the large diamond brooch which she is seen wearing in the picture. Their son was destined to become William III of England. Once again Van Dyck solves the problem of combining dignity with informality: the embroidered silken clothes and solemn poses only emphasize the sitters' rather pathetic youth. They seem to look out of the picture with rather uncertain gaze, conscious of their importance but still timid. Van Dyck seizes the opportunity to heighten the decorative effect by recording every gleam of satin, and by contrasting the effect of the Prince's red-and-gold dress with his bride's cool green one. A few months after completing the picture, Van Dyck was dead.

JACOB JORDAENS (1593–1678) *The Painter's Family* · Oil on canvas · 71¼ × 73⅝″ · The Prado, Madrid

Jacob Jordaens was Rubens' most distinguished pupil after Van Dyck. The boisterous Baroque side of his master's art was developed by him in pictures which are rarely as sensitive and as attractive as this group portrait. Jordaens was able to capture the straightforward aspect of reality, without any of the psychological nuances of Van Dyck. Here he manages to solve the difficulty of organizing a group portrait so that it appears spontaneous and yet not awkward. Although all the sitters look out at the spectator— as if looking at a camera—they also fuse together to suggest a charming, domestic group of the different generations.

CORNELIS DE VOS (1584–1651) *A Family Group* · 1631 · Oil on canvas · 70 × 92¼″ · Royal Museum of Fine Arts, Antwerp

Cornelis de Vos was an Antwerp portrait painter, concerned especially with the depiction of prosperous bourgeois families such as the one in this painting. It is more formal than Jacob Jordaens' *The Painter's Family* but it has its own quiet charm. De Vos stems from a tradition older than Rubens, and his sitters have none of the relaxed air and naturalness projected by that great artist. The present group would be rather stiff without the presence of the children—so much more spontaneous and unconscious than their soberly dressed, dignified parents. De Vos had a particular rapport, it would seem, with children. His portraits of children by themselves are attractive and interesting for the sympathy which the painter feels for them. The same quality is noticeable in this portrait group.

DAVID TENIERS the Younger (1610–90) *Still Life* · c. 1645–50 · Oil on canvas · 20⅝ × 27″ · Royal Museum of Fine Arts, Brussels

David Teniers, the son of a painter and the most famous member of a family of artists, worked at Antwerp and Brussels. He is chiefly associated with peasant scenes in the style of Brouwer, but was capable of painting a wide variety of subjects. The present picture is rather unusual. It is a comparatively early work and shows Teniers' ability to make a satisfying picture out of no more than a few books and a globe. The tonality is deliberately sober and restrained, but in this brownish atmosphere the heavy volumes take on a life of their own.

234

DIEGO VELÁZQUEZ (1599–1660) *Prince Baltasar Carlos*, and detail of his sash · c. 1634 · Oil on canvas · 82¼ × 68⅛″ · The Prado, Madrid

This picture was intended for Buen Retiro, to hang in the same hall as *The Surrender of Breda* (page 235) and with an equestrian portrait of the Prince's father, Philip IV. There is a certain pathos in this grandiose equestrian portrait of a boy—hardly more than six years old when this picture was executed. The Prince was born in 1629. All the hopes of his father, and Spain, were concentrated on him, but already here his pale, unformed face seems doomed; he was to die in 1646. Since the picture was to hang high, Velázquez has painted the pony with an almost exaggerated

curve of belly; this pony is doubtless that sent to Baltasar Carlos as a gift from Flanders in 1633. The Prince is raised up, a miniature rider on a miniature horse, but treated with full Baroque swagger. The result is probably the first equestrian portrait of a child.

Only gradually did Velázquez evolve a technique of impressionism, but the painting of the sash here shows that by the mid 1630s he had found the way to suggest rather than record reality. The rapid brush strokes are almost rough in application, but the effect is at once vivid and convincing. The few marks on the canvas are fused by the eye to form a sash of crumpled silk.

Detail is shown on next pages

235

DIEGO VELÁZQUEZ (1599–1660) *Pope Innocent X* · 1650 ·
Oil on canvas · 55⅛ × 47¼″ · Doria Pamphili Gallery,
Rome

Diego Velázquez became court painter to Philip IV of
Spain in 1623 and served the king until his death in 1660.
In all those years he was permitted to leave Spain only
twice, and both times he visited Italy. On the second visit
he was in Rome in 1650, where he painted this portrait of the
Pope—a portrait instantly famous and ever since admired.
By this date Velázquez' mastery was supreme. The splendid
whites and crimsons of the costume only serve to set off
the flushed, almost angry, saturnine features of the Pope.
Contemporaries found him difficult to fathom, but Velázquez seems to have probed to his very heart.

DIEGO VELÁZQUEZ *The Rokeby Venus* · Oil on canvas
48¼ × 69¾″ · National Gallery, London

Velázquez takes his place among the very greatest painters
not just of the seventeenth century, but of all time. Few
painters have achieved anything approaching his dispassionate realism, in which everything seems to obey an
inevitable law and where gravity (in every sense of the
word) reigns supreme. Although he painted several mythological pictures, and other nudes, *The Rokeby Venus* is his
only surviving painting of a female nude. Venus is hardly
a classical goddess here, but simply a woman lying on a
bed. Only the winged Cupid suggests a mythological note.
The picture is quite unsensual, almost unsensuous, in the
simplified form of the woman's body and the very restrained
coloring. It is not so much a homage to Venetian art and
Titian (so splendidly represented in the Spanish royal collection) as a puritanical reworking of a Venetian theme.

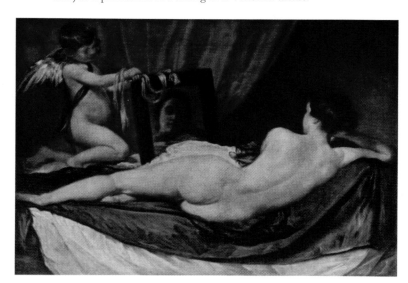

DIEGO VELÁZQUEZ *Sebastian de Morra* · c. 1643–44 · Oil on
canvas · 41¾ × 31⅞″ · The Prado, Madrid

The Spanish court lives most memorably, and horribly,
in the series of portraits painted by Velázquez of the
dwarfs who served as objects of ridicule and humor for the
royal family. Velázquez treats them with great dignity, and
even perhaps with compassion. The present dwarf seems
to have come to Madrid in 1643 to serve the heir to the
throne, Prince Baltasar Carlos, and he lived until 1649.
Unlike some of the other pitiful creatures painted by
Velázquez, De Morra does not appear mentally afflicted.
Only his pose on the ground, and the stunted legs, betray
that he is a dwarf. The head has a directness of gaze—intense and black—which scrutinizes the spectator with
great penetration. It is the humanity of this dwarf that gives
a noble impact to the portrait; and the picture is also a
tribute to Velázquez' humanity.

DIEGO VELÁZQUEZ *The Surrender of Breda* · Finished 1635 ·
Oil on canvas · 121⅛ × 144¾″ · The Prado, Madrid

The scene represented took place in 1625, when the Dutch
city of Breda was surrendered up by Justin of Nassau to the
Spanish General Spinola. Velázquez did not, of course,
witness this scene; he painted his picture about ten years
later. It was one of a series of battle pictures by different
artists commissioned for a hall in the palace of Buen Retiro
at Madrid. Velázquez' famous picture is very different in
conception, as well as technique, from the other pictures. It
makes the Spanish victory no triumphant moment over a
humiliated enemy. The two generals meet almost like host
and guest. War is seen not as splendid, but as a tiring
struggle, and both parties seem glad it is concluded. Thus,
to the plastic realism of the painting, Velázquez adds a
psychological realism that makes the picture poignant.

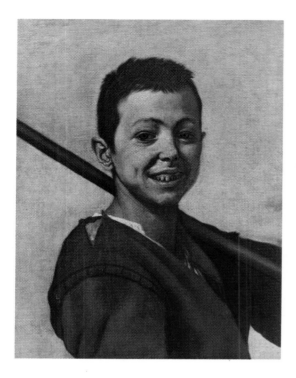

JUSEPE RIBERA (1591–1652) *Boy with a Club Foot* (detail) ·
1652 · Oil on canvas · 64⅝ × 36¼″ · The Louvre, Paris

Although born in Spain, Jusepe Ribera worked in the
Spanish-dominated city of Naples. From him derives the
whole Neapolitan School of tenebrist painting, with its
emphasis on dramatic chiaroscuro and its strongly individualized saints and beggars. *Boy with a Club Foot* is typical
of Ribera's harsh realism, more pungent than Caravaggio's,
rougher in handling than Velázquez'. There is even
something grotesque about the boy's head, and perhaps
Ribera intended to shock by the honesty of his portrayal of
a boy both poor and deformed.

FRANCISCO DE ZURBARÁN (1598–1664) *St. Jerome with
St. Paula and St. Eustochia* · Oil on canvas · 96½ × 68⅛″ ·
National Gallery of Art, Washington, D.C.

Francisco de Zurbarán worked in Madrid but more
especially in Seville, and represents a withdrawn private
world of austere compositions and clear hand coloring. He
is at his best in depicting events in the lives of the saints,
not as miraculous and visionary, but as moments of such
intensity that they take on a suprareality. The three figures
here have all the firmness and clarity of statues carved
from wood and then boldly but austerely colored. Their
clothes fall with few folds; their faces are simple forms; and
there is hardly any movement. Everything has a pious
contemplative air that suits the subject of a sacred conversation.

FRANCISCO DE ZURBARÁN *St. Dorothy* · c. 1645–50 ·
Provincial Museum, Seville

Zurbarán painted several pictures of single female saints
wearing the ordinary Spanish clothes of the seventeenth
century and having about them an almost rustic charm.
St. Dorothy has little of the obviously saintly in her appearance, but Zurbarán gives her that quiet, meditative air
which marks out so much of his art. The silhouette pose is
highly effective, and with bold chiaroscuro Zurbarán builds
up the solidity of the figure. His gift for highly original
color is revealed in the juxtaposition of the striped yellow-
and-black scarf to the plum-colored dress with its thick,
heavy folds—contrasting with the wispy black veil that
floats from the saint's head. Finally, there is an intensely
satisfying weight given to the beautiful still life of fruit.

FRANCISCO DE ZURBARÁN *Still Life of Fruit* · c. 1633 · Oil on
canvas · 23⅝ × 42⅛″ · Collection Contini Bonacossi,
Florence

What had been merely an accessory in Zurbarán's *St.
Dorothy* becomes here the whole subject of a picture,
recalling the still life painted more than thirty years before by
Caravaggio (see page 225). There is something almost naïve
in Zurbarán's study: yet, at the same time, it has a tremendous conviction and an almost mystical intensity. It is as if
by concentrating on these few carefully arranged objects
the painter has discovered something about the nature of
reality. What he paints is completely free of the trivial.
Three sets of objects are placed with geometrical precision
in relation to each other and to the spectator; scrupulously
recorded, they seem to tell us something not only about
their external appearance, but also about their inward
essence.

239

Bartolomé Estebán Murillo (1617–82) *Madonna and Child* · c. 1670 · Oil on canvas · 65¼ × 45¼″ · State Picture Gallery, Dresden

Bartolomé Estebán Murillo, the third great seventeenth-century Spanish painter, is very much less powerful and intense than either Velázquez or Zurbarán. He is more interested in feelings, even to the point of sentimentality. The actual paint is softer in its application, laid on with a graceful feathery touch which—allied to his pale vaporous coloring—makes him already a Rococo artist. He is particularly the painter of gentle religious pictures, obvious devotional images like this *Madonna and Child* which is attractive, pious, but rather empty out of religious context.

Bartolomé Estebán Murillo *Beggar Boys Playing Dice* · Oil on canvas · 58¾ × 43¼″ · The Old Pinakothek, Munich

Murillo could not escape the genre interest of his century, an interest particularly strong in Spain. The contrast there between the showy splendor of the nobility and the desperate poverty of the ordinary people was also particularly strong. Murillo's beggar boys are poor and ragged enough, but their poverty seems invested with a certain sentimentality. They themselves are well-washed children, shown as appealing, contented gamins. Murillo's tendency to glamorize reality makes these pictures now rather difficult to appreciate, but for a long time they represented one of the most popular aspects of his art.

Bartolomé Estebán Murillo *St. Diego* · Detail from *The "Angel-Kitchen" of St. Diego of Alcalá* · c. 1645 · Oil on canvas · 70⅞ × 177⅛″ · The Louvre, Paris

Murillo's early work shows a stronger fiber than his later pictures. Though religious subjects are already his chief output they are treated with Ribera-like realism, as this head of St. Diego reveals. The *"Angel-Kitchen"* was painted for the Franciscans in Murillo's home town of Seville and shows the Franciscan lay brother St. Diego—the humblest of men—raised in ecstatic prayer while his kitchenwork is being done for him by angels. Harsh and unidealized, he represents that pungent actuality which is at the root of all Spanish seventeenth-century painting.

Simon Vouet (1590–1649) *Wealth* · Oil on canvas · 66⅞ × 48⅞″ · The Louvre, Paris

Simon Vouet stands for the most courtly, decorative side of art in France under Louis XIII. At the same time his free handling and brilliant coloring look forward to the decorative achievements of the following century; to some extent, he anticipates Boucher. *Wealth* is a fine example of his fluent allegorizing and graceful painting, in which the mood is seldom particularly serious. The very subject suits Vouet in its suggestions of prodigality, its elaborate vases and jeweled chains. But under all this are reminders that Vouet had worked in Italy as a young man and been influenced by Caravaggio; it is easy too to see some influence of Gentileschi, who had worked in France.

NICOLAS POUSSIN (1593/4–1665) *The Lamentation of Christ* ·
Oil on canvas · 41 × 59⅜″ · The Old Pinakothek, Munich

Nicolas Poussin is perhaps the key figure for appreciating
the oscillation of the seventeenth century between Venice
and Rome, between Baroque and classicism, between
colore and *disegno*. Though French by birth, he was Roman
by adoption, and it was in Rome that he finally achieved
that synthesis of opposing tendencies that is his art. *The
Lamentation* is a comparatively early picture which still
possesses some wild Venetian poetry. Grief is a cry of pain,
as St. John sits in rigid agony and the Virgin swoons over
the extended corpse of Christ. At the same period Poussin
painted in similar pose the dead Adonis, mourned by
Venus. The two worlds of religion and mythology remain
symbolically close for him.

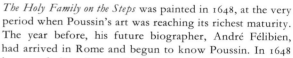

NICOLAS POUSSIN *The Holy Family on the Steps* · Oil on
canvas · 27 × 38½″ · National Gallery of Art, Washington,
D.C. (The Samuel H. Kress Collection)

The Holy Family on the Steps was painted in 1648, at the very
period when Poussin's art was reaching its richest maturity.
The year before, his future biographer, André Félibien,
had arrived in Rome and begun to know Poussin. In 1648
he records listening to the painter who spoke of the importance of the intellect in art, and the value of reflecting
about the subject rather than directly imitating nature.
This solemn *Holy Family* might have been painted to
illustrate Poussin's ideas. The group forms an equilateral
triangle, with its base the long line of the first step. Formalized, almost Cubist architecture rises behind—obviously
an idealized construction. A few calm verticals mark off the
intervals across the composition which is bathed in light
and given a sense of infinity by the staircase which leads
straight into the cloudy sky.

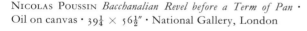

NICOLAS POUSSIN *Bacchanalian Revel before a Term of Pan* ·
Oil on canvas · 39¼ × 56½″ · National Gallery, London

Poussin's response to classical antiquity was intense, to the
point where it could be said to be more Romantic than
classical in its feeling. Gradually, however, he curbed the
more spontaneous aspects of his art, organizing it with
almost mathematical precision. This order has its own
poetry, the poetry of harmony. In *Bacchanalian Revel* the
figures are all carefully related to each other, so that the
eye is led in and out of the dance. The most elaborate and
beautiful pattern is formed by the left-hand trio whose
arms are entwined in a way that is calculated and yet seems
spontaneous. This chain of nymphs and satyrs is like a
classical frieze that has come to life. Wine and blood have
brought vivacity to these marble forms, and they dance
gaily in a Titianesque landscape of heavy-foliaged trees.

NICOLAS POUSSIN *Summer* (detail) · 1660–64 · Oil on canvas ·
46½ × 63″ · The Louvre, Paris

This picture is one of the *Four Seasons* painted by Poussin
for the Duc de Richelieu, begun in 1660 and finished only
two years before Poussin's death. Each season is also a
scene from the Old Testament. *Summer* is thus Ruth and
Boaz in the cornfield, symbolizing the world since Christianity, with the marriage of Ruth and Boaz standing for the
mystic marriage of Christ and the church. These layers of
meaning are typical of the complexity of Poussin's very late
pictures. At the same time Poussin was able to develop
such symbolism without any diminution of his artistry.
Even the detail of the landscape background in *Summer* is
sufficient to show how responsive he remained to Italian
scenery. Across the cornfield the eye is led along the
winding road, to rest on the beautiful blue mountain
range that lies along the horizon.

241

CLAUDE LORRAIN (1600–1682) *Acis and Galatea* · Oil on canvas · 39⅜ × 53⅛″ · State Picture Gallery, Dresden

Claude Lorrain lived most of his life in Rome, like Poussin—with whom he was friendly. Passionately attached as Claude was to Italy, it was less its classical past than its romantic suggestions which formed the essence of his art. He chose to restrict himself to landscape, observed atmospherically and constructed by him on his own principle of *coulisses* and melting distances where sky and water merge. All Claude's pictures approximate dreams: dreams of a world which never was, where people have hardly any significance, where there is always mellow light and few seasonal changes. Above all, there is no hint of winter weather. *Acis and Galatea* captures the lyrical freshness of sunlight over the wide sea while the fond lovers embrace in the foreground.

CLAUDE LORRAIN *Landscape with the Marriage of Isaac and Rebecca* · 1648 · Oil on canvas · 58¾ × 77½″ · National Gallery, London

Once again, the "subject" is really unimportant for Claude. His dancing figures might be ordinary country people rather than illustrations of an incident in the Old Testament; and the setting is again Italy. It is a perfect pastoral scene in which ground and trees and water have all been disposed to make a landscape more ideal than any in fact. The trees are grouped at either side of the composition, leaving the center for the action and also for the suggestion of depth. Just enough interest is provided by the figures, and then the land breaks into the large, limpid stretch of lake which reflects the calm sky above. In Claude the landscape interest already expressed at Rome by Elsheimer in the first decade of the century reaches its fullest and most sophisticated development.

CLAUDE LORRAIN *Embarkation of St. Ursula* · 1646 · Oil on canvas · 44½ × 58½″ · National Gallery, London

It was particularly during the decade of the 1640's that Claude devised a whole series of seaport scenes. Sometimes it is simply a seaport without classical or religious subject; sometimes (as in this picture of 1646) there is a definite subject, but hardly more than an excuse to animate the cloud-capped architecture. No seaport was ever like Claude's imagined scene, where water laps gently against the splendid stone steps that descend from fantastic marble palaces. Early morning light is dissolving the mist, and the ships that are to carry St. Ursula and her virgin companions float like phantoms in the liquid atmosphere.

LOUIS LE NAIN (c. 1593–1648) *The Cart* · 1641 · Oil on canvas · 22 × 28¼″ · The Louvre, Paris

There were three brothers Le Nain, but there can be no doubt that the greatest was Louis. Pictures can only be ascribed to him on grounds of quality, however, since none is individually signed by him. *The Cart* explains the nature of the Le Nain revolution, with its uncompromisingly humble, rustic subject and its straightforward "Dutch" manner of depicting people and things. There is even less attempt at storytelling than in comparable Dutch genre, and a very powerful sense of dignity. Poverty is not made something picturesque, still less something humorous. The life of these peasants in their farmyard is like a rebuke to the ostentatious court world evoked by Vouet (p. 237). Already in France there are two nations—poor and rich. Perhaps it is not too fanciful to see in Le Nain's people the ancestors of those who were to rise in 1789 to take revenge for years of penury.

GEORGES DE LA TOUR (1593–1652) *St. Joseph, the Carpenter* ·
Oil on canvas · 52 × 38⅜″ · The Louvre, Paris

The realism of Georges de La Tour is different from that
of Le Nain, though he shares the predilection for humble
life. His genre and religious scenes are very similar to each
other, and his treatment must have been inspired by
Caravaggio. Probably he knew nothing directly of Caravaggio's work but was influenced by Dutch followers
of Caravaggio, notably Honthorst. It was probably
from them that he derived his fondness for indirect or
concealed lighting effects, like the dramatic single candle
that illuminates St. Joseph. La Tour worked all his life in
Lorraine and was quite unknown in Paris. His art has a
somewhat uncouth but impressive power and originality.
St. Joseph's toil at night is more than just a pictorial
device. He really is a worker, and the carpenter's tools—
even the spiral of shavings—help to emphasize this point.
Daily life and a Biblical subject are fused in a way that must
have powerfully struck home to La Tour's provincial
contemporaries.

GEORGES DE LA TOUR *The Newborn Child* · Oil on canvas ·
29⅞ × 35⅞″ · Museum of Fine Arts, Rennes

In this picture La Tour achieves greater subtlety than in the
St. Joseph, and there is a more vigorous control of reality.
This time the actual candle flame is concealed and light too
is more restricted. Shadow makes the simple figures look
like forms of varnished wood, almost recalling the figures
of Zurbarán, and perhaps the two painters have something
in common in their grave and dignified realism. La Tour
has restricted his colors here, making the woman holding
the candle merge into the dark background, so that it is the
warm vermilion of the mother which attracts the eye.
Mystery hovers round the composition and even around
the subject, for it may or may not represent Christ's
nativity. For La Tour the birth of *a* child and of the Christ
Child became confounded. And the picture's moving power
remains the same for us, whichever subject is intended.

PHILIPPE DE CHAMPAIGNE (1602–74) *Omar Talon* · Oil on
canvas · 88½ × 63⅝″ · National Gallery of Art, Washington,
D.C. (The Samuel H. Kress Collection)

Philippe de Champaigne was Flemish by birth although
working and living in France. There is a vein of powerful
Flemish-style realism in his work from the first and this
emerges with an increasing intellectual austerity which
gives his pictures their grave air. Although he worked for
royalty and for Cardinal Richelieu, Champaigne was really
a painter of the middle classes—the lawyers and merchants
—painting for them and portraying them. His sitters are
posed quietly and with dignity. There is no accompanying
Baroque apparatus. Instead they are seen in their ordinary
environment, studied with simple directness and painted
with scrupulous attention. They remind us that seventeenth-century Paris was more a bourgeois than a royal
city, and that its citizens were proud of their independence
from the court. Champaigne himself had a natural affinity
with this level of society with its practicality, honesty, and
deep religious feelings.

CHARLES LEBRUN (1619–90) *Chancellor Séguier* · Oil on
canvas · 116⅛ × 137¾″ · The Louvre, Paris

Charles Lebrun represents the public triumph of the arts
under Louis XIV and inspired by Colbert. Colbert was the
instigator of Lebrun's success not only as painter and
decorator, but as virtual dictator of all artistic enterprises
at the French Court. The grandiose nature of Lebrun's
decorations at Versailles represents the very opposite
world from that of Champaigne. And his protector Chancellor Séguier represents the typical envious and ambitious
courtier. He was to persecute the Jansenists, the very sect to
which Champaigne was attracted. Lebrun's portrait shows
the Chancellor in his formal robes, proceeding in state like a
miniature monarch, with his attendant pages. Although
the result cannot be a penetrating portrait of an individual,
it remains an impressive statement of power.

HYACINTHE RIGAUD (1659–1743) *Cardinal de Bouillon*
Oil on canvas · 107⅞ × 85⅜″ · Rigaud Museum, Perpignan

Hyacinthe Rigaud carried on the tradition of the French
state portrait well into the eighteenth century. Rigaud's
craftsmanship is allied to considerable feeling for the character of his sitters—particularly when they are not great
personages. But he always made something exciting out of
the commission for a state portrait, and here the opportunity
for grandeur given by the Cardinal's robes has been seized
on by Rigaud with impressive effect. The Cardinal sits very
much a grand seigneur and a prince of the Church. For
him, however, life was to prove less calmly elevated than
art. Although he was the French ambassador to Rome, of
noble blood, and doyen of the cardinals, he clashed with
Louis XIV and was banished from France.

NICOLAS DE LARGILLIÈRE (1656–1746) *The Family of
Louis XIV* · Oil on canvas · 50 × 63″ · The Wallace
Collection, London

Nicolas de Largillière was the rival of Rigaud and is
usually thought of as the painter of the middle classes. His
portraits are more relaxed than the formal splendors of
Rigaud. Largillière has something more Flemish and
direct in his depictions, even of the royal family. In this
picture—which contains the king and his male heirs—there
is a domestic mood, despite the grand setting in which the
four generations are gathered. Largillière records their
features without flattery and concentrates on the details
of costume and furnishing to enliven the scene. Attention
focuses finally on the child in leading strings who is the
future Louis XV.

244

REMBRANDT VAN RIJN (1606–69) *Titus Reading* · c. 1656 ·
Oil on canvas · 27⅞ × 24¼″ · Kunsthistorisches Museum,
Vienna

Rembrandt shares with Rubens the revolution whereby
painting came to depict the more personal aspects of
the painter: his own home and his family. While Rubens'
depictions of such intimate scenes are glowing tributes to
vitality, with healthy children and handsome wives, Rembrandt's are necessarily less joyful and exuberant after the
first triumph of his marriage to Saskia. Their only surviving
child was Titus, who was born in 1641 and lost his mother
the subsequent year. There is great tenderness, as well as
intimacy, in Rembrandt's portrait of his son here, painted
about 1656. The artist's style had become a perfect instrument for sympathetic response to personality and
atmosphere. A smoky twilight is brushed on to the canvas
and out of it emerges only the sitter's face—itself absorbed
—and the single hand holding the book. It is this very
simplicity which makes such an impressive picture.

REMBRANDT VAN RIJN *Danaë* · 1636 · Oil on canvas ·
73 × 79″ · The Hermitage, Leningrad

Painted in 1636, the so-called *Danaë* is a picture which
probably represents another scene from mythology, but
one with the same type of incident of Jupiter's love for a
mortal woman. The subject is most likely that of Semele
who, misled by the deceit of Juno disguised as her nurse,
made Jupiter appear by her bed in all his majesty—and was
destroyed by the lightning and thunderbolts. Rembrandt
transforms the classical story into this depiction of a nude
woman bathed in light, her flesh set off by the sheer white
of the bed's draperies. The composition is tense from
Semele's upraised half-apprehensive hand and the direction
of the two women's gaze which suggests the god is already
coming. Rembrandt has wonderfully combined the eminent sense of tragedy—above the bed a cupid weeps—
with the sensuous study of a reclining female nude.

REMBRANDT VAN RIJN *Self-Portrait in Old Age* · Oil on canvas · 33⅞ × 27¾″ · National Gallery, London

No artist has painted himself so often as did Rembrandt. His concept of himself continued to deepen in grasp and subtlety, while his technique grew more daring. The present portrait must be among the very last, painted when the artist was about sixty but had suffered the many vicissitudes which have marked his features. Poverty and loneliness have eaten away at him and yet he manages to stand here simply, hands clasped, and look out with a sort of agonized resignation. Not content with this moving concept of himself, Rembrandt gives the actual paint almost expressionistic handling.

REMBRANDT VAN RIJN *A Woman Bathing in a Stream* (Hendrickje Stoffels?) · 1654 · Oil on wood · 24⅜ × 18½″ · National Gallery, London

The picture is dated 1654 and is very likely to represent Hendrickje Stoffels, who was living with Rembrandt during the decade of the 1650s and bore him a daughter, Cornelia. Although there is no documented portrait of Hendrickje she seems to be the model for several pictures by Rembrandt, and that model in turn has affinities with the woman of the present picture. Small in scale, and probably rapidly painted, it is a brilliant sketch. The forms are almost harshly brushed in, with quick, stab-like splashes of paint to suggest the folds of the white shift. As it stands, the picture is a piece of pure genre, with no subject except a woman bathing. Possibly it was originally executed as a study for some composition of Susannah and the Elders, but it is not connected with any surviving one.

REMBRANDT VAN RIJN *The Flayed Ox* · 1655 · Oil on wood · 37 × 26½″ · The Louvre, Paris

All the tendencies of seventeenth-century art toward realism are united in Rembrandt. Despite some early Baroque pictures, he was from the first the great master of revolutionary naturalism, with a preference for the life and sights of his own experience. Everything was a legitimate subject for painting; in recognizing this Rembrandt was a pioneer of modern art. Perhaps no painter before him would have dared to paint such a picture as *The Flayed Ox*. The subject remains disgusting but is transfigured by Rembrandt's art. The animal's stripped carcass is painted with an astonishing bravura and tonal range.

REMBRANDT VAN RIJN *Woman with a Pink* · 1665–69 · Oil on canvas · 36¼ × 29¼″ · Metropolitan Museum of Art, New York

In the 1630s Rembrandt was a highly successful portrait painter in Amsterdam and his portraits are brilliant, polished likenesses of prosperous people. Thirty years later Rembrandt was portraying only a few sitters, and in a very different style. *Woman with a Pink* is one of these very late pictures, painted in the last four or five years of Rembrandt's life. In place of brilliance and polish there is now diffusion and softness. The sitter does not confront the spectator, but seems lost in private meditation. Almost like a musician Rembrandt creates this mood around her, letting the shadows absorb her, while light picks out a few jewels, the fine pleated chemise, and the bright color of the flower which glows against the dark background.

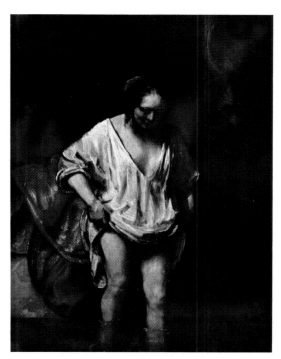

CAREL FABRITIUS (1622–54) *The Goldfinch* · 1654 · Oil on wood · 13¼ × 8⅞″ · Mauritshuis, The Hague

Carel Fabritius was killed in an explosion at Delft in 1654—the year that this picture was painted. He was probably the most talented artist to have passed through Rembrandt's studio and in turn he was to exercise a decisive influence on such artists as Jan Vermeer and Pieter de Hooch. Paintings definitely attributed to him are few in number and most of them show some revolutionary aspect of his art. *The Goldfinch* is not only remarkable for its *trompe l'oeil* realism and its simplicity, but also for the typical Fabritius device—the reverse of Rembrandt's custom—of setting dark objects against a light background. Here the bird and cage absorb the darkness while the rough wall behind is bathed in light. The result is to bring the spectator unexpectedly into contact with the composition: instead of receding, the bird and cage seem to jut forward.

JAN VERMEER (1632–75) *Young Woman Standing at a Virginal* Oil on canvas · 20⅜ × 17¼″ · National Gallery, London

Jan Vermeer seems to have passed his whole life in the quiet atmosphere of Delft. His art was influenced by the Utrecht Italianate artists and also by Carel Fabritius. But he developed the interior as a complete category of art, preferring to reduce the strong daylight of Fabritius into the pearly tone that light has in this picture, where it filters coolly through the window. There is never any drama in Vermeer's compositions, which are rather studies in silence and intimacy. Light is always the protagonist. It fills whole cubes of space with liquid effect. Here the girl, the instrument, the chair are each arranged almost like abstract shapes.

JAN VERMEER *The Little Street at Delft* · c. 1658 · Oil on canvas · 21⅜ × 17⅞″ · Rijksmuseum, Amsterdam

Occasionally Vermeer moves outside into the streets of his native town. He is the creator of the townscape panorama of Delft (in the Mauritshuis) and also of the intimate "close-up" scene here, which shows the influence of Carel Fabritius. The technique is less brash than Fabritius' and the paint has a pellucid quality as it creates the varying textures of the street, the warm brick of the houses and the soft sky. With Vermeer's response to the bricks and mortar goes his feeling for the buildings as lived-in: they are people's houses and he is concerned not only with the architecture of Delft but with ordinary life in Delft. Yet this genre interest is beautifully control d. The scene is at once realistic and heightened; it is an ideal Delft created by the artist.

PIETER DE HOOCH (1629– after 1684?) *Interior with Woman Holding a Glass* · Oil on canvas · 29 × 25½″ · National Gallery, London

Pieter de Hooch was not born at Delft, but many of his best pictures originate during the period he lived there—after having married a Delft woman—in the 1650s, and he has left many pictorial records of its life. This *Interior* must date from this time and probably represents a tavern scene. Like Vermeer, De Hooch is fascinated by effects of light and this is more truly the subject than the ostensible genre scene. The effect is less pearly and muted than one finds in Vermeer, but an equally complete room—showing both floor and ceiling—is modeled and given recession. The woman makes an effective dark silhouette against the pale wall and window and it is in the glass that she holds up like a prism that all the room's luminous brightness seems concentrated.

JAN VERMEER (1632–75) *The Painter's Studio*, and detail of the candelabra · c. 1665 · Oil on canvas · 47¼ × 39⅜″ · Kunsthistorisches Museum, Vienna

Vermeer's interest in effects of light, and in all optical effects, probably reaches its culmination in this picture of himself (?) painting in his studio a model who poses for the allegorical figure of Fame. But the picture's importance is not so much for what it tells us about seventeenth-century artists' studios as for its formal beauty: an almost abstract beauty of the pattern of the black-and-white tiles, the patterned curtain, and the geometrical precision of the glittering candelabra hanging from the beamed ceiling. The studio seems an ideal room, carefully ordered and plotted,

lifted outside time and placed in a tranquil dimension of its own. The painter sinks his individuality into being simply this figure—also of black and white—who is seen from the back. He becomes only one more object in the beautifully planned space where each surface has been caressed by light until it is as smooth and glowing as if made of pearl. Over natural appearances Vermeer has spread the bloom of his wonderful technique.

Paint as handled by Vermeer is like some thick glaze applied to porcelain. The glitter of light on the candelabra is only the final touch of verisimilitude, for the paint seems to have been modeled into solidity: it *is* the candelabra.
Detail is shown on next pages

247

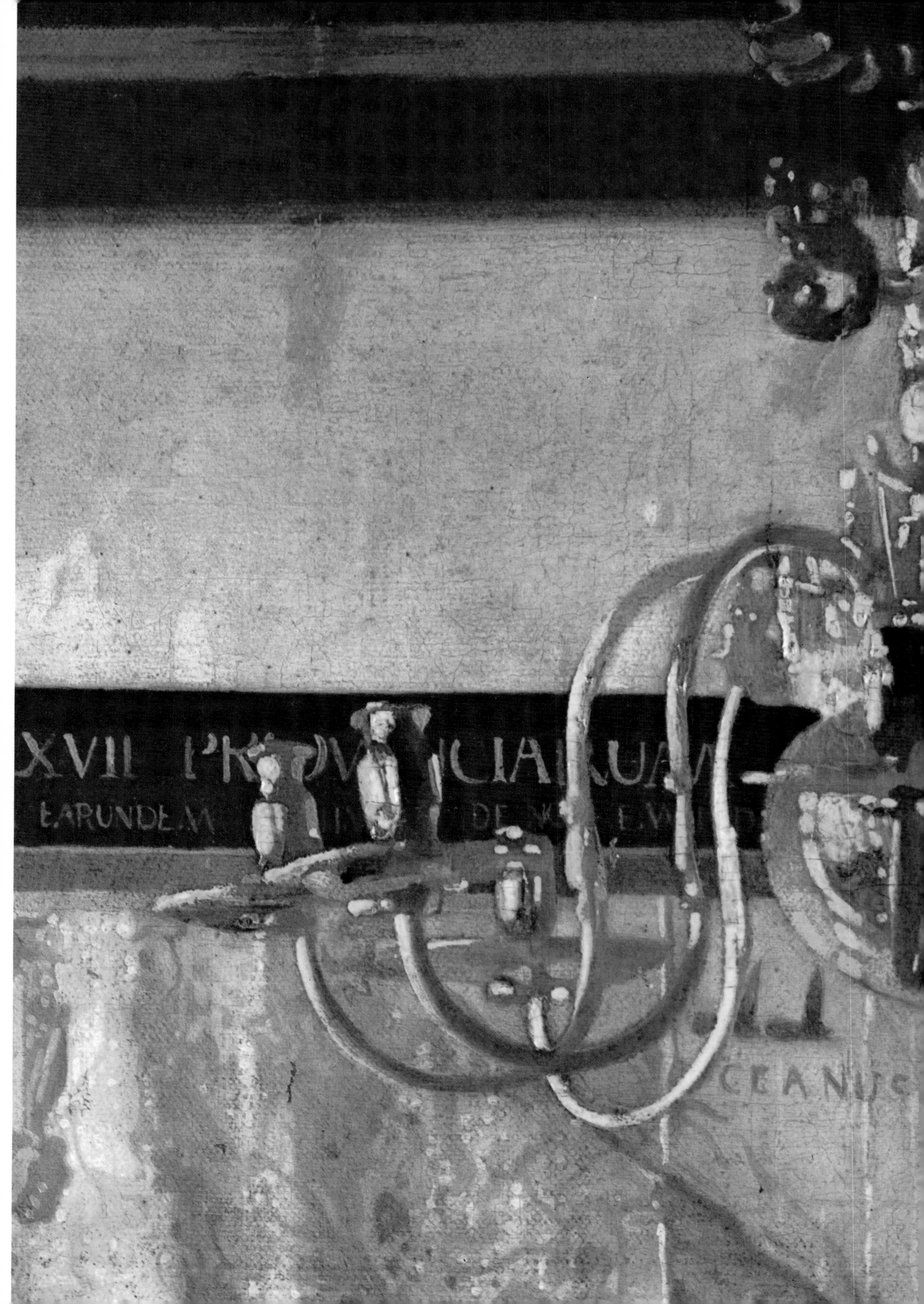

PIETER DE HOOCH *A Dutch Courtyard* · c. 1656 · Oil on canvas · 26¾ × 23⅛″ · National Gallery of Art, Washington, D.C. (Mellon Collection)

In his outdoor scenes De Hooch seems to come less close to Vermeer, and to suffer less by comparison. He is fond of open-air light effects—as in this picture—which seem to be more closely related to Carel Fabritius than to Vermeer. There is less intense concentration than in Vermeer, and perhaps more of sheer charm. The painter is particularly responsive to the texture of tiles and weathered brick, wooden shutters and fences—all bathed in strong sunlight. The mood is more convivial too, and suitably open-air. Two cavaliers enjoy the spectacle of the woman drinking wine from a tall glass, watched by the solemn figure of the child at the right. A moment of ordinary life is recorded by the artist, attached deeply to his period. In place of Vermeer's timelessness we have a sense of actuality.

PIETER JANSSENS (active after 1650) *A Woman Reading* · Oil on canvas · 30 × 23¾″ · The Old Pinakothek, Munich

Pieter Janssens shows how it was possible for the comparatively minor Dutch artist to achieve at least a single masterpiece. This picture is certainly Janssens'. Without the example of Vermeer it would not have been possible, and yet the result is something very different. Its air of tranquillity is more homely than Vermeer's. Part of the picture's charm is in the air of deep domestic intimacy which it suggests—cleverly emphasized by turning the woman away from the spectator. She sits reading in a sparsely furnished room, with its bare floor made to seem yet more bare because of the pair of shoes that stand on it, making one of the few color notes in the restricted tonality. Everything breathes simplicity, silence, preoccupation.

GERARD TERBORCH (1617–81) *The Concert* · Oil on wood 22 × 17⅞″ · State Museums, Berlin

Gerard Terborch is one of the leaders in the evolution of a new type of genre picture in seventeenth-century Holland, under the influence of Gabriel Metsu. The interior itself is of less importance than its inhabitants, who are usually engaged in some polite occupation—very often, as here, in music-making. But even the figures themselves are really of less importance than the new insistence on the decorative effect of materials, particularly clothes. *The Concert* is memorable, above all, for the sumptuous colors and the varied textures of the clothes worn by the woman in the foreground. Paint has created the soft brown fur at her neck and the shiny folds of her white satin skirt—itself a marvel of eye-deceiving virtuosity. Technically brilliant though the picture is, it is perhaps rather slight in content, and there is an almost dangerous emphasis on the merely decorative.

GERARD TERBORCH *Boy Picking Fleas from a Dog* · Canvas on oak · 15 × 11¼″ · The Old Pinakothek, Munich

Simple scenes of ordinary life are perhaps handled by Terborch with more feeling than his compositions of ladies in polite society. The simplicity of the *Boy Picking Fleas* extends to the much quieter color range and restricted tonality. Terborch makes very effective use of the simple elements of the composition, giving the spectator a close-up sense of the foreground table where the boy's hat lies, and thus bringing us into contact with the whole scene.

GABRIEL METSU (1629–67) *A Man Writing a Letter* · Oil on canvas · 11 × 10¼″ · Museum of Montpellier

Gabriel Metsu was probably a pupil of Gerard Dou and was to concentrate in his later years entirely on genre subjects, remarkable for their virtuosity of handling. He settled in Amsterdam and probably the present picture dates from this, the most mature period of his career. He combines the ultimate in interior-painting with artificial lighting so that, for all its quiet subject matter, the picture is a drama of light and darkness. The painter is no longer concerned with daylight, but uses the light thrown by a single candle to make of the interior something at once dusky and glowing. The soft darkness increases the sense of intimacy. One's eye is even more drawn to the tenderly painted servant girl who patiently stands waiting for the letter to be finished, than to the man seated writing. As well as the drama of light, there is also a miniature drama of humanity.

GERARD DOU (1613–75) *The Doctor* · Oil on wood · 19⅜ × 14⅝″ · Kunsthistorisches Museum, Vienna

Gerard Dou was as a young boy a pupil of Rembrandt, but his art was to evolve in a very different direction: toward the creation of small, highly finished anecdotal genre pictures which were to have tremendous success. Dou was indeed one of the most successful artists of the period and his reputation extended beyond Holland. *The Doctor* is very typical, especially in the device of seeing the interior through, as it were, a window. These "niche" pictures were, in fact, derived from Rembrandt but popularized by Dou. The bas-relief of children playing with a goat, which occurs in the present composition, is a favorite motif in Dou's paintings and seems to be copied after a lost work by the famous Flemish sculptor Duquesnoy.

JAN STEEN (1626–79) *The Skittle Players* · c. 1652 · Oil on wood · 31¼ × 23¾″ · National Gallery, London

Jan Steen represents the livelier, and ruder, aspects of low life in seventeenth-century Holland. His pictures are often intended to be both satirical and funny. But there are other aspects to Steen—who as a painter nearly always handled the actual medium with great delicacy. There is nothing rowdy about the beautifully painted *Skittle Players* which has something of the bloom of Vermeer. The skittle players hardly disturb the peaceful atmosphere, with the trio seated at the left enjoying repose in the garden of a country inn ("The White Swan," to judge from its signboard at the left of the picture). Steen's response to natural scenery is exquisitely shown in the glowing foliage of the tall trees which rise into a sunny sky and seem to screen the inn and its visitors from all intrusion by the outside world.

ADRIAEN BROUWER (1605/6–1638) *The Card Player* · Oil on wood · 13 × 16⅞″ · The Old Pinakothek, Munich

Adriaen Brouwer is the link between low-life genre painting in Flanders and Holland. He himself was Flemish by birth and he is in some ways the inheritor of the subject matter of Bruegel. But he lived part of his short life in Holland and may even have been a pupil of Frans Hals at Haarlem. His chief subject is the inn interior, usually with peasants carousing or playing cards. The present picture is typical of his ability to combine this sort of uncouth subject matter with extremely sensitive handling of paint and nuances of color—for instance, the man in green and the crumpled tablecloth.

ADRIAEN VAN OSTADE (1610–54) *The Fiddler* · Oil on wood · 17⅝ × 16½″ · Mauritshuis, The Hague

Adriaen van Ostade is said to have been a pupil of Brouwer and there is great affinity of subject matter between the two painters. Like Brouwer, he preferred to depict the life of merrymaking peasants; and here the visit of a wandering fiddler to a village inn provides him a subject. His pictures are usually small in scale and he was enormously prolific and popular. A whole stream of imitations and copies began to flow already at that period, and his work remained in vogue—especially in France—during the eighteenth century.

HENDRICK TERBRUGGHEN (1588?–1629) *Shepherd Playing a Flute* · c. 1621 · Oil on canvas · 27⅝ × 21⅝″ · State Picture Gallery, Cassel

Hendrick Terbrugghen studied in Italy and is the first important northern Caravaggist to return and settle in Holland. No dated pictures by him are known before 1620 and the present one is of the following year. He concentrated chiefly on religious subjects and pastoral Arcadian figures, such as this shepherd. All his work shows a very individual interpretation of Caravaggio's manner, particularly in his color schemes and his fondness for over-life-size studies—as here—of a half-length single figure. The picture is half realistic and half fantasy—perhaps rather a boy posing as a shepherd, and equipped also with a fancy-dress hat. Terbrugghen had brought back from Italy a bold handling and revolutionary realism which were to become established especially at Utrecht and to lead to a whole group of Caravaggesque artists there.

GERARD VAN HONTHORST (1590–1656) *The Procuress* (detail) · c. 1625 · Oil on wood · 28 × 41″ · Centraal Museum, Utrecht

Gerard van Honthorst was one of the principal channels for the dissemination of Caravaggio's style in northern Europe. Probably younger than Terbrugghen, he lived much longer and became an internationally famous figure. He trained in Rome and was particularly to popularize the night scene (in Italy he was called *Gherardo della notte*) and highly realistic candlelight effects similar to that in *The Procuress*, which dates from after his return to Utrecht. The scene is a typical one of genre, but very carefully planned—the device of the dark shape of the pleading man silhouetted in profile at the left, which throws into vivid relief the smiling woman, so provocatively illuminated. In this way the dramatic contrasts of extreme light and darkness are paralleled by the psychological drama of the subject itself.

FRANS HALS (c. 1580–1666) *The Gipsy Girl (La Bohémienne)* · Oil on wood · 22¾ × 20½″ · The Louvre, Paris

Frans Hals was Flemish by origin and was probably born at Antwerp. But early in his life his parents settled at Haarlem and Hals was to remain active there for the whole of his long career. Besides painting portraits, he was the creator of genre studies, usually of single figures as in *The Gipsy Girl*. While the subject recalls Terbrugghen and Honthorst, the striking difference is Hals's lively handling of paint—which has something of Rubens in its rapid sketch-like brilliance. In this picture the girl's white chemise is painted with dazzling broken touches, jagged strokes of paint which give the material as much vivacity as her face. Everything gives the feeling of having been seized as an "impression"—a fleeting moment as transitory as the girl's expression. The color is deliberately restricted and simple. Hals was to have many pupils and exert great influence—not least on Manet and the Impressionists in the nineteenth century.

252

FRANS HALS *Banquet of the Officers of the Guild of St. George* (detail) · 1627 · Oil on canvas · 70½ × 101¼″ · Frans Hals Museum, Haarlem

Although this is only a detail from a much larger group portrait, it gives sufficient idea of the crowded group portraits of guilds and military companies that were to be a speciality of Hals's work. Such portraits raised a number of problems—among them the need to give a good likeness and equal prominence to each sitter in the group. Hals was able to solve this by very full lighting of the sitters and by giving an almost snapshot air of actuality to all the varying poses. The result manages to be informal and yet coherent, as well as dignified. The opportunities offered for color and decorative effect were chiefly restricted to the sashes and banners of the companies. Hals cleverly makes use of these as the final enlivening touch to the large composition. The air of gay improvisation is misleading because, to achieve this apparent spontaneity, the artist had to work very hard.

FRANS HALS *The Women Regents of the Haarlem Almshouse* · 1664 · Oil on canvas · 67¼ × 98″ · Frans Hals Museum, Haarlem

Despite his great productivity, Frans Hals suffered for many years from financial difficulties. In his very last years he and his wife were dependent on public charity at Haarlem and perhaps it is no accident that in these years his art took on a new depth. He now portrayed not gay military companies but the rather severe-looking groups who managed the charitable institutions of the city. *The Women Regents* was painted in 1664, not long before his death, and shows an almost Rembrandtesque profundity in its depiction of five plainly dressed women in a very simple setting. There is no suggestion of movement, but an intense gravity in these sober faces which reflect age and wisdom.

JOHANNES VERSPRONCK (1597–1662) *A Little Girl in Blue* · Oil on canvas · 32¼ × 26¼″ · Rijksmuseum, Amsterdam

Johannes Verspronck is not a major painter, but the creator at times of memorable portraits. He was a Haarlem artist who studied under Frans Hals. His brushwork is less showy than that of Hals, but he has at least equal receptivity to the character of the sitter—and this sensitive portrait is a demonstration of it. The child is dressed up in finery—beautifully painted white lace and unexpected, pale blue stiff silk—but yet retains the touching appeal of childhood. Though so simple and effective in presentation, the portrait indicates a revolution in accepting children as subjects for pictures. The social and family side of Dutch life at the period is summed up in this minor masterpiece.

HERCULES SEGHERS (1589/90–1633) *Landscape with the Meuse* · c. 1625–27 · Canvas on panel · 11½ × 18″ · Boymans van Beuningen Museum, Rotterdam

Hercules Seghers is an important pioneer of landscape in seventeenth-century Holland, both as a painter and etcher. There is likely to have been an exchange of influence between him and Rembrandt (who owned as many as eight pictures by Seghers). Seghers represents also the transition from the Flemish fantasy landscapes of the later sixteenth century to the more powerful realistic seventeenth-century landscapes which were to be created in Holland. Seghers himself retains some elements of romantic feeling in his panoramic mountainous scenes, with thundery effects and bold monochromatic handling. In the present picture, the foreground is heavily shadowed, and its oppressive effect is broken only by the gleam of distant water. The feeling of wildness is accentuated finally by the absence of human figures.

JACOB VAN RUISDAEL (1628/9–1682) *Wheatfields* · c. 1670 ·
Oil on canvas · 39⅜ × 51¼″ · Metropolitan Museum of
Art, New York

Jacob van Ruisdael is probably the greatest of the Dutch
seventeenth-century landscape painters. As well as distinguished pupils like Meindert Hobbema, he had many pupils
and imitators. Strong pride in the landscape of Holland is
expressed in his work, with its response above all to the
shifting patterns of light and shade in a northern country
so often overcast and cloudy. Ruisdael's wonderful skies
are never quite still. Indeed, he prefers the ominous atmospheric effect that broods over the *Wheatfields*, where
light turns livid the strips of the fields and the patch of
road where a man walks. While the actual landscape has
nothing remarkable or grand about it, the sky is an agitated
pageant of streaming clouds which makes the spectator
feel—almost physically—the weather depicted.

JACOB VAN RUISDAEL *The Mill near Wijk-bij-Duurstede*
(detail) · c. 1670 · Oil on canvas · 32⅝ × 39¾″ · Rijksmuseum, Amsterdam

Though this is only a detail, it conveys enough of the
tremendous power of Ruisdael—especially in his later
work. With his response to the varied moods of nature
there went perhaps an instinctive feeling for dark, almost
melancholy days. In Ruisdael's best pictures, the ever-
changing pattern of light and shade seems almost to mirror
the artist's character, and he is never better than when
catching an oppressive, thundery atmosphere. Here the
tall shape of the mill stamps itself boldly against the overcast sky, while a patch of red roof gleams with sinister
brightness. With his sensitivity to atmosphere goes Ruisdael's feeling for the textures of wood and foliage and stone.

PHILIPS KONINCK (1619–88) *Extensive Landscape with a
Hawking Party* · Oil on canvas · 52¼ × 63⅛″ · National
Gallery, London

Philips Koninck seems to have been influenced as a
landscape painter by both Rembrandt and Seghers. Although now thought of largely as a landscape painter,
Koninck in his own period was better known for his
portraits and genre scenes. *Extensive Landscape* shows a vast
panorama, apparently seen from a very high viewpoint.
Indeed, landscape is subordinated to the vast area of
cloud-filled sky where heavy cumulus lies almost threat-
eningly over the flat countryside. The dramatically dark
band of shadow that wraps the middle distance is broken by
distant gleams over the town and far hills—a device recalling
Segher's *Landscape with the Meuse* (page 253).

MEINDERT HOBBEMA (1638–1709) *The Avenue, Middelharnis* · c. 1689 · Oil on canvas · 40¾ × 55½″ · National
Gallery, London

Meindert Hobbema represents a more prosaic world than
Ruisdael's, though he was Ruisdael's pupil and very much
indebted to the older artist's example. *The Avenue* is Hobbema's masterpiece—a masterpiece of effectiveness which,
once seen, is always remembered. Neither the sky nor the
landscape is painted with the sensitivity of Ruisdael.
Hobbema is much more the recorder of actual topography—
and this view of Middelharnis is remarkably accurate. But
thanks to the presence of the tall trees that line the avenue,
Hobbema has a perfect subject: the eye is led for a walk up
the perspective of the narrowing road, to encounter the
man strolling with his dog. The composition is bold and
instantly memorable. Hobbema has produced a picture
which is the quintessential landscape of seventeenth-
century Holland.

PAULUS POTTER (1625–54) *Landscape with a Boar* · 1650 ·
Oil on canvas · 11⅜ × 11″ · Collection Van Beuningen,
Vierhouten

Paulus Potter was the son of a painter and clearly precocious during his brief lifetime. He concentrated on small
pictures, almost always of animals in landscapes, painted
with great care and delicate aerial effects—as in the subtly
colored sky of the present landscape. Once so famous, and
now rather neglected, Potter is one of those painters with
the equivalent of nearly perfect pitch. There is an uncanny
accuracy of tone in the warm light that here bathes the
hillside with the deer and the clump of trees at the left. It
is a softer and more lyrical atmosphere than that of either
Ruisdael or Hobbema. An almost southern sunshine makes
the whole picture glow with warmth.

JAN VAN GOYEN (1596–1656) *Haarlemmermeer* · 1656 · Oil
on canvas · 15⅝ × 27¼″ · Staedel Institute, Frankfurt

Jan van Goyen was one of the most prolific of Dutch
landscape painters, working all over Holland. The present
picture was painted in the year of his death and shows the
final evolution of his style. He is particularly the painter, not
so much of Dutch landscape, as of Dutch seascape—perpet-
ually reminding the spectator of the ever-present water that
intersects and partly surrounds Holland. With Van Goyen
water is a mirror of the sky. He creates stormy effects—as
in the present picture—in which people and land dwindle to
mere black dots and strips, and only a few boats drift
somberly, their sails dark against the lurid sky with its
scudding, ragged clouds.

ALBERT CUYP (1620–91) *A Herdsman with Cows by a River* ·
Oil on wood · 17⅞ × 29⅛″ · National Gallery, London

Albert Cuyp began to paint first in the style of Jan van
Goyen but gradually his pictures became flooded with a
golden light such as in the present view. Though the
subject and setting are typically Dutch, there is an Italian
warmth and brightness which Cuyp probably derived
from such artists as Jan Both who had lived in Italy. With
Cuyp the landscape and the cattle are hardly more than
objects to diversify the buoyant atmosphere—all liquid sky
and crystalline water. In this atmosphere everything is
washed into soft tones of caramel and golden-brown. The
figures are like corks—stubby like them, too—which seem
to float between sea and sky. The elements are Cuyp's
subject and in his pictures seem always calm and domestic,
a fitting environment for country people going about their
daily life.

WILLEM VAN DE VELDE (1633–1707) *The Cannon Shot* · Oil
on canvas · 30⅞ × 26⅜″ · Rijksmuseum, Amsterdam

Willem van de Velde turns the seascape increasingly into
a representation of shipping or of actual naval events. The
present picture shows his attention to the minutiae of the
structure and rigging of vessels—though no particular
historic moment is depicted. The man-of-war at the right
fires a cannon shot probably as a salute and this explosion
alone disturbs the placid calm of the scene. Historically
Van de Velde represents the rise of two great maritime
empires—those of Holland and England. It is no accident
that, having worked in Holland as a young man, he settled
in England and found considerable employment there.

255

AMBROSIUS BOSSCHAERT (c. 1565–1621) *Vase of Flowers* · Oil on canvas · 12⅝ × 10⅜″ · Collection Perman, Stockholm

Ambrosius Bosschaert was Flemish by birth but was to live and work in Holland. He is one of the first painters restricting himself to the new category of the flower piece, and Flemish and Dutch styles agreeably combine in his pictures. He is fond of setting the flowers in a glass vase placed on a ledge—as here—and with a very Flemish-style landscape extending behind. The flowers themselves are painted with an almost primitive directness, which is part of the picture's charm. As well as being decorative, the picture stands for the seventeenth century's developing interest in the natural world: in botany, and even in insects and shells. All are recorded with scientific fidelity and the picture may be said to instruct as well as to please.

WILLEM KALF (1619–93) *Still Life* · 1662 · Oil on canvas · 25¼ × 20⅞″ · State Museums, Berlin

Willem Kalf is the Vermeer among painters of still life, with a deep, glowing sense of color and feeling for light-bathed textures that probably do derive from the great Delft artist. In Dutch seventeenth-century painting, the still life becomes a category of picture, and in Kalf the arrangement of a few objects on a table is not so much a reflection of ordinary domestic life as a completely artistic invention. He chooses his objects very carefully: here a Chinese bowl and lid are set off in tone by the orange and the unpeeled lemon, and they in turn by the richly colored Turkish rug. The light falls warmly on all these different surfaces and Kalf achieves a sensuous effect from juxtaposing the various textures of hard porcelain and glass, soft rug, and mat surface of the fruits.

WILLEM CLAESZ HEDA (1593/4–1680/82) *Still Life (Breakfast Table)* · Oil on wood · 21¼ × 32¼″ · State Picture Gallery, Dresden

Willem Claesz Heda represents a more austere and cooler-toned version of the still-life picture when compared with Kalf. If Kalf is always seeking strong sunlit effects, Heda prefers almost moon-blanched tones of gray and greenish-silver. In place of Kalf's rich rug this *Still Life* shows a plain white tablecloth, with a few pewter plates. The background is Heda's typical plain one, colored very much the same as the grayish glasses of pale wine. The whole atmosphere is as if bathed by northern light. In its cold clarity Heda depicts everything with great precision and delicacy. Like Kalf, he transcends the mere recording of objects and achieves an abstract, nearly geometrical, beauty of shapes.

PIETER SAENREDAM (1597–1665) *Interior of the Church of Assendelft* · Oil on wood · 19⅝ × 29⅞″ · Rijksmuseum, Amsterdam

Pieter Saenredam, one of the leading painters of church interiors, was not only interested in architectural effects in pictures but was in touch with important architects of the period—such as Jacob van Campen, the builder of the Town Hall at Amsterdam. In Saenredam's drawings there is an architectural accuracy which accords well with the artist's practice of noting the actual day and month, as well as the year, when the drawing was executed. But in his paintings Saenredam is freer and can modify for compositional reasons the actual structure of a building. The result is to give a timeless quality to his blond church interiors where the eye is led serenely through a succession of arches and vaults, all honey-colored, as if into infinity.

JAN VAN DER HEYDEN (1637–1712) *Imaginary View of the Church at Veere* · Oil on canvas · 12½ × 14⅛″ · Mauritshuis, The Hague

Jan van der Heyden is more than a recorder of the urban scene in seventeenth-century Holland. He is the creator of scenes where the actual and the imaginary are blended for artistic effect. Even when his pictures seem entirely accurate topographically they are often full of slight fantasy elements which give to them an almost ideal air—the air of being perfect towns. Van der Heyden's response to light gives everything a crystal clarity: serene skies arch over luminously glowing buildings and streets. His townscapes seem as miniature and clear as if captured in a glass paperweight. There is always about them a peepshow effect, reminding one that painted peepshows were a specialty of Holland at the period.

JAN ASSELYN (1610–52) *A Roman Bridge* · Oil on canvas · 32 × 46⅛″ · Collection Duke of Bedford, Woburn Abbey, Bletchley

Jan Asselyn lived and worked for some years in Italy before settling in Holland. He was certainly influenced by the achievements of several artists in Rome, most outstandingly by Claude. It is a warmer version of Claude's light that floods his pictures—and in *A Roman Bridge* it has become a deep sunset glow that lends the final suggestion of romance to the scene. Italy is seen not so much literally as in a dream-like haze, with all the associations of country, ruins, southern light, fused into an almost visionary whole. It is a view of Italy very consciously seen through the eyes of a northern artist.

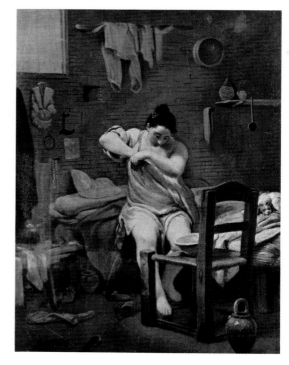

GIUSEPPE MARIA CRESPI (1665–1747) *Girl with a Flea* · c. 1707–9 · Oil on canvas · 18 × 13⅜″ · Uffizi Gallery, Florence

Giuseppe Maria Crespi bridges the gap between the Bolognese tradition of the seventeenth century and the revived Venetian School of the eighteenth century. Himself born within Guercino's lifetime, he lived to train both Piazzetta and Pietro Longhi. In Crespi there is carried on a response to the actual medium of oil paint, as well as a Caravaggesque love of dramatic effects of light, and an intensive realism of setting. The natural and the undignified appeal to Crespi; he invests them with his own sense of human dignity. *Girl with a Flea* is a deliberate piece of humble, even squalid, genre. It asserts the truth of the individual and shows also that art can take any subject and make a picture out of it.

ALESSANDRO MAGNASCO (1677–1749) *Punchinello and His Son* · Oil on canvas · 13⅜ × 12¼″ · Collection Hoine Gatte Casazza, Venice

Alessandro Magnasco is still a rather mysterious figure whose highly personal style of painting seems the reflection of a strange, haunted character. His rapid calligraphic handling of paint looks forward to the Guardi, but his color is much more sober than theirs. His elongated figures are agitated and shaken as if by fever and the mood of his pictures is melodramatic. *Punchinello and His Son* is in a more tender vein than is usual with Magnasco. In place of hysterically praying monks there is only this simple group of father and child sitting eating in a kitchen. The picture is, in one sense, ordinary genre, but genre heightened by the figures, which are from the *commedia dell'arte* yet are shown not acting, but at a private and domestic moment.

SEBASTIANO RICCI (1659–1734) *Esther before Ahasuerus* ·
Oil on canvas 18½ × 13″ National Gallery, London

Sebastiano Ricci was the oldest of the creators of the
Rococo at Venice and one of the most important figures in
the dissemination of the style all over Europe. Probably
under the influence of Luca Giordano, Ricci turned
back to the great Venetians of the sixteenth century,
particularly Veronese. Veronese's brilliant colors and
superb decorative effects were to inspire Ricci to such
pictures as *Esther before Ahasuerus* which is probably a late
work and shows the painter at his most accomplished—
but still with echoes of Veronese in design and color. It is a
typically operatic, Rococo moment of drama which is
shown—a drama that centers on a woman—as Esther
dares to appear before Ahasuerus and the king extends in
mercy toward her his golden scepter.

SEBASTIANO RICCI *The Resurrection* · Fresco · Chapel of the
Royal Hospital, Chelsea

As well as working in Vienna and visiting Paris, Sebastiano Ricci traveled to England. He was tempted to go by the
prospect of decorating the dome of St. Paul's, but he failed
to get the commission. However, he did decorate the apse
of Chelsea Hospital Chapel with *The Resurrection*. Here he
revealed to English eyes a new lightness of palette and an
almost gay drama even in a religious subject. His
decorative gifts enabled him to solve the problem of filling the apse
with an animated and effective composition. It is into a
golden heaven radiant with hosts of clustering angels
that Christ triumphantly rises. Everything sweeps about
him and he is like the conductor of some colossal orchestra
who sets the whole composition in motion.

258

GIOVANNI ANTONIO PELLEGRINI (1675–1741) *Musicians* ·
Oil on plaster · Kimbolton Castle School

Giovanni Antonio Pellegrini was the most traveled of
all the peripatetic Venetian Rococo decorators and the
first to come to England. For the Duke of Manchester's
country house, Kimbolton, he painted several decorations
including, on a staircase, the *Musicians*. The picture is
painted in oils on the plaster of the wall and has a brilliance
of color partly achieved by heavy impasto. As so often
with these artists, the inspiration derives from Veronese
who had already made marvelous use of oriental costumes.
Pellegrini treats the problem of decoration in a thoroughly
lighthearted manner and with the playful piece of illusionism whereby the boy leans out of the composition to
feed the dog. No story is told. Three brilliantly clad musicians enchantingly play on a feigned balcony; they and the
boy are the only "subject."

GIOVANNI ANTONIO PELLEGRINI *Rebecca at the Well* · Oil on
canvas · 50 × 40″ · National Gallery, London

There is a sense of improvisation about all Pellegrini's
compositions, even when they have a subject such as this
Biblical scene. The setting is seldom more than a feathery
tree—virtually a theatrical property—and the figures too
have a feathery insubstantiality as if made up from twists
of colored drapery. Pellegrini simply makes the occasion
an opportunity to paint one of his favorite blond women—
her blondness set off by ravishing blue and white clothes—
and pose her in a faintly exotic atmosphere. Above all, the
picture is intended to be decoration and Pellegrini never
forgets that intention. Light and air and shimmering color
all go to serve his purpose and contribute to the final
decorative effect.

GIAMBATTISTA TIEPOLO (1696–1770) *Temptation of St. Anthony* · Oil on canvas · 15¾ × 18½″ · Brera Gallery, Milan

Giambattista Tiepolo is the culmination of all the decorative tendencies of Venetian art, going back to Veronese and including Ricci and Pellegrini. He is also the end of that splendid tradition. When he died in Madrid the Rococo movement, already under attack for several years, was over. The climate of pure imagination which he represents was being replaced by serious Neoclassic "truth." History was replacing mythology, and the dreams and visions devised by Tiepolo were to seem frivolous to a more sober generation. *Temptation of St. Anthony* is an early work but it already reveals Tiepolo's imaginative gifts. The huddled dark figure of the saint is less important than the delightful Temptation herself, almost a hallucination.

GIAMBATTISTA TIEPOLO *The Holy House of Loreto* · Oil on canvas · 48⅞ × 33½″ · Academy of Fine Arts, Venice

No surface was too huge for Tiepolo to decorate, but his decorations have much less flippancy than Pellegrini's. He believes utterly in his own art and is able to create a completely valid imaginative world where nothing is impossible. Instinctively attracted to the miraculous—to all those moments when nature's law is broken—he was able to serve the Church magnificently. For churches all over North Italy, as well as at Venice, he frescoed and painted glorious visionary moments, like this of the Holy House being swept through the sky from Bethlehem to Loreto. This is the sketch for the ceiling decoration, now destroyed, in the church of the Scalzi, which gave the illusion of dissolving the vault, replacing it by an airy sky which deceived the spectator into experiencing a vision.

GIAMBATTISTA TIEPOLO *Rinaldo and Armida* · Oil on canvas · 39¼ × 55″ · Bavarian State Galleries, Munich

Again and again Tiepolo returned to the story, told by Tasso in *Gerusalemme Liberata*, of how the wicked enchantress Armida carried off the hero Rinaldo to her magic gardens where he forgot everything in his love for her. But the story was told in the eighteenth century by others besides Tiepolo. It was one of those stories of man beguiled by woman—like that of Anthony and Cleopatra—that the century loved. It was an opera, a ballet, the subject for numerous painters of all countries. And Tiepolo captures all the ingredients of the story, paying his tribute too to his century's obsession with the power of women.

DOMENICO TIEPOLO (1727–1804) *The Minuet* · Oil on canvas · 30⅞ × 43⅝″ · Catalan Museum of Fine Arts, Barcelona

Domenico Tiepolo was the devoted collaborator of his father whom he loyally served until the latter's death. But Domenico himself was really a very different artist, attached not to the world of imagination but to the solid world of fact. This appealed to his sense of the ludicrous, the satirical, and the topical. He is at home with clowns and mountebanks and masked dancers—figures recognizably from the Venice of his own period, wittily observed and set down in sparkling paint. Above all, he is linked to the new spirit of realism which pervaded the art of Goldoni. The dancing figures in Domenico's pictures might be characters strayed from a Goldoni comedy.

259

POMPEO GIROLAMO BATONI (1708–87) *Time Destroying Beauty* · 1746 · Oil on canvas · 53¼ × 28″ · National Gallery, London

Pompeo Girolamo Batoni stands as one of the leading exponents of the new Neoclassic style which took root in Rome and was to oppose successfully the Venetian Rococo. However, Batoni did not altogether understand the Neoclassic and he was certainly not a seriously "engaged" artist of the caliber of David, nor, intellectually, could he equal his German contemporary, Mengs. But his coldly sculptural art is grave and still, after the airy movement of the Rococo.

GIAMBATTISTA PIAZZETTA (1683–1754) *Assumption of the Virgin* · 1735 · Oil on canvas · 203 × 96⅞″ · The Louvre, Paris

Giambattista Piazzetta was older than Tiepolo and exercised considerable influence on him. Trained under Giuseppe Crespi, Piazzetta was not naturally sympathetic to the rainbow colors and movement of the Venetian decorators. The son of a woodcarver, he seems always to have been conscious of form and volume, and to prefer to model his figures in thick paint and in deliberately restricted tones of gray and white and brown—all used with exquisite effect. The *Assumption* is one of his largest altarpieces and was painted in 1735 for the Archbishop-Elector of Cologne, a great patron of Venetian artists.

GIAMBATTISTA PIAZZETTA *Rebecca at the Well* · Oil on canvas · 40⅛ × 53⅞″ · Brera Gallery, Milan

The contrast with Pellegrini's treatment of the same theme (page 261) tells something about the individuality of Piazzetta's art in the Venice of his day. Unlike Pellegrini and Tiepolo, Piazzetta was a slow worker. He was a rather withdrawn personality, though a teacher with many pupils. There is in his *Rebecca* a sense of drama that Pellegrini's completely lacks. Rebecca is a peasant girl surprised by the advances of a well-dressed, dashing gentleman who dangles a pearl necklace to attract her. Two rather sly girls at the right seem to be quite amused by the situation, and the whole picture breathes an unexpected air of countrified humor. The scene is treated not in terms of dignity, or charm, but in terms of plain humanity.

PIETRO LONGHI (1702–85) *The Dancing Lesson* (detail) · Oil on canvas · 23⅝ × 19¼″ · The Academy of Fine Arts, Venice

Pietro Longhi was to satisfy the interest of his century in ordinary humanity by painting small pictures of prosperous life as it was lived behind the façades of Venetian palaces. He is the devoted recorder of the daily existence there—and nowhere else. His people are usually engaged in amusing themselves, but the sentiments expressed are always very tentative. Not a great deal is happening and there is a general sense of "nothing too much." A man and woman may dance decorously—as here—watched by the fiddler and chaperoned by another woman. As documents of the life of the day, Longhi's pictures have a prettiness and charm which does not always avoid the trivial.

Antonio Canaletto (1697–1768) *Ascension Day at Venice*, and detail of a boat · Oil on canvas · 71⅝ × 102″ · The Crespi Collection, Milan

Antonio Canaletto did not invent the view picture *veduta*, but with him it became a new and quite definite category of picture. Its popularity and his fame resulted in a host of imitators and followers who fed on the picturesqueness of Venice and supplied souvenir paintings to generations of tourists. Venice is the subject of much of Canaletto's best work. Here the city is seen in the most splendid and important of all its festivals—that of Ascension Day, when the Doge rowed across the Lagoon for the Wedding of the Sea, symbolized by a ring dropped into the waters of the Adriatic. Canaletto not only conveys the bustling scene in the Bacino before the Doge's Palace but also responds to the whole atmosphere with passages of marvelous painting which suggest the water, the boats, the hangings, and finally the calm shapes of the buildings that are quintessentially Venice.

The crispness of Canaletto's technique is part of the secret of his ability to animate what would otherwise be mere topography. Working with quite a heavily loaded brush, he creates these figures who have their own reality—for all their miniature scale. Light, water, and air are all conveyed by the brilliant handling which captures a vivid moment of life in Venice.
Detail is shown on next pages

261

PIETRO LONGHI *The Rhinoceros* · 1751 · Oil on canvas ·
23⅞ × 19⅛″ · The Rezzonico Palace, Venice

The coming of a rhinoceros to Venice, for the carnival of
1751, created a great stir and a demand for paintings of the
animal. Longhi's picture is a record of it, done—as the
inscription tells—for the patrician Giovanni Grimani. It is
quite likely that Grimani is the man standing in the center of
the composition, between the showman and the woman in
carnival dress. A certain blankness in the spectators' reaction
to the rhinoceros seems part of a curious vacuity in Longhi
himself. He seldom bothers to organize his picture properly
and convinces us more by his attention to detail than by
his powers of composition. But he is part of Venice's
obsession with itself in the last years of the Republic when
its power had dwindled and it had become a show place.

ANTONIO CANALETTO (1697–1768) *View of the Thames*
(detail) · Private collection, London

Canaletto was from the first much patronized by English
visitors to Venice and it was probably inevitable that he
should finally come to England. With brief visits back to
Venice, he spent about ten years in England after 1746,
painting one or two other places but concentrating on
London. The Thames offered him the best substitute for
his native city's Grand Canal and he seems to have preferred
rather distant views which allowed him to present a panorama of London and the river. English light did not have
the sparkle of Venetian, and the architecture in London
clearly did not appeal very much to him. But water and
boats and bridges could still be painted with the detail, and
affection, that came from Canaletto's knowledge.

BERNARDO BELLOTTO (1720–80) *View of the Gazzada*
1744 · Oil on canvas · 25⅝ × 39¼″ · Brera Gallery, Milan

Bernardo Bellotto was the pupil of his uncle, Canaletto,
and his early work betrays the debt. But Bellotto was
basically a rather different painter, though he continued
the tradition of the view picture. When quite young he left
Italy forever, and painted at Dresden, Vienna, and—
eventually—Warsaw, where he settled. *View of the Gazzada*
is one of his rare early paintings of an Italian scene, but
already the tonality is distinct from Canaletto's, as is the
technique. Cool shades of blue and green give an almost
subaqueous effect to Bellotto's pictures and he seems to
have more affinity with northern than with southern
light—even in his early work.

FRANCESCO GUARDI (1712–93) *Ascension Day at Venice* ·
Oil on canvas · 26¼ × 39½″ · The Louvre, Paris

Francesco Guardi is inevitably compared with his contemporary Canaletto, by whom he was certainly influenced.
Although this picture represents a different moment
from that in Canaletto's picture (page 258), together they
make a fascinating comparison and neatly reveal how
very diverse was the two painters' attitude to depicting
the Venetian festival. Guardi's is a much more airy scene,
more loosely composed and more impressionistic in handling. Everything is subordinated to the almost equal expanses of sea and sky. Between these two elements the
boats seem frail structures, and people dwindle to being
hardly bigger than ants. Buildings are pushed well away
into the distance. And sparkling light blends water and
air into one atmospheric whole.

FRANCESCO GUARDI *Venice: The Doge's Palace* · Oil on canvas · $22\frac{3}{4} \times 30''$ · National Gallery, London

The miracle of Venice remains its rising from the waters of the Lagoon—a sight that can never fail to surprise and enchant. Guardi seems always moved by it, always responsive to the ubiquitous water which laps at the base of the buildings and makes them all become like boats. His view of the Doge's Palace and the buildings along the Molo emphasizes the jumbled effect, and the straggling line of buildings receding into the distance. It is a different truth from Canaletto's, more wayward and perhaps more poetic. Guardi is the last great interpreter of the city. And four years after his death the Republic came to an end.

FRANCESCO GUARDI *Venice: Piazza San Marco* · Oil on canvas · $11\frac{5}{8} \times 17\frac{3}{4}''$ · Kunsthistorisches Museum, Vienna

In Guardi's late work he is completely emancipated from Canaletto. His style has become the complete expression of his artistic personality and it is well summed up in the present picture. Even the architecture of Piazza San Marco seems to have changed, because Guardi shows the Piazza with the elaborate wooden arcading designed by Macaruzzi in 1776 and from that time on erected in the Piazza during the Ascension Day carnival. This graceful structure breaks the familiar rectangle of the scene, and Guardi enjoys the sweeping curves which have a Rococo vivacity. The same vivacity animates the tiny figures which are mere squiggles and drops of paint and which yet communicate a lively sense of life.

FRANCESCO GUARDI *Venice: Piazza San Marco* (detail) · Oil on canvas · $24 \times 39''$ · The Carrara Academy, Bergamo

Where Canaletto recorded Venice with precision, asserting the firm verticals and horizontals of its edifices, Guardi exaggerates the drama of the city. His *Piazza San Marco* is seen in steep perspective, with the campanile of San Marco rising tall and needle-thin—taller and thinner than in Canaletto's views, but the drama and shade here remind one of Canaletto's early pictures. From him Guardi has borrowed the effective device of plunging the Procuratie buildings at the right into deep shadow and then showing the patch of Doge's Palace beyond bathed in warm sunlight.

FRANZ ANTON MAULPERTSCH (1724–96) *The Holy Family* · Oil on canvas $50 \times 33\frac{3}{8}''$ Kunsthistorisches Museum, Vienna

Franz Anton Maulpertsch is only one of the great Rococo painters produced in Austria and Germany during the eighteenth century. It could be said that the Rococo was really most at home there, and certainly nowhere else were buildings so beautifully designed to accommodate altarpieces and frescoes. The tendency toward dissolution of forms is shown at its most extreme in the sweet mists of bright color which drift across Maulpertsch's pictures. The figures pose with affected grace, gesticulating with elegant, fluid hands, all reminiscent of Bavarian Rococo sculpture, in their gestures and in the sugar pinks and blues and gold of their flowing draperies.

265

ANTOINE WATTEAU (1684–1721) *The Judgment of Paris* ·
1720 · Oil on canvas · 18½ × 12¼″ · The Louvre, Paris

Antoine Watteau does more than represent the emancipation of French art from officialdom in the early eighteenth century. He stands for the completely personal mood in art—as much as Giorgione, if not more—and for a typically eighteenth-century interest in the psychology of love. Virtually a Fleming by birth, he had a native affinity to Rubens, whose health and vigor he must have envied. He himself was, in handling of paint, a Rubens turned miniaturist. It is significant that *The Judgment of Paris* was a subject painted several times by Rubens, and Watteau's composition is full of reminiscences of Rubens. But Watteau's scene is much more intimate.

ANTOINE WATTEAU *Fête Vénitienne* (detail) · 1718/19 · Oil on canvas · 22 × 18″ · National Gallery, Edinburgh

This detail shows the central figure, the woman dancing in a park, in the so-called *Fête Vénitienne*. It probably dates from late in Watteau's brief career, when his wonderfully sensitive handling of textures had reached the pitch revealed by the painting of the white silk dress here—which is set off by the rusts and purples of the background clothing and by the woman's own short blue cloak.

ANTOINE WATTEAU *La Gamme d'Amour* · Oil on canvas ·
20 × 23½″ · National Gallery, London

In Watteau's pictures music is the food of love—and also its language. Here the duet of the singer and her accompanist becomes more than a musical harmony, as they exchange glances. The pair of lovers is detached from the group in the background, isolated in the moment of discovering their own emotions. Watteau uses landscape in the same way that he does music, to suggest the natural and the free. Out of doors there is no constraint, no formality. His clothes too are easier than the actual clothes of the period—their fancy-dress version of seventeenth-century costume represents one more emancipation from convention. His people naturally prefer to sit at their ease, in flowing, graceful costumes, in sheltered parks and gardens. Yet, with all this beauty, there goes some sense of the passage of time. Love will not last forever. And here the antique stone bust seems a reminder that stone can survive when human beings and their passions have passed.

ANTOINE WATTEAU *The Concert* · c. 1716 · Oil on canvas ·
25⅝ × 36⅝″ · The Wallace Collection, London

Although he was never to visit Italy, Watteau was haunted by the great Italians—the Venetians, above all. He may well have known Giorgione's *Concert Champêtre* which was already in the French royal collection. That picture is the first large-scale statement of the twin theme of music and the countryside. It is, as it were, restated by Watteau's *Concert* where now a whole family are music-making or at least sharing in the musical atmosphere. The curled-up dog is certainly borrowed from Rubens—Watteau's other great source. But whereas it had been used by Rubens in his pageant of the *Coronation of Marie de Medicis*, Watteau places it in this relaxed, informal scene. This is how society now sees itself: placed as it were between interior and exterior, between art and nature. Watteau's are the most civilized pictures in a highly civilized century.

ANTOINE WATTEAU (1684–1721) *Gilles*, and detail of the background figures · 1719–21 · Oil on canvas · 72½ × 58¾″ · The Louvre, Paris

This is one of Watteau's rare pictures on a large scale. Probably it was painted as a sort of signboard for the comedians whom it depicts, and it seems to have been lost sight of from Watteau's own day until the early nineteenth century when a keen collector spotted it. In the picture Watteau manages to suggest both the lively atmosphere of the comedians' performances and also something of the life—even the private life—of a comedian. The noisy fun of the background, where a clown is pulled along on a

donkey, is abruptly silenced by the complete detachment and stillness of Gilles himself, a motionless figure in white, at once dignified and poignant. His expression is inscrutably blank. Yet he seems to communicate to the spectator an intense and moving sense of existence.

Watteau had studied Rubens' pictorial technique. His work on a large scale shows how superbly he could handle oil paint, with a more nervous energy but with no less mastery than Rubens. Paint conveys with liquid vivacity these wide-eyed faces and the shimmering material of their clothes. The brush seems to draw with the paint—beautifully sure and in its result utterly individual to Watteau.

Detail is shown on next pages

267

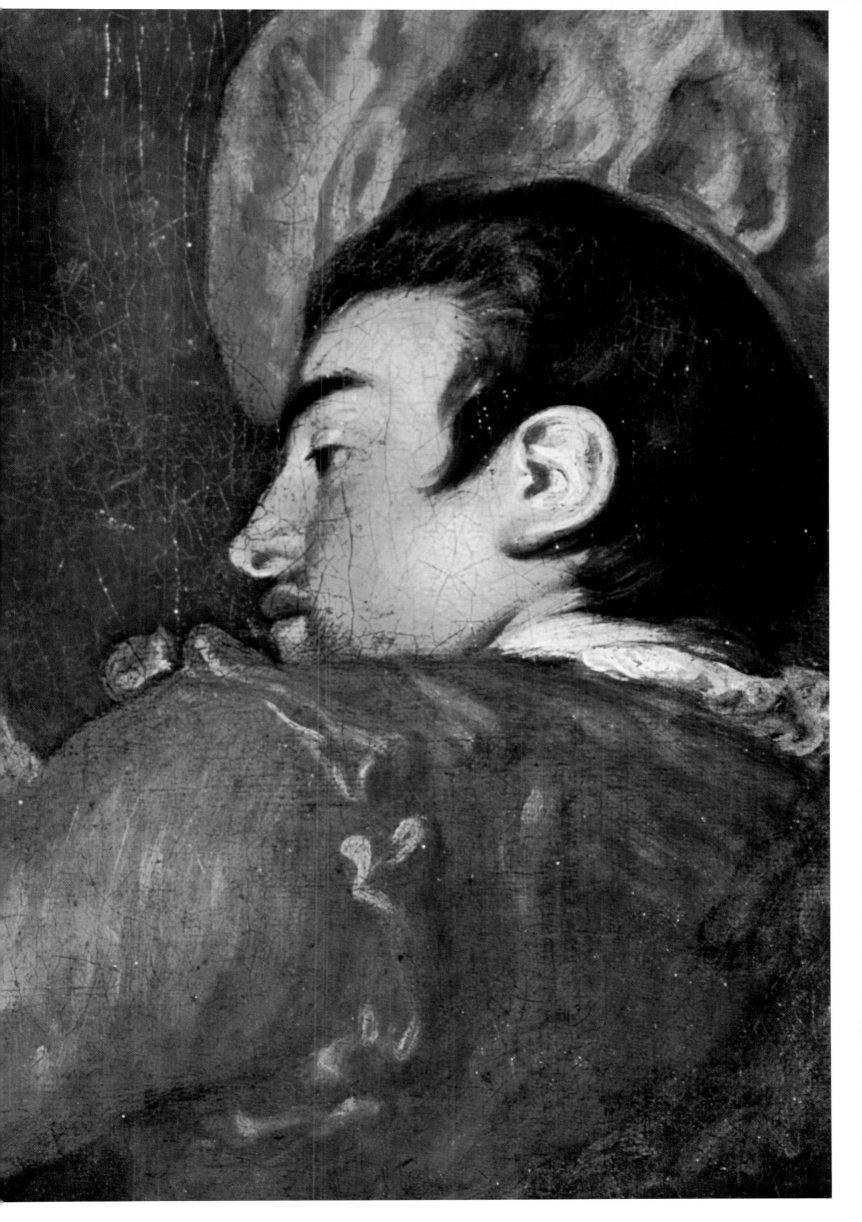

NICOLAS LANCRET (1690–1743) *Scene from the Italian Comedy* · Oil on canvas · 11 × 14⅛″ · The Wallace Collection, London

Nicolas Lancret pays tribute to the popularity of Watteau, whose style of picture he was to continue. Lancret is a charming painter, but most of Watteau's intensity and conviction has been lost from his work and the content becomes rather anecdotal. *Scene from the Italian Comedy* suffers from the fact that Watteau had interpreted such scenes with pure enchantment. Lancret remains a lively artist, with sensitive handling of the medium and his own attractive color harmonies. The theater continued to fascinate society during the period, and there was a natural preference for amusing, amorous plays, as opposed to the somewhat stilted, high-flown world of tragedy.

FRANÇOIS BOUCHER *The Bath of Diana* · Oil on canvas · 22½ × 28¾″ · The Louvre, Paris

The patrons of Boucher, whether men or women, expected him to pay tribute to the century's obsession with women. He is virtually the inventor of a certain female type, with prettified baby features and a body at once slim and mature. His mythological pictures revolve around this type of woman, shown either titillatingly half-dressed or—as here—quite frankly nude. Boucher's response to blond flesh was very real, and here he sets it off ravishingly with the great expanses of blue drapery and green foliage. The picture is quite consciously artificial, but it is also enchanting. Firmly planned and firmly executed, it is one of Boucher's most serious masterpieces.

FRANÇOIS BOUCHER *Nude on a Sofa* · 1752 · Oil on canvas · 23⅝ × 25⅞″ · The Old Pinakothek, Munich

For a long while this picture was supposed to represent an Irish girl, Louise O'Murphy, who was one of the many mistresses of Louis XV. Her identity is of little importance, but Boucher has given her the ideal sensuousness, and sensuality, of an ideal mistress. Her pose and the disarray of clothes and sofa on which she lies might all have been thought up by Colette, so intense is the delight in the juxtaposed textures and so deep the sense of abandonment. Boucher is frank in his enjoyment of the subject. He means us to confound art and nature in this provocative portrait of a naked girl. She is not shown in any mythological guise but simply as herself. Boucher localized the picture in his own period and produced one of the finest nudes painted in the eighteenth century.

FRANÇOIS BOUCHER (1703–70) *Birth of Venus* · Oil on canvas · 31½ × 53⅞″ · The Wallace Collection, London

François Boucher is more than the contemporary of Tiepolo. He is the Tiepolo of France, substituting fancy for imagination, but remaining a great decorative painter unjustly despised in the Neoclassic period in which he lived. His *Birth of Venus* tells us nothing about classical mythology. It is as a subject only the pretext for an attractive woman to recline in some not very realistic water. The light touch and delightful color enhance its pleasurable effect. What had originally been a rather brutal story of how Venus was born, became in Renaissance times an idyl of a goddess-woman floating over the water and eventually, with Boucher, the story is told in intimate, boudoir terms.

JEAN HONORÉ FRAGONARD *The Washerwoman* · c. 1756–67 ·
Oil on canvas · 18½ × 25⅝″ · The Picardy Museum, Amiens

JEAN HONORÉ FRAGONARD (1732–1806) *Rinaldo and Armida* · Oil on canvas · 28¾ × 35⅞″ · Private collection

Jean Honoré Fragonard leads inevitably toward the dissolution of the Rococo style. Pictures like *Rinaldo and Armida* fracture the firm world of Boucher under new impact of light which sparkles and breaks up all the surfaces—rather as Canaletto's world is broken up by the light and rapid calligraphy of Guardi. With nervous feathery strokes Fragonard creates a flickering composition in which everything seems excited. The figures are so many curving strokes that reel and bound toward each other in a frothy woodland setting. Rinaldo is led forward into the bowers of the enchantress Armida. It is the same subject that Tiepolo had already painted (page 262), and Tiepolo was one of the significant influences on Fragonard.

There is another aspect of Fragonard's art besides his cheerfully erotic vein. He won the Prix de Rome in 1752 and lived in Italy for some years. The romantic associations of Italy, its climate, its gardens, its statues, made a deep impression on him and he recorded them in wonderfully evocative drawings and paintings. *The Washerwoman* seems redolent of southern life with its sense of sunshine and dark trees, statues and a steep overgrown staircase. Everything is conveyed with sketch-like rapidity and the result is like a drawing in paint.

JEAN HONORÉ FRAGONARD *Bathers* · Before 1756 · Oil on canvas · 25¼ × 32½″ · The Louvre, Paris

Although Fragonard pays tribute, like Boucher, to his period's preoccupation with the feminine, it is with more dynamic effects. Where Boucher, for example, had painted Diana almost pensively at her bath (page 267), Fragonard conceives this animated and erotic scene of bathers who tumble and fall about in the water. Even the trees seem agitated by gusts of passion, and yet the whole picture is lighthearted. Fragonard seems to go on painting with tremendous verve and gaiety, keeping clear of too solemn subject matter, and unaware that he would live on in penury and neglect to see Napoleon on the throne of France.

HUBERT ROBERT (1733–1808) *The Pont du Gard* · c. 1787 ·
Oil on canvas · 95 × 95 ″ · The Louvre, Paris

Robert influenced Fragonard (in such pictures as the one above) and was in turn influenced by him. Robert, too, studied in Rome and became, in effect, a French version of the Roman view-painter, Panini. But there is in him also a fully developed Romantic feeling which looks forward to the nineteenth century. The grandeur and the melancholy of ruins became his special subject. It was in front of one of his pictures that Diderot was to be led into musing on all the ideas that ruins evoked: "*Tout s'anéantit, tout périt, tout passe.*" The double arches of the Pont du Gard seem to dwarf people into insignificance, stretched dramatically across the picture under a boldly colored sky.

271

JEAN-BAPTISTE-SIMÉON CHARDIN (1699–1779) *The Morning Toilet* · Oil on canvas · 19¼ × 15⅜″ · National Museum, Stockholm

Jean-Baptiste-Siméon Chardin must have studied Dutch seventeenth-century pictures, but his own still lifes and genre scenes have a dignity and power of composition that link them to Poussin. Chardin manages to cut away all the trivial, anecdotal qualities from his pictures and present us with much more than a mere "slice of life." He prefers the interior on a small scale, usually with only one or two figures who are occupied in some simple domestic task. Here a mother gives the finishing touches to her daughter's toilet before church. But the spell of the picture is in its grave preoccupation and in the beautifully applied paint which gives weight, as well as color, to each object.

JEAN-BAPTISTE-SIMÉON CHARDIN *The Kitchenmaid* · Oil on canvas · 18⅛ × 14¾″ · National Gallery of Art, Washington, D.C. (The Samuel H. Kress Collection)

Chardin, the contemporary of Boucher, takes us behind that gallant, Rococo façade and shows us the actual facts of existence of the period. Like the Rococo painters, he places the emphasis upon women—but with what a difference. Women are seen in the humblest circumstances, occupied in domestic tasks in the kitchen. Here a maid simply sits peeling turnips, or rather pauses for a moment in her work. This stillness is part of Chardin's quiet power. He checks the Rococo tendency to movement and dissolution, and makes all his pictures become literally still lifes. With immense gravity he examines each object, its essence and its surface, and records the vegetables, the pots and pans, the shape of the woman's white apron.

JEAN-BAPTISTE-SIMÉON CHARDIN *Pipes and Drinking Vessels* · Oil on canvas · 12⅝ × 16½″ · The Louvre, Paris

Chardin began as a painter of still lifes and only gradually went on to deal with genre compositions. In his later work he largely left aside genre and turned back with new virtuosity to still life. The actual elements remain simple and very much the same. The composition is restricted to a few objects, usually placed—as here—on a plain stone ledge that runs parallel with the bottom of the picture. On this the objects are arranged with scrupulous care; their varied shapes are plotted with exactness. The result is the tremendous authority which exhales from Chardin's still lifes. A few commonplace objects are lifted into a timeless plane.

JEAN-BAPTISTE-SIMÉON CHARDIN *Girl with a Racket and Shuttlecock* · 1741 · Oil on canvas · 37⅞ × 24¼″ · Private collection, Paris

By the 1740s Chardin's art had become completely confident. Only then did he paint several pictures in which the human figure takes on, for him, a new and important scale. But the mood remains very much the same. He still concentrates on private domestic moments. Even when his subject is a child, it is the child's gravity which is portrayed. There is a touching solemnity about the girl who is absorbed in her own thoughts as she clasps the racket and shuttlecock. These shapes, like that made by her dress and by her profile against the cool background, are all explored and expressed with intense conviction. Only Vermeer has approached Chardin in that sense of light which saturates as it falls, building up surfaces of beauty like that of the girl's skirt.

JEAN ETIENNE LIOTARD (1702–89) *Self-Portrait* · Pastel · 24¾ × 20⅝″ · Museum of Art, Geneva

Jean Etienne Liotard was perhaps the most gifted in sheer virtuosity of all the eighteenth-century practitioners in the popular medium of pastel. He was Swiss by birth but traveled all over Europe, as well as to Turkey. His adoption of Turkish dress and growth of a beard added to his notoriety and in this portrait he well conveys a sense of his own eccentricity. The medium of pastel encouraged dexterity and speed—those qualities so much admired by the eighteenth century—and the pastel portrait was popular throughout Europe. Liotard aimed not so much at a lively touch as at *trompe l'œil* realism in conveying textures, combined with a powerful honesty in portraying his sitters —not least in this portrait of himself.

JEAN MARC NATTIER (1685–1766) *Madame Henriette* · 1742 · Oil on canvas · 37⅛ × 50⅝″ · Uffizi Gallery, Florence

Jean Marc Nattier began his career as court portraitist with this composition of Louis XV's daughter, painted in 1742. The eldest of the king's children and much loved, she was to die at twenty-four years of age in 1752. For this first of his portraits of her, Nattier has lightly allegorized her into Flora or, rather, a nymph who is weaving a crown of flowers. Portrayed like this, Madame Henriette is able to adopt an unconventional but elegant pose, very different from that of formal court portraiture. Nattier is able to combine grace with a tolerable likeness. It is not surprising that the portrait pleased the royal family, and the painter was to go on to portray Madame Henriette's sisters as well as the king and queen.

MAURICE QUENTIN DE LA TOUR (1704–88) *Self-Portrait* · 1751 · Pastel · 22 × 17⅝″ · The Louvre, Paris

Maurice Quentin de La Tour was the leading French pastelist of the period, approached only by Perronneau (below). Originally influenced by the success of the Venetian, Rosalba Carriera, La Tour was to carry much further the vivacity of handling and grasp of character. He was capable of great elaboration and finish—in which pastel almost becomes paint—but it is in the more relaxed and direct sketches and informal portraits that he is at his best. Here he poses without any pretense—without wig or formal cravat—simply as the artist-workman. He is able to catch too the smiling, no-nonsense air of his own face, a good guide to his character. An anecdote tells how, when painting Madame de Pompadour, he undid his collar and took off his wig, so as to feel completely at ease.

JEAN-BAPTISTE PERRONNEAU (1715–83) *Charles Lenormant du Coudray* · 1766 · Pastel · 24⅜ × 19″ · Cognacq-Jay Museum, Paris

Jean-Baptiste Perronneau cannot really equal La Tour in penetration as a portrait painter, but he was a successful artist of the period and worked in oils as well as pastel. Unlike La Tour, he was Parisian by birth but his later years took him wandering—perhaps to seek clients beyond La Tour's reach. He visited Italy and Russia and spent considerable periods in Amsterdam, where he died. The Lenormant portrait shows his ability as interpreter of character and physiognomy, and also contains a brilliant passage of that blue that Perronneau was so fond of introducing into his portraits.

JEAN-BAPTISTE GREUZE (1725–1805) *Head of a Child* · Oil on canvas · 16¼ × 12⅝″ · Kenwood Collection, London

Jean-Baptiste Greuze is an example of the artist whose historical importance is greater than his artistic merit. Launched by Diderot's high praise for his sentimental genre pictures, Greuze represents the triumph of bourgeois feeling and the rejection of the Rococo. But while it is still hard to appreciate the painter of the tearful village scenes which made him so famous (such as *The Village Bride*), and even less the creator of rouged girls posed with doves and jugs, it is necessary to recognize that Greuze was always an admirable portraitist. At his best and most straightforward, he was able to respond to children with real feeling, and their popularity in his work is part of the new urge toward a more natural code of manners. Greuze heralded the Revolution without being aware of doing so. He survived it, living on neglected and impoverished; and one of his very last letters tragically speaks of being "without a single commission."

ELISABETH VIGÉE-LEBRUN (1755–1842) *Queen Marie-Antoinette* · Oil on canvas · 35⅜ × 28⅜″ · Collection H.R.H. The Prince of Hesse and the Rhine

Elisabeth Vigée-Lebrun became famous for her portraits of Marie-Antoinette which represent a minor revolution in the portrayal of royalty. Friendly with the Queen, Madame Vigée-Lebrun was easily able to convey a simplicity and intimacy in her portraits of a sovereign whose lack of formality shocked the French court. In 1783 Marie-Antoinette adopted a new fashion by wearing simple dresses of white muslin. It is in this costume that she appears here, wearing a straw hat which adds a further suggestion of the pastoral. In fact the portrait is a tacit recognition that queens are really only ordinary women under the trappings. But this recognition was too abrupt a break with tradition; the portrait had to be withdrawn from public exhibition after its informality had caused a scandal.

PIERRE-PAUL PRUD'HON (1758–1823) *The Empress Josephine* · Oil on canvas · 96 × 70½″ · The Louvre, Paris

Pierre-Paul Prud'hon, born only three years later than Madame Vigée-Lebrun, carries further those hints of a new feeling which her portraits contain. It is positively as an escape from rationality and regal convention that Prud'hon's Josephine has seated herself in this romantic, lovely spot. Josephine patronized him generously, clearly preferring the mysterious penumbra of his art to the somewhat chilly daylight of his contemporary artist, David. She herself is an attractive if shadowy figure—somebody whose charm still exerts itself over the years. Prud'hon catches her easy elegance and natural grace, while the woodland setting he places around her has the glowing beauty of a landscape painted by Corot.

JACQUES-LOUIS DAVID (1748–1825) *The Oath of the Horatii* (detail) · 1785 · Oil on canvas · 152 × 204¾″ · The Louvre, Paris

Jacques-Louis David painted *The Oath of the Horatii* in 1785, four years before the French Revolution. The picture created a sensation first at Rome—where it was painted—and then on its exhibition in Paris. Its stern republican sentiment is foreboding, both artistically and politically, and it is a pleasing irony that the commission for it came from the Crown. The subject was inspired by Corneille's tragedy, *Horace*. Although there is some lingering theatricality in David's treatment, he has aimed at a dramatic moment interpreted by a static composition. It is a solemn moment of action frozen in the uplifted arms, the static folds of the draperies, and the regular series of arches that enclose the background. All the nascent and confused ideas of Neoclassicism are suddenly given complete, coherent expression.

JACQUES-LOUIS DAVID *Madame Récamier* · Oil on canvas · 67 × 94½″ · The Louvre, Paris

Significantly, it was in 1800 that David began this famous portrait of a famous beauty, which he never completed. The picture is exactly balanced between two centuries. Despite the classic severity of the composition, it places an almost Rococo feminine emphasis upon woman herself: Madame Récamier seems to incarnate womanhood, so beautiful, so tantalizing, so consciously exerting her charm. In the masculine, politically realistic world of Napoleon, she still remains a goddess and an enchantress. No longer posed as Cleopatra or Armida, she is simply one ordinary woman, Jeanne-Françoise Récamier. And it is in this sense of being "modern" that David is a revolutionary. The bareness of the room, the austerity of the clothes and furniture, all symbolize rejection of the Rococo.

JACQUES-LOUIS DAVID *Napoleon in His Study* · Oil on canvas · 80¼ × 49¼″ · National Gallery of Art, Washington, D.C.

The Napoleonic legend, created so assiduously by Napoleon, needed pictorial expression, and it was fortunate for the Emperor that a perfect court artist-cum-propagandist was available in David. Not only did David respond with complete loyalty to Napoleon, but he has enshrined the man and his ideals in a whole series of portraits. This one is the least rhetorical and probably the most successful. The Emperor stands in his study in his habitual pose. It is a deliberately private scene, an intimate view of the man who early in the morning—the clock shows it is nearly a quarter past four—is still at work. The candles have burned low, but France's destiny requires the constant toil of her master. Thus David combines a scrupulous portrayal of fact with the propagandist dissemination of a myth.

WILLIAM HOGARTH (1697–1764) *The Shrimp Girl* · c. 1750–60 · Oil on canvas · 26 × 20¾″ · National Gallery, London

William Hogarth began by painting small portraits and conversation pieces, but was led from these to the idea of depicting "modern moral subjects" in a way that anticipates Greuze. Hogarth's deep attachment to the ordinary life of the period is summed up in this "portrait" of an itinerant shrimp girl—a cockney character rather like the painter himself. The picture is only a sketch and is perhaps unfinished. Nevertheless, it is completely realized and painted with almost Impressionist freedom.

WILLIAM HOGARTH *The Graham Children* · 1742 · Oil on canvas · 63¾ × 71¼″ · The Tate Gallery, London

Hogarth's lively attitude made him a naturally sympathetic portraitist of children. In *The Graham Children* he paints them in a group portrait on a large scale. He aims at the informality of a moment of their daily life, here focused on the pet bird in the cage which has caught the attention of the baby at the left. Round the children is depicted a complete interior of the period, where the only contrived element is a swag of curtain. Amid the bright-eyed, eager-looking children there is also set the bright-eyed cat which—equally attracted by the bird—has popped up from behind the chair. It is perhaps the liveliest sitter of all.

GEORGE STUBBS (1724–1806) *Mares and Foals* · c. 1760–70 · Oil on canvas · 40 × 63¼″ · The Tate Gallery, London

George Stubbs is one of those artists of the eighteenth century who reveal how deeply imbued the period was with scientific interests. In Stubbs art serves knowledge, and for him it is knowledge especially of the animal kingdom—and particularly, knowledge of the horse. He dissected horses and drew the results of his study, in addition to painting many horse portraits. Behind all of them is a sense of bone and structure which helps to give tremendous conviction to the individual studies here; at the same time, together they make up a delightful decorative frieze, which is charming as well as natural, true to the facts and yet essentially poetic.

RICHARD WILSON (1713/14–82) *View of Snowdon* · Oil on canvas · 39⅝ × 48⅞″ · The Walker Art Gallery, Liverpool

Richard Wilson was to move from portrait painting to the depiction of landscapes, influenced by several seventeenth-century masters and also by his contemporary Zuccarelli. Wilson's visit to Italy in the 1750s resulted in this switch of subject matter and his Italian views have a strong sense of classical nostalgia—as well as a classical gravity in their design. The same Italian and classicizing vein was to be utilized by him in approaching scenes in England and in his native Wales. A glowing light gives dignity to the landscape where some simple feature of grandeur—as here the peak of Snowdon—takes its place boldly in the composition. Wilson's elevated view of nature found fewer patrons at the time than the sugary and more flimsy landscapes painted by Zuccarelli.

SIR JOSHUA REYNOLDS (1723–92) *The Strawberry Girl* · Oil on canvas · 29¼ × 24¾″ · The Wallace Collection, London

Sir Joshua Reynolds is the leading figure, historically, in the eighteenth-century English School. He painted nothing but portraits and nearly every leading figure of the period sat to him. He represents a tremendous advance in the social prestige of the painter, accelerated by the creation of the Royal Academy in 1768. The following year Reynolds, its first President, was knighted by George III. He received an honorary degree from Oxford and was made mayor of his native town, Plymouth. As well as attempting every variety of treatment of his sitters, Reynolds was attracted to the "fancy-picture" with a possible classical or genre interest. *The Strawberry Girl* is at once portrait and genre, painted with clear recollections of Murillo, and patently sentimental when compared with Hogarth's depiction of children.

SIR JOSHUA REYNOLDS *Nelly O'Brien* · c. 1760–62 · Oil on canvas · 49¾ × 39¼″ · The Wallace Collection, London

Although Reynolds was quite capable of classicizing his sitters—especially female ones—and providing them with classical draperies, he could also create startlingly direct and "modern" portraits. *Nelly O'Brien* is a supreme example of this more sympathetic vein and her portrait may be contrasted with the elaborate full-length of Lady Bampfylde (below). Reynolds was a friend of Nelly O'Brien's, who was a courtesan of the period. The portrait breathes affection and simplicity. The pose is deliberately direct and straightforward, in a manner very unusual for Reynolds. Equally unusual is his sensitive recording of the varied textures of her clothes, from the lace at her sleeves to the striped dress—partly covered by a black shawl—and the beautifully painted quilted skirt which fills the foreground.

SIR JOSHUA REYNOLDS *Lord Heathfield* · 1787 · Oil on canvas · 56 × 44¾″ · National Gallery, London

There is something retiring in Reynolds' concept of Nelly O'Brien. Lord Heathfield was a public and important person, and this aspect of him is seized on in Reynolds' impressive portrait. Lord Heathfield was the governor of Gibraltar and had sustained a famous siege of the island. He holds the key of the fortress, while in the background there smoke the cannon which defended Gibraltar. Bluff, confident, a hero but not posing in any conventionally heroic way, Lord Heathfield is presented as no more than a man—but also as a personality. It is with this kind of dominating male sitter that Reynolds was probably most successful.

SIR JOSHUA REYNOLDS *Lady Bampfylde* · 1776/77 · Oil on canvas · 93¾ × 58¼″ · The Tate Gallery, London

An anecdote tells how Gainsborough once exclaimed of Reynolds, "Damn him, how various he is." Whether true or not; the story pays tribute to the variety of concept of which Reynolds was capable, always changing to suit the type of sitter and the purpose of the portrait. *Lady Bampfylde* is the aristocratic extreme: a full-length of contrived grace, attired in those mock-simple clothes that were sometimes stigmatized by Reynolds' contemporaries as "nightgowns." Everything about her is perhaps rather too fluid and beautiful to be true—from the sinuous line of her white scarf to the profusion of lilies so surprisingly growing in a wood. The sitter herself seems not positive enough to carry off all these trappings, despite all Reynolds' contrivance.

THOMAS GAINSBOROUGH (1727–88) *The Painter's Daughters Chasing a Butterfly* · c. 1755/56 · Oil on canvas · 44½ × 41⅜″ · National Gallery, London

Thomas Gainsborough is in eternal contrast to Reynolds. Contemporaries, portraitists, acquaintances, and at the end virtually friends, they had very different aims and ambitions. It can be said that Reynolds is all talent, Gainsborough genius. While Reynolds continually strives, Gainsborough achieves his effects with easy mastery. He is the creator of a whole series of felicitous masterpieces, but even among them few reach the lyrical level of this portrait of his two daughters, Mary and Margaret. The picture shows a completely absorbed moment of childhood, as the children run through the trees, intent on the butterfly. The paint runs too, rapidly conveying the shadowy wood, the silver-lemon tone of the girls' dresses, and their solemn, dark-eyed faces.

THOMAS GAINSBOROUGH *Mary, Countess Howe* · Oil on canvas · 96 × 60″ · The London County Council, Iveagh Bequest, Kenwood

Gainsborough was a countryman by birth, and he kept a sort of rustic disrespect before even his grandest sitters. And he brings with him a country air which is as fresh as a breeze on one's face. Lady Howe, the wife of a distinguished sailor also painted by Gainsborough, is dressed for the country, with gloves and a wide-brimmed straw hat. Over her marvelously painted raspberry-pink dress, she wears a nearly transparent muslin apron, very slightly agitated. The same slight current seems to shake the slender trees of the delicate landscape where she stands. All these details are part of Gainsborough's spontaneous delight in costume and in motion. Faced with the problem of the full-length portrait, he chooses ravishing clothes to adorn the sitter, painted with a graceful delicacy which is equaled only by Watteau.

THOMAS GAINSBOROUGH *The Morning Walk* · 1785 · Oil on canvas · 93 × 70″ · National Gallery, London

This portrait is among Gainsborough's last pictures and shows a young, newly married couple, Mr. and Mrs. William Hallett. They stroll in a wood which Gainsborough has turned into an enchanted bower of silk and feathers—rather like the plumes and ribbon of Mrs. Hallett's hat. There is a graceful sense of movement as the couple walk along, arms interlinked, and accompanied by their elegant, silky-furred dog. By this date Gainsborough's handling of oil paint had become even more fluent. He worked with long brushes and achieved effects almost like penciling. This technique, which is part of the secret of the freshness of his pictures, was well described by Reynolds after Gainsborough's death. He spoke of how, out of what seem random marks of paint, there assembles the final form "by a kind of magic."

278

THOMAS GAINSBOROUGH *The Ford* · Before 1786 · Oil on canvas · 38⅞ × 49″ · Collection Mrs. H. Scudamore, London

Gainsborough differed in yet another way from Reynolds in being a painter of landscapes as well as portraits. Already as a boy he was painting, under Dutch influence, scenes of his native Suffolk. Later in life he preferred to paint half-imaginary landscapes, concocted from pieces of twig and stones which he would arrange in his studio. A haze of enchantment gradually comes over his landscapes, just as it does over his portraits. The sober depiction of actual reality is replaced by a lighter and more graceful interpretation in which the trees group themselves elegantly and the peasants take on almost the grace of dancers. In these landscapes it is easy to see affinities with Fragonard—whose work Gainsborough probably did not know.

WILLIAM BLAKE (1757–1827) *The Simoniac Pope* · c. 1825 · Pen and watercolor · 20⅝ × 14¼″ · The Tate Gallery, London

William Blake seems to fit into the eighteenth century no more easily than does David or Goya. Certainly he was violently antagonistic to all the Rococo and divine-right-of-kings paraphernalia. He asserts the artist's right to his own private visions, reinforced in his own case by great poetic gifts—arguably greater than his gifts as an artist. Most of his work was executed in watercolor or engraving, and with an increasing attachment to the purely visionary. His subjects were taken either from his own poems, or from the Book of Job, or—as here—from Dante. Imagination gives its force to a technique which, though often perhaps academically weak, is yet in its idiosyncrasy more than sufficient to convey the blazing intensity of the artist.

SIR THOMAS LAWRENCE (1769–1830) *Queen Charlotte* · Oil on canvas · 94¼ × 58″ · National Gallery, London

Sir Thomas Lawrence was brilliantly precocious, and he was still a young man when he painted this portrait of Queen Charlotte. It reveals his bravura qualities and also his ability to invest his sitters with glamour as well as dignity. The homely queen is not flattered as she sits high up in a room at Windsor Castle, looking out over Eton—the chapel of which is visible among the russet autumn trees. Yet there is a stateliness in the presentation which suits the sitter. Out of her basically simple dress, Lawrence makes a beautiful piece of crisp painting, a sweep of pale lilac which heightens the effect of distance and dignity.

SIR HENRY RAEBURN (1756–1823) *The Drummond Children* · Oil on canvas · 94¼ × 60¼″ · Metropolitan Museum of Art, New York

Sir Henry Raeburn was to become the leading portrait painter in Edinburgh, influenced by Reynolds and living on into the age of Lawrence. He seems to have received little early training, but developed a virtuoso handling of oil paint which often becomes rather monotonous in its slick application. Already there is a hint of Victorian sentimentality in his portraits of children, although *The Drummond Children* is more elaborately worked out than usual and an extremely effective group.

Luis Meléndez (1716–80) *Still Life with Pears and a Melon* ·
Oil on canvas · 15⅞ × 20½″ · Museum of Fine Arts, Boston

Luis Meléndez was probably ambitious to be known as a
history painter and in his own self-portrait he shows himself holding an academic drawing. However, he is famous
for his still-life pictures which in many ways continue the
tradition of Velázquez and Zurbarán. At the same time, it
is interesting to find him insisting on the sheer facts of
objects—concentrating deeply on their appearance—in the
very years that Chardin was at work in Paris. There is a
conscious austerity about Meléndez' pictures. Here each
pear seems scrutinized and recorded with minute accuracy,
and in the same way the tough texture of the melon skin is
explored. The fruit is placed in full light and set off by the
very simple vessels and the basket, with its sharp white
drapery, which have an almost inexplicable, innate dignity.

Francisco Goya (1746–1828) *The Duchess of Alba* · 1795 ·
Oil on canvas · 74¾ × 51⅛″ · Collection Duke of Alba,
Madrid

Francisco Goya not only revives the great tradition of
Spanish painting but positively leads painting into the
nineteenth century. That his death was in France is almost
symbolic, as if in recognition of the country that was to
continue in the creation of modern art. From Goya it is a
logical step to Géricault and Delacroix. This portrait of
the Duchess of Alba was painted in 1795 and is only one
testimony to the artist's fascination with a woman who was
described as "outstanding for her beauty, popularity, charm,
riches, and rank." After the death of her husband in 1796
Goya accompanied her to her country estate—and the
countryside is already suggested in this portrait. Its almost
naïve effect is deliberate and there is something witty not
only in the black-eyed Duchess' appearance, but also in
that of her toy dog with its absurd red ribbon.

Francisco Goya *Still Life with Salmon* · Oil on canvas ·
17⅝ × 24⅜″ · Collection Dr. Oskar Reinhart, Winterthur

It is a part of Goya's modernity that he tackled all subjects.
Though his still-life pictures are few they provide further
testimony to his delight in the topical subject. He was least
successful in the world of myth and allegory, and superb
when it came to grasping in paint or ink the world of
actuality. Out of a few collops of salmon he is able to make
this impressive picture which conveys the raw red flesh of
the fish and the mottled shiny grayish skin which so
vividly contrasts with it. There is hardly any arrangement
of the three pieces: they are simply laid in the center of the
composition and then painted with tremendous respect for
the sheer facts. The boldness of the concept and the execution once again prelude the entire nineteenth century and,
here especially, Courbet.

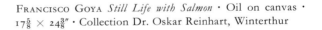

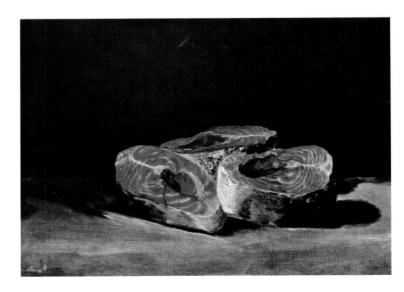

FRANCISCO GOYA (1746–1828) *The Third of May, 1808*, and detail of the soldiers' feet · c. 1814 · Oil on canvas · 104¾ × 135⅞″ · The Prado, Madrid

The confused events which followed on France's invasion of Spain are made almost intolerably vivid by two pictures which Goya painted some five years after the actual events. On May 2, the Spanish rose against Napoleon's troops and attacked them in the streets of Madrid. Goya painted that scene. The following day French reprisals resulted in the scene depicted here when hostages were shot. In a dark night, these pitiful figures cluster together before the level, lethal line of French rifles. One man screams in defiance, and despair perhaps, as the soldiers shoot. Already blood stains the ground where the first victims have fallen. Goya's attachment to reality continued even before such spectacles as this. He does not seem to indict the French so much as he does man's brutality to man. The eighteenth century, which had thought to laugh man's follies away, was condemned to see its civilized system collapse. Goya shows its death agony.

Goya carries further the impressionistic technique of Velázquez. He handles the paint with a boldness that leads straight to the achievements of Manet. The menacing shapes of the soldiers' heavy boots are rapidly drawn with sweeps of dark pigment, summary but utterly convincing. The artist feels free to jettison old styles of painting, becoming revolutionary in technique as well as in subject matter.

Detail is shown on next pages

281

FRANCISCO GOYA *Majas on a Balcony* · c. 1810–15 · Oil on canvas · 76¾ × 49½″ · Metropolitan Museum of Art, New York

The life of his own time fascinated Goya and the present picture shows an almost idyllic and charming scene of social life in the Madrid of about 1800. It was probably painted simply for the artist himself and may well be one of the two pictures of "young people on a balcony" which are mentioned in an inventory of Goya's effects in 1812. There is really no subject. It is merely an impression of contemporary life—as if the artist had glanced up in a Madrid street and seen these four people sitting out on a balcony. The actual painting is direct and vivid, with masterly touches just suggesting the women's veils. Not only does its technique prelude Manet, but even its subject is likely to have inspired his famous picture *Le Balcon*.

FRANCISCO GOYA *Self-Portrait* · 1785 · Oil on canvas · 16½ × 10″ · Collection of the Count of Vallagonzalo, Madrid

Goya's interest in life around him naturally included himself. Indeed, his highly conscious art depends on a great deal of self-awareness and probably no artist has probed as deeply as did he into the mind and its mental states. He was still comparatively young when this full-scale self-portrait was painted—a completely revolutionary conception in its silhouetting of the figure against the light expanse of the window. It shows Goya as he supremely thought of himself: as an active artist. Part of the moving quality of his life is his devotedness to that vocation, despite infirmities and banishment and old age. In him, as in Rembrandt, there is a tenacity and integrity which is expressed not only in his art but in his features. He convinces us, as he stands at his easel painting, that this is exactly what he was like.

FRANCISCO GOYA *The Colossus (Panic)* · 1809 · Oil on canvas 76¾ × 41⅜″ · The Prado, Madrid

In his later years Goya did not retreat from reality but he turned from man's exterior behavior to study more intensely man's mind. Always interested in, and aware of, the basic irrationality which is waiting to engulf the structure of reason, Goya was increasingly preoccupied by dreams and by visions of nightmarish intensity. Many of the resulting "black paintings" he intended for the decoration of his own house—extensions as it were of what his mind had already dreamed. The subjects of these pictures are horrific and mysterious. Sanity seems to have deserted the earth and it is inhabited by giant forms like this one which has terrified a great crowd of people. Men are reduced to panicky little creatures—ants frightened by the colossal figure which rises so huge into the clouds. Thus the last eighteenth-century artist ends not with charming pictures, or graceful decorations, but with this dreadful vision of the world gone mad.

the nineteenth
and twentieth centuries

Hans L. C. Jaffé

Let it be said right from the outset that nineteenth- and twentieth-century painting constitutes a single entity. How can we justify this, what is the common denominator?

The historical period with which we are concerned is clearly and unmistakably delimited: on the one side by the French Revolution and its obviously inevitable break with an old tradition and on the other by nothing more than the date at which these pages are written. This span of more than a century and a half can be viewed as a whole for the simple reason that, in this time, painting went through a single and highly characteristic process of development that permits all of it to be considered from one fixed point of view. When we ask ourselves what has been the essence of painting for the past 150 years, we are really asking what was the unique principle that set it off and shaped its further development.

The best definition of that principle seems to be the problem of reality. No previous epoch ever posed that question so clearly and so consciously. No epoch ever made it the focal point of the painter's thinking and seeking. That task was left to the nineteenth and twentieth centuries.

Certainly the Netherlandish painters in the fifteenth century as well as the Spanish and Dutch in the age of the Baroque had discovered and mapped out reality with magnificent enthusiasm, and their voyages of exploration in an unknown realm influenced painting for centuries thereafter. But the painting of their times respected other rules, never asked with such a single voice as ours: What is reality?

In our historical period, painting's time-honored ties to religion, to kings and their dynasties, to the mythology of the ancients have largely fallen away. That is why it can—indeed, must—ask itself such a cogent question. For the first time in history, men lack the sure lodestars of religion, mythology, and dynastic hierarchies, and stand naked face to face with reality. Reality itself has become, so to speak, just another kind of subject matter, something for men to think about, to have feelings about either for or against. For the first time, painting has truly become the expression of a *Weltanschauung*, a view of the world in the most literal sense of the term; the artist views the world in order to explain, to account for its *real* content, its truth. What is reality?

The question, like Ariadne's thread, runs through the painting of the nineteenth and twentieth centuries as the principle determining its development, the laws of its growth and unfolding. And precisely for that reason, many themes that in the past had seemed the very stuff of painting have been jettisoned in our age: religious altar paintings, biblical episodes, narrative pictures, and with them the whole freight of

mythology. In their place new types of pictures have been brought into being: first of all, landscape, the great form in which men compete and come to terms with nature; then, the glimpse of everyday life that, though it has its origins in Dutch genre painting of domestic and peasant scenes, has completely discarded that art's concern with picturesque effects: finally, once again but in a new way, the still life—and still life goes to the very heart of the question concerning the essence of reality.

Right at the beginning of the past century and a half of modern art there appeared two great painters who proposed diametrically opposite solutions to the problem of reality: Ingres and Delacroix. In their entirely contrary ways of working there was revealed the polarity that for the next 150 years was to pull art first one way, then another: Ingres tried to solve the problems through his intelligence, through reasoning, whereas Delacroix dared to unleash his emotions on the question before him—head or heart, both approaches were opposite and opposing. But both sought their answers in Nature herself. Delacroix claimed Nature as his "dictionary," and Ingres once wrote, "In Nature resides that beauty which is the proper study of painting, there must we seek it and nowhere else."

This was the starting point for all the painting of our time, though the path finally led to other climes that Ingres and Delacroix could not imagine, to remoter horizons. And yet, despite their temperamental differences, a common trait links these two great forerunners to the work of their successors. The basic question is already set down in their paintings, however their answers may differ, for both ask: What is reality?

For such men of the early nineteenth century, reality was no longer the mythology of the Greeks —though Ingres painted it because it was still the fashion—nor could it be the world of biblical stories, although these are the subjects of some of Delacroix's finest pictures. For them reality was nothing less than Nature herself, looked at by nineteenth-century man with new eyes that plumbed her secrets, unraveled her mysteries.

From that point on, the rediscovery of nature was carried out methodically, step by step. First of all, the painters of the Barbizon School fled the noisy cities to seek refuge in the countryside, where they thought true reality was to be found in the simple life of men who worked the soil. Beside these painters of country innocence, of unspoiled sentiments—Millet, Théodore Rousseau, Daubigny—stood two truly great artists, Daumier and Corot, who in their separate ways pursued a similar problem. In his oil paintings of washerwomen and the humble occupants of third-class railway carriages, Daumier, the great master of caricature, caught slices of everyday reality and, in them, sought to reveal a truth both in and above our daily drabness. This he did with a fully aroused social awareness, with a militant participation that explains how the social experience of reality can make of it a problem: it is not only things in themselves his paintings depict but also —as in his pamphleteering lithographs— the whole question of the vindication of reality.

Corot was Daumier's contemporary. The landscapes Corot painted in Italy and France portray nature as a realm that transcends the social concerns of the moment. The peacefulness and pure poetry of nature belong, for him, to a paradisiac reality as yet uncontaminated by man's Fall. Trees and clouds, green fields, and films of haze, these are the protagonists of his idyl—elemental things of quotidian reality, to be sure, but transfigured by the poetry of an innocent heart. Corot's pictures tell us that there truly is a reality where men still live in concord, in which man has his place.

The first great and conscious shift in the conception of reality was engineered by Courbet. Unflinchingly and methodically, he swept out all the old dust heaped up around man's notions of reality; the broom he used he called Realism. Out went every scrap of tattered literary, religious, storytelling subject matter. He brooked no nonsense, and his orders read, "Painting is an essentially concrete art and can only consist in the representation of things that are real and that really exist. Abstract objects, invisible and without existence, simply have nothing at all to do with painting." With Courbet, philosophical positivism influenced the painter's point of view: only what exists positively, what is objectively visible, can be portrayed in paint.

Courbet's Realism is an extreme reply to the question—what really is reality?—that nags at our entire epoch. It is an answer that springs from a fully optimistic attitude toward life, an attitude that puts its trust in man's powers of observation, that sees precisely in this observation of individual things the one and only basis for painting and flatly turns its back on all the things that defy the evidence of the senses, banning them as alien intruders in the painter's world. Courbet, one of the great masters of all time, fully embodied this polemical position in his paintings and thereby laid down a new point of departure for later generations. He charted out in black and white, so to speak, the frontiers of the reality his own time recognized, and he created pictures that speak out boldly with a new awareness of what reality means and is.

And yet at the very time that Courbet was realizing in paint his most advanced position, pinning down with utmost rigor his positive interpretation of reality, the way was being paved for another and completely contradictory conception. In the art criticism of the great poet

Charles Baudelaire there was voiced, for the first time, the presentiment that beside or even beyond such an objective, tangible reality there might lie another—the reality of the immaterial, incorporeal world that neither hand nor eye can perceive, that imagination and fantasy alone can decipher. In his aesthetic concern with the nonnatural, with art that is art because an artist makes it, Baudelaire laid down in the middle of the nineteenth century, in the very years of Courbet's Realism, the basis for a development that was not to be realized until the end of the century. Meanwhile, Courbet's virile, positivist feeling for reality held sway; landscapes, portraits, scenes from daily life flourished under the banner of his Realism that tolerated nothing but what was visible and concrete.

The next step in this process was to be the subjection of reality to that which the eye can perceive. It was Manet who took that step. He liberated himself from the traditional conventions that governed observation and made the eye the sole judge of reality. This meant that since painters must by the nature of their art confront reality in a different way from the run of men, reality was to be painted not according to what we know but rather according to what we can see of it. Manet gave up modeling forms in volume and, instead, juxtaposed directly colors, tones, and gradations to give a suggestion, an impression of form. What he knew about form seemed to him to open the way to dangerous temptations; he accepted as valid truth only what his eye could perceive and register as in a lightning flash. His conception of reality was therefore somewhat more extreme than Courbet's, since he limited the apprehension of reality to those appearances that can be grasped by the senses.

But soon, in the next generation, that of the Impressionists, this line of development took a new turning. True, the Impressionists are always thought of as exponents of an optimistic delight in things as they are, as painters who rejoice over the good things of life in luminously bright colors. Of this there can be no question. And yet the art of the Impressionists, that of Monet, Pissarro, Renoir, and Sisley, has another side; with it begins the ineluctable devaluation of objects as things in themselves. This is most evident in Claude Monet's late works, the series of variations on a single theme, such as haystacks, the portal of Rouen cathedral, poplar trees, or water lilies. In these series, a single subject is painted over and over again, each time in a different light. But such a procedure proves that the subject itself, the object that serves as motif, has lost any value beyond providing the occasion for a study in light. The true subject matter of all these pictures is light alone, the most impalpable, immaterial phenomenon in all of nature; the material object involved merely lends its name to the picture. Things in these pictures are dissolved in light, are no more than shadows awakened by always changing light to transient and never fixed life. Of the concrete character of things, of their own autonomous existence, little indeed survives in these paintings. Once before it had happened, when the long night fell on the age of antiquity, and now it was happening again with Impressionism: the devaluation of the world of things was the first step in the further decline of a long-held picture of the world. It was also the first step in decisively summoning forth new forms, for when Impressionism translated a subjective kind of perception into a dematerialized, disembodied impression, it opened the gates to the self-assertion of the human spirit that refused any longer to be slave and victim of material things.

Yet, no sooner had Impressionism begun to make its presence felt outside of a limited circle than critical opposition to its principles arose, above all from the ranks of painters themselves. Typical of this reaction was the half-admiring, half-critical characterization of Monet pronounced by no less a one than Cézanne: "Monet is nothing but an eye—but what an eye!" This short, sharp summing up indicates that contemporary artists, or at least the most progressive among them, objected to the prédominant materialism of Impressionist art, to the lack of any spiritual basis in an art in which the painter strove to record every nuance of the fleeting moment by his senses alone without feeling any need to incorporate the experience into a broader spiritual context. It was, in fact, men of the same generation as the Impressionists—Cézanne, Van Gogh, Gauguin, Redon, Seurat—who dared the venture of seeking a basis for reality that would go beyond what the eye can say about the passing moment.

Cézanne and Van Gogh were together the founding fathers of modern painting, and in them was repeated the polarity we found at the outset of our historical epoch in Ingres and Delacroix. Each sought in his own way a reality that would transcend the appearances of a brief moment— Cézanne through intellectual discipline, Van Gogh through the quickening power of the emotions. With their respective choices, the two great masters of the end of the nineteenth century broke open the way that twentieth-century painting was to take in its own voyage of self-discovery.

Cézanne overcame the element of chance and accident that was Impressionism's Achilles' heel by rigorous, clear, and uncomplicated method, as befitted a man of Latin stamp determined to equip reality with comprehensible structures and laws. This meant infusing reality with the "permanence of reality," and his tool was the discipline of which the human mind is capable. To this end he took as basis the abstract laws of geometry and reduced natural forms to their simplest stereometric prototypes—sphere, cone, prism. With these means, he formed a skeleton for the new art, hewed a scaffolding and architecture for pictorial composition; in doing so, this new type of painting acquired its own autonomous right to exist. Cézanne himself defined his art as "a harmony running parallel to nature," meaning that the creations of the human spirit could now take their place as peers of equal distinction beside the laws of nature. Cézanne's painting is an initial triumph of the human intellect over the arbitrary choices reality offers, bringing them to heel and so ordering them as to make them accessible to human comprehension.

Van Gogh's road led elsewhere. For him true reality is revealed only through the warmth of human compassion. Characteristic of his attitude toward the things of life is this sentence from a letter to his brother: "May it not be that one can perceive a thing better and more accurately by loving it than by not loving it?" This loving fusion with all things—a kind of *unio mystica*— determined even the special way he used his colors and forms. Indifferent to what things look like from the outside, his entire concern was with their inner, invisible truth, and so he aspired to learn "to make such distortions, such aberrations, deformations, alterations of reality that, if you will, they must all end up as lies—but as lies that have more truth in them than literal reality." Emotions, excitement, profound sympathy— these are what Vincent wanted to paint; he wanted to give visible form to the very subject matter that according to Courbet's rigorous doctrine had nothing to do with painting, because for Van Gogh the things of the spirit were just as real as the things of the world, were, in fact, what was ultimately most real. The rhythm of his brushwork was for him the expression of his inner agitation, and in the heat of his passion his forms became charged with movement. Cypresses lick the sky like black flames, sun and stars whirl in violent alarm, his whole universe becomes the symbol of a dynamic, passion-laden way of looking at the world. It is the man himself, the artist, who stirs the world to life by the fullness of his heart, and in so doing he gives sense and significance to reality. Van Gogh was the creator of this new and meaningful and vital reality; he lived it in both his life and his art.

Along with these two great masters who set the way for others, there were in the same generation other painters who helped go beyond the Impressionists' notion of reality. In his flight from European civilization to the South Sea islands, Paul Gauguin discovered another kind of reality, the reality of myth, and through it he too was to make a great contribution to painting. The magical rites of so-called primitive peoples, the immediacy of their relations to men and things, stirred in Gauguin a feeling for reality long forgotten by Europe. In unmixed colors and large unbroken surfaces, he pinned down the directness of this experience of a life whose real essence still lay so close to hand; it is the mysterious power of this experience which speaks so vividly in his pictures.

But to find such primitivism, such a direct bond with reality, it was not necessary to escape to the tropics. In the heart of Paris and in its suburbs another artist of the same generation was revealing the unspoiled paradise of a still-innocent reality: the customs clerk, Rousseau. For him, nature, the natural setting for man, was magic and miracle enough, disclosing itself over and over and always as fresh as if newly minted before his astonished eyes. And this is why his vision of reality was in no way affected by any of the new theories of painting. Naïve and artlessly amazed, he spelled out the things he saw around him and put them together into astonishing words and sentences. His pictures contain a whole world in itself, a world of things that, familiar as they may be, take on something of the ever-renewed miracle in the painter's personal and peculiar vision; in the directness of their contact with life they reach out to the beholder and move him wonderfully.

In the generation of the discoverers of a new reality there was also Odilon Redon, a contemporary of Monet but a citizen of a world infinitely remote from the nature the Impressionists cherished. Redon was the explorer of that indefinable realm bounded on the one side by dreams, on the other by the waking eye's adventures. He painted faces, landscapes, events as no man had ever seen them with open eyes; in his world reality is what we see behind closed eyelids, the realm of vision, of illusion, of fairy tale and fable. After its exile of several hundred years, painting was led back by Redon to that land so fertile in images that lies beyond the farthest horizon our eyes can reach; images plowed up from memory, forms and colors that imagination alone can know float up into the light out of the uncharted depths of human experience. What was revealed by these pictures of our inner existence pushed infinitely far the horizons of reality, for such forms and colors—whatever Courbet may have said against them—are just as much a part of our own human reality as Courbet's "facts." With the sensitive eye of an Impressionist painter, Redon set down in his pastels and oils these images of dream with all the iridescent luster of their colors and the inexhaustible flux of their forms. In this he enriched the vocabulary of his generation with new ways to pin down new truths.

And finally, in the generation of founding fathers, there was Georges Seurat. The reality he discovered, which enabled him to go beyond the prevailing norms of the Impressionist picture of the world, was the reality residing within the art work itself. By dogged, systematic work in his own studio, he found that a painting, a work of art, is not only a depiction of nature but also,

in its way, adds to the stock of nature by creating a new fragment of reality—the composition of rising and falling lines, the harmonies of contrasting and related colors all build a new reality that is independent of nature, and this is so because forms and colors obey not natural but, instead, aesthetic laws like those of music. Because of this, men are able to create a new reality freed from all contingencies and natural accidents, a reality in the form of a picture that they can hold up—unshakably permanent, refined of every dross—before the eyes of other men.

Thus, even before the century's end, what people considered to be reality had undergone a great change. Beginning as a positive affirmation of the realness of objects, it had come under the sway of the Impressionists' purely sensory perception and finally transformed itself into something fraught with problems—from the question as to what reality really is arose the problem of whether there truly is a reality that men can grasp and how they may lay hold of it. Neither mere knowledge of facts nor the simple sensory appearances of objects were enough for the new generation: with the beginning of the new century the whole problem of reality was thrown open for discussion. A new generation made itself heard, and it looked with skeptical eyes on the standards the nineteenth century had bequeathed to it. Scientific and technological discoveries and the consequences the human mind was able to draw from them had opened up vast new prospects in the realm of reality, but by the same token they shook men's faith in the truth of sensory perception. Moreover, in the last years of the century an event had taken place that made the relations between painting and the sensory apprehension of reality even more complicated. This was the invention and exploitation of photography. It brought about what may justly be called the "Industrial Revolution" of painting.

What really happened? Earlier, in the centuries before mankind's technological advances, a man who wished to perpetuate something, to preserve at least a record of its outer semblance, had no one to turn to save the painter; the portrait, as soon as its possibilities dawned on man, became the concern and task of the artist. By portrait we mean, of course, the preservation in effigy of the individual features of any object whatsoever—men, houses, ships, landscapes, or even still lifes of fruit, flower, or fish heaped on a table. But then, with the coming of the camera, anyone who wished to preserve such a likeness could turn to the photographer as well. Thus, through man's technical progress came about also a change in the limits of what had been the painter's special domain. The whole field of portrait painting, exclusively reserved until then to artistic communication in the truest sense of the word, was now opened up to what can be called mere reporting. Many artists at the turn of the century, especially the younger ones, took this expropriation of their freehold as a challenge. In this light we must view a declaration by Paul Klee that is symptomatic of twentieth-century painting and its new conception of reality: "Art does not imitate the visible, it *makes* visible."

So we see that the painter's notion of reality underwent a profound change that was to be decisive for all the art of our epoch. Painting broke with the visible aspects of reality precisely because it could no longer find in such external appearances the substratum of truth upon which an art must base itself if it wishes to provide something more than accurate documents of real existing things. Certainly this break with the past was not due only to the changed situation as regards appearances and likenesses, that is, to the invention of the camera; there were equally decisive grounds in the universal breakdown of confidence in reality and in the crisis in standards and certitudes that were sapping all Europe in those years. Painters and sculptors sought the new reality on a plane that lies behind, beneath, and beyond appearances—a plane on which the appearance of things is more likely to be concealed than revealed. What had to be done was to pierce the veil of visible appearances—not passive reporting of the eye's experience but instead, through intellectual and spiritual effort, the construction of a new conception of reality.

The artist was then forced to become a creator, spokesman for the only kind of reality in which his fellow men could recognize themselves.

The first step on this climb to a more spiritual and more passionate picture of the world was taken by the Expressionists, in the wake of Vincent van Gogh; everything in their world was made subject to human emotion. Van Gogh's pictures taught them how to embody an unbounded, liberating subjectivity; his trees flicker up to the sky as if filled with some wild urge to grow still higher, and his colors shout out the immense ecstasy of living that in his pictures impregnates the entire universe with spirit. This feeling for life subjects even things themselves to its sway; it juggernauts triumphantly over the world of things. This triumph of life dominates in Expressionism, whether it be the French "Fauves" —Matisse, Derain, Vlaminck, Rouault, and the others—or the Dresden "Brücke" group— Kirchner, Heckel, Nolde, Schmidt-Rottluff—or the Munich "Blaue Reiter" painters—Kandinsky, Jawlensky, Macke, Marc, Klee. The forebear of all of them, though, was the Norwegian Edvard Munch. In Expressionist pictures, trees and men alike cringe in petrifying fear or rack themselves in ecstasy as high as heaven; the space itself in which the events take place (in Expressionist art there are only events in the act of happening, never dead facts) is sometimes breath-takingly narrow, as if even space had shrunk in on itself in fear, or it explodes suddenly outward so far that one wonders how a picture frame can hold it.

Every form, every color is crammed with a supernatural inner vitality that subjugates objects and twists them out of shape. That vitality is the true content of these pictures, and their ostensible subject matter is no more than an excuse. It was this demon-driven feeling for life that suggested to painting the possibility of incorporating elements from the magic art of primitive peoples, for Expressionist art finds much in common with things and themes from exotic worlds. For the Expressionists, the immediacy of experience, the special way they knew the world, dominated all their work, everything they created. They were the first to bring the men of their time to the point where they could understand the truth concealed in deformations of form and exaggerations in color—the truth Van Gogh defined as "lies that have more truth in them than literal reality."

Pitted against this picture of a world ravaged by unbridled subjectivity was another current, Cubism; Cubism stood for law and order. Its basis lay in Cézanne, but it did not share his interest in nature. Certainly Cubism used objects as its point of departure; violins, guitars, and bowls of fruit are always cropping up in its pictures, but they are there only as demonstrations of how a clear and rigorous system works. Braque, one of the founders of Cubism along with Picasso and Léger, neatly summed up the relationship of this art to reality: "The senses conceal form, the mind creates it." The approach of the Cubists was therefore not based on sensory perception but rather on the virtually mathematical cognizance of the intellect. And such cognizance is superior to subjective experience, to the accidents of appearance: it possesses objective validity in itself. For this reason, Cubism completely did away with the individual viewpoint. It made perception of the object entirely independent of the easily deceived eye. In Cubist pictures an object is seen—or, more accurately, considered—from every vantage point, from above, below, behind, from all its sides. This approach to objects not only means the rejection of any individual's particular way of perceiving reality, but it was also a step forward in capturing a fourth dimension, that of time. It was the Italian Futurists—Balla, Boccioni, Carrà, Russolo, Severini—who pushed furthest on this typically modern road.

But the great achievement of the Cubists was the invention of a new vocabulary and syntax entirely independent of sensory perception, by means of which an intellectual, objective conception of the world could at last be set down in paint.

Both Expressionism and Cubism were products of the years before World War I. During the war and in the immediate postwar years, a new movement sprang up, Surrealism. Surrealism was, in every sense of the word, a child of the war. The incredible, irrational, and meaningless happenings so much a part of a world conflict could not help but give rise to a new attitude toward reality. The illogical cohabitation of contradictory objects within a single contradictory space, the shock effect of such haphazard mixed marriages between unlike things all made sense only in the world of nightmares and anxiety-ridden visions. The realm Odilon Redon had unlocked, the half-world of dreams, lay close; it was in the works of Redon and James Ensor, the painters of masks and spooks, that the war generation found its models. Chirico, Dali, Max Ernst, and Tanguy stripped the husk off the subconscious, held up to the light (at much the same time as psychoanalysis) images that before then had slumbered formless in the dark domains of the human soul. This was a new reality behind reality, and for the most part it was terrifying to behold. Only a few—Chagall for one—knew how to find and paint in happier fashion the less grim corners of the new realm: the provinces of fairy tale, fable, and folk song.

The common ground of all these painters was the unfamiliar, the sur-real wonderland through the looking-glass. In this they were joined by the so-called primitive, or naïve, painters—Bauchant, Bombois, Vivin—who with unsophisticated directness beheld and painted this wonder-studded side of reality as Rousseau had before them.

On the climb to a representation of reality entirely independent of the senses' evidence, the last, most recent rung is Abstraction. In abstract art, images of things, the reality our eyes can grasp, are entirely exiled from a territory for which sensory perception holds no visa. Comprehending by the intellect outdistances completely whatever information the eye is capable of providing. And yet the fact remains, these pictures give answers that strike to the heart of the basic question of our epoch: What is reality? Rather than fob off on us a simulacrum of reality's pieces and parts, the painters of abstraction—Kandinsky, Kupka, Malevich, Mondrian—devise symbols for reality entire. The most consistent abstractionist of them all, Mondrian, defined his art and the path that led to it as a "clear vision of reality." Mondrian, like many others, was not interested in portraying random fragments of reality. Such painting, he said, does no more than distort the real essence. What he was after was the perdurable law behind the passing accident of outward aspects, and this law he found in the principle of universal harmony. To embody this,

to bring an abstract principle before our eyes, the only means he could possibly use were themselves abstract, and so he reduced his vocabulary to straight lines, right angles, the three primary colors, red, yellow, and blue, and the three primary noncolors, black, gray, and white. With such meager means he created a symbol for the essence of all reality, for the law behind the individual phenomenon.

All these abstract pictures give meaning to the world, to a reality. Whether they present themselves as a sternly ascetic, highly disciplined theorem, as with Mondrian, or as a stormily ecstatic dance of forms and colors, as in Kandinsky's works, all of them are decodable ciphers of a reality experienced. Again, just as at the beginning of our historical epoch, we find the same polarity between the two masters Kandinsky and Mondrian that set Delacroix against Ingres, Van Gogh against Cézanne. The most recent painting, that of the years since World War II, has taken that same storm-lashed road where reality is experienced to the fullest, the road trod by Delacroix, Van Gogh, and the Expressionists. Action Painting in America, led by Jackson Pollock, as well as the work of the "Cobra" group of Appel, Corneille, Alechinsky, and Jorn, contains a spirit that rides roughshod over all discipline, and flings onto canvas the wild and boiling experience of an inner or outer reality. Their pictures, with their thickly laid-on glaring colors and their vortex of frantically ribboning forms, are in their way too a chemical precipitate of reality distilled out of experience. And this is so because these painters do not feel themselves in opposition to reality. They are sensible to reality as something born out of man's contact with that opposition; reality exists for them only as reality experienced, as our human reality.

The paintings reproduced here trace the history of art through the last 150 years. They show that history to be the visible token of the central problem of the modern age, the quest for a meaningful image of reality. This problem has ruled the destinies of painting in our time. It has, likewise, been the goad of modern literature, philosophy, and science. It asks what the essential nature of reality really is, and this is the question all men—not painters alone—have asked themselves in this epoch, the question with which today's man wrestles and whose answer determines and decides no less an issue than man's fate itself.

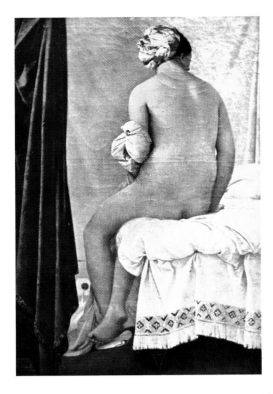

JEAN AUGUSTE DOMINIQUE INGRES (1780–1867) *Nude from the Back*. Oil on canvas · 57⅛ × 46½″ · The Louvre, Paris

An uncompromising Classicist, Ingres stands at the opposite pole to Delacroix. His mythological compositions are infused with a spirit of dignified repose, and his portraits confer on the sitter an air of austere self-control. His ideal was a transfigured nature, purified of all earthly dross. The values he sought transcended time, were eternal—Phidias and Raphael were his legitimate ancestors. Cool, disciplined, objective, his painting is the source of all those modern movements that deny to the art work any part of the subjective temperament. And yet his paintings are charged with a remarkable strength of will entirely focused on attaining a completely impersonal style.

THÉODORE GÉRICAULT (1791–1824) *Horse Reined In by Slaves* · 1817 · Oil on canvas · 18½ × 23¼″ · Museum of Fine Arts, Rouen

Géricault was the pioneer of the Romantic movement in France, and his *Raft of the Medusa* of 1819 paved the way for the realism that was to come later. In it, he went so far as to take an event of his own time—the more terrible, the more gruesome in that it affected men and women of no heroic distinction—as subject for a monumental tragic painting: the despair and vain hope of the shipwrecked huddled on a raft after their boat, the *Medusa*, had gone under. The pathos and agitation of the figures was not taken from plaster models as was the custom of the period but studied from live models, and this innovation was enough to throw the art world of his time into an uproar. His pictures of horses were likewise taken from life. In his works can be glimpsed the future course of nineteenth-century painting.

EUGÈNE DELACROIX (1798–1863) *Liberty Leading the People* · 1830 · Oil on canvas · 102⅜ × 128″ · The Louvre, Paris

In Delacroix modern painting found its beginnings. Van Gogh wrote of him that "he labored to revive passion." To restore to painting the element of passion, Delacroix looked back to Rubens and the Venetians. The agitated glow of his colors, the nervous excitement of his brush strokes, instill a passionate animation into his paintings that, in the best sense of the word, can be called Romantic and that belongs unequivocally to his own time, that of the July Revolution of 1830. The turbulence of the surfaces of his paintings, which results from the way he used color, chiaroscuro, and brushwork, reflects his own inner turmoil. In all his compositions, whether he drew the subject from mythology, history, or elsewhere, he strove to pin down the tumult of life in all its drama and colorful intensity. At a time that others sought inspiration in Classical antiquity, Delacroix turned to the Arabian world.

HONORÉ DAUMIER (1808–79) *The Washerwoman* · Oil on panel · 19¼ × 12¾″ · The Louvre, Paris

Daumier was the greatest master of caricature of his age, and as such his lithographs made him known, famed, and feared. But his painting and sculpture win for him a place among the great artists of his century; through them he converted Romanticism into Realism. He was the first to restore to painting a subject matter drawn from the simple facts of daily life, but on those drab facts he conferred the pathos and heroism that is mankind's abiding dignity. In Daumier's work is embodied the spirit of the Revolution of 1848; his paintings link the common happenings of everyday life with the great tradition of man's innate worth that had dominated art since the close of the Middle Ages.

THÉODORE ROUSSEAU (1812–67) *Storm Effect Seen from the Plain of Montmartre* · Oil on canvas · 9 × 14⅛″ · The Louvre, Paris

Rousseau, along with Millet, was part of that group which sought refuge in the woods of Barbizon near Paris from the inexorable onrush of the Industrial Revolution. There he learned what landscape is and that the hours of the day have each their own mood, and how colors are transformed with the seasons' change. His landscape paintings cling to traditional modes of depicting space in orderly planes of foreground, middle distance, and background, but in their play of light and color he revealed a new understanding of atmosphere and mood that was part of the Romantic feeling for the world. He thereby opened to landscape art new realms of poetry and imagery.

JEAN FRANÇOIS MILLET (1814–75) *Spring* · Oil on canvas · 33½ × 43¼″ · The Louvre, Paris

With Millet, landscape painting regained its place in French art. Classicism and Romanticism had both taken as their ideal the human figure and the large-scale composition; Millet and his circle rediscovered nature when they fled to the woods around Barbizon to escape the ugliness of the new industrial world. Their single subject was the magic of nature and the way in which it was attuned to the poetry of the human soul. But this view of nature, still essentially Romantic, led also to the kind of close observation of landscape that revealed new possibilities to the generations that were to come.

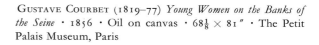

GUSTAVE COURBET (1819–77) *Young Women on the Banks of the Seine* · 1856 · Oil on canvas · 68⅛ × 81″ · The Petit Palais Museum, Paris

Courbet was the master and champion of Realism in painting. In opposition to both Classicism and Romanticism, he considered as worthy subjects for painting only those things the painter can see with his own eyes. In Courbet the scientific spirit of the nineteenth century found its greatest advocate, one who did not hesitate to cast off the dreams and fables of earlier generations and to fix all his attention on what lay around him. But he conferred on the real world in which he lived a grandeur and a dignity that, before his time, were reserved to religious and mythological subjects. He was the first painter of modern times to take visible reality—and this alone—as the subject matter for his art and, by means of art, to elevate it to a new significance.

JOHAN JONGKIND (1819–91) *In Holland: Boats near a Mill* · c. 1867 · Oil on canvas · 20⅞ × 32″ · The Louvre, Paris

With Jongkind French landscape painting of the nineteenth century forged a link with the landscape art of seventeenth-century Holland. A product of the Dutch Romantic School, which consciously harked back to the great period of art in its own country, Jongkind's fine original talent matured in the course of his travels; he deeply studied the changes of landscape in atmosphere, character, and light, from one place to another. His sensitivity to the fascination of light was made keener by his work in the more immediate and spontaneous technique of watercolor. In this way Jongkind became the painter of light, its changes and its varied effects on the colors of things, and this achievement accounts for his important influence on the next generation, that of the Impressionists.

EUGÈNE BOUDIN (1824–98) *The Jetty at Deauville* · 1869 · Oil on panel · 9 × 12½″ · The Louvre, Paris

Together with the painters of the Barbizon School, Boudin stands out as a discoverer of the landscape, but his is a quite different kind of landscape with its innumerable views of sand and sea. The dominant theme in his work is the atmosphere itself, the moisture-laden air that sucks up light. Things lose their solidity, swim in the light-drenched atmosphere, and earth, sea, and sky, men and objects, all melt into a single fluid colorful image. In contrast to the modeling construction of the Barbizon painters, Boudin's free and flexible brush strokes suggest the never-still animation of the seashore climate. His discoveries made possible the innovations of the Impressionists and pointed the way to them.

JOSEPH MALLORD WILLIAM TURNER (1775–1851) *The Fighting Téméraire* · 1839 · Oil on canvas · 35½ × 47½″ · The Tate Gallery, London

Turner was the master painter of English Romanticism. That school, unlike its French equivalents, was not primarily concerned with the human figure; its feeling for life was placed under the aegis of the workings of nature. But here too the decisive theme is heroism and tragic grandeur. In Turner's picture, the antiquated battleship that sets forth on its last journey in the glow of the setting sun is made to appear a tragic hero haloed by the heavens' colors. Nature, for Turner the mighty sounding board of human feeling, takes part in the last great act of the heroic ship—the world is an indivisible unity. This Romantic world-embracing sense impelled Turner to a spiritual conception of nature that opened the eyes of the Impressionists to the vivid fresh beauty of the world.

RICHARD PARKES BONINGTON (1802–28) *Picardy Coast* · Oil on canvas · 13¾ × 19¼″ · The Wallace Collection, London

Bonington, the precursor of English Realistic painting who died so young, opposes a quiet, restrained lyricism to Turner's heroic dramaturgy. Not for him such exalted declamation but rather a quiet meditation on the simple poetry of nature. His pictures breathe a fresh naturalism, an entirely new attitude toward nature, and they seek after no effect but only to disclose the beauty and the magic of the everyday natural world about us. The easy familiarity with which the English approach nature, their independence of all artistic traditions, enter into landscape painting for the first time in the works of Bonington, the earliest in a line of great "prosewriters" of landscape.

JOHN CONSTABLE (1776–1837) *Salisbury Cathedral* · 1829 · Oil on canvas · 20¾ × 30¼″ · The National Gallery, London

Constable's work represents the first really great step forward in art's discovery of landscape. With a free improvisatory technique, he pins down the basic motifs of landscape in seemingly random slices of reality that convey to the viewer a feeling of great immediacy. Not for England alone but also for France Constable was a pioneer of landscape art because of the freedom he achieved in the relaxed composition of his paintings as well as in the refreshing independence with which he used color. Delacroix, the master of French Romanticism, was indebted to him for a completely new conception of landscape background and for a heightened feeling for color. Above all, Constable's paintings embody the unaffected spontaneity of an Englishman's companionship with nature.

CAMILLE COROT (1796–1875) *Chartres Cathedral* · 1830 · Oil on canvas · 25¼ × 20⅜″ · The Louvre, Paris

Corot's paintings grew out of his calm, dispassionate contemplation of his own surroundings. But as a painter Corot knew how to infuse this orderly middle-class point of view with so much poetry that he could transform a casual glimpse of a church or dwelling into a novel pictorial experience. He disposed the house or monument that was his subject in the far distance, treated it as a natural part of the landscape, and thereby caught in his painting that artless spontaneity characteristic of the middle-class view of the world in the first half of the nineteenth century.

PHILIPP OTTO RUNGE (1777–1810) *The Artist's Parents* · Oil on canvas · 76⅜ × 51½″ · Kunsthalle, Hamburg

Out of this portrait of his parents Runge made a kind of Romantic allegory. It portrays not only the two people he knew best but also the Road of Life—from childhood, burgeoning carefree as green plants, all the way to the ripe spiritual flowering of old age. The meaning of the painting far transcends the forms in which it is expressed; the picture becomes the embodiment of a vision of the world which draws into the personal orbit of the individuals he portrayed the greater fact of the nature and growth of creation itself. Such intellectual idealism, first introduced into German painting by Runge, is characteristic of German Romanticism in contrast to that of France and England.

CASPAR DAVID FRIEDRICH (1774–1840) *Forest Pathway* · Oil on canvas · 19¼ × 13¾″ · Kunsthalle, Hamburg

Friedrich created a new kind of landscape painting; in his pictures landscape becomes a symbol of human feeling. The special trait of his approach to landscape is that the eye is pulled into the far distance, as the path here is lost in the farthest depths of the forest. This compositional peculiarity originates in the predominant sentiment of his period —longing, aspiration toward the unknown and the illimitable. Nature for Friedrich is a mirror held up to man's soul, and it can become this because he himself has no doubts of the quintessential oneness of nature and man.

EDOUARD MANET (1832–1883) *The Fifer* · 1866 · Oil on canvas · 63 × 38⅛″ · The Louvre, Paris

A trip to Spain in 1865 had led Manet to employ sparingly his artistic means. It was precisely this economy, however, that repaid him with a new strength in his work: his young fifer, life-size and set in an unusually narrow format, speaks to the viewer with all the immediacy of a playing card, with extreme clarity and simplification. Without a trace of sentimentality or rhetoric, the figure of the boy in his red trousers and blue jacket is installed directly in front of a simple background. Manet was not concerned with telling a story; this portrait is no more than a fragment snatched from the life around him. Here all excess is rejected; forms and colors speak coolly, clearly in this picture, poised as it is between the Romantic and the Realistic.

295

EDOUARD MANET *Luncheon on the Grass* · 1862 · Oil on canvas · 83⅛ × 106½″ · The Louvre, Paris

Manet was the pacemaker for the new painting in France. He had a single aim: to make art belong to his own time. This early painting is a clear declaration of this spiritual position, for Manet translated a composition of the sixteenth century into the costumes and atmosphere of his modern age. The gathering of river gods in his Renaissance prototype is metamorphosed by Manet into a picnic party of young artists and their models in the fields. The joys of outdoor life are proclaimed here with all the self-evident satisfaction of the age that discovered them. All the colors sing more strongly in the sunlight; the artist has escaped from his studio-prison into the light of day, into the core of life of his own times.

EDOUARD MANET *Peonies* · 1864/65 · Oil on canvas · 36 × 27″ · The Louvre, Paris

Manet was, after Courbet, the second great pioneer in the development of French painting. Like Courbet he limited himself, with utmost self-awareness, to the realm of everyday fact. Anything that smacked of literature or mythology he translated promptly into the language of his times, as in the picnic scene based on a Renaissance original. Manet cared only to speak for his own age, and rejected from his painting anything that might be problematical, which is why he relied above all on his own eyes. For the first time a painter painted what he saw, not what he knew. Shadows take on color, colors reflect other colors and are thereby altered. What can be perceived by the senses—visible, verifiable phenomena—becomes the only ultimately valid reality for art.

296

ALFRED SISLEY (1839–99) *Road at the Edge of the Woods* · 1883 · Oil on canvas · 23⅝ × 28¾″ · The Louvre, Paris

Sisley was a pure landscape painter who consistently and with much charm applied the principles of Impressionism to the variegated aspects of French scenery. His English ancestry may perhaps explain his special sensitivity to the loveliness of the French terrain, so much like that of English parks. This charm he owed directly to the new technique: the nervous, thin application of paint and the tiny bits of pure colors laid next to each other make his canvases tremble with the warm breath of the wind, and his colors contribute to the impression of an idyllic gentleness that seems to quiver delicately in his paintings. Sisley's work fully realized the feeling for nature of the Impressionists, the pleasure they took in mere light and air.

CAMILLE PISSARRO (1830–1903) *The Red Roofs* · 1877 · Oil on canvas · 21 × 25¼″ · The Louvre, Paris

Pissarro was the oldest member of the generation that raised the banner of Impressionism. In his early works his approach was that of Corot, a simple unproblematic observation of nature. But he came to understand that this was not the way to paint light and the color of life, that this was not how to capture the fleeting moment, ultimate source of all illumination. Under Monet's influence he joined the Impressionist group and adapted its methods, a spontaneous technique that trusted only in the evidence of the eyes in juxtaposing tiny particles of pure color directly on the canvas, instead of the earlier practice of mixing paint on a palette. By these new means he achieved a new clarity, and his colors came to vibrate like the atmosphere itself.

CLAUDE MONET (1840–1926) *Rouen Cathedral* · 1894 · Oil on canvas · 39½ × 25⅜″ · Museum of Fine Arts, Boston

In his later pictures Monet pushed Impressionism to its furthest limits. Real things no longer have any value in themselves; what matters is only the impression they make on the eye, which is significant only because of what Monet does with it in paint. The thing in itself no longer interests Monet but only its accidental appearance. Thus, in his later life he did entire series of pictures that record the effects of different lighting on the same subject. One of the first of these series focused on the façade of the cathedral in Rouen—the changing appearances of its architecture under the changing light of different times of day. In these variations on a theme, the point of departure, the subject itself, is of less importance than the art of variation, and in this respect these paintings anticipate the abstract art of more recent times.

Detail is shown on next pages

CLAUDE MONET (1840–1926) *Impression, Sunrise* · 1872 · Oil on canvas · 19⅝ × 25½″ · Marmottan Museum, Paris

Monet was the leading spirit of the Impressionist School. It was he and his friends who conceived the notion of carrying over into landscape painting the lessons learned from Realism. Monet himself went even farther: not only did he explore and put down in paint the everyday world around him but, what is more, he painted it exactly as he saw it. What mattered to him was not what he knew about a thing but, rather, the impression it made on his eyes. He seized upon the appearances of things and set them down in minute particles of color loosely brushed in. By this new technique he was able to capture the vibration of light, the quivering of the atmosphere. The vision of the world that Monet proposed was so fresh, so brimming with vitality, that it can be said to be a true expression of his age.

PIERRE AUGUSTE RENOIR (1841–1919) *Her First Evening Out* · c.1880 · Oil on canvas · 25½ × 19¾″ · The Tate Gallery, London

Renoir's work parallels that of his Impressionist friends, although landscape painting was of less interest to him and the focus of his art is on the human figure. His means are the same as theirs: animated brush strokes that set the atmosphere into movement. His pictures likewise achieve a casualness, an apparently accidental vitality, that makes the fleeting moment grasped on canvas seem deliberately snatched while still fresh from the passing stream of daily life. Above all else, Renoir is the painter of the joy of living. His figures are impregnated with a feeling of healthful healing well-being, and his hymn to life is sung in the invigorating glow of his shimmering delicate palette.

300

EDGAR DEGAS (1834–1917) *The Blue Dancers* · 1890 · Oil on canvas · 33½ × 29½″ · The Louvre, Paris

Degas belonged to the group of Impressionists, but he was above all a painter of the human figure, unlike his friends who devoted themselves chiefly to landscape. His artistic aims, however, were the same: in his pictures of ballet dancers and jockeys, bodies flash by in a vision of light and color that speaks to the viewer of the transitoriness of the moment captured there. Yet behind his radiant vision of what colors mean and do there lurks a solid feeling for classical formal construction. In this he carries on the tradition of an Ingres, but he brings to it a new and startling way of seeing things, a masterly keenness of observation.

HENRI DE TOULOUSE-LAUTREC (1864–1901) *Women* · 1893 · Pastel on board · 23⅝ × 19⅝″ · Private collection, New York

Toulouse-Lautrec, the crippled offspring of an ancient and noble French family, viewed his models and objects without a trace of sentimental indulgence; like an anatomist he analyzed what he saw before him. There is nothing equivocal about the brothel scenes he painted; they are merely one more aspect of the reality he had set himself to discover. This unsentimental attitude left him perfectly free to do whatever he, as a painter, wished to do: his figures sliced off by the edge of the painting may produce an astonishing play of lines, and this device can be justified on other grounds—they are a slice of life caught as it happens. The movement his Impressionist friends suggested through light and color Toulouse-Lautrec attained by the tension and animation of his lines.

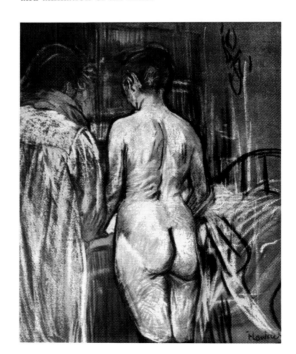

Pierre Puvis de Chavannes (1824–98) *The Toilette* · Oil on canvas · $27\frac{5}{8} \times 24\frac{3}{4}''$ · The Louvre, Paris

Puvis de Chavannes remained faithful to the French Classical tradition, but to it he added a sentimentality typical of the late nineteenth century. In that age of booming industrialism, the Classical manner with its high respect for the human figure no longer conformed to reality—it could inspire no more than nostalgic yearning. Puvis' figures are idealized, remote from life, but the Classical tradition gave his work architectonic strength and logical construction. The form and color he used transcend what he found in nature, and he obeyed underlying principles of organization that go back to the laws of earlier mural painting.

Dante Gabriel Rossetti (1828–82) *Ecce Ancilla Domini: The Annunciation* · 1850 · Oil on canvas, mounted on wood · $28\frac{1}{2} \times 16\frac{1}{2}''$ · The Tate Gallery, London

Rossetti and the English Pre-Raphaelite School deliberately turned their backs on the painting of Realism, and were indifferent to open-air painting and to landscape. Their ideal was a return to early Italian art, to a highly stylized representation of noble and elevated subject matter. Such sentimental nostalgia for the remote past is not unconnected with the times in which these artists lived. Typical of Rossetti's disdain for Realism and for the depiction of contemporary truth is his insistence on painting in a completely flat manner: figures and backgrounds are woven into a purely decorative pattern.

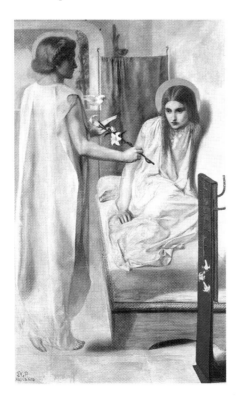

Arnold Böcklin (1827–1901) *Naiads at Play* · 1886 · Tempera on canvas · $59\frac{1}{2} \times 69\frac{1}{4}''$ · Kunstmuseum, Basel

In Böcklin's works the flight from the modern world of facts and figures into a realm of mythology is aided and abetted, quite remarkably, by the technical advances of Realist painting. The passion for the fabulous and legendary reveals clearly the Romantic roots of this kind of art so closely related to Richard Wagner's music dramas. The mythical and fantastic scenes are depicted in a technique taken over directly from Courbet's untrammeled observation of actuality. The dual character of this art—symbolic content in realistic form—is symptomatic of the *fin de siècle*, the waning of the nineteenth century, but it also points toward a development still to come, Surrealism.

James Abbott McNeill Whistler (1834–1903) *Mother of the Artist* · 1871/72 · Oil on canvas · $57 \times 64\frac{1}{2}''$ · The Louvre, Paris

Whistler was America's first contribution to modern art, although from 1855 on he lived mostly in Europe, where he was linked with the Impressionists through ties of friendship. He sought a musical quality and even entitled his paintings —mostly portraits—"Arrangements" or "Symphonies," often going so far as to designate the specific key in which they were composed. Thus, the portrait of his mother is also known as "Arrangement in Gray No. 1." His attempt to think of his paintings in terms of music was, moreover, paralleled by the fact that he took as model the perfection of craftsmanship to be found in Japanese prints. From these influences emerged quite surprising compositions which combine a spontaneous feeling for form with carefully calculated effects.

JOZEF ISRAELS (1824–1911) *Homeward Going* · 1868 · Oil on canvas · 17¾ × 22⅞ ″ · Stedelijk Museum (on loan from the Rijksmuseum), Amsterdam

Jozef Israels belongs to the generation of the Barbizon painters. He too, distressed by the industrial inroads of his time, turned to country scenes and the life of the peasantry. But in his work landscape plays scarcely any role; man is his basic theme, man in his natural setting. In this his great sympathy with the poor and downtrodden has a part, as well as his virtually biblical solidarity with the persecuted of the earth. The warmth of his love for mankind, so much like that of Charles Dickens, is reflected in the warm tones of his pictures and in his manner of infusing his figures and their surroundings with the breath of life. There is in his work a mood, an atmosphere, in which man and his environment become a single whole.

ADOLF MENZEL (1815–1905) *Staircase with Night Lighting* · 1848 · Oil on canvas · 14½ × 8⅝ ″ · Folkwang Museum, Essen

In Germany it was Menzel who opened the way to Realism. With him, that style so firmly based on material facts took on a new and special character: intimacy. In his entire rich body of work, Menzel was preoccupied with grasping the truth of his subjects, and he left a great treasure of studies and sketches from nature. Despite this passion for accurate depiction, what concerned the painter most was to achieve the greatest possible insight—empathy even—into his subject: this was his own very personal conception of the nineteenth-century insistence on scientific accuracy. From this sympathetic identification with the subject arises the intimate quality of his pictures, enhanced by his subordination of all factors to his single-minded quest for authenticity.

WILHELM LEIBL (1844–1900) *Kitchen in Kutterling* · 1898 · Oil on canvas · 33⅛ × 25⅜ ″ · Wallraf-Richartz Museum, Cologne

Leibl's realism was the answer of the German contemporaries of Impressionism to the high-flown Romantic exuberance of the preceding generation. His thoroughgoing objectivity allowed no room for fantasy but sought, instead, to explore to the fullest the reality of daily existence and to render a proper account of it in paint. This passion for plain unvarnished fact was carried to the point of fanatical insistence on accuracy, as shown in his minute observation of every detail, although all the isolated factors are united in the firm, clearly articulated construction of his pictures. Leibl was not concerned with the beauty of forms but only with making them immediately recognizable as true to life. He linked the earnest single-mindedness of the scientific approach with the impressive eloquence of pictorial construction based wholly on clarity and truth.

GEORGE HENDRIK BREITNÉR (1857–1923) *Brouwersgracht* · 1923 · Oil on canvas · 37⅞ × 71¹⁄₁₆ ″ · Stedelijk Museum, Amsterdam

Breitner, the master of Dutch Realism, was four years younger than Vincent van Gogh but did not follow him in his epoch-making rejection of Impressionism. Not that Breitner's somber colors and broad heavy brush strokes relate him to that school; his art, in fact, has more in common with the spirit of Courbet's Realism. Like Courbet, he looks reality square in the face and has a profound feeling of solidarity with the facts of existence he portrays. Breitner created the modern Dutch cityview, in which the subject is not only the architecture of the houses but, above all, the lives and doings of common men.

HANS VON MARÉES (1837–87) *Horsedriver and Nymph* ·
1881–83 · Oil on canvas · $73\frac{5}{8} \times 56\frac{1}{4}''$ · Kunsthalle,
Hamburg

Hans von Marées' pictures begin with the observation of
reality but aim at a quite different ideal. Like Paul Cézanne,
his junior by two years, Marées strove to elevate reality to a
significance beyond mere time and place; from the play of
naked bodies in natural surroundings he built solid architectonic structures of Classical style, in which the pride of
mankind and the majesty of nature sound together in full
diapason. German painting before or since never came so
close to the Classical ideal of Greece, and Hans von Marées
remains as one of the masters of the nineteenth century,
a painter who portrayed reality with a spiritual dignity.

HENRI ROUSSEAU (1844–1910) *The Wedding* · 1905 · Oil on
canvas · $63\frac{3}{8} \times 45''$ · Collection Mrs. Jean Walther, Paris

The customs clerk Rousseau was the pioneer among
"Sunday painters," those we now call "naïve" or "primitive." After he was pensioned off from the Paris customs
bureau in 1885, painting dominated his life. In their naïve
self-assuredness, his paintings capture a kind of reality;
childlike and self-confident at one and the same time, they
define the world not as he saw it but rather as his mind and
experience told him it was. Even dreams and legends take
on, in his world of images, a clarity and palpability they can
have only for a man who, in full innocence, unhesitatingly
places his trust in reality.

PAUL SIGNAC (1863–1935) *Port of Marseilles* · 1911 · Oil on
canvas · $49 \times 53\frac{1}{2}''$ · Museum of Modern Art, Paris

Signac is second only to Seurat as the leading figure of
Neo-Impressionism, and after Seurat's early death he became
the most authoritative exponent of that highly methodical
approach. The harmony that Seurat set up as the ultimate
goal of his art and that he achieved in his figure paintings,
Signac caught primarily in landscapes. While in these there
is less opportunity for architectonic construction than in
figure paintings, even Signac's landscapes with their harbor
towers and ships are articulated according to architectonic
principles and create a homogeneous décor whose planes
overlap and reinforce each other. Now and again, it is true,
his method becomes too obvious; what had been original
discovery in the early years of this style later hardened into
an inflexible system and Pointillism, in its turn, became a
new dogma.

GEORGES SEURAT (1859–91) *Bathers at Asnières* · 1883–84 ·
Oil on canvas · $79 \times 118\frac{1}{2}''$ · The Tate Gallery, London

Seurat's painting stems from Impressionism but transcends that style. In the spontaneous, predominantly hedonistic work of the Impressionists Seurat found there was
lacking an intellectual method, an architectonic skeleton.
This systematic structure he added to the Impressionist
technique by imposing on its haphazard particles of color
a grammar, so to speak, based on solid scientific grounds—
a dense system of tiny dots of pure color organized in the
plane of the canvas with rigorous respect for architectonic
principles. By these means, along with a heightened luminosity, Seurat achieved a new monumentality in striking
contrast to the snapshot-like results of the Impressionists.
His pictures seem to dwell beyond time, in their own world
of peace and order.

PAUL CÉZANNE (1839–1906) *Aix: Rocky Landscape* ·
1885–87 · Oil on canvas · 25½ × 32½″ · The Tate Gallery,
London

Although Cézanne's painting has its roots in Impressionism, he is one of those who went beyond that art so subject
to the tyranny of the eye, so obsessed by the fleeting moment.
The purely visual experience of Impressionism no longer
satisfied him, and the whole truth, he felt, was not to be
found in mere visual sensation. He wanted his pictures to
have an air of timelessness, a universal significance like that
of the masterworks of the past. The means to this end lay in
formal construction; firmly articulated, his compositions
are based on forms derived from fundamental geometric
figures. With Cézanne, order returned to painting, and it is
this which makes him the ancestor and patron saint of much
of modern art.

PAUL CÉZANNE *Man with Crossed Arms* · 1895–1900 · Oil
on canvas · 36¼ × 28¾″ · Private collection, U.S.A.

Even in figure painting Cézanne strives for something
more than portraiture; the particular and immediate data of
the sitter are elevated to a universal value. For this reason,
he is indifferent to the psychological possibilities of the
portrait: what he is after is the superhuman value inherent
in man. In his portrait of a man with crossed arms, the
essential theme is the inner peace of his sitter far more than
his individual traits. The human figure for Cézanne is as
much a part of nature as trees and mountains, and it is this
common bond in all of creation he seeks to depict. Color
and drawing work together to give this figure its monumental character, its timeless unagitated repose.

PAUL CÉZANNE *Apples and Oranges* · c.1895–1900 · Oil on
canvas · 28¾ × 36½″ · The Louvre, Paris

Cézanne's still lifes are the clearest expression of his fundamental goal: to reveal the order and the unity of all nature.
Tablecloth, plates, cups, fruit, all lose their accidental character to become vehicles of color and geometrical form
brought together into a common order. The artist strives
to penetrate the secret heart of nature, and it is in his
still lifes that he comes closest to creating "a harmony
parallel to that of nature." The rigor and discipline of his
pictorial construction, the imposing authority of his work,
make him the greatest pioneer of that art of the twentieth
century which seeks the essential reality behind the casual
appearance.

VINCENT VAN GOGH (1853–90) *The Potato Eaters* · 1885 ·
Oil on canvas · 32½ × 44⅞″ · Vincent van Gogh Foundation,
Amsterdam (Collection V. W. van Gogh)

Vincent van Gogh together with Paul Cézanne did most
to renew art in the latter part of the nineteenth century. For
him also merely sensory impressions of reality were not the
true ones, but as a man of northern Europe his way could
not be that of Cézanne, with its reliance on intellectual
clarity; the unfettered passion of the human heart was the
guiding principle in Van Gogh's renewal of art. The
Potato Eaters is the outstanding work of his early, Dutch,
period. In it he has already found the way to liberate himself
from the merely visual impression and to make his real
theme the emotional quality of the subject depicted. The
resulting picture is a social document, evidence of his deep
feeling for the peasantry, for simple men—a profoundly
persuasive declaration of his love for his fellow creatures.

PAUL CÉZANNE (1839–1906) *Mount Ste. Victoire* · c. 1885/86 ·
Oil on canvas · $21\frac{1}{4} \times 25\frac{5}{8}''$ · Stedelijk Museum, Amsterdam

In paintings that were to become the foundation stones of
modern art, Cézanne sought for the truth in the world
around him. Mere semblance no longer satisfied him;
beyond the limits of what the eye can observe, he strove to
decipher the true essence of reality. In his landscapes,
especially those very beautiful ones of the mountains near
his native town, Aix, he attempted to track down the
fundamental laws of nature's structures, reducing natural
forms to the geometrical prototypes of sphere, prism, and
cone. Color too, he found, could be employed according to
principles, like the tones of a musical scale. The severely
intellectual method of his painting reveals itself in every
single brush stroke: his pictures are tightly woven fabrics of
color in which each brush stroke is conceived in contra-
puntal relation to all the others.
Detail is shown on next pages

VINCENT VAN GOGH *Self-Portrait with a Gray Hat* · 1887 · Oil on canvas · 17⅝ × 14¾" · Vincent van Gogh Foundation, Amsterdam (Collection V. W. van Gogh)

During the two years between 1886 and 1888, Van Gogh lived and worked in Paris, where his brother Theo was an art dealer. During that time he taught himself everything he needed to know about the Impressionist technique; the man from provincial Holland was determined to acquire for himself the newest technical conquests of his French friends in order to paint, like them, the varicolored world about him. From this period dates this self-portrait in which paint is laid on in a web of streaks and points so as to capture color in all its innate vitality. The years in Paris equipped Van Gogh with a foundation on which to build his more mature art; this was also to be an art of color, but color used as a means of personal expression.

VINCENT VAN GOGH *Memory of Mauve* · 1888 · Oil on canvas · 28¾ × 23⅜" · Kröller-Müller Museum, Otterlo

In 1888 Van Gogh left Paris for Arles, in the south of France. There, under the southern sun, he found new potentialities in his painting: he became a colorist, using color as a vehicle for expression. Color no longer served to define the object he painted but, instead, to express the artist's own innermost feelings. Thus, a picture of a flowering tree beneath the clear blue sky meant, for Van Gogh, a recollection of his dead teacher, the painter Mauve. Human emotions became for him the key to the world, and they are embodied in his color and brush strokes. This concept of the world as spirit, as the expression of man's passions, constitutes Van Gogh's legacy to the new art of the twentieth century.

PAUL GAUGUIN (1848–1903) *Nave, Nave Moe: The Spring of Delight* · 1894 · Oil on canvas · 28¾ × 38¾" · The Hermitage, Leningrad

Paul Gauguin was no longer a young man when he discovered his vocation for painting. At thirty-five he kicked over the traces, quit his stockbroker's job, and devoted himself entirely to art. Although the roots of his art lie in Impressionism, painting the objective appearance of things according to what the eye can understand of them did not content him. He sought a world beneath the surface, the world of myth in which the elemental experiences of human existence are embodied. Such a primitive world he found in Tahiti, to which he had fled in his Romantic disgust with the dubious delights of civilization. In his pictures of the life of the simple half-primitive natives, there is revealed all the feeling of modern man who seeks to rediscover a lost paradise at the very source of human life.

PAUL GAUGUIN *The White Horse* · 1898 · Oil on canvas · 55½ × 35¾" · The Louvre, Paris

Gauguin sought to pin down the uncomplicated innocence of life in a latter-day paradise not simply within his subject matter but, even more, by his entire approach to a picture. He tried to create a worthy replacement for the religious art that had deteriorated so grossly in the nineteenth century. Toward this end, he worked with firm outlines and flat planes; he did not seek to draw the viewer into a world forever locked within the confines of the picture frame, but instead he spread forms and colors on the surface of his canvas to create an impact as direct as that made by altar paintings in an earlier period. *The White Horse*, from his last years, is conceived as flatly as mural painting, an ancient tradition revived to express a wholly modern view of the world.

VINCENT VAN GOGH (1853–90) *Street in Auvers* · 1890 ·
Oil on canvas · 28¼ × 35¾″ · Athenaeum Gallery of Art,
Helsinki

Van Gogh, in his late pictures, stands beside Cézanne as the
great forerunner of modern art, though their respective
interpretations of reality stand at opposite poles. Whereas
Cézanne strives to discover the essence of reality in basic
laws arrived at intellectually, Van Gogh seeks to impart
spiritual significance to nature by means of his own passions, through the intensity of his own emotions. Thus, he
could write, "May it not be that one can perceive a thing
better and more accurately by loving it than by not loving
it?" The exaltation, the ardent verve of his overpowering
emotion, is visible even in the way he painted; color is
used as a means of expression, and his brushwork betrays
the vehemence of his passionate love for life. His brush
courses over the canvas with the sure determination of a
visionary who sets down directly and without fear, as if in
a state of holy possession, what his vision dictates.
Detail is shown on next pages

ODILON REDON (1840–1916) *The Chariot of Phaëton* · c. 1900 ·
Pastel on paper · 19 × 22⅞" · Stedelijk Museum,
Amsterdam

Odilon Redon rediscovered a world poised between
reality and dream, that half-real world of forms and colors
we glimpse with eyes shut. Even before psychoanalysis
charted the world of dream images, Redon had set down its
forms in paint. To bring this realm of fantasy to life for the
viewer, he made use of the Impressionist palette, and the
light and color in his pastels and oils reveal an eye trained in
that school—except that Redon did not use his eyes to see
what all of us can see; his images are dredged up out of the
deepest world of dreams where what is seen is the unseeable.

Although he was born in Belgium and died as a refugee in
Holland during World War I, Wouters had much in common with the Nabis group in France. His forms and colors
combine in a musical harmony in which the subject depicted
is no more than an incidental motive. There is in his works
an invigorating youthful pleasure in living, and his forms
and colors sing joyfully of the beauty of a world whose
charm transcends mere material facts. To us today, the
pictures of this painter who died too soon seem like a last
message from that happier, less hectic world so brutally
snuffed out by World War I.

EDOUARD VUILLARD (1868–1940) *Interior* · 1899 · Watercolor on paper · 23 × 37" · Private collection, Zurich

Vuillard belonged to the group called the Nabis, who, at
the end of the century, drew the logical consequences from
the development of Impressionism: indifference to subject
matter, a new feeling for color and decoration, the play of
lines and color—these were the basis for this group's art.
In their pictures, forms and colors cooperate to create an
animated design that is not the product of the objects
portrayed but rather of the artist's own way of bringing line
and color into a harmonious whole. These decorative
patterns are the key to Vuillard's special intimate charm:
colors are toned down to a placid, lyrical harmony and,
under the influence of Japanese prints, the entire surface is
organized in a quiet, euphonious rhythm.

PIERRE BONNARD (1867–1947) *Nude Taking a Bath* · Before
1937 · Oil on canvas · 36⅝ × 57¾" · Private collection

Bonnard shared with Vuillard the leadership of the Nabis
group at the turn of the century. In his art, too, there are
reminiscences of Impressionism, especially in the loose
pointillist texture of his paint. Unlike the Impressionists,
however, he cared nothing for the vibration of the atmosphere and the play of light. He weaves his loosely disposed
particles of pigment into a carpet-like flat surface of pure
color and flickering arabesques that fascinates the viewer
not for the object portrayed but for the intimate charm of
its lines and colors. The treatment of flat surfaces, which
he had achieved by the first years of the new century,
opened vast new horizons to the art of the future.

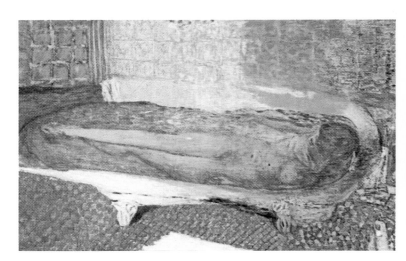

MAURICE UTRILLO (1883–1955) *Sacré-Coeur* · 1924 · Oil on canvas · 57¼ × 39¼″ · Collection Mrs. Jean Walther, Paris

The painting of Utrillo, the self-taught son of the painter Suzanne Valadon, was based on Impressionism, but he himself was too simple-hearted to deny the importance of his subject matter and place his trust entirely in the glitter of visual impressions. For this man of untutored taste and feeling, reality possessed a charm that transcended appearances, and this charm he sought to capture with the Impressionists' technique. He painted the reality he was most familiar with—the houses, streets, and churches of Montmartre, where he lived—for only that reality had any meaning for him. Utrillo was no pathfinder, but he looked at the real things he knew with a fresh and gentle vision and communicated to them something of his own innocence.

JULES PASCIN (1885–1930) *The Two Friends* · 1924 · Oil on canvas · 32¼ × 26″ · Collection Robert Ducroquet, Paris

Pascin came from a Bulgarian Jewish family and after studying at the Vienna Academy, became one of the most brilliant young illustrators for the famed weekly *Simplizissimus*. At twenty he went to Paris where he found the subject matter that appealed most to his particular personality, the world of dispirited girls and women in brothels. Their sadness and hopelessness he transmuted into a sorry world of quiet, resigned melancholy in which there sounds a distant echo of his native ghetto. The colored grounds of his paintings, over which soft tones and lines flow peacefully, lend them a dreamlike air in which harsh reality dissolves into a meek elegy for things as they are.

WALTER RICHARD SICKERT (1860–1942) *Interior of St. Mark's, Venice* · 1901–3 · Oil on canvas · 26⅞ × 18⅝″ · The Tate Gallery, London

Sickert translated into English the achievements of European painting of the beginning of the twentieth century. As a pupil and friend of Whistler, he learned his manner of treating form and color as music. In this his art resembles that of the Nabis, but the Japanese quality that influenced Bonnard's art came to Sickert from Whistler. Sickert's pictures are cooler and more undemonstrative than those of his French friends, but with him, too, colors and forms remain on the surface plane to form a poster-like design that owes its vitality, above all, to the artist's individual way of dealing with his materials.

FERDINAND HODLER (1853–1918) *Lake of Geneva from Chexbres* · 1905 · Oil on canvas · 32⅜ × 41″ · Kunstmuseum, Basel

Hodler belongs to the generation of the forerunners of twentieth-century art; he was born in the same year as Vincent van Gogh. Being of Swiss origin, he never joined the Impressionist movement, and drew his inspiration, instead, from Courbet's brand of French realism. Soon, however, he too came to grips with the problem of the picture surface, and his greatest preoccupation became the organization of the world within the plane of a canvas. Around the turn of the century, Hodler worked out his principle of Parallelism; by means of parallel lines of movement, he aimed at strengthening the organization within the plane of the picture and at expressing to the fullest the inner unity of the things depicted. His mural-like landscape paintings opened the way to a new pictorial feeling for the vastness of nature.

313

AMEDEO MODIGLIANI (1884–1920) *Seated Nude* · 1917 ·
Oil on canvas · 39⅜ × 25⅝″ · Private collection, Paris

In the Mediterranean countries, it was Modigliani who led
the shift from the nineteenth century's traditional way of
looking at things to the twentieth century's revolution in
vision. His models—the placid, almond-eyed girls he loved
—were the point of departure for a process of transmutation;
he did not try to make accurate portraits of them but instead infused their languid bodies with a lyrical melancholy,
a bittersweet worldweariness like that of the earlier Italian
poet Leopardi. This melancholy was the more intense
because of the secret sense of differentness he felt as a Jew.

PAULA MODERSOHN-BECKER (1876–1907) *Portrait of Rainer
Maria Rilke* · 1906 · Oil on canvas · 13⅜ × 10¼″ · Collection Ludwig Roselius, Bremen

Paula Modersohn-Becker helped bring about in Germany
a breakthrough to a new conception of reality; she was one
of those who first created a new art of expression at the
beginning of this century. In Paris near the end of her short
life, she discovered the new potentialities in French art
of the time, above all in Cézanne's firm constructions and
simple direct forms. Those forms, with their monumental
stillness, found a responsive note in the strength and power
of her own sensibilities. Thus in her mature work she
sloughed off every nonessential detail in order to concentrate all her force of expression on the ultimate human
values she wished to express; her portrait of Rilke probes
far beyond contingency and appearances.

JAMES ENSOR (1860–1949) *Carnival* · 1888 · Oil on canvas ·
21¼ × 28¾″ · Stedelijk Museum, Amsterdam

Ensor's masquerade world is the earliest and, indeed, the
most profound evidence of the ambiguity inherent in
reality that men at the end of the nineteenth century had to
face up to—a symptom of the crisis of confidence in the
truth of the visible world. Like Redon, Ensor painted a
half-world that lies beyond the familiar frontiers of fact, and
he painted it with bright, gleaming colors inherited from
Impressionism. But the people in his world have themselves
become one with their masks, they have stepped out of the
world we know, and they huddle together, cramped, in the
tiny acre of world left them. In Ensor's pictures, despite
their Impressionistic coloring, we perceive how, at the turn
of the century, the age which had delighted in the good
things of life became metamorphosed into the age of
anxiety.

EDVARD MUNCH (1863–1944) *By the Bed* · 1906 · Oil on
canvas · 24¾ × 23⅝″ · Collection Stenersen, Oslo

The Norwegian Munch introduced into European art the
demoniac element and visionary psychology that were
making their startling bow at the same time in Scandinavian
literature. For Munch the world is no longer merely a
familiar place to live in; it has become a nightmare that
crushes and suffocates soul and body. So painting for him is
no longer observation of reality, but penetration into that
reality; his eyes bore through the appearances of things to
grub out hidden fears and terrors. And the appearances of
things themselves take on a new meaning; lines and colors
unveil the psychic state of things, make visible hitherto
invisible aspects of them, and with visionary clairvoyance
unearth the spiritual needs of an entire generation, thrusting
them up into light and consciousness.

LOVIS CORINTH (1858–1925) *Walchensee and Yellow Prairie* · 1921 · Oil on canvas · 27⅝ × 33½″ · Bavarian State Picture Gallery, Munich

Corinth's painting grew out of the German form of Impressionism, but in his mature years his own unbridled temperament kicked over the traces; he strode roughly over the barriers imposed by his preoccupation with subject matter and made colors and lines express his own over-brimming vitality. Brush strokes no longer traced the contours of objects but coursed across the canvas in dynamic rhythms. Corinth's works belong among the first manifestations of a new feeling for life that no longer seeks the order and solid structure of nature but, instead, surrenders to the intoxication of unrestrained passion in order to seize what is most significant, most pregnant in reality. This explains why Corinth's importance has been acknowledged only in recent years.

MAURICE DE VLAMINCK (1876–1958) *The Seine at Le Pecq* · 1905 · Oil on canvas · 35⅛ × 45⅝″ · Private collection, Paris

Vlaminck was one of the first revolutionaries at the beginning of our century, one of the "Fauves," the self-proclaimed "savage beasts," who aimed to rip painting free of the bonds of rigorous grammatical discipline and set it loose as an act of pure instinct, a scream of drunken passion. The obstacle to be overcome was not formal structure but rather the arbitrary laws governing color. Vlaminck was early fascinated by Van Gogh's work, but he and his circle understood it only in part; they isolated from it what was pure passion and intensified its colors to the point of Dionysiac delirium. Vlaminck's landscapes testify to this ecstatic feeling for life, which, in revolt against cool thought and calm reflection, placed all its trust in instincts and the *élan vital*, the vital impulse.

ALBERT MARQUET (1875–1947) *Le Pont Neuf* · 1906 · Oil on canvas · 19⅝ × 24″ · National Gallery of Art, Chester Dale Collection, Washington, D.C.

Marquet likewise belonged to the group of Fauves, the first revolutionary movement of this century, and his early work has in common with them a passionate vehemence of color and construction. With the years, however, he acquired a calmer outlook that led him to cooler colors and more solid composition. A conscious influence from Far Eastern drawing may have helped quell the agitation of his painting, although he never completely denied his origins. He carried over from his stormy revolutionary beginnings the use of heavy lines and antirealistic color, and he achieved the feat of adapting the style of his youth to the more settled temperament of his mature years.

ANDRÉ DERAIN (1880–1954) *Westminster Bridge* · 1907 · Oil on canvas · 31⅞ × 39¼″ · Private collection, Paris

In his early work Derain was one of the foremost fighters in the revolution instigated by the Fauves. Colors took on un-suspected emotional significance, and he himself considered them to be so much dynamite. It was not only his colors which were loaded with emotional content, but his linear drawing also bore witness to a starkly dynamic feeling for life; every form was ripped out of balance and set whirling. He reached his high point in those early pictures; in later years he bowed out of his revolutionary commitments and merely followed the changing fads of European art without again attaining the compelling power of his early works.

ERNST LUDWIG KIRCHNER (1880–1938) *Nude in a Room: Fränzi* · 1907 · Oil on canvas · 47¼ × 35½″ · Stedelijk Museum, Amsterdam

Kirchner was the leader of the Brücke group, which in 1906 paved the way in Germany for Expressionism. Their aesthetic revolt was a protest against the exaggerated respect both painting and society as a whole paid to everyday fact; they claimed that the task of all men, including artists, is not merely to mirror reality but, instead, to transform it. To this end, Kirchner treated his models as symbols, signs of a new and more elemental humanity. The art of primitive peoples proved a potent stimulus to his efforts; the unequivocal directness and the supernatural force of South Sea sculpture pointed the way to portraying human beings in forms and colors that reveal their most deeply hidden emotions.

ERICH HECKEL (1883–1970) *In the Woods* · 1910 · Oil on canvas · 37¾ × 47¼″ · Collection Buchheim, Feldafing

Along with Kirchner and Schmidt-Rottluff, Heckel was one of the founders of the Brücke group that created German Expressionism. He too made his painting a sounding board for human passions; form and color became adjuncts to the human will for expression rather than mere means of imitation. Heckel is distinguished from his two friends in the Brücke by the lyrical, minor-key mood of his pictures as well as by his subdued colors and brittle forms that somehow suggest something of the Gothic. His intensely personal vision transformed images drawn from reality into an expression of this feeling for the world.

KARL SCHMIDT-ROTTLUFF (1884–1976) *Landscape in Dangast* · 1910 · Oil on canvas · 30⅜ × 33½″ · Stedelijk Museum, Amsterdam

Schmidt-Rottluff was the landscape painter of the Brücke group, although for him landscape is neither subject nor motif; instead, it poses a question he strives to answer in paint. He is not enslaved by factual details, but conceives a whole out of a fragment of nature, intensifies his colors, lets space expand. Nature for him is not a matter for imitation, it is in itself a dramatic happening. In this his work is typical of German Expressionism, which did not seek to describe reality but to flood it with human and cosmic emotion. Schmidt-Rottluff's robust appreciation of nature lends his pictures a fresh, vital spontaneity and a new, almost barbaric monumentality.

HENRI MATISSE (1869–1954) *Portrait of the Artist's Wife* · 1913 · Oil on canvas · 57⅞ × 39 9/16″ · The Hermitage, Leningrad

Matisse was the first revolutionary among the French painters of the early twentieth century to break completely with the representation of observed reality. Revolutionary as he was, he was nevertheless highly disciplined, with nothing of the anarchist about him. The visible appearances of reality—for so long the standard and goal of painting—were for him no more than raw material to be distilled into their essence, their ineffable perfume. Form and color were what he used to set going the fires of the distillery from which he extracted the purified essential features of the world rather than the dross of accidental appearances.

HENRI MATISSE *The Large Studio* · 1911 · Oil on canvas · 67⅝ × 80¾ · Pushkin Museum, Moscow

In the pictures Matisse painted before World War I—most of which are in Russian collections—he blended the forms and colors of reality into a reposeful harmony, a virtual symbol of one aspect of man's being; Apollonian calm and clarity infuse his pictures and radiate from them. The objective aspects of a fragment of reality concerned him little; perspective, anatomy, and the like had meaning for him only in so far as he could transform them. Matisse liberated himself and the painting of his time from that tyranny of realism that is no more than the imitation of appearances, and—secure in his own sovereign skill—he played as he willed with the stuff of the world.

HENRI MATISSE *Flowering Ivy* · 1941 · Oil on canvas · 28½ × 36½" · Collection Mrs. Albert D. Lasker, New York

In Matisse's old age, his formal language became more concise and economical. A still life might consist of no more than a few contrasting colors and ornamental lines and yet embody the nobility and simplicity he sought. He could do this because his very personal way of drawing combined with forms and colors to create a meaningful whole; the essence of his pictures was determined not by the objects depicted but by the character and frame of mind of the artist himself. The logic and intellectuality of his pictures reflect something that lay deep in Matisse—that clarity and sense of value characteristic of the French, who, secure in these values, are able to penetrate into the true essence of reality.

CHAIM SOUTINE (1894–1943) *Choirboy* · c. 1928 · Oil on canvas · 24½ × 19⅜" · Collection Mrs. Jean Walther, Paris

Soutine was one of the group in Paris to whom self-expression meant more than representing what things looked like. For him, the son of a poor Jewish tailor in a Lithuanian village, that expression was from the outset tragic, and this sentiment tinged the things and people he painted. His Dionysiac transports were born not out of joy but piercing sorrow; in his paintings there are decadence, decay, and corruption—not that of the model he happened to choose but of a world in crisis whose truths he saw as lies. Coruscating colors and slashing brush strokes make of his pictures apocalyptic visions.

GEORGES ROUAULT (1871–1958) *The Old King* · 1937 · Oil on canvas · 30⅜ × 21¼" · The Carnegie Institute, Pittsburgh

Another prophet of the Apocalypse was Georges Rouault but his vision stemmed from a different source: the horror of a deeply devout Catholic at the decay and disorder of the modern world. Like others of this generation, Rouault demanded of his visions some universal meaning, some potent symbol. He found it in a style of painting based on heavy black contours, like the lead flanging in stained-glass windows, which both tie together and hold apart great fragments of gleaming color. The violent emotion that erupted in painting everywhere in Europe in those years became, in Rouault's art, a desolate, heartsick accusation against the world.

OSKAR KOKOSCHKA (1886–1980) *Portrait of Herwarth Walden* · 1910 · Oil on canvas · 39¼ × 26¾″ · Collection Nell Walden, Switzerland

PABLO PICASSO *Woman with a Fan* · 1908 · Oil on canvas · 59⅝ × 39⅞″ · Pushkin Museum, Moscow

Kokoschka's art likewise is Expressionistic; feeling dominates over fact, and the message is tragic despair over the world's ways. But what in Rouault is prophetic lamentation and in Soutine is slashing outcry becomes with Kokoschka biting criticism. The Austrian-born painter views corruption and collapse as an event that transcends any one man's acts and seeks some explanation for it. At the same time as Freud, Kokoschka pried into man's confused and anguished soul and, with furious brush strokes and livid colors, held up before our shocked gaze the disintegration of a world trembling on the brink of collapse.

In 1907 Picasso together with Braque invented a new style of painting: Cubism. What matters in a Cubist painting is the carefully constructed form; what gives it lasting value is how objects are conceived in volume. The bases of the style were Cézanne's revelation of the underlying geometrical principles in nature and, along with this, the magical directness of primitive sculpture. Picasso and his band smashed the last lingering respect for visual sense data in order to rebuild pictorial reality on a quite different intellectual foundation. His *Woman with a Fan* is a masterly example of this sculpturesque style in which the simplified concentration on what is essential, characteristic of primitive art, cooperates with Cézanne's geometrical grammar to create a new, powerful, and noble monumentality.

PABLO PICASSO (1881–1973) *Girl on a Ball* · 1905 · Oil on canvas · 55½ × 37⅞″ · Pushkin Museum, Moscow

Since the early years of this century, the great painter Picasso has been our guide through the many meanderings of an ever-changing world picture. At the outset he was concerned with realistic depiction of human beings, not as an end in itself but rather as the means to communicate his own compassion for the outcasts of society. The small gaunt figures of his acrobats, in pale quiet shades of rose and light blue, bear witness to those feelings.

PABLO PICASSO *Pigeon with Baby Peas* · 1912 · Oil on canvas · 25⅝ × 21¼″ · Museum of Modern Art, Paris

In the years after 1910, Picasso and Braque, working in close association, devised a new modification of their contemporary approach to painting: Analytical Cubism. The forms of things were dissected into bits and then separated; a fixed viewing point was abandoned, and the painter looked at objects not from a single point but from above, below, front, back, everywhere. In this way, a picture came to take on an essential reality that has nothing to do with the eyes' illusions.

PABLO PICASSO *Woman in a Chemise* · 1921 · Oil on canvas · $28\frac{3}{4} \times 23\frac{3}{8}''$ · The Tate Gallery, London

After World War I, Picasso devised a new style for himself. The Cubist experiments were abandoned, and, after a series of still lifes, he went back to the human figure. In the paintings of female figures of this period some have hailed a return to the imitation of reality, to the old reliable world of recognizable forms. But the inspiration for these works lay in the secret, self-absorbed stillness of Classical figures and in the firm intellectual discipline that Classicism—above all that of Ingres, its last great exponent in France—had set up as the ultimate concern of painting. Picasso's Classical period grew out of a personal quest for self-discipline especially impressive in our times.

PABLO PICASSO *Muse* · 1935 · Oil on canvas · $51\frac{1}{8} \times 63\frac{5}{8}''$ · Museum of Modern Art, Paris

Hard upon the Classical style of the 1920s Picasso's art took another turning; beginning in 1925, he did a series of paintings in which the human figure is treated as a symbol of unleashed passion. After bringing into pictorial existence a world founded on order, Picasso himself ripped the veil off the Janus face of that world, proclaiming its tragic disarray in distorted and demoniac figures. In those years he invented a personal mythology to express the disorder of our age. The series of such paintings, to which belongs this nude woman drawing, was climaxed by the grandiose mural painting *Guernica*, Picasso's reply to the Nazi aerial bombardment of an open city in Spain.

PABLO PICASSO *Portrait of a Woman* · 1938 · Oil on canvas · $38\frac{1}{2} \times 30\frac{1}{2}''$ · Museum of Modern Art, Paris

During World War II, the Expressionist element became more important in Picasso's work; the ordeals of the preceding decade intensified the painter's compassion for man's fate and trials. This feeling emerges in the paintings of women he did about that time, figures steeped in the dramatic atmosphere of the time. One of the means of this pictorial dramaturgy is the stretching of form to its limit in the portrayal of faces in a half-profile, half-front view; another is the contrast—conflict even—between figure, chair, and background.

GEORGES BRAQUE (1882–1963) *Composition with the Ace of Clubs* · c. 1911 · Gouache and charcoal on canvas · $31\frac{1}{2} \times 23\frac{1}{4}''$ · Museum of Modern Art, Paris

Braque was Picasso's co-worker in the invention of Cubism. Both sought an art whose truth would be as objective as possible and largely independent of accidental semblance, an art that would reveal the quintessential truth of reality. Braque concentrated above all on formal problems; color plays a secondary role in his pictures, a mere adjunct to the essential definition of the form. For this reason, Braque—with his inborn love for the craft element in art—attributed great importance to the treatment of the picture's surface. By imitating to perfection the grain of wood and other such elements, he succeeded in introducing a new dimension, that of textural value. Such innovations in technique led to the invention of *collage* and thence to a further revolution in art.

319

FERNAND LÉGER (1881–1955) *Contrast of Forms* · 1913 ·
Oil on canvas · 39⅜ × 31⅞″ · Museum of Modern Art,
Paris

Léger opened a new horizon to the Cubists. From the outset
he was fascinated by machinery, its impersonal construction
and metrical movement; he became the portraitist and
spokesman for the Machine Age, for the Brave New World
of engineers. Even his human figures resemble machines,
and his entire world is placed under the sign of a forceful
formal anonymity. But the machine for him was a positive
value, an aid to mankind's striving for a sounder future,
and so there is a hearty optimism about his painting; solid
simplified lines and planes combine with the cheerful harmonies of primary colors to express, in an energetic and
virile language, a joyous satisfaction in well-being.

JACQUES VILLON (1875–1963) *Soldiers on the March* · 1913 ·
Oil on canvas · 25⅝ × 36¼″ · Gallery Louis Carré, Paris

Villon introduced into Cubism a new accent, movement.
In a sense, movement became his dominant subject matter,
while his means remained those of the Cubists; he constructed his pictures out of small overlapping flat planes,
rejected the seductions of color, and brought space and
figures into a single whole. Where he differs from the
Cubists is in turning all this into movement. The flat planes
are no longer merely superimposed but take on life; they
push and shove for position, their contour lines become
direction signals, symbols of movement. Villon's work
approaches that of the Italian Futurists in his use of the
formal language of Cubism to embody movement, the
phenomenon so significant for his time.

ROGER DE LA FRESNAYE (1885–1925) *Man Seated*, or *The
Architect* · 1913 · Oil on canvas · 51⅛ × 64⅞″ · Museum of
Modern Art, Paris

Within the Cubist ambience, Roger de la Fresnaye and the
entire group of "Orphists" occupy a special position. The
distinguishing mark of this minority faction is their concern
with color as opposed to the almost monochromatic painting of Picasso, Braque, and Juan Gris, where the focus is on
form. With Roger de la Fresnaye, color, laid down in large
geometrical, well-defined slabs, becomes the architectonic
basis of his pictures, and the forms themselves are stylized
into their elementary geometrical configurations. This kind
of art, with its colorful large surfaces conceived cubistically,
brought about a revival of the long-neglected art of mural
painting.

ROBERT DELAUNAY (1885–1941) *Circular Forms* · 1912–13 ·
Oil on canvas · 39⅜ × 27″ · Collection Sonia Delaunay,
Paris

Delaunay's painting grew out of Cubism. In opposition to
all the Cubists whose primary concern was with formal
construction, Delaunay concentrated doggedly on the analytical dissection of color and the new unity to be gained
thereby. Just as the Cubists disarticulated form and dissected its elements, so Delaunay split light into its stable
components, which he then synthesized into a new whole.
In this way, color became at one and the same time his form
and content. These experiments, in which he broke down
light in order to obtain a new dynamics of color, were of
great importance in freeing color from its associations with
actual objects and became another significant step toward
abstract painting.

PABLO PICASSO (1881–1973) *Portrait of the Art Dealer Vollard* · 1910 · Oil on canvas · 36¾ × 26″ · Hermitage, Leningrad

The three portraits that Picasso painted in 1910, of Wilhelm Uhde, Ambroise Vollard, and Daniel-Henry Kahnweiler, belong among the major works in the Cubist style that Picasso and Braque together had been developing since

1907. The Cubist technique is based on the splitting of forms into prismatic facets, which are then laid one upon the other in overlapping planes, the so-called *plans superposés*. The aim of this rigorous method is the greatest possible objective comprehension of the thing depicted, entirely independent of the viewing point of the beholder and even of his personal frame of mind. In these portraits, Picasso almost entirely rejects color to the profit of form. *Detail is shown on next pages*

321

JUAN GRIS (1887–1927) *Still Life with Grapes* · 1914 ·
Pencil and gouache with collage on canvas · 31⅞ × 23⅝″ ·
Private collection, Paris

The true classicist among the Cubists was Juan Gris. It was
he who pushed farthest Cubism's rigorously intellectualistic
discipline, rooted in universally valid principles. He brought
about a decisive transformation in the relationship of the
object depicted to reality; instead of taking an object as his
point of departure and breaking it down into its geometrical,
formal elements, as the early Cubists did, he began with the
play of geometrical forms and only then, in the course of the
creative process, permitted them to metamorphose themselves into objects: a cylinder grows into a bottle, a right
angle into a tablecloth. In the crystal-clear grammatical construction and the classical rigorous syntax of Gris's paintings
lies the secret of their eminently convincing power.

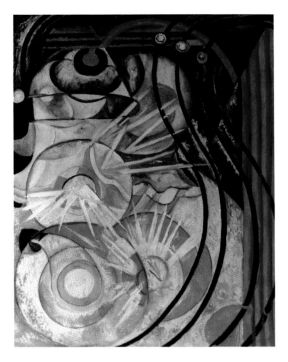

NATHALIE GONTCHAROVA (1881–1962) *Electric Lamps* ·
1912 · Oil on canvas · 41⅜ × 31⅞″ · Formerly the artist's
collection, Paris

Gontcharova worked beside Larionov in prewar Russia
to carry further the innovations of Cubism. Unlike the work
of the French Cubists, her painting is not based on the
analysis of form; as with Larionov, the foundation from
which she worked was the analysis of light. Light in movement was her chief interest, and she translated its radiation
into dynamic lines, which, it must be admitted, often betray
their kinship with the serpentine twistings of Art Nouveau.
Through her absorbing concern with light in movement,
over and beyond any association with real objects,
Gontcharova contributed much to the development of
abstract art, although her role as a forerunner is not yet
sufficiently appreciated.

MICHAEL LARIONOV (1881–1964) *Rayonism* · 1911 · Oil on
canvas · 21¼ × 27⅝″ · Formerly the artist's collection, Paris

At the beginning of the century, Russia was a thriving
center of artistic and intellectual activity. All new trends in
painting were quickly brought to Moscow and there carried
to their ultimate consequences. Very early, before 1913,
Larionov devised a kind of painting he called Rayonism,
which, on the basis of the Cubist analytical method, constructed pictures out of nothing other than sheaves of
colored light rays. This was one of the first approaches to
the principle of abstraction, which, in those years, was
agitating the younger generation of painters throughout
Europe. In Larionov's work was laid down the basis for a
Constructivist art.

GIACOMO BALLA (1871–1958) *Little Girl Running on a
Balcony* · 1912 · Oil on canvas · 51⅛ × 51⅛″ · Gallery of
Modern Art, Milan

For the Italian Futurists, movement was as much the central problem in painting as it was for their Russian contemporaries. The achievements of both Pointillism and Cubism
were exploited to this end; in order to create the effect of
fleeting, flashing movement, colors and forms were de-
composed ruthlessly. In this painting by Balla, showing
simultaneously the various phases of a young girl's running
movement, the influence of the newly invented cinema is
obvious; it is as if successive quick snaps of the same model
were copied out one above the other in order to combine the
static gestures caught by the camera eye into a dynamic
succession as in a motion picture film.

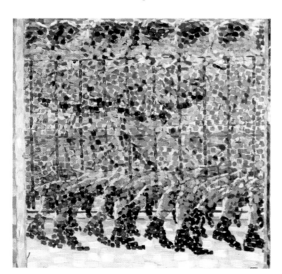

EMIL NOLDE (1867–1956) *Candle Dancers* · 1912 · Oil on canvas · 39⅜ × 33¼″ · Nolde-Stiftung, Seebüll

A member of the Brücke group in Dresden, Nolde was the most convincing exponent of German Expressionism. His work, like that of his German colleagues, stems from Van Gogh's; it attempts to breathe new spirit into the familiar world by means of a personal Dionysiac outpouring of passion. Color was the chief means of this new art of ex-

pression. It was used not for depiction of things as they are but rather to infuse those things with its own innate energy. Above all, the emotional power of his color transforms every picture by Nolde into a violently ecstatic drama, but the stirring animation of his forms also plays its part. This drama is evoked in large measure by the special way paint is laid on; impetuous brush strokes jerk across the canvas like flickering tongues and transform the rectangle of the picture into a field where contradictory forces of movement war.

Detail is shown on next pages

CARLO CARRÀ (1881–1966) *The Funeral of the Anarchist Galli* · 1911 · Oil on canvas · 77¼ × 101¾″ · Museum of Modern Art, New York

Nineteenth-century Italy took almost no part in the development of modern painting; the enormous prestige of classical Renaissance art nipped all such ambition in the bud. When in 1910 modernism finally broke through, exasperation had made its form so much the more extreme. Under the leadership of the poet Marinetti, who had already shaken up the literary world in like manner, five young artists published a manifesto of Futurist painting. The manifesto extolled dynamic movement as the most meaningful factor in modern culture and proposed it as the basis of painting. Partisans of any kind of revolution, Futurism took on a political character, first with anarchism, then Fascism. Carrà's picture is an outstanding example of both the subject matter and treatment of this kind of painting.

UMBERTO BOCCIONI (1882–1916) *Female Figure* · 1909 · Oil on canvas · 51⅝ × 37⅜″ · Gallery of Modern Art, Milan

The chief theme of Futurist painting was movement. The young Italian artists, among whom Boccioni was by far the most gifted, found a new way of incorporating movement into their works, and time itself became an essential factor in their pictures. There were two ways to do this: either the successive phases of a movement could be presented simultaneously, like a series of action photographs placed one on top of the other, or, alternatively, the movement of both the figures and their environment could be made to interpenetrate. Inspired by Cubism, Boccioni thus achieved a simultaneity that enriched the world of Futurism by a new dimension, that of time and movement.

GINO SEVERINI (1883–1966) *Dynamic Hieroglyphic of the Bal Tabarin* · 1912 · Oil on canvas · 63½ × 61⅜″ · Museum of Modern Art, New York

The Futurist who stood closest to the Cubists was Gino Severini. He was less concerned than his Italian friends with unbridled movement, with the dynamic vibration and oscillation of all existence. For him, the principal theme was the dance, with its controlled and orderly movement within the conventional bonds of rhythm. But he too presented the various phases of an action simultaneously, creating the effect of a rhythmically controlled kaleidoscope, suggestive of movement in space and time. This kaleidoscopic approach lends his paintings a decorative effect that became ever more prominent in the work he continued to do after the death of Futurism in 1916.

ALEXEJ VON JAWLENSKY (1864–1941) *Portrait of a Girl* · 1909 · Oil on canvas · 36¼ × 26⅜″ · Kunstmuseum, Düsseldorf

Jawlensky's art has its roots in the brilliantly colored folk art and icon painting of his native Russia. The focal point of his painting is color, with all its power of sensuous suggestion, and he intensified this element far beyond its purely objective significance. Matisse pointed the way to this superb treatment of color, but it was above all the influence of his compatriot Kandinsky, whom Jawlensky came to know in Munich, that led him to use colors in all their intensity and without regard to their factual connotations. Jawlensky's is an art of expression in which color itself is the vehicle of a kind of mysticism.

RAOUL DUFY (1877–1953) *Regatta* · 1938 · Oil on canvas · 13 × 32¼″ · Stedelijk Museum, Amsterdam

At the beginning of the century, Dufy took part in the revolutionary upheaval of the Fauves, sharing their enthusiasm for the expressive power of color. The passion and vehemence of his early period were toned down with the years, but color remained his chief and most significant concern. In the 1920s, he worked out a highly personal calligraphic style, a kind of pictorial stenography; subject matter drawn from life was jotted down in an ingenious, light, and dexterous shorthand that was combined with strong primary colors to communicate an unruffled delight in existence. This deft and quick pictorial script proved an ideal vehicle for his masterly intuitions.

KEES VAN DONGEN (1877–1968) *Portrait of Pierre Lafitte* · 1919 · Oil on canvas · 51⅛ × 31⅞″ · Stedelijk Museum, Amsterdam

As early as 1905, Kees van Dongen became an enthusiastic partisan of the Fauves and soon formed a link between the French group and the Dresden Brücke movement. The expressive power of his pictures was developed through his youthful experience as a satirical cartoonist, and when he discovered the emotional possibilities of color, his early work took on even stronger and sharper accents. With his mature years, after World War I, when the polemical passions of his youth had worn themselves out, he retained his keen powers of observation and of swift, striking notation. In the best works of his later period, Van Dongen succeeded in translating into his own terms the Expressionist belief in the superiority of feeling over faithful imitation.

FRANZ MARC (1880–1916) *Deer in Forest II* · 1913–14 · Oil on canvas · 45¼ × 39¾″ · Kunsthalle, Karlsruhe

Together with Kandinsky, Marc helped found the Blaue Reiter—Blue Horsemen—group in Munich. He was one of those painters who revitalized art through a deep religious feeling for nature. However influenced he may have been by Cubism and Italian Futurism, what is new and personal in his painting is an all-pervading pantheistic love for the natural creatures and environments of the world. In his work man and nature are brought into a single harmony, the mystic unity of all creation. This feeling for life he expressed through the symbolic power of color. It was in the animal world that he found his chief subject matter: through it he could convey the dream of a return to a lost paradise and the hope of man's redemption, which is the ultimate message of his art.

HEINRICH CAMPENDONCK (1889–1957) *Man with Flower* · 1918 · Oil on canvas · 23⅝ × 22″ · Stedelijk Museum, Amsterdam

In the years before World War I, Campendonck was the youngest member of the Blaue Reiter group. All of his work, from youth to maturity, combines glowing, warm colors with a solid sense of composition. His contemplative lyricism and sensitive, intuitive feeling for nature are manifested in pictures such as this *Man with Flower*, with its masterly color and form. In later years, after fleeing to Amsterdam from Nazi terror, he became the mentor of an entire generation to whom he revealed the secrets of formal construction, thereby paving the way for a revival of mural painting.

329

LASZLO MOHOLY-NAGY (1895–1946) *A II* · 1924 · Oil on canvas · 44½ × 52¾″ · Solomon R. Guggenheim Museum, New York

Among the Constructivist painters Moholy-Nagy stands out as the most versatile and inventive. He assimilated into his work every new technical advance—photography, montage, collage, and the like. From such experimentation he came to understand the autonomous laws inherent in materials themselves, and this led to his formulating a kind of theory of harmony for the visual arts. His painting, graphic work, montage, and the rest were, in fact, all experiments in the behavior of pictorial materials and led him, inevitably, to complete abstraction. Moholy-Nagy's influence was first felt in the Bauhaus, the school in Weimar where the fine and applied arts were set on the same plane, but he did not become really significant and effective until his mature years, when he emigrated to the United States.

WASSILY KANDINSKY (1866–1944) *Arrows* · 1927 · Oil on canvas · 35⅛ × 30¾″ · Private collection, Paris

Kandinsky was the first to arrive at the goal that, ever since the beginning of the century, had become for many painters an unshakable obsession—the truly abstract picture. Such an image is entirely independent of any association with objects in the existing world and is, instead, the expression of a purely human truth, of quintessential reality. Kandinsky took his first steps in this direction in 1910 in his oils and water colors, in which he poured forth a veritable flood of rhapsodic feelings in richly orchestrated forms and colors. In later years, when he became associated with the Bauhaus School, he disciplined his outpouring; through geometry he achieved a visual counterpoint that served as a symbol for the new world that science had opened up to man.

AUGUST MACKE (1887–1914) *Large Lighted Shop Window* · 1912 · Oil on canvas · 41⅜ × 33½″ · Landesgalerie, Hanover

Macke helped found the Blaue Reiter group together with Marc, Klee, and Kandinsky. Like his friends, he strove to bring out in painting a conception of the world that, for him, was based on the mystic concordance of the untroubled but deeply sentient soul with the forces of nature. Macke, a Rhinelander in origin, felt closer to the clear, salubrious formal beauty of French art—that of Delaunay, in particular—than to the mystical transports of other German artists. His pictures have the precision and conciseness of polished gems. By means of such clarity in the organization of form and color, Macke's painting transcends the material facts of his subject matter to aspire to the condition of music, thereby strongly suggesting the possibilities inherent in purely abstract art.

PAUL KLEE (1879–1940) *Structural II* · 1924 · Oil on canvas · 12½ × 9″ · Collection Mr. and Mrs. Burton Tremaine, Meriden, Connecticut

Klee too was a member of the Blaue Reiter movement and shared its aspirations to heal the gaping wound that separates man from his environment, to weld again our splintered unity. He achieved this goal by suffusing in equal measure every element of his paintings with spiritual energy. His point of departure was those elements themselves: point, line, plane, form, color, texture. All were subjected to the same searching inquiry, until, purified, they could finally be brought together into his tiny pictures—glimpses of a world where miracles still occur.

PAUL KLEE *Sinbad the Sailor* · 1923 · Watercolor on paper and board · 14⅞ × 20⅝" · Private collection, Basel

The artistic core of the Bauhaus School at Weimar was made up of Klee, Feininger, Kandinsky, and Schlemmer. Invited to Weimar in 1922, Klee made great efforts to clarify his own ways and means of working in order to guide his students to deeper understanding of their work. The results of this self-analysis were set down in a sketchbook designed to aid his teaching. His works of those years reveal a firmly disciplined approach that nevertheless was at the service of his free-flowering imagination. In these tiny pictures, Klee brings out all the miracle of man's creative fancy, and his penetrating, concentrated power of expression and invention makes these images understandable and believable in spite of their whimsicality.

PAUL KLEE *Portrait of Gaia* · 1939 · Oil on canvas · 38⅛ × 27⅛" · Collection Felix Klee, Bern

Toward the end of his life, already a prey to fatal illness, Klee made a radical change in his work. His colors became earthier and more subdued, his lines harsher and heavier; a tragic element appeared, glooming over the lighthearted fantasy world of his earlier years. Now, in the shadow of death, there fell upon his work the shadow also of deep earnestness, and with thoughts turned inward he found no place for flights of fancy. His life work was crowned by these tragic pictures, ultimate manifestation of his adventure beyond the frontiers of the visible into a new realm of inner experience. His maxim—"Art does not imitate the visible, it *makes* visible"—was amply proven by his own work.

FRANÇOIS KUPKA (1871–1957) *Architectural Study III* · 1925 · Oil on canvas · 43¼ × 35½" · Gallery Louis Carré, Paris

The concept of abstract painting sprang up in two centers: in the Slavic world of Kandinsky and Larionov, and in French Cubism as represented by Delaunay. The Czech Kupka, who had been living in Paris since 1895, united both worlds in a single person. As early as 1912 he began to paint pictures in the spirit of architecture and of rigorously constructed music. Out of the hues of the prism he built color compositions which seem to make visible the play of musical forms in Johann Sebastian Bach's fugues. The strength and conciseness of his structures, their architectonic compactness, make these works a microcosm of the great world picture laid out in those same years by mathematicians and physical scientists.

KASIMIR MALEVICH (1878–1935) *Supreme* · Before 1915 · Oil on canvas · 26 × 38¼" · Stedelijk Museum, Amsterdam

Malevich strode with seven-league boots through all the movements of his lifetime, from Impressionism to Cubism and finally to Abstraction. In 1913, as a polemical demonstration of completely nonfigurative art, he painted a black square on a white ground, nothing more, and therewith inaugurated a new movement, Suprematism. In his pictures after that date and in his book on "the nonfigurative world," he completely liberated painting from imitation of reality, which, he felt, had become so fortuitous as to have lost any significance it might once have had. Through the interplay of geometrical forms and bright colors, his painting embodies a new feeling for the world that, dissociated from any gravitational hold, floats unconstrained and free as air.

ELIEZER LISSITZKY (1890–1941) *Proun* · 1920 · Oil on canvas · 22¾ × 18¾″ · Collection H. L. Winston, Birmingham Michigan

Lissitzky was another Russian artist who approached painting as construction. The perfection of manufactured products, the precision of the machine, became for him a source of inspiration; he aimed to give painting a comparable logical consistency in order to express the spirit of our age of technique. His pictures are therefore often put together out of new materials whose artistic possibilities he explored and exploited with enthusiasm. The exactness and solidity of industrial products take on in Lissitzky's works a new form independent of their utility, that is, an aesthetic form, while on the other hand his pictures enriched industrial design with many happy discoveries and solutions.

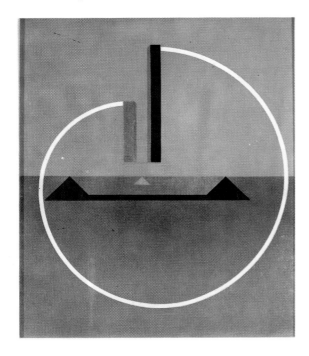

PIET MONDRIAN (1872–1944) *Composition with Red, Yellow, and Blue* · 1920 · Oil on canvas · 20½ × 23⅝″ · Private collection, Amsterdam

Mondrian and the other Dutch painters of the De Stijl group went furthest in freeing painting from all connection with the external world. For Mondrian, the goal of human development is liberation from the irrationality of nature; just as Holland's landscape is a product of man's labors, so he wished to shape his painting only in obedience to its own inner laws. For this, he banned the world of appearances from his art and rigorously reduced the arsenal of his artistic means to a few essential factors: straight lines, right angles, the three primary colors—red, yellow, and blue—and the three primary noncolors—white, gray, and black. Using nothing but these elementary means, he attained the goal of his art and of his conception of the world: to give visible form to the absolute harmony and fundamental logic that govern both art and the universe.

THEO VAN DOESBURG (1883–1931) *Russian Dance* · 1918 · Oil on canvas · 53½ × 24½″ · Museum of Modern Art, New York

The intellectual driving force of the Dutch group De Stijl was Theo van Doesburg. In 1917, together with his friends Mondrian and Van der Leck and certain progressive architects, he founded the group and the magazine, *De Stijl*. The magazine became the spokesman for those who wished to break completely with everything naturalistic, and the group worked to realize—in a rigorous, almost Calvinistic manner—the ideal of a human equivalent to that harmony which is entirely independent of the accidents of nature. In Van Doesburg's painting and architecture there is revealed an indomitable will to change the face of the world, to build for men a radiantly serene environment, a new earthly paradise.

BART VAN DER LECK (1876–1958) *Composition* · 1918 · Oil on canvas · 39¾ × 39⅜″ · Stedelijk Museum, Amsterdam

From 1917 on, Van der Leck belonged to the De Stijl group along with Mondrian and Theo van Doesburg. Starting out as a naturalistic artist, he had simplified his forms and colors in a manner related to mural painting and finally arrived at a thoroughgoing liberation of his pictorial means from all naturalistic associations. In 1917, at the same time as Mondrian and Van Doesburg, he achieved complete abstraction, the rejection of everything suggestive of the external world. The composition of 1918 reproduced here shows with what clarity and uncompromising discipline he attained the ideal of the De Stijl group—an objective image of suprapersonal harmony—while employing only the most limited means.

MARC CHAGALL (1887–   ) *The Violinist* · 1912/13 · Oil on canvas · 74 × 62⅛" · Stedelijk Museum, Amsterdam

One of the first artists of our time to explore the realm between dream and reality, Chagall looks with simple frankness at the miracles that crop up ever and again in the daily life of the real world. His village violinist is one of those miracles: weightless he soars above the rooftops of the village locked in winter, while down below, to the right,

doves perch in a summer-flowering tree. Over Chagall's world lies a magic spell, an enchantment poetic and fantastic and warm with human sentiment; it is reality as experienced by devout Jews in the villages of old Russia. Ever and again the magician Chagall lets us glimpse this real-unreal universe. Whether it be in his paintings or in his illustrations for La Fontaine and the Bible, he always conjures up a world mere mortals know only in dreams and fairy tales.

Detail is shown on next pages

333

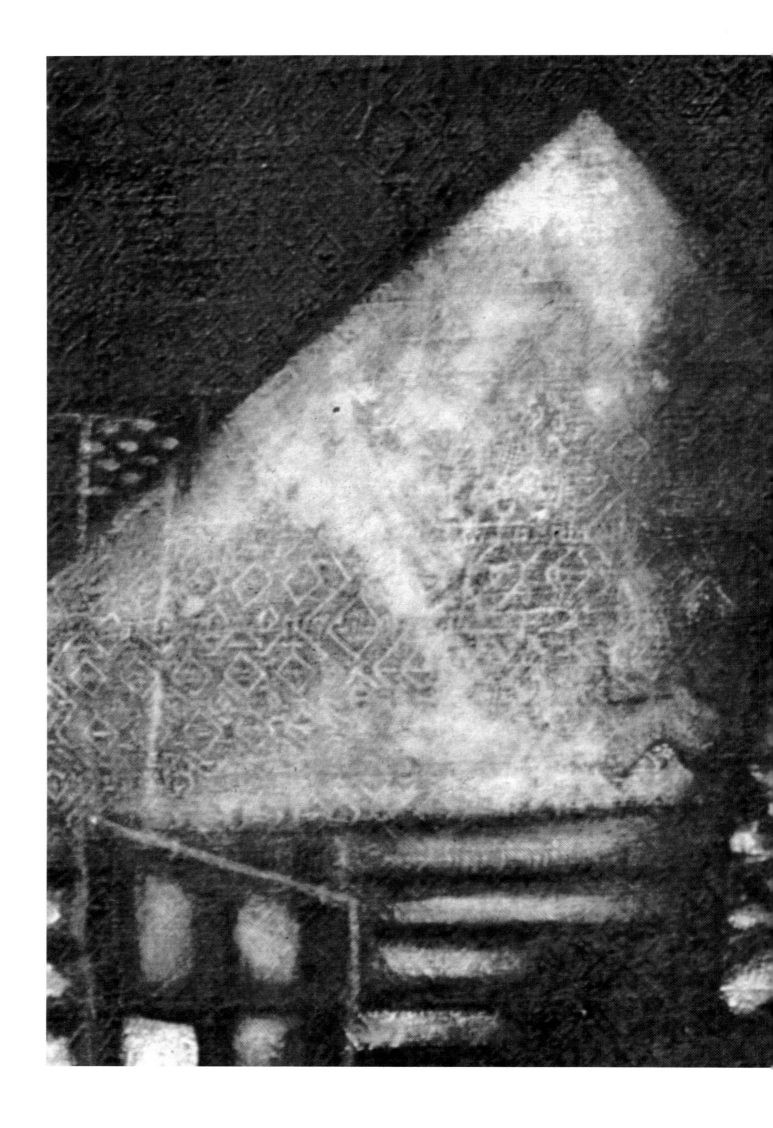

AMÉDÉE OZENFANT (1886–1966) *Flask, Guitar, Glass, and Bottles on the Gray Table* · 1920 · Oil on canvas · 31⅞ × 39⅝″ · Kunsthalle, Basel

In 1920 Ozenfant founded the Purist group together with Le Corbusier, who was both painter and architect. Both artists, as Fernand Léger had been, were fascinated by the new culture of the twentieth century, and they took as model and ideal the machine and its precision products. Ozenfant and his circle aimed at the same objectivity as the Bauhaus, and at the same time. They adapted the discoveries of Cubism to a style in which flat planes predominated and whose chief traits were lucidity and order. Through this insistence on large flat surfaces, Ozenfant exercised great influence on industrial design and especially on poster art.

OSKAR SCHLEMMER (1888–1943) *Group of Fifteen* · Oil on canvas · 70¾ × 39¼″ · Stedelijk Museum, Amsterdam

Through the Bauhaus School in Weimar, founded by the great architect and pedagogue Walter Gropius, the ideas of the Cubists, of the De Stijl group, and of Russian Constructivism all took root in Germany. Uppermost in the Bauhaus circle was the notion of the *Gesamtkunstwerk*, the completely coordinated union of all branches of art in a single all-embracing project; this was held to require a purified and cleansed contribution from each of the branches. Schlemmer directed the stage design workshop in the Bauhaus, and this familiarity with man in theatrical space carried over into his paintings; the human figure, with every individualistic trait sloughed off, becomes a component in the architectonic order to which it owes its existence.

MARCEL DUCHAMP (1887–1968) *Nude Descending a Staircase II* · 1912 · Oil on canvas · 58⅛ × 35″ · Philadelphia Museum of Art, Philadelphia

Duchamp's art stems from Cubism and was also influenced by Italian Futurism. As early as 1911 he became fascinated with the disarticulation of objects and with the movement that inhered in their isolated fragments. But for Duchamp fragmentation was not a means to a new order, as it was for the Cubists, but rather something mysterious and even phantasmagoric. This way of looking at the world led him in 1917, together with a few like-minded friends, to launch the experiment of Dada: art in a world of accident, unreason, and improbability. As a tireless and masterly chess addict, Duchamp believed in rules and laws—but they were the rules of a game, the formulas of play. It was in art as a great game that Duchamp and his Dadaist friends found the key to the truth of reality.

LYONEL FEININGER (1871–1956) *Gelmeroda VIII* · 1921 · Oil on canvas · 39¾ × 31¼″ · Whitney Museum of American Art, New York

Feininger and Schlemmer deserve the credit for the clearest demonstration of the ideal of order set up by the Bauhaus. For Feininger the point of departure was not the human figure but, instead, architecture, the austerely geometrical formal structure he observed in Gothic churches and admired in the music of Johann Sebastian Bach. He was not content to reduce to mere constructed forms the structural order he found throughout nature—in the sea, in old towns, in sand dunes; instead, he permitted the lines of force of the architectonic principles at work in the objects he depicted to radiate out beyond the objects themselves.

FRANCIS PICABIA (1879–1953) *Rubber* · 1909 · Watercolor on paper · 17⅞ × 24½″ · Museum of Modern Art, Paris

Picabia joined up with the Cubists in their years, but exploited their innovations in his own way and with his own scheme of values. His eccentric temperament impelled him to a highly fantastic view of reality. In 1917, at the time the Dada movement was born in Zurich, Picabia, who was living in the United States, organized a similar group in New York, which was soon assimilated into the parent body. His pictures combine abstract images with fantastic apparitions to unsettle and haunt the viewer with their bizarreness. Picabia conceives reality as bristling with improbabilities and impertinent surprises, a reality in which miracles are the rule, not the exception.

GIORGIO DE CHIRICO (1888–1978) *The Silent Statue* · 1913 · Oil on canvas · 39¼ × 49⅛″ · Private collection, Paris

Simultaneously with Dada, a trend sprang up in Italy that likewise was based on the meaninglessness and horrifying improbability of modern life. This was so-called Metaphysical Painting, of which Giorgio de Chirico was founder and spiritual father. The theme of this art was man's fatal alienation from the everyday objects that had once been the reliable landmarks of his daily existence. The artists who had served in the war suddenly saw these familiar things with different eyes, upon their return to civilian life: they found them nonsensical, but terrifyingly so, and terrifyingly devoid of meaning. It was this panicky anxiety they tried to set down in paint. Precisely because they had come to see that the things men know and use are the enemies of man—a lesson learned again in World War II —their paintings inevitably pinned down with great exactitude the character of things, what it is that makes them so terrible.

KURT SCHWITTERS (1887–1948) *Merz-Picture* · 1922 Collage · 6⅞ × 5¾″ · Collection Mr. and Mrs. Burton Tremaine, Meriden, Connecticut

Schwitters enriched Dada with a technique by which the oddness of things could be better depicted. This was summed up in his "Merz-Pictures"—the name goes back to one of his early collages in which only the letters MERZ survived from the word KOMMERZIELL—which were composed of bits and scraps of all sorts of materials picked up in the street and pasted together. The inner meaning of these pictures lies in the artistic order imposed on the useless, meaningless detritus of modern life. The fascination of Schwitters' exciting pictures lies not in their esthetic effect but in the magical potency that such a montage of shabby refuse assumed in his hands; indeed, their magic is so much the greater for having been built from fragments discarded in everyday life.

MASSIMO CAMPIGLI (1895–1971) *Women on the Beach* · 1935 · Oil on canvas · 19¼ × 23⅝″ · Formerly Collection Regnault, Stedelijk Museum, Amsterdam

Metaphysical Painting marked the turning point from movement, which had been the Futurists' great concern, to classical repose—though in Chirico's pictures such repose is precisely what is so disquieting and alarming. A younger generation seized on this tendency to give modern expression to Italian nostalgia for the solemn dignity and classical form of the Italian past. Campigli turned to Etruscan and Roman prototypes to realize the dream of reviving the lost art of mural painting; he hoped thereby to satisfy the hunger for peace, for the Arcadian simple life, that gnawed at men throughout Europe in the years after World War I. His paintings are all conceived in the spirit of great wall decorations destined to be seen by multitudes of men.

337

GIORGIO MORANDI (1890–1964) *Still Life* · 1957 · Oil on canvas · Private collection, Paris

Morandi's art grew out of Metaphysical painting, with its horror-filled, panicky attitude towards objects, but he overcame the enmity of things for man through his warm, affectionate sympathy for them. His chief theme was the still life, the assemblage of familiar objects in everyday use, flasks, glasses, cups. These things he contemplated with such tranquil humility, with such a Christian spirit of *devotio moderna*, that they all but lost for him their identity as things to become symbols of a brotherly order. Like Schwitters, Morandi was concerned with the search for an eventual order, and his quest for harmony, for the universal unity of all things, was similar to Mondrian's. Thus, in the careful disposition of small things, like and unlike, Morandi found the secret of the greater order of the universe.

YVES TANGUY (1900–55) *A Smile Lingers* · 1936 · Oil on canvas · $25\frac{5}{8} \times 21\frac{1}{4}''$ · Private collection, Paris

Tanguy belonged to the Surrealist group organized in 1924 by the poet André Breton. His approach to painting was quite traditional, using painstaking brushwork to bring out the form of objects. But the objects themselves have nothing to do with reality; they are images like those of our wildest dreams—cartilaginous growths spread out in an unending desolate landscape losing itself at the horizon's edge. It is precisely the rigorous exactitude with which these dream objects are painted that makes the viewer feel so strongly their very real menace. Tanguy's picture of the world—a modern Apocalypse—embodies the anxiety and oppression of which modern man has become painfully aware.

MAX ERNST (1891–1976) *Landscape* · c. 1941 · Oil on canvas · Private collection, Paris

In Max Ernst's paintings the consciousness of our age's terrors is held up ruthlessly before our eyes. Images that seem survivals from a time before man become symbols of a world the artist views with dismay and revulsion. World War I, with its horrors and unimaginable disasters, left Max Ernst and other artists baffled in the face of such a triumph of unreason. It is that world which Ernst depicts, and through the painstaking precision of his technique the weirdness of his forms becomes doubly disturbing to the viewer, the menacing handwriting on the wall of history.

JEAN LURÇAT (1882–1966) *Masts and Sail* · 1930 · Oil on canvas · $47\frac{3}{4} \times 56\frac{1}{2}''$ · Stedelijk Museum, Amsterdam

The insecurity, the all-pervading anxiety, the doom that hung over Europe in the 1930s brought Lurçat close to Surrealism. The themes of his lapidary, highly expressive art took on new significance; they became stage settings for the drama of a world in collapse. Sails lashed by the wind whip around masts that bend to their pull, but sails and masts propel no ship; they stand in sand beneath a bilious yellow sky. Strength unemployed, energy dissipated, the gnawing knowledge of the world's illusion—these are what his pictures confess to, and their message is made doubly forceful by the concise, concentrated forms that Lurçat was to exploit in quite different ways in later years, for his revival of large-scale tapestry-making.

RENÉ MAGRITTE (1898–1967) *The Dawn of Liberty* · 1929 ·
Oil on canvas · 44¾ × 57¼″ · Museum Boymans-van
Beuningen, Rotterdam

Surrealism found an especially favorable reception in
Belgium, the country that had fallen unprepared and defenseless before the surprise attack of World War I and that
therefore had more reason than other countries to feel
clearly and deeply the shock of the unimaginable. Surrealism is the art of the illogical, the unexpected, the im-
plausible. To convey such improbability and make the
viewer experience a surprise not only shocking but also
magically enthralling, the Belgian Surrealists resorted to the
technique of the old masters, depicting the objects in hallucinating clarity and precision. This photographic accuracy
intensified the weirdness of unrelated objects brought into
incongruous relationship and made reality seem doubly
ambiguous.

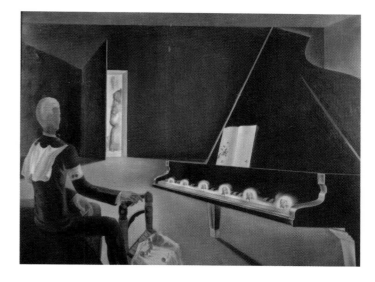

SALVADOR DALI (1904–   ) *Composition* · 1931 · Oil on
canvas · 45 × 57″ · Museum of Modern Art, Paris

The supreme master of the synthesis of Surrealist content
and naturalistic technique is Dali. His aim is in no way to
depict a possible reality. Quite the opposite: by painstakingly accurate attention to the finest details, he succeeds
in discrediting reality, in making it impossible. His manner
of depicting the components of his pictures is faithful to
reality, but in their startling unions they turn out to be fantastically improbable. It is precisely by arranging this shocking
cohabitation of dissimilars that he reveals the strangeness of
the dream world of man's mind. There is nothing novel
about Dali's way of painting, but in his attitude toward
reality he is a spokesman for modern man, who views with
mistrust what his eyes reveal to him of the world he lives in.

PAUL DELVAUX (1897–   ) *Hands* · 1941 · Oil on canvas ·
43¼ × 51⅛″ · Collection Claude Spaak, Choisel

In the Surrealist pictures of Paul Delvaux, the painter lets
us glimpse an arcadian dream world—and then promptly
casts doubt on the very existence of such a world. With a
virtually Classical, old-master technique, he depicts figures
from some still innocent paradise consorting with the dull
denizens of our everyday prosaic world of fact. This mélange
of Classical ideals and contemporary banality displaces his
elegiac dream of primordial innocence into some never-
never land of absurdity. Moreover, Delvaux invites us into
those realms opened up by psychoanalysis in the course of
our century: erotic complexes and repressions are dangled
before us in the daylight of his pictures. Like most exponents
of naturalistic Surrealism, Delvaux reveals his novelty of
thought in his subject matter, not in his techniques.

MARC CHAGALL (1887–   ) *Rabbi with Torah* · Gouache
and watercolor on paper · 29 × 21″ · Stedelijk Museum,
Amsterdam

Chagall comes from a poor Jewish family of Vitebsk, in
Russia, and carries with him, wherever he lives, this in-
heritance from his past. His native world is rich in images of
folk tales and legends that flowered out of the ancient
beliefs of a Jewish community ghettoed off from modern
society. Chagall was the first to capture in paint the fairy-
tale wonder of those legends, those waking dreams. His
universe is filled with men and beasts who seem to hover in
a realm between dream and waking, and we take that realm
on faith because of Chagall's glowing colors and the warmth
of his human sympathies. This picture of a rabbi in a wintry
village street exemplifies Chagall's own spiritual feeling.

339

MARC CHAGALL *Interior of Synagogue, Safad* · 1931 · Oil on canvas · 28¾ × 36¼″ · Stedelijk Museum, Amsterdam

In 1931 Chagall visited Palestine, Israel's Land of Promise. From this trip he brought back a few pictures such as this interior of a synagogue in Safad, an ancient house of worship with its venerable atmosphere of humble piety and unshakable belief. Chagall metamorphosed the actual vault of the synagogue into something dreamlike; lighter than air, the building soars up, and from the three red-curtained niches for the holy scrolls radiates a light that glows and warms. Chagall the magician's special gift is to cast a legendary spell over the dull facts of life; in his pictures the great treasure of ancient traditional Jewish lore, which has always transcended the here and now, takes on pictorial reality.

LASAR SEGALL (1890–1957) *Brazilian Landscape* · 1925 · Oil on canvas · 25¼ × 21¼″ · Private collection

Segall, like Chagall, came from a Russian ghetto but first learned his art in Germany, from the Expressionists. In 1910 he emigrated to Brazil, where he laid the foundations for a native modern painting, bringing together the European tradition and the first stirrings of art in a new land rich in promise. His own style combines construction in planes in the Cubist manner with the warm, eloquent coloring of Expressionism. In their strong mural-like simplicity, Segall's paintings satisfied the needs of his adopted country and prepared the way for a new native art.

MORRIS GRAVES (1910–   ) *Bird Searching* · 1944 · Water-color on paper · 53½ × 27″ · The Art Institute of Chicago

Graves has a special place in American painting. He rejected everyday reality, which for so long had been the chief concern of American art, and concentrated instead on the magical world of nature and creation. Out of this great unity he chose for motifs the phenomena that sum up nature's enigmas: birds who build their nests in secret places, the mysterious growth of plants, and the like. His work communicates a feeling for nature that links profound observation of nature's miracles with an awareness that such puzzles are not for man to solve—a philosophical conception characteristic both of Graves's generation and of the American tradition.

CONSTANT PERMEKE (1886–1952) *View of Aertrijke* · 1930 · Oil on canvas · 39¼ × 47¼″ · Stedelijk Museum, Amsterdam

In Flanders and the Netherlands, the years after World War I saw a revival of Expressionism. Painters turned back to the old Netherlandish tradition as exemplified by Bruegel and also to those early works of Van Gogh in which he portrayed peasant life with heavy, somber colors. Permeke was the leader of the Flemish Expressionist group for whom, in the years following the enemy occupation of Belgium, their native earth and the peasants' lot became symbols of a new myth. Not the imitation of landscape as such but rather the mythlike pathos of man's ties to the land lends to these pictures their great and impressive monumentality.

WASSILY KANDINSKY (1866–1944) *Improvisation 33 for "Orient"* · 1913 · Oil on canvas · $34\frac{3}{4} \times 39\frac{1}{4}''$ · Stedelijk Museum, Amsterdam

At the start of our century, Kandinsky was the active heart of the circle of German artists in Munich who created Expressionism, and he himself was the founder of the Blaue Reiter group. In that spiritual climate Kandinsky painted the first abstract pictures and thereby took the initial decisive step that had tantalized so many less daring painters before him. At the same time he brought out his book, *On the Spiritual in Art*, a perceptive declaration that art could be revitalized by rejecting external semblances. His picture *The Orient* of 1913 embodies his new principles: colors and forms, liberated from all association with existing things, are brought together in a resonant, energyfull harmony that works directly on the viewer's emotions and conveys to him the spiritual content of the picture in all its rich density.

Detail is shown on next pages

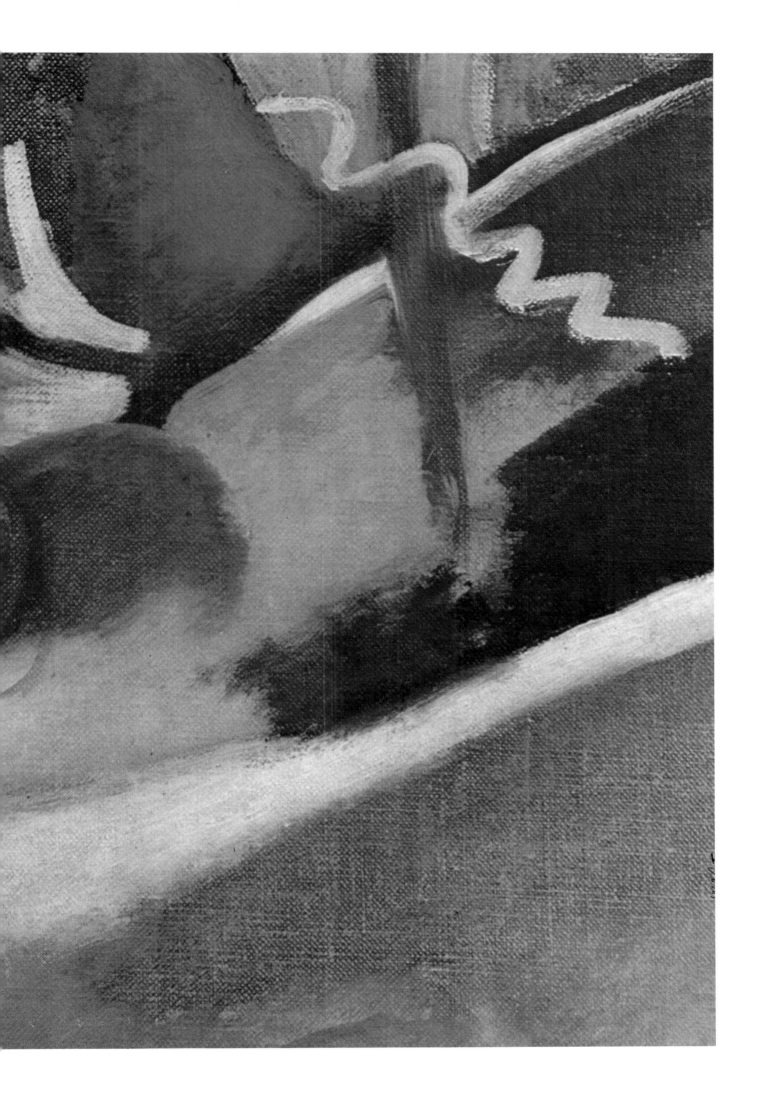

JAN SLUYTERS (1881–1957) *Autumn Landscape, Laren* · 1910 · Oil on canvas · $19\frac{5}{8} \times 23\frac{5}{8}''$ · Collection Mrs. Sluyters

The first impetus to Dutch and Belgian Expressionism came from the French Fauves, appropriately so since the Fauves themselves took their initial inspiration from the Dutch Van Gogh. Sluyters led the new Expressionist art back to the land of its origins and thereby opened the way to modern art in the Netherlands. Around 1907 he was already the first in the Netherlands to lend his color that expressive value which results from rejection of the too familiar colors of nature. In his early landscapes, after around 1910, he was the pioneer of a new ecstatic feeling for life expressed through the brilliant sonorities of new color harmonies.

FRITS VAN DEN BERGHE (1883–1939) *Genealogy* · 1929 · Oil on canvas · $57\frac{1}{4} \times 44\frac{7}{8}''$ · Kunstmuseum, Basel

Frits van den Berghe carried Flemish Expressionism further in his own way. Along with Permeke and the De Smet brothers, he was among the founders of the second Group of Latem, the rallying point of Flemish Expressionism. Through his transcendent spirituality and his wide-ranging imagery, he differed essentially from his colleagues, whose inspiration was drawn chiefly from peasant life and a primitive bond with nature. Van den Berghe, with his deeper awareness of the terrible aspects of his time, introduced into his work a visionary view of contemporary events, thereby linking the tendencies of Expressionism with the Surrealist realm of the subconscious and fantastic.

CHRISTIAN ROHLFS (1849–1938) *Red Roofs* · 1913 · Oil on canvas · $31\frac{1}{2} \times 39\frac{1}{4}''$ · Kunsthalle, Karlsruhe

In terms of age, Rohlfs belonged to the generation of the Impressionists—he was eight years younger than Renoir, four years older than Van Gogh—and only relatively late in life revealed an artistic personality and developed his own Expressionistic style. Once he had been introduced to the problems of modern painting by Van de Velde and the group around Osthaus in Hagen, he pushed forward with astonishing results to the very borders of abstraction, farther than even his German colleagues had ventured. His dramatic cityscapes are a surging tissue of colors; the subject is no more than a pretext for the artist's expression of his deep emotion in the face of nature and the works of man.

MAX BECKMANN (1884–1950) *Self-Portrait with Saxophone* · 1930 · Oil on canvas · $55\frac{1}{8} \times 27\frac{1}{4}''$ · Kunsthalle, Bremen

The master of post-World War I Expressionism was Beckmann. The war had revealed to him how reality, its essence and its meaning, can be thrown into question by men's behavior, and he accepted the charge of reconstituting that reality in his pictures. Thus, his painting became an answer to his times, an act of self-assertion that, to all intents and purposes, Beckmann was literally compelled to perform. In his pictures, things emerge from the mass as if to proclaim: "Here we are, it is we who can and will take possession of space." Beckmann's pictures are weighed down by a monumentality through which speaks the destiny of an entire generation, but to it they owe also their inner conviction, their spiritual value as documents of a world in peril.

JOHN MARIN (1870–1953) *Maine Islands* · 1922 · Watercolor on paper · 16¾ × 20″ · Phillips Collection, Washington, D.C.

Expressionism, which had sprung up in Europe as a pictorial answer to the challenge of a cultural crisis, was a long time sinking its roots in America. In the United States it turned up in personalities like Marin and Marsden Hartley, and precisely at the moment when, there too, the first cracks in a seemingly faultless structure were appearing. In Marin's small watercolors the structure of the landscape begins to totter; one scarcely notices it at first, but forms are jerked out of joint—somewhere the earth has quaked. This earthquake was, indeed, a fact—spiritual, not physical—and throughout the world it was above all the Expressionists who like seismographs registered it through the medium of paint.

MARCEL GROMAIRE (1892–1971) *Portrait of a Man* · 1925 · Oil on canvas · 31⅞ × 25⅝″ · Collection Burki, Paris

After World War I a younger generation of painters sought to rediscover the way to a more humane expression. In France, the formal discipline of Cubism had preoccupied an entire generation who had been trained to look at their surroundings with the penetrating vision of scientists and to go about their work like analytical chemists. Now a reaction set in against that approach. The leader of the new generation was Gromaire, and he was well enough grounded in Cubism not to discard that school's great discoveries— overall formal construction, the power inherent in volume and mass. But his essence lies closer to the Flemish Expressionism of a Permeke in the way in which he places man and man's labors at the center of his mythical conception of the world.

TADE MAKOVSKY (1882–1932) *Children with Japanese Lanterns* · Oil on canvas · 38¼ × 51½″ · Museum of Modern Art, Paris

In Poland, Makovsky was the exponent of an Expressionism that, there as elsewhere, sought to uncover the sources of human emotions. For him, simple unsophisticated feelings, the primary stirrings of the soul, constituted the fundamental core of reality. Such natural sentiments he found among peasants and artisans but also, above all, in children. To give appropriate expression to the primordial purity of that world, he employed highly simplified forms that with childlike naïveté conveyed his experience of this humble innocence of soul. Makovsky's last years were spent in Paris, which explains why his influence was slow to affect his own country.

CHARLEY TOOROP (1891–1955) *Self-Portrait with Hat* · 1938 · Oil on canvas · 15⅞ × 14⅛″ · Stedelijk Museum, Amsterdam

If anyone came close to the spiritual position of Beckmann, it was Charley Toorop, daughter of the painter Jan Toorop, who had led the Symbolist movement in the Netherlands at the start of the century. The striving for self-assertion evident in her pictures has less to do with the times in which she lived than with her own personality; the painter's daughter insisted on equal rights with her father and his colleagues. Charley Toorop's friendship with Mondrian and her admiration for Léger brought into her pictures a clarity and strength that were already part of the Dutch tradition. But unlike those painters, she focused on reality, which, in her pictures, is raised to quintessential truth.

Vaclav Späla (1885–1946) *On the Otava River* · 1929 · Oil on canvas · 35 × 45⅝″ · Private collection, Prague

In the first forty years of this century, the influence of the various artistic innovations extended to every corner of Europe; later, after World War II, they reached the other parts of the globe. For the young republic of Czechoslovakia after World War I, Späla was the spokesman for a modernism opposed to the older formal tradition of Austria. Here the basic premises of Cézanne's work were combined with their later developments through Cubism. As in all the new countries created after the armistice of 1918, the principles of modern art were linked to a strong love for the native land to create a highly expressive and colorful art of landscape painting.

André Dunoyer de Segonzac (1884–1974) *The Canoers* · 1924 · Oil on canvas · Private collection, Paris

The Expressionism of the years after World War I had little impact on France. Beside Gromaire, with his somber colored, heavily constructed figure compositions, the chief representative of the trend in France was Dunoyer de Segonzac. Landscape was his principal concern, but in place of the ecstatic sweep of color of the Fauves or the passionate vehemence of Soutine, there is in his pictures a heavy oppressive mood that links them with the northern schools. Segonzac strove to revive a Classical style on the basis of a return to Cézanne, but his romantic northern temperament stamps his work with his own peculiar individuality.

Herman Kruyder (1881–1935) *Village Street* · Oil on canvas · 26 × 26⅛″ · Stedelijk Museum, Amsterdam

In the Netherlands, as in other northern countries, the second wave of Expressionism, after World War I, looked to the home soil for the simplicity and primitivism Gauguin had found in Tahiti. Kruyder discovered among the peasants of his own country that childlike state of innocence, that unspoiled humanity. His formal sense and use of color were conceived in this spirit—forms as simple as those of children's art, pure colors not broken down—and with the sense of immediacy typical of the direct statements that children make.

Camille Bombois (1883–1970) *Country-Fair Athlete* · Oil on canvas · 51⅞ × 35″ · Museum of Modern Art, Paris

In the European crisis in conceptions of reality, the existence of so-called primitive, or naïve nonprofessional painting is a most revealing symptom. This kind of painting stands entirely outside the mainstream of modern developments, impervious to all recent innovations, but it is precisely this quality which accounts for both its existence and its extraordinary popularity within the context of the art of the last fifty years. Only these nonprofessional "Sunday painters," most of them plain uncomplicated people, believe that visible appearances suffice to define reality. By means of such an art, blissfully unaware that reality presents pictorial problems, Bombois—originally a circus athlete and weight-lifter—captures his kind of reality with all the confidence of naïveté.

346

SÉRAPHINE DE SENLIS (1864–1934) *Clusters of Grapes* · 1928 · Oil on canvas · $57\frac{1}{2} \times 44\frac{7}{8}''$ · Private collection, Paris

Séraphine de Senlis has a special place in the ranks of "modern primitives." A charwoman by occupation, she never studied painting but made her pictures for her own pleasure until the collector and art expert Wilhelm Uhde discovered her in 1912 and gave her his advice and support. Séraphine painted only flowers, plants, and fruit, but on these she lavished her very personal fancy. The fantastic vegetable world of her pictures is thought through and worked out to the finest detail, so that these strange plants strike the viewer as oddly plausible. Most of all, their vivacious play of colors gives these pictures an entirely personal enchantment, the charm of a fairy-tale world.

EDGAR TYTGAT (1879–1957) *Side Show* · 1923 · Oil on canvas · $44\frac{1}{8} \times 53\frac{1}{8}''$ · Collection Oscar Mairlot, Lambermont, Belgium.

The art of the Belgian Edgar Tytgat has much in common with that of the naïve painters. It is folklike and illustrative in the same way as are popular broadsheets or the pictures in old peasant almanacs. The relationship is marked in another trait, the naïve pleasure the artist takes in setting down every last detail. Tytgat's homespun joviality enhances his and his viewers' delight in the real things of life, but the things in his pictures are really more than prosaic facts; they seem snatched from some delightful fairy-tale world with seven Sundays a week. In his art the age of Tyl Ulenspiegel lives again, but it is an age that has nothing to do with the developments of modern art.

ANDRÉ BAUCHANT (1873–1958) *Flowers* · 1950 · Oil on canvas · $29\frac{1}{8} \times 36\frac{5}{8}''$ · Private collection, Stockholm

The lovable side of naïve painting is displayed by André Bauchant in particular. He painted reality, true, but it was his own reality, that of a gardener and peasant. It was quite by accident that he discovered painting in the course of his military service as a surveyor, and at first it was no more than a hobby for his hours of leisure. With loving care he chose from reality the things closest to his heart—a basket of flowers, the flowers he himself grew—and painted them with the comprehension of a man who feels himself akin to the things of nature. More than a painter of reality, Bauchant was above all the painter of his own close bond with real things, even when he strayed into the realm of Greek mythology he loved so much.

BEN SHAHN (1898–1969) *Ave* · 1950 · Tempera · $31 \times 52''$ · Wadsworth Atheneum, Hartford, Connecticut

Ben Shahn was a satirist and critic in paint, a moralist who painted his prophetic passion for truth and justice. He thought of his art as a weapon in the struggle against injustice and deceit, and toward this end he often had recourse to markedly illusionistic depiction of reality in pictures that are built up starkly in flat planes. The simplified means of poster painting, the surprising effects achieved by the use of various techniques within a single picture, all this served his purpose of criticism of the world he lived in. The case of the two Italian anarchists Sacco and Vanzetti inspired him to paint a series of pictures, including this one, in which sharp social criticism is born of love for his fellow man and profound faith in human values.

GEORGE GROSZ (1893–1959) *Homage to Oskar Panizza (Vision Macabre)* · 1917–18 · Oil on canvas · 55 × 43¼″ · Staatsgalerie, Stuttgart

Grosz also aims at popular expression, but he has assimilated all the techniques of modern painting the better to denounce the disorder and misdeeds of his time. He heaps biting scorn on injustice, above all social injustice, which together with the loathsome quagmire of politics provides him with ever-new subjects for social criticism. From Futurism he adopted the principles of simultaneity and movement to fill his street scenes with tumultuous pushing-and-shoving rhythms in which protest marches and parades ring weirdly hollow. If Grosz limits himself to realism, depicting it at times with Futurist distortions, at others with virtually photographic accuracy, it is because, as a preacher of repentance and doom, he wishes to expose and scourge out human degradation, human misery.

IVAN GENERALIC (1914–   ) *Burial of Stef Halachek* · 1934 · Oil on canvas · 19⅝ × 18½″ · Gallery of Modern Art, Zagreb

Generalic, who began to paint entirely without instruction, is now the leading spirit of the school of Hlebine in Croatia. His art, and that of his disciples, differs from that of the so-called Modern Primitives or Sunday Painters because Generalic is able to draw on a still lively folk tradition in Yugoslavia. In both form and content his art is folklike. Peasant life is almost always the theme of his pictures, and his pictorial treatment is broad, however carefully all details are set down. In their color likewise, the pictures reveal their debt to the bright gay colors of folk art, like embroidery on peasant dresses.

OTTO DIX (1891–1969) *Portrait of My Parents* · 1924 · Oil on canvas · 46⅜ × 51½″ · Landesgalerie, Hanover

With Dix's pictures, art appears to return to naturalistic imitation of reality, to that approach so consciously and resolutely rejected by modern art. But this effect only seems to be so; it is true that Dix painted every detail in a brush technique learned from the old masters and even tried to compete with photography, but this kind of naturalism is no longer the old self-evident art based on an unshakable confidence in the truth of appearances. Quite the contrary: Dix went beyond naturalism precisely because things and their appearances had seemed to him unworthy of his faith ever since World War I. For all its harshness and cynicism, Dix's style, which has been called New Realism or New Objectivity, is an attempt to exorcise reality.

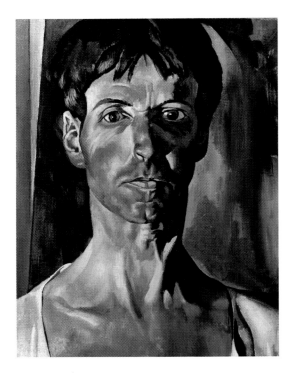

STANLEY SPENCER (1892–1959) *Self-Portrait* · 1936 · Oil on canvas · 24½ × 18″ · Stedelijk Museum, Amsterdam

Among the English, Spencer is the most open spokesman for New Reality. For him, as for other partisans of this trend, what counts is the focus on the visible facts of reality. This emphasis does not in any way imply a return to the realistic painting of the nineteenth century but, instead, a rejection of everything rhetorical, a new asceticism, and a deliberate sobriety in the face of our contemporary spiritual climate. Elements of Cubism and Expressionism have no doubt been incorporated in Spencer's straightforward, objective self-portrait, but the most significant trait of this kind of painting is still its deliberate limitation to the simple daily language of form and color in order to confer new value on everyday reality.

DIEGO RIVERA (1886–1957) *Mother's Helper* · 1950 ·
Watercolor on paper · $10\frac{1}{2} \times 15\frac{1}{4}''$ · Collection Anton
Schutz, New York

Rivera was the pioneer of the renaissance of Mexican art.
His style depends much on the experiments of modern
European art, which Rivera came to know in his years of
study in Paris, where he became acquainted with Picasso,
Braque, and Gris and their work; but he reworked all these
European innovations into a grandiose national style rooted
in Aztec and Mayan forms. In the service of the Mexican
Revolution, he created a monumental style intended to be
worthy of recording the great historical events and, at the
same time, through its broad simplifications, to be understandable to the masses. Rivera's monumental realism is a
hymn to a reality that he himself and his generation had
first to create for themselves.

JOSE CLÉMENTE OROZCO (1883–1949) *The Menaces* · 1936 ·
Mural painting. Cabanas Orphanage, Guadalajara, Jalisco,
Mexico

Orozco stands with Rivera and Siqueiros among the
pioneers of twentieth-century art in Mexico. He was less
influenced than Rivera by European trends and developed a
dramatic and expressive style with bold coloring and rugged
forms. Orozco's art, like that of his two companions-in-
arms, found and proved itself in mural painting especially.
On the broad walls of public buildings, the stark raw speech
of his forms finds its proper setting. His grandiose art
serves to mold the political consciousness of the Mexican
people by bringing before their eyes, in the broad images of
mural painting, their own history and historical destiny.

DAVID ALFARO SIQUEIROS (1896–1974) *Revolution against the
Dictatorship of Porfirio Diaz*, detail from *The Strike at
Canarica* · Mural painting, pyroxiline on Masonite ·
National History Museum, Mexico City

Of the three masters of the new Mexican mural art,
Siqueiros has the most revolutionary temperament.
Compared with Rivera's classically equilibrated composition and Orozco's controlled drama, Siqueiros' murals impress by the vehemence of their passionate movement,
which often seems almost to burst out of the architectural
framework. This potent vitality of form and color stems
from the artist's ardent participation in the social and
political problems of his country. His murals were conceived in the service of the nation, and from that fact they
derive the magniloquence of their language and the explosive force that their themes assume.

BEN NICHOLSON (1894–   ) *Still Life: Nightshade* · 1955 ·
Oil on canvas · $38 \times 50''$ · Collection Hans C. Bechtler,
Zurich

The De Stijl group in Holland created an art entirely independent of the objects in the environment, and of their
appearances. The achievements of that group were taken up
only slowly in other parts of Europe. Finally, in 1931, the
Abstraction-Creation group was organized in Paris to work
with pure pictorial means toward the creation of a pro-
totypal significance, an ideal harmony owing nothing to
anything already in existence; their aim was not representation but presentation, creation. To this quest for a harmonic
order, Nicholson brought an English contribution. As is
typical of his native heritage, he worked with cool, reserved
colors and clear, discrete forms to create in his pictures a
world symbolizing only its own tranquil self-contemplation.

349

ALBERTO MAGNELLI (1888–1971) *Confrontation* · 1952 · Oil on canvas · 45¼ × 63⅝″ · Collection Fernand C. Graindorge, Liège

Magnelli's painting went through a long painful process of development parallel to that of other types of modern art. Before World War I, he was in contact with Cubism in Paris, and in the spirit of Cubist experimentation he soon worked out the geometrical principles that were to become the basis of his art. During the war he ventured as far as total abstraction; then in 1931, after an interlude of figurative painting, he turned to systematically exploiting geometrical abstraction. For the Italian Magnelli, geometry no doubt meant something other than for painters of northern countries; it is the same geometrical structure that underlies the great fresco art of the Italian Renaissance and gives it such high dignity.

VICTOR VASARELY (1908–   ) *Donan II* · 1958 · Oil on canvas · 26 × 20″ · Gallery Denise René, Paris

Vasarely was led to art and to his rigorously ordered conceptions by his compatriot Moholy-Nagy. After studying in his native Hungary, where he became acquainted with the principles of the Bauhaus, he emigrated to Paris in 1930 to join other painters who were making rigid geometrical construction the basis of their art. In his abstract pictures Vasarely seeks to pin down the harmony and orderly laws of the reality in which he lives. Recent years have seen him more and more occupied with experiments in movement, which he captures in exciting and often astonishing works by exploiting exclusively optical means.

350

FRANCIS BACON (1910–   ) *Lying Figure* · 1966 · Oil on canvas · 78 × 58″ · Marlborough Fine Art Ltd., London

More than any other, Bacon's work conveys the anxiety and oppression of our times obsessed by the menace of total extinction through the weapon we ourselves created. By means of their peculiar manipulation of space and livid ghostly colors, his pictures evoke that panicky paralysis of fright that our age has good reason to know. Space in Bacon's pictures is like a locked cage sprung on figures that, aghast and desperate, seek to flee the trap. By limiting his technique to bold sinuous contours twisting on themselves and to broad areas of flowing color, he enhances the terrible force of themes that in themselves harrow the viewer.

GRAHAM SUTHERLAND (1903–1980) *La petite Afrique III* · 1955 · Oil on canvas · 56½ × 48″ · Private collection, London

Even in Sutherland's most freely conceived pictures, nature remains the supreme source of his inspiration. But the natural forms he selects are transmuted into something entirely personal and given an archetypal significance. Thorns, prickles, and spikes crop up ever and again and take on magical meaning; since early in his career, Sutherland has been fascinated by the image of the Crown of Thorns. His aggressive, starkly expressive forms and the often venomous dissonances of his colors confer on his pictures a life that at times recalls the dream world of the Surrealists. This feeling is carried over even into his portraits, in which his world of images seems to fend off the viewer's easy comprehension.

BERNARD BUFFET (1928–   ) *Still Life* · 1952 · Oil on canvas · $25\frac{3}{4} \times 19\frac{3}{4}''$ · Collection Mrs. Albert D. Lasker, New York

At the end of World War II there was a psychological reaction among artists to what those years had brought. Many painters, most of them young, sought in their canvases to exorcise the hollowness of existence, the despair voiced by all the things of the world. They thrust before the viewer a niggardly reality stripped to its ugly bones and painted in apathetic colors with hard stark lines. The silence in these pictures is the muteness of despair, born from disillusionment, from the avowal that hope is dead. Such a romantic sentiment—hopelessness—was communicated by Buffet in particular, as it was also, and at the same time, by the Existentialist writers.

JOAN MIRÓ (1893–   ) *Bullfight* · 1945 · Oil on canvas · $44\frac{7}{8} \times 57\frac{1}{2}''$ · Museum of Modern Art, Paris

In Miró's art the various trends of the time intersect. This man, so richly endowed with an inner fantasy life, has looked with unclouded eyes on all that European painting has to offer, but he has been able to preserve intact his innocence of heart. His early years were influenced by Surrealism; in time he fixed his attention on the miraculous element in nature that only the most sensitive eyes can see, on the poetic and fabulous. The real essence of such a world defies the painter's art; set down on canvas, it quickly loses its poetic power. But Miró has transformed it into symbols laid on a ground so transparent as to suggest unbounded space—hieroglyphs from the deepest primordial sources of man's feelings, which leave every viewer free to interpret them as he will and can.

ANDRÉ MASSON (1896–   ) *Genesis I* · 1958 · Oil on canvas · $63\frac{3}{4} \times 51\frac{1}{8}''$ · Collection Louise Leiris, Paris

Among the paintings that convey their message by calligraphic symbols, those of Masson bear witness to a turbulent, hunted, world of feeling. At the outset, through his friendship with the poet Émile Verhaeren, he became engrossed in symbolism; when he later came under Cubist influence, he was led to seek some kind of order for his unruly feelings. But ever and again in the course of man's development the experience of passion erupts; out of the forgotten depths of the unconscious where forms live their secret lives surge up calligraphic signs that form symbols of compassion for the world. These hieroglyphs have a movement of their own, an almost chaotic motion. Masson, who has long felt oppressed by the things of reality, experiences the chaotic whirling of the world as a menace; in his pictures, it is this imminent threat that he places before our eyes.

ROBERTO MATTA (1911–   ) *Who's Who* · 1955 · Oil on canvas · $23\frac{5}{16} \times 29\frac{1}{2}''$ · Private collection, New York

Matta's work introduces the viewer into a world where natural science and technology work hand in hand to reveal the oppressive aggressiveness of nature. Matta, a native of Chile, turned to painting of a Surrealist character after having studied architecture with Le Corbusier. There remains with him from his architectural studies a feeling for the technical construction of his phantasmagoric images; the terrifying world he depicts metamorphoses beetles, grubs, and strange insects into machines of war to produce a nightmare world of hostility and destruction, a world that leers menacingly at the viewer from behind the reality he thinks he knows.

351

Renato Guttuso (1912–   ) *Still Life* · 1961 · Oil on canvas · 76⅝ × 63⅜″ · Stedelijk Museum, Amsterdam

Guttuso comes from Sicily, one of the few regions left in Europe that preserves, in the paintings on its peasants' carts, an authentic folk art. This folk style influenced Guttuso's early work; then his opposition to the official art of Italian fascism led him first to Expressionism and then to the influence of Picasso. Since 1937 he has found a personal idiom that has made of him a leading personality among the Neo-Realists. The forceful realistic depiction of everyday reality, his chief subject, is not for him an end in itself but rather a means of denouncing injustice with emotional conviction.

Mordechai Ardon (1896–   ) *The House of the Maggid* · 1954 · Oil on canvas · 57¾ × 44¾″ · Royal Museum of Fine Arts, Brussels

Israel has made a contribution to modern art in Ardon's work. Ardon was trained at the Weimar Bauhaus by Klee and Feininger, but in Israel, where he has lived since 1934, his painting slowly came to take on the character of the Holy Land; the mystical poetry of the Jewish tradition has filtered into his pictures to purify them of their vestiges of European formalism. Forms and colors, laid on canvas in strongly rhythmic counterpoint, pose a riddle to the viewer, conceal a deeper meaning that is disclosed only when the viewer reaches out to the brooding but wonderful content.

Rufino Tamayo (1899–   ) *The Singer* · 1950 · Oil on canvas · 76¼ × 51⅛″ · Museum of Modern Art, Paris

Tamayo's contact with European painting occurred only when most of the modern developments were already well established. But Tamayo's art is also based on the Mexican tradition, especially its native folklore, to which he has devoted much study. In his large figure compositions he makes use of the achievements of European painting, especially the expressive distortion of the human body, but he incorporates these innovations in pictorial structures derived essentially from mural painting and therefore folk-like and possessed of immediate impact. In contrast to the dramatic and epic art of the other Mexican painters, he is above all lyrical.

Nicolas de Staël (1914–55) *Sicilian Landscape* · 1954 · Oil on canvas · 35⅛ × 51⅛″ · Private collection, Paris

The work of De Staël lies on the border between abstraction and realism. Over and over it moves to one side, then the other, oscillating between realistic depiction and abstract color harmonies. For the most part, however, De Staël takes color as his starting point, laying it out in large glowing blocks; then out of those resounding color surfaces and their harmonies he evokes objects—landscapes or figures. Color is his basis, just as form was earlier for Juan Gris; out of abstract color he brings forth, as if by magic, images of things, and this metamorphosis lends his pictures a significance that comes eventually from a pantheistic feeling for life. Color is the raw material out of which the artist creates his worlds.

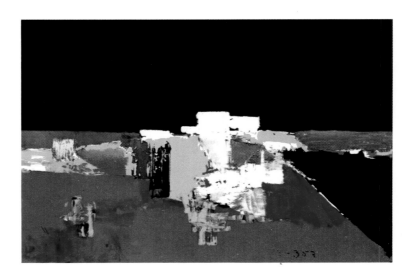

ROGER BISSIÈRE (1888–1964) *Gray and Violet* · 1957 · Oil on canvas · $36\frac{1}{4} \times 28\frac{3}{4}''$ · Museum of Luxembourg, Collection Grand Duchess of Luxembourg

After a slow and difficult development, Bissière became, in the years after World War II, a leading personality in a non-objective art whose origins lie in an intimate knowledge of nature and whose formal vocabulary is based on flexible, lively, painterly brush work. His pictures are made up of colored fragments woven together in an animated web, and they recall in their contemplative view of nature the small works by which Klee gave visual expression to his thoughts about creation and growth. Nature—not as a product of creation but rather as a mysteriously effective force in creation—fills Bissière's pictures with the magic of that reverential vision with which he puzzles out the riddle of reality.

GERRIT BENNER (1897–) *Farmhouse* · 1954 · Oil on canvas · $23\frac{1}{2} \times 31\frac{1}{2}''$ · Stedelijk Museum, Amsterdam

The Dutch painter Benner likewise uses color as a starting point and builds his harmonies from it. His world is that of the child's wonder at man and beast, at the harmony his rejoicing spirit discovers in the simple world of every day. Like the Blaue Reiter painters, he seeks to know the unity that binds together all the things of nature to each other and to man. This unity he finds in the consonance of the simplest colors, a consonance that unfolds in his paintings with utmost richness and fullness. Even his color harmonies are simple, as uncomplicated as a folk song, like the land in which Benner's paintings are rooted; the world of men with simple hearts, the wonder world all men can see who look with eyes of innocence.

SAM FRANCIS (1923–) *Composition* · 1960 · Oil on canvas · $25\frac{5}{8} \times 31\frac{7}{8}''$ · Gallery Jacques Dubourg, Paris

Francis is one of the young Americans who after World War II discovered their own artistic personalities in Paris. From his homeland he brought with him the need to express himself on very large surfaces. This he does by spreading loosely and freely rhythmic successions of light-toned color areas over a white ground. The paint runs in threads or streams over the canvas, leaving tracks of the fast-moving hand, of the brush that seems to give its own orders. Francis' rhythmic splashes of color are, however, above all the visible traces of a lyrical emotion that—as they do in Turner's pictures—streams out in mists and patches of color whose rhythm echoes the painter's inner vision of rhythm.

MARIA ELENA VIEIRA DA SILVA (1908–) *Composition* · 1956 · Oil on canvas · $11 \times 7\frac{7}{8}''$ · Private collection, Paris

The central concern of all Vieira da Silva's pictorial thinking is space itself, perhaps because this Portuguese painter started as a sculptress, studying under Bourdelle. Space for her is that phenomenon through which things first achieve reality—and yet, space can also bear down, enclose as in a prison. Her spatial visions start out mostly as views of cities, but the external appearances of the cities disappear completely when translated into her pictorial language. Nothing survives except a scaffolding of color and rhythm that, through its virtually weightless structure, clearly suggests the boundlessness and power of absorption characteristic of space.

353

AFRO (Afro Basaldella) (1912–) *Villa Horizon* · 1960 ·
Oil on canvas · 33½ × 39½″ · Galerie de France, Paris

As far as its symbolic language is concerned, Afro's
painting inhabits a frontier between abstraction and figuration. Starting with a subject, the works always denote some
aspect of reality that is often summed up significantly in
their titles. The painter does not, however, limit himself to
depicting that reality but seeks the essence beneath the
appearance, the true core. For this special approach to
reality, we as yet have no generally recognized common
vocabulary, and every viewer must decipher the words for
himself. Despite their strong bright colors and assured
treatment, Afro's symbols seem somewhat tentative; the
calligraphic signs he sets down come from no language
learned or taught but only from an intuition that strives to
grasp reality.

WILLI BAUMEISTER (1889–1955) *Two Lanterns* · 1955 · Oil
on canvas · 25½ × 21¼″ · Private collection

In Germany, before it was overwhelmed by the Nazi
dictatorship, Baumeister had already made an important
contribution to the development of new artistic trends.
Like Schlemmer, he came from Hoelzel's school, where he
learned how painting and architecture are related. His early
works were consequently conceived as mural paintings;
their surfaces are like walls, and the forms depicted have the
clarity and potential of architectural materials. Before
World War II his style had already become more fluent; the
configurations of his paintings assumed a more organic
form, giving rise to vitalized signs that embody some idea or
feeling. With their broad planes and simple colors, these
pictures seem predestined for walls.

ALFRED MANESSIER (1911–) *Composition* · 1956 · Oil
on canvas · 10⅜ × 18″ · Private collection, Paris

Manessier is another of those who conceive their pictorial
forms in terms of flat planes, in his case either walls or
stained-glass windows. His images make no attempt to
duplicate appearances and are therefore so much the more
significant in their sure grasp of an all-embracing reality.
Manessier was brought to this profound sense of reality
by his religious beliefs; as a devout Catholic he has an
innate sensitivity to the spiritually significant image. He has
given visual form to the entire world of faith—a sphere both
visible and real—which he has infused with the warmth of
his own religious feeling. He deserves credit for discovering
for himself the abstract symbols of a language with which
to speak to others who have faith, a language he has elevated to a virtually liturgical dignity.

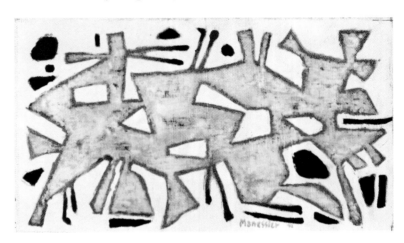

PETAR LUBARDA (1905–) *Mediterranean* · 1952 · Oil on
canvas · 44¾ × 57¼″ · Gallery of Contemporary Art,
Belgrade

Lubarda's painting has its sources not only in the imagery
of his bustling Montenegrin homeland but also in the
principles of mural decoration. From his feeling for his
native landscape come his animated, sharply contrasting
forms, from mural art his way of locking and controlling
those forms within a plane. Behind this treatment of surfaces stands the entire great tradition of medieval southern
Slavic mural painting as well as the responsibility, imposed
on him by his active participation in a Socialist system, to
turn out art not for the homes of private citizens but rather
for the general public. The way in which Lubarda orders
and masters his animated forms is, in this sense, another act
of faith, of faith in art.

FRANZ KLINE (1910–62) *Brass and Red* · 1959 · Oil on canvas · 68 × 39″ · Collection Mr. and Mrs. Burton Tremaine, Meriden, Connecticut

The paintings of Kline, all of very large dimensions and with forms made of broad bold strokes, are built around signs that no longer have any association with external reality. For this reason they are so much the more suggestive of an inner reality, a personal experience. The vehemence of the broadly slapped-on forms involves the viewer directly in the slashing gesture of the brush to which they owe their existence—gestures of an unleashed Dionysiac primordial violence. "Action Painting," a rallying cry of the young generation in America, proclaims that painting is no longer to be performed as a means of saying something or revealing something but, instead, as an act in itself, as pure physical gesture. In this act Kline's art has its basis and significance.

FRITZ WINTER (1905–1976) *Yellow Luminosity* · 1951 · Oil on canvas · 29½ × 39¼″ · Private collection, Darmstadt

Before he studied painting at the Bauhaus in 1927, Winter was a miner in his native Westphalia. From this he acquired the fundamental experience that was later to take form in his paintings—the building up and stratification of stone, the petrification of ancient life—the processes by which nature takes shape. He turned away from the representation of the forms that nature had already created and chose instead to work in a way parallel to nature's creative acts. Structures of growth, the eternal patterns that lie at the foundations of inorganic matter, became the themes of his pictures, which are more than a mere play of forms; they are a revelation of the essence and laws of nature itself.

BRAM VAN VELDE (1892–   ) *Painting* · 1960 · Oil on canvas · 51⅛ × 63¾″ · Collection Henri Samuel, Paris

Born in the Netherlands, Bram van Velde has lived and worked in Paris since 1925. His style has changed slowly from an Expressionism rooted in the School of Paris to a personal world of forms, in which the appearance of reality is no more than the soil from which forms spring. The recognition that Van Velde has received in recent years owes much to the sympathetic interest of the writer Samuel Beckett; in Van Velde's pictures Beckett's strange and special world is made visible. Van Velde's graphic signs are volatile and seem never to come to rest. Through his use of flowing paint, they become symbols of the many-sidedness of a reality that ever and again slips from man's unsteady, hesitant grasp.

PIERRE SOULAGES (1919–   ) *Painting 3-11-'56* · 1956 · Oil on canvas · 21⅝ × 14⅞″ · Collection Madame Prévot, Paris

The ponderous configurations in Soulages' work are the direct natural expression of their creator. Soulages comes from a peasant background and brought with him to Paris the heavy robust character of his origins. His pictures are all variations on a simple, somber basic theme; a black form, with a feeling of inner strain as of great weight in movement, is set heavily over a scaffolding of dark streaks. The black forms heave up before a lighter background like fateful omens. By means of thick, viscid paint dragged on with a broad brush, the artist intensifies the impression of something crushing, nocturnal, and fraught with destiny, a monumental vision of a simple but oppressive reality.

355

CORNEILLE (van Beverloo) (1922–   ) *Hostile City* · 1954 · Oil on canvas · 35⅞ × 50½ʺ · Stedelijk van Abbe Museum, Eindhoven

Corneille is one of the young painters who in 1949 founded the Cobra group as an international rallying point for artists of experimental orientation. The origins of his art are therefore to be found in an intensified Expressionism employing abstract means, but very soon he broke with the orthodox trend of the group in order to realize his own potentialities. Using the same spontaneous and direct means as the others in the group, he recoiled from their extreme dramatic emphasis to his own more lyrical, poetically intense nexus of lines and colors. Through absorbed attention to things, he has learned how to capture the rhythm of nature and of landscapes and cities. The firm construction of his pictures is the hallmark of his poetic sensitivity.

SERGE POLIAKOFF (1906–1969) *Abstract Composition* · 1957 · Oil on canvas · 38⅛ × 51⅛ʺ · Private collection, Paris

The pictures of the Russian-born Poliakoff are constructed out of large slabs of pure color in simple, almost geometrical forms set one against the other. They are completely devoid of all objective association. These straightforward compositions built from the simplest of elements appear closely related to Magnelli's geometrical abstractions and similar works by Nicholson. Poliakoff's rejection of strict geometry reveals, however, his lyrical and sensitive individuality; to the puritanical rigor of geometrical abstractions he opposes the flowing rhythms of more supple forms, whose effect is further heightened by glowing color harmonies and rich materials.

JEAN DUBUFFET (1901–   ) *Reddish Nude*, or *Woman Casting Spell* · 1945 · Oil on canvas · 28¾ × 23⅝ʺ · Collection Carlo van den Bosch, Antwerp

Dubuffet was one of the first painters in Europe to define his link with reality by drawing inspiration directly from the materials he used. Thus, the agitated surfaces of his pictures —like crusts or tree bark—take on special meaning. In addition, Dubuffet uses as point of departure the drawings of the mentally ill and the scribbles found on billboards and walls, the so-called *graffiti*, which constitute a direct uncensored definition of reality. He is especially fascinated by the diverse forms matter can assume (he has even painted a series of beards!), recognizing and exploiting this magical power of suggestion in pictures put together out of sand, iron filings, leaves, and the like, to make what he calls "texturologies" and "matterologies."

ERNST WILHELM NAY (1902–1968) *Parabola* · 1958 · Oil on canvas · 45⅝ × 31⅞ʺ · Collection P. Peilli, Düren, West Germany

Nay made his way from Expressionism to Abstraction slowly and with great independence. What remained constant, however, in this progression from exterior depiction to abstractions like music was his fundamental point of departure—color. In his early pictures, where objects and space are still defined, it is color that fulfills this function. After the war, Nay discarded all suggestion of real objects and let color lead an autonomous life; in a series of pictures he let the rich chromaticism of his palette flower, and he found ever-new ways to orchestrate his harmonies.

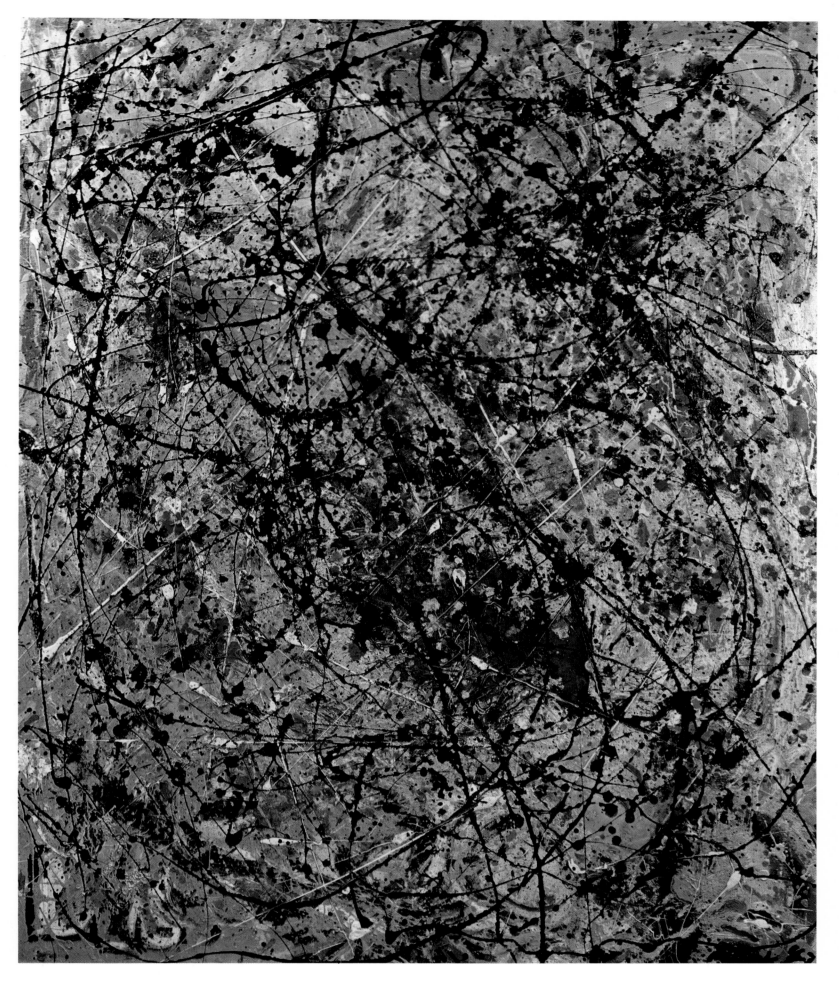

JACKSON POLLOCK (1912–56) *Reflection of the Big Dipper* · 1946 · Oil on canvas · 43⅝ × 36¼″ · Stedelijk Museum, Amsterdam

It was Pollock in America who was responsible for the decisive revolution in postwar painting. He broke with the traditional notion that a picture is the end product of an idea first conceived in the mind and then slowly and painstakingly worked out on canvas. For Pollock, a painting was in itself a spontaneous creative act. Action Painting— painting as a physical act—was the result of his revolutionary innovation; the picture grows out of the unpremed-

itated, uncontrolled gestures of the painter himself. In Pollock's paintings one can follow the tracks of the wild, unbridled, demoniac dance of the painter's gestures as his hand shoots across the canvas. We viewers can and must translate those tracks back into the outpouring discharge of the painter's energy and thereby ourselves experience the fiercely vital movement that brought them into being. For this reason, brushwork itself takes on an entirely new importance; it is the direct notation of the painter's own excitement communicated directly to the beholder's eyes and emotions without the obstacle or the aid of any recognizable image.

Detail is shown on next pages

357

JEAN BAZAINE (1904–) *Composition* · 1956 · Oil on canvas · 36¼ × 23⅝" · Private collection, Paris

Bazaine's abstract compositions take their feeling for color from nature and in this respect owe much to Monet's late works. But quite unlike late Impressionism, Bazaine does not limit himself to optical impressions of the external color of objects but instead seeks to decipher the laws that determine the special characteristics of their surfaces. He aims to embody in images those laws obeyed by both nature and man, and he distills them out of his experience of the colors of nature. Abstraction for him is not mere rejection of figuration but rather its translation into the language of color. As a Frenchman, his pictorial construction is more methodical than Nay's, also clearer and more concise in syntax, but he lacks Nay's intoxicating, ecstatic resonance.

GEORGIA O'KEEFFE (1887–) *Black Iris* · 1926 · Oil on canvas · 36 × 30" · Metropolitan Museum of Art, New York

O'Keeffe's paintings place objective semblances before the viewer's eyes and invite him to let his imagination play over them, to penetrate into the broader significance of the forms depicted. Flowers, mountains, skull bones are her intermediary symbols for the universal formal power of nature, which the artist herself comprehends through her ever-renewed contact with it. Her remarkable capacity for experience elevates simple natural forms into world-embracing symbols; a flower comes to mean fertility, a bull's skull the visible shape of suffering.

ARTHUR DOVE (1880–1946) *Moon* · 1935 · Oil on canvas · 35 × 27" · Private collection, Los Angeles

Dove was the pioneer of nonfigurative art in America though today most of his pictures seem quite representational. Very early, soon after his visit to France in 1907–1908, he went beyond the external aspects of objects to seek the formal principles that lie at the heart of the world of forms. Slowly and inexorably, he worked out his own style, first in geometrical shapes, later with flowing animated clusters of lines. Still, his pictures remain linked to his insight into nature, which is often embodied in metaphorical images of great simplicity, such as this vision of the moon hanging in a tree.

ARSHILE GORKY (1904–48) *The Liver Is the Cock's Comb* · 1944 · Oil on canvas · 73 × 98" · Albright Knox Art Gallery, Buffalo

In the United States, Gorky opened the way to a free abstract vocabulary of forms. The effervescent richness of his colors and forms was his heritage from his homeland, Turkish Armenia. For centuries, the art of the East—folk art in particular—was indifferent to depiction of the external world, exercising its fantasy on adorning houses, furnishings, and clothing with decorative motifs brilliant in colors and inexhaustible in form. It was that art that Gorky found closest to his own feelings. His forms and rich colors often recall Kandinsky's early work. His imagination disports itself in a wild dance of forms, in landscapes of the subconscious, in a world of symbols bursting with color.

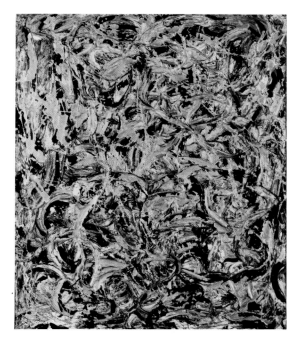

JACKSON POLLOCK (1912–56) *Eyes in the Heat II* · 1947 ·
Oil on canvas · 24 × 20½ ″ · Gallery Berggruen, Paris

Pollock pointed a new direction for a thoroughgoing
renewal of painting; he was the first to break with the conventional notion of a consciously worked-out picture. By
letting his brush run over the canvas in free rhythmic movement, or by dribbling paint from brush or can onto a canvas
laid flat on the floor, he allowed the painting to paint itself
without the calculating control of a prior conception. This
extreme spontaneity, which records the fluctuations of the
artist's feelings unhampered by the conscious will, is truly
the ultimate form of an art of expression of Dionysiac
origin. It made visible and communicable those impulses of
the inner reality which surge up in man ever and again.

MARK ROTHKO (1903–1970) *No. 8* · 1952 · Oil on canvas·
80½ × 68″ · Collection Mr. and Mrs. Burton Tremaine,
Meriden, Connecticut

Another of those who took a long and painstaking road to
abstraction was the Russian-born American, Mark
Rothko. Beginning with impressions of landscapes, he
converted these into colored motifs; clouds and damp fogs
dissolved into patches of color. His personal style and
individual concept of reality were not, however, achieved
through observation of nature but, rather, by long meditation over the movements of clouds and the splintering of
light. Thus, like Turner, he came to translate his vision of
nature, his cosmic mysticism, into a pure play of colors,
whose dreamlike imprecision holds the viewer in a mood of
quiet reflection.

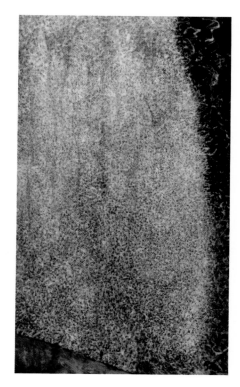

MARK TOBEY (1890–1976) *Edge of August* · 1953 · Casein
on composition board · 48 × 28 ″ · Museum of Modern
Art, New York

Through Tobey, American painting came to be influenced
by Far Eastern calligraphy. In 1934, on a visit to Shanghai,
Tobey, who had begun as a portrait painter, became aware of
the possibilities of abstract imagery offered by Chinese
script. Out of that animated but superbly controlled calligraphy he developed the fleet brushwork of his "white
writing" to express the vibrancy of life in great cities and in
nature.

HANS HARTUNG (1904–   ) *Painting T57–17E* · 1957 ·
Oil on panel · 18 × 13″ · Private collection, Paris

Hartung transmitted to Europe the shock wave set off in
America when Jackson Pollock spontaneously created a
painting without the intermediary steps of conscious will or
deliberate control. But in their pictures, in the way their
pictorial organisms grow, can be recognized the difference
between the American Pollock and the European Hartung.
Pollock flings his entire self into the restless spurting stream
of his creative activity, whereas Hartung shows pauses,
restraints, ebbs and flows. An art such as Hartung's inevitably has much in common with drawing, since the inner
tensions of the artist are released through the energetic
movement of lines and slashing brush strokes.

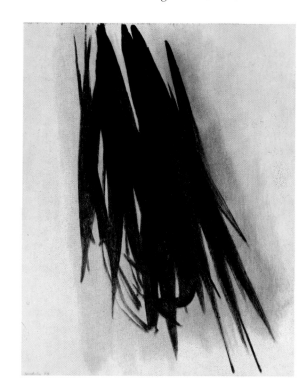

361

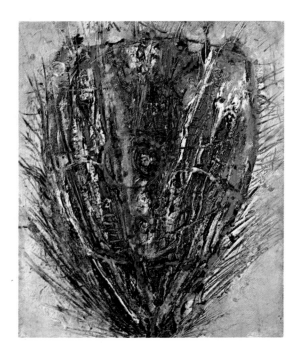

OTTO WOLS (1913–51) *Composition* · 1946 · Oil on canvas · 16½ × 13⅜″ · Private collection, Paris

Wols belongs among the Abstract Expressionists. The oils and the many small paintings on paper he did in his short creative life have an entirely personal individuality. The pictorial signs formed by his automatic calligraphy of nervously jotted dots, streaks, and spots let us glimpse a world of tragic despair, of fathomless depths. The world of Wols is like the anxiety-laden obsessions of Kafka, whose books he illustrated. In its total surrender to an inner vision, Wols's work gropes toward hidden realms of the subconscious never before revealed, which he holds up before the viewer in demon-haunted scribblings.

JEAN FAUTRIER (1898–1964) *Informal Pastel* · 1928 · Pastel on paper · 6¼ × 10½″ · Private collection, Paris

After World War II, the notion gained currency that, at the beginning of his creative act, the artist has no clear conception of what is to emerge from his canvas. This is totally unlike the practice of earlier generations who worked from an initially laid-out concept to the clearest possible realization of it. Here what is implied is that only in the course of the artist's work does a pictorial idea take shape. Many artists, Wols and Pollock among them, have been driven by their inner tension to set down a highly expressive kind of calligraphy; others, and in particular Fautrier, give themselves over completely to the material they work with and voluntarily permit it to dictate what they are to do. In both cases, creativity springs from unplumbed realms of human feeling and the conscious will plays no part. Fautrier was one of those who chose to explore and to exploit the richly expressive possibilities of their materials.

362

ANTONI TAPIES (1923–   ) *Brown and Ocher* · Oil on canvas · 46½ × 52″ · Collection Henry Markus, Chicago

Among the various painters primarily concerned with materials, such as Fautrier, Burri, and Wagemaker, a special place is held by Tàpies because of his Spanish heritage. What appeals to him is not the richness of materials but rather their stark economy. Because of this, his art is not one of superabundance and resonant harmony; rather, through an austere, almost melancholy meditation he allows his materials to speak, as if by miracle, of something deeply true to experience. Forms borrowed from reality—crumbled old walls, rotted wooden doors, and the like—are no more than the remote starting point for pictures whose true content is the human problem of decay and dissolution. At the heart of his work, with its poetic nuances, lies the eternal Spanish warning of *memento mori*—remember death—expressed in contemporary Existentialist terms.

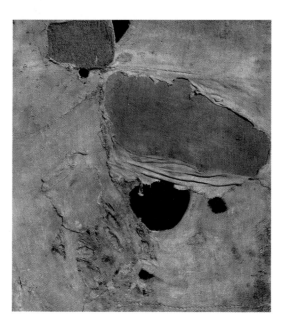

ALBERTO BURRI (1915–   ) *Sacking 56* · 1956 · Oil on burlap · 39⅜ × 33⅛″ · Galerie du XXe Siècle, Paris

After studying and practicing medicine in his Italian homeland, Burri turned to painting in 1944 while a prisoner of war in the United States. In his pictures, the most ordinary, unlikely seeming materials are given pictorial significance. Using burlap, wooden planks, or iron bars, he constructs broad-surfaced compositions in which such decayed materials reveal astonishing new expressive possibilities. Ragged, torn sacking, singed wood, and burnt scraps of plastic evoke oppressive visions of a doomed world, and yet, despite the repulsiveness of the means he uses, Burri's strong compositional sense reveals the classical order of his native Italian tradition.

ROBERT MOTHERWELL (1915–   ) *Afternoon in Barcelona* ·
1958 · Oil on canvas · 53½ × 72″ · Sidney Janis Gallery,
New York

Motherwell is the leader of the school of younger
American painters who seek a new solution to the riddle of
reality in the symbolic content of their pictorial vocabulary.
Surrealism led them to this discovery, and Miró and Matta
pointed the way. Forms risen to the surface from the subconscious become meaningful signs that thrust their hidden
significance before our conscious understanding. By his
studies in philosophy and psychology, Motherwell has
deepened his grasp of these processes; what he has learned
from these sources he uses to pin down the image of a
reality wrenched from those deepest strata of human experience where man and universe are still as one.

ASGER JORN (1914–1973) *Letter to My Son* · 1956–57 ·
Oil on canvas · 51⅛ × 76⅝″ · Collection Albert Niels,
Chaussée de la Grande Espinette, Rhode-St. Genèse

Asger Jorn, a Danish painter who lived in Paris, was the foremost exponent of a contemporary frame of mind whose
roots reach back to Expressionism and even to Romanticism.
His stormy fantasy world is Nordic, akin to the earthy,
Dionysiac Expressionism of Nolde. But Jorn's origin does
not wholly explain the inner message of his paintings nor
their technique, which so closely derives from their content;
it is an art that expresses the emotions of all men of our day,
their nostalgia to be one again with nature, their revulsion
against the threat of compulsion from without, their con-
tempt for stultifying familiarity. The true message of his
pictures is the human right to self-expression, and this ideal
he communicates in fully convincing pictorial images.

WILLEM DE KOONING (1904–   ) *Woman I* · 1950–52 ·
Oil with charcoal on canvas · 75⅞ × 58″ · The Museum
of Modern Art, New York

In 1926 De Kooning emigrated to the United States from
his native Netherlands, bringing with him the unquiet,
turbulent temperament that has been one side of his country-
men's nature, from Frans Hals to Van Gogh. To this,
present-day life in America added further fire to his protest
against slick perfection and conformism. In the series of
female figures, his pictures are in part representational, but
their greatest significance lies rather within the realm of
abstraction, in their frenetic agitated brush strokes, the
chaotic tangle of their crooked, gnarled lines. The savage
restlessness of his brushwork seems to fight against the
chaos that lies so close in his paintings and threatens to
engulf them. The real content of De Kooning's art lies
precisely in this struggle against the menace of existence.

KAREL APPEL (1921–   ) *Personage* · 1958 · Oil on
canvas · 51⅛ × 38⅛″ · Collection Madame Willy Grubben,
Brussels

Appel was one of the founders of the international Cobra
group, which first made its mark in 1949 in an exhibition at
the Stedelijk Museum in Amsterdam. Their work conveyed
the feeling of a young generation in enthusiastic revolt
against any attempt to stifle spontaneous expression,
against the hidden compulsions of rules, taboos, conventions, and formulas. The explosion of vitality and pictorial
fury in Appel's pictures is a protest against numb stagnation,
but it is also a shout of joy for the new horizons opening
before man. Through the years Appel has been able to
preserve the energy of his first volcanic outpourings.

363

far eastern art

H. Hetl-Kuntze

This survey of painting of the Far East is designed to give some idea of the rich diversity of artistic creation in that part of the world. In a development spanning more than two thousand years, not all of which has even yet been thoroughly studied, it provides us with innumerable examples that demonstrate the relationship of the Far East to the art of color—color so much the more interesting for having its own unique and characteristic traits.

All painting depends on color, however restrictive that definition may seem. Even in grisaille—the monochromatic painting often used for frescoes or stained glass—the gradations of a single color inevitably suggest coloristic effects. This makes all the more understandable the Oriental insistence that India ink, with its all-inclusive range from palest gray to deepest black, contains within itself all the colors of the world. India-ink painting is one of the chief glories of Far Eastern art, and it was at the very moment when the range of vision of the West first began to conceive the world in impressionistic terms, with a new concern for light and atmosphere, that India-ink painting made its most universal impact. Today, in the perspective of time, that impact seems so immense that no one can any longer ignore or deprecate Oriental art.

But instead of coming to grips on its own terms with this still little-known but, for all that, no less interesting medium of Far Eastern art, the West has tended to imitate its aesthetic effects while employing a range of colors entirely alien to its basic character. Those of us who love India-ink painting find that it loses its significance when transposed into color. The tonal values are all too often debased and often enough quite simply falsified. Any color juxtaposed to ink distorts: the cinnabar red of certain wax seals stamped on pictures in the Orient to indicate ownership creates such an intense color contrast that often the total impression of the picture is disturbed. (Unfortunately, Emperor Ch'ien-lung was not alone in his mania of so marking every picture in his collection.) However, we need not limit ourselves to such a special case to see just how important and objective a role color plays in Oriental painting.

Even a comparatively modest example of early Chinese art, the fragment of a lute dating from the fourth century B.C. (page 372), is characterized not only by the animated rhythms of its figures in silhouette but also by a secure instinct for the use of a few related colors. The twisting contours of the figures are typical of the style of the time, though they were exploited most fully in jade and bronze. As for the painting of that early era, we know something about it from the poems of Ch'u-yuan (c. 300 B.C.) which describe the wall paintings in the ruined palaces of his native state of Ch'u in Central China. The paintings on the walls of those wooden palaces have not come down to us, but their subject matter is known not only from Ch'u-yuan's poems but also from later versions of the same themes found in tomb chambers of the Han period (206 B.C. to A.D. 220).

It is to that period, the first century or the beginning of the second of our era, that the lacquer painting on the lidded pannier unearthed at Lo-Lang in northern Korea belongs (page 372). Northern Korea was a Chinese colony at that time, and most of the inscriptions incised on the bottoms of lacquered objects indicate the imperial workshops in Szechwan as their place of fabrication. The figures on the pannier lid, illustrating the subject of filial piety, are painted with a wealth of detail inside the contours, with finely harmonized colors, and with animated expression. Such art makes us regret so much the more the loss of all large-scale paintings.

The situation is no better for the next few centuries. For any idea of Chinese painting we still must depend on examples from provincial regions, such as the frescoes in tombs and cave temples from the outer borders of the vast empire. Yet, we do know something at least about the great artists of the time and the works they made to adorn palaces and temples, because they are spoken of in literary sources which, in China more than elsewhere, have survived in great numbers and from very early times. Even from the T'ang Dynasty (618–906), one of the truly brilliant periods of Chinese art and culture, scarcely a single noteworthy work of fine art, as distinguished from applied art, has survived through the ages, though it was precisely this epoch that had such great influence on the art of Japan.

Nara, the first stable capital of Japan, was patterned after Ch'ang-an, the capital of the T'ang Dynasty, and the same city served as the model for Kyoto which was founded in 794 and remained the chief city of Japan right up to 1868. In those Japanese centers, Chinese objects were used, some of which were imported, others turned out by native artists in strict imitation of Chinese prototypes. That is why, today, we often find it difficult to identify objects from the Shosoin, the treasure house founded in 756 in honor of Buddha by the widow of Emperor Shomu, which contained the entire domestic furnishings of the imperial household. Thanks to dedicated care through the centuries, its rich collections have survived to our time. Even though the most recent research has decided that most of the objects were Japanese in origin, these collections give us the best idea possible under the circumstances of what Chinese work of the same period was like, and with some justification we can disregard the question of precisely where the objects were, in fact, made.

The rich repertory of subject matter of the time—Buddhist scenes like that on the Tamamushi shrine, landscapes, and figures (pages 373–74)—

would never again appear simultaneously to such an extent. After the persecution of Buddhism in 843–45, when among other artworks the frescoes of Wu Tao-tzu (c. 690–760), famed as unique in their kind, were destroyed, religious art using many figures disappeared almost entirely from China. It was supplanted, in the Sung period especially, by the restrained India-ink painting of the meditative form of Buddhism called Ch'an in China and in Japan, Zen. The outstanding examples of that art were often done by monks and were Japanese in origin. The Chinese themselves did not accord such great significance to this kind of painting, and in contemporary accounts there is little or no mention of the artists who made it. Be that as it may, in the classification of Emperor Hui-tsung's collection, Taoist and Buddhist themes take first place, even though they are outnumbered by pictures of flowers and birds. Hui-tsung was himself an excellent painter of such themes, as we can see in the small leaf from an album with a quail and narcissus (page 375). With Hui-tsung and the Southern Sung Academy, the decisive factor in landscape painting, as in that of flowers and birds, was asymmetrical composition in which the principal subject was placed not in the center but in a corner of the picture. This formal peculiarity, however, was less frequent in pictures on domestic themes and in those done for hand scrolls. Compare, for instance, Su Han-ch'en's *Children Playing* (page 377) or the anonymous *Homecoming of Wen-chi* (page 378) with Hui-tsung's *Quail and Narcissus* (page 375) or Li Ti's *Herdsman Returning Home* (page 377). In the former, the entire scenes are depicted in detail, in the latter there is only an intimation of the essential inner meaning. The distinction is summed up in a saying of Confucius: "I point out one corner, and for the man who cannot find the other three I will not repeat myself."

Beginning with the Southern Sung period, landscape became one of the chief subjects of Chinese painting; thenceforth no painter could ignore it. Even the greatest artists of the Yuan period, those who carried on the ideals of the Sung Academy, did their best work in landscapes which, as a part of the whole of nature, became a symbol of the free man. After the passing of the Mongols who had ruled China as the Yuan Dynasty, the native Chinese house of Ming acceded to the throne in 1368. It was at the court of Peking especially that the effort was made to pick up where the Sung Academy had been forced to leave off. This, then, became a time for the restoration of old values, and it was painters like Tai Wen-chin and Lu Chi (page 380) who rose to fame then. The former specialized in India-ink landscapes in the style of the Southern Sung Academy, the latter in birds and flowers. Had he lived under the Sung Dynasty, Lu Chi's carefully observed and naturalistic birds would have earned him great honor at the court of Hui-tsung, but his gleaming colors have much more in common with the decorative fashions of his own time.

Alongside this academic circle there was another and brilliant group of utmost importance: the so-called Four Great Painters of the Ming Dynasty—Shen Chou (page 380), Wen Cheng-ming, T'ang Yin, and Ch'iu Ying (page 381). These men merit as high a place in world art as their Western contemporaries Leonardo, Michelangelo, Grünewald, and Dürer. Although he passed all the state examinations with the highest distinction, Shen Chou declined to accept an official post in Ho where all attention was concentrated on the revival of the old styles. He lived apart from the world, though not averse to the company of friends, in his country place near Soochow in the old district of Wu. Forbidding as the towering mountain seems in his conception, his soft colors tone down the ruggedness of the place and the tiny figures he introduces lend a human dimension to an awesome landscape. Wen Cheng-ming, Shen Chou's friend and pupil, was subtler and more sensitive in both brushwork and color. For a short time he held an official post which only later, after many difficulties, he was able to secure definitively. Most of his life was spent as a freelance teacher in Soochow where he wrote poetry, painted, and dedicated himself to literary studies. His brushwork is never bold and challenging like that of Shen Chou or the younger T'ang Yin, but rather has an unobtrusive delicacy and seems secondary to his interest in color. T'ang Yin's was the most unbridled personality of the group, and he painted not only landscapes but also remarkably fine figures. In the picture reproduced here, there is an enchanting still life of flowers in the foreground, and the rocks and landscape on the screen in the background are done in soft ink washes. In addition, the subtle, effective drawing of the figure and plum branch is skillfully combined with a restrained but fresh approach to color. Through intrigues, T'ang Yin never obtained an official post but, instead, passed his days in the company of beautiful women (it is said of him that he would paint a picture merely for a cup of wine). The youngest of the circle, Ch'iu Ying, was the only one not from a well-to-do family. Obliged to earn his daily bread by his art, it is a tribute to his native endowments that he is reckoned among the great artists of his country. His figures and landscapes are executed with delicate brushwork, though his colors tend to be vivid. Unfortunately, his works have been so often imitated and counterfeited that it is difficult to discern the qualities which his contemporaries admired in his pictures.

At the end of the sixteenth century appeared an artist whose overpowering personality set the tone for China's artistic life for a long time to come: Tung Ch'i-ch'ang (page 382). His brushwork is relatively easy to recognize: he is always concerned with exposing clearly the structure of a tree or crag and uses color only to emphasize the form and to intensify the effect of his ink drawing. The principles he laid down—the most significant of any of the old masters'—were followed more literally by his circle of friends and students than by the great painter himself, although many of his authentic works remain to be identified and may possibly contradict this. Not only was he painter, calligrapher, theorist, tutor to the prince, and minister, but he was also esteemed as one of the finest connoisseurs of painting: a work that he saw or an inscription he praised was and still is considered of greater value than any other. His high reputation and fame were due also, in part, to his friends and students. These included the four Wangs, Yun Shou-p'ing, and Wu Li who collectively are known as the Six Famous Masters of the Ch'ing Period. Contemporary with Tung Ch'i-ch'ang and his circle was the quite different school of Che, followers of the almost two-centuries-old tradition of Tai Wen-chin. They are represented here by two fresh and lively pictures by Li Shih-ta and Lan Ying (page 383).

In the seventeenth century the Manchus overran the country and, as a sign of submission, ordered the Chinese to wear the pigtail. Many of the best and most independent spirits of the time turned their backs on the new rulers and withdrew from public life: they became monks and had their heads shorn so as not to have to wear the pigtail. Many of them entered monasteries, like Shih-ch'i and Hung-jen, while others, such as Shih-t'ao and Pa-ta-shan-jen, took to wandering about the country. The latter two were related to the imperial house of Ming (their official names were Chu Jo-ch'i and Chu Ta) and spent their later years in Yangchow where, upon occasion, they collaborated on the same work. In time, these four highly independent artists came to be known as the Individualists. The two pages from albums by Shih-t'ao seen here (page 387) use blue and red as intensifying colors. Considered the colors of the free spirit, blue and red were used first in landscapes of the Yuan period and are strikingly prominent in pictures by the Individualists.

Contemporary with these impassioned spirits, who felt themselves rejected and so chose voluntary exile, were the so-called Six Famous Masters of the Ch'ing Period (or, more precisely, of the seventeenth century) and they enjoyed the highest social standing. Wang Hui, one of the two younger of the four Wangs, is represented here by two characteristic landscapes (pages 384–86 and 388) and his younger friend Yun Shou-p'ing by a page from an album with a delicate branch of flowers (page 389). Yun Shou-p'ing's flower pictures are for the most part done entirely in color without any preliminary skeleton of ink. This "Western" technique was known and practiced in China as far back as the sixth century, as literary sources tell us, but no early examples have survived. It was not until the eighteenth century, however, that with the Emperor's support European influence actually made its impact felt, though commercial relations had begun in 1517 and through them European objects and books had been introduced into China.

But there was no real effect on the upper strata of society until the arrival of the Jesuit missionaries, especially Castiglione who was awarded the post of privy councilor under his Chinese name of Lang Shih-ning (not the least part of his success was due to his proficiency in the Chinese language). Emperor Ch'ien-lung was interested in everything new and was ready for any experiment (unfortunately, not in painting alone). He had himself portrayed many times with his horse and attendants (page 389) and also required Castiglione to execute for him studies from nature of plants and birds. To Chinese eyes most of these works seemed uncouth, deficient in brush technique and so heavily shaded as to disturb the total impression. Nevertheless, the Emperor insisted that his court painters study under Lang Shih-ning and vice versa. What such docile students turned out can be seen in pictures by Wang Ch'eng-p'ei (page 391) and Tsou I-kuei (page 390). Tsou I-kuei's picture is at least plausible, what with the fine shading of ink, especially in the rocks, and the animated movement of the crane, but Wang Ch'eng-p'ei's shows what happened to a too impressionable student.

A number of important painters kept aloof from the academic circle around Emperor Ch'ien-lung. Of these, the group called the Eight Fauves of Yangchow stands out for the unconstrained way they manipulate ink and for their highly witty compositions. Despite their name, these painters had only the vaguest ties with Yangchow—only Kao Hsiang was actually born there. They took up again the style of the Individualists but coarsened it in a somewhat humorous manner and without the passionate awareness of self so remarkable in their revered predecessors. Besides Kao Hsiang, the group is generally said to comprise Cheng Hsieh, Huang Shen, Li Fang-ying, Wang Shih-shen, Li Shan, Lo P'ing, and Chin Nung, and only the last-named is represented here, although with one of his best works. His *Lo-han* (page 391) shows better than words just what the Chinese mean by a "wild beast of a painter," what we call a Fauve. That these painters, in spite of their coarse brushwork (often they laid on paint with their fingers or a twist of paper), really knew how to wield the instrument is proved by the subtle brush-drawing in the remarkable face of Lo-han. In any case, "wild" and "unorthodox" do not imply any lack of capability. It was this style of free and independent character which Chinese painters took up again in the middle of the last century, above all Jen Po-nien who left a number of paintings full of humor. Like his predecessors of the seventeenth century, he too made use of blue and red, the colors of freedom, particularly in his album of portraits of poets. The portrait of T'ao Yuan-ming reproduced here (page 391) lacks the witty exaggeration of a painter like Chin Nung, though it does reveal a highly individualistic use of the brush.

Jen Po-nien's generation also included Wu

Ch'ang-shih (1844–1927), the teacher of Ch'i Pai-shih (page 392). These men rediscovered, in a somewhat similar situation and with a similar spirit, the seventeenth-century Individualists. That the nineteenth and twentieth centuries produced no fewer great painters than the past is attested by the few examples given here of Jen Po-nien, Ch'i Pai-shih, Hsu Pei-hung, Chao Shao-ang, and Chang Ta-ch'ien (pages 391–94), artists who are in every sense modern but who nevertheless belong to an ancient and still vital tradition.

* * *

The beginnings of Japanese art date from the same time as Japan's appearance in history, the sixth century of our era, when Chinese Buddhism made its way through Korea to gain influence in the island nation. The Regent Shotoku Taishi (552–621) adopted the new religion and gave his support to the Chinese missionaries. Although the early Buddhistic painting and sculpture of China have come down to us only in provincial examples of lesser quality, Japan has conscientiously preserved the art that China, its great master, rejected. To our great loss, the earliest paintings known, the seventh-century frescoes from the Kondo (Golden Hall) of the Horyuji in Nara, were burned after World War II through carelessness. Japan at the outset imitated fairly closely Chinese prototypes on all levels: public administration, city planning, temple architecture, sculpture, and painting. But with the passing of the T'ang Dynasty in China, such close relations declined and by the end of the ninth century contacts were limited to the formal exchange of ambassadors. In the centuries that followed, Japan, quite independently of China, developed its own more refined artistic conceptions.

The earliest Japanese painting reproduced here, which shows Buddha's entrance into Nirvana (page 395), was probably done after a Chinese prototype by Wu Tao-tzu whose depiction of this subject was famous in Eastern Asia. The Heian period (794–1185) was the most fruitful for Buddhist painting in Japan: esoteric Buddhism had become the dominant religion, and its artistic creations were still imbued with the force of conviction. The picture of Red Fudo (page 395) is one of the most significant works of that type.

With the close of the Heian period—also called the Fujiwara period (897–1185) after the most powerful family in the country—art acquired a courtly elegance in which subject matter became almost secondary to manner of treatment. The noble enthroned Buddha Shakyamuni (page 396), with his majestic bearing and elegant gold and red robe, is one of the most impressive works from that time. But then there arose the first completely original style of Japanese painting, the Yamato-e (the name devised to distinguish true Japanese painting from what preceded it).

Buddhist texts from the Sutras, often with particularly beautiful title pictures, as well as non-religious novels were illustrated on hand scrolls intended to be read from right to left in the same way as the script itself. China had known such hand scrolls, but they had never won the significance they enjoyed in Japan where they became the medium for the very finest narrative painting. The Genji-Monogatari scroll (page 397), which recounts the story of Prince Genji, numbers among the most beautiful works of this kind. The artist inserted the text of the novel in a fluent script between the individual illustrations, and these fragments of manuscript are the earliest texts known of the Tale of Genji. Not only do these pictures recount the story, but they also afford us a glimpse of the manners, costumes, and dwellings of the court circles of the time. The painter removes, as it were, the roofs from houses to permit us to look in on the events taking place indoors, and this compositional device makes it possible to present several actions within a single picture. In similar scrolls of later periods, the illustrations became much more numerous and the text was separated from them. Such narratives in pictures were still being done in the Kamakura period (1185–1392) as is shown by the pictorial biography of the priest Ippen (page 399). But the figures were reduced in size and took second place to the landscape, and landscape itself became an independent subject, although it continued to have special significance. The *Nachi Waterfall* (page 400) is such a picture, at one and the same time a view of an actual place and a symbol of the divinity of nature.

The Kamakura period was marked by wars which began with Minamoto Yoritomo, who was named shogun or imperial field marshal, and who transferred the seat of government from Kyoto to Kamakura. During this time, relationships with China were resumed and Zen Buddhism was given an enthusiastic reception, by the military caste above all. Zen called for rigorous discipline and spiritual submission and taught, moreover, that enlightenment could be attained even in the daily round of practical living. Along with this Buddhist sect there came also from China a type of painting whose highest achievement was deemed to be tersely conceived pictures in India ink, either of landscapes or of themes drawn from the Zen teachings. Such an art corresponded to the spirit of the times in Japan and was taken up eagerly, even though it scorned all outward show. The greatest artist in this style of painting in ink, called by the Japanese Sumi-e, was beyond question Sesshu (1420–1506), who himself made several trips to China. The new style notwithstanding, it was the very realistically oriented Kamakura period which also produced the finest and most beautiful portraits. In China, ever since the Sung period, portrait painting was considered fit only for those who were merely painters by trade, and we know practically no examples of it. This is so much the more surprising in that, around 500, Hsieh Ho had laid down the classical formulation for Chinese aesthetics and art criticism, and it was equally applicable to portrait and figure painting. His theory was summed up in his famous Six Canons: (1) animation through spirit consonance, (2) structural method in the use of the brush, (3) fidelity to the object in portraying forms, (4) conformity to kind in applying colors, (5) proper planning in the placing of elements, (6) transmission of the experience of the past in making copies.

Just as ancient Rome especially favored portraiture and achieved its highest perfection in that form, so too there are outstanding examples in Japan. The most significant is certainly that of Yoritomo painted by a distinguished nobleman of the house of Fujiwara, then already in decline (page 398). With a realism carefully held in check, the painter produced a completely convincing portrait of the first imperial marshal in Japanese history. An earlier example, from the Heian period of the middle of the eleventh century, the portrait of the Chinese priest Jion Daishi (page 396), was painted after a Chinese prototype. Still in the courtly tradition of the Fujiwara is the portrait of Kobo Daishi sunk in profound meditation but nevertheless presented as a charming child (page 396). The idealized portrait of the poetess Ko-ogimi (page 398), attributed to a son of Fujiwara Takanobu, is one of the most enchanting of the series of portraits of the thirty-six poets most highly honored and often depicted in Japan. This portrait is quite rightly numbered among the finest of its kind, with the refined woman poet in a graceful pose, her garments decoratively displayed. The last of the outstanding portraits reproduced here is that of the poet Sogi (page 401): very close to the portrait of Yorimoto in its realistic conception, it is fully the equal of that masterwork in the subtlety of its means. The portrait did not die out in Japan but continued to be done right into the period of the great masters of the colored woodcut with their remarkable depictions of actors.

India-ink painting, which began in the Kamakura period, reached its perfect consummation in the Muromachi period (1392–1572), also known as the Ashikaga period. The shoguns of the house of Ashikaga returned the seat of government to Kyoto where they took up again the old traditions of court life. Two Ashikaga shoguns, Yoshimitsu (1358–1408) and his grandson Yoshimasa (1435–90), played a most important role in Oriental art through their passion for collecting. Both were lay priests of the Zen sect and sent monks and painters to China for the purpose of acquiring Zen ink paintings. To their particular affection for the art of the Southern Sung Academy we owe a number of outstanding Chinese pictures which the late Professor Speiser published in his *Meisterwerke chinesischer Malerei aus der Higashiyama Sammlung*. The Ashikagas'

admiration for Chinese Zen painting was to have an enduring effect on Japanese art. Painters were urged and encouraged to try their hands at similar subjects. Sesshu is considered the most famous master of this style, and alongside him is ranked the somewhat younger Kei Shoki (c. 1478–1523) (page 401) who did not himself visit China but, as director of the Geiami Gallery for Ashikaga Yoshimasa in 1478–80, had ample opportunity to study and copy the paintings there. Favorite subjects included not only landscapes but also the patriarchs of the sect, above all Daruma, its founder, whose powerful portrait by Soga Jasoku is reproduced here (page 401). Jasoku, a member of the warrior caste and a lay priest in the Zen sect, retired to a monastery in his old age, as did also the two Ashikaga shoguns.

Whereas the Ashikaga period was under the influence of China, the brief Momoyama period (1573–1615) led to a revival of purely Japanese art. Successors to the effete Ashikagas, the powerful generals Nobunaga and Hideyoshi ruled the country with iron fists. Nobunaga himself did not live to enjoy the power he fought for, but Hideyoshi survived to build for himself, in the vicinity of Kyoto, the Momoyama Palace from which this brief but brilliant period takes its name. To embellish this and other palaces Hideyoshi brought in the finest artists of his time, and they produced those impressive decorative paintings which have become world-famous. The Kano masters excelled in making gleaming blue and gold folding screens, especially Eitoku who had learned how to work with ease on large surfaces from his teacher Motonobu, the founder of the Kano school. Flowers, birds, figures, and landscapes were the themes which in constantly renewed variations were used to cover the walls, utilizing rich gold backgrounds not only for their impressive splendor but even more to cast a shimmering light over everything.

A high point of this kind of painting was reached in the work of Sotatsu whose talent for decorative conceptions was not confined to large-scale paintings. In contrast to the often somewhat stiff and cold effect of the pictures of the Kano school, he introduced a new style of soft but colorful surfaces. In collaboration with his friend Koetsu, today famed chiefly as a calligrapher, he created pictures of extraordinary charm, one of the finest of these being the scroll with deer in the Seattle Art Museum.

If Sotatsu, with his pictures which revived the tradition of Yamato-e (page 404), was the perfect expression of Kyoto, his pupil Korin was the ideal painter of Edo and is acclaimed by many as the greatest genius in Japanese art. Edo—the present-day Tokyo—was the capital of the shoguns of the house of Tokugawa, and the time of their reigns, 1603–1868, is known as the Edo or Tokugawa period. It was a dynasty which brought the country three hundred years of peace and prosperity but, at the same time, isolation from the outside world and nearly the most efficient police state known through the years since then. The middle classes of Edo became wealthy and, lacking the special convictions peculiar to the warrior caste and the intellectuals, they found their pleasure in the things of daily life. They commissioned and bought pictures which corresponded to their own interests: actors, beautiful women, theater, and historical pictures as simple as those in popular illustrated books. The colored woodcut was introduced, and with it came painters who exploited the Ukiyo-e themes, subjects drawn from the transitory world of human life. The first painter to turn out pictures that also satisfied the popular taste in woodcuts was Hishikawa Moronobu (page 405), whose portraits of beautiful women were used as models by many other artists.

But once again a wave of Chinese influence had a decisive effect on Japanese painting. This came from two sources: painters who were seduced by European realism, and others who admired the works of Wen-jen-hua which exemplified the literary art of the late Ming and early Ch'ing periods. The realists made the acquaintance of European copperplate engravings through the Dutch settlement in Nagasaki. Their foremost exponent was Maruyama Okyo who found the way to harmonize fidelity to nature with purely decorative conceptions, although this is perhaps less obvious in the picture of wild geese over the sea (page 407) than in the large pair of portable screens with snow-covered pines in the Mitsui Collection, Tokyo. Rosetsu was the most noteworthy of his pupils and can almost be classed as a master of witty realism (page 408).

The Bunjingwa painters, on the other hand, were conservatives for whom the traditional literature and painting of China sufficed and who used that older style to liberate themselves from the stifling disciplines of the studios. They championed a highly individual way of painting which is perhaps most evident in the works of Gyokudo (page 409) and whose last great master in more recent times was Tomioka Tessai (page 412). Japan's "modern era" began with the Meiji reforms of 1868 when the confining barriers fell and the country was opened to the outside world. When that happened, there was a passionate eagerness to adopt everything new from the West, and many Japanese would have been ready to sell their centuries-old treasures of art. Happily, an American, Ernest Fenollosa, appeared on the scene and succeeded in convincing the authorities to take legal measures for the protection and preservation of the culture of the past. The first public art school was founded—the Academy in Tokyo—and it was there that tradition and modernism were reconciled. An outstanding product of the Academy was Yokoyama Taikwan (pages 411–12). Because of his perpetuation and mastery of the classical Japanese brush techniques he has come to be ranked among the most highly esteemed of modern artists.

In summary, then, China and Japan used the same means: India ink, a paint similar to our tempera, silk, and paper. With these, they both created superb and at the same time very different works of art. The two cultures were most closely related in two specific types of art, early Buddhist painting and India-ink painting, but in spite of all the influences from China the Japanese decorative sense produced a thoroughly indigenous art which belongs unmistakably to Japan itself.

Connoisseurs and scholars may perhaps regret the absence from these pages of many outstanding works known to them, but in assembling these examples it was the aim of the late Professor Speiser to give special prominence to the role played by color in painting of the Far East. For that reason he was particularly concerned that the painting of modern and recent times should be represented here in order to counter the notion that no significant art was produced in the Orient after the seventeenth century. He deliberately chose his examples from among those less frequently reproduced, and this conscientious approach was characteristic of all his work.

Two Hunting Scenes on a Fragment of a Lute · China, 4th century B.C. · Lacquer on wood · From an excavation in Hsin-yang, South Hunan, China

The wood of the lute was first covered with a black lacquer ground, then, on this fragment, painted in lacquer with a scene of two hunters carrying their quarry suspended from a staff slung across their shoulders. Above them are two dogs, to the right an animal resembling a bear, with a dog squatting on its back and the point of a spear pressing into the bear from the front. The painter's means were limited to flat silhouette style with only three colors—bluish violet, flesh red, and yellow. Here and there he laid one color over the other and then rubbed the top one away to make a subtle transition from red to yellow, as in the bear's head. The taut curves and silhouette style have much in common with objects of the time in jade or bronze.

Filial Piety · China, 1st century A.D. · Lacquer on wood · Length, 15⅜″ · From an excavation in Lo-Lang, Korea · National Museum, Seoul

This small pannier with separate lid was made in a lacquer manufactory in Szechwan and probably served as a gift to a minor colonial official. Geometrical motifs in red on a black ground are painted on the borders, and some of the corners are decorated with figures. The lid is ornamented by a frieze of figures depicting a theme much favored in the Han period, that of filial piety. The figures, in their colorful patterned garments, are well individualized. They are no longer rendered merely in profile and silhouette, but face each other in a diversity of positions and express themselves in lively gestures. From this product of an artisan's workshop we can glean some notion of what figure painting of the time must have been like.

Carriages and Horsemen · China, 2nd century A.D. · Fresco (detail) · Height, 42⅞″ · From a tomb in Liao-yang, Manchuria, near Port Arthur

Carriages with court dignitaries attended by outriders gallop across a landscape. The dominant colors are red and black. To give an impression of depth, of nearness and distance, the figures are disposed one above the other. Although the carriages are drawn in three-quarter profile, thus allowing us to see their passengers, some of whom are likewise in three-quarter profile, the horses are rendered in pure profile. This limitation, combined with their sweeping contour lines, recalls the earlier silhouette style. However, similar depictions of carriages and horsemen are found on the molded tiles and relief-plaques from tombs of the same period, especially in northern China.

Hunting Scene · China, c. 400 · Detail of a fresco in the Tomb of the Dancers · T'ung-kou on the Yalu River

Until 427, the capital of the North Korean Kokuryo dynasty was located in T'ung-kou on the middle Yalu. In the environs were many splendidly painted tomb chambers whose contents were despoiled long ago. The frescoes remain, however, and show the things that delight men in death as in life. Here, for example, are hunters on horseback, aiming their bows both forward and backward at deer and beasts of prey. Their horses seem to fly as they gallop, and this peculiarity, along with the special technique of aiming the bow, suggests some connection with the Near East. New in Chinese painting was the depiction of landscape through semicircular flat mountain forms rising directly from the ground, like flat pieces of stage scenery. We can be quite certain that fresco painting in China at the same period must have been much like this, even if this highly animated though modest example does not allow us to draw conclusions about the work of Ku K'ai-chih, reputed to be the most famous figure painter of the time.

The Good Deeds of Buddha · Northwest China, c. 450 ·
Detail of a fresco in the Caves of the Thousand Buddhas,
Tun-huang

In many frescoes of the Caves of the Thousand Buddhas
near Tun-huang we find depictions of the Jataka, the fables
of the good deeds accomplished by Buddha before his birth
into our world. Here, in the so-called Ruru-Jataka, he
appears as a golden gazelle rescuing a despairing man who
had thrown himself into the water. At the left we see the
rescued man astride the gazelle; at the right he kneels in
gratitude before the fabulous creature. The landscape is
built out of a number of elements like stage flats which,
for all their unrealistic coloring, clearly represent small
stratified mountain peaks. This kind of symbolic representation of landscape belongs to an ancient Near Eastern
tradition, and is found in Sassanian silver work of a later
period.

Buddha and the Wild Animals · Northwest China, early 6th
century · Detail of a fresco in the Caves of the Thousand
Buddhas, Tun-huang.

The cave temples of Tun-huang lie on the overland route
to India used by the Chinese Buddhist pilgrims. Along with
innumerable Buddhist statues, they contain brightly colored
frescoes. The surfaces are divided into horizontal bands
by means of fantastically colored trees and stage-wing-like
rocky peaks. The pictures must be read from right to left,
like the later hand or transverse scrolls so familiar in
Eastern Asiatic art. In this detail, the middle band shows
two episodes from the earlier existence of Buddha: in the
first scene, impelled by his deep compassion for all creatures, he throws himself off a rock as food for the hungry
young of a tigress; in the second, the tigress creeps up on
the lifeless body. The rocks serve not only as a horizontal
division but also to create a certain feeling of space.

Landscape · Japan, first half of 8th century · Box lid ·
Painted in gold and silver on persimmon wood · $7\frac{1}{8} \times 15\frac{1}{4}''$ ·
Shosoin, Nara

The upper surface was first colored with a dye from the sap
of the sapan tree and then painted in gold and silver (the
plain strip of the upper border is an addition). The decoration of the lid is designed to be viewed from all four sides, at
each of which is a separate small composition, complete in
itself, but combining to form a single large composition.
At each of the four sides there are rocky peaks in the conventional stage-flat shapes, but well articulated. These are
painted in gold, as are the trees, mostly pines, whose tips
are touched with silver. The landscapes are enlivened by a
diversity of birds and by ruffling clouds rising up between
the peaks. The handling of the birds and clouds reveals a
kind of playful pleasure in animated brush drawing of a
mastery we have not met with before this. Such painting
would scarcely have come into being without Chinese
prototypes. Most probably the Japanese artists who did this
kind of work were pupils of Chinese or Koreans, if the latter
themselves did not execute it.

Jataka Scene · Japan, beginning of 7th century · Side of the
Tamamushi Shrine · Lacquer on wood · Height, $25\frac{5}{8}''$ ·
Horyuji, Nara

The episode from the earlier existence of Buddha depicted
here is the same as that in *Buddha and the Wild Animals*
(at left), but here the sequence must be read from top to
bottom: Buddha hangs his garment on a tree, then plunges
down, and is devoured in a bamboo grove by the tigress
and her young. The Buddha has pronounced Indian
features, but the rocky cliffs recall Chinese decoration of the
Han period (200 B.C.–A.D. 200). The filigreed fittings at the
corners were originally underlaid with iridescent wings of
the Tamamushi beetle—which is how the shrine came by its
name. The entire altar is about six and a half feet high and
resembles a two-storied temple. Certainly the shrine and its
lacquer decoration are Japanese work, though whether it is
as closely connected with Chinese painting as Professor
Speiser proposed must remain an open question.

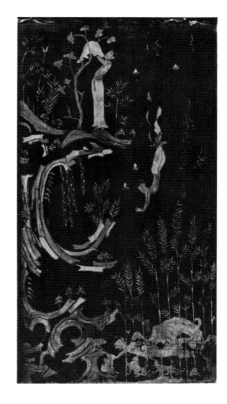

373

Music in the Mountains · Japan, 8th century (traditional dating) · Painting on leather · Maximum dimensions, 16 × 6½″ · Shosoin, Nara

This painting comes from the central part of the soundboard of a large four-stringed lute *(biwa).* To protect the soundboard from the blows of the heavy plectrum used to pluck the strings, a band of leather was glued across it which, as here, was then decorated. On the white ground *(gofun)* of the leather, we see in the foreground a white elephant ridden by a bearded man of Indo-Iranian type who beats a drum while three children dance and play flutes. Through a cleft in the steep crags, in the center background, runs a watercourse, and behind it we see the sun setting over the high horizon. A flock of birds flies toward the setting sun. Because the painting was covered with a coat of varnish to protect it from the strokes of the plectrum, the more delicate shades of green, yellow, and various reds can scarcely be made out. The sensitively conceived landscape with its animated painting gives us a foretaste of what the finest Chinese painting of the T'ang period was to be, and it is highly likely that this work was done by a Chinese master.

Woman under a Tree · Japan, middle of 8th century · Detail of a wall screen · India ink and pale color on paper · Length of the face, 4½″ · Shosoin, Nara

This proud beauty with her rouged lips and rosy cheeks has tiny green beauty spots strategically placed on her forehead and on either side of her mouth to enhance the colors and animation of the face. She exemplifies the aristocratic ideal of beauty of the T'ang period in China, as we know it from many tomb figures. Even if the artist was himself Japanese, he followed Chinese models so closely that we can almost speak of a copy, perhaps of one of the unfortunately badly damaged pictures found in the oasis of Turfan in Central Asia.

The Tejeprabha Buddha and the Genii of the Five Planets · China, dated 897 · India ink and color on silk · 27⅛ × 20½″ · From the Cave of the Thousand Buddhas, Tun-huang · British Museum, London

The Tejeprabha Buddha, surrounded by a gold-rayed glory, sits on a high two-wheeled chariot drawn over the clouds by two white oxen. The figures around the chariot represent the planets: Mercury in the background, an ape perched on his crown, holds up a brush and a writing tablet; to his left is Jupiter with a white boar's head as his chief ornament; the bearded, dark-skinned oxherd is Saturn; Venus plays a lute and wears a cock on her head; to her right stands Mars, a four-armed warrior-demon with sword, spear, and bow in his hands. The rayed glory behind the Buddha suggests influence from the Near East with which China had commercial relations in the seventh and eighth centuries. It was in that period, also, that the figure of Buddha Tejeprabha as Lord of the Planets was popular in China, and so it may be that this picture was done earlier than the date indicates.

Domestic Scene · China, dated 1099 · Detail of a wall painting · 49¼ × 39⅜″ · Pai-sha, Honan Province, China

The tile-faced tombs in Pai-sha contain innumerable frescoes whose scenes from daily life were intended to guarantee happiness for the deceased in the other world. This detail comes from the west wall of the first tomb, which was discovered and excavated in 1951–52. A distinguished couple sit on high stools at a table. Behind each is a portable screen with lacquered frame and gilded angle braces. On the table are wine cups with high saucers and a tankard with ribbed body, very narrow neck, and modeled lid. Objects like these, and like the vessels held by the male and female servants, can be found in numerous collections of Chinese and Korean ceramics of that period. In the Sung period, lifelike genre scenes with figures were a favorite subject of even the famous painters, though we know few original works of the time.

Autumn Landscape · Northern China, 1031 · Detail of a wall painting from the mausoleum of Emperor Sheng-tsung · Total dimensions, 142⅞ × 119¼″ · Ch'ing-ling (Balin), Mongolia

The Liao or Khitan people who founded an independent kingdom in northern China were horsemen and hunters. One of the favorite hunting regions of Emperor Sheng-tsung (d. 1022) was in the Ch'ing-ling Mountains, and his son and grandson built him there a subterranean mausoleum of tiles. In the foreground of this wall painting of an autumn landscape, there is a bellowing stag on a knoll, birds in flight, and red-leafed trees. The rather naïve conception of the landscape, with all its elements distinct and separate, resembles that of the T'ang period. The lively coloring in the fantastic cloudbank, the trees and animals outlined in firm though not very vigorous brush strokes, both reveal the hand of a well-schooled painter.

Attributed to EMPEROR HUI-TSUNG (1082–1135) *Quail and Narcissus* · China · Leaf of an album · India ink and color on paper · 10⅝ × 16½″ · Collection Asano, Kanagawa, Japan

Emperor Hui-tsung of the Sung dynasty, who ascended the throne at nineteen and reigned from 1101 to 1127, is not only the most famous but also the most significant of China's emperor-painters. Moreover, he is the first of the Chinese artists whose names we know and whose paintings have survived, though many more works have been attributed to him than one can be sure are from his hand, among them this quail near a narcissus plant. There exist many anecdotes about what a scrupulous observer of nature Hui-tsung was, and about how his attentive eyes never missed any detail. Nevertheless, no one would be tempted to consider as merely a realistic study from nature this picture done in a classical style characterized by confining the principal subject to a single corner of the composition. With the subtlest of brush techniques the artist contrasts the strong colors of the quail with the gentle sway of the narcissus to create an indelible impression of springtime. Had he been as secure and skillful a sovereign as he was painter and patron of the arts, his country might well have been spared war and conquest.

375

Attributed to CHAO CH'ANG *Bamboo and Insects* (detail) ·
China, c. 1000 · Color on silk · Total dimensions, 39 × 8¾″ ·
Collection Asano, Kanagawa, Japan

Chao Ch'ang, whose exact dates are unknown, is among the
most highly esteemed flower painters of China. This picture
and another on the same subject appear to have been
formerly in the Higashiyama Collection in Japan, and the
attribution to Chao Ch'ang rests at least on a long tradition.
Chao Ch'ang did not belong to the Sung Academy, though
he could not entirely resist the appeal of the subject matter
and style of those masters. It is said of him that he painted
the souls and not merely the outward forms of plants. In the
varicolored profusion of insects and plants of this picture,
the richly nuanced color is linked with a delight in detail and
with a sure feeling for the distribution of colors. The
gleaming red of the flowers and the white of the butterflies
are not just accents of color in and for themselves, but also
confer on the various shades of green an extraordinary
brilliance which has survived intact through the centuries.

Mandarin Ducks beneath Peach Blossoms · China, late 12th
century · India ink and color on silk · 41½ × 19¼″ · Museum,
Shanghai

From early times in China, mandarin ducks in pairs have
been a symbol of marital concord, and this has been a
favorite motif in the various arts and crafts. Here, with a
scrupulous precision that must certainly be the work of one
of the best painters of the Southern Sung Academy, the
ducks are placed together with peach blossoms to symbolize not only connubial bliss but also springtime. In the
finely balanced composition, the dry grass blades and first
green leaves of spring lead into the picture like the first line
of a stanza in poetry, the pair of ducks express the inner
meaning of the theme, and the peach tree branches with
their delicate pink blossoms round off the image and carry
the eye up to the upper margin.

Attributed to LI AN-CHUNG (c. 1090–1160) *Quail* · China ·
Leaf of an album · Color on silk · 9½ × 10⅝″ · Nezu Museum,
Tokyo

Li An-chung is one of the artists rather neglected in China,
but in Japan, since quite early times, he has been very
highly regarded, especially as a painter of quails. Many
paintings in Japanese collections are attributed to him, and
the present one is certainly among the finest of its kind.
Whether it is correctly attributed to Li An-chung remains an
open question, but there is no doubt that it is a brilliant
example of the painting of the Southern Sung Academy,
and it was not out of place in the great Higashiyama
Collection to which it once belonged. In the division of the
picture surface, almost half is left free, but the center is more
emphasized than in the painting on the subject by Hui-
tsung (page 375). Secure mastery in brush technique is
revealed in the veins of the leaves as much as in the ebb and
flow of the lines of the wavy ground on which the bird
stands. The red of the buds, introducing a note of animation
into the picture, shows the artist's subtle feeling for color.

376

LI TI (1089–after 1174) *Herdsman Returning Home through the Snow with a Hare* · China · India ink and color on silk · 9⅜ × 9⅝″ · Yamato-Bunka-kan Museum, Osaka

Li Ti was among the painters who, together with Kao-tsung, the nephew of the unfortunate Emperor Hui-tsung, fled across the Yangtse to the south, where they carried on the work of their academy in the new residence city of Hangchow. Kao-tsung, himself a painter, encouraged the arts at least as much as his uncle. Of the innumerable works of the Southern Sung Academy, a few found their way into the Higashiyama Collection, among them two pictures by Li Ti. These latter were painted as a pair, though each is complete and artistically valid in itself, as the example given here, the left-hand panel, proves. The composition left open on one side as well as the displacement of the center of gravity to a corner are entirely typical of the feeling for style of the period. The gray-toned empty sweep of the sky filled by the white of the snow-laden branches admirably expresses the chill and hostile winter's day, as does the humble figure of the herdsman with his ox.

Winter Landscape · China, late 12th century · India ink and pale color on silk · 50 × 21½″ · Konchi-in, Kyoto

In the past, as today, Chinese landscape painters were particularly fond of the seasons as a subject, and especially the cycle of all four seasons. Thus there is an autumn landscape from the hand of the same master who did this winter scene. Both works were once in the Higashiyama Collection and for a long time were attributed to Emperor Hui-tsung. Whoever the artist really was—probably a member of the Southern Sung Academy—there can be no doubt that he was a landscape painter of importance. The wanderer, in dark cowl and carrying a staff, has stopped in his path for a last look at the waterfall plunging down from snow-covered rocks and to listen to the cry of the apes in the tree above the water. The figure serves to lead our eye on, but is also an inseparable part of the landscape, as much so as the rocks and water. This is so not only because it is viewed from the back but, even more, because of its tiny proportions in relation to the whole. Unfortunately, no reproduction can possibly capture the delicate coloring which emphasizes even more the gleaming snow on the bamboo trees.

Attributed to SU HAN-CH'EN (c. 1119–63) *Children Playing* · China · India ink and color on silk · 53⅞ × 29¾″ · Formerly Collection Kawasaki, Kobe

Su Han-ch'en was a famous member of the Academy in Kaifeng at the time of Hui-tsung. He was one of those who "crossed the river," that is, he fled with the Emperor's nephew to Hangchow where his presence is documented even after the abdication of Kao-tsung in 1163. Hangchow's gardens were famous; because of them it was called the Heavenly City. Something of this paradisical feeling carries over into the painting done there. Such a garden is seen here, with its flowering trees, decorative rocks, and peonies. The artist was no less skillful in depicting the children in their gay-colored, richly patterned garments. One of them tries vainly to disentangle his playmate's kite from the willow branches while another helps him by steadying the stool on which he stands, and at the same time teasingly holds up the youngest child's puppet. Though it is possible that this picture may be only a copy, it gives us, nevertheless, an excellent notion of the lively coloring and kind of subject matter which brought fame to Su Han-ch'en in his own time.

The Homecoming of Wen-chi · China, 12th century · Detail of a hand scroll · India ink and color on silk · Height, 9⅞″ · Museum of Fine Arts, Boston

This scroll showing four episodes from the life of Lady Ts'ai Wen-chi is among the finest of the four surviving scenes from daily life by the Sung Academy painters. During the invasion of the Huns in 195, Lady Wen-chi was taken prisoner and deported. In captivity she married a Hun prince and bore him two sons. After twelve years she was permitted to return home. There exists a cycle of eighteen poems, traditionally ascribed to the Lady herself, which describe her life in the other land, her sorrowful farewell to her children, and the return to the cultured environment of her homeland. The detail shown here, her arrival at her own home, affords a glimpse of the busy life of a street in China: at the right, the dwelling of Wen-chi, in front of which the people who came to greet her are gathered in excited conversation; her carriage is hauled by oxen, and street vendors offer food to the men of the Lady's escort. The artist shows great subtlety in his use of the black of India ink to accent and enliven the colors.

LIU SUNG-NIEN (c. 1174–1230) *Palace Ladies in a Garden* · China · Leaf of an album · India ink and color on silk · 10⅛ × 10⅝″ · Formerly Collection Kuroda, Tokyo

Liu Sung-nien came from the south, from Hangchow, and was first a pupil and later a high official of the Academy which awarded him the high honor of the Golden Girdle. Along with Ma Yuan and Hsia Kuei he is reckoned among the greatest painters of the turn of the century, and his fame was based equally on his landscape and figure painting. This small page from an album shows once again the popularity of scenes from domestic life in China at that period. In this glimpse of a garden in Hangchow, we sense something of the loveliness for which that city was renowned. The very subtle painting of the ladies in their delicately patterned gowns with flowing shawls recalls an artist like Chou Wen-chu (c. 970), who treated the same subjects, though scarcely any original works of his have come down to us. The figures are outlined with such precise brushwork that it would not be difficult to cut them out with scissors. This by itself suffices to prove the artist's control and mastery of his medium, but it is matched by a beautifully balanced use of color such as can be expected only from a very great artist.

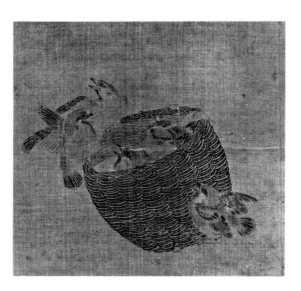

Attributed to SUNG JU-CHIH (c. 1260–80) *Sparrows in a Basket* · China · Leaf of an album · India ink and pale color on silk · 8⅝ × 8⅝″ · Collection Asano, Kanagawa

Sung Ju-chih was another who came from Hangchow and was a member of the Academy there. At the beginning of the Yuan dynasty, in 1278, he entered a Taoist monastery. It is said that he painted landscapes, figures, flowers and birds, but very few of his works are known. This small page from an album, belonging to an exquisite Japanese collection, may very well be ascribed to him. In any case it is a precious example of the painting of the late Southern Sung Academy done in the best academic style as laid down by Hui-tsung. The finely balanced composition built on a diagonal axis with its center of gravity almost in the middle still leaves enough room on the tiny page to avoid any impression of crowding. The basket and birds are depicted in animated fashion by strong, precise brush strokes, and the brown of the sparrows' plumage is subordinated to the delicate shadings of the black India ink.

378

Attributed to CH'IEN HSUAN (1235–c. 1302) *The Flute Player Huan Yeh-wang* · China · India ink and color on silk · 34 × 11¾" · Formerly Collection Kawasaki, Kobe

Here we have one of the greatest of China's painters. He was a friend of Chao Meng-fu who was some twenty years his junior, but unlike the latter he accepted no official position under the Mongols of the Yuan dynasty. He held himself aloof from the court, and it is believed that his friendship with Chao ended because of political differences. It was said of Ch'ien Hsuan that he aspired to revive the art of the Northern Sung and T'ang periods, and among the paintings ascribed to him with some certainty, some at least are on subjects frequent under the T'ang dynasty. To what extent we have authentic works by Ch'ien Hsuan cannot as yet be proved. Certainly this portrait of Huan Yeh-wang corresponds to his period and style, and one need only observe the delicacy with which the loop of gauze on the hood is painted to know that it is a masterpiece. Huan Yeh-wang was a courtier of the fourth century famed for his flute playing. Here his instrument is tucked into his girdle while the gentleman busies himself with his fingernails. His red garment stands out most effectively against the brown ground, and the tiny blue brooch on his hood lends liveliness to the other colors.

FANG TS'UNG-I (documented 1338–77) *After the Rain* · China, dated 1349 · India ink and pale color on paper · 39 × 17" · Collection King Kwei, Hongkong

Fang Ts'ung-i came from Kuei-ch'i in Kiangsi province. He was a Taoist and lived most of his life withdrawn from the world in the Shang-ch'ing temple on Lung-hu Mountain near his native town. At the upper left of the landscape is an inscription by the artist recounting that he painted this picture on the sixteenth day of the third month of spring in 1349. The longer inscription in two parts is a poem by the famous painter Wen Chen-ming (1470–1559) written in 1535. The rain has stopped, but its haze lingers on above the river and twines like veils around the base of the mountain on the far bank. Despite its isolated prominence, the tiny figure in red on the shelf of rock in the foreground is there only as one more aspect of nature. The pagoda rising between trees on the left may belong to the Shang-ch'ing temple, and the view over the river may well be one familiar to Fang Ts'ung-i during his many years of seclusion; however, the artist's aim was to portray not any specific place but rather the essence of nature as revealed in the landscape.

379

SHEN CHOU (1427–1509) *The Mighty Mount Lu* · China, dated 1467 · India ink and pale color on paper · 76¼ × 38⅝″ · Palace Museum, Taichung, Taiwan (Formosa)

Shen Chou, one of those known as the Four Great Painters of the Ming period, belonged to a prominent family in Suchow. He passed the state examination, but disdained an official position, preferring instead to remain in Suchow and indulge his inclinations. He became famed as a calligrapher, painter, and poet, and was friendly with most of the scholars and artists of his time. This mountain landscape embodies a powerful compositional scheme which begins with the topmost peak and runs down in a bold S-curve to come to rest in the splendid clump of pines in the lower foreground. The energetic, transcendent spirit of a great painter is revealed in the brushwork of the extremely subtle calligraphic lines in the trees, the contours of the separate crags, and the waves of the stream. It appears also in the powerful accents of stippling such as that on the highest mountain peak (the latter a technique for which Shen Chou was especially famed). The tiny spots of color on the trees jutting out between the rocky crags are subordinate to the wide scale of tonal values of India ink which is the basic medium of the painting, because they intensify the suggestion of color inherent in that scale.

LU CHI (documented 1477–1505) *Winter* · India ink and color on silk · 69 × 39¾″ · National Museum, Tokyo

Lu Chi, who came from Ning-po in Chekiang, was only twenty when he was called to the court in Peking where he rose to high honors. His specialty was decorative flower and bird pictures—his teacher was Pien Wen-chin—done in the style of the Sung Academy, in accord with the prevailing taste at the imperial court. His pictures are for the most part of large dimensions, intended less for the appreciation of small groups of connoisseurs than for display in the great halls of palaces. This winter scene belongs to a cycle of the Four Seasons with birds and flowers. A pair of pheasants is seen on the snow-covered bank of a stream, and there are plum trees in blossom with sparrows, bamboo plants, red camellias, and barberry shrubs. Energetically drawn, the stream winding through the mountains divides the composition asymmetrically. While the hatched drawing of the cliffs, which seem to be hewn by an ax, may be related to the restrained India-ink landscapes of the Southern Sung Academy, the gleaming colors lend the picture a quite extraordinary decorative character. Lu Chi was one of the most famous artists of his time at the court of Peking, a highly skilled painter who came to exert great influence, especially on the eighteenth century.

YAO SHOU (1423–95) *Red Plum Blossoms* · China · Hand scroll · India ink and color on paper · 15⅝ × 48″ · Collection King Kwei, Hongkong

The family of Yao Shou was of some importance in Chiashan in Chekiang province, and his father, Yao Fu, had a certain reputation as a painter. Yao Shou passed the highest state examinations and for a time, in his mid-sixties, had an official position. But he left public service and returned to his native place where he built a house whose name came to be identified with his, so that he was called the Master of the Cinnabar Hill. He belongs among the painters of the early Ming dynasty who continued to work in the tradition of the Yuan period, and the three great painters of that period, Wu Chen, Wang Meng, and Chao Meng-fu, were the models he chose. Besides being a painter he was also a poet and an excellent calligrapher. In China, plum blossoms together with bamboos and pines constitute the "Three Friends of the Cold Season," since their flowering begins when snow is still on the ground. Even without an inscription, the artist's skill as a calligrapher shows in every line of the energetically curving branch which, with the delicate rose of its blossoms, is in contrast with the gnarled tree trunk the artist has painted by overlaying areas of wet color.

CH'IU YING (c. 1500–1550) *Two Houseboats with Gentlemen and Ladies* · China · Leaf of an album · India ink and color on silk · 9½ × 9½″ · Formerly Collection Kuroda, Tokyo

Of the "Four Great Painters of the Ming Period"—Shen Chou, T'ang Yin, Wen Cheng-ming, and Ch'iu Ying—the latter was the youngest. Unlike the other three, he did not come from landed gentry and earned his bread mostly as a lacquer painter and a copyist of T'ang and Sung pictures. He came from T'ai-ts'ang in the outer environs of Shanghai but, like his three associates, lived most of his life in Soochow. T'ang Yin's teacher, Ch'en, discovered the young man's talent and took him as a pupil, as did later T'ang Yin himself, with whom Ch'iu Ying enjoyed the deepest friendship. Ch'iu Ying's preference for scenes from everyday life may derive both from his teacher and from prototypes of the T'ang and Sung periods. The excellence of this small painting, which bears the artist's seal, explains why he is ranked alongside the famous figure painters Chou Wen-chu (c. 961–75) and Su Han-ch'en (page 377).

WEN CHENG-MING (1470–1559) *The Studio at Chen Shang* · China, dated 1549 · Detail of a hand scroll · India ink and pale color on paper · Total dimensions, 14⅛ × 42½″ · Museum, Shanghai

Wen Cheng-ming (Wen Pi) belonged to a family of scholars and public officials in Soochow. He lived for a time in the capital, Peking, where, as an associate of the Han-lin Academy of Literature, he helped compile and edit the official history of the Yuan dynasty. Soon, however, he returned to his homeland to devote the rest of his long life to painting, poetry, and calligraphy. He had a large circle of students and friends, and his painting continued to be influential right up to the late sixteenth century. For his friend Lord Hua Hsia, a famous collector of the time, Wen Cheng-ming painted this scroll showing his own studio, a subject he took up again eight years later. This detail shows the house open on the garden, and in it two distinguished gentlemen looking at some writing while a boy serves them. The weirdly shaped garden rocks and the gnarled pine trees are a good indication of this artist's fine brushwork. The tiny red spot of a stool suffices to intensify the delicate blue of the rocks and mountains, the green of the pines, and the brown of the tree trunks.

T'ANG YIN (1470–1524) *Domestic Scene* · China · India ink and color on paper · 58¾ × 26″ · Palace Museum, Taichung, Taiwan (Formosa)

Like Wen Cheng-ming, T'ang Yin came from Soochow. His father was a modest tradesman, but the father of Wen Cheng-ming was willing to sponsor his son's gifted friend who had passed his examinations brilliantly but who, at the last moment, lost all chance of a position because of a scandal involving cheating. Disillusioned, the young man returned home and lived by painting. There he enjoyed the friendship of Shen Chou, Wen Cheng-ming, and Ch'iu Ying, and a life of wine and beautiful women—his reputation rests especially on his portrayals of the latter. The subject of this painting is a story of the T'ang period about the beautiful courtesan Li Tuan-tuan of Yangchow who attracted the attention of a poet and was praised by him in his poem "The White Peony Who Walks." Here she stands holding the white flower while the poet and her serving woman gaze at her. Two portable screens, set up to protect the beauty from the eyes of the curious and from the wind in the garden, reveal T'ang Yin's great talent as a landscape painter.

TUNG CH'I-CH'ANG (1566–1636) *The Winding Valley* · China · Detail of a hand scroll · India ink and pale color on silk · 16 × 267⅛″ · City Art Museum, Osaka

Tung Ch'i-ch'ang was a member of an eminent family of Hua-t'ing who lived in Peking and on the Western Sea near Hangchow. He was a minister, tutor to the crown-prince, outstanding painter and calligrapher, writer on art, collector, and connoisseur. The influence of his powerful individuality can still be traced in the following century. As a highly placed official he was often beseeched by friends for a picture—a practice quite common in China. Naturally, he could not easily refuse these requests, which is why not every work that bears his authentic signature is, in fact, by his hand. Two of his pupils and friends, themselves recognized painters, Chao Tso and Shen Shih-ch'ung, often furnished him with a way out of such embarrassing situations. This scroll, in linear style, is considered authentic and typifies his classical insistence that each and every brush stroke be complete and traceable from its beginning to its end. Such completely linear drawing, especially that of the trees which are only slightly emphasized by added color, reveals the hand of a brilliant calligrapher.

TUNG CH'I-CH'ANG *Hut beneath Crags* · China · Leaf of an album · India ink and pale color on silk · 10⅞ × 10⅜″ · National Museum, Tokyo

This landscape from an album containing six landscapes and ten examples of calligraphy belongs, like the preceding scroll, among the authentic works of this artist. When we examine these two pictures, we can understand why Tung Ch'i-ch'ang's two "ghost" painters had to divide their tasks into their separate specialties: Chao Tso did the calligraphy, Shen Shih-ch'ung the painting. Unlike the scroll in the previous plate, what dominates in this landscape is less the linear than the formal element. It has a freshness of conception often lacking in the drier calligraphic approach. The foliage of the trees, delicately touched with color, contrasts markedly with the broadly washed-in mountains of the background. Yet, even at his most painterly, Tung Ch'i-ch'ang never abandons his linear style, as shown by the contrasts of the tree trunks and by the brush line which outlines the silhouette of the great mountain to the rear.

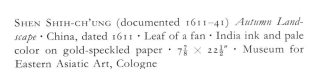

SHEN SHIH-CH'UNG (documented 1611–41) *Autumn Landscape* · China, dated 1611 · Leaf of a fan · India ink and pale color on gold-speckled paper · 7⅞ × 22½″ · Museum for Eastern Asiatic Art, Cologne

Like the preceding artist, Shen Shih-ch'ung also came from Hua-t'ing. His exact dates are not known, but he was a friend and pupil of Chao Tso and of Tung Ch'i-ch'ang, for whom he often painted pictures which the latter signed and gave as gifts. Shen Shih-ch'ung ranks among the most charming artists of the early seventeenth century, and in his calligraphically delicate and yet strong linear drawing he shows himself a worthy pupil of his master. In this clear autumn landscape, the open hut on the foothill at the opposite side of the stream puts one in mind of the great Yuan painter Ni Tsan (1301–74) whose unpeopled landscapes are characterized by such motifs.

LI SHIH-TA (documented 1574–1620) *Landscape with Figures* · China · Leaf of a fan · India ink and pale color on gold-speckled paper · 7⅛ × 22″ · Museum for Eastern Asiatic Art, Cologne

Li Shih-ta was a native of Soochow and passed the state examination, although it is not known if he ever held any official position. Even in his lifetime he was famed as a figure and landscape painter. Narrative subjects like this were strictly taboo for the classicists such as Tung Ch'i-ch'ang and his circle, but had been familiar ever since the Sung period. Accompanied by two servants carrying books, scrolls, and a parasol, the tall gentleman rides toward his house where another servant waits for him at the open door and where his books are already laid out for him on the table. The landscape is impregnated with a feeling of clarity and contemplativeness whose mood is well expressed by the double line of writing at the edge of the fan: "In the distance I see the weary-hanging willows of evening. In the house I feel autumn enter in the midst of old mountains."

LAN YING (1585–c. 1664) *Autumn Landscape* · China, dated 1642 · Leaf of an album · India ink and color on gold-speckled paper · 14⅛ × 13¾″ · Collection Hoshijima

Another painter from a prominent family was Lan Ying of Hangchow. He is considered the last follower of Tai Wen-chin (c. 1430–50), who had revived the Sung style of painting and founded the Chekiang school. Lan Ying never sat for any examination or held any official position. He painted figures and landscapes, flowers and birds, bamboos and rocks, often in the style of the Southern Sung Academy though the great Yuan masters were also his models. It is said of his pictures that the trees seem as if the scurfy flesh of old witches had been pulled over them. He was, in fact, a thoroughly independent painter, and all the rather exaggeratedly theoretical objections to his art one reads in the Chinese literature are confuted by this single precious page of an album. According to the inscription, the picture is meant to be in the style of the Yuan painter Chao Meng-fu (1254–1322), but it has about as much resemblance to its prototype as a statue by Rodin has to one by Michelangelo. Compared with the works by Tung Ch'i-ch'ang, the pontiff of art of his time, this picture impresses one by its strong color. The malachite green of the patches of moss on the stones combined with the gold of the heavily speckled paper creates an immediate effect of brilliance such as was vigorously banned by the classicistic circles of the period.

383

SHEN SHU-YU (documented 1667) *Winter Landscape* · China · Leaf of an album · India ink and pale color on paper · 10⅝ × 12⅛″ · Museum for Eastern Asiatic Art, Cologne

Shen Shu-yu lived in Hangchow, but practically nothing is known of his life. The single date we have for him—1667, when he received a commission for a painting—tells us nothing about his age or his position in the new Manchu dynasty of the Ch'ing. What is more, scarcely enough works have survived to make it possible to sum up his creative activity. Nevertheless, we can recognize a painter of deep feeling in this leaf from an album formerly containing eight landscapes, two of which are now in Cologne. The verse inscription contains an allusion to a poem about snow by Su Tung-p'o (1036–1101), the most famous poet of the Sung dynasty and also a painter, statesman, historian, and writer of high rank. But we have no need of the poem to explain this winter landscape. The gray sky heavy with snow fills the entire surface so that we cannot tell where the sky leaves off and the sea begins. A man sits in the pavilion enjoying his solitude and the view of the Western Sea which is among Hangchow's many beauties. The green of the pines makes one feel, by contrast, the cold of the snow whose whiteness is further emphasized by the black patches against the ice in the foreground.

TAO CHI (SHIH-T'AO) (1630–c. 1707) *Landscape* · China · Leaf of an album · India ink and pale color on paper · 10⅝ × 15¼″ · City Art Museum, Osaka

Tao Chi came from a side branch of the Ming Imperial House (family name, Chu), and is best known under the name he used as an artist, Shih-t'ao. Born in Chuanchow in Kwangsi province, he became a monk in 1644 after the overthrow of the dynasty and undertook many voyages which led him into far-flung regions of China. In 1697, toward the end of his life, he settled in Yang-chow where he died around 1707. Along with Shih-ch'i, Pa-ta Shan-jen, and Hung-jen, he is reckoned among the "Individualists" of the seventeenth century, who refused to serve the new rulers and to wear, as a sign of subjection, the pigtail, and so had their heads shaved and became Buddhist monks. In a different time, they might all have pursued official careers; now, instead, they withdrew into monasteries and painted. Shih-t'ao was perhaps the most free and forceful personality among them. This painting from an album with twelve pictures reduces the landscape to its essential components. According to the stylistic criteria worked out by Victoria Contag, it must be a late work, painted with very powerful, even hard, but highly economical brush strokes. The predominant reds and blues—the colors of the free spirit— are contrasted with the strong accents of black in the trees on the right and in the cliffs.

TAO CHI (SHIH-T'AO) *The Glimmering Peak* · China · Leaf of an album · India ink and pale color on paper · 9⅝ × 6⅞″ · Museum for Eastern Asiatic Art, Cologne

This picture belongs to an album with twelve views of Mount Lo-fou in southern China, each of which is accompanied by a written description on the facing page. The album was probably painted by Shih-t'ao on one of his voyages between 1660 and 1670. The very loose brushwork and the light coloring give no more than a hint of the powerful accentuation of his later work and suggest a relatively early date for the album. Three travelers melt into the landscape and become so much a part of the whole that at first one hardly notices them. Again there are black accents in the pines and other trees which draw the eye to the most remote chain of hills beyond the opposite bank.

WANG HUI (1632–1717) *Deep in the Mountains* · 1692 ·
India ink and pale color on paper · 43¾ × 19⅛″ · Museum
for Eastern Asiatic Art, Cologne

Wang Hui was a native of Ch'ang-su in Kiangsi province.
His father was an art dealer, and so the young man had
ample opportunity to see and copy paintings of the old
masters. His teachers were Wang Shih-min (1592–1680)
and Wang Chien (1598–1677), friends of Tung Ch'i-ch'ang
whose classicistic conception they perpetuated. To this
circle belonged also Wang Yuan-ch'i (1642–1715)—the
youngest of the "Four Wangs" and grandson of Wang
Chien—as well as Yun Shou-p'ing and Wu Li (1632–1718),
the first educated Chinese to become a Catholic priest. The
group came to be known later as the "Six Famous Painters
of the Ch'ing Period," that is, of the seventeenth century.
Wang Hui was the most prolific among them, and a great
many of his pictures have come down to us. In his youth he
was obliged to earn his living by painting, and that meant
mostly copying, which probably explains how he came by
the skill of imitating old masters so perfectly. The present
picture, done in his old age, nevertheless betrays no hint of
the facile routine of which he is often accused. The wry informative inscription reads: "Deep in the mountains fleet
water falls; two old temples and hidden red wells. I saw
such a picture by Chu-jan (c. 970) in the house of the
Wu family in Ch'ing-hsi. The old Po-shih (Shen Chou)
imitated the original perfectly. So I did likewise." This is a
landscape to wander about in and to live in, as Kuo Hsi
once expressed it. The figures, seen from the rear, with
their soft red color which creates a bright point of contrast, not only invite us to observe the waterfall but also
lead the eye along the path through the ravine up to the
temple. The thoroughly worked-out forms of the separate
parts of the landscape become especially clear in the detail
reproduced, and what is meant by mastery of brushwork is
revealed by the animated play of thick and thin strokes
with which the waves and the contours of the figures are
rendered.

Detail is shown on next pages

WANG HUI (1632–1717) *Mountains, Streams, and Autumn Trees* · Dated 1670 · India ink and color on paper · Palace Museum, Peking

This great landscape is identified as a work by Wang Hui in a long complimentary inscription by Wang Shih-min. Of Wang Hui himself no signature or seal has come down to us. The inscription is dated 1670, which can be taken as the date of the picture. Up to the middle ground, the landscape is densely filled with red-leaved autumn trees, between which there opens at the left a steep path leading up to a mountain village with straw-roofed houses. On the right the landscape becomes more precipitous, and above the trees rises a temple enclosure with fish-tail roofs and a pagoda. The picture is dominated by the extraordinary mushroom-shaped mountain on the left which towers above the valley and foothills. Its completely formed shape, accented by the sparse vegetation, is the salient element of the landscape and draws the eye up to it, while the counter-movement of the red-leaved trees below leads toward the temple at the middle right.

KAO YANG (documented 1623–36) *Spring Landscape* · Dated 1623 · Leaf of a fan · India ink and pale color on gold-speckled paper · $6\frac{1}{4} \times 19\frac{1}{8}''$ · Museum for Eastern Asiatic Art, Cologne

Kao Yang came from Ning-po, the harbor city on Hangchow Bay in the province of Chekiang. He is known as a painter of landscapes, birds, and flowers, but is especially famed for his garden rocks. He collaborated on the "Collection of Calligraphies and Paintings of the Ten-Bamboo-Hall" ("Shih-chu-chai shu-hua p'u"), a compendium of woodcuts for the student of painting, and many of the examples for copying in it are by him. Late in life he moved to Nanking where he specialized in landscapes. His exact dates are not known, though he was probably still alive at the beginning of the Ch'ing period in 1644. It can be presumed that this fan comes from his years in Nanking. The tall gentleman on the left, crossing a bridge which leads to a temple, is a common motif in Chinese landscape painting. But this figure does not invite us to join him in contemplating nature's beauties, but instead to follow his wanderings, though the path he must take soon disappears behind the cliffs. Indeed, the wanderer taking his first step across the bridge is so peripheral to the broad landscape that one scarcely notices him as one's eye travels over the mountain spurs to the gleaming pale blue distance.

YANG CHIN (1644–1728) *Landscape* · Dated 1674 · Leaf of an album · Gold on blue paper · 8⅝ × 6″ · Museum for Eastern Asiatic Art, Cologne

Yang Chin was from Ch'ang-shu in Kiangsi province like Wang Hui (see pages 384–86 and opposite), with whom and for whom he worked. In his last years, Yang Chin was called to Peking as court painter for Emperor Yung-cheng (1722–36). His subjects were landscapes, birds and flowers, figures and portraits. This picture is from an album with five landscapes and calligraphies done in gold on a gleaming cobalt blue background. Though it is painted in the style of Wu Chen (1280–1354), the latter did not turn out such highly decorative landscapes. What is imitated mostly is the composition: the two tongues of land separated in the middle ground of the picture by water, and the bold contour lines whose movement is emphasized by the tiny blobs of flat color. Two islets of reed and a boat headed toward land soften the effect of emptiness of the broad surface of water. Even more than the figure in the boat, the house half-hidden by the trees in the foreground shows that the homecomer is no simple fisherman but a great gentleman. The gold used for this picture is difficult to apply, and the technique of shading is borrowed from that of India ink to achieve similar effects of rich tonal gradation.

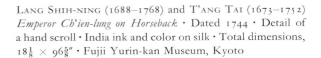

YUN SHOU-P'ING (1633–90) *Flowering Branch* · Leaf of an album · India ink and color on paper

Yun Shou-p'ing was a native of Wu-chin in Kiangsi province. His uncle Yun Hsiang (1586–1655) was a recognized landscape painter, and his teacher Wang Shih-min also taught Wang-hui, Yun Shou-p'ing's lifelong friend. Yun Shou-p'ing is the most sensitive in feeling of the "Six Famous Painters of the Seventeenth Century." Landscapes are rare among his production, and his fame rests on the special style of his flower pictures which, even in his lifetime, were counterfeited. For the most part he painted only in pale colors without the "bony framework" of outlines in India ink; this technique was known in China as far back as the sixth century although no early examples have survived. The flowering branch seen here is done in the "boneless" style, which explains the almost fragrant delicacy of the blossoms. The leaves are painted with such control and subtle rhythm as to make us not even miss the usual "skeleton" of ink, and their green and orange coloring makes a delightful contrast to the rose and gray of the flowers such as only a great painter can achieve.

LANG SHIH-NING (1688–1768) and T'ANG TAI (1673–1752) *Emperor Ch'ien-lung on Horseback* · Dated 1744 · Detail of a hand scroll · India ink and color on silk · Total dimensions, 18⅛ × 96⅝″ · Fujii Yurin-kan Museum, Kyoto

Lang Shih-ning, whose real name was Giuseppe Castiglione, was an Italian Jesuit missionary who came to China in 1719. His talents in painting won him the respect of Emperor Ch'ien-lung who named him court painter, especially for portraits. Lang's collaborator T'ang Tai was, like him, a foreigner, a high Manchu dignitary (the Manchu invaders had occupied the Chinese throne for barely thirty years at his birth). T'ang learned his art with some success from Wang Yuan-ch'i and himself wrote a treatise, "A Demonstration of Fine Subtleties in Painting." To this scroll, done together with Castiglione, whose full title is "The Emperor's Inspection of His Horses on a Meadow in Spring," T'ang Tai contributed his specialty, the landscape, while the Italian painted the dignified portraits of the Emperor on horseback and his attendant. Lang's figures, painted directly without any ink drawing, appear against T'ang's colorful background in shades of green and both delicate and strong rose.

TUNG PANG-TA (1699–1769) *Landscape* · Fan · India ink and pale color on silver paper · 9½ × 26¾″ · Museum for Eastern Asiatic Art, Cologne

Tung Pang-ta belonged to the Fu-yang circle in Chekiang, took the state examinations, and became court painter under Emperor Ch'ien-lung (1736–96). He was also curator of the imperial collection of paintings and bronzes and one of the compilers of its catalogue. His pictures are often in the style of the great artists of the tenth century: this fan, with its dense profusion of mountains and trees leaving almost no free space, recalls the work of Tung Yuan. However, his models were taken just as much from the Yuan painters, in accordance with the express wish of his imperial employer. Thus, in only a few pictures did he reveal that his talents extended beyond this sort of imitation of the past.

TSOU I-KUEI (1686–1772) *Cranes and Peonies* · India ink and color on paper

The family of Tsou I-kuei were officials and scholars in Wu-hsi in Kwangsi province. After passing the examinations with highest honors, he became not only court painter but also the Emperor's adviser on questions of taste. As inspiration for his landscapes he chose the Yuan painters Ni Tsan and Huang Kung-wang, but his flower paintings—the chief source of his fame—are said to be in the style of Yun Shou-p'ing (page 389). But, at the wish of the Emperor, he also studied European painting with the Jesuits, and as a result he rendered flowers with virtually scientific accuracy. His own gifts and his schooling in an old tradition lend his pictures a unique charm with their happy use of color and their animation.

WANG CH'ENG-P'EI (c. 1725–1805) *Two Birds on a Plum Tree with Bamboo* · Color on blue-painted paper · $22\frac{1}{4} \times 6\frac{7}{8}''$ · Museum for Eastern Asiatic Art, Cologne

Wang Ch'eng-p'ei was a member of a family of officials and scholars in Hsiu-ning, Anhwei province, and his father was a well-known painter and poet. He himself passed two examinations and, like Tung Pang-ta, was called to the court as a painter. There he did figures, landscapes, flowers and birds, and followed his father also as poet and writer. Only a few of his pictures are known. Just as Emperor Ch'ien-lung desired Castiglione to learn the Chinese way of painting, so also did he require his own Chinese court painters to acquaint themselves with European techniques. The product of this double training was painting such as this, in which Wang Ch'eng-p'ei tried to reconcile the two worlds of art. Despite its evident European traits, this plum branch recalls the compositions of the Sung school: almost two-thirds of the background is left blank, though the white of the birds seems to raise the center of gravity above the lower left corner.

CHIN NUNG (1687–1764) *Lo-han* (detail) · India ink and pale color on paper · Dimensions of entire scroll, $37\frac{1}{4} \times 10\frac{3}{4}''$

Although he lived in Yangchow, Chin Nung came from Hangchow. He was a poet and writer and famed as a calligrapher of seal inscriptions, but at fifty he began to paint. He is counted among a group of painters who, because of their unorthodox and expressive style, are called the Eight Eccentrics of Yangchow or the Yangchow Fauves. They were in open opposition to the fastidious though not unexperimental circle at the court, which explains why none of their paintings are in the imperial collection. The models of the Yangchow group were, without doubt, the "Individualists" of the seventeenth century with their powerfully expressive landscapes and bitter opposition to the foreign invaders. Such bitterness was no longer a trait of the "Yangchow Fauves": their disdain was directed against the smugness of the native society. With coarse, bold brush strokes Chin Nung has outlined this figure of Lo-han, a disciple of Buddha, seated on a throne of leaves before a wall of rock. The rock is thinly washed in, its form implied but not set down in detail. Colors which are soft but clear contrast with the heavily accentuated black of the contour drawing and the inscription, while the leaves, though stylized and disciplined, are painted with an almost delicate verve. All the subtlety of drawing is concentrated on the face to reveal its extraordinary, grotesque but spiritual humorousness.

JEN PO-NIEN (1840–95) *The Poet T'ao Yuan-ming* · Dated 1887 · Leaf of an album · India ink and pale color on paper · $10\frac{1}{8} \times 13\frac{3}{8}''$ · Museum for Eastern Asiatic Art, Cologne

Jen I, better known under his name as an artist, Jen Po-nien, came from Shao-hsing in Chekiang province but lived mostly in Shanghai. He was among those who rediscovered the "Individualists" of the seventeenth century and is acclaimed as a pioneer of modern art in China—his grandson and pupil is Ch'i Pai-shih. This picture belongs to an album which formerly had eight paintings, six of which are now in the Cologne museum, all of them portraits of China's famous poets. Here we see the poet T'ao Yuan-ming (365–427) returning home in a boat with chrysanthemums. Over and beyond the imaginary portrait there is a clear allusion to the often quoted poem "Homewards," one of the perennial themes in Chinese art. The figure of the poet is outlined in somewhat nervous brush strokes, whereas the boy behind the gnarled tree trunk seems to be painted with dabs of ink. Blue and red in both delicate and strong tones lend animation to the figures set against the broad empty expanse of water in the middle ground.

CH'I PAI-SHIH (1863–1957) *Lemons* and *Persimmons* · Both
1926 · India ink and color on paper · Each 52 × 13″ ·
Museum for Eastern Asiatic Art, Cologne

Ch'i Huang, who as an artist used the name Ch'i Pai-shih,
came from the small town of Hsing-tse-wu in Hunan
province. Of poor family, he worked as a carpenter. But
already in his early years he painted for his own pleasure,
though he did not learn to write until later—an unusual
sequence in China—when the scholar Wang Hsiang-chi
taught him his letters and the painter Wu Ch'ang-shih his
art. Ch'i Pai-shih learned more, in fact, from nature than
from the classical models. In early manhood he was able to
give up his carpenter's trade and support his family by
selling his pictures. Fame reached him, however, only after
showing in the Berlin Sezession exhibition of 1930, when
word of his European triumph filtered back to China. His
unusual personal background and unconventional way of
painting have made him a model for the recent and present
generations of painters in China. These two pictures, now
in Cologne, were acquired directly from the artist by
Professor Otto Fischer in 1926 in Peking where Ch'i
Pai-shih lived from 1920 until his death. Their fascination
lies in their gleaming colors, a quality for which this artist
has always been acclaimed. In contrast to the graduated
tones of ink used for the leaves, the fruit is painted in the
"boneless" manner as bright and undetailed globes of
yellow and red.

HSU PEI-HUNG (JU PÉON) (1894–1953) *Horse under Willows* ·
Dated 1936 · India ink and pale color on paper · 41¾ × 14″ ·
Collection Mrs. Renate Berk, Neuhemmerich bei Köln
(Cologne)

Hsu Pei-hung was born in I-hsing in Kiangsi province, an
ancient center of ceramic-making, and studied in Shanghai
and Japan. After the first World War, he attended the
École des Beaux-Arts in Paris between 1919 and 1923, and
then traveled much in Europe, spending considerable time
in Berlin and Vienna. In 1932 he again traveled about
Europe, presenting exhibitions under his French name Ju
Péon, and in 1937–38 he visited southern and southeastern
Asia. He became a professor in Nanking, and from 1947 to
his premature death he was president of the Academy in
Peking. He harmonized European modes of seeing with
Chinese technique to make a highly personal style which,
nevertheless, is not false to the classical traditions in which
he was trained. His pictures of horses have become known
throughout the world as examples of modern Chinese
painting. In this picture of a young horse, which is dedicated
to the elder brother of the painter Chang Ta-ch'ien, the
mastery of brushwork as seen in the bare branches and
boughs of the willow tree reveals the hand of a great
painter. By graduating the ink from pale gray to deep black,
the horse is made to stand out strikingly against the colored
ground at its feet.

CHAO SHAO-ANG (1904–   ) *Kingfisher on a Flowering Branch* · Dated 1934 · Leaf of an album · India ink and paint on paper · 11½ × 14⅝″ · Collection Mrs. Renate Berk, Neuhemmerich bei Köln (Cologne)

Chao Shao-ang comes from the cosmopolitan city of Canton and studied under the painter and writer Kao Chien-fu. After many years spent in western China, he now lives in Hongkong. In his paintings, as in those of his teacher, French Impressionism is blended with the ancient traditions of China. Here, on a gnarled tree, a kingfisher perches, and from the right projects a branch of blossoms. The theme itself is an old one, typical of the Sung Academy. Chao's picture is notable for the way paint and ink are used, with shadings which give form to the tree, flowers, and leaves and which make the kingfisher stand out brightly and prominently. The delicacy of the buds and flowers is balanced by the strong accents of the tiny spots of black ink on the trunk and leaves. The tension of the small bird is conveyed by its eye and beak which are outlined by forceful brush strokes. Although this small picture may seem no more than a quick sketch, every stroke of the brush is exactly right and could not be improved on. There is nothing accidental, nothing unnecessary in the composition; everything is executed with a sure and masterful hand.

CHANG TA-CH'IEN (1899–   ) *Landscape* · Dated 1945 · India ink and pale color on paper · 31⅞ × 15⅜″ · Museum for Eastern Asiatic Art, Cologne

A native of Neikiang in Szechwan province, Chang Ta-ch'ien now makes his home in South America after having traveled extensively in China, Japan, Europe, and America and gained international fame. He owes most to the seventeenth-century "Individualists" but has not ignored the lessons of the Sung and T'ang masters—he has copied the frescoes in Tun-huang with such skill that his copies almost surpass the originals in general favor. He is also a collector of pictures of every style and period, though there have been rumors that some of them were painted by the master himself. His is a completely cosmopolitan spirit, and there is a vast diversity of expression in his pictures. Even when he seems to be painting in the style of Shih-t'ao, he gives his own creative character to the spirit and brushwork of that master. Among his friends are many outstanding painters, including Picasso with whom he exchanges pictures and ideas. This picture combines the delicacy of a Yuan landscape with the artist's own feeling for color as expressed in the pale blue-green mountains and trees and the brown of the sand bar. The tiny figures of the wanderer and his servant under the trees in the foreground are seen from the rear and blend with the vegetation to such an extent that they give no pause to the eye as it travels to the distant hill.

Death of Buddha · Dated 1086 · India ink, color, and gold on silk · 105⅜ × 106¾″ · Kongobu-ji, Koyasan

This composition of the death of Buddha, or his entry into Nirvana, is the most ancient surviving painting on this moving theme in Japan. Buddha lies in the center beneath blossoming Sala trees; at his head kneel Bodhisattvas; the entourage of Devas (watchmen and demi-gods) surrounds him, with figures from the human world nearby and, in the foreground, a lion as symbol of the animal kingdom. Above the trees appears Maya, mother of Buddha Shakyamuni, who has been resting in the abode of the gods since her death. There is a contrast between the restrained mourning of the Bodhisattvas and the vivid grief of the other figures; one can go so far as to say that the expression of grief increases from left to right, and that the use of color corresponds to this expression. Buddha, as the center of interest, is painted in pure, brilliant gold, with contours and internal drawing rendered in a soft purple which we also find in the Bodhisattvas, while the other figures are painted with lines in India ink and bright colors which lend them a special accent.

Fudo Myoo (Red Fudo) · 10th–12th century · India ink, color, and gold on silk · 65 × 36⅞″ · Myoo-in, Koyasan

Of the five tutelary Buddhist gods Fudo is the most important. He is regarded in Japan as the manifestation of the principal Buddha of the mystic sects, the Dainichi-Buddha. As a champion against Evil, he counteracts it by assuming an even more frightening appearance. As the "Indestructible One" he is seated on crags from where he binds and slays Evil with his dragon-encompassed sword and rope; his halo is a blaze of flames. The youthful companions at the lower right are Seitaka and Konkara. The painting is intended as a liturgical object which is honored and supplicated at specific ceremonies. Paintings such as this were not done by ordinary professional artists, but were the result of long meditation on the part of devoted monks; they were painted to be worshiped, not to be looked at. Mystical Buddhist religious paintings are subject to the strictest iconographic rules which were nonetheless infringed by the artists. This representation of Fudo is among the most vigorous paintings of the Heian period.

Nagarjuna at the Iron Stupa · First half of 12th century · Color and gold on silk · 70 × 55⅝″ · Fujita Museum, Osaka

Nagarjuna is one of the patriarchs of mystical Buddhism (Shingon), to whom, according to the legend of the Iron Stupa in South India, the esoteric doctrine of Vajrasattva was revealed. The painting refers to the legend: the Stupa is set in an unreal landscape such as we know from the Chinese T'ang paintings. Layerlike mountain formations shift from shades of green to pale blue—colors to which unfortunately no reproduction can do justice—and the delicate flowering plants and trees suggest spring. The effect of the landscape is produced above all by its stratified forms which seem to be achieved almost without brush strokes, while the artist reveals an extremely fine use of line in the details, in the blossoms and leaves of the plants, in the superstructure of the Stupa, and in the sensitive delineation of the figures and the folds of their costumes.

395

Portrait of Jion Daishi · Middle of 11th century · Color and India ink on silk · 63⅜ × 50⅜″ · Yakushi-ji, Nara

Jion Daishi was a famous Chinese priest of the T'ang dynasty, who was especially honored by the Japanese Hosso sects. On the anniversary of the death of the patriarch the temple of Yakushi-ji, a center of this Buddhist cult, organized ceremonies at which special prayers were recited before the present picture. Many portraits of Jion Daishi were done in China during the T'ang and Sung dynasties, some of which were doubtless brought to Japan by pilgrims. We can thus assume a Chinese model for this portrait, a fact that is demonstrated by such details as the small table on the right with the writing implements and, on the left, the water jug, which give us an insight into the life of a Chinese monk of the T'ang dynasty. Despite such influences, this painting impresses us as an entirely individual work of art; crowning the starkly contrasting colors of the robe, we see the powerfully modeled face of a dominating personality, with eyes which lend vitality to the whole figure.

Buddha Shakyamuni · c. 1000 · Paint, India ink, and gold on silk · 62¾ × 33⅝″ · Jingo-ji, Kyoto

The exalted Buddha on his lofty lotus throne, with the red robes which give the picture its alternative title *Aka Shaka (Red Shaka)*, is a noble representation which, though perhaps lacking in forcefulness, prevails all the same by virtue of its gentle beauty. The soft red of the robes is overlaid by a delicate pattern in incised gold leaf *(kirikane)*, which is given a particular luminosity by the vivid green border. Rays from the head of the Buddha break through the halo of painted golden flowers encircling his face, which expresses graceful serenity. The whole figure awakes in us the impression of that courtly though perhaps somewhat effeminate elegance peculiar to the period.

Kobo Daishi as a Boy (detail) · Late 13th. century · Paint, silver, and India ink on silk · 30⅜ × 16¾″ · Collection Maruyama, Mikage

According to a legend, Kobo Daishi, when a boy, dreamed that he was sitting on an eight-leafed lotus throne in discussion with various deities about the principal features of Buddhism. Characteristic of the courtly style, the legend inspired paintings such as this showing one of the most important priests of his time, the founder of the Shingon sect, as a child (Chigo Daishi). Here we see him as a delightful, bright-faced boy sharply delineated and with a vitality which is emphasized by the severe frame of dark hair. Black trousers and a white robe, the silver flower-pattern of which has oxidized to gray, accentuate the elegant figure. The picture belonged originally to the Koyasan where it hung among the tutelary deities of the temple.

Title-picture of the Yakuso-Yubon Scroll · Completed 1141 · India ink, color, and gold on paper · 10 × 8⅜″ · Collection Muto, Kobe

As well as Buddhist religious paintings, the late Heian period also gave us the E-Makimono (hand scrolls with narrative content), which were commissioned or even created by lords and ladies of the court. A few Buddhist sutras, the title-pictures of which have for the most part only a very loose connection with their pious texts, have been preserved and give us an insight into the court life of the time. The Yakuso-Yubon scroll belongs to the Hokkekyo Sutra series, which was donated in 1141 by nobles and ladies of the court of the Emperor Toba to the no longer preserved Kunoji temple in Suruga. The title-picture represents the realm of Buddha compared with that of man. With his rain, Buddha gives new life to the parched earth and the plants. In the foreground a noble gentleman sits under his umbrella enjoying the rain which hovers in tiny golden droplets over the riverbank scene, lending a decorative luster to the restrained colors of the page.

The Scroll of the Sicknesses (Yamai-no-soshi) · Late 12th century · India ink and color on paper · 5½ × 7″ · Yamato Bunka-kan Museum, Nara

In addition to the representation of the refined world of the court, there also exists among the Yamato-e scrolls a number of paintings which deal with the perils and needs of human existence. Among these are the Sickness Scrolls where the people represented are generally of humble station. This small fragment shows acupuncture being applied to a corpulent man whose pain can be read in his face. The "doctor" wields his instrument with an aloof expression, refusing to be influenced by the priest holding the prayer beads or the woman in the background. Compared with the other existing Yamai-no-soshi Scrolls, the figures are too large in relation to the height of the paper, though the original measurements of the fragment cannot be reconstructed. There is no doubt that this painting is not the work of the artist who did the other scrolls, even if in liveliness of expression it does not fall short of the other representations of this theme.

Genji Scroll, chapter 39: Yugiri (detail) · First half of 12th century · India ink and color on paper · Dimensions of detail, 8⅝ × 11⅝″ · Collection Masuda, Tokyo

The Genji-Monogatari, or the Tale of Prince Genji, was written around 1000 by the lady-in-waiting Murasaki Shikibu. Of the scrolls illustrating the novel (the Genji-Monogatari-Emaki) four are in existence today, and they rank among the finest of the Yamato-e. Here we see Yugiri, the son of Prince Genji, who has fallen in love with the widow of his friend. The latter's mother writes to him that she wishes to give her daughter to him. But his wife, Kumoi-no-kari, has begun to have suspicions and surprises him as he reads the letter. From the black writing-case open in front of him one can suppose that he intended to reply to the letter at once. The artist lets us see into the house from above; he has, as it were, removed the roof, with the result that we can also look into the adjoining room. The contours in India ink display, in the figures especially, a delicate play of line, but this is subordinated to the careful balance between gray and red.

Nezame Scroll (detail) · Late 12th century · India ink, color, gold, and silver on paper · Total dimensions of scroll, 10⅛ × 200″ · Yamato Bunka-kan Museum, Nara

The Genji Scrolls and the Nezame-Monogatari-Emaki number among the finest achievements of the Yamato-e style (the "Japanese" style). The Nezame Scroll, with its clear coloring and rich use of patches of gold and silver—in part made from cut-out foil (kirikane)—tends perhaps more toward decorative effect. The Nezame-Monogatari is related to a collection of short novels, the original form of which has not been preserved, and this explains why the exact subject matter in the illustrations cannot be pinned down. The figures tend to be smaller than in preceding scrolls, and take second place to the landscape. For this reason it is certain that the painting was done later than the Genji Scroll. This title-picture for the first scene gives us a glimpse of a Japanese landscaped garden of the time. Blossoming cherry trees and meadows are decoratively but naturalistically presented, while the blue and brown costumes of the lady playing the flute and her attendant form a lively contrast to the enchanting garden.

Kitano Tenjin Engi (detail) · First half of 13th century · India ink and color on paper · Total dimensions of scroll, 20½ × 372⅛″ · Kitano Temman-gu, Kyoto

In this scroll, the life of the loyal statesman Sugawara no Michizane (845–903) is portrayed. He was deified as Temman Tenjin and the Kitano Temman-gu was consecrated to him. This detail is from the first of eight scrolls and shows a discussion between the young Michizane and his father Sugawara Koreyoshi. We look down on the carefully laid-out garden surrounded by buildings. In the background, on the outer porch, the boy sits facing the Prince who is in an open room. The unknown artist meticulously depicted the garden with a dark blue stream running zigzag through it. Stepping stones and rocks overgrown with moss make bridges and rock crannies, while tiny low chains of hillocks form the boundary in the foreground. Trees in blossom tell us that it is spring, while a few dark pines, such as are invariably included in Japanese paintings, make a lively point of emphasis in the background.

FUJIWARA TAKANOBU (1142–1205) Portrait of Minamoto Yoritomo · India ink and color on silk · 55½ × 44¼″ · Jingo-ji, Kyoto

Fujiwara Takanobu was not only a prominent nobleman in Kyoto, but also a brilliant portrait painter. This portrait is one of a series which originally included four—all of friends of Emperor Goshirakawa—commissioned for the palace erected in 1188 for the abdicated ruler. The portrait of Minamoto Yoritomo is one of the most famous not only in Japanese painting but in all of art. Yoritomo (1147–99) was the founder of the house of Minamoto, the organizer of the palace stewardship (Baku-fu), and belonged to a military regime which had its seat in the new capital of Kamakura. Yoritomo is portrayed seated in the ceremonial dress (Sokutai) of a senior court official. His pale face rises like a sharp accent above the angularly defined black figure, and pale lines delineate nose and eyes above a full mouth. It is the face of an energetic man accustomed to giving orders.

Attributed to FUJIWARA NOBUZANE (1176–1265) The Poetess Ko-ogimi (detail) · 13th century · India ink and color on paper · 14⅛ × 23¼″ · Yamato Bunka-kan Museum, Nara

The poetess Ko-ogimi, better known as Kodai-no-kimi, numbers among the thirty-six poets and poetesses considered as the classical writers of the Heian period and profoundly admired in Japan for many centuries. This picture belonged originally to a series of thirty-six portraits of poets in two hand scrolls which were cut up a few years ago and are now scattered among several collections. The artist Fujiwara Nobuzane was one of Takanobu's sons and shares his father's fame as a portraitist. More than a portrait of a person we see here an extravagant profusion of magnificent robes such as the women of those times wore layer over layer, as many as twenty-five at a time. The gradation of colors evident on the sleeves and borders was an expression of the taste and culture of the wearer. Fine locks of long black hair frame her white-powdered face with its blackened teeth and high-arched eyebrows. There is here a symphony of colors which almost obscures the figure and yet forms a charming frame for the face.

Leaf of a fan from the Hokkekyo-Sutra · 12th century · India ink, color, gold, and silver on paper · 10⅛ × 19⅜" · Fujita Museum, Osaka

Late in the Heian period a series of decorative copies of the Hokkekyo-Sutra appeared (the Sutra of the Lotus of the Good Doctrine, cf. also page 397, top), which were done by noble ladies and gentlemen. Of these copies a great many are painted and written on fans, some of which still exist in various collections. This fan-shaped album leaf with a gnarled tree, birds, and bamboo on paper sprinkled with gold and silver and spots of cut out gold leaf (kirikane) has a sumptuous effect and is technically interesting: the contours were printed from a woodblock, while the strong colors were painted in by hand. The text of the Sutra is on the reverse side of the leaf.

EN-I *The Priest Ippen on a Journey* (detail) · 1299 · India ink and pale color on silk · Total dimensions of scroll, 14⅞ × 427¼" · Kankiko-ji, Kyoto

As early as ten years after his death, the life of the wandering priest Ippen (1239–89) was portrayed by the artist En-i in twelve scrolls. The biographical text that accompanies the pictorial scrolls is the work of the priest Shokei, and it is likely that En-i was also a monk. Several versions of the biography of Ippen (Ippen-Shonin-Eden) have been preserved in Japan, but the 1299 version by En-i is probably the most important. Ippen was one of the most outstanding wandering priests, a missionary for the Nembutsu movement (the invocation of the Amida Buddha "Namu Amida Butsu"). For many years he traveled through all parts of Japan winning numerous disciples. Here he is journeying to Dazaifu on the southern island of Kyushu with his pupil Shokei in search of his instructor. Ippen and Shokei are dressed simply and carry umbrellas; they are followed by three monks and two luggage-bearers. Well-balanced, vigorous lines delineate the contours of the promontory, on the far side of which dark pines rise up from the cliffs and a flock of birds flies over the water. Even if we know nothing of the artist, he must surely be counted among the leading early landscape painters of Japan.

GYOGEN (documented 1286–1300) *Shinto Goddess* · Dated 1295 · Paint on panel 75⅝ × 20⅛" · Yakushi-ji, Nara

This picture belongs to a series of thirty-six deities represented on six panels set between the columns in the Shinto shrine of Hachiman-jinja which is consecrated to the patron deities of Yakushi-ji. On one of the panels are given the date 1295 and the name of the artist. Gyogen was a Buddhist painter who belonged to the workshop of a temple (e-dokoro) in Nara which was set up to replace older and, by that time, damaged paintings done around 1087. According to the Honchi Suijaku, a doctrine that merged Buddhist with Shinto deities, it was quite customary to paint Shinto portraits for Buddhist temples and vice versa, and these were often done by the same artist or at least by the same workshop. For this reason, these religious paintings frequently depict a mixture of Shinto and Buddhist deities. The Shinto gods of Yakushi-ji are mostly dignified figures in the ceremonial costume of high court officials (Sokutai). The goddesses, as this example illustrates, were portrayed as voluptuous beauties with pleasing faces, wearing crowns and long-sleeved decorative robes in accordance with the aesthetic ideal and the fashions of the Chinese T'ang dynasty.

The Nachi Waterfall · c. 1300 · India ink and color on silk · 62¾ × 22¾″ · Nezu Museum, Tokyo

This grandiose view of the Nachi Waterfall is not just a landscape; it is at the same time a religious painting symbolizing the deity of this waterfall, even if the deity himself is not portrayed. During the Kamakura period many pictures of Shinto shrines in their natural environment *(Mandara)* were produced, pictures in which the landscape increasingly supplanted the shrine and became the actual subject. At the end of that development is this painting of the Nachi Waterfall, the fundamental idea of which is still rooted in the religious worship of nature practiced by the Japanese, as is indicated by the golden semi-orb of sun visible over the mountains. The force of the waterfall plunging steeply downwards is stressed by the dazzling whiteness, beside which the structure of the rocks recedes and only the bluish green of the pines stands out.

MINCHO (1352–1431) *Ten Rakan* · Dated 1386 · India ink and color on silk · 68⅛ × 35⅜″ · Nezu Museum, Tokyo

In the fourteenth century, relations with China once again became close, particularly in the monasteries of the Zen Buddhists, and the style of the Chinese ink-painting of the Southern Sung Academy was enthusiastically taken up by Japanese artists. Mincho, known also as Chodensu because of his priestly office, was a monk in the Zen monastery of Tofuku-ji in Kyoto. He produced pure ink-paintings in the style of the Southern Sung Academy and became famous for his colorful portraits of Buddhist saints. In 1386 he created a series of fifty paintings portraying the 500 Rakan (pupils of Buddha). These are closely derived from Chinese proto-types of the same period. This picture is from that series, which is still preserved almost complete in Tofuku-ji. The colorful robes of the disciples of Buddha form a strong contrast to the delicate mountainous landscape and clouds of the background. Mincho was the first artist to adapt themes from Zen Buddhism, and his works repeatedly reveal the technique of a professional painter.

SOGA JASOKU (documented 1452–83) *Daruma* · India ink and pale color on paper · 26⅜ × 15¾″ · Yotoku-in, Kyoto

Jasoku came from Echizen, lived in Kyoto and belonged to the Samurai class. He was the pupil of the artist and monk Shubun who was celebrated for his ink-paintings in the Sung style. Jasoku is an example of the transitional period during which Zen Buddhist painting passed more and more from the hands of priest-painters into military circles which, as lay fraternities, adhered to this Buddhist school or were at least very close to it. Jasoku was a close friend of the priest and artist Ikkyu, whose portrait of 1452 is Jasoku's first authenticated picture. The portrayal of Daruma (Bodhidarma), the first patriarch of Chinese Ch'an (Japanese Zen) Buddhism, was a favorite motif of Japanese Zen painting in the fifteenth century. Bodhidarma, the son of an Indian prince, came to China as a missionary. Once, according to legend, his eyes closed while he was in meditation, and in his fury he ripped off his eyelids and threw them to the ground; later, on the spot where they fell, a tea plant sprang up. Daruma is consequently portrayed with large eyes (in fact, lidless), which dominate his face, and a red cloak drawn over his head covers his body and hands. Eyes and nose and the folds of the cloak gave the artist an opportunity to demonstrate his mastery of powerful brush drawing.

KEI SHOKI (documented 1478–1523) *Landscape* · Leaf of a fan · India ink and pale colors on paper · 13¼ × 14⅛″ · Museum for Eastern Asiatic Art, Cologne

Kei Shoki (Shokei) was a priest at Kencho-ji in Kamakura where he held the office of scribe *(Shoki)*. In 1478 he traveled to Kyoto, remained there three years as a pupil of the famous painter Geiami (1431–85) and then returned to Kamakura with its many Zen monasteries. The small leaf of a fan, mounted as a hanging scroll, shows that Kei Shoki was accomplished in the art of classical Chinese landscape painting. The crags on the right, which seem to be hewn by an ax, and the wiry trees are in the best Sung tradition of Ma Yuan and Hsai Kuei. The soft green of the leaves and pine needles, the fading blue of the distant mountains between the cloudbanks, and the touch of red in the servant's hat to intensify all the other colors prove Kei Shoki to be a lyrical composer in color.

Portrait of Sogi · 16th century · India ink and color on silk · 41 × 16¾″ · Collection Nambu, Tokyo

The monk Sogi (1421–1502) was a well-known poet who had a great love of nature and wandered widely throughout the country. He is particularly famous for his series of poems (Renga), which he brought out as a collection in 1495. Sogi is portrayed seated and dressed in the violet, black, and brown habit of a priest; his finely featured head stands out above the white undergarment. The face is shaped by delicate lines. The accentuated brows above his lively eyes and the fine flourish of his mouth make this the portrait of a dignified, sensitive man. This portrait is on a level with the outstanding works of other epochs of Japanese painting.

Kano Eitoku (1543–90) *Pine Trees and Eagle* · Screen ·
India ink, color, and gold on paper · 63¼ × 138″ · Academy
of Art, Tokyo

Kano Eitoku was a grandson and probably also a pupil of
Kano Motonobu (1476–1559); he was court painter to the
most powerful men of his time, Oda Nobunag and Toyotomi
Hideyoshi, who had their new palaces decorated in splendor
but without pretension. Eitoku evolved a style which made
it possible to cover large spaces decoratively. Many screens
and sliding doors were painted by him, but only a few that
can be attributed to him with any certainty have been
preserved. Among these is the pair of screens with pine
trees and eagles—this one among them—which were
attributed to Eitoku by Kano Eino, one of his great-
grandsons. As with all the existing works, this is unsigned,
but it shows all those features for which Eitoku was
famous. He links the brilliant blue and green of the Yamato-e
—the Kitano-Tenjin scroll (page 398)—with the vigorous
brush strokes of the Kano school. The decorative background of clouds in dull-finished gold leaf gives the colors
even greater luminosity.

Attributed to Hasegawa Kyuzo (1568–93) *Cherry Blossoms* ·
Sliding doors · Color, India ink, and gold on paper ·
Height, 69½″ · Chishaku-in Monastery, Kyoto

The four sliding doors, two of which are illustrated here,
belonged originally to the Shoun-ji temple which was
erected by Hideyoshi in 1591 to the memory of his deceased
favorite son; they came into the hands of the Chishaku
Monastery at a later date. These doors have often been
attributed to Hasegawa Tohaku, the father of Kyuzo, whose
pair of screens in a similar style still exists. But the *Cherry
Blossoms* panels are definitely the work of another hand,
being more delicate in conception and less emphatic in their
realization. It is quite possible, however, that the young
Kyuzo helped his father with the Shoun-ji screens and that
these doors were painted in collaboration with him. While
one can sense the influence of Eitoku, what is lacking here is
the courage to tackle large forms. The blossoms are finely
detailed, painted in gouache, and stand out from the gold
background as if in relief.

The Four Seasons · 16th century · Pair of screens · Color, India ink, and gold on paper · Each 58⅝ × 124″ · Kongo-ji, Osaka

KANO SANRAKU (1559–1635) *The Three Laughing Men of the Valley of the Tiger* · Screen · Color, India ink, and gold on paper · National Museum, Tokyo

Kano Sanraku came from Omi and was the son of the painter Kimura Nagamitsu. He studied under Kano Eitoku in Kyoto and worked for Hideyoshi. The latter esteemed the young painter so highly that Eitoku adopted him. Sanraku later became his son-in-law and successor as head of the Kano school in Kyoto. There are some magnificent ink paintings by Sanraku and equally decorative works on screens and doors. Here he takes up the theme of a Chinese legend: a hermit in the Valley of the Tiger had made up his mind never again to cross the small bridge; one day, accompanying two friends with whom he was deep in conversation, he crossed the bridge without noticing it. When they realized what had happened they all three roared with laughter. The landscape with its strong colors still preserves the energy of Eitoku, even if the latter's masterly freedom in covering large surfaces has given way here to a more subtle draftsmanship in individual shapes.

The method of composition of the Yamato-e scrolls is applied here to screens. The passing of the seasons from spring to summer, then to autumn and winter, is depicted on two six-sectioned screens. There is a bold use of color: green and blue on a gold base in the summer screen, and for autumn and winter extraordinarily cold colors such as brown, green, white, and dark blue, and then the entire surface sprinkled with gold and silver. The mountains rise disk-shaped behind one another, while extremely clever brushwork is displayed in the waves and tree trunks. Such boldness of composition and coloring does not appear again until the art of Sotatsu.

KANO SANSETSU (1589–1651) *Seabirds on a Winter Coast* ·
Screen · Color, India ink, and gold on paper · 61 × 143¼″ ·
Collection Hosotsugi, Kyoto

Kano Sansetsu was the pupil of his father-in-law Kano
Sanraku, whose name he took, as was usual in cases of
adoption. He came from Hizen, lived in Kyoto, and
inherited the leadership of the Kano school in Kyoto from
his master after many members of the painter's family had
drifted away to the new capital Edo (Tokyo). It is difficult
to distinguish the works of Sanraku from those of
Sansetsu, and opinions differ, especially with regard to
screens and sliding doors, most of which are unsigned. The
pair of screens with waterfowl—one of which is illustrated
here—belong to those works which have been attributed
with some certainty to Sansetsu. Sansetsu combines asymmetrical composition and highly skillful, finely detailed
draftsmanship with decorative brilliance, elements similar to
those we find also in the applied arts of the time.

Attributed to TAWARAYA SOTATSU (early 17th century) ·
Picture constructed with fans · Color, India ink, and gold
on paper · Height, 7″ · Sambo-in, Kyoto

Very little is known of Sotatsu's life; the only certain dates
are 1602 and 1630. He was a friend of Koetsu (1558–1637),
the greatest calligrapher of his day, and worked in collaboration with him. According to tradition he is reputed
to have been a painter of fans by profession. The exceptionally free composition of the straw-covered farmhouses
in the semicircle of the fan seen here demonstrates his
unusual gift for composition. Consider too the sensitive
use of cold colors which gives the picture a painterly charm.
This fan is part of a two-sectioned gold-backed screen on
which the fans have been newly mounted. Because the
screen is in the possession of the Sambo-in in the Daigo-ji
temple, where Sotatsu lived for some time, one can consider it his work with certainty, even though the individual
fans are unsigned.

Attributed to TAWARAYA SOTATSU *Ise Monogatari, Akutagawa*
· Leaf of an album · India ink, color, and gold on paper ·
9⅝ × 8¼″ · Yamato Bunka-kan Museum, Nara

It was not only in his use of color that Sotatsu returned to
the tradition of Yamato-e painting, for he also took as
models the classical narrative pictures of the tenth, eleventh,
and twelfth centuries and, indeed, "copied" them, although
in his own individual style. His great achievement lies
firstly in his revival of Yamato-e art and secondly in his
treatment of color, which he used in the same way as India
ink. He was thus able to depict classical themes in a highly
decorative manner, even on large surfaces. This small leaf
from the tenth-century tale of *Ise Monogatari* shows Prince
Narihara carrying a beautiful lady across dewy fields by the
river Akutagawa. With great skill the artist paints strongly
colored areas over a gold background and integrates the
written text into the composition. Sotatsu developed the
style which reached its consummation perhaps in the hands
of Korin and which achieved enormous popularity,
particularly in lacquer work for which Sotatsu himself
sketched the designs, if no more.

Genre Scene · 17th century · Detail from a pair of four-sectioned screens · India ink, color, gold, and silver on paper

A series of screens portraying scenes from everyday life has been preserved from the seventeenth century, the beginning of the Edo period. Such themes, however, were not considered worthy to be treated in painting, and these works are unsigned because the authors did not wish to risk their reputations. Customers for such "glimpses of this transitory world" (Ukiyo-e) were to be found among the wealthy upper middle classes, which, particularly in Edo (Tokyo), were coming to exert considerable influence on artistic activity and whose ideals were focused on the pleasures of this world. It is understandable, then, that the pair of screens from which this detail is taken is not signed. Like the well-known Yuna screen in the Atami Museum, it portrays men and women of no particular distinction, dressed simply and carrying on in a most relaxed manner. The artist lavished special care on the patterns of the clothing and caught on paper the wealth of color characteristic of Japanese fashions. To these he added gold leaf and sprinkled silver to give an impression of luxuriousness.

OGATA KORIN (1658–1716) *Irises* · Screen · Color on gold-ground paper · 59⅝ × 141¼″ · Nezu Museum, Tokyo

Ogata Korin, son of a kimono manufacturer in Kyoto, was related to Koetsu and consequently from an early age was familiar with painting. His family's wealth made it possible for him to live freely as an artist. Even during his lifetime his artworks, whether in lacquer, ceramics, silk, India ink, or gold, were valued most highly, and craftsmen of all kinds adopted his forms as models. In a pair of screens painted with irises—only one is illustrated here—he achieved one of his most beautiful decorative works. The motif, taken from the *Ise Monogatari*, can also be found in his lacquer work. It comes from the "Yatsubashi" Chapter (the Eightfold Bridge) in which the hero Narihara writes a poem about the irises alongside the Yatsubashi bridge (a bridge made out of eight simple planks placed together to form a zigzag leading across the marsh). There is neither water nor bridge on this screen, but the thick clumps of iris, with the full splendor of their blooms, suffice to awaken the memory of this poem. With simple means—flat unshaded green juxtaposed with lapis lazuli on a shimmering gold ground—Korin was able to achieve a superb decorative effect.

HISHIKAWA MORONOBU (d. 1694) *Beauty with Attendant* · India ink and color on paper

Hishikawa Moronobu was the first artist to turn out Ukiyo-e pictures in the exacting form suited to the woodcut. He lived in Edo and was a tapestry worker by profession. It is not known whether he was ever the pupil of any established painter or whether he belonged to some workshop. In his work, which does not only portray beautiful women, we are reminded of the styles of both the Yamato-e and the Kano school. He created a large number of book illustrations for a public that found its entertainment in popular literature. Besides these, he also painted pictures of the beautiful women of Yoshiwara, the red-light district of Edo.

405

MIYAGAWA CHOSHUN (1682–1752) *A Beauty* (detail) · India ink and color on silk · Total dimensions, 44⅛ × 23½″

Miyagawa Choshun came from Owari, went to Edo, and there became one of Moronobu's best pupils. Unlike his master, Choshun never worked at the woodcut, although those on Ukiyo-e subjects depicting beautiful women provided his favorite themes. The beautiful woman here fanning herself to keep cool is one of Choshun's classical works. She is gracefully seated on the bench. The design on her kimono is evidence of Choshun's pronounced sense of color. The main tone is a subdued brownish red against which gleams the white of the chrysanthemums. Black tresses of hair tumble in a gentle rhythm round her head, which is inclined to one side; her white-powdered face stands out above the red of the collar, while strong regular lines mark the folds and contours of her robe.

KAIGETSUDO ANDO (c. 1700) *Courtesan and Maid* · c. 1713 · India ink and color on paper · 38⅝ × 17½″ · Collection Takeoka

Kaigetsudo Ando's dates are not known with any accuracy. He was the leader and perhaps also the most important artist of the Kaigetsudo group, the members of which can barely be distinguished from each other by their styles. It was Ando who created the type of large figure with sharp contours and broad flat areas of kimono decorated with a diversity of patterns typical of the fashions of the time. He painted the beauties of the day for the sake of fashion and vice versa. His works were very popular and attracted many imitators. This picture of a courtesan with her servant is considered one of Kaigetsudo Ando's best works. The delicacy of color in the robes is achieved by applying wet paint over a moist surface, and the details of the pattern can be made out in the wide expanse of the sleeves and borders. The splendid kimono seems to be the real subject of the painting more than its gracious wearer herself.

TORII KIYONOBU I (1664–1728) *Pantomime* · c. 1726 · India ink and color on paper · 13 × 17″ · Collection Kuwahara

Torii Kiyonobu I came to Edo in 1687 with his father, an actor who also painted posters for the theater. In the same year his first book illustrations appeared, modeled after those of Moronobu. His intimate contact with the theater made him the first artist in that genre: he painted large-scale portraits of actors as well as scenery and posters to be reproduced in woodcuts, a medium that began to be used in 1695. This small picture draws its subject from the theater, depicting a dancer in the "Tsuri Kitsune" pantomime. Disguised as a man, a fox who has been ravaging the area dances around the trap a farmer has set. While the fox-man urges the farmer to destroy the snare, the scent of the bait—a roasted rat—is wafted to his nose and, unable to resist, his disguise is revealed, and he is caught by the farmer. With few but forceful lines Kiyonobu delineates the dancer, and the lively movement is emphasized by the bright colors of the costume.

KATSUKAWA SHUNSHO (1726–96) *April* and *August* · India ink and color on silk · Height, 40¼″ · Collection Nakano, Niigata

Katsukawa Shunsho is doubly famous as a Ukiyo-e painter and as a woodcut designer. He was a pupil of Miyagawa Choshun, whose influence can still be traced in Shunsho's portraits of women. These two narrow pictures belong to a series of ten (formerly twelve) paintings of the months in which the customs of their festivals are represented by beautiful women. April (the third moon) is the time to admire the cherry blossom and to play a kind of football: here the ball has got caught in the tree, and the ladies are trying to dislodge it with a small stick. In August (the seventh moon) the Tanabata festival is celebrated, where the Heavenly Weaver and the Shepherd, the two constellations that meet only once a year in the Milky Way, are honored. For the occasion, small strips of paper with poems are hung from the trees. The artist had a masterly comprehension of how to arrange his colors and figures in this narrow format, and these paintings certainly have their place among Shunsho's most significant works.

KO SUKOKU (1730–1804) *Yorimasa Slays a Monster* · Dated 1787 · Paint on wood · 116⅞ × 147⅞″ · Senso-ji, Tokyo

Sukoku lived in Edo and was a pupil of the well-known Hanabusa Itcho; he later studied Yamato-e painting, the techniques of which he applied to his genre paintings and, above all, to the historical pictures for which he became especially famous. He was particularly apt in historical paintings with several figures, as this picture shows. With the help of his attendant Inohayata, Yorimasa—one of the heroes of Japanese mythology and often portrayed as the hero in plays—is slaying a monster which has been prowling round the Emperor's palace. Energetic brushwork together with finely detailed patches of color are the outstanding characteristics of this picture. The fierce expression of the hero and the violence of the depiction may have prepared the way for Kuniyoshi, one of the later masters of the Japanese woodcut.

MARUYAMA OKYO (1733–95) *Wild Geese* · Dated 1767 · India ink and color on paper · 58¼ × 54¾″ · Emman-in, Otsu

In the eighteenth century, under the influence of Europe and China, there occurred an outburst of realism in Japanese art, and Maruyama Okyo is rightly regarded as its most important exponent. The center of the movement was Nagasaki, which attracted many painters, and Okyo lived there for some time. From European copperplate engravings he studied vanishing-point perspective, and from the work of the Chinese painter Shen Nan-p'in, who was also under European influence, he learned to depict animals and plants realistically. Many anecdotes have been handed down about the preciseness of his observation and drawing. This painting of wild geese over the sea is one of the best examples from which to understand his conceptions: the diverse movements of the geese are brilliantly observed and set down, and the use of color is true to nature and full of life; yet this is saved from being a mere nature study by virtue of the skillful composition. The energetic drawing of the waves demonstrates the classical tradition of Okyo's painting, and the bright red foliage, forming a stark contrast to the rocks and birds, reveals his sense of decorative values.

407

NAGASAWA ROSETSU (1754–99) *Yamauba and Kintoki* · India ink, color, and gold on silk · 66 × 33¼″ · Itsukushima-jinja, Akinokuni

Rosetsu lived in Kyoto and was probably the most original pupil of Maruyama Okyo. In his paintings, the realism of his master is softened by wit and humor, as in this depiction of Yamauba with Kintoki. Mountain witch and foster mother of the boy-hero Kintoki who has the strength of a bear, Yamauba is portrayed in splendid but somewhat tattered garments, with a torn parasol and the furrowed face of an old crone. With her left hand she clutches Kintoki, who is generally painted red as a symbol of his extraordinary physical strength. The colors are a composition of brown and red on a shaded background against which gleam the gold of the calligraphic inscription, the chrysanthemums, and the figwort leaves. The gathered robes cascade down to their hem in jagged brush strokes, while the face of the boy is outlined with finely rhythmed India-ink drawing.

YAMAGUCHI SOKEN (1759–1818) *Young Woman under a Pine Tree* · India ink and color on silk

Like Rosetsu, Yamaguchi Soken was a pupil of Okyo and lived in Kyoto. He is famous particularly as a painter of beautiful women. The young woman standing under a pine tree completely justifies this reputation. Her posture and movement are full of natural charm. Her right hand points into the distance while with a bamboo switch in her left hand she gathers mushrooms. The rhythm of the green and yellow patterned *obi* (sash) corresponds to the curve of her body. The violet kimono with its red undergarment and white collar stands out in strong contrast against the lightly shaded background, and all this makes the small face seem all the more animated. The contours and folds of the garment are emphasized by fine lines. What counted for the artist, was his portrayal of the young woman, and so he treated everything else in the painting rather schematically, though not without precision.

SAKAI HOITSU (1761–1828) *Summer Grass in the Rain* · Wall screen in two folds · India ink, color, and gold on silver-ground paper · 55⅛ × 72″ · Commission for Protection of Cultural Properties of Japan, Tokyo

Hoitsu is regarded as the last great artist of the Sotatsu-Korin school, although there is evidence in his pictures of the realism which Okyo had introduced into Japanese art. In the pair of screens called *Summer Grass in the Rain* and *Autumn Grass in the Wind* (the former is illustrated here), he paints grass and flowers very accurately and naturalistically, catching the way they bend heavily under the rain. Across the upper right corner of the screen meanders a dark blue stream with golden waves, while the red and white of the flowers on the dull silver background give the picture a lively brilliance. This pair of screens make up the reverse side to Korin's celebrated pair with the gods of thunder and of wind, the summer grass in the rain corresponding to the god of thunder. While this example of Hoitsu's work is decorative in effect, it lacks the broad sweeping mastery with which Korin or Sotatsu fills large surfaces.

URAGAMI GYOKUDO (1745–1820) *Autumn Landscape* · Leaf of an album · India ink and pale color on paper · 11⅜ × 8⅞″ · Collection Umezawa, Tokyo

Gyokudo was a Samurai in the service of the Ikeda family in the province of Bizen. His love of music made him quit that service after forty-nine years, in order to be free to wander around the country with his *koto*, a kind of thirteen-stringed zither. Later he began to paint in a free and very unconventional style which recalls the seventeenth-century "Individualists" in China. With short strokes of an almost dry brush, he sketches in the hill in the background, and for the trees and rocks of the foreground he makes the separate strokes firmer and heavier. The patches of undergrowth are freely distributed, as are the yellow and red of the autumn foliage. It is understandable that Gyokudo's work was received with enthusiasm in Europe, however much it may differ from our Western way of looking at things.

YOSA BUSON (1716–83) *Autumn Landscape* (detail) · Dated 1780 · Sliding door · India ink and pale color on silk laid on gold · 13 × 17⅛″ · Museum for Eastern Asiatic Art, Cologne

Together with Gyokudo, Buson was one of the most important exponents of the stylistic tendency called in Japan *Bunjin-gwa* (in Chinese, *Wen-jen-hua*, "literary painting," whose foremost exponent around 1600 was Tung Ch'i-ch'ang, see page 382). Like the realistic school of the beginning of the eighteenth century, this trend likewise came from China. Its enthusiastic reception by a great many artists was due to the fact that this subjective landscape painting allowed the individual artist greater freedom than the traditional schools. This sliding door of a small wall-cupboard is the third in a series of four: the four sections making up a single landscape were designed to hang like hand scrolls over four doors. In the foreground is a group of rocks with gnarled trees; a path leads past them to Chinese-style peasant dwellings huddled together in a village. The touches of blue on some of the rocks and the russet of the foliage stand out delicately against the dull shimmer of the gold background.

YOSA BUSON *The Narrow Path into the Back Country* (detail) · Dated 1778 · Hand scroll · India ink and pale color on paper · Height, 11⅜″ · Nagao Museum, Tokyo

Buson was not only an important painter but also a *Haiku* poet of some fame (*Haiku* are short poems of seventeen syllables). He came from a small community near Osaka and in 1737 moved with his family to Edo where he became a pupil of Hayano Bajin (1677–1742), the *Haiku* poet. In this period, his main interest was probably in poetry. After his master's death, he wandered through Japan, visited friends, and eagerly acquainted himself with Chinese painting. Along with the *Bunjin-gwa* style of painting, he practiced another style, one which was related to his poetry. This was *Haigwa*, concise short poems illustrated in painting. The present picture, one of his best-known works, belongs to this tendency. Buson here depicts the wanderings of Basho, the most famous of the Japanese *Haiku* poets. With short, pregnant brush strokes and discreet colors he portrays the various phases of the journey with wit and poetry.

409

AOKI MOKUBEI (1767–1833) *Morning Sun over Uji* · Dated 1824 · India ink and pale color on paper · 19⅝ × 31¾" · Commission for Protection of Cultural Properties of Japan, Tokyo

Like Buson in his later years, Mokubei lived in Kyoto and was a pupil of Ike-no Taiga (1723–76). He is perhaps the last great master of literary painting *(Bunjin-gwa)*, and he lived well into the nineteenth century. In addition to his other talents, he was a famous amateur potter. Like many intellectuals of his time, he was very interested in the art and literature of China and learned much from the paintings of the Ming and early Ch'ang dynasties (sixteenth and seventeenth centuries). His paintings are characterized by their cool colors and a feeling for spatial depth. They are quite comparable to the works of his master Taiga, even if they do not perhaps have the spontaneity which is the special charm of Buson's work. The picture seen here is justifiably regarded as one of his most important paintings. It is more a pictorial conception of an ideal landscape than a realistic portrait of some particular place, and it is executed with lovely brushwork and dots of color introduced here and there as accents.

UTAGAWA KUNIYOSHI (1798–1861) *Young Woman* · c. 1855 · India ink and pale color on silk · 36⅝ × 13¼" · Museum for Eastern Asiatic Art, Cologne

Born in Tokyo, Kuniyoshi was the son of a silk-dyer. At the age of thirteen he came under the instruction of Toyokuni, then the most popular master of the woodcut on theatrical subjects. At nineteen he was already an independent artist famous for his paintings of heroes and battles. His woodcuts with their energetic use of color were highly appreciated and sought after in the nineteenth century when they first came to Europe, but today are somewhat looked down upon as crude and garish, though they are full of expressive dramatic qualities in composition. Be that as it may, this picture of a young woman is restrained in color. The twist of the head, however, with the hair ruffled by the wind still shows something of the painter's expressive vitality. Although elsewhere he is lavish in his use of powerful accents of color, here he makes do with a light red for the undergarment and black for the collar and sandal straps to create a carefully balanced color composition.

SHIBATA ZESSHIN (1807–91) *Blossoming Branches and Bamboos* · Leaf of an album · Lacquer on paper · 7¼ × 6⅜" · Herbig-Haarhaus Lacquer Museum, Cologne

Shibata Zesshin was the last great artist working with lacquer. He rose to great fame in the new Japan of Emperor Meiji, and is credited with preserving the art of lacquer in an industrial age. Determined to free himself from the standardized designs for lacquer furnished by the painters and woodcut artists, he went to Kyoto in 1825 to study painting for himself under various masters. He thus became known not only as an independent artist in lacquer work but also as a painter who adapted many of the lacquer techniques to painting on paper. This picture is taken from an album with five leaves which were all painted on paper in lacquer colors. Bold in composition and subtle in execution, it achieves a decorative effect, which is further emphasized by the bright colors laid over the delicate gold bands of cloud.

KATSUSHIKA HOKUSAI (1760–1849) *Duck with Watermelon* ·
1847 · Leaf of an album · India ink and color on silk ·
Collection Sakata, Tokyo

Due to his innumerable woodcuts, Hokusai is probably the
Japanese artist best known to the West. There, no less than
in the East, he has been much written about. But Hokusai the
painter is less known, although rich material is in existence
and he was hardly less productive as a painter than as a
woodcut designer. His work is so extensive that, even though
it was the product of a long life, one can hardly imagine it
to have come from the hand of a single painter. He bubbled
over with brilliant ideas which he pinned down with a
rapid brush. This small leaf, painted at the age of eighty-
seven, is a good example of his self-confident gift of
imagination. The duck is captured in its natural movement
on the water, its plumage is painted with great subtlety,
while the slice of melon like a sickle-moon echoes the
pattern of the waves. The result is a decorative one,
accentuated by the cold colors to which, unfortunately, no
reproduction can do full justice.

YOKOYAMA TAIKWAN (1868–1958) *Red Maple* · Dated 1931 ·
Screen · India ink, color, gold, and silver on paper ·
$63\frac{3}{4} \times 142\frac{5}{8}''$ · Private collection, Japan

Taikwan lived in Tokyo and is regarded as one of the
leading figures among modern Japanese artists. He was
a pupil of Hashimoto Gaho (1835–1908) and Kakuzo
Okakura. The latter founded the School of Art in Tokyo
and together with the American Ernest Fenollosa did a
great deal toward preservation of Japanese works of art of
the past at a time when Japan was plunging headlong and
with enormous enthusiasm into the new culture of the West.
Taikwan, who worked right through his old age, was
firmly opposed to all innovations and practiced and handed
on the traditional forms. The pair of screens in six sections
depicting red maple trees (only one reproduced here)
shows for all its naturalism (reminiscent of Maruyama
Okyo) a decorative brilliance whose effect is made by the
use of gleaming colors. This screen follows the best tradition of the late sixteenth century, the Momoyama period.

YOKOYAMA TAIKWAN *Fujiyama at Dawn* · 1955 · India ink, pale color, and gold on silk · $17\frac{3}{4} \times 22\frac{1}{2}''$ · Museum for Eastern Asiatic Art, Cologne

If the screen done by Taikwan in 1931 (page 411) is in the tradition of the late sixteenth century, here the artist expresses quite the opposite side of his personality and of Japanese art by his masterly use of ink. The radiant whiteness of Fujiyama rises up over clouds and pine trees in the golden light of sunrise. Taikwan is regarded as one of the greatest masters of India-ink technique in the twentieth century, and if one examines the finely shaded tones of the trees and clouds one understands why he has enjoyed such high esteem in Japan.

TOMIOKA TESSAI (1836–1924) *Journey to the Red Wall* (detail) · India ink and color on paper · $61\frac{3}{8} \times 16\frac{7}{8}''$ · Kiyoshi-Kojin Temple

While Tokyo was the center of all modern tendencies in the nineteenth century, Kyoto jealously perpetuated the enchantment of an imperial palace rich in traditions. It was there that Tessai lived, withdrawn into his library to study Chinese literature, painting strictly for his own pleasure and for that of his friends. He is regarded as the last master of the *Bunjin-gwa* style, was self-taught, and obstinately restricted himself to India ink and colors. The Journey to the Red Wall, based on the prose poem of Su Tung-p'o (1036–1101), is a recurrent theme in Chinese painting. During his exile the poet often sailed to these cliffs in his boat to meditate on the naval battle that had taken place there in A.D. 208. Here Tessai portrays one of Su Tung-p'o's expeditions: with his friends he stands on the shore, accompanied by a servant with food for a picnic slung over his shoulder in two hampers. The artist has captured this cheerful gathering with lively colors and boldly powerful brushwork.

ISHIKAWA BIHO (1902–   ) *Walk in the Fields in Autumn* · Screen in two sections · India ink and color on paper

Biho is one of the modern Ukiyoe painters who have taken the masters of the early seventeenth century as models. With sharply defined contours the figures are placed prominently in the foreground. Their colorful kimonos stand out decoratively against the background of autumn plants and bright maple leaves. As in the early Ukiyoe paintings, the dark hair forms a severe frame around the white faces and also creates a lively contrast of colors. The outlines and folds of the garments are clearly and finely drawn without any particular emphasis. This pair of screens, one of which is illustrated here, demonstrates how the finest aspects of the Japanese tradition live on in the painting of today.

index

415

Acknowledgements

The following photographers, photographic agencies, and publishers have co-operated in the making and gathering of the color photographs for this book:

Joachim Blauel, Munich; Hirmer Verlag, Munich; Carlfred Halbach, Ratingen, Germany; Hans Hinz, Basel; Editions Pierre Tisné, Paris; La Photothèque, Paris; Photographie Giraudon, Paris; Scala Istituto Fotografico Editoriale, Florence; Thames & Hudson Ltd., London.

All reproduction rights, where applicable, are reserved by Beeldrecht, Amsterdam.

The Publisher and the authors express their gratitude and appreciation to all the museums, galleries, cultural authorities, and private collectors who so graciously made available for this book the works in their custody or possession. All such sources are acknowledged in the captions for the individual reproductions.